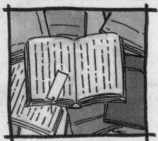

Recently, the people around me tell me they have been reading books. I rarely read books, so I'm thinking about picking one up for the first time in a while. I'm considering either a mystery or a fantasy work.

—*Masashi Kishimoto, 2006*

岸本斉史

Author/artist Masashi Kishimoto was born in 1974 in rural Okayama Prefecture, Japan. After spending time in art college, he won the Hop Step Award for new manga artists with his manga **Karakuri** (Mechanism). Kishimoto decided to base his next story on traditional Japanese culture. His first version of **Naruto**, drawn in 1997, was a one-shot story about fox spirits; his final version, which debuted in **Weekly Shonen Jump** in 1999, quickly became the most popular ninja manga in Japan.

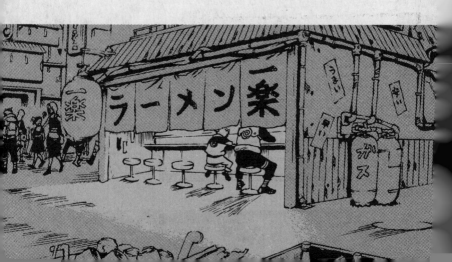

NARUTO

3-in-1 Edition
Volume 12
SHONEN JUMP Manga Omnibus Edition
A compilation of the graphic novel volumes 34–36

STORY AND ART BY MASASHI KISHIMOTO

Translation & English Adaptation/Mari Morimoto
English Adaptation/Deric A. Hughes, Benjamin Raab
Touch-up Art & Lettering/Sabrina Heep, Inori Fukuda Trant
Design/Sean Lee (Original Series)
Design/Sam Elzway (Omnibus Edition)
Editor/Joel Enos (Manga Edition)
Managing Editor/Erica Yee (Omnibus Edition)

NARUTO © 1999 by Masashi Kishimoto. All rights reserved.
First published in Japan in 1999 by SHUEISHA Inc., Tokyo.
English translation rights arranged by SHUEISHA Inc.

The stories, characters and incidents
mentioned in this publication are entirely fictional.

Printed in the U.S.A.

Published by VIZ Media, LLC
P.O. Box 77010
San Francisco, CA 94107

10 9 8 7 6 5 4 3 2 1
Omnibus edition first printing, September 2015

SHONEN JUMP MANGA EDITION

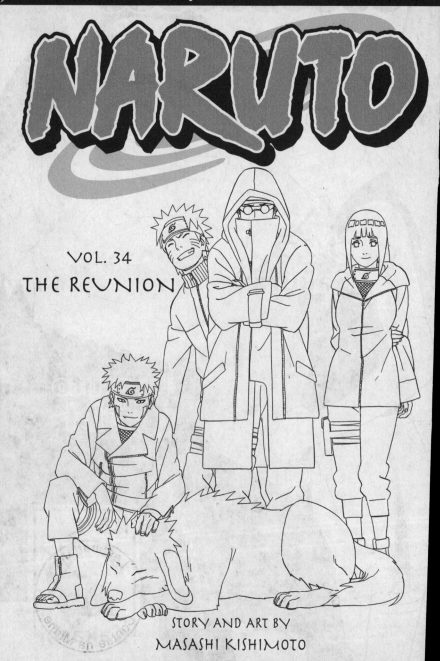

NARUTO

VOL. 34

THE REUNION

STORY AND ART BY

MASASHI KISHIMOTO

CHARACTERS
サクラ
Sakura
Naruto
ナルト
はたけカカシ
Kakashi

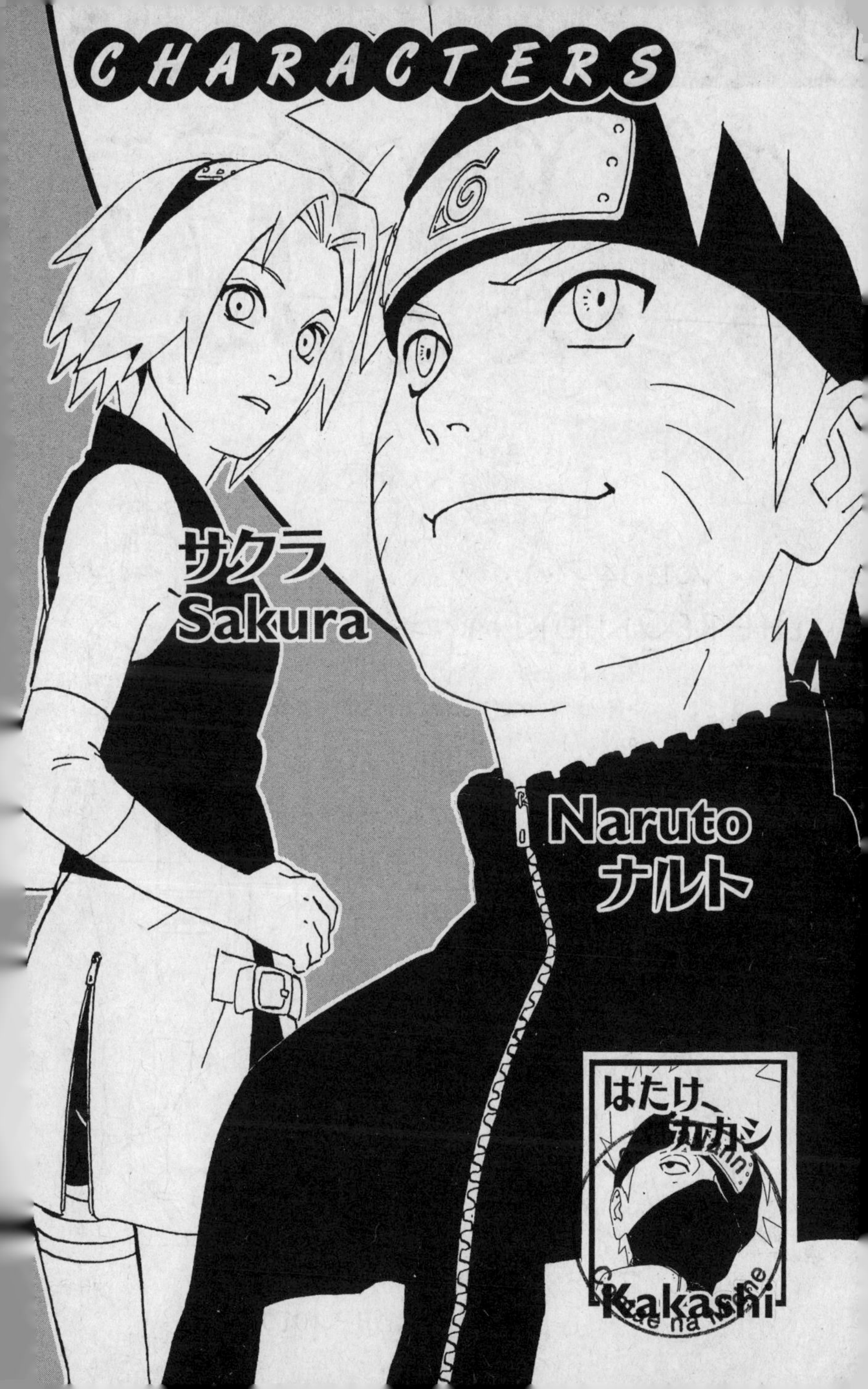

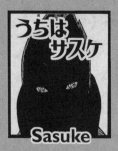

うちはサスケ
Sasuke
綱手
Tsunade
サイ
Sai
薬師カブト
Kabuto
大蛇丸
Orochimaru
ヤマト
Yamato

The Story So Far...

With the aftershocks of *Operation: Destroy Konoha* still reverberating throughout their elite shinobi corps, the new Team Kakashi, under the substitute leadership of Captain Yamato, and joined by the enigmatic, emotionless Sai, sets out on a mission to rescue Sasuke from Orochimaru.

But their mission is soon jeopardized. First, by Orochimaru and his henchman, Kabuto... Then, by Naruto himself as he succumbs to the power of the Nine-Tailed Fox demon hidden inside him and goes on a rampage... And finally by Sai who is secretly working for Danzo, leader of the military organization The Foundation.

But with Sai's private picture book now in their possession, Naruto, Sakura and Yamato regroup in an attempt to unravel the secrets of Sai's *real* mission...

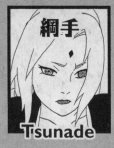

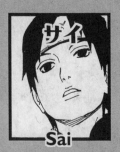

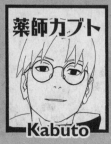

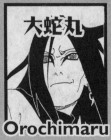

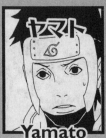

Number 300: Sai's Picture Book!!

in the case of
with a probability

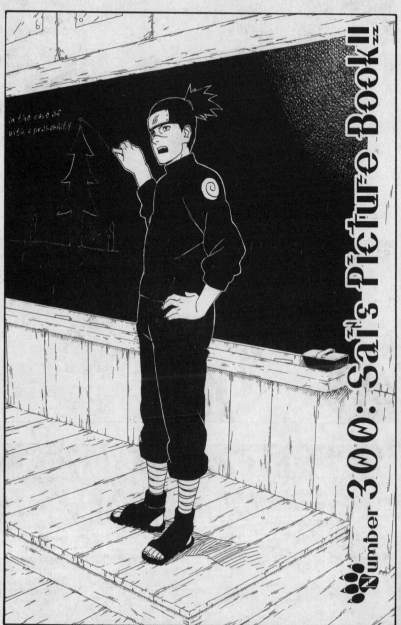

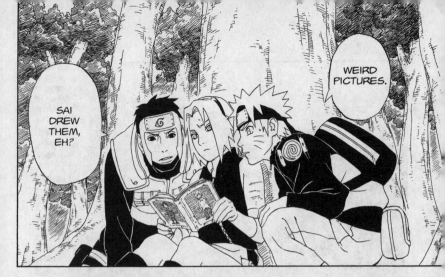

SAI DREW THEM, EH?

WEIRD PICTURES.

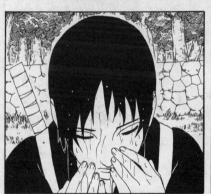

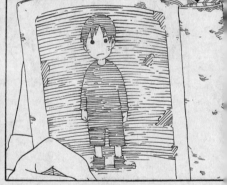

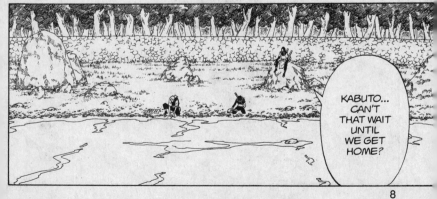

KABUTO... CAN'T THAT WAIT UNTIL WE GET HOME?

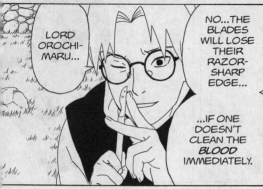

READ THIS WAY
NO...THE BLADES WILL LOSE THEIR RAZOR-SHARP EDGE...
...IF ONE DOESN'T CLEAN THE *BLOOD* IMMEDIATELY.
LORD OROCHI-MARU...
...?!
WHEN WE RETURN...
...MAY I HAVE ANOTHER MALE CORPSE?
DON'T YOU HAVE SOME?
SHH
HF
OH, I HAVE *MANY*...
...JUST NO MORE 15- OR 16-YEAR-OLD MALES, LIKE THIS ONE.
IF I DON'T ALWAYS HAVE AT LEAST ONE OF EACH AGE RANGE STORED IN CHRONOLOGICAL ORDER IN MY SCROLL, I GET... *ANXIOUS*.

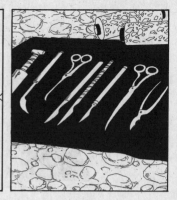

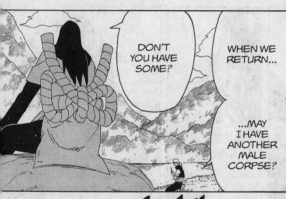

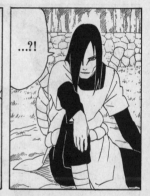

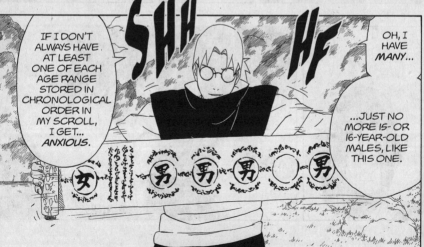

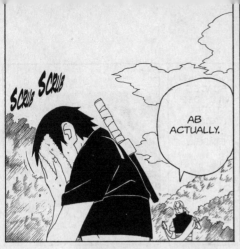

SCRUB SCRUB

AB ACTUALLY.

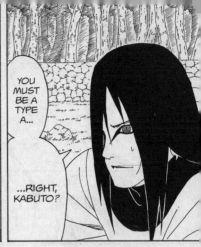

YOU MUST BE A TYPE A...

...RIGHT, KABUTO?

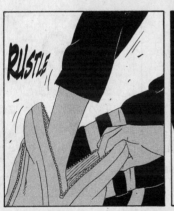

RUSTLE

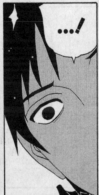

....!

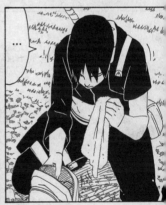

...

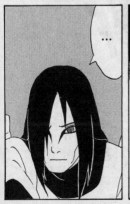

...

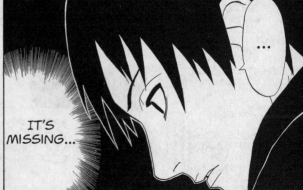

IT'S MISSING...

...

10

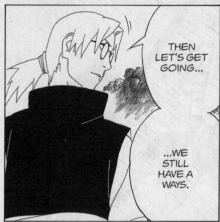

READ THIS WAY

SOME-THING WRONG, SAI?
IT'S... IT'S NOTHING ...
THEN LET'S GET GOING...
...WE STILL HAVE A WAYS.
...
STRANGEST THING ABOUT SAI'S PICTURE BOOK...?
THE CENTERFOLD. IT SEEMS REALLY OUT OF PLACE.
YEAH...
...AND REALLY CREEPY...

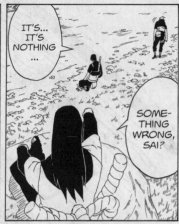

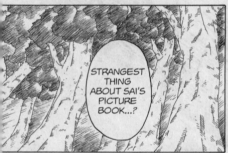

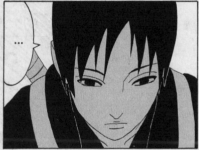

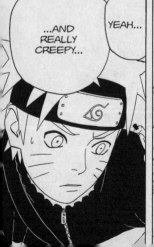

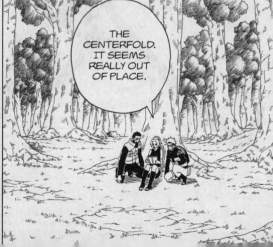

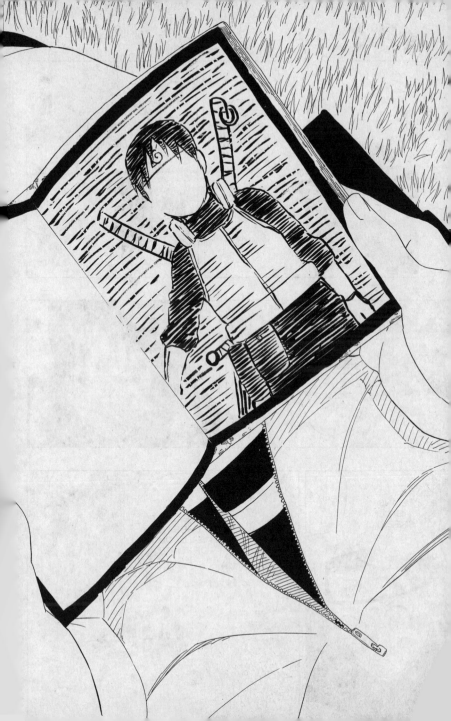

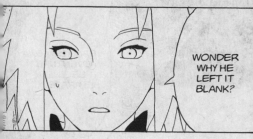

READ THIS WAY
WONDER WHY HE LEFT IT BLANK?
ARTISTS REVEAL SECRETS ABOUT THEM-SELVES THROUGH THEIR ART.
PERHAPS SAI'S WORK WILL TELL US WHAT WE NEED TO KNOW ABOUT HIM.
GOOD POINT. LET'S SEE...
THIS SEEMS TO BE THE TALE OF THE TWO BOYS DRAWN ON THE COVERS...

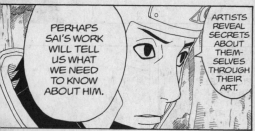

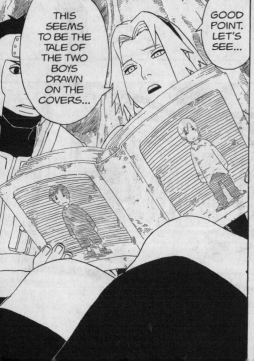

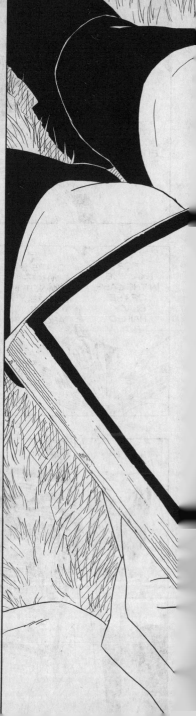

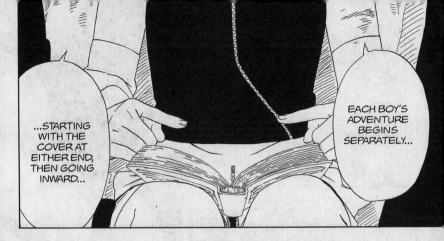

EACH BOY'S ADVENTURE BEGINS SEPARATELY...
...STARTING WITH THE COVER AT EITHER END, THEN GOING INWARD...
BUT THERE'S NO DIALOGUE OR TEXT AT ALL.
NO WORDS? JUST PICTURES? WHAT KINDA STUPID STORY IS THIS?
THAT'S... WHAT I'M NOT ENTIRELY SURE ABOUT...
FOR EXAMPLE, IN THE CASE OF THE BLACK-HAIRED BOY...
FLIP
FLIP
FLIP

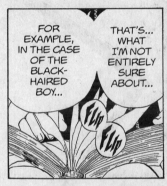

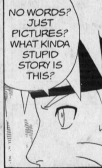

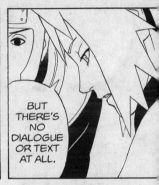

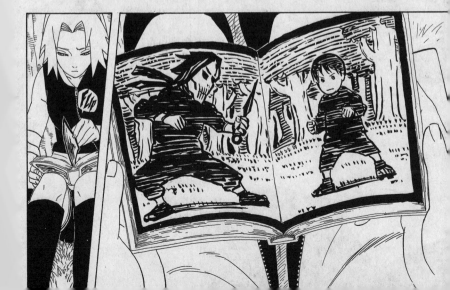

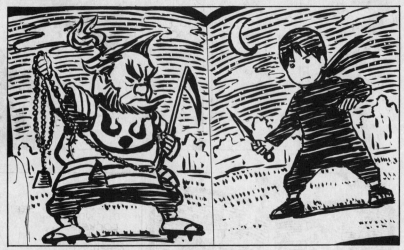

READ THIS WAY
THE RIGHT-HAND PAGE ALWAYS SHOWS THE BOY...
...AND THE LEFT-HAND PAGE HAS A DIFFERENT CHARACTER ON IT EACH TIME...
...
SEE...

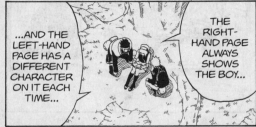

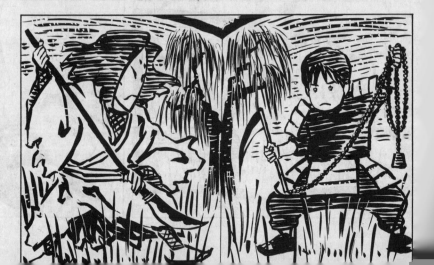

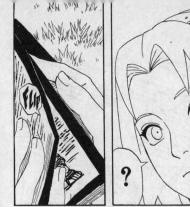

GO BACK TO THAT LAST PAGE FOR A SEC!

WAIT!

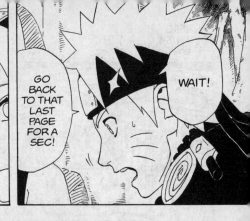

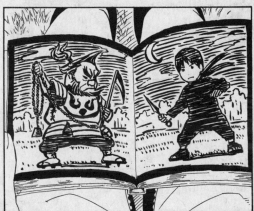

SEE!

ON EACH PAGE, THAT KID LOOKS A LITTLE DIFFERENT.

AND NOT ONLY THAT...

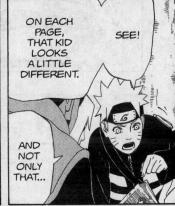

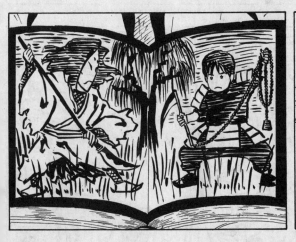

...HE'S HOLDING THE SAME WEAPON AS THE CHARACTER FROM THE PREVIOUS LEFT-HAND PAGE...

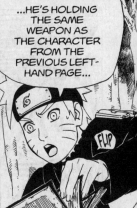

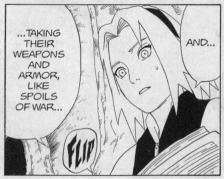

READ THIS WAY

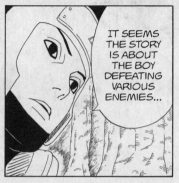

IT SEEMS THE STORY IS ABOUT THE BOY DEFEATING VARIOUS ENEMIES...
AND...
...TAKING THEIR WEAPONS AND ARMOR, LIKE SPOILS OF WAR...
FLIP
SEE? IT'S THE SAME EVERY TIME.
WITH EACH BATTLE, THE BOY MATURES... GAINS KNOWLEDGE, WISDOM, STRENGTH...
THE ORIENTATION IS FLIPPED...
...BUT THE PREMISE IS THE SAME FOR THE WHITE-HAIRED BOY TOO.

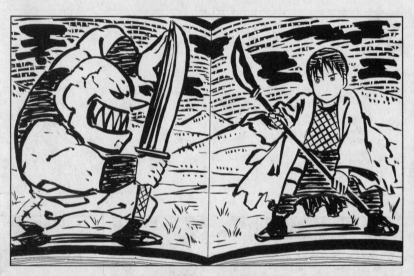

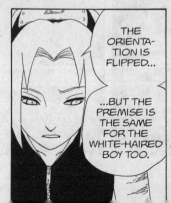

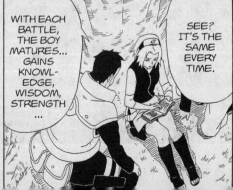

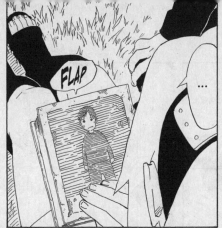

FLAP
...
HEY!
DOESN'T THE BLACK-HAIRED KID LOOK AN AWFUL LOT LIKE SAI?
BUT THEN WHO'S THE OTHER BOY...?
PERHAPS HE WAS DRAWING HIS OWN STORY.
...YOU'RE RIGHT...
...BECAUSE IT BELONGS TO MY OLDER BROTHER.
PLUS, I DON'T REALLY SHOW IT TO OTHERS...
...IT'S NOT FINISHED YET.
....!

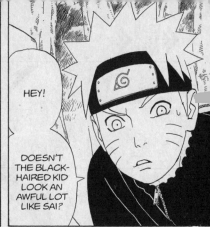

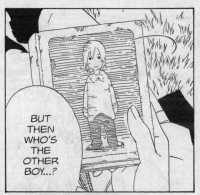

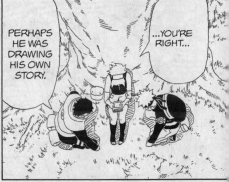

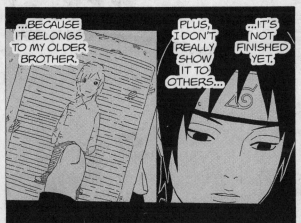

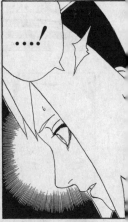

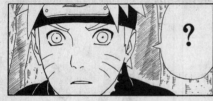

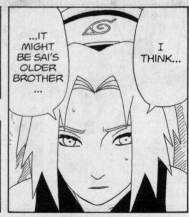

READ THIS WAY

I THINK...
...IT MIGHT BE SAI'S OLDER BROTHER...
?
...
MY BROTHER IS *DEAD.*
...
WHICH WOULD MEAN...
...THE CENTER-FOLD...
...WAS MEANT TO BE SAI... AND HIS BROTHER TOGETHER...

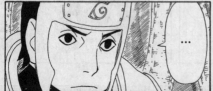

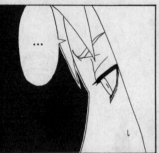

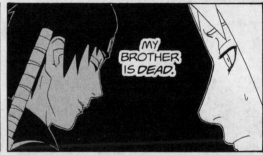

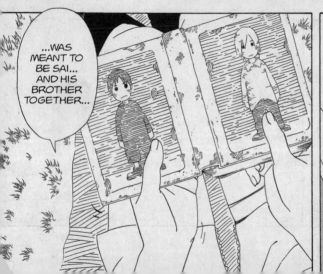

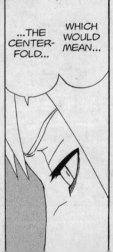

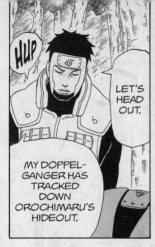

HUP

LET'S HEAD OUT.

MY DOPPEL-GANGER HAS TRACKED DOWN OROCHIMARU'S HIDEOUT.

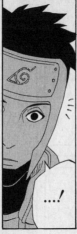

....!

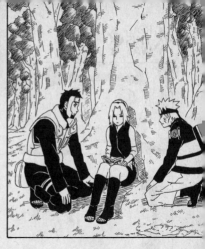

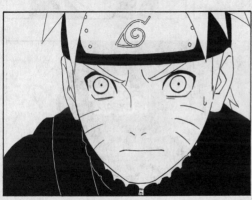

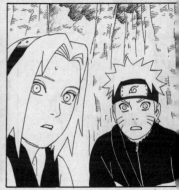

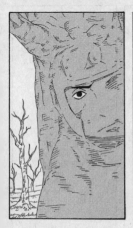

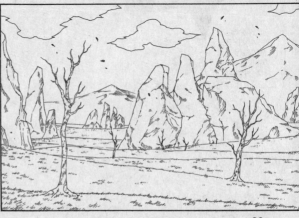

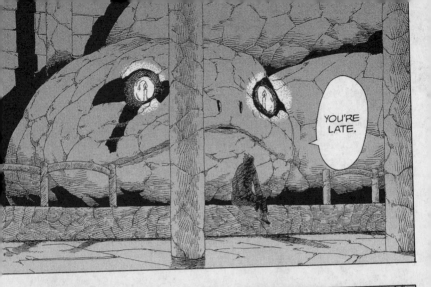

YOU'RE LATE.
YOU SAID YOU WERE GOING TO HELP ME HONE A NEW JUTSU THIS AFTERNOON... OROCHIMARU.
IF I WERE YOU, BOY, I'D TAKE A MORE RESPECTFUL TONE...
ENOUGH, KABUTO.
OUR EFFORTS TODAY HAVE BEEN REWARDED WITH A LITTLE GIFT.
SOMEONE FOR OUR FRIEND HERE TO REMINISCE WITH...
...A SHINOBI FROM HIS DEAR KONOHAGAKURE...
HNNH...

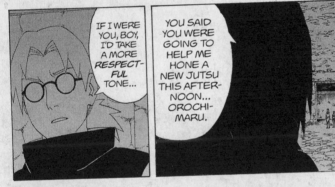

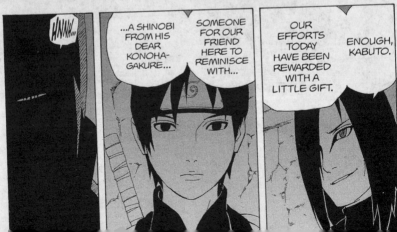

HUMPH...

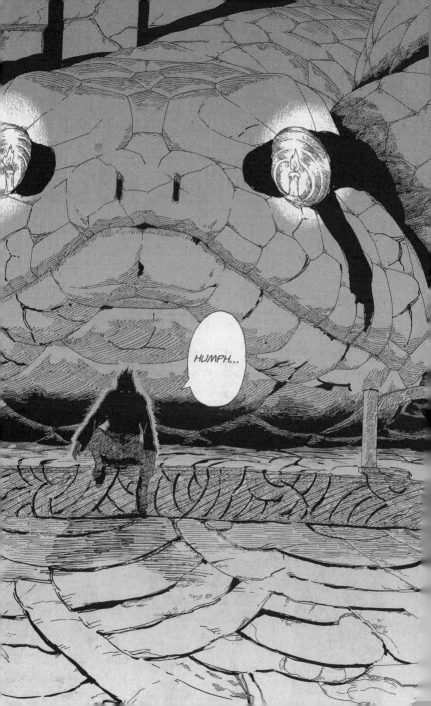

...
FINALLY... UCHIHA SASUKE...

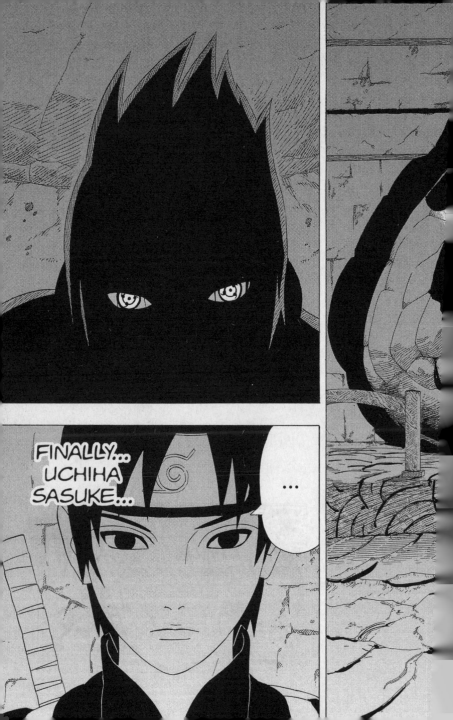

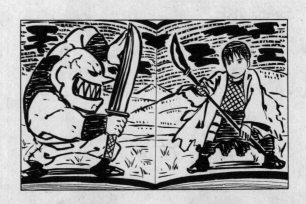

Number 301: Sai & Sasuke!!
四代目火影

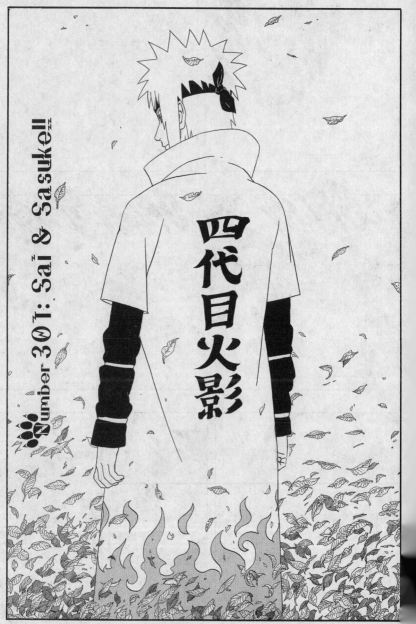

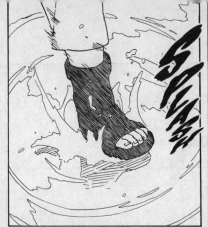

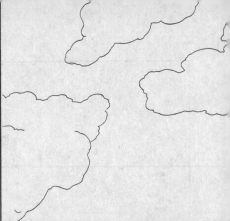

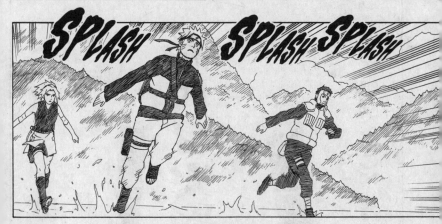

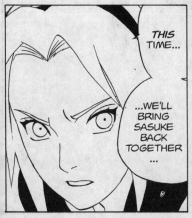

SPLASH
SPLASH
SPLASH
SPLASH
NARUTO.
?
THIS TIME...
...WE'LL BRING SASUKE BACK TOGETHER ...

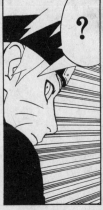

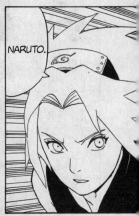

READ THIS WAY

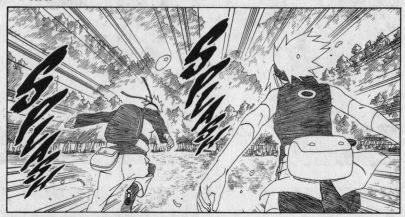

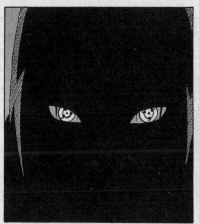

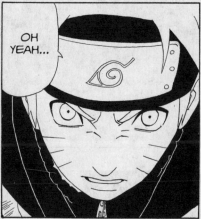

OH YEAH...

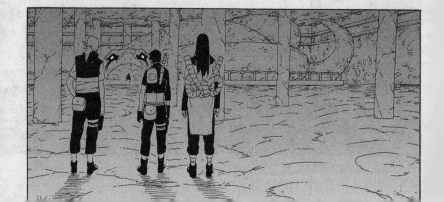

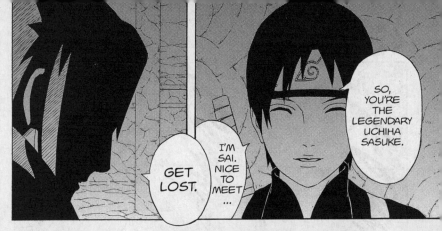

SO, YOU'RE THE LEGENDARY UCHIHA SASUKE.
I'M SAI. NICE TO MEET...
GET LOST.
...
...
NO MATTER HOW MUCH I SMILE...
...EVERY-ONE SEEMS TO DISLIKE ME RIGHT AWAY...
EVEN NARUTO...

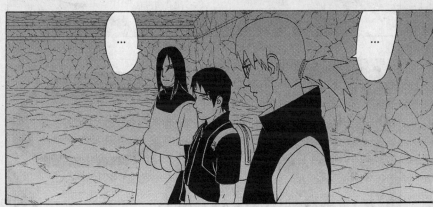

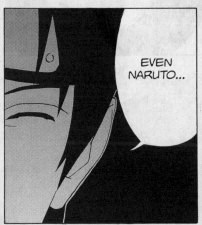

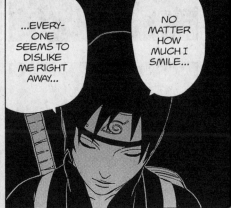

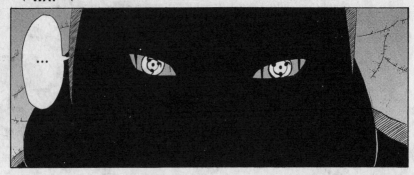

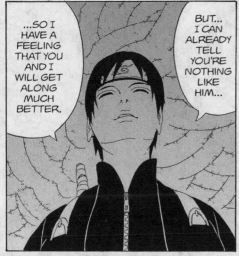

READ THIS WAY

...
...
BUT... I CAN ALREADY TELL YOU'RE NOTHING LIKE HIM...
...SO I HAVE A FEELING THAT YOU AND I WILL GET ALONG MUCH BETTER.
...
!

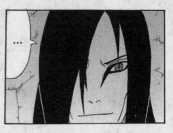

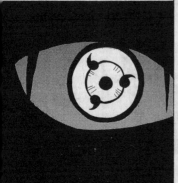

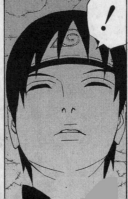

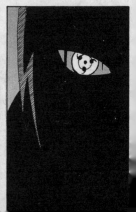

OM

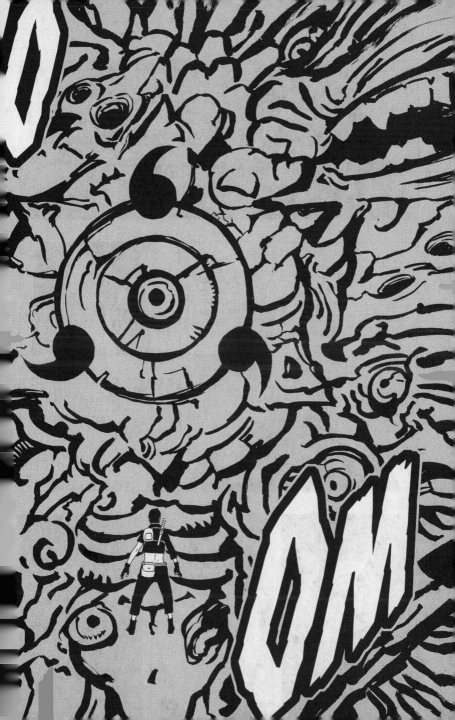

GASH
CRNNCH
THUMP
SASUKE!!

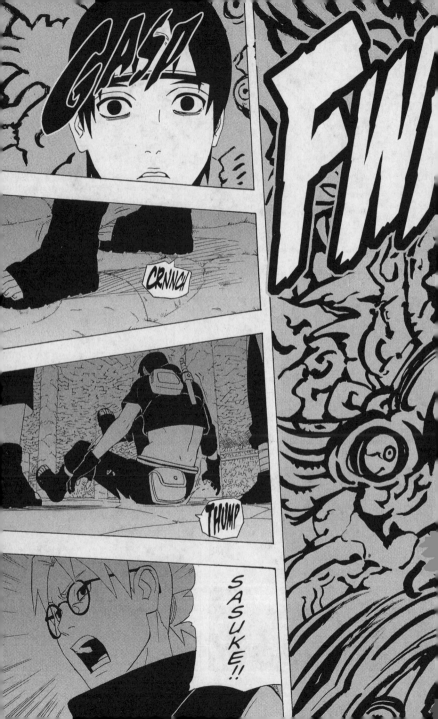

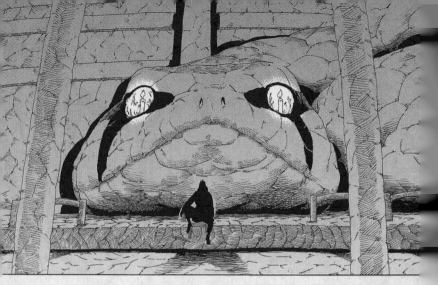

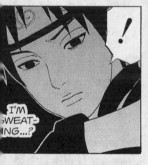

!
I'M SWEAT-ING...?
I HAVE NO EMOTIONS, I FEEL NOTHING...
...AND YET, JUST BY MEETING HIS EYES... SOMEHOW EAR SASUKE FROM THE OTTOM OF A HEART THOUGHT I IDN'T HAVE...

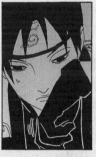

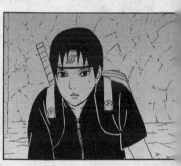

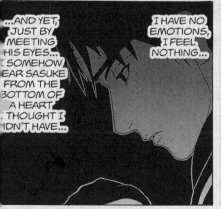

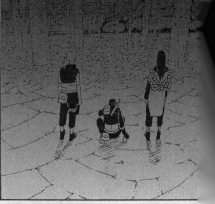

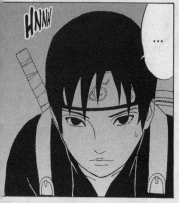

READ THIS WAY

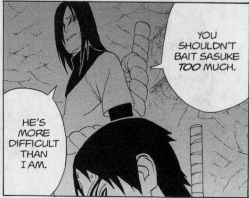

YOU SHOULDN'T BAIT SASUKE *TOO* MUCH.
HE'S MORE DIFFICULT THAN I AM.
HNNH
...
I DON'T CARE ABOUT HIM.
COME ON OROCHI-MARU, LET'S GO...
HSSS
NARUTO'S TOLD ME A LOT ABOUT YOU.
NNNH
THESE LAST THREE YEARS...
HE'S BEEN LOOKING FOR YOU THIS WHOLE TIME, YOU KNOW.

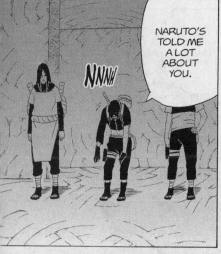

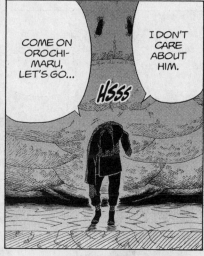

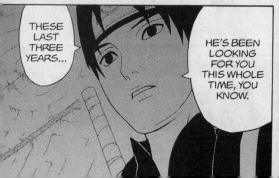

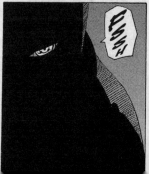

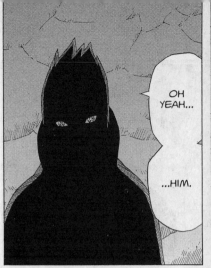

OH YEAH...
...HIM.
...
LET'S GO, OROCHIMARU...
NARUTO...
...HE THINKS OF YOU AS A BROTHER...
...OR SO SAKURA SAYS.
...

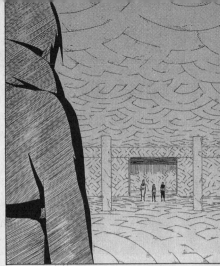

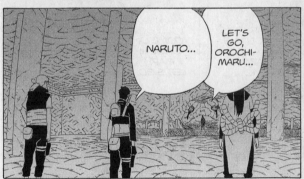

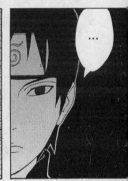

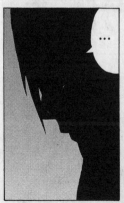

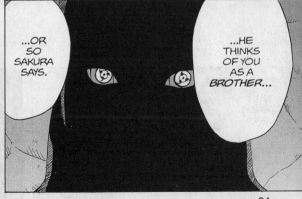

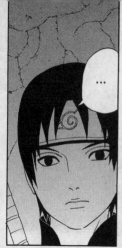

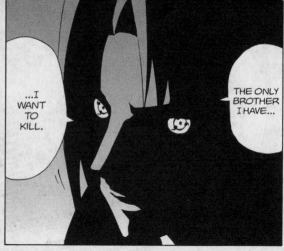

THE ONLY BROTHER I HAVE...
...I WANT TO KILL.
...
WHISP
I'M GOING TO JOIN HIM.
KABUTO... WHY DON'T YOU COMPILE A BINGO BOOK WITH THESE.
SHUFF SHUFF
KRRNKLE
THIS IS...!

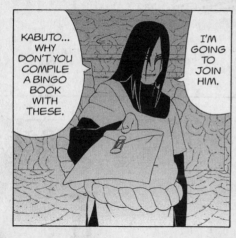

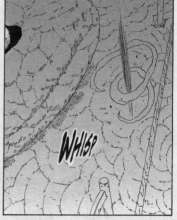

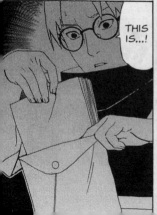

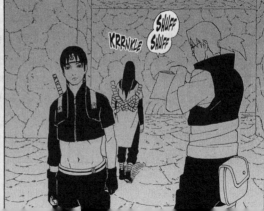

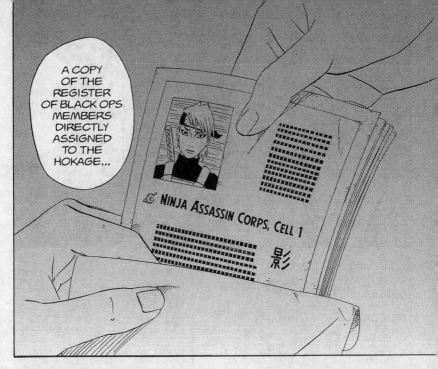

A COPY OF THE REGISTER OF BLACK OPS MEMBERS DIRECTLY ASSIGNED TO THE HOKAGE...

NINJA ASSASSIN CORPS, CELL 1

影

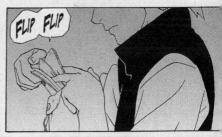

FLIP FLIP

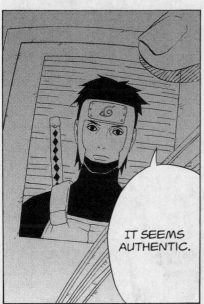

IT SEEMS AUTHENTIC.

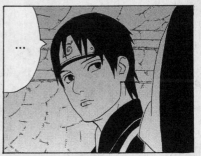

...

36

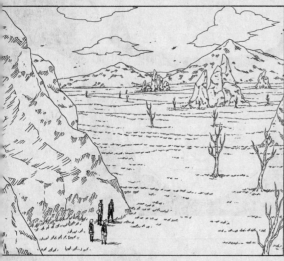

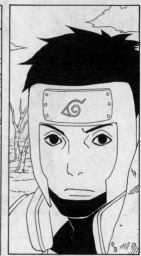

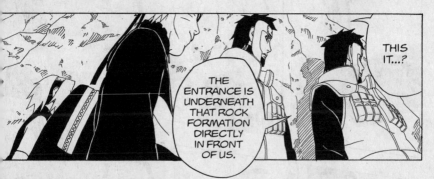

THIS IT...?

THE ENTRANCE IS UNDERNEATH THAT ROCK FORMATION DIRECTLY IN FRONT OF US.

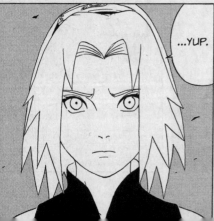

...YUP.

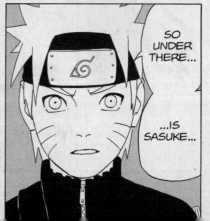

SO UNDER THERE...

...IS SASUKE...

...LET'S GO.

ALL RIGHT...

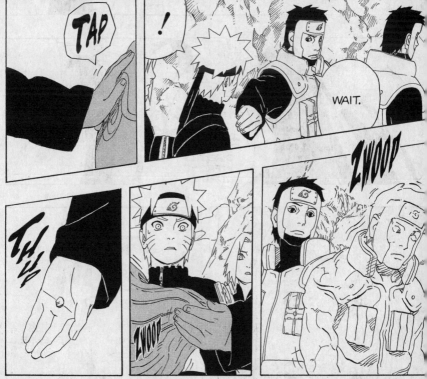

TAP

!

WAIT.

ZWOOP

THVP

ZWOOP

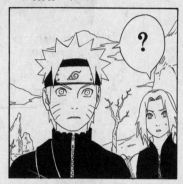

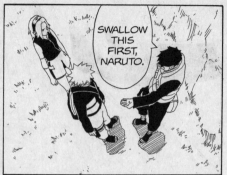

READ THIS WAY
SWALLOW THIS FIRST, NARUTO.
?
YOU TOO, SAKURA.
SWISH
SO THAT IF WE GET SEPARATED...
...I CAN LOCATE YOU RIGHT AWAY.
WHAT IS THIS ...?
THESE SEEDS ARE TRANS- MITTERS FOR TRACKING.
IT'S A NINJA TOOL THAT ONLY RESONATES TO MY CHAKRA.

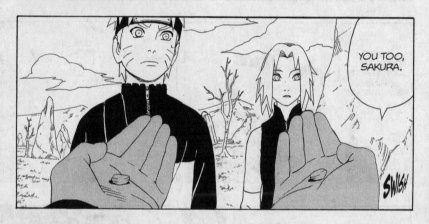

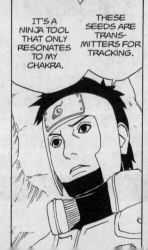

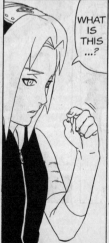

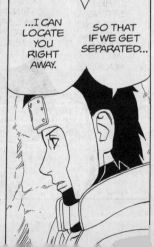

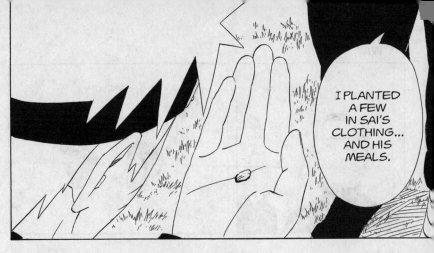

I PLANTED A FEW IN SAI'S CLOTHING... AND HIS MEALS.
...!
SO...
...THAT'S HOW YOU WERE ABLE TO FOLLOW HIM.
BUT WHEN ...?
I GOT OUT FIRST AT THE HOT SPRINGS, REMEMBER?
WELL, THAT'S ENOUGH BONDING FOR ME...
...BUT BEFORE I GO, LET ME SHARE A FUNNY STORY WITH YOU, NARUTO.
SNEAK
NOW DO YOU UNDERSTAND WHY I SPLURGED FOR THOSE LUXURIES...
...THE HOT SPRINGS, THE FINE DINING... OUT OF MY OWN POCKET?

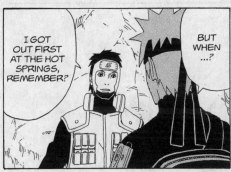

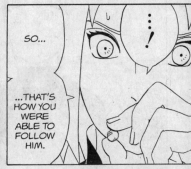

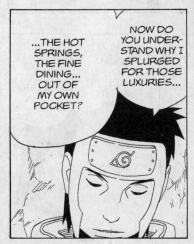

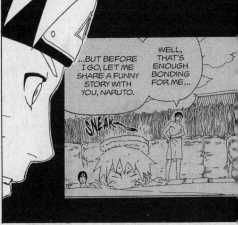

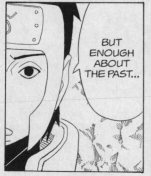

READ THIS WAY

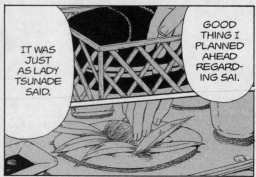

GOOD THING I PLANNED AHEAD REGARDING SAI.
IT WAS JUST AS LADY TSUNADE SAID.
BUT ENOUGH ABOUT THE PAST...
GULP
FOCUS ON WHAT'S AHEAD.
READY, YOU TWO?
SASUKE... HERE WE COME!
YES, SIR!

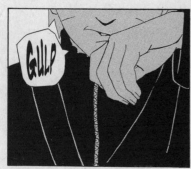

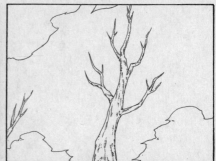

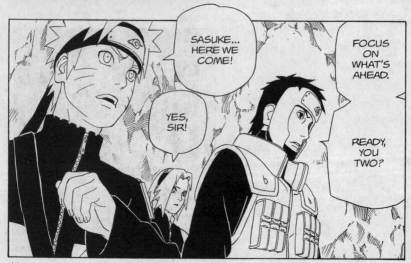

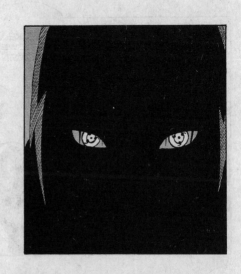

Number 302: Infiltration...!!

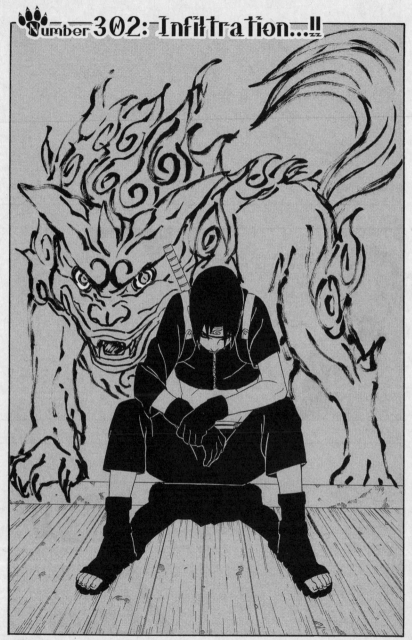

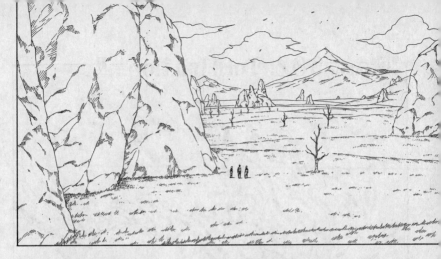

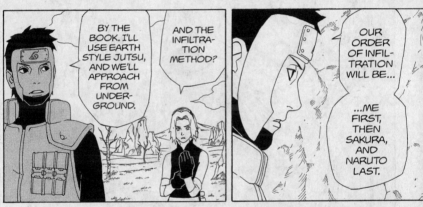

OUR ORDER OF INFIL-TRATION WILL BE...
...ME FIRST, THEN SAKURA, AND NARUTO LAST.
AND THE INFILTRA-TION METHOD?
BY THE BOOK. I'LL USE EARTH STYLE JUTSU, AND WE'LL APPROACH FROM UNDER-GROUND.
...
WE'VE FINALLY FOUND YOU...
...SASUKE...

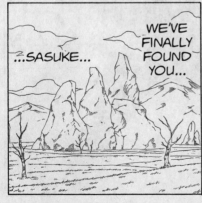

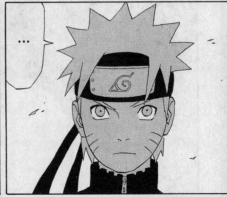

READ THIS WAY

SHUFF
SHUFF
KA-CHINK
CREAK
HERE YOU GO...

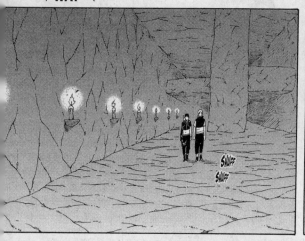

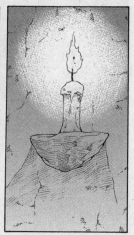

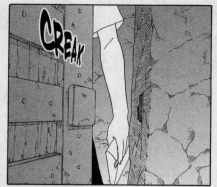

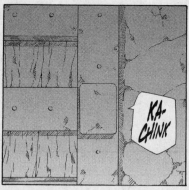

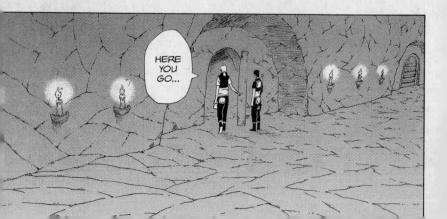

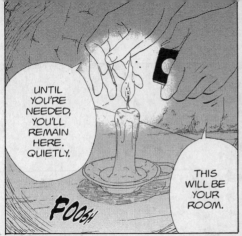

THAP
THIS WILL BE YOUR ROOM.
UNTIL YOU'RE NEEDED, YOU'LL REMAIN HERE. QUIETLY.
FOOSH
IF SOME-THING COMES UP, WE'LL LET YOU KNOW.
...
CREAK
SORRY, BUT I'M GOING TO HAVE TO LOCK YOU IN.
BECAUSE YOU'RE... WELL...
...YOU KNOW...

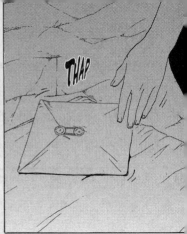

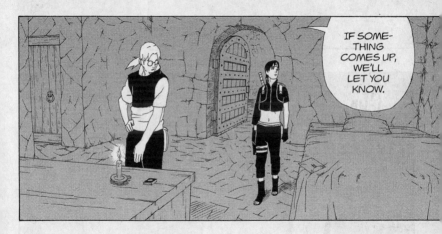

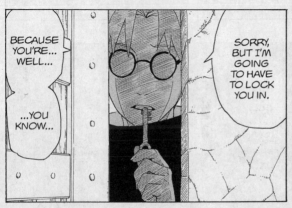

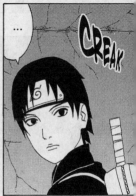

READ THIS WAY
KA-CHINK
...
...
HUP

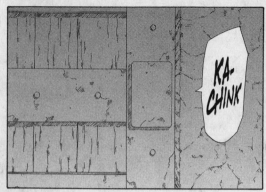

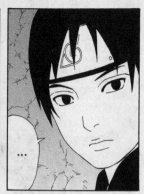

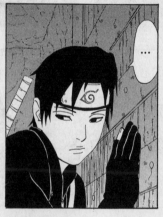

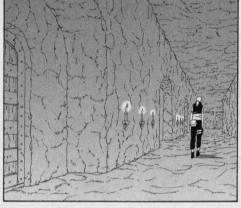

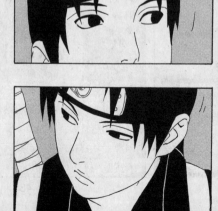

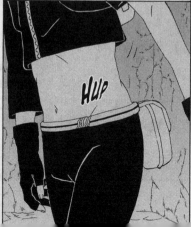

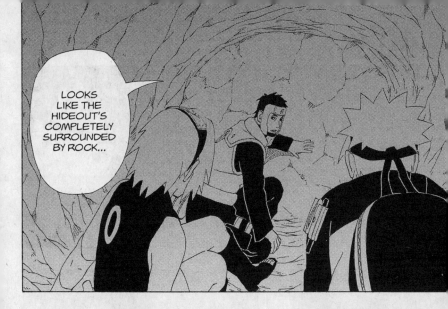

LOOKS LIKE THE HIDEOUT'S COMPLETELY SURROUNDED BY ROCK...
...
LET ME BLAST A HOLE THROUGH WITH MY RASENGAN!
WAIT!
IF YOU USE SUCH A FLASHY JUTSU, YOU'LL ALERT THE ENEMY!
WHAT WE NEED RIGHT NOW IS *STEALTH...*
THEN HOW...?
...

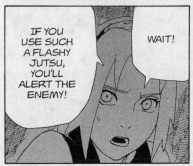

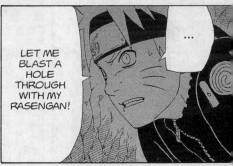

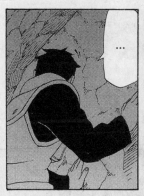

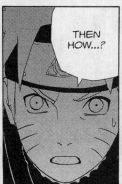

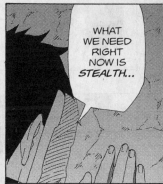

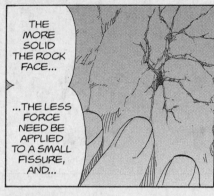

READ THIS WAY

FOUND IT...
?
THE MORE SOLID THE ROCK FACE...
...THE LESS FORCE NEED BE APPLIED TO A SMALL FISSURE, AND...
ZWOOP...
ZWOOP...
SPLISH
CRACK CRACK CRACK
ZWOOP...
CLACK CLACK CLACK
VOILA! THERE YOU GO.

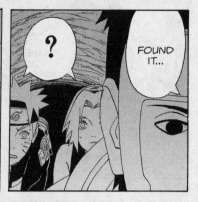

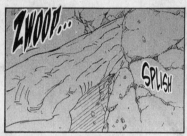

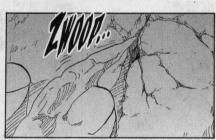

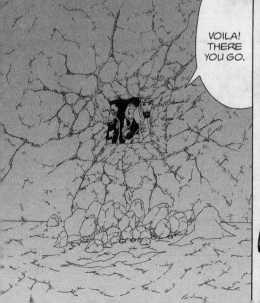

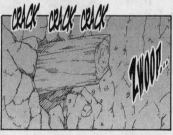

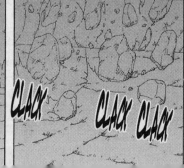

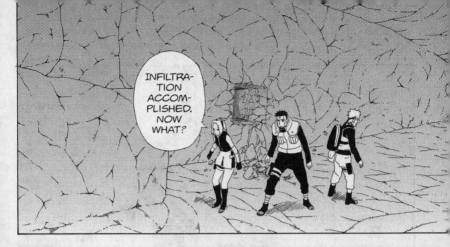

INFILTRATION ACCOMPLISHED. NOW WHAT?

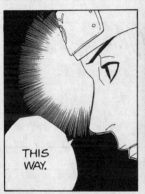

THIS WAY.

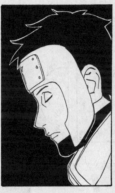

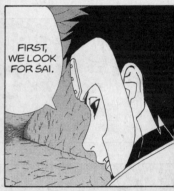

FIRST, WE LOOK FOR SAI.

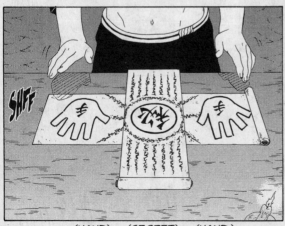

SHFF

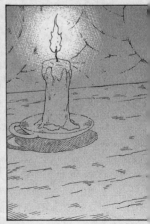

(HAND) (SECRET) (HAND)

READ THIS WAY
FLIP FLIP FLIP
BOOF
SHUP
SHUP
ALL CLEAR... KEEP MOVING...
SWISH

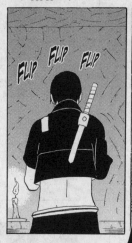

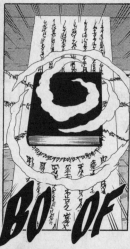

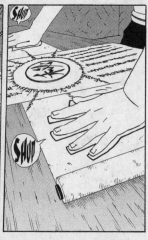

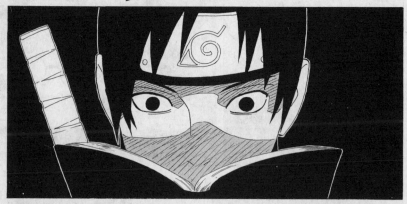

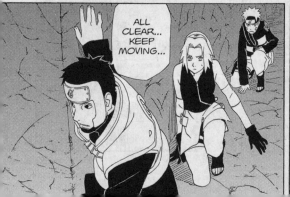

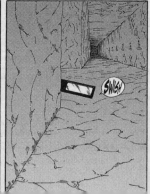

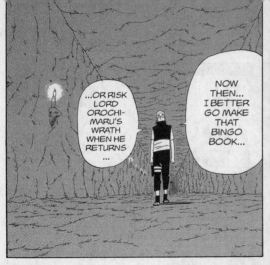

NOW THEN... I BETTER GO MAKE THAT BINGO BOOK...
...OR RISK LORD OROCHI-MARU'S WRATH WHEN HE RETURNS ...
...
!
HMMM, IF I WAS A TYPE A, I'D BE BETTER AT THIS...
WHIRL
SHUFF
SHUFF

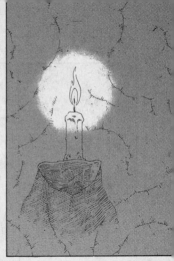

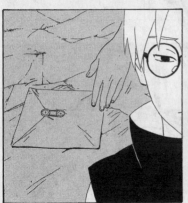

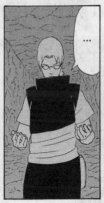

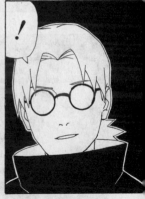

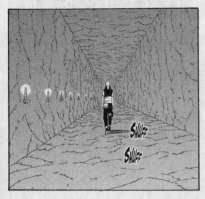

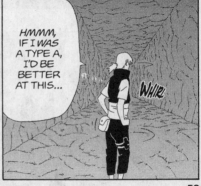

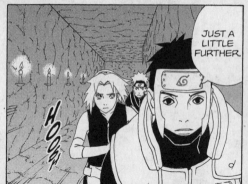

JUST A LITTLE FURTHER.

HOOO

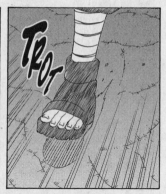

TROT

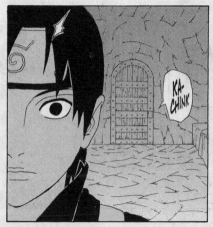

KA-CHINK

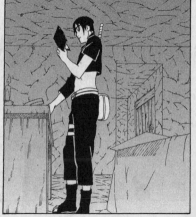

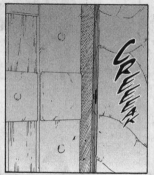

CREEEEAK

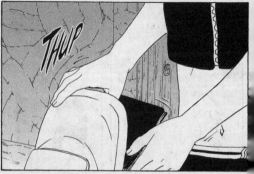

THUP

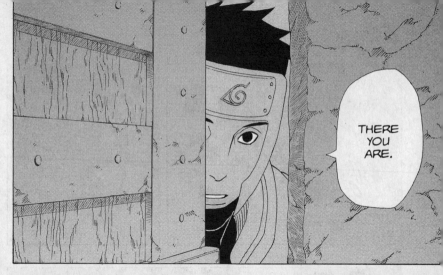

THERE YOU ARE.
SWISH SWISH
...!
TRUST A BLACK OPS MEMBER DIRECTLY LINKED TO THE HOKAGE...
...NOT TO BE FOOLED BY THAT CORPSE...
NOW, WHY DON'T YOU TELL US WHAT'S GOING ON.
ZWOOP...

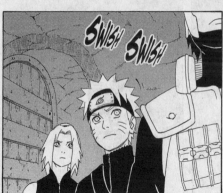

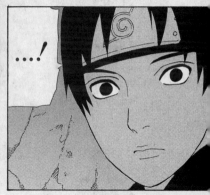

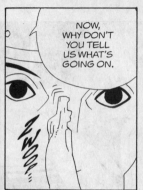

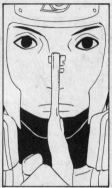

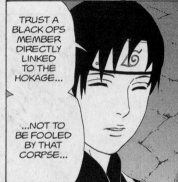

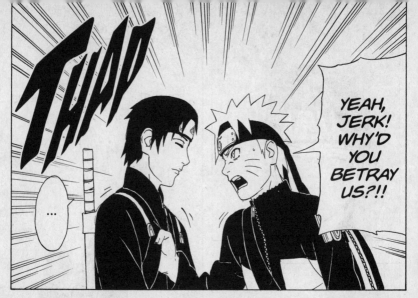

YEAH, JERK! WHY'D YOU BETRAY US?!!

...

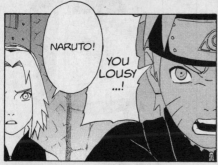

NARUTO!

YOU LOUSY ...!

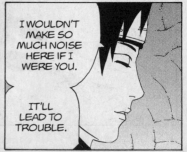

I WOULDN'T MAKE SO MUCH NOISE HERE IF I WERE YOU.

IT'LL LEAD TO TROUBLE.

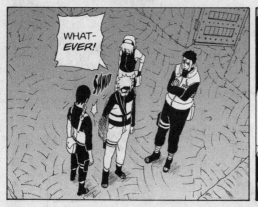

WHAT-EVER!

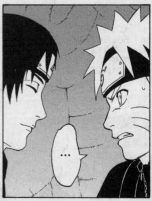

...

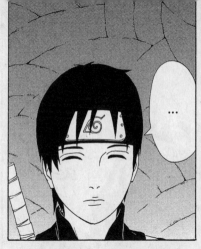

HERE...
...THIS IS YOURS, ISN'T IT?
...
THANKS.
FAP
DANZO GAVE YOU ORDERS, DIDN'T HE...?
HE'S TRYING TO ALLY WITH OROCHI-MARU FOR SOME PURPOSE...
...AND YOU WERE SELECTED TO BE THEIR GO-BETWEEN...

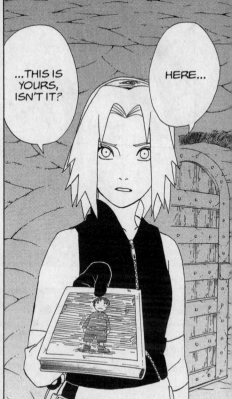

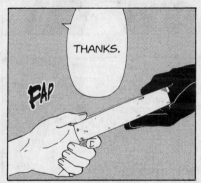

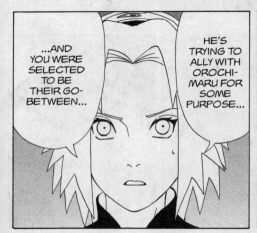

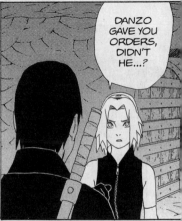

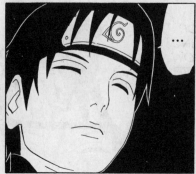

...

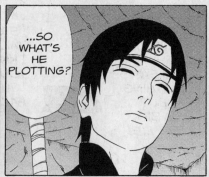

...SO WHAT'S HE PLOTTING?

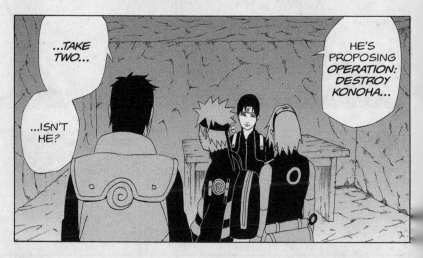

...TAKE TWO...

...ISN'T HE?

HE'S PROPOSING *OPERATION: DESTROY KONOHA*...

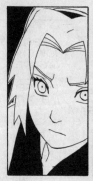

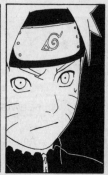

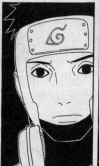

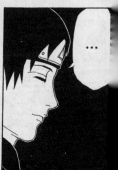

...

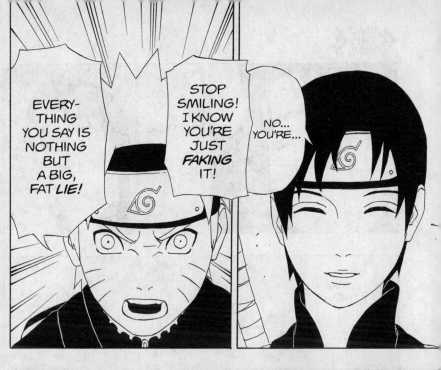

NO... YOU'RE...
STOP SMILING! I KNOW YOU'RE JUST FAKING IT!
EVERY-THING YOU SAY IS NOTHING BUT A BIG, FAT LIE!
WELL, NOW THAT YOU'VE FINALLY FIGURED ME OUT...
...SEEMS MY MISSION IS OFFICIALLY A FAILURE.
BUT SINCE I CAN'T TAKE ON ALL OF YOU TOGETHER...

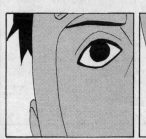

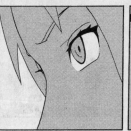

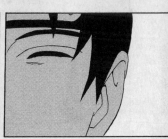

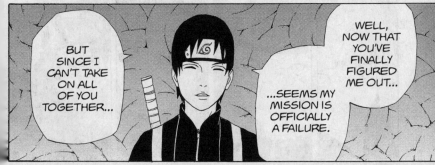

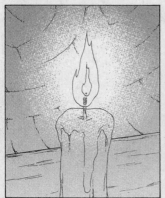

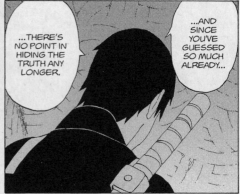

READ THIS WAY

...AND SINCE YOU'VE GUESSED SO MUCH ALREADY...
...THERE'S NO POINT IN HIDING THE TRUTH ANY LONGER.
YOU ARE CORRECT.
THE PLAN WAS TO GET RID OF KONOHA AS WE KNOW IT.
SHUFF SHUFF SHUFF

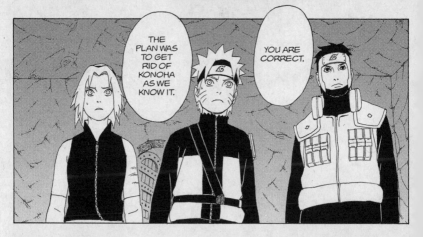

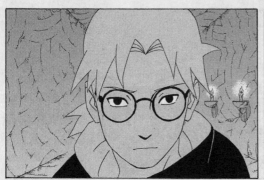

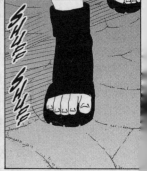

NARUTO

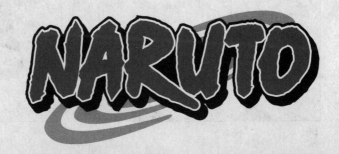

Number 303: Sai's Betrayal!!

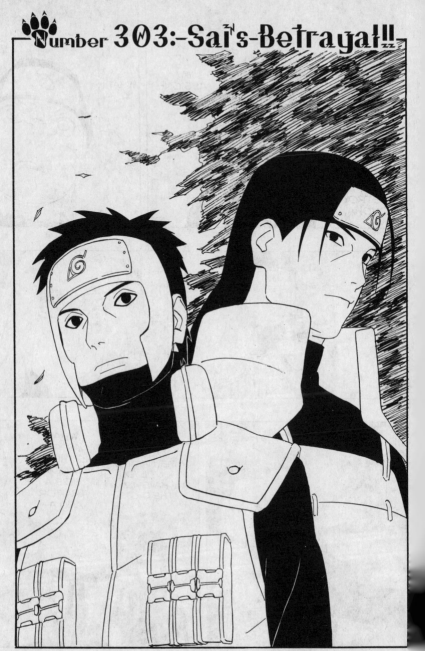

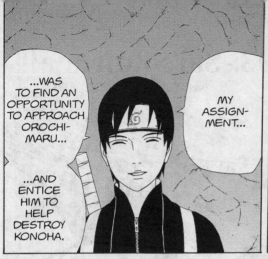

WHAT ...?!
MY ASSIGNMENT...
...WAS TO FIND AN OPPORTUNITY TO APPROACH OROCHIMARU...
...AND ENTICE HIM TO HELP DESTROY KONOHA.
...
KEEP TALKING.
I WANT *ALL* THE DETAILS.
WHAT MORE IS THERE TO KNOW?! HE'S A TRAITOR AND A—
DO NOT RUSH TO JUDGE ME, NARUTO, UNTIL YOU HAVE *ALL* THE FACTS.
...!

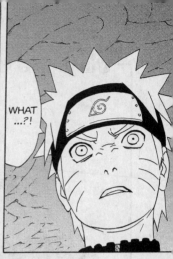

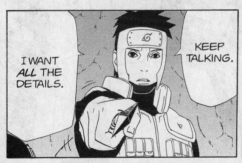

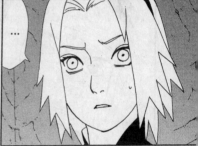

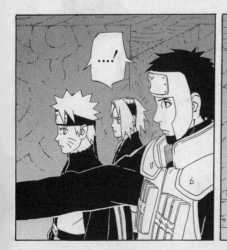

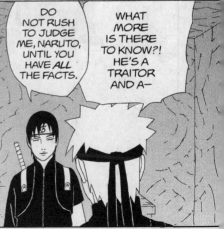

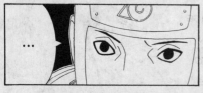

READ THIS WAY

I WAS ALSO ORDERED TO SECRETLY REPORT BACK OROCHIMARU'S ACTIVITIES TO LORD DANZO...
IN SHORT, TO ACT AS HIS SPY.
...
ENTER A CONSPIRACY WITH OROCHIMARU...
...WHILE PLAYING HIM AT THE SAME TIME?
THAT'S AN EXTREMELY DANGEROUS GAME...
...
WELL, IF KONOHA *DID* FALL, WE EXPECTED OROCHIMARU TO TRY TO BETRAY US AT SOME POINT, SO...
...CONSIDER THIS OUR WAY OF MAINTAINING THE UPPER HAND.
SO DANZO WANTS KONOHA FOR HIMSELF.
AND YOU WERE SENT IN, ALONE, TO SET ALL THIS IN MOTION...
I WAS SPECIFICALLY CHOSEN FOR THIS MISSION BECAUSE OF MY ABILITIES.

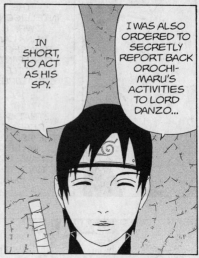

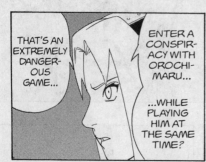

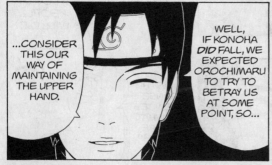

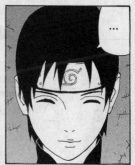

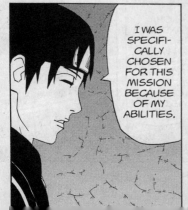

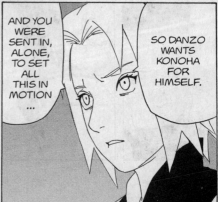

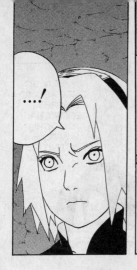

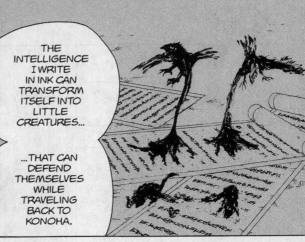

THE INTELLIGENCE I WRITE IN INK CAN TRANSFORM ITSELF INTO LITTLE CREATURES...
...THAT CAN DEFEND THEMSELVES WHILE TRAVELING BACK TO KONOHA.
...!
IF KONOHA FALLS, A LOT OF PEOPLE WILL DIE!
DO YOU HAVE ANY IDEA...
...OF THE CONSE-QUENCES OF WHAT YOU'RE DOING?!
...WELL ...
I'M JUST FOLLOW-ING ORDERS.
SAI... HOW CAN YOU...
OH, AND SAI IS JUST A NAME I WAS GIVEN FOR THE PURPOSES OF THIS MISSION...
I'M ACTUALLY *NOBODY*.
...

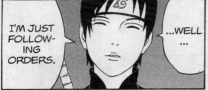

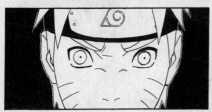

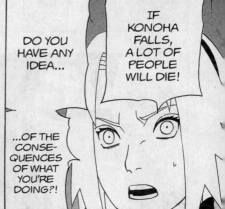

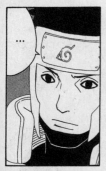

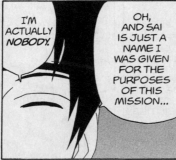

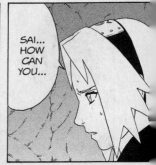

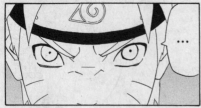

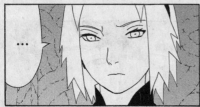

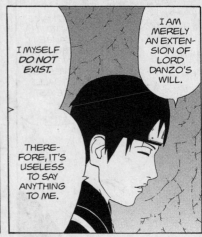

READ THIS WAY

I AM MERELY AN EXTENSION OF LORD DANZO'S WILL.
I MYSELF DO NOT EXIST.
THEREFORE, IT'S USELESS TO SAY ANYTHING TO ME.
...
...
THEN...
...WHY DO YOU CARRY AROUND THAT PICTURE BOOK?!
...

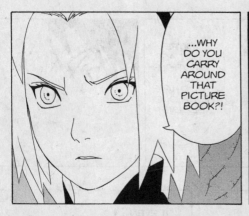

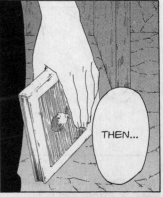

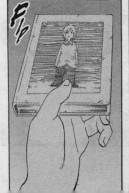

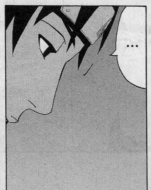

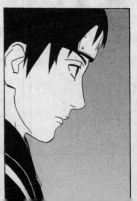

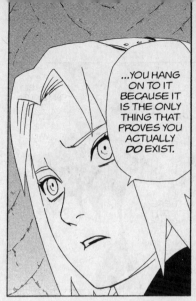

THE TWO BOYS ON THE COVERS ...
...ARE YOU AND YOUR BROTHER, RIGHT?
...YOU HANG ON TO IT BECAUSE IT IS THE ONLY THING THAT PROVES YOU ACTUALLY *DO* EXIST.
...
...?
YOU'RE NOT AS EMOTION-LESS AS YOU'D HAVE EVERYONE BELIEVE.
NOT EVEN SHINOBI CAN CUT OFF THEIR FEELINGS COM-PLETELY, YOU KNOW.
...
...

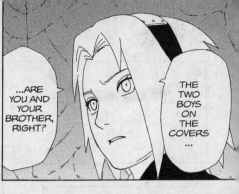

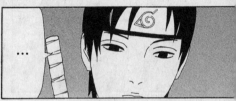

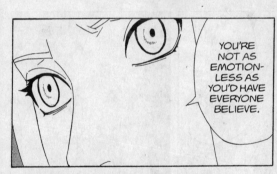

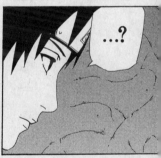

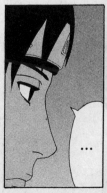

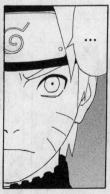

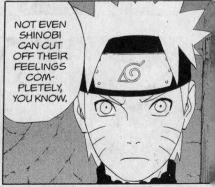

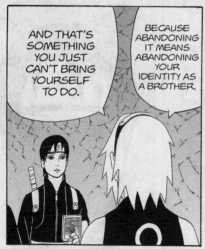

READ THIS WAY

HOW DOES POSSESSING THIS BOOK...
...TRANSLATE INTO PROVING MY EXISTENCE...?
BECAUSE ABANDONING IT MEANS ABANDONING YOUR IDENTITY AS A BROTHER.
AND THAT'S SOMETHING YOU JUST CAN'T BRING YOURSELF TO DO.
DO YOU KNOW WHY...?
...
...
BECAUSE YOUR BOND WITH YOUR OLDER BROTHER STILL MATTERS TO YOU. IT'S THAT IMPORTANT.

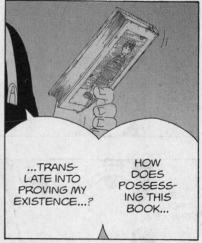

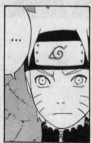

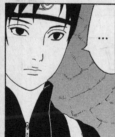

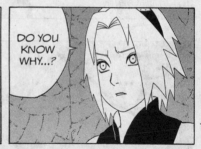

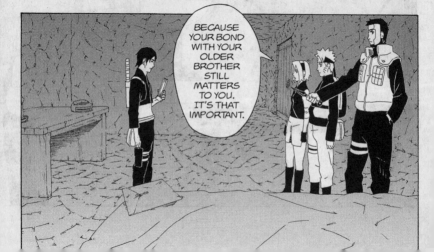

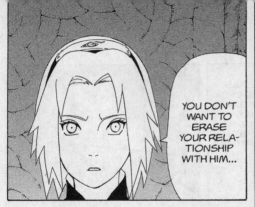

YOU DON'T WANT TO ERASE YOUR RELATIONSHIP WITH HIM...
...
...RELATIONSHIP...?
SORRY, BUT WE FLIPPED THROUGH YOUR PICTURE BOOK.
THE CENTERFOLD IS THE ONLY ILLUSTRATION THAT'S INCOMPLETE.
....!

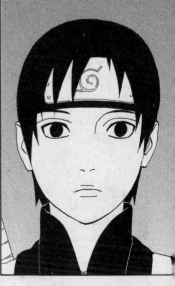

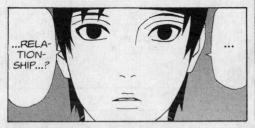

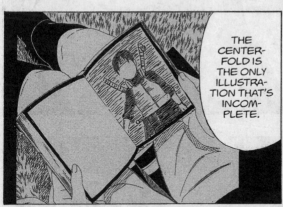

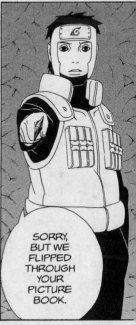

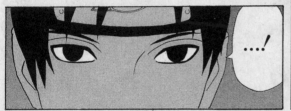

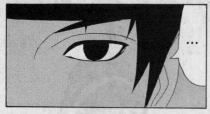

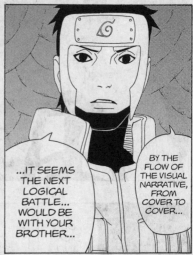

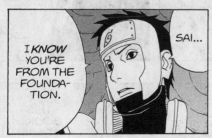

READ THIS WAY
BY THE FLOW OF THE VISUAL NARRATIVE, FROM COVER TO COVER...
...IT SEEMS THE NEXT LOGICAL BATTLE... WOULD BE WITH YOUR BROTHER...
...
SAI...
I KNOW YOU'RE FROM THE FOUNDATION.
YOU'VE RECEIVED SPECIAL TRAINING FROM DANZO TO KILL ALL EMOTIONS.
EVIL EXERCISES ...
...SIMILAR TO THAT WHICH USED TO BE PRACTICED IN KIRIGAKURE, THE VILLAGE OF BLOODY MIST.
...
SO, DID YOU DO IT? DID YOU KILL YOUR BROTHER ...?

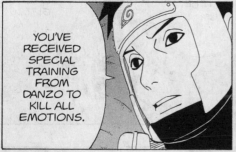

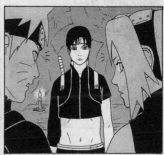

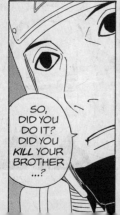

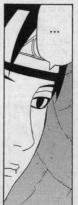

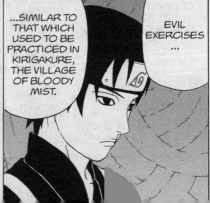

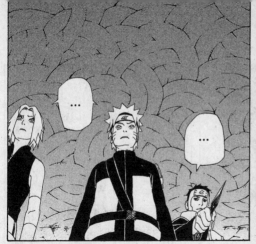

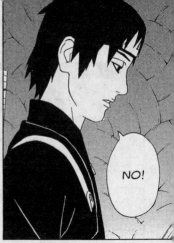

NO!
...
...
THIS BOOK... IT WAS SUPPOSED TO BE A GIFT...
BUT JUST BEFORE I COMPLETED IT, HE...
...GOT SICK AND DIED.
...
WE MAY NOT HAVE BEEN RELATED BY BLOOD...
...BUT HE WAS THE CLOSEST THING TO *FAMILY* I EVER HAD.

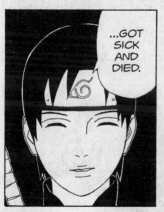

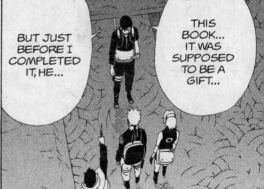

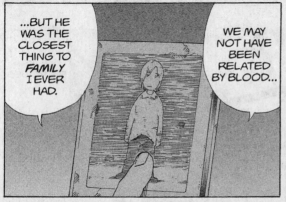

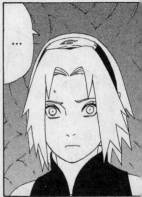

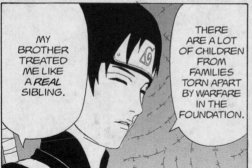

READ THIS WAY
...
THERE ARE A LOT OF CHILDREN FROM FAMILIES TORN APART BY WARFARE IN THE FOUNDATION.
MY BROTHER TREATED ME LIKE A *REAL* SIBLING.
THIS PICTURE BOOK... WHAT I WANTED TO SHOW HIM THE MOST WAS THE FINAL CENTERFOLD...
...BUT AFTER HE DIED...
...I COULDN'T REMEMBER WHAT I HAD BEEN PLANNING TO DRAW.
...
SHUFF
SHUFF
CLACK

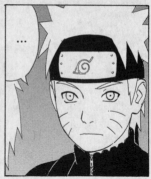

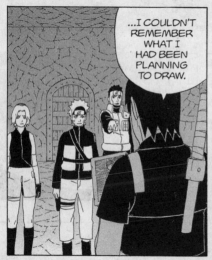

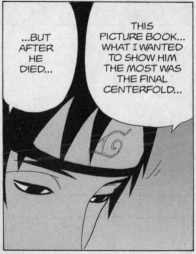

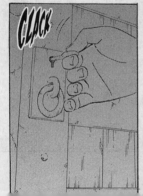

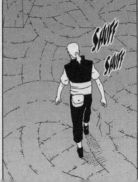

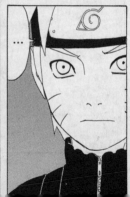

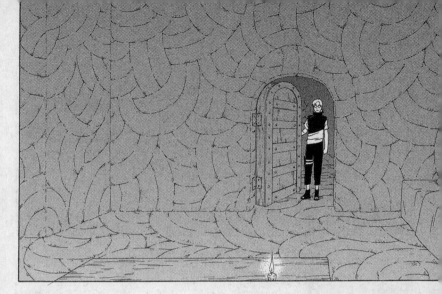

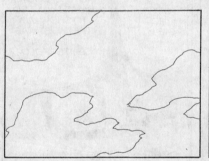

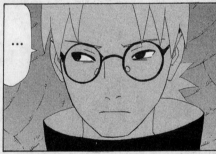

...

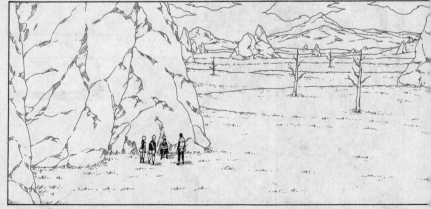

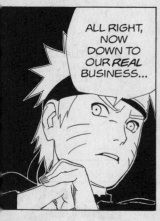

READ THIS WAY
SORRY, SAI...
...BUT I'M GOING TO HAVE TO LEAVE YOU HERE WITH MY DOPPELGANGER STANDING WATCH.
ALL RIGHT, NOW DOWN TO OUR REAL BUSINESS...
...LET'S GO RESCUE SASUKE!
...
AND WHAT IF HE DOESN'T WANT TO BE RESCUED?
...
...!

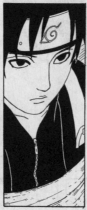

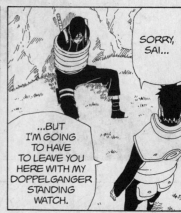

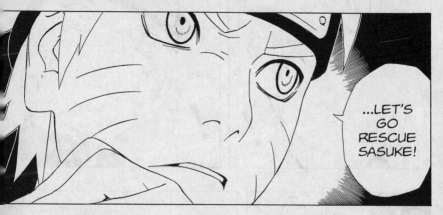

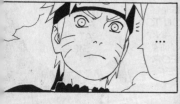

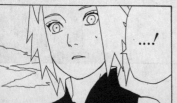

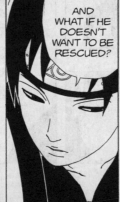

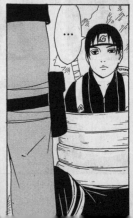

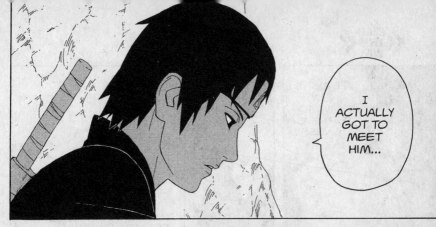

I ACTUALLY GOT TO MEET HIM...
!
!
...BUT OROCHI-MARU IS ALWAYS AT HIS SIDE.
CROSS HIM AND HE'LL TEAR YOU TO PIECES AND USE YOUR BODY FOR HIS EXPERI-MENTS.
BESIDES ...
...

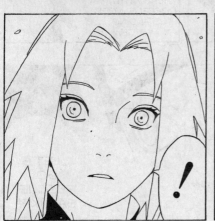

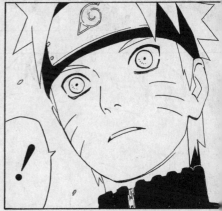

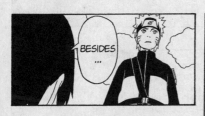

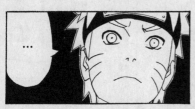

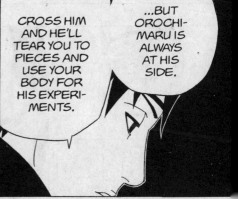

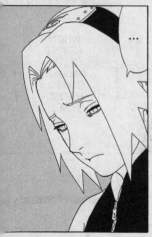

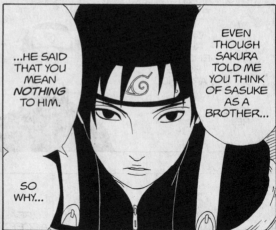

READ THIS WAY

EVEN THOUGH SAKURA TOLD ME YOU THINK OF SASUKE AS A BROTHER...
...HE SAID THAT YOU MEAN *NOTHING* TO HIM.
SO WHY...
...
...DO YOU STILL CARE SO MUCH?
WHY STAND UP TO THE LIKES OF OROCHIMARU AND RISK YOUR OWN LIFE...
...TO SAVE SOME-ONE WHO DOESN'T WANT TO BE SAVED?
WHY?
IT'S NOT LIKE ANYONE'S ORDER-ING YOU TO...
...

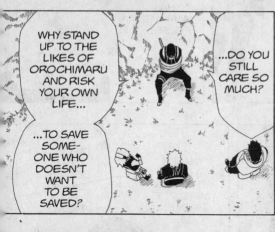

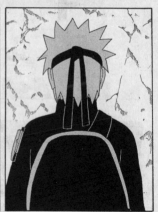

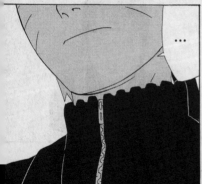

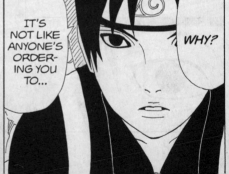

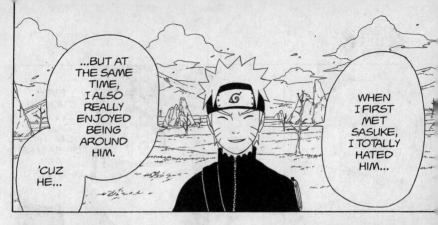

WHEN I FIRST MET SASUKE, I TOTALLY HATED HIM...
...BUT AT THE SAME TIME, I ALSO REALLY ENJOYED BEING AROUND HIM.
'CUZ HE...
...REALLY ACCEPTED ME MORE THAN ANYONE ELSE.
I'M DOING THIS BECAUSE SASUKE IS MY *FRIEND...*
...AND THAT'S A BOND THAT CAN *NEVER* BE BROKEN.
...
BOND...

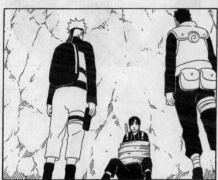

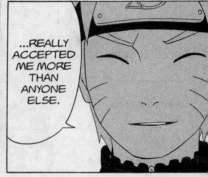

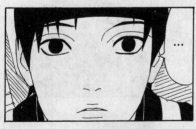

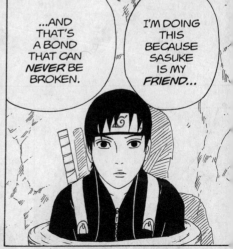

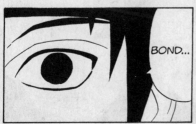

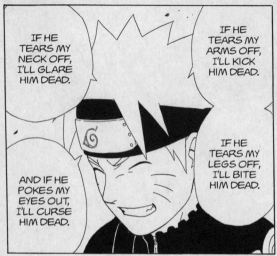

READ THIS WAY

BUT STILL...
...TO GO UP AGAINST OROCHI-MARU...?
IF HE TEARS MY ARMS OFF, I'LL KICK HIM DEAD.
IF HE TEARS MY LEGS OFF, I'LL BITE HIM DEAD.
IF HE TEARS MY NECK OFF, I'LL GLARE HIM DEAD.
AND IF HE POKES MY EYES OUT, I'LL CURSE HIM DEAD.
...
LET OROCHI-MARU TRY AND CUT ME TO PIECES...
...I'LL STILL FIND A WAY TO STEAL SASUKE BACK!

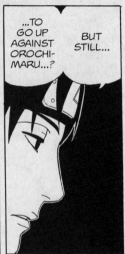

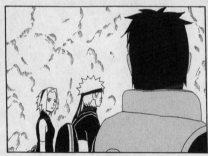

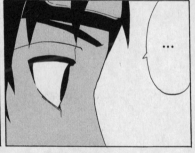

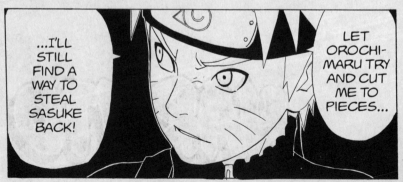

NARUTO

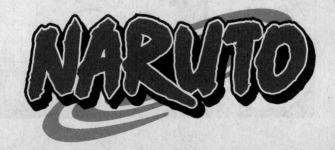

Number 304: Behind the Betrayal!!

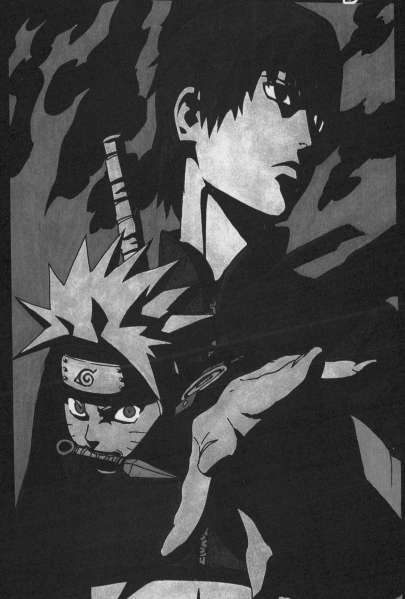

NARUTO

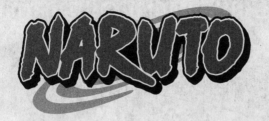

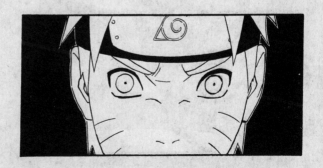

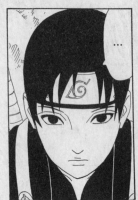

...

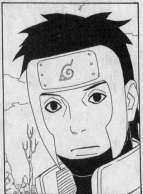

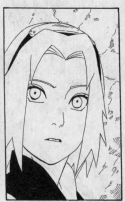

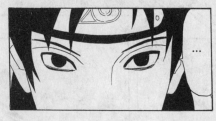

...

LET ME
CREATE
THE
LOOKOUT
SO WE
CAN GO
BACK IN.

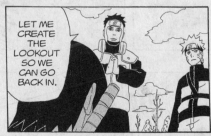

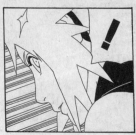

!

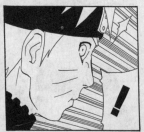

!

!

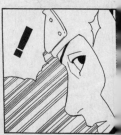

!

81

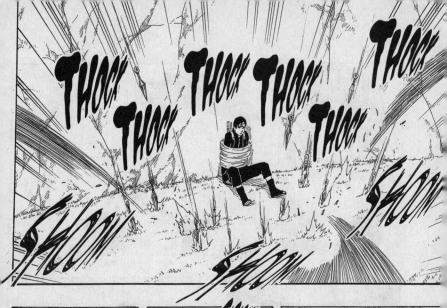

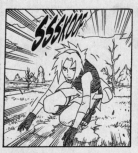

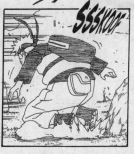

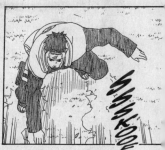

THOCK
THOCK
THOCK
THOCK
THOCK
THOCK
SHOOM
SHOOM
SHOOM
SSSKOOF
SSSKOOF
SSSKOOF
FROM THE LOOKS OF IT, SAI...
TAP
!
...YOU'VE BEEN CAPTURED.

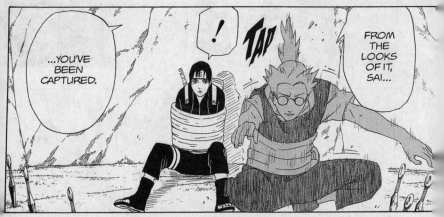

READ THIS WAY

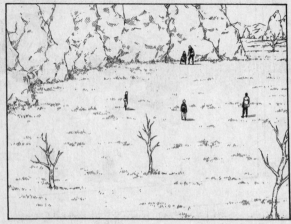

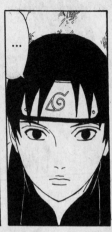

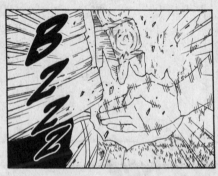

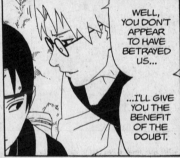

...
WELL, YOU DON'T APPEAR TO HAVE BETRAYED US...
...I'LL GIVE YOU THE BENEFIT OF THE DOUBT.
BZZZZ
THAT KABUTO... SUCH A PEST...
SHMP
IF YOU TRY TO STOP US, SAI...
...WE WON'T HOLD BACK!
...

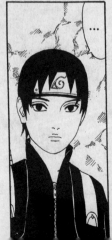

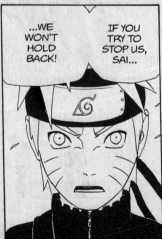

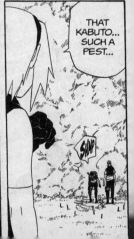

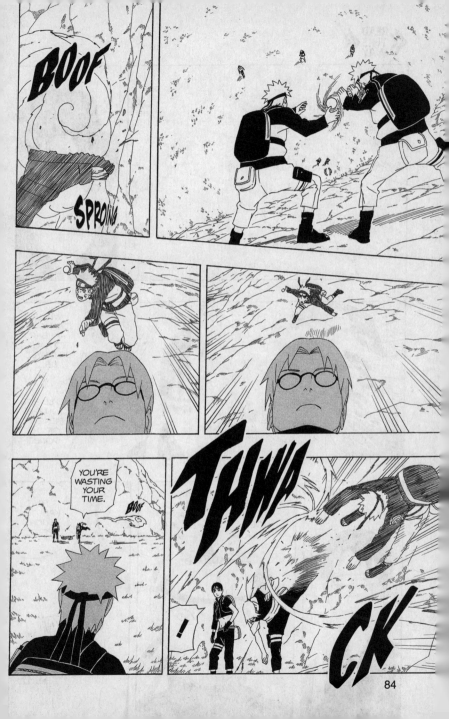

BOOF

SPROING

YOU'RE
WASTING
YOUR
TIME.

BOOF

THWA

CK

84

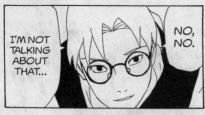

READ THIS WAY

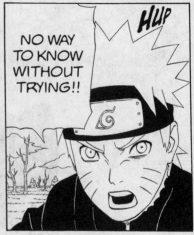

HUP
NO WAY TO KNOW WITHOUT TRYING!!
NO, NO.
I'M NOT TALKING ABOUT THAT...
...WHEN I LOOK AT YOU, IT'S REALLY PATHETIC...
PEOPLE CHANGE.
SASUKE IS NO LONGER THE BOY YOU KNEW.
...
...
?!

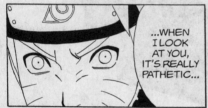

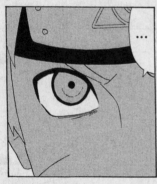

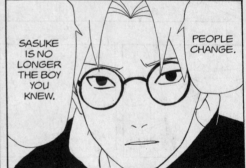

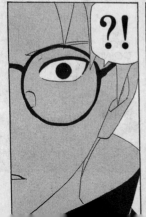

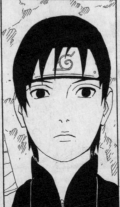

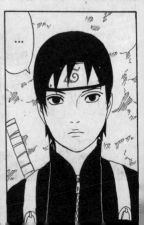

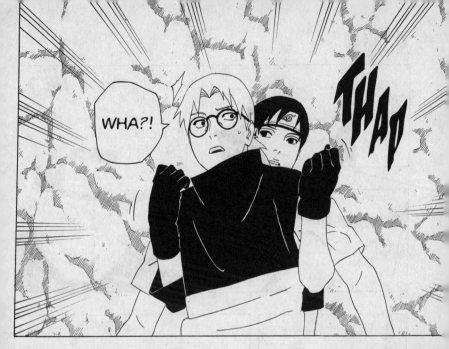

THAP
WHA?!
?!
?!
...!
WHAT ARE YOU DOING ...?!
IF PEOPLE CHANGE ...
...THEN SO CAN I.
WHAT?!

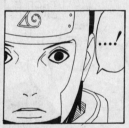

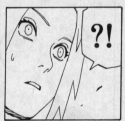

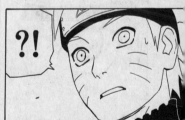

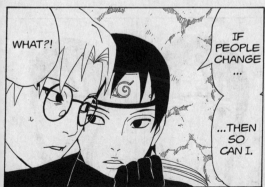

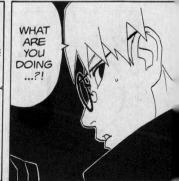

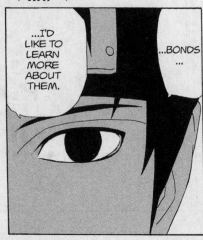

READ THIS WAY

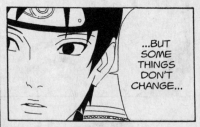

...BUT SOME THINGS DON'T CHANGE...
SAI...
...YOU ...
...BONDS ...
...I'D LIKE TO LEARN MORE ABOUT THEM.
...SAI...
THAT'S IT, SAI! HOLD HIM LIKE THAT A LITTLE LONGER ...
ZWOOOP

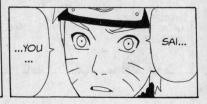

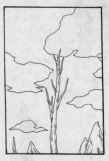

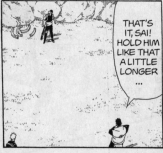

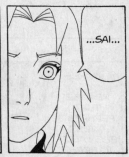

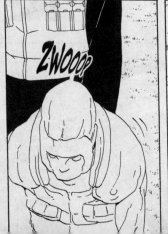

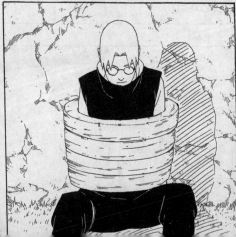

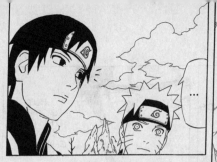

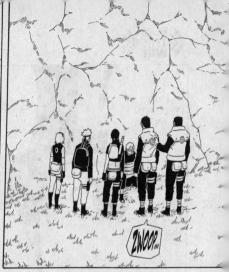

ZWOOP...
...
SAI...
WHAT'S... UP WITH YOU...?!
I'M CURIOUS ABOUT THIS BOND YOU AND SASUKE SHARE...
...THAT KEEPS YOU GOING AFTER HIM...
THE HOW AND WHY...
...
WATCHING THE TWO OF YOU...
...MAKES ME REALIZE THAT PERHAPS I HAVEN'T BEEN ABLE TO ERASE MY BOND WITH MY BROTHER.
AND IF SAKURA IS RIGHT...
...IF THAT REALLY IS SUCH AN IMPORTANT THING TO ME...
...PERHAPS I CAN FIGURE OUT WHY BY OBSERVING THE BOND BETWEEN YOU AND SASUKE.
THAT'S ALL...

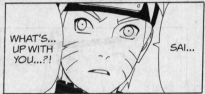

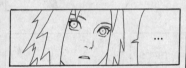

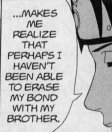

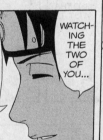

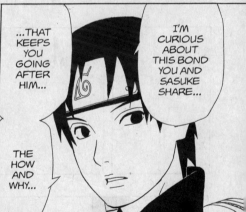

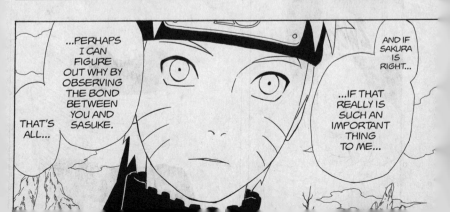

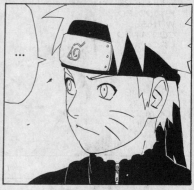

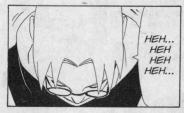

HEH... HEH HEH HEH...

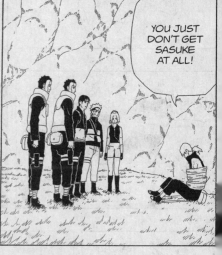

YOU JUST DON'T GET SASUKE AT ALL!

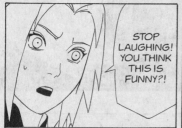

STOP LAUGHING! YOU THINK THIS IS FUNNY?!

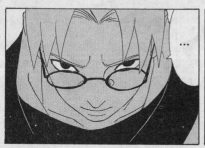

...

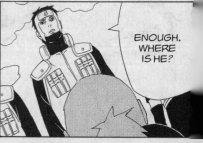

ENOUGH. WHERE IS HE?

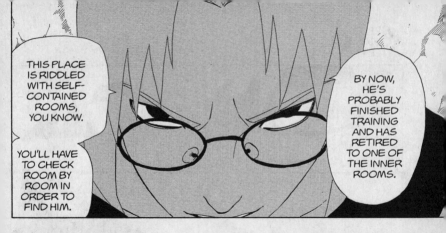

BY NOW, HE'S PROBABLY FINISHED TRAINING AND HAS RETIRED TO ONE OF THE INNER ROOMS.
THIS PLACE IS RIDDLED WITH SELF-CONTAINED ROOMS, YOU KNOW.
YOU'LL HAVE TO CHECK ROOM BY ROOM IN ORDER TO FIND HIM.
BUT IF YOU'RE NOT CAREFUL, POKING THE WRONG BUSH WILL FLUSH OUT SOME SNAKES.
FOR LORD OROCHIMARU'S PRIVATE QUARTERS ARE LOCATED NEAR THERE AS WELL.
...
THANK YOU FOR YOUR HONESTY.
OH NO, NO NEED TO THANK ME.
BECAUSE WE'RE GOING TO GET KILLED ANYWAY?
YES.
...
AS NARUTO SAID, NO WAY TO KNOW WITHOUT TRYING...

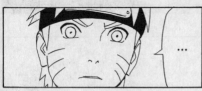

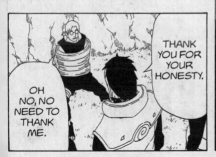

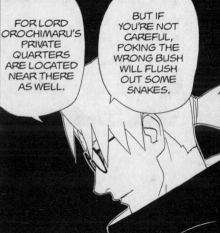

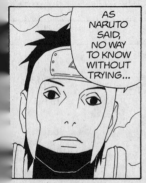

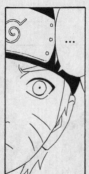

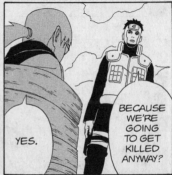

READ THIS WAY

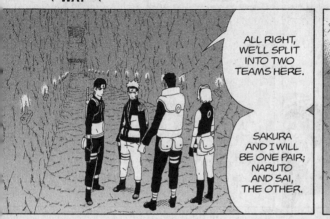

ALL RIGHT, WE'LL SPLIT INTO TWO TEAMS HERE.
SAKURA AND I WILL BE ONE PAIR; NARUTO AND SAI, THE OTHER.
IF ANYTHING GOES WRONG, JUST MANIPULATE YOUR CHAKRA.
IT'LL ACTIVATE THE TREE SEED INSIDE YOU AND ALERT ME.
I'LL COME RUNNING RIGHT AWAY.
...
SASUKE ...

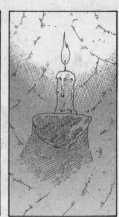

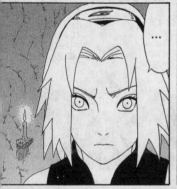

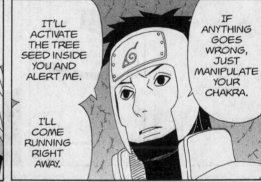

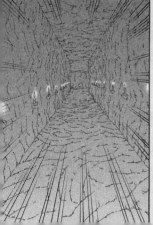

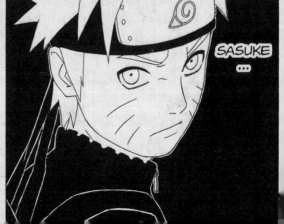

CLACK
HUF
HUF
HUF
HUF
...
NOPE NOT HERE EITHER...
THAT'S IT FOR THIS LEVEL.
LET'S CHECK THE NEXT ONE.
YUP!
WHUMP
OWW!
HOOSH

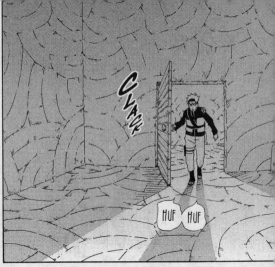

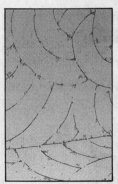

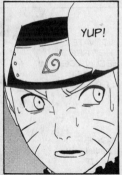

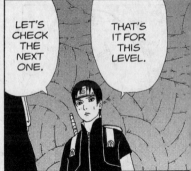

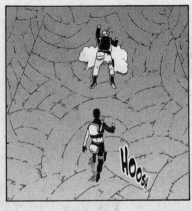

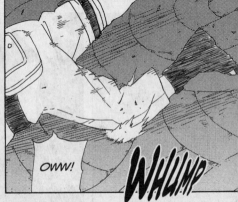

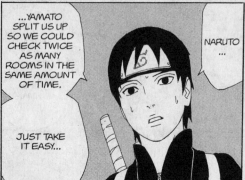

READ THIS WAY

HUF
HUF
...
NARUTO ...
...YAMATO SPLIT US UP SO WE COULD CHECK TWICE AS MANY ROOMS IN THE SAME AMOUNT OF TIME.
JUST TAKE IT EASY...
SHUT UP...! THERE'S NO TIME TO REST!
WE'VE GOT TO FIND SASUKE...
HUP
HUF
HUF
THUMP
I'M STILL WEAK FROM BEING IN THE NINE-TAILS STATE...
...
FAP

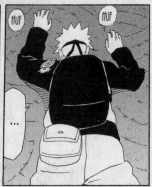

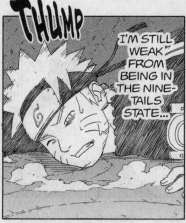

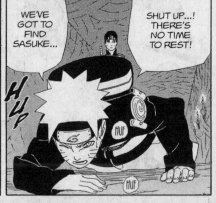

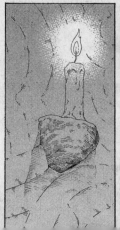

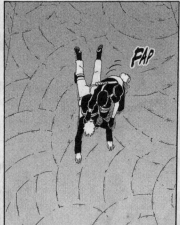

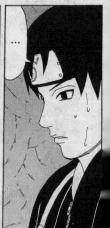

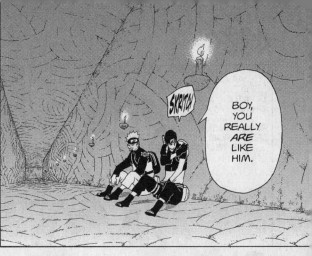

SKRITCH
BOY, YOU REALLY ARE LIKE HIM.
?
THIP
MY OLDER BROTHER.
HE WAS LOUD-MOUTHED AND IMPATIENT TOO...
...UN-REFINED... UNCOUTH...
...THE LIST OF HIS SHORT-COMINGS GOES ON AND ON...
...
BUT YOU KNOW... WHEN HE DID SOME-THING...
...HE ALWAYS GAVE IT HIS ALL, JUST LIKE YOU.
WATCHING YOU HAS HELPED ME REMEMBER HIM...

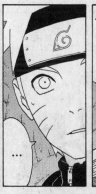

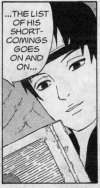

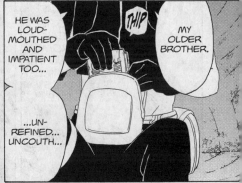

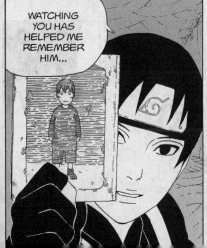

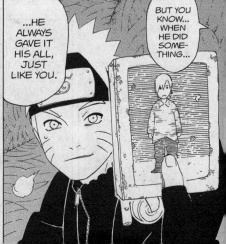

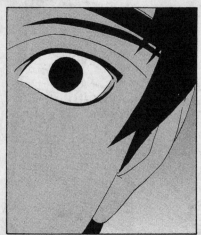

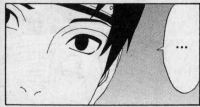

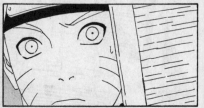

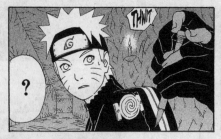

READ THIS WAY

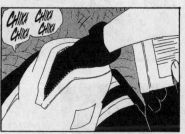

...
CHIKA CHIKA
CHIKA CHIKA
THWIT
?
SCRITCH SCRITCH
HEY!
DRAWING?! NOW?!
I REMEM-BERED...
I FINALLY REMEM-BERED...!

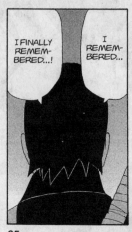

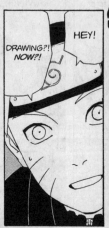

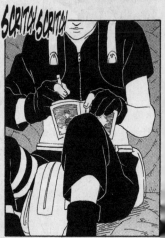

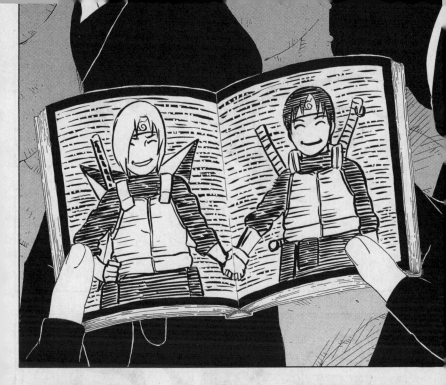

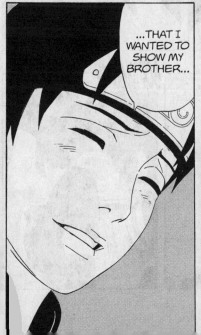

THE DREAM DRAWING...
...THAT I WANTED TO SHOW MY BROTHER...

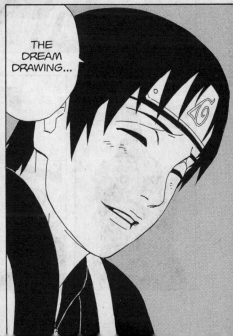

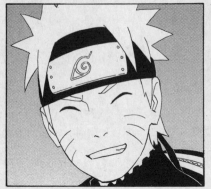

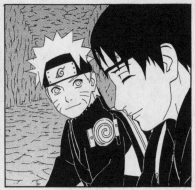

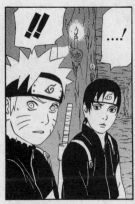

!!

....!

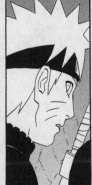

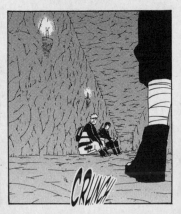

CRUNCH

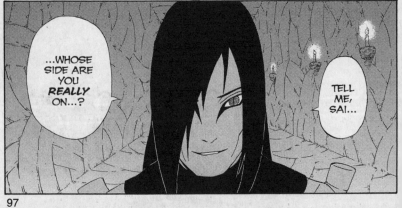

...WHOSE SIDE ARE YOU *REALLY* ON...?

TELL ME, SAI...

NARUTO

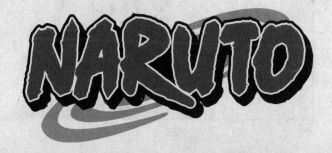

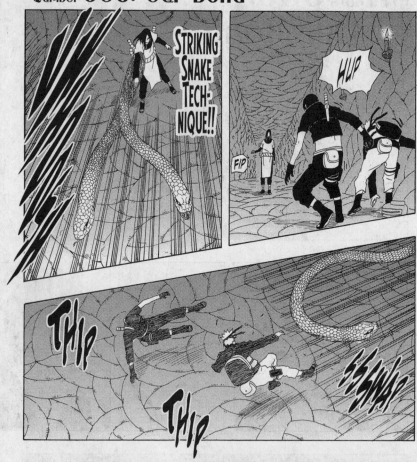

STRIKING SNAKE TECHNIQUE!!

HLIP

FIP

THIP

THIP

SSSNAP

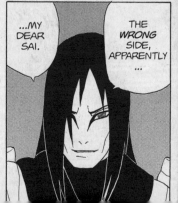

...MY DEAR SAI.

THE *WRONG* SIDE, APPARENTLY...

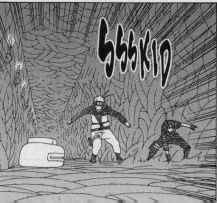

SSSKID

Number 305:
Our Bond
!
YOU GO FIND SASUKE, SAI...
...LEAVE OL' SNAKE FACE TO ME!
...
GO!
ALL RIGHT.
WE'LL MEET YOU OUTSIDE... ...GOOD LUCK...
HOOSH

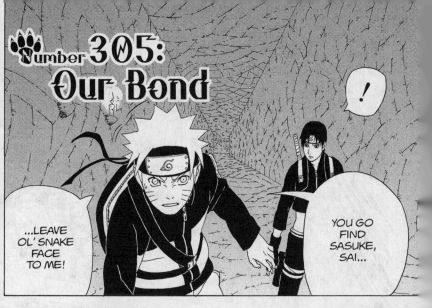

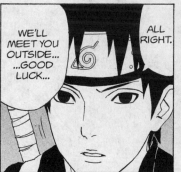

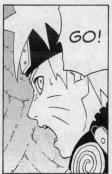

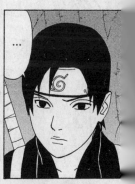

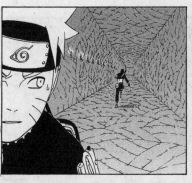

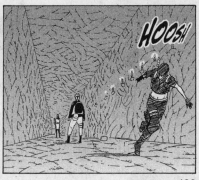

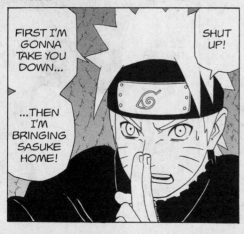

READ THIS WAY

SO YOU CAME HERE TO RETRIEVE SASUKE, EH?
I COMMEND YOUR ZEAL, BUT I ASSURE YOU, THE OUT-COME OF THIS WILL NOT BE IN YOUR FAVOR...
SHUT UP!
FIRST I'M GONNA TAKE YOU DOWN...
...THEN I'M BRINGING SASUKE HOME!
HE'S NOT HERE EITHER...
?!

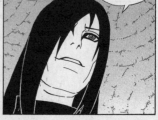

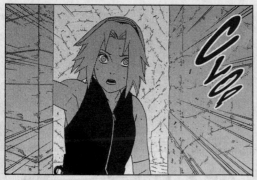

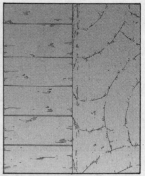

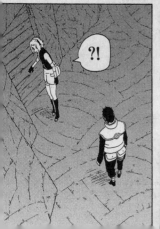

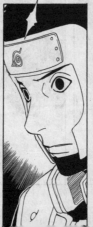

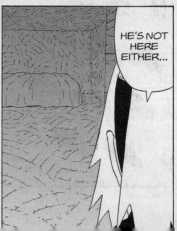

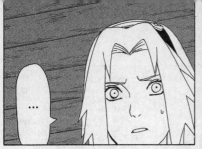

...

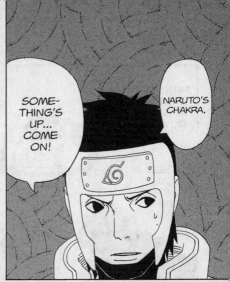

NARUTO'S CHAKRA.

SOME-THING'S UP... COME ON!

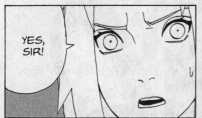

YES, SIR!

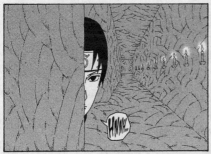

HNNH...

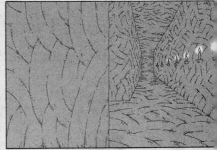

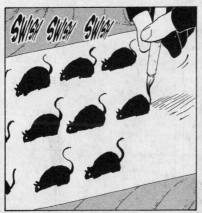

SWISH SWISH SWISH

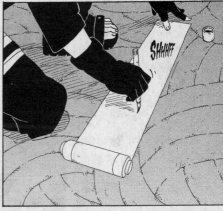

SHHHFF

READ THIS WAY

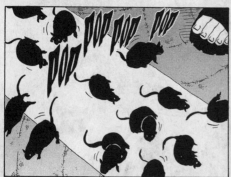

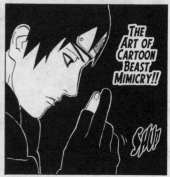

THE ART OF CARTOON BEAST MIMICRY!!
SHOP
POP POP POP POP POP
WHOOSH
HUF
HUF
WHAT HAPPENED TO ALL YOUR ENERGY?
HUF
BOOF
HUF
!

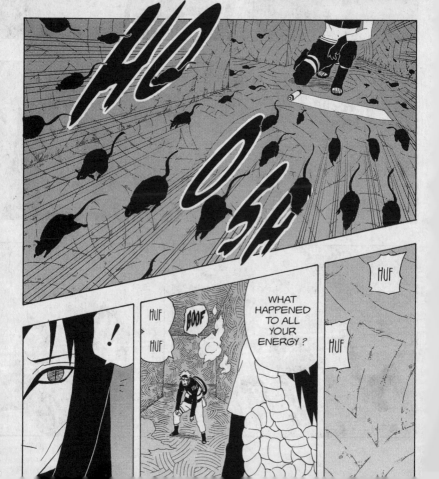

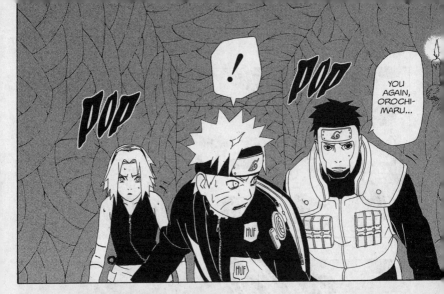

YOU AGAIN, OROCHI-MARU...
POP
!
POP
...
HUMPH...
REMEMBER, NARUTO... THIS MAKES TWICE THAT I'VE LET YOU LIVE.
...A DEBT I HOPE YOU'LL SOMEDAY REPAY BY ELIMINATING AT LEAST ONE MORE AKATSUKI MEMBER FOR ME...
AND NOW, IF YOU'LL EXCUSE ME, I'VE GOT SOME UNFINISHED BUSINESS...
...WITH SAI...
WHISP

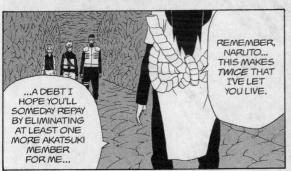

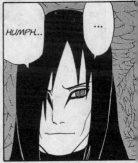

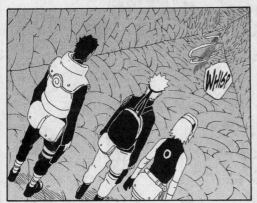

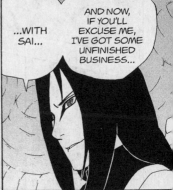

READ THIS WAY

JERK ...!
PHEW ...
!
NARUTO, WHERE'S SAI?
OH NO... HE WENT TO LOOK FOR SASUKE!
WE'VE GOT TO FIND THEM BEFORE OROCHI-MARU DOES.
SQUEEEEZE
SLIP...

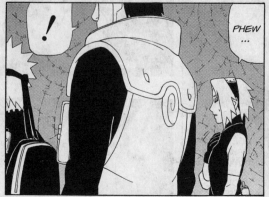

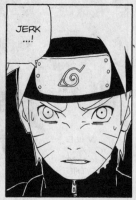

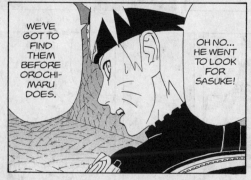

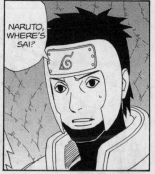

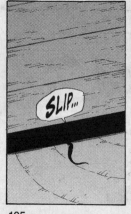

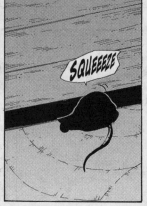

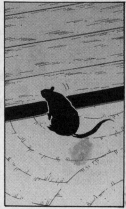

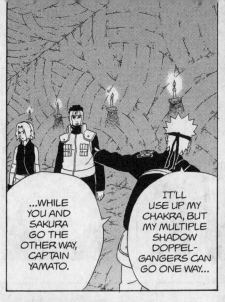

IT'LL USE UP MY CHAKRA, BUT MY MULTIPLE SHADOW DOPPEL-GANGERS CAN GO ONE WAY...
...WHILE YOU AND SAKURA GO THE OTHER WAY, CAPTAIN YAMATO.
!
THE CENTER-FOLD...
YEAH...
HE FINALLY REMEM-BERED...
HE SAID THAT WAS THE DREAM DRAWING OF THE TWO OF THEM...
...THAT HE HAD WANTED TO SHOW HIS BROTHER.

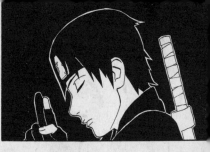

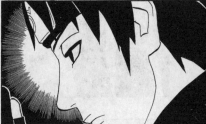

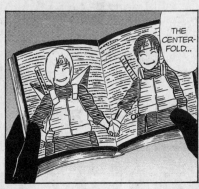

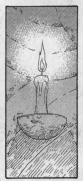

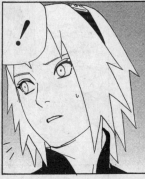

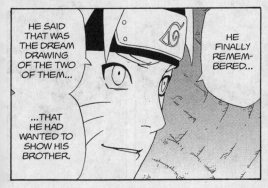

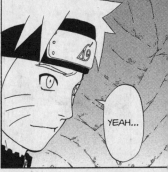

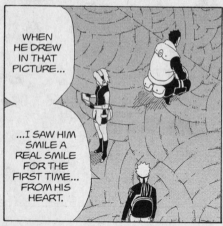

READ THIS WAY
THEY'RE BOTH SMILING ...
WHEN HE DREW IN THAT PICTURE...
...I SAW HIM SMILE A REAL SMILE FOR THE FIRST TIME... FROM HIS HEART.
!

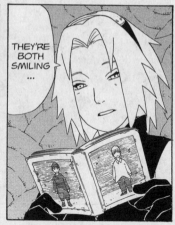

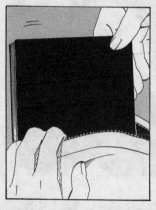

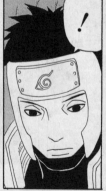

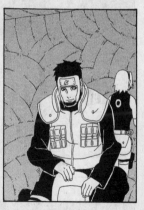

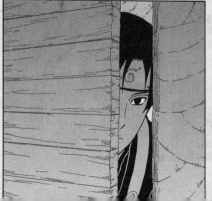

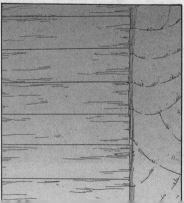

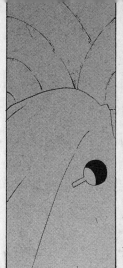
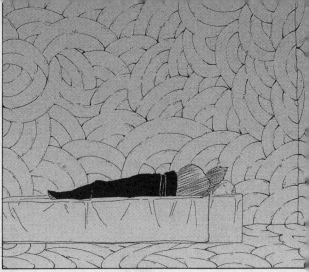

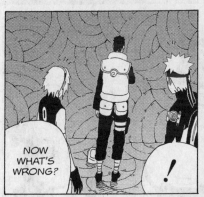

NOW
WHAT'S
WRONG?

!

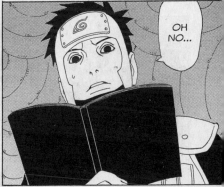

OH
NO...

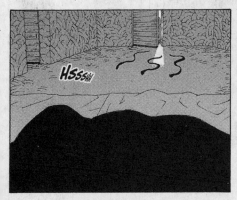

HSSS

ร ร

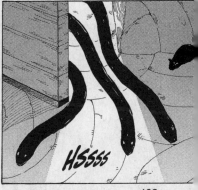

HSSSS

READ THIS WAY

...I FOUND THIS IN SAI'S PACK...
THIS TYPE OF BINGO BOOK IS STANDARD ISSUE FOR BLACK OPS MEMBERS.
IT LISTS ONE'S TARGETS FOR ASSASSINATION.
AN ASSASSINATION LIST?
...SO WHAT DO THE X MARKS REPRESENT?
THE PEOPLE HE'S ALREADY KILLED.
...
BUT WHY WOULD SAI HAVE SOMETHING LIKE...
FLIP FLIP
!
?!

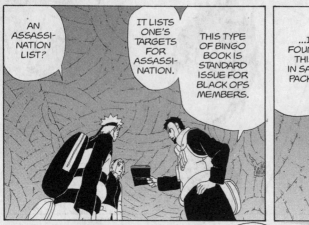

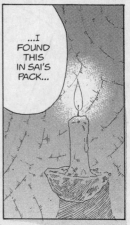

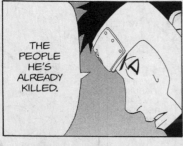

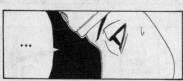

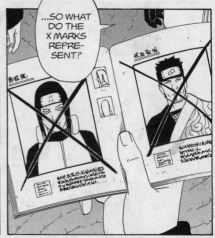

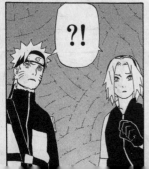

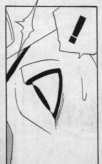

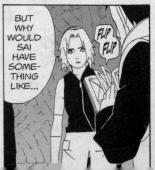

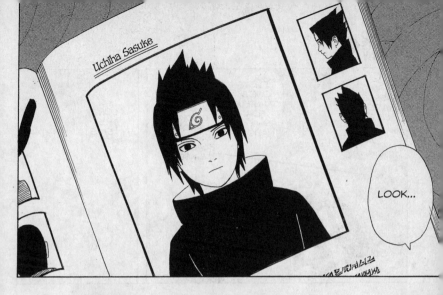

Uchiha Sasuke
LOOK...
N-
NO...
WAIT...
...WHY IS SASUKE ON SAI'S ASSASSINATION LIST?
HIS FACE ISN'T X'ED OUT YET...
...HMNNN ...
...SO *THAT'S* WHAT THIS IS ABOUT...!
WHAT IS?! WHAT'S THIS ABOUT ...?!
...
SAI'S MISSION... WASN'T TO BECOME THE CONDUIT BETWEEN DANZO AND OROCHIMARU...
...HIS *REAL* TOP-SECRET MISSION...

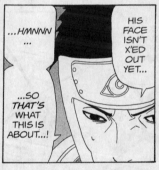

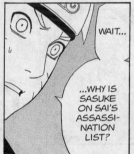

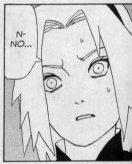

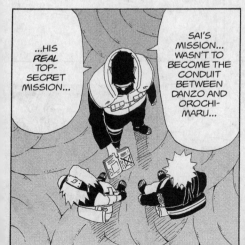

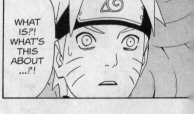

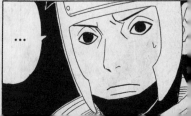

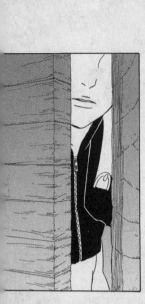

...IS TO ASSASSINATE SASUKE.
HSSSS
BUT...
...BUT THAT'S NOT POSSIBLE!
I MEAN, JUST NOW HE SAID HE WAS GOING TO RESCUE SASUKE...!
AND I SAW HIM SMILE FROM HIS HEART...
...I REALLY THINK HE'S CHANGED...
UNLESS IT WAS ALL JUST AN ACT TO DRAW YOU OUT...

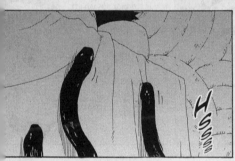

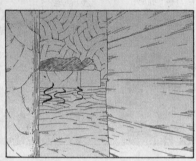

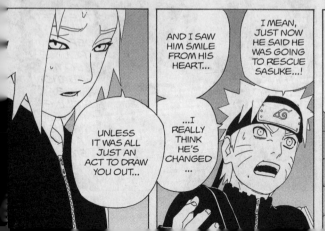

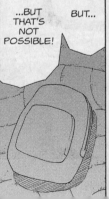

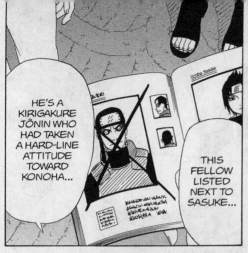

THE OWNER OF THIS BINGO BOOK COULD DO IT.
LOOK AT THIS...
THIS FELLOW LISTED NEXT TO SASUKE...
HE'S A KIRIGAKURE JÔNIN WHO HAD TAKEN A HARD-LINE ATTITUDE TOWARD KONOHA...
Uchiha Sasuke
SO SAI SEEMS TO HAVE BEEN ASSIGNED TO DISPOSE OF INDIVIDUALS WHO POSE A THREAT TO KONOHA...
...AND SASUKE IS ONE OF THOSE TOO...
...
A SMILE CAN HELP ONE ACHIEVE ONE'S GOALS...
THAT REMINDS ME... THAT TIME I SLUGGED SAI...
THE BEST WAY TO DEFUSE A TROUBLE-SOME SITUATION IS BY SMILING. ...EVEN IF IT IS A FAKE SMILE...
...IT WILL FOOL MORE PEOPLE THAN YOU THINK ...OR SO I'VE READ.
...

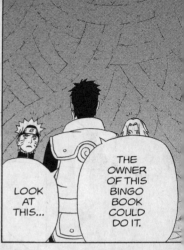

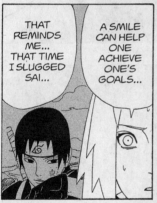

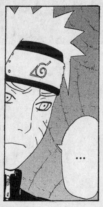

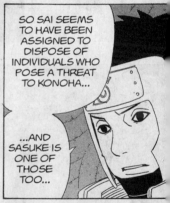

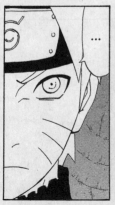

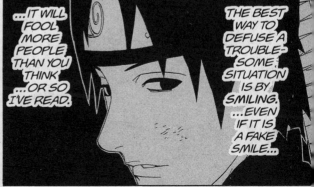

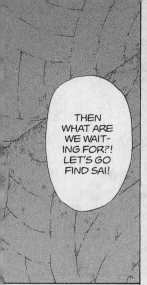

DANZO'S ULTIMATE GOAL IS TO DESTROY OROCHIMARU'S FUTURE HOST BODY.
THAT'S WHY SAI WAS TRYING TO GET CLOSE TO OROCHI-MARU.
THEY WEREN'T GOING TO BETRAY KONOHA. IN FACT, QUITE THE OPPOSITE...
...IT'S PRECISELY THE KIND OF TACTIC THE FOUNDA-TION WOULD EMPLOY.
THEN WHAT ARE WE WAIT-ING FOR?! LET'S GO FIND SAI!
...WHO'S THERE?
MY COVER'S BEEN BLOWN...
...BUT I CAN STILL TAKE ACTION...
WHAT DO YOU WANT?
...I HE TO

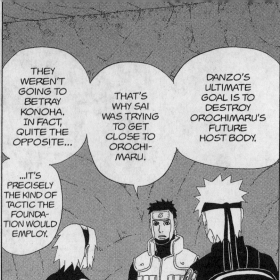

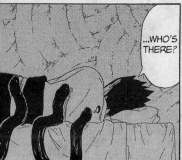

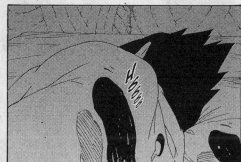

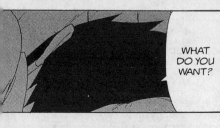

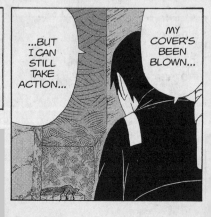

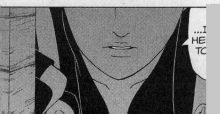

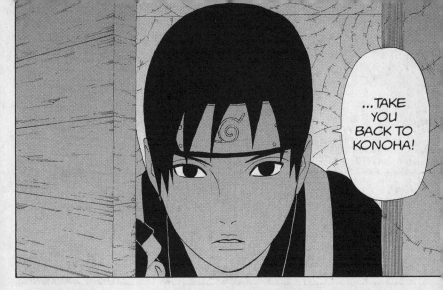

...TAKE YOU BACK TO KONOHA!
...
MY MISSION WAS TO KILL YOU.
AT FIRST, I WAS GOING TO, BUT...
...
'CUZ HE...
...REALLY ACCEPTED ME MORE THAN ANYONE ELSE.
NARUTO...
...THINKS OF SASUKE AS A BROTHER.

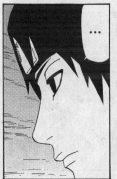

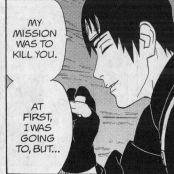

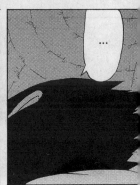

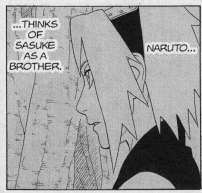

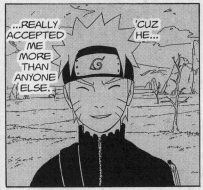

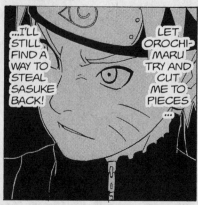

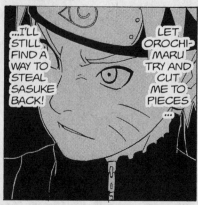

...I'LL STILL FIND A WAY TO STEAL SASUKE BACK! LET OROCHIMARU TRY AND CUT ME TO PIECES...

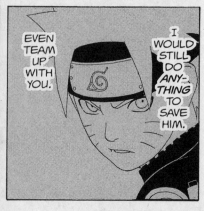

EVEN TEAM UP WITH YOU. I WOULD STILL DO ANYTHING TO SAVE HIM.

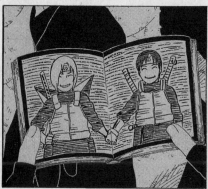

...AND THAT'S A BOND THAT CAN NEVER BE BROKEN.

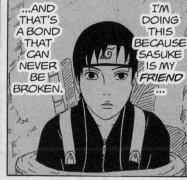

I'M DOING THIS BECAUSE SASUKE IS MY FRIEND...

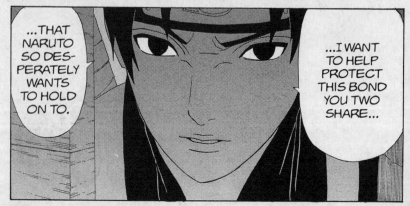

...THAT NARUTO SO DESPERATELY WANTS TO HOLD ON TO. ...I WANT TO HELP PROTECT THIS BOND YOU TWO SHARE...

115

NARUTO

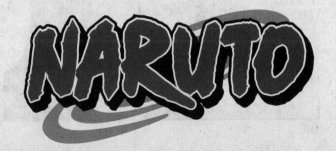

Number 306: The Reunion...!!

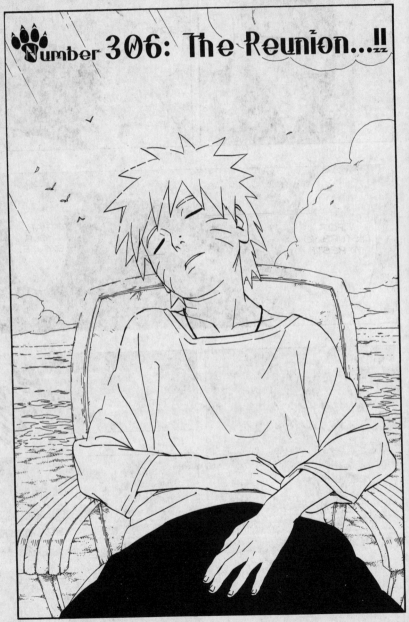

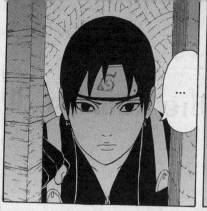

A BOND ...?
...
THAT'S YOUR EXCUSE...
...FOR DISTURBING MY REST?
HOOSH
WHSSH
BOOF

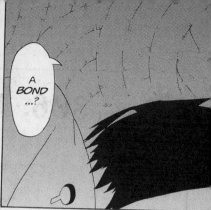

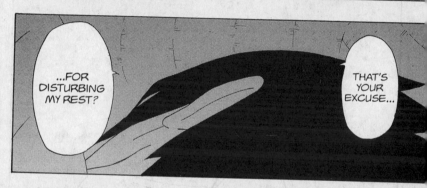

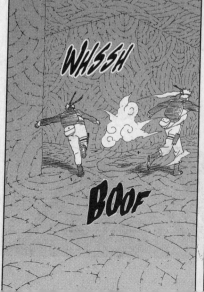

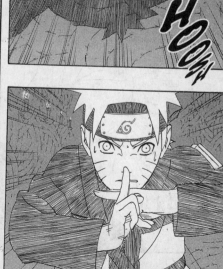

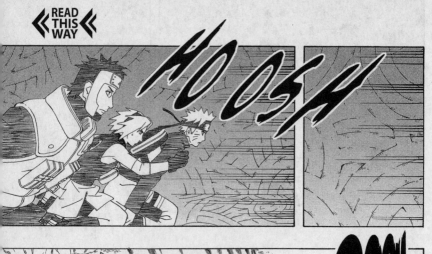

READ THIS WAY
WHOOSH
BOOM
KA
IT MUST BE SASUKE...
...HE'S SO GRUMPY WHEN HE FIRST WAKES UP...
WHAT WAS THAT ...?
!
!

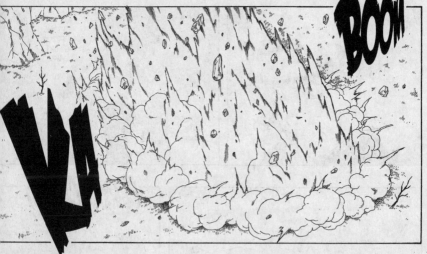

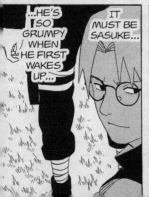

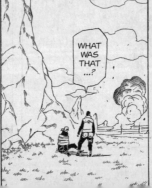

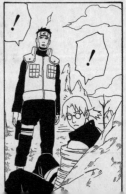

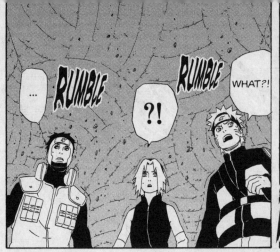

... RUMBLE RUMBLE WHAT?!

?!

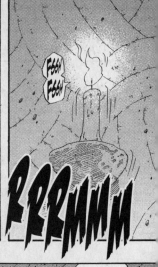

FSSH FSSH

RRRMMM

....!

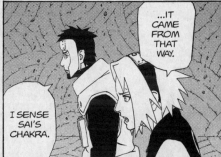

...IT CAME FROM THAT WAY.

I SENSE SAI'S CHAKRA.

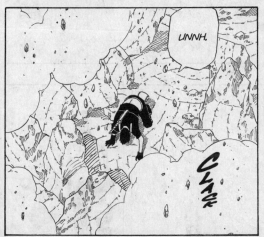

UNNH.

CLACK

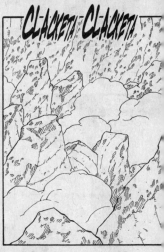

CLACKETA CLACKETA

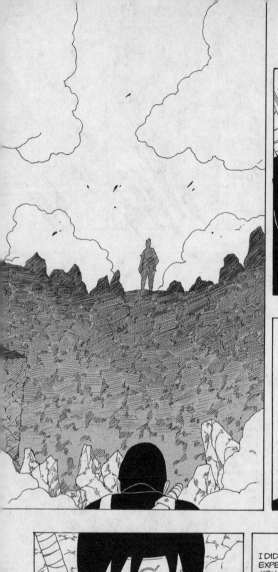

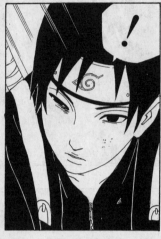

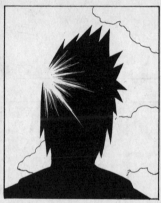

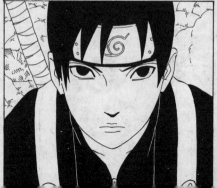

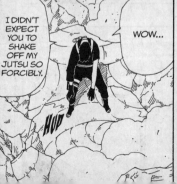

I DIDN'T EXPECT YOU TO SHAKE OFF MY JUTSU SO FORCIBLY.

WOW...

HOP

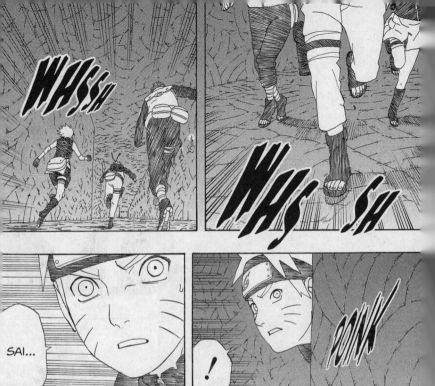

WHSSH

WHSSH

SAI...

!

POINK

FOUND YOU...

TAP

TAP

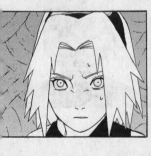

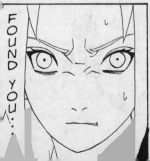

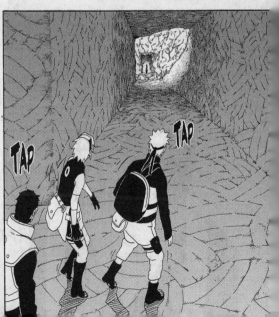

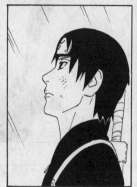

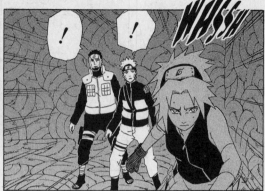

READ THIS WAY

WHSSH
!
!
CRUNCH
FAP
SAKURA! WHAT'RE YOU DOING?!
QUIET, YOU! I'M ASKING THE QUES-TIONS HERE!
AND THIS TIME, YOU BETTER NOT LIE!
WELL, WELL, WELL... IF IT ISN'T SAKURA...
!

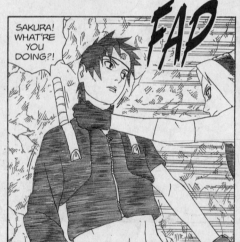

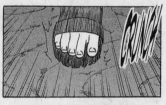

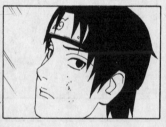

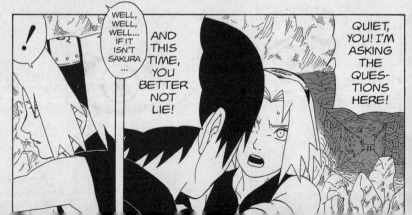

...THAT VOICE!...

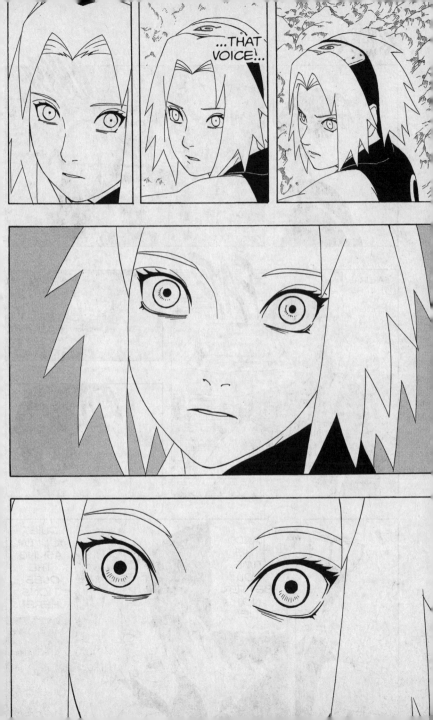

READ THIS WAY

FUP
?!
?!
...
...S-
SASUKE
...?

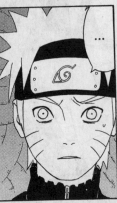

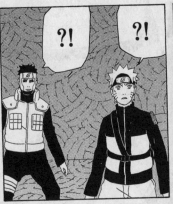

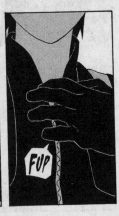

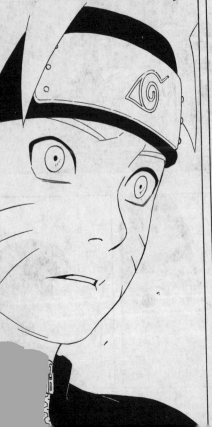

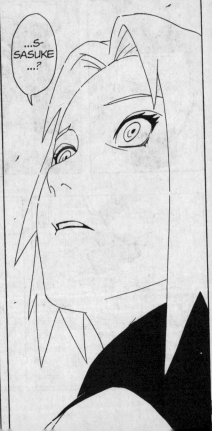

...
WHSSH
...
...
...!
HUF!
HUF!

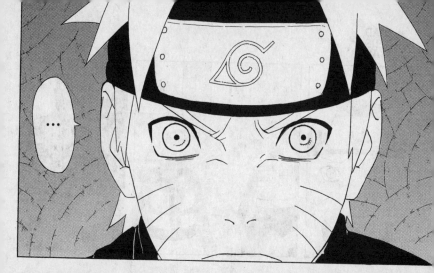

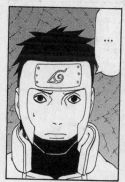

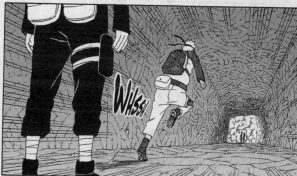

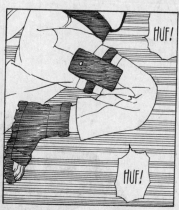

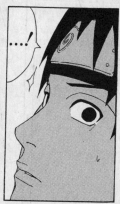

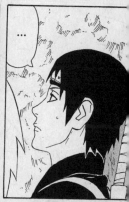

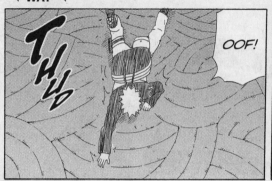

OOF!

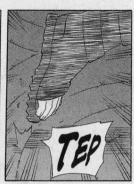

TEP

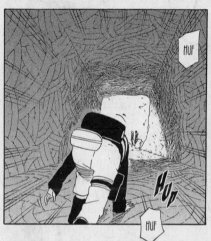

HUF

HUF

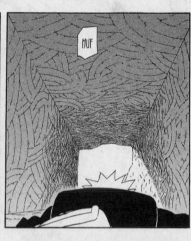

HUF

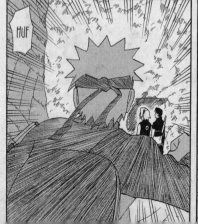

HUF

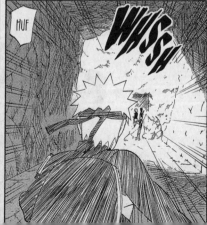

HUF

WHSSH

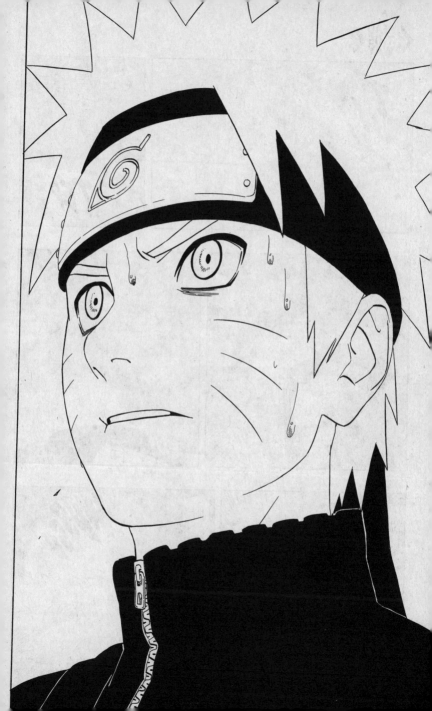

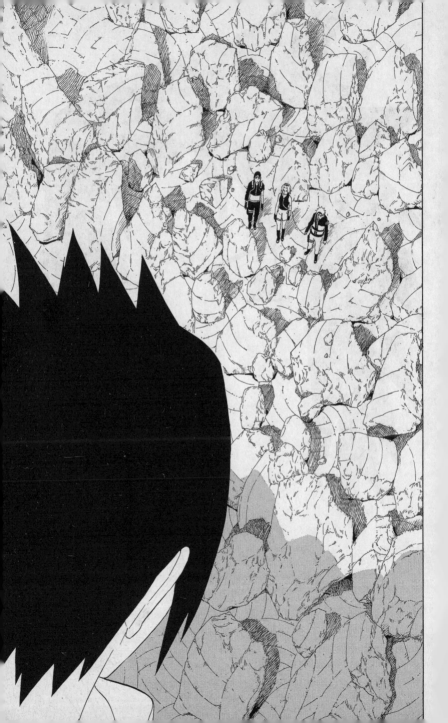

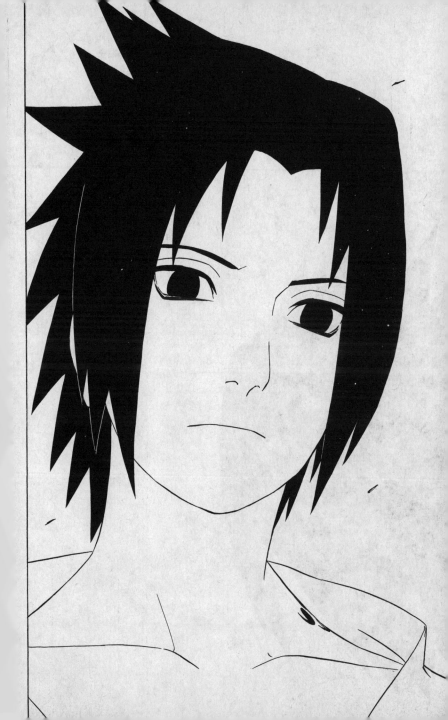

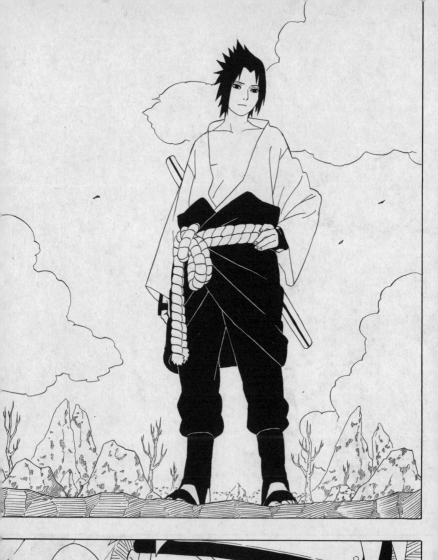

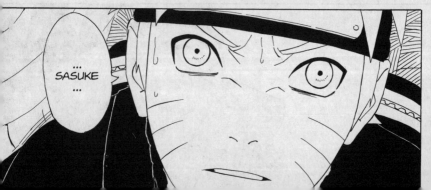

...SASUKE...

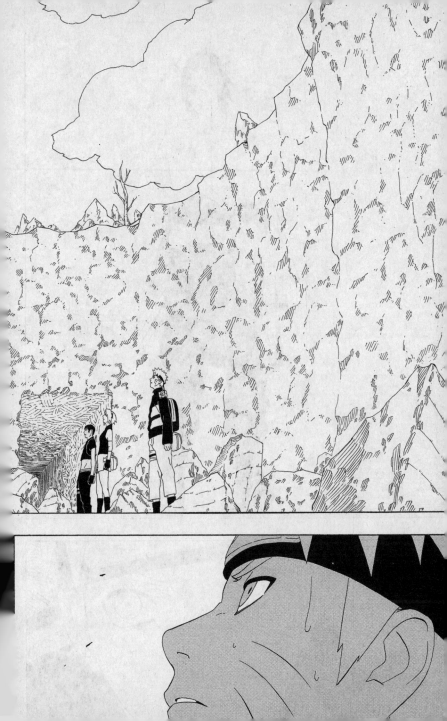

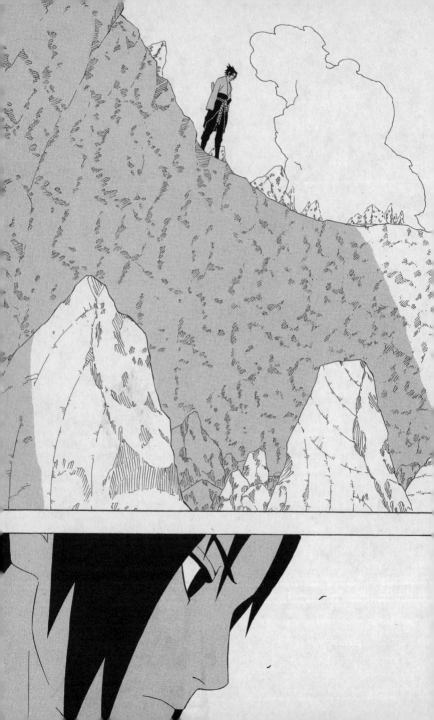

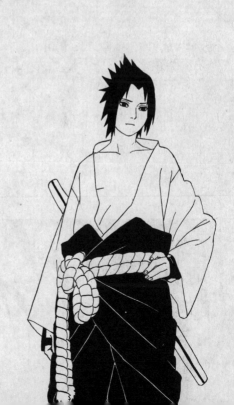

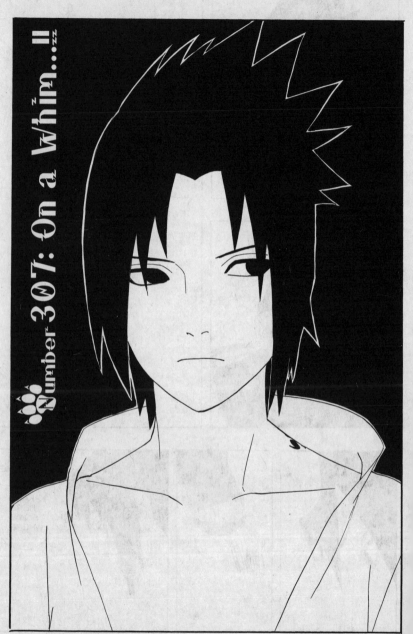

Number 307: On a Whim...!!

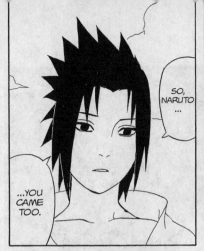

SO, NARUTO...

...YOU CAME TOO.

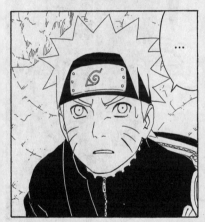

...

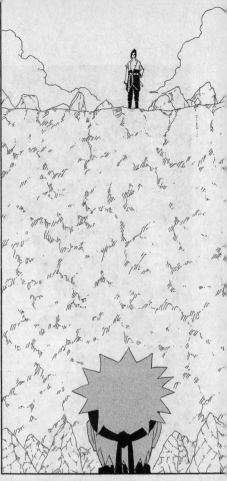

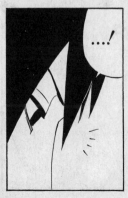

....!

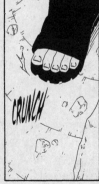

CRUNCH

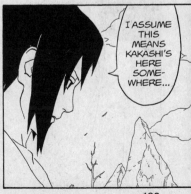

I ASSUME THIS MEANS KAKASHI'S HERE SOME- WHERE...

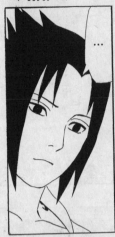

...

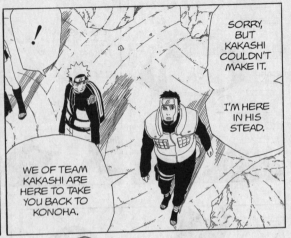

!

SORRY, BUT KAKASHI COULDN'T MAKE IT.

I'M HERE IN HIS STEAD.

WE OF TEAM KAKASHI ARE HERE TO TAKE YOU BACK TO KONOHA.

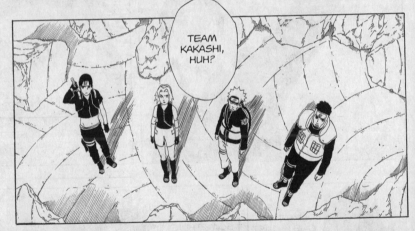

TEAM KAKASHI, HUH?

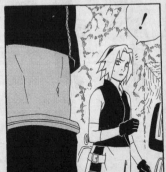

!

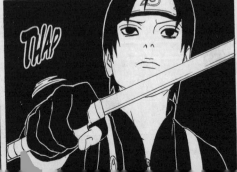

THAP

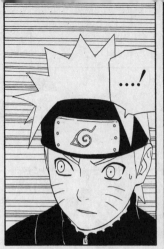

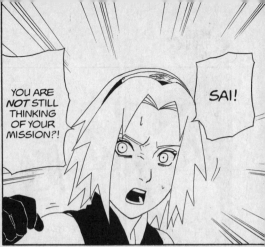

SAI!
YOU ARE NOT STILL THINKING OF YOUR MISSION?!
...!
!
IS HE MY STAND-IN...?
HE SAID SOMETHING ABOUT WANTING TO PROTECT THE BOND BETWEEN ME AND NARUTO, BUT...
... LOOKS LIKE THIS ONE IS JUST ANOTHER WEAKLING TOO.

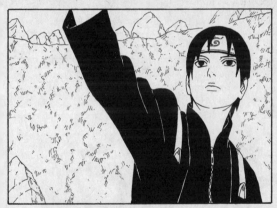

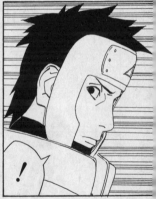

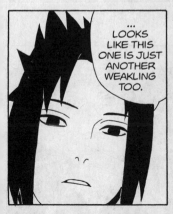

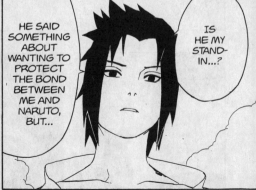

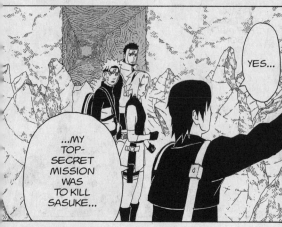

READ THIS WAY

WHAT?
YES...
...MY TOP-SECRET MISSION WAS TO KILL SASUKE...
...BUT I'M DONE FOLLOWING ORDERS.
FROM NOW ON, I WANT TO THINK FOR MYSELF.
I FEEL LIKE YOU CAN HELP ME REMEMBER, NARUTO...
...BRING BACK THOSE OLD FEELINGS I THOUGHT WERE LOST...
THE THINGS THAT WERE ONCE REALLY IMPORTANT TO ME...
AS FOR YOU, SASUKE...

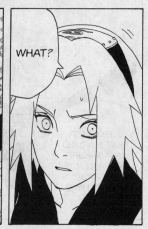

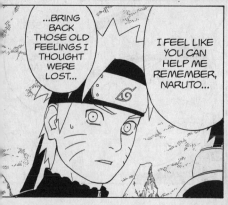

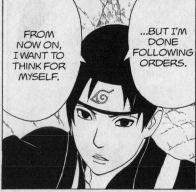

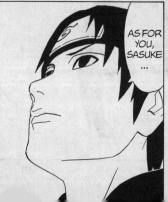

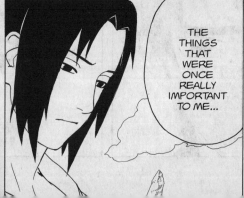

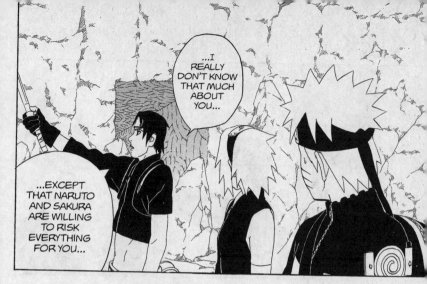

...I REALLY DON'T KNOW THAT MUCH ABOUT YOU...
...EXCEPT THAT NARUTO AND SAKURA ARE WILLING TO RISK EVERYTHING FOR YOU...
...TO KEEP THAT SPECIAL BOND YOU ALL SHARE ALIVE...
...IN THE NAME OF FRIEND-SHIP.
I STILL DON'T UNDER-STAND IT FULLY...
...BUT I THINK *YOU* DO, SASUKE.
DON'T YOU?

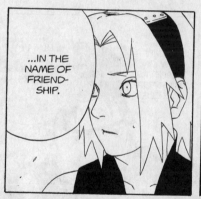

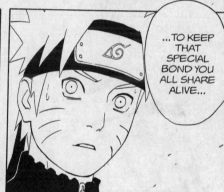

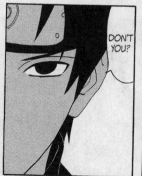

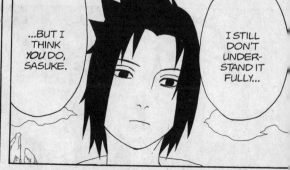

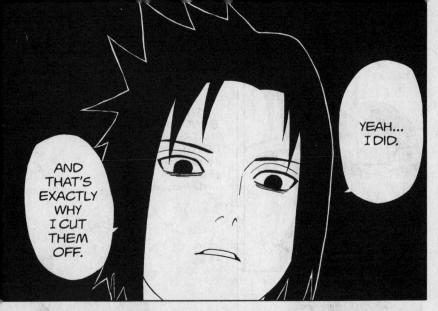

YEAH... I DID.

AND THAT'S EXACTLY WHY I CUT THEM OFF.

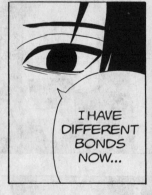

I HAVE DIFFERENT BONDS NOW...

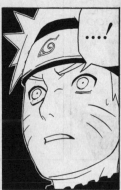

....!

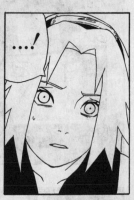

....!

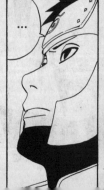

...

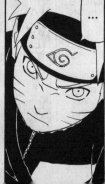

...

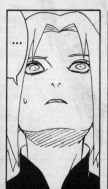

...

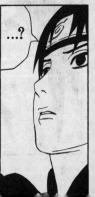

...?

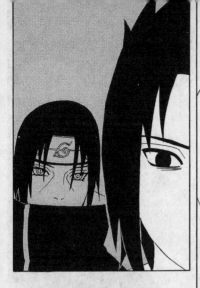

THE BOND OF HATRED BETWEEN MY OLDER BROTHER AND ME...
YOU'RE STILL TOO WEAK...
YOU DON'T HAVE ENOUGH...
...HATE...
PERSONAL TIES CAUSE CONFUSION.
PRECIOUS MEMORIES ONLY MAKE YOU WEAK.

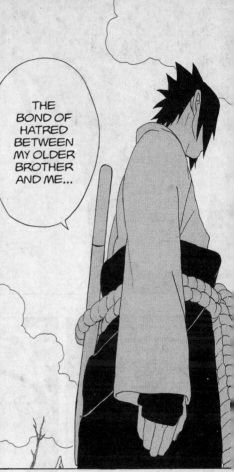

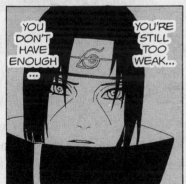

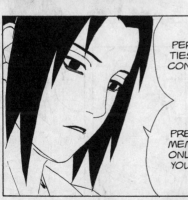

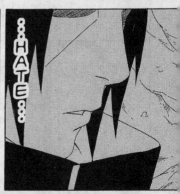

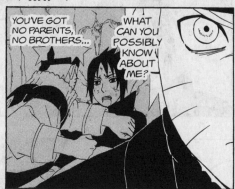

READ THIS WAY

...
WHAT CAN YOU POSSIBLY KNOW ABOUT ME?
YOU'VE GOT NO PARENTS, NO BROTHERS...
YOU WERE ALONE TO BEGIN WITH...
WHAT CAN YOU KNOW ABOUT ME?! HUNH ?!!
THIS PAIN IS BORN FROM MY FAMILY BONDS!
HOW COULD YOU EVER KNOW WHAT IT MEANS TO LOSE ANYTHING!!
IT'S TRUE, I DON'T KNOW A THING...
...ABOUT HAVING BROTHERS OR REAL PARENTS.
WHY, SASUKE ...?

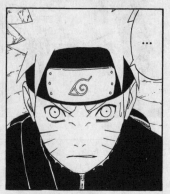

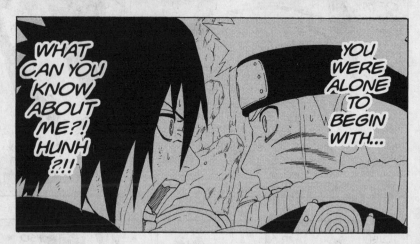

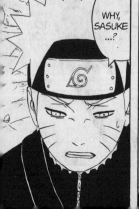

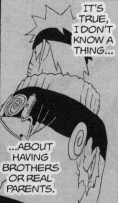

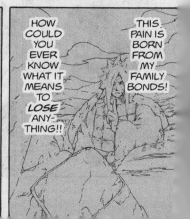

WHY?
WHY DO YOU WASTE SO MUCH EFFORT ON...ME?
...?!
BECAUSE... FOR ME...
...YOU WERE PART OF MY FAMILY.
SO. THAT'S WHY... I HAVE TO STOP YOU!
WHY, ON THAT DAY...
IF THAT'S WHAT YOU THINK, THEN ALL I HAVE TO DO...
...IS SEVER THAT BOND!

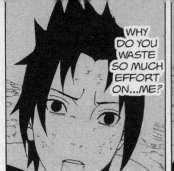

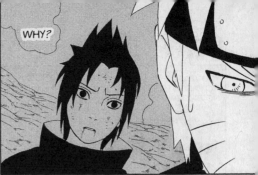

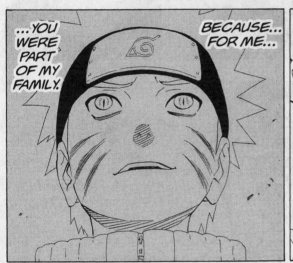

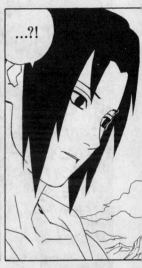

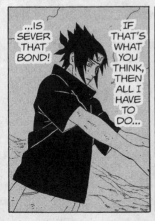

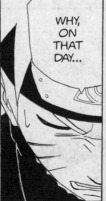

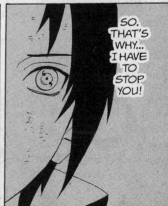

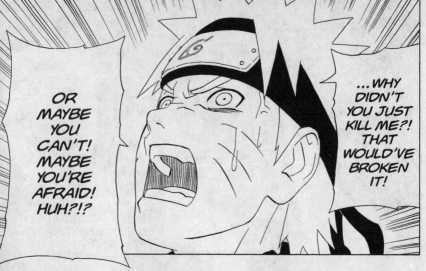

...WHY DIDN'T YOU JUST KILL ME?! THAT WOULD'VE BROKEN IT!
OR MAYBE YOU CAN'T! MAYBE YOU'RE AFRAID! HUH?!?
...
NARUTO ...
IT'S NOT THAT I COULDN'T BREAK THE BOND BETWEEN US...
...THERE'S A SIMPLE EXPLANATION...
JUST LIKE ME, YOU HAVE THE POWER...
...TO AWAKEN THE MANGEKYO SHARINGAN ...
BUT THERE'S A CATCH.
YOU HAVE TO KILL...
...YOUR CLOSEST FRIEND.

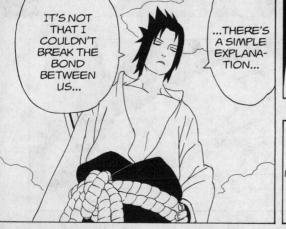

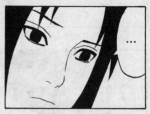

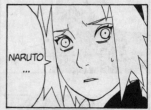

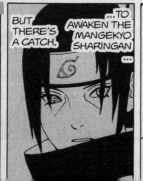

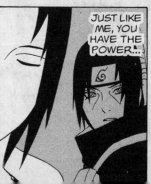

I WAS SIMPLY DOING AS MY BROTHER DID BEFORE ME.
IT WAS JUST A STRATEGY TO GAIN POWER.
?!
WHAT DO YOU MEAN?!
I DON'T NEED TO EXPLAIN ANY-THING TO YOU...

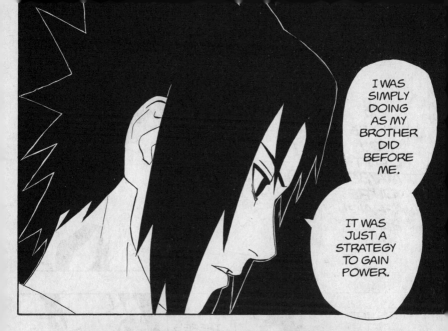

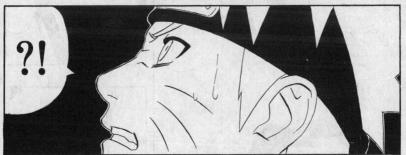

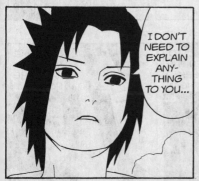

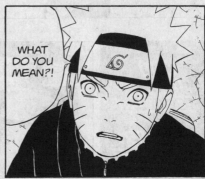

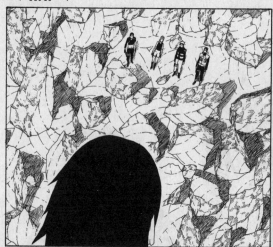

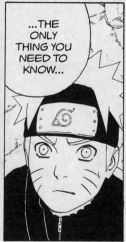

...THE ONLY THING YOU NEED TO KNOW...

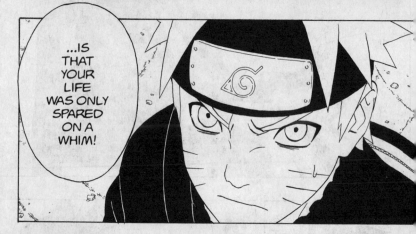

...IS THAT YOUR LIFE WAS ONLY SPARED ON A WHIM!

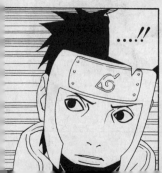

....!!

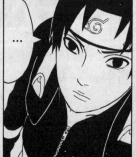

...

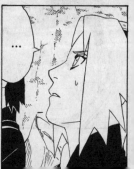

...

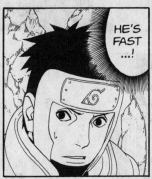

HE'S
FAST
...!

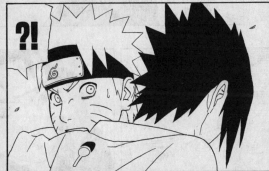

?!

READ THIS WAY

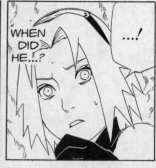

...!
WHEN DID HE...?
THAT REMINDS ME...DIDN'T YOU USED TO SAY YOUR DREAM WAS TO BECOME HOKAGE?
INSTEAD OF WASTING ALL THAT TIME CHASING ME, YOU SHOULD'VE BEEN *TRAINING.*
DON'T YOU THINK?
S... SASUKE ...!
BECAUSE THIS TIME...

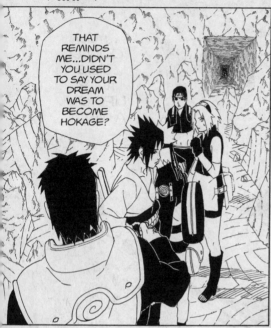

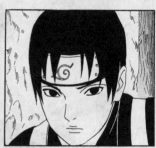

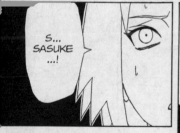

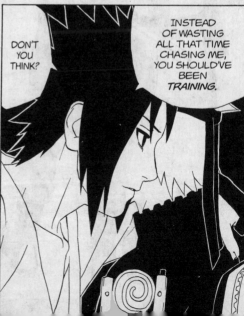

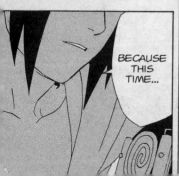

...YOU COULD LOSE YOUR LIFE ON A WHIM.
SHING

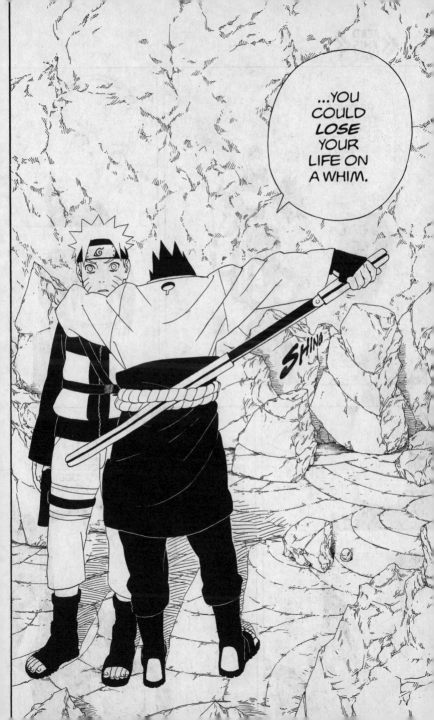

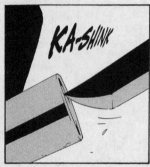

KA-SHINK

...

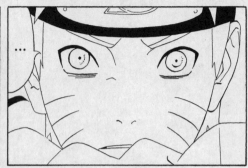

...DO YOU...

...SASUKE?

IF SOMEONE CAN'T EVEN SAVE A FRIEND, THEN I DON'T THINK THEY DESERVE TO BE HOKAGE...

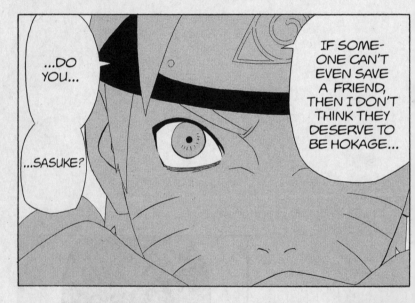

HUMPH ...

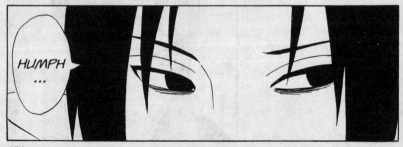

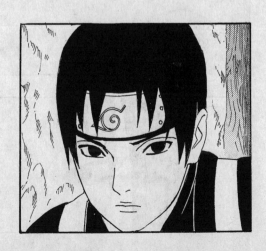

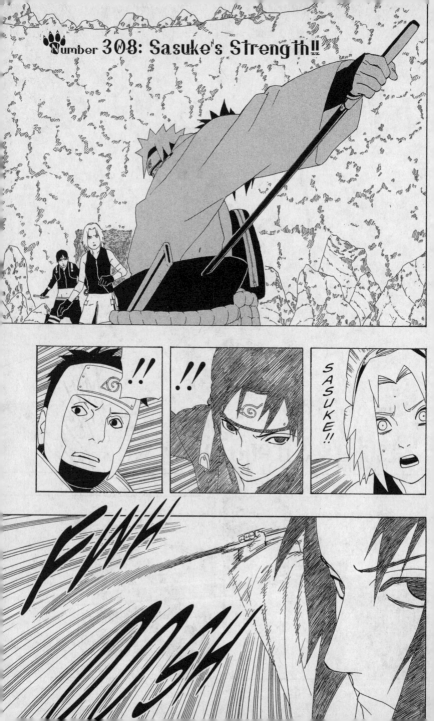

Number 308: Sasuke's Strength!!

SASUKE!!

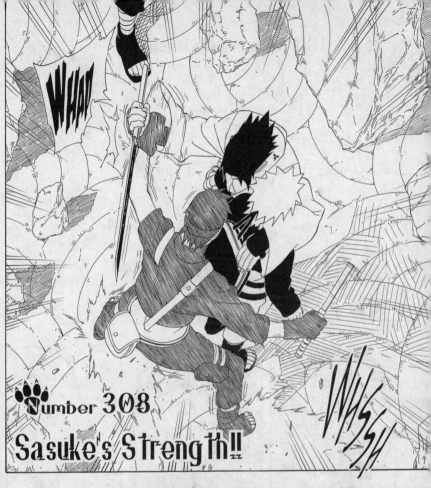

WHAM

Number 308
Sasuke's Strength!!

WHASH

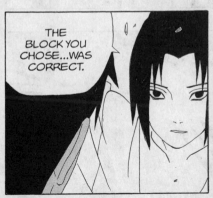

THE BLOCK YOU CHOSE...WAS CORRECT.

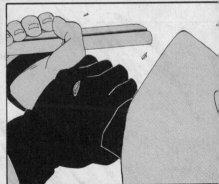

154

?!
SHUP
GOOD!

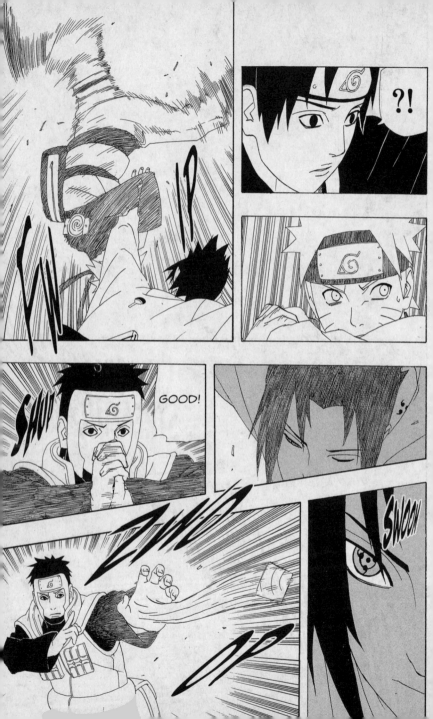

ARGH!
!!
CHIDORI STREAM!!
!!
UNH!
CHIRP CHIRP CHIRP CHIRP

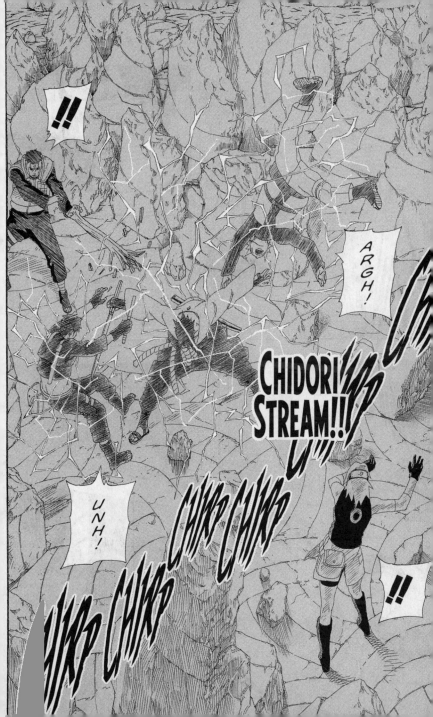

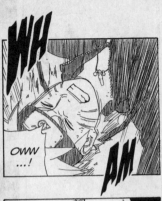

WH
AM

OWW
....!

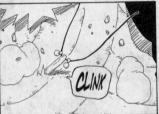

CLINK

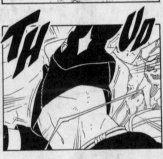

TH UD

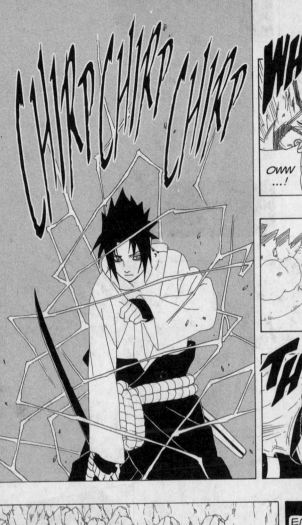

CHIRP CHIRP CHIRP

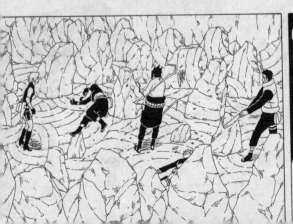

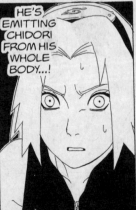

HE'S EMITTING CHIDORI FROM HIS WHOLE BODY...!

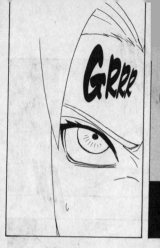

GRRR

BUT NEXT TIME, I'M COMING WITH YOU!

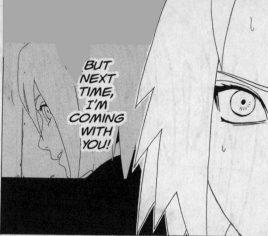

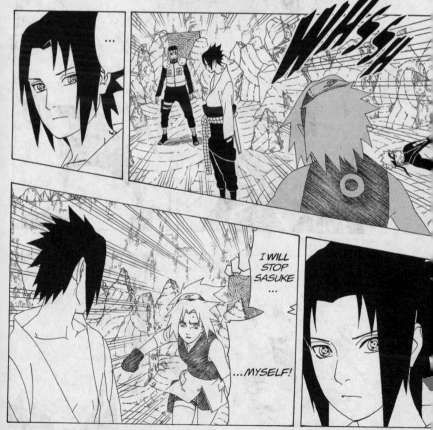

...

WHSSH

I WILL STOP SASUKE...

...MYSELF!

158

WATCH OUT, SAKURA ...!

HIS EYES...

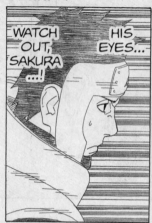

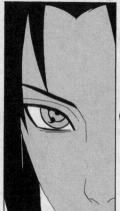

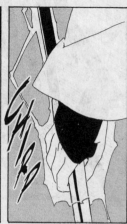

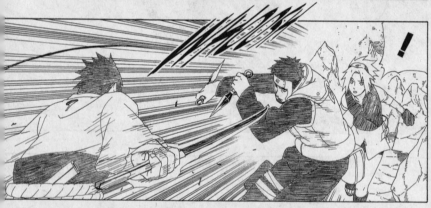

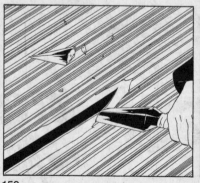

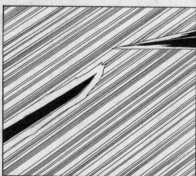

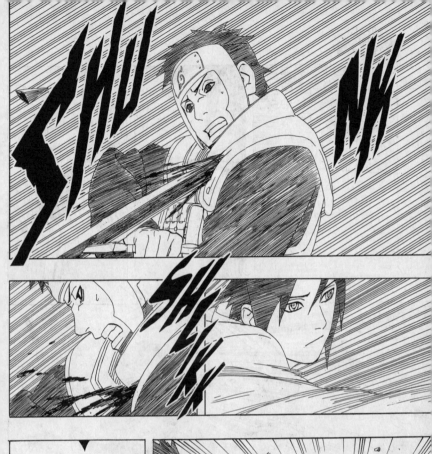

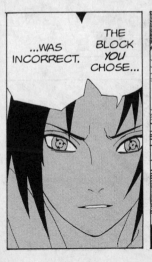

THE BLOCK *YOU* CHOSE...

...WAS INCORRECT.

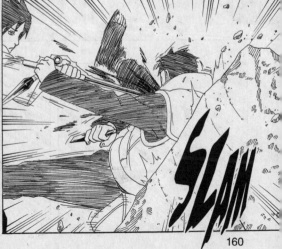

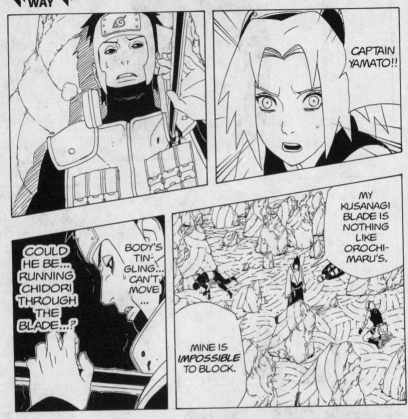

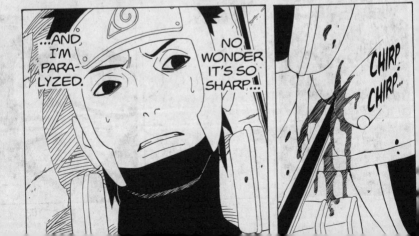

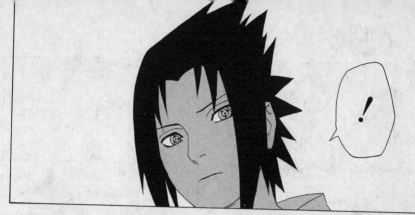

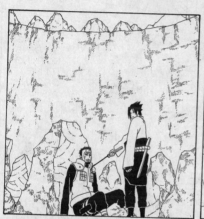

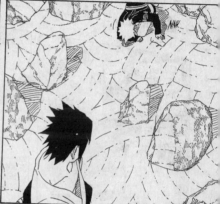

THIS IS
YOUR
CHANCE...
NARUTO...

HEH
HEH...

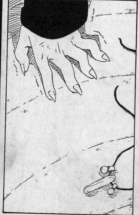

AHH...

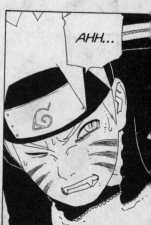

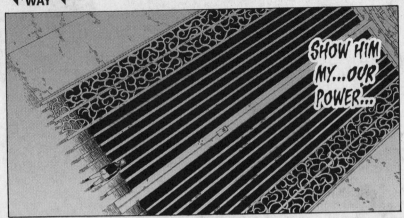

SHOW HIM, MY...OUR POWER...

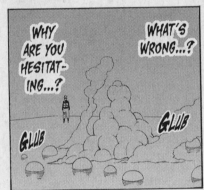

WHY ARE YOU HESITATING...?

WHAT'S WRONG...?

GLUB

GLUB

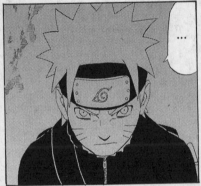

...

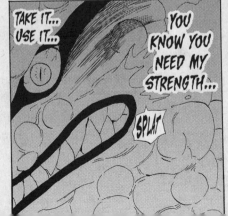

TAKE IT... USE IT...

YOU KNOW YOU NEED MY STRENGTH...

SPLAT

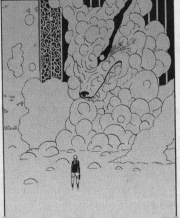

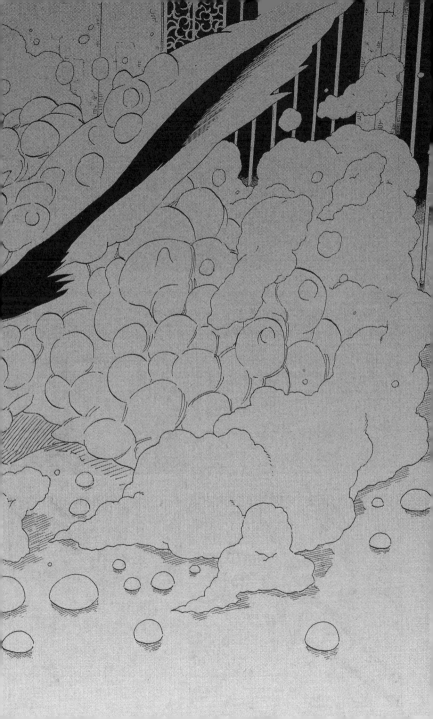

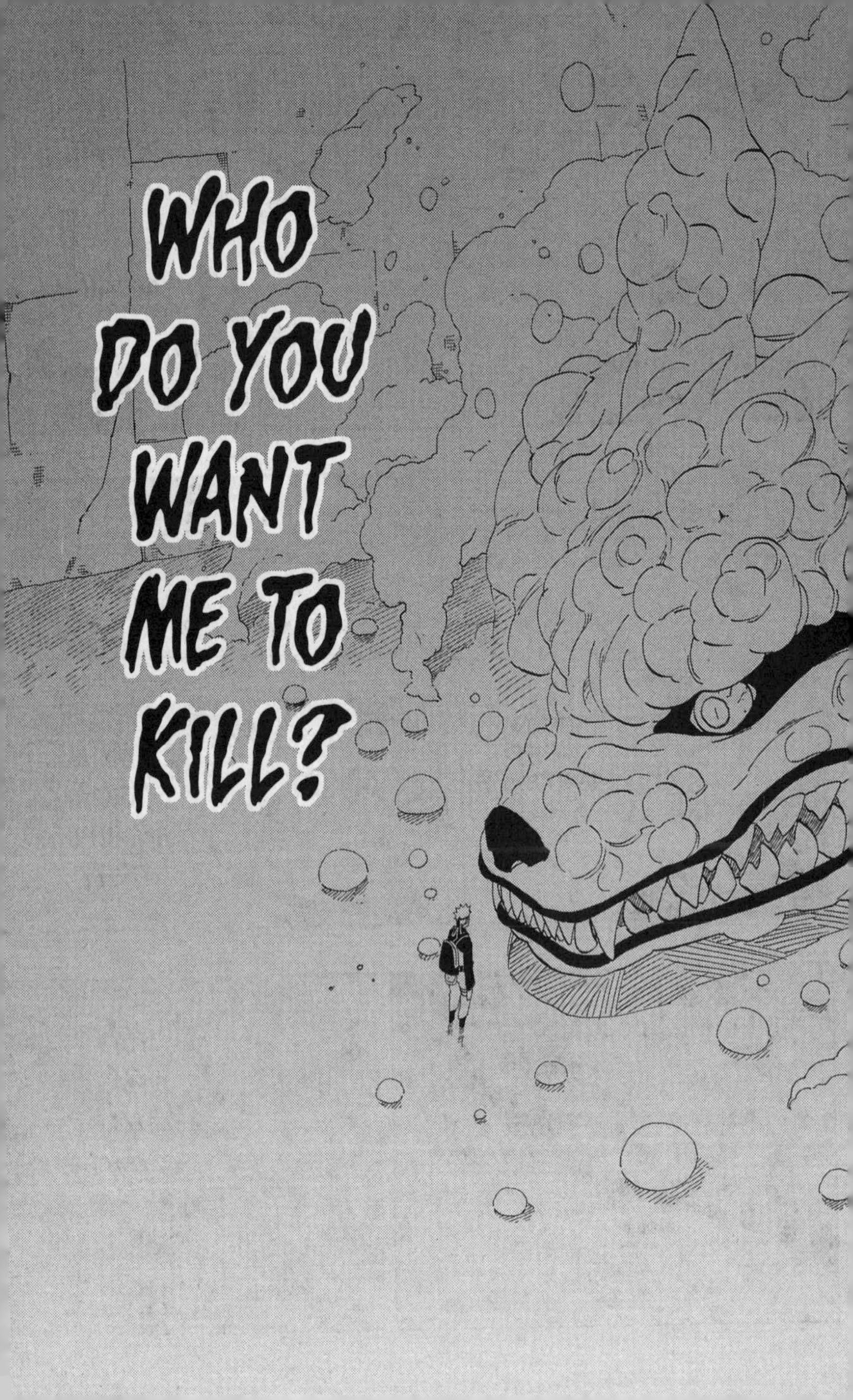
WHO DO YOU WANT ME TO KILL?

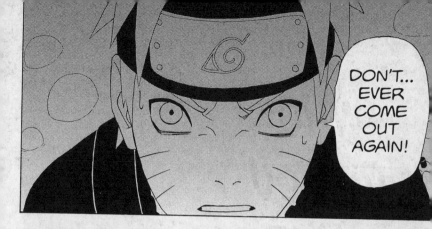

DON'T... EVER COME OUT AGAIN!
...
WHAT ARE YOU SO AFRAID OF, BOY?
SHUT UP! I'M NOT AFRAID!
I DON'T NEED ANYTHING FROM YOU!
HA HA HA HA HA!

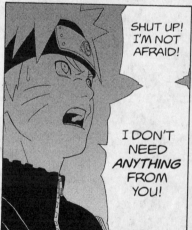

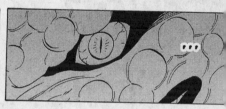

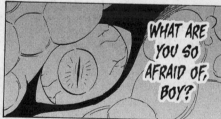

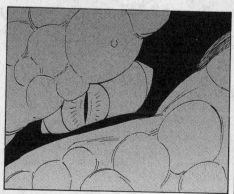

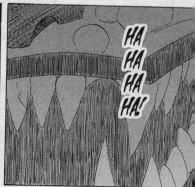

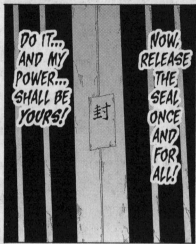

READ THIS WAY

THIS ISN'T THE FIRST TIME YOU'VE COME TO ME FOR HELP!
YOU'RE NOTHING WITHOUT ME... AND YOU KNOW IT!
NOW, RELEASE THE SEAL ONCE AND FOR ALL!
封
DO IT... AND MY POWER... SHALL BE YOURS!
...
GET LOST...!
?!
...
WHO ARE YOU ...?!

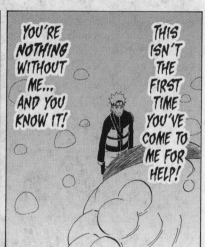

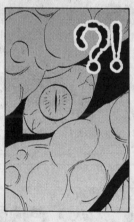

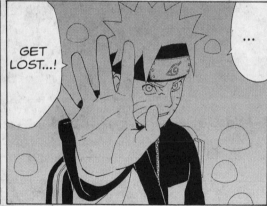

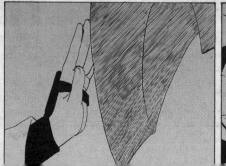

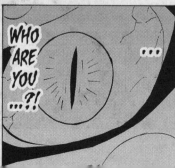

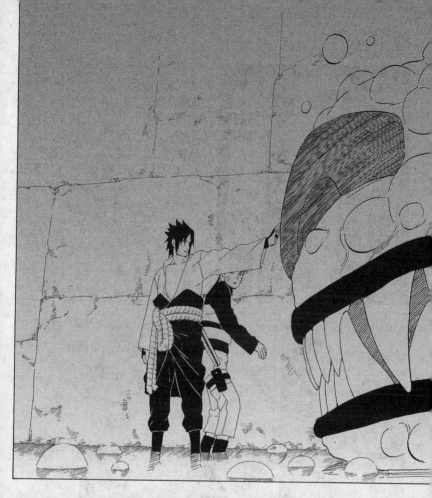

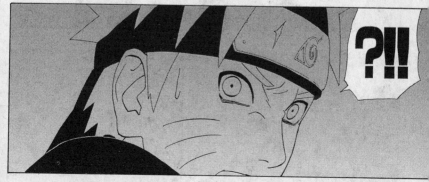

?!!

168

READ THIS WAY

I SEE... AN UCHIHA.
YOU'VE COME QUITE FAR...
WHAT ARE YOU DOING HERE?
I CAN SEE IT NOW...
...THE SOURCE OF YOUR STRENGTH...
I NEVER IMAGINED YOU HAD SUCH A THING INSIDE OF YOU.

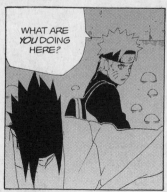

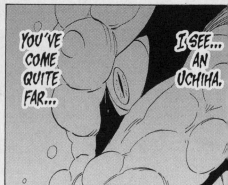

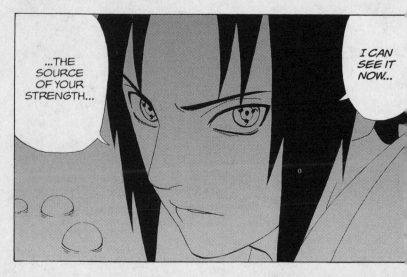

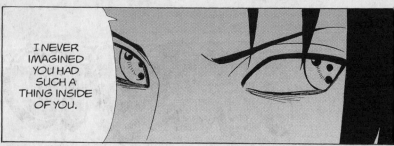

NARUTO

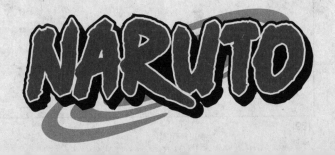

Number 309:
A Conversation with Nine Tails!!

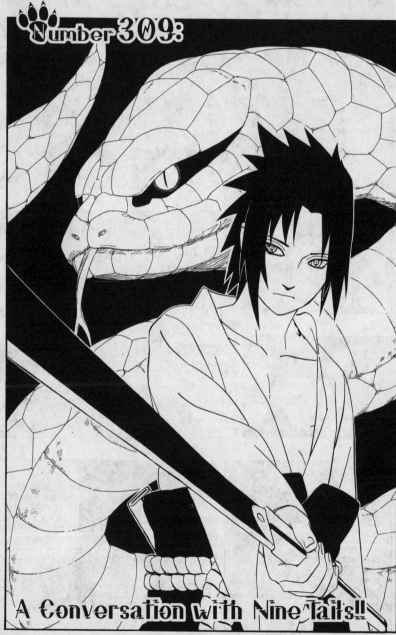

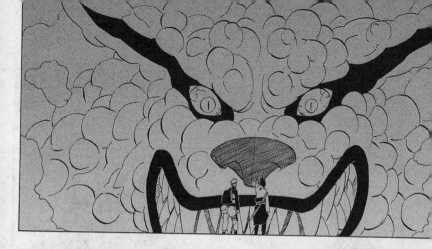

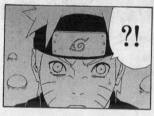

YOU CAN ACTUALLY SEE ME...
...THANKS TO THAT ABOMINABLE SHARINGAN... A PRODUCT OF YOUR ACCURSED BLOODLINE.
?!
SEEMS THIS ISN'T YOUR FIRST ENCOUNTER WITH THESE EYES...
...WHICH MEANS...

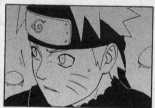

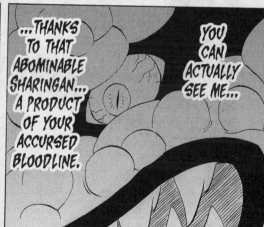

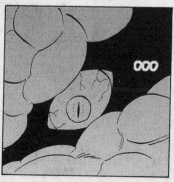

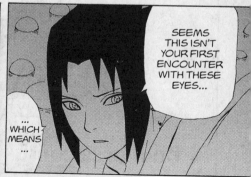

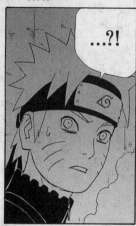

...?!

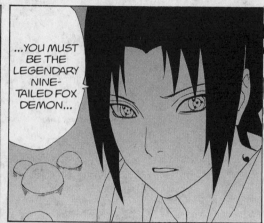

...YOU MUST BE THE LEGENDARY NINE-TAILED FOX DEMON...

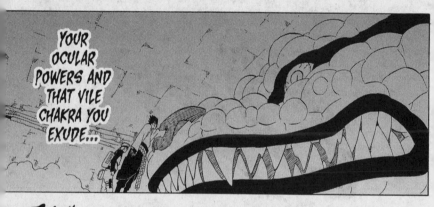

YOUR OCULAR POWERS AND THAT VILE CHAKRA YOU EXUDE...

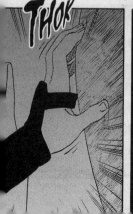

THOK

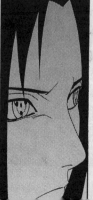

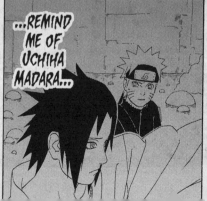

...REMIND ME OF UCHIHA MADARA...

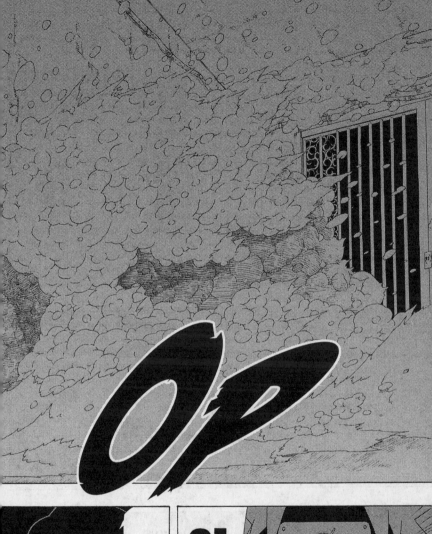

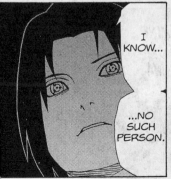

I KNOW...

...NO SUCH PERSON.

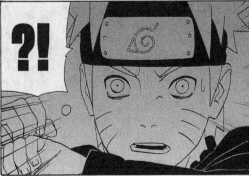

?!

174

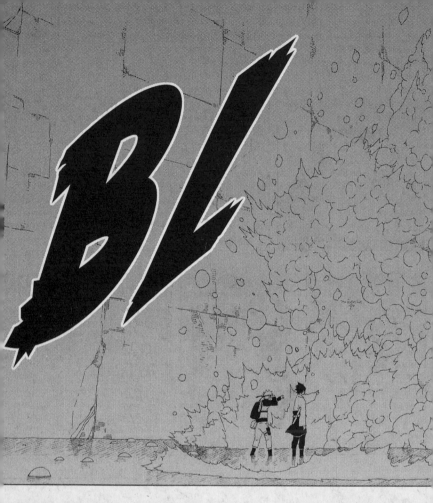

BL
I CAN'T BELIEVE YOU ARE EVEN ABLE TO SUPPRESS MY POWER...
GLUB
FIZZLE
...
...IT MAY BE MY UNDOING, BUT...
...LET ME... TELL YOU... ONE THING...

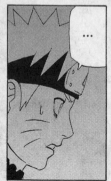

....!

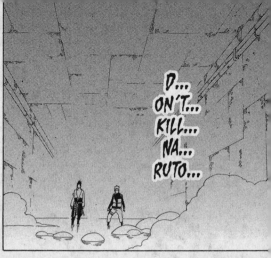

D... ON'T... KILL... NA... RUTO...

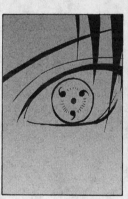

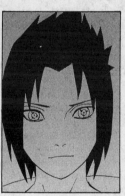

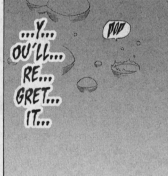

...Y... OU'LL... RE... GRET... IT...

POP

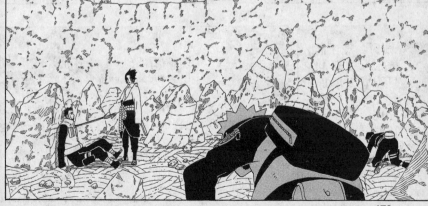

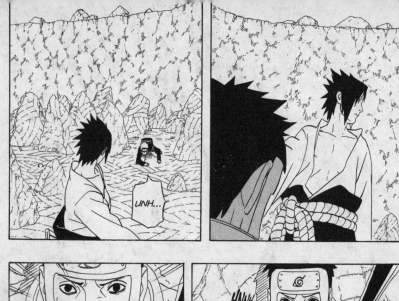

UNH...

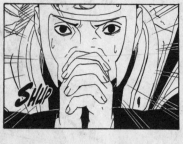

SHUP

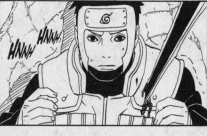

HNNH! HNNH!

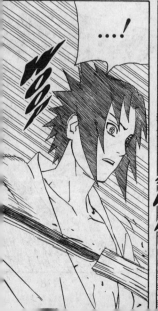

....!

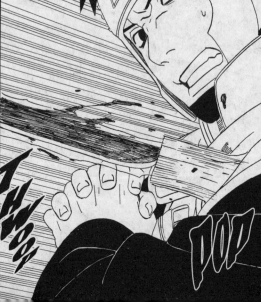

THWOO!

POP

ZWHOOSH
!
WOBBLE
BZZ
WHSSH
SKRAKK

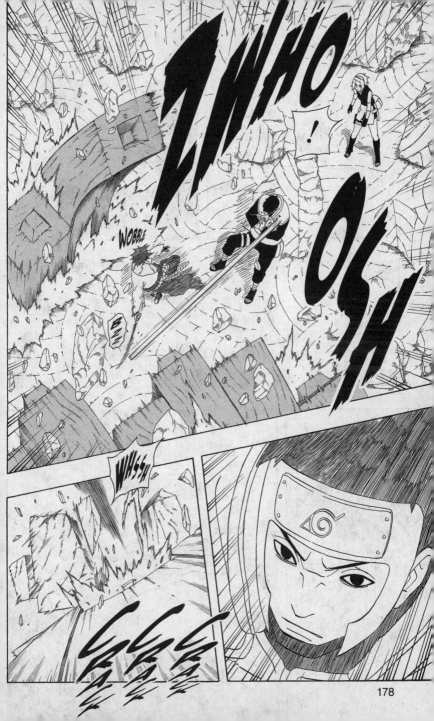

READ THIS WAY

TAP
NNH...
...
SASUKE ...
HUP

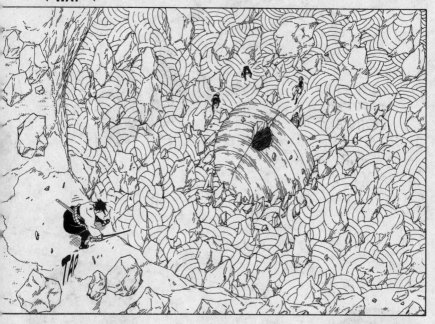

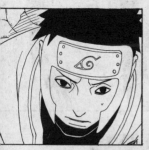

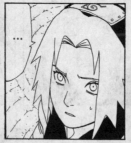

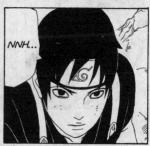

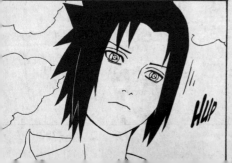

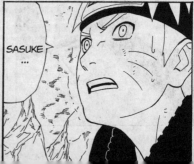

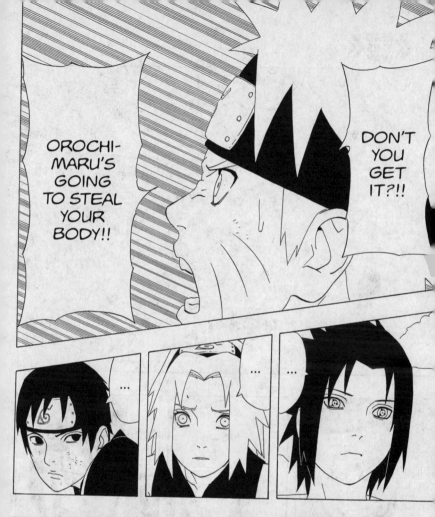

DON'T YOU GET IT?!!
OROCHI-MARU'S GOING TO STEAL YOUR BODY!!
...
...
...
IF IT HAPPENS, IT HAP-PENS... SO BE IT.
?!

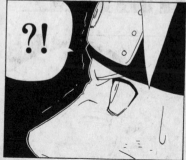

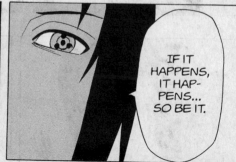

READ THIS WAY

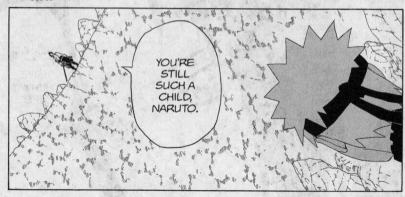

YOU'RE STILL SUCH A CHILD, NARUTO.
I DON'T CARE WHAT HAPPENS TO ME OR TO THE REST OF THE WORLD...
...SO LONG AS I CAN GET MY REVENGE.
NOTHING ELSE MATTERS.
TO BE HONEST...
...NEITHER OROCHIMARU NOR I ARE STRONG ENOUGH TO DEFEAT ITACHI ON OUR OWN.
BUT IF I CAN OBTAIN THE POWER TO DEFEAT ITACHI...
...BY GIVING MYSELF OVER TO OROCHI-MARU...

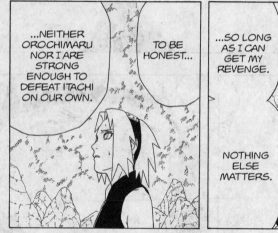

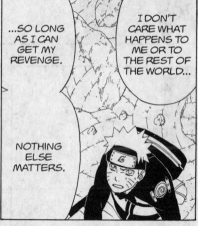

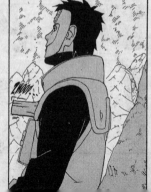

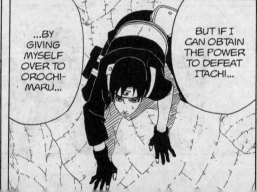

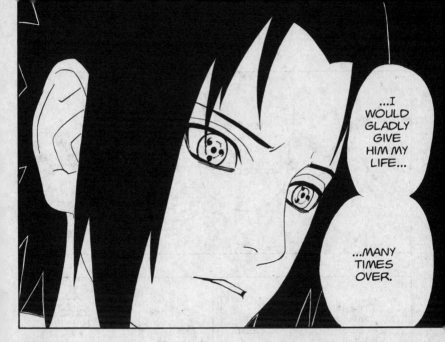

...I WOULD GLADLY GIVE HIM MY LIFE...

...MANY TIMES OVER.

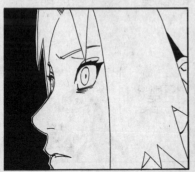

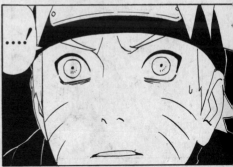

....!

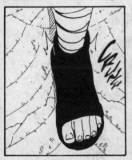

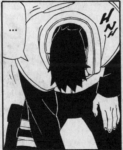

...

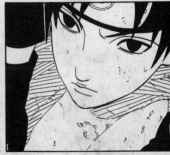

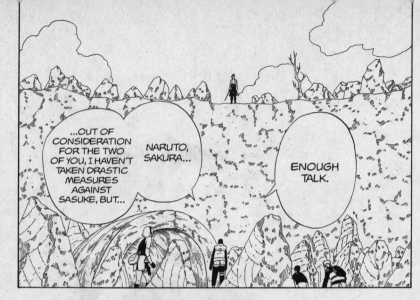

NARUTO, SAKURA...
...OUT OF CONSIDERATION FOR THE TWO OF YOU, I HAVEN'T TAKEN DRASTIC MEASURES AGAINST SASUKE, BUT...
ENOUGH TALK.
CAPTAIN YAMATO ...!
...I SEE I CAN'T HOLD BACK ANY LONGER... I'M SORRY...
I'M DONE WITH YOU...
KONOHA...
THAP
BEGONE!
SHOOP

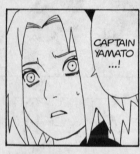

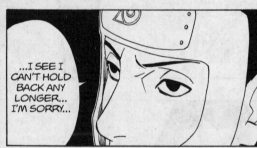

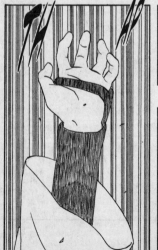

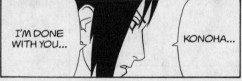

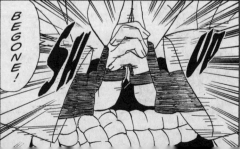

WHOOSH
FAP
!
I WOULDN'T USE *THAT* JUTSU... SASUKE.
!
!
LET GO.
...

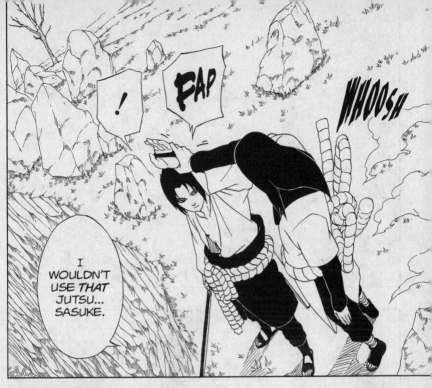

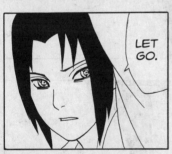

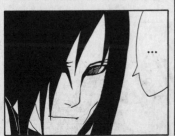

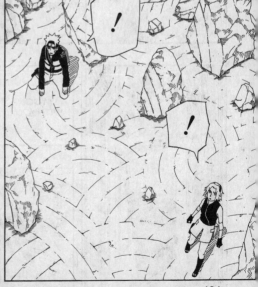

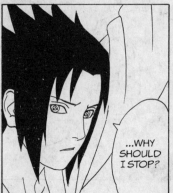

READ THIS WAY

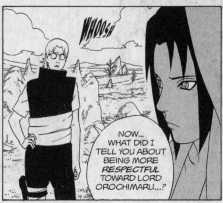

WHOOSH
NOW... WHAT DID I TELL YOU ABOUT BEING MORE *RESPECTFUL* TOWARD LORD OROCHIMARU...?
...WHY SHOULD I STOP?
YOU KNOW THAT THE AKATSUKI'S ON THE MOVE.
WE WANT THESE KONOHA PEOPLE TO GET RID OF THE AKATSUKI FOR US.
AS MANY OF THEM AS POS-SIBLE...
BECAUSE IF OTHER AKATSUKI MEMBERS INTER-FERE...
...IT WOULD PREVENT YOU FROM GETTING YOUR PRECIOUS REVENGE...
...THAT'S A PITIFUL EXCUSE.

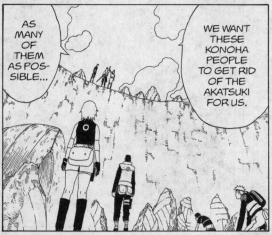

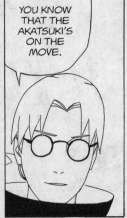

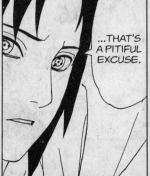

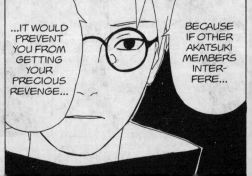

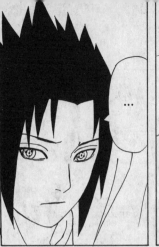

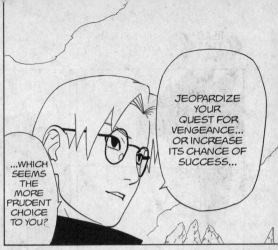

...
JEOPARDIZE YOUR QUEST FOR VENGEANCE... OR INCREASE ITS CHANCE OF SUCCESS...
...WHICH SEEMS THE MORE PRUDENT CHOICE TO YOU?
FUP
BRIGHT BOY.
...
...

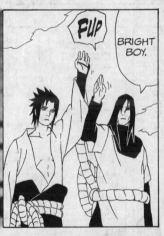

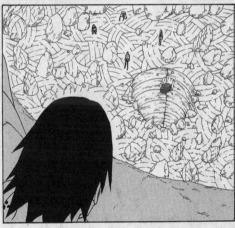

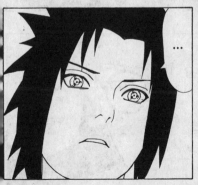

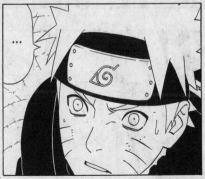

READ THIS WAY

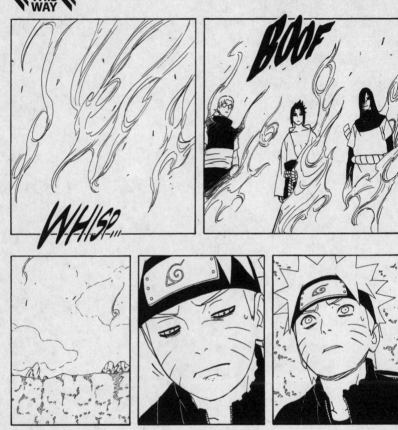

BOOF
WHISP...

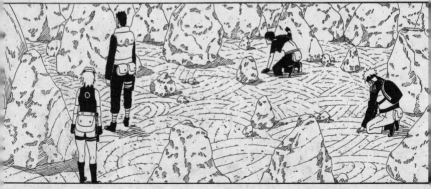

NARUTO

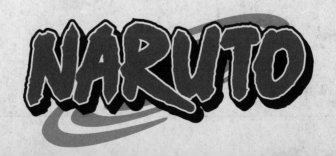

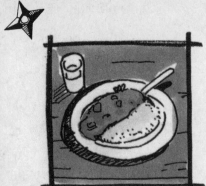

Curry rice or rice curry... I have no idea what the difference is...

—*Masashi Kishimoto, 2006*

岸本斉史

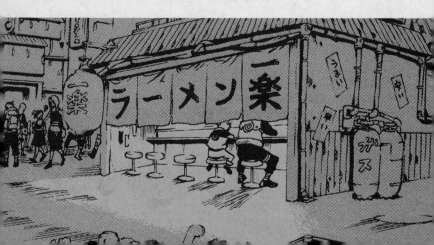

NARUTO

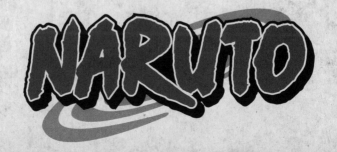

NARUTO
VOL. 35
THE NEW TWO
STORY AND ART BY
MASASHI KISHIMOTO

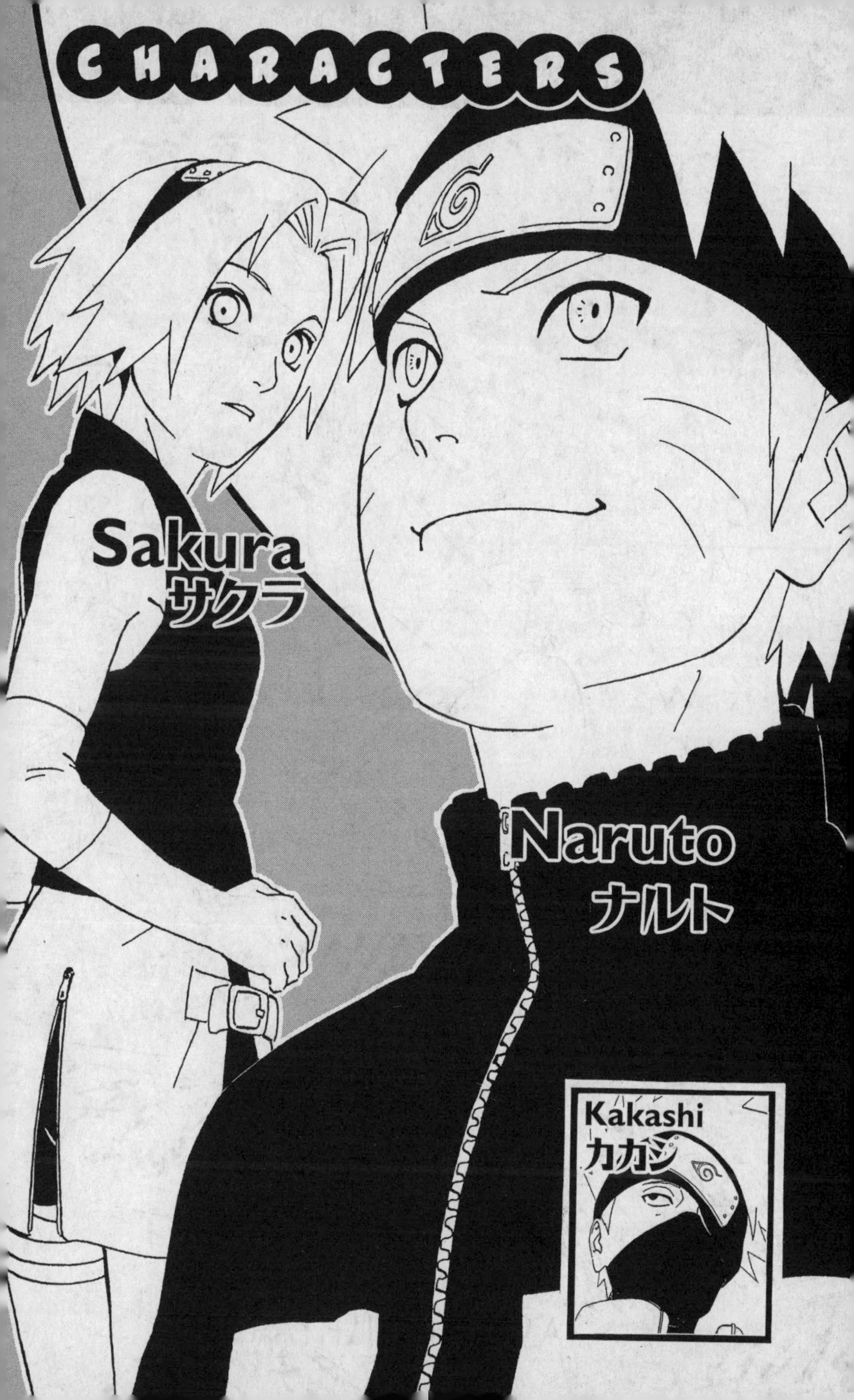

CHARACTERS

Sakura
サクラ

Naruto
ナルト

Kakashi
カカシ

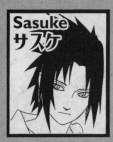

Sasuke
サスケ

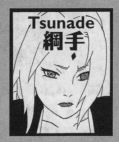

Tsunade
綱手

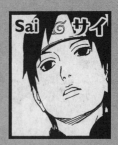

Sai
サイ

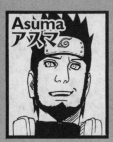

Asuma
アスマ

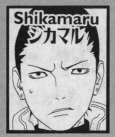

Shikamaru
シカマル

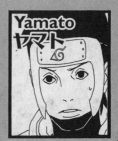

Yamato
ヤマト

The Story So Far...

Team Kakashi's mission to rescue Uchiha Sasuke from the sinister Orochimaru continues! While Captain Yamato's doppelganger searches for the villain's secret hideout, Naruto and Sakura pore over Sai's mysterious picture book and finally learn the truth about their treacherous teammate's troubled origin...

Sai, meanwhile, remains in the company of Orochimaru where he at last comes face to face with Sasuke. But the young man he meets bears little to no resemblance to Naruto's friend of the past. Gone are any traces of the light that was once inside him. All that remains is a being of darkness bent on destruction...

Team Kakashi finally infiltrates Orochimaru's lair and goes toe to toe with Sasuke. Now more powerful than ever, he leaves his former friends in the dust, picking up the pieces of their failed mission...

NARUTO

VOL. 35
THE NEW TWO

CONTENTS

NARUTO

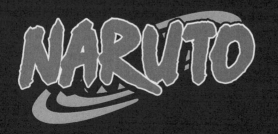

Number 310: The Title
NARUTO

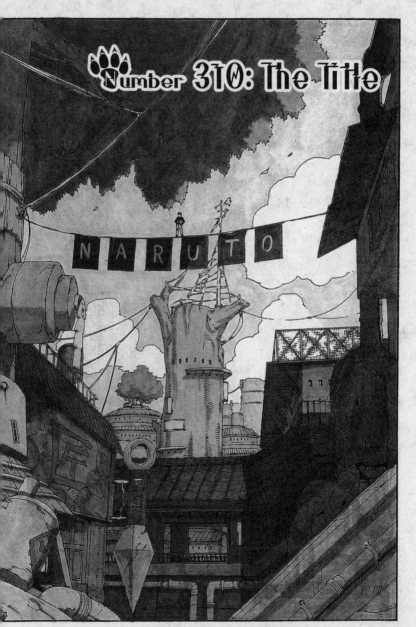

NARUTO

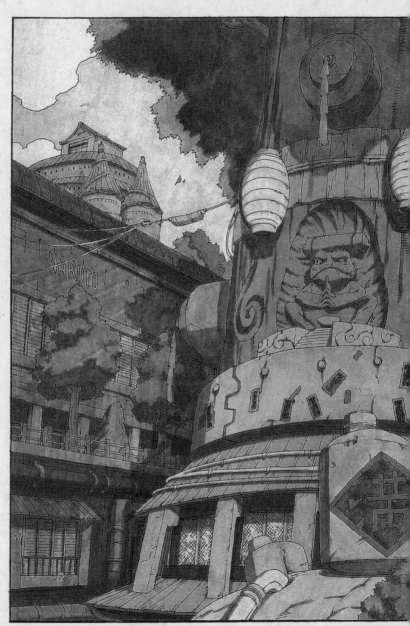

NARUTO

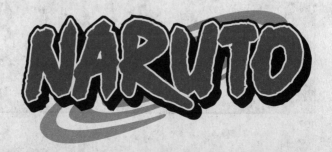

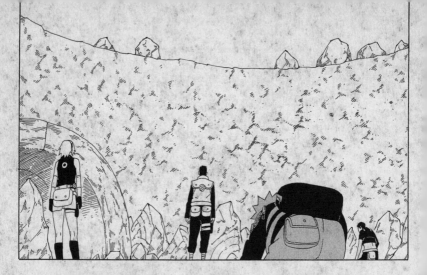

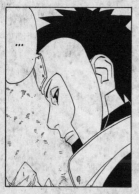

...

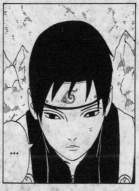

...

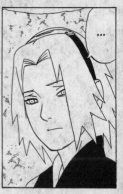

...

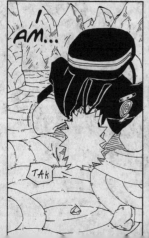

I AM...

TAK

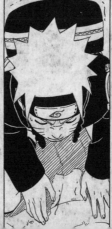

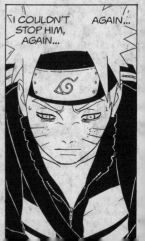

I COULDN'T STOP HIM, AGAIN...

AGAIN...

...SO WEAK...

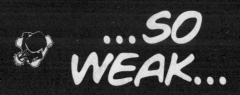

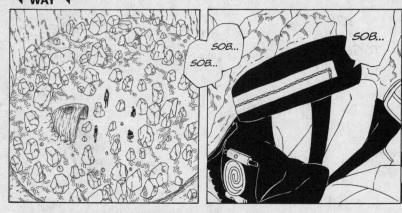

SOB...

SOB...

SOB...

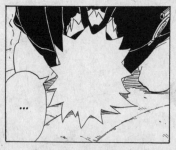

...

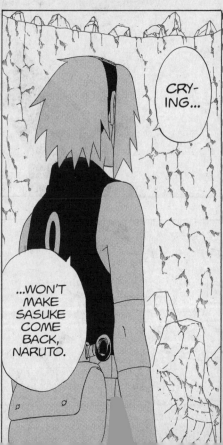

CRY-ING...

...WON'T MAKE SASUKE COME BACK, NARUTO.

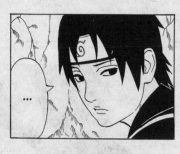

...

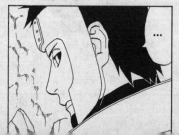

...

WE HAVE TO BE STRONG.
YOU AND ME. TOGETHER.

...

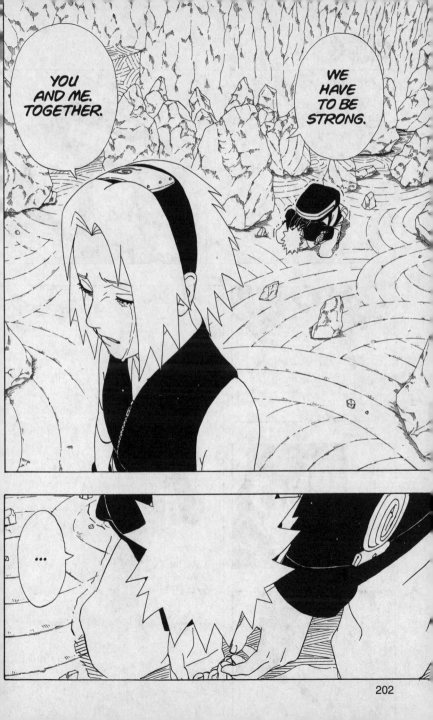

READ THIS WAY

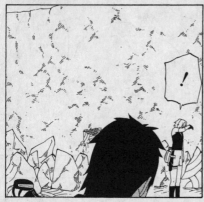

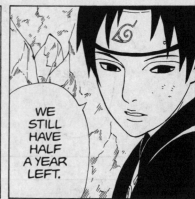

WE STILL HAVE HALF A YEAR LEFT.
!
THREE MAKES FOR BETTER ODDS THAN TWO.
AND I'M PRETTY STRONG, TOO.
...
SCRUB
SCRUB

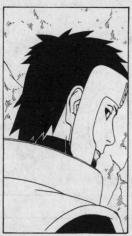

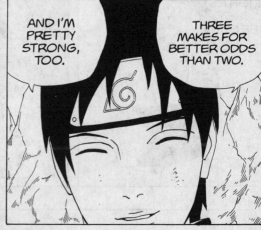

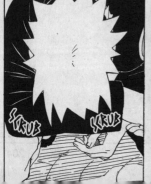

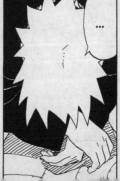

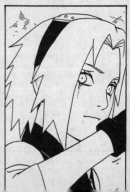

...
...THANKS ...GUYS...
NOW THEN ...
THE FIGHT'S JUST BEGUN ...

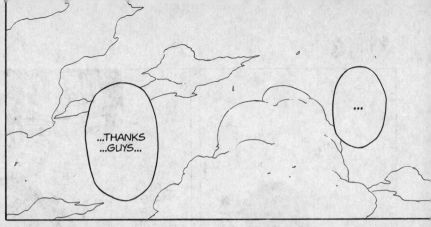

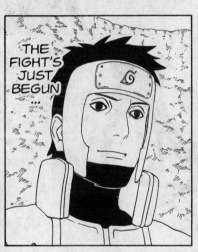

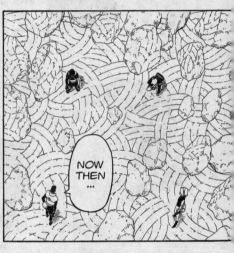

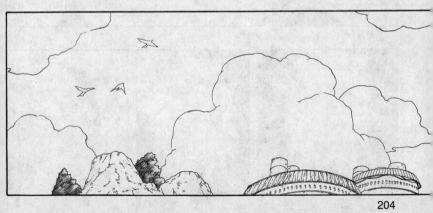

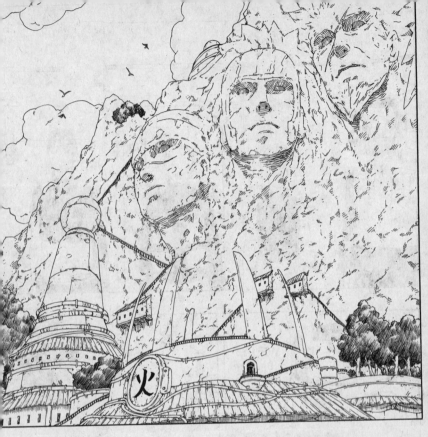

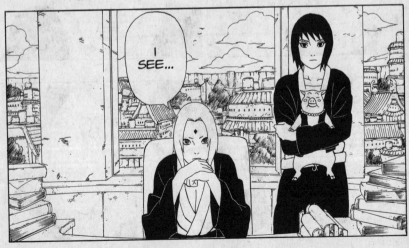

I SEE...

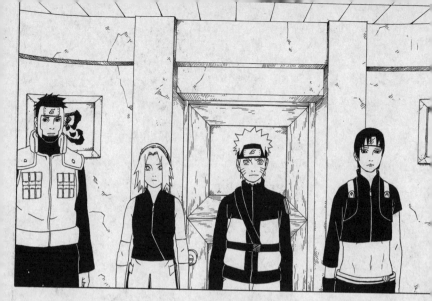

WE'RE NOT GIVING UP!

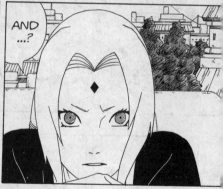

AND ...?

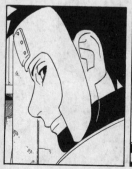

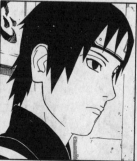

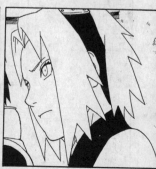

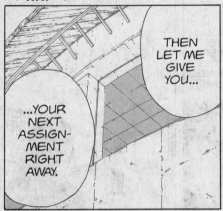

THEN LET ME GIVE YOU...

...YOUR NEXT ASSIGNMENT RIGHT AWAY.

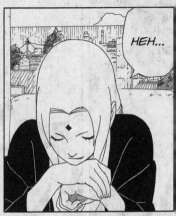

HEH...

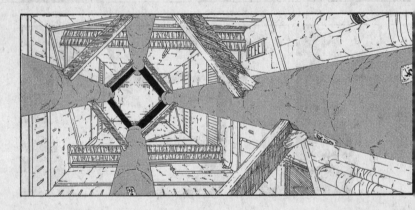

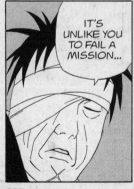

IT'S UNLIKE YOU TO FAIL A MISSION...

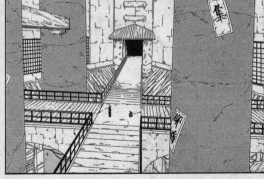

207

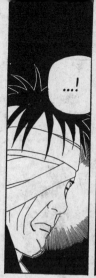

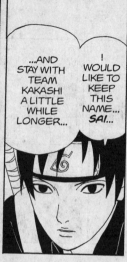

...IF I MAY MAKE A REQUEST.
A REQUEST ...?
YES...
I WOULD LIKE TO KEEP THIS NAME... SAI...
...AND STAY WITH TEAM KAKASHI A LITTLE WHILE LONGER...
...!
THAT SMILE ...
TSUNADE HAS ALSO APPROACHED ME ABOUT THIS.
BUT UNDER-STAND THIS, SAI...
...EMOTIONS GENERATE HATRED...
...AND HATRED BREEDS CONFLICT...

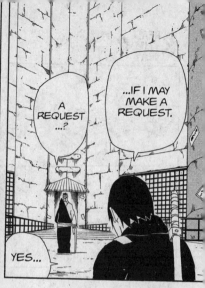

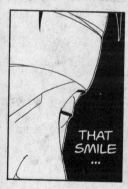

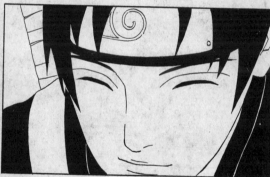

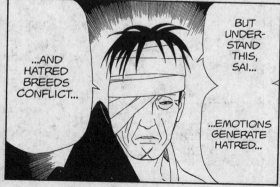

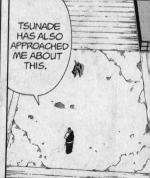

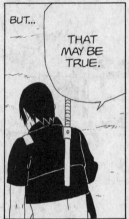

READ THIS WAY
...
THE BOND OF HATRED BETWEEN MY OLDER BROTHER AND ME...
BUT...
THAT MAY BE TRUE.
'CUZ HE... REALLY ACCEPTED ME MORE THAN ANYONE ELSE.
I'M DOING THIS BECAUSE SASUKE IS MY FRIEND...
...AND THAT'S A BOND...
...THAT CAN NEVER BE BROKEN.

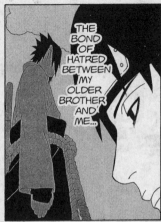

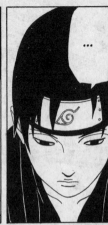

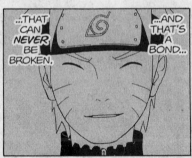

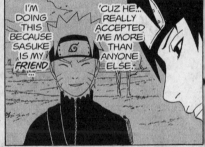

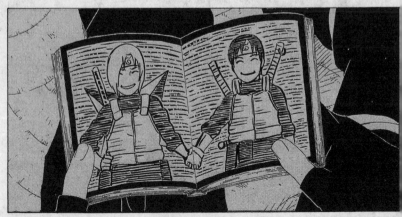

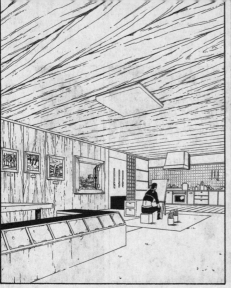

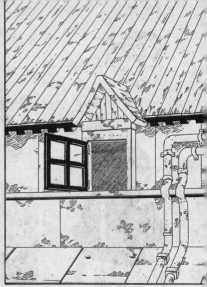

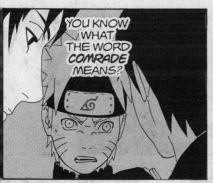

YOU KNOW WHAT THE WORD **COMRADE** MEANS?

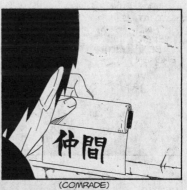

(COMRADE)

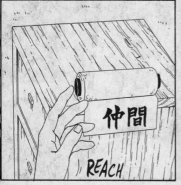

REACH

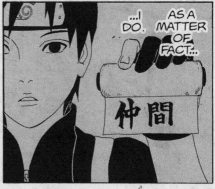

...I DO.

AS A MATTER OF FACT...

READ THIS WAY
THP...

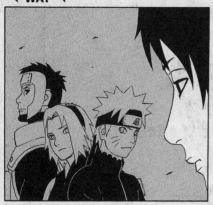

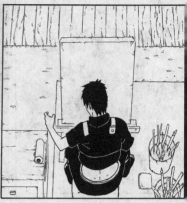

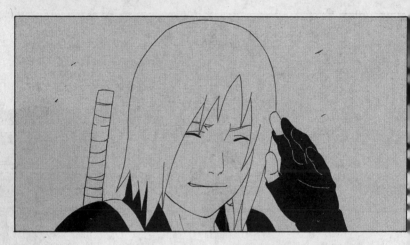

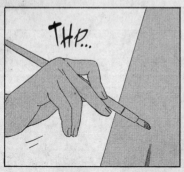

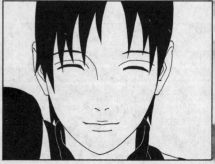

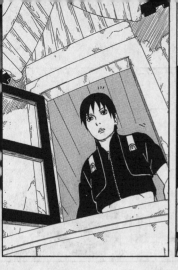

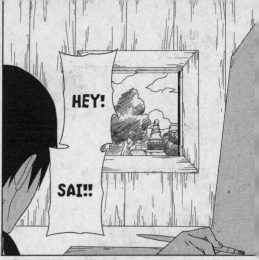

HEY!

SAI!!

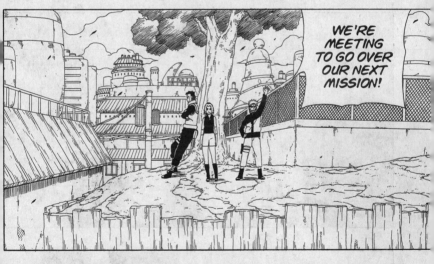

WE'RE MEETING TO GO OVER OUR NEXT MISSION!

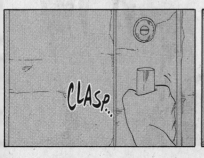

CLASP...

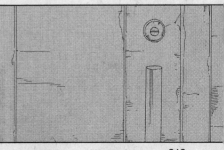

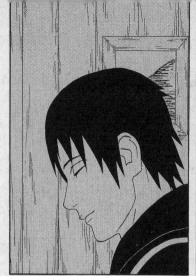

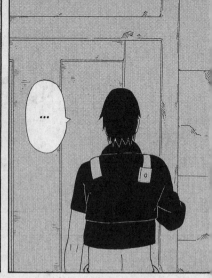

…

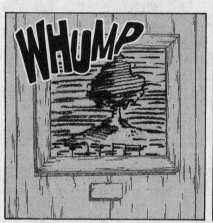

WHUMP

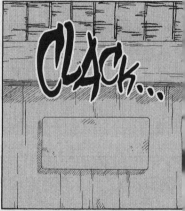

CLACK…

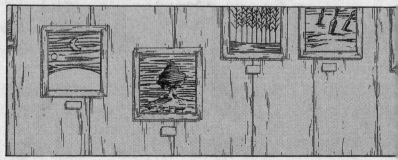

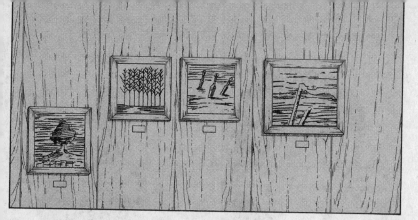

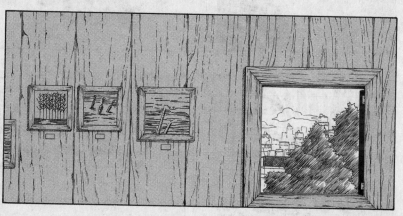

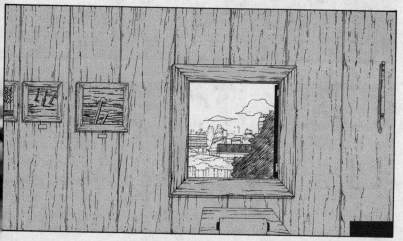

214

READ THIS WAY

仲間

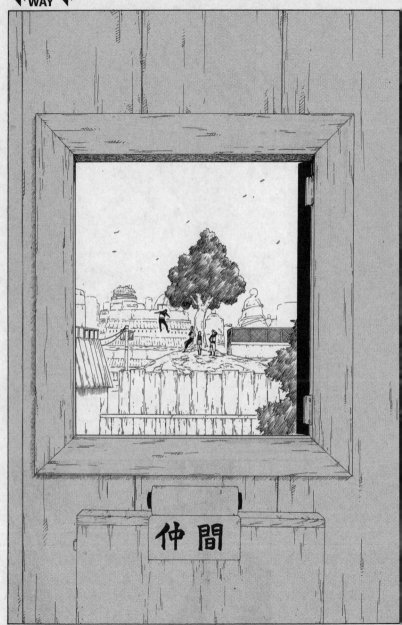

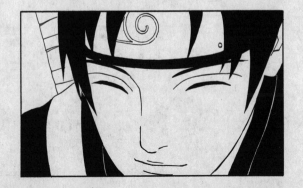

Number 311: Nicknames

Make-Out
TACTIC

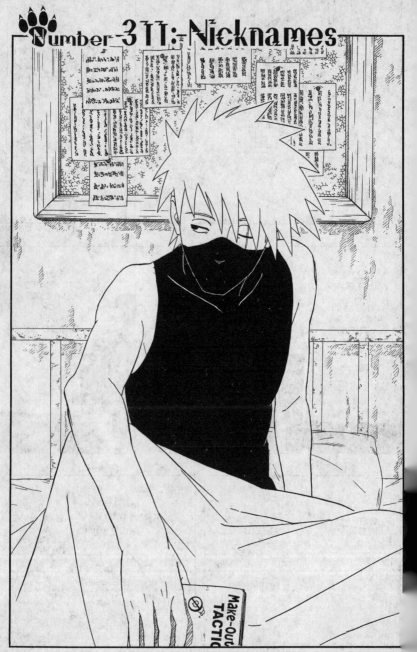

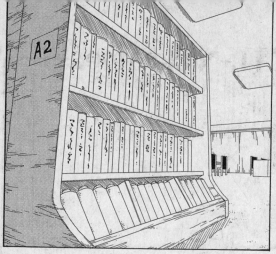

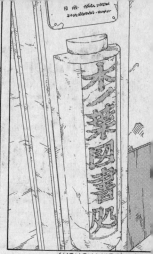

A2
木ノ葉図書館
(KONOHA LIBRARY)
"...IN ORDER TO BE MORE QUICKLY UNDER-STOOD BY OTHERS..."
"...ONE MUST FIRST DRAW THEM IN AND WARM THEM TO YOU."
How to Build Better Interperso Relationships
"FOR EXAMPLE, WHEN ADDRESSING OTHERS..."
"...IF YOU PERSIST IN CALLING THEM 'MISTER' OR 'MISS'..."
Communication
"...IT MAINTAINS A RESERVED AIR AND NEVER ALLOWS THE GAP TO BE BRIDGED."

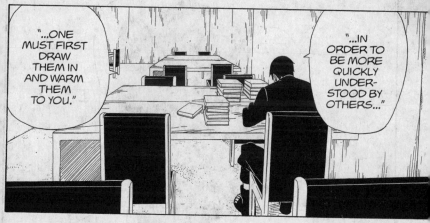

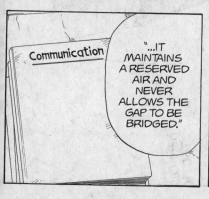

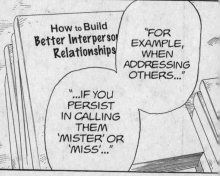

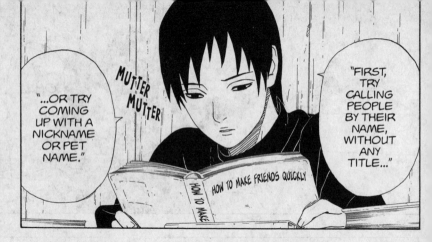

"FIRST, TRY CALLING PEOPLE BY THEIR NAME, WITHOUT ANY TITLE..."
MUTTER MUTTER
"...OR TRY COMING UP WITH A NICKNAME OR PET NAME."
HOW TO MAKE FRIENDS QUICKLY
HOW TO MAKE
"THIS WILL MAKE THEM FEEL SPECIAL..."
"...AND BRING THEM CLOSER TO YOU..."
... HUH ...
The Effects of Medicinal
Powerful Drugs and Their Uses
PREPARING MEDICINES
GREEN FUNGUS AND SUN GRASS
GREEN HERBS AND RED HERBS
HERE IT IS...
!

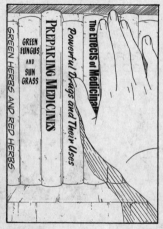

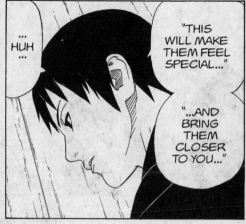

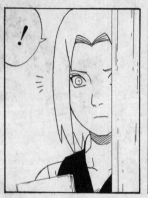

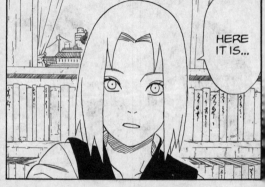

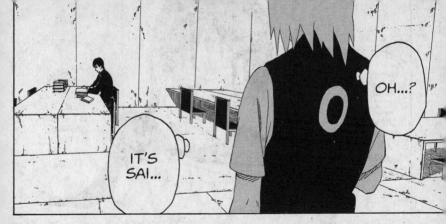

OH...?
IT'S SAI...
DID YOU COME LOOKING FOR ART BOOKS?
!
SAKURA ...
NEVER PEGGED YOU FOR A READER.
CLATTER
OCCA-SIONALLY ...

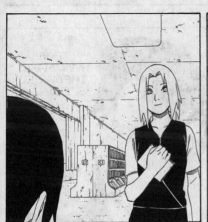

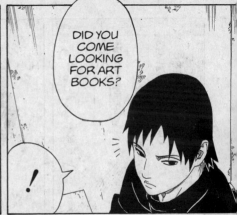

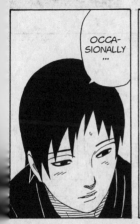

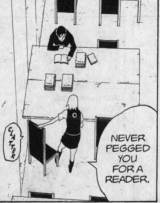

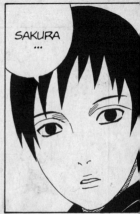

READ THIS WAY

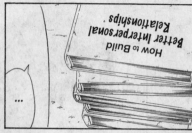

...!
How to Build Better Interpersonal Relationships
...
SAI'S ACTUALLY GOT QUITE A HUMAN SIDE TO HIM...
OH, I ALMOST FORGOT!
?!
NARUTO AND I ARE GOING TO GO VISIT MASTER KAKASHI IN THE HOSPITAL.
WANNA COME WITH US?
MASTER... KAKASHI...
WELL, YOU *ARE* PART OF TEAM KAKASHI...
...SO YOU OUGHT TO AT LEAST MEET HIM.

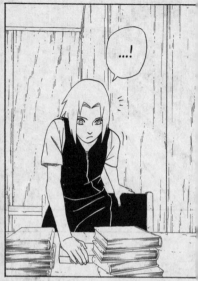

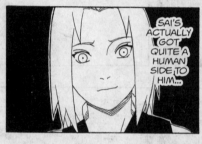

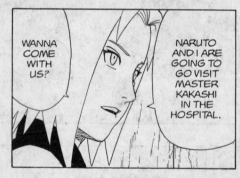

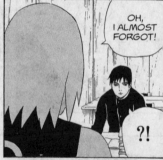

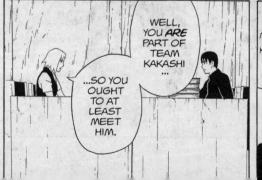

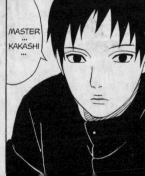

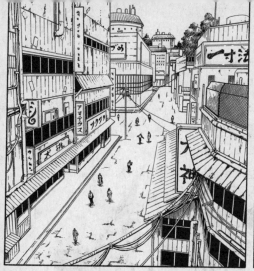

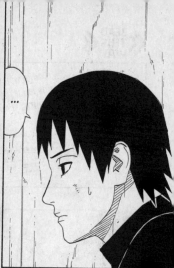

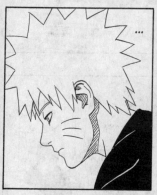

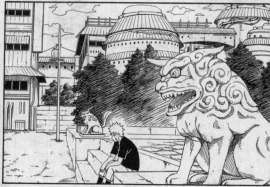

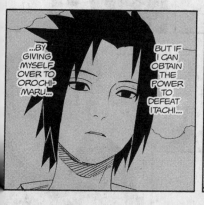

...
...
I DON'T CARE WHAT HAPPENS TO ME OR TO THE REST OF THE WORLD...
...SO LONG AS I CAN GET MY REVENGE. NOTHING ELSE MATTERS.
BUT IF I CAN OBTAIN THE POWER TO DEFEAT ITACHI...
...BY GIVING MYSELF OVER TO OROCHI-MARU...

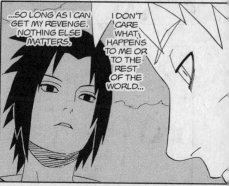

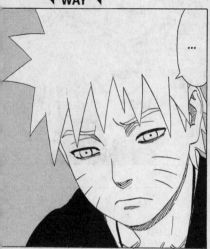

...

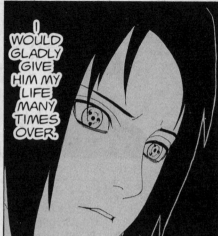

I WOULD GLADLY GIVE HIM MY LIFE MANY TIMES OVER.

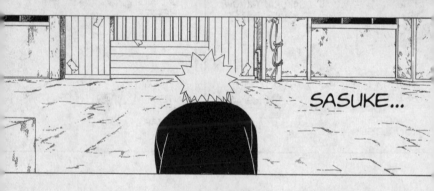

SASUKE...

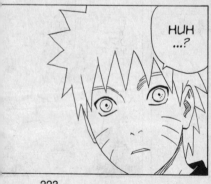

HUH ....?

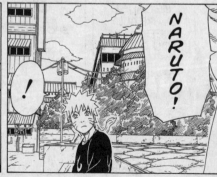

!

NARUTO!

223

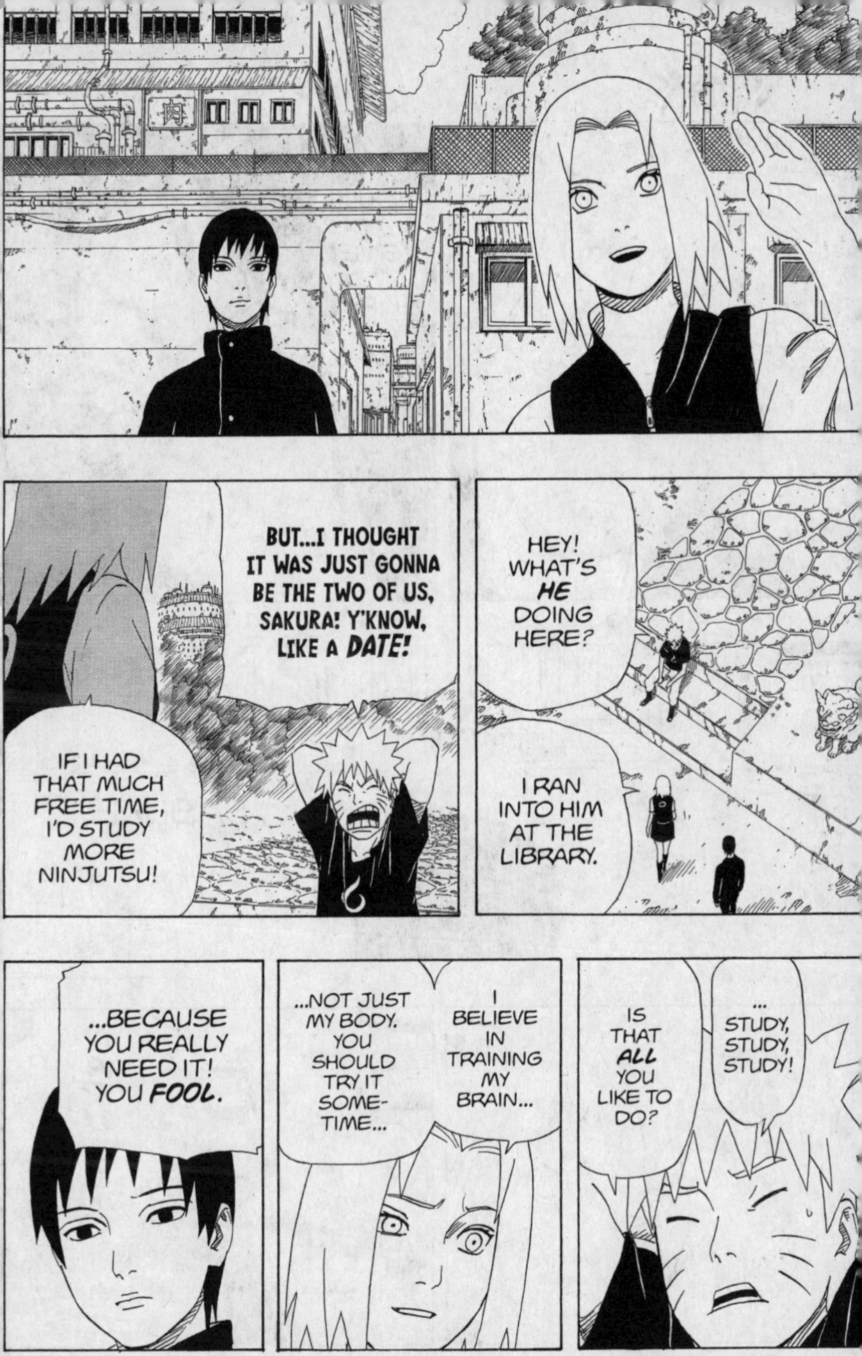
HEY! WHAT'S HE DOING HERE?
I RAN INTO HIM AT THE LIBRARY.
BUT...I THOUGHT IT WAS JUST GONNA BE THE TWO OF US, SAKURA! Y'KNOW, LIKE A DATE!
IF I HAD THAT MUCH FREE TIME, I'D STUDY MORE NINJUTSU!
... STUDY, STUDY, STUDY!
IS THAT ALL YOU LIKE TO DO?
I BELIEVE IN TRAINING MY BRAIN...
...NOT JUST MY BODY. YOU SHOULD TRY IT SOME-TIME...
...BECAUSE YOU REALLY NEED IT! YOU FOOL.

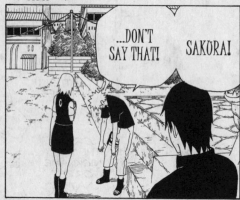

...DON'T SAY THAT!

SAKURA!

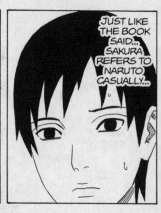

JUST LIKE THE BOOK SAID... SAKURA REFERS TO NARUTO CASUALLY...

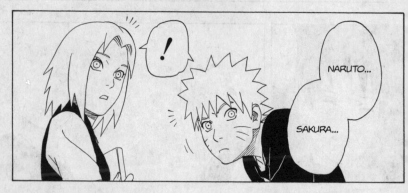

!

NARUTO...

SAKURA...

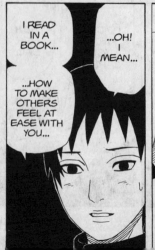

I READ IN A BOOK...

...HOW TO MAKE OTHERS FEEL AT EASE WITH YOU...

...OH! I MEAN...

....?

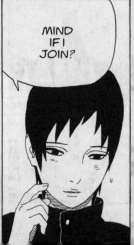

MIND IF I JOIN?

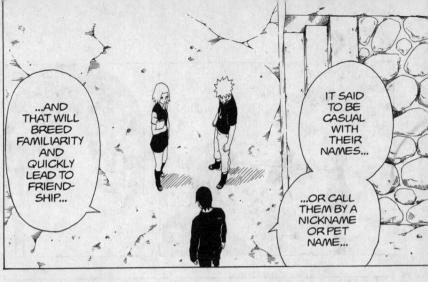

IT SAID TO BE CASUAL WITH THEIR NAMES...
...OR CALL THEM BY A NICKNAME OR PET NAME...
...AND THAT WILL BREED FAMILIARITY AND QUICKLY LEAD TO FRIEND-SHIP...
...
HEH HEH. SAI...
I DIDN'T KNOW YOU CARED.
SO THAT'S WHY YOU WERE AT THE LIBRARY ...
...
...YES.

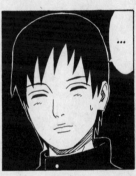

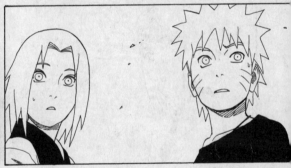

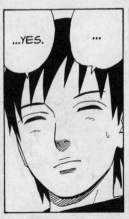

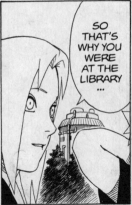

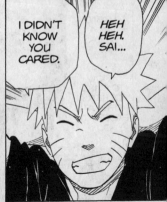

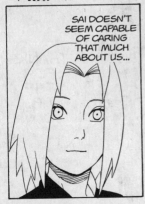

READ THIS WAY

SO...I WAS TRYING TO THINK OF NICKNAMES OR PET NAMES FOR THE TWO OF YOU...
...AND I COULDN'T REALLY THINK OF ANY, SO I DECIDED TO JUST GO WITH REFERRING TO YOU CASUALLY...
SAI DOESN'T SEEM CAPABLE OF CARING THAT MUCH ABOUT US...
DON'T THINK SO HARD. JUST LET IT COME NATURALLY!
PET NAMES AND NICKNAMES OFTEN REFER TO THAT PERSON'S PERSONALITY TRAITS.
TAKE NARUTO, FOR EXAMPLE...
...YOU COULD CALL HIM *STUPID NARUTO*! OR *DIMWIT NARUTO*!
SAKURA! YOU DID IT AGAIN!
SLUMP
I SEE... PERSONALITY TRAITS, HUH...
WOW, SAI'S...
...SO DIFFERENT FROM WHEN WE FIRST MET HIM...

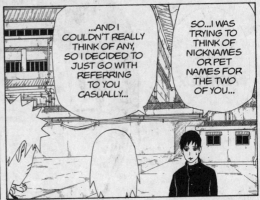

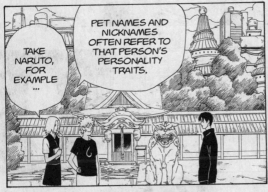

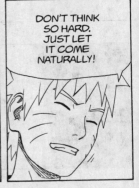

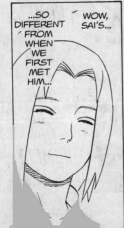

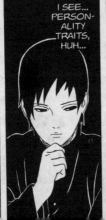

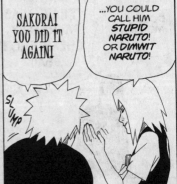

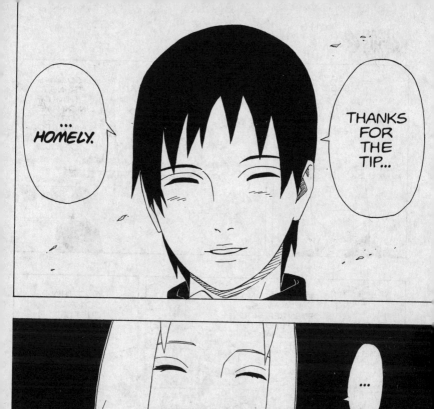

THANKS FOR THE TIP...
... HOMELY.
...
HOMELY III WHO ARE YOU CALL-ING HOMELY ...???
RAARR!
NOW THAT WAS A REALLY CHEAP SHOT, SAI!
...HUH? WHAT DO YOU MEAN?

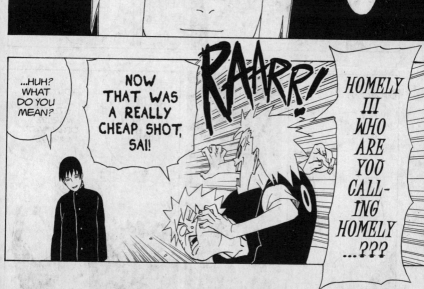

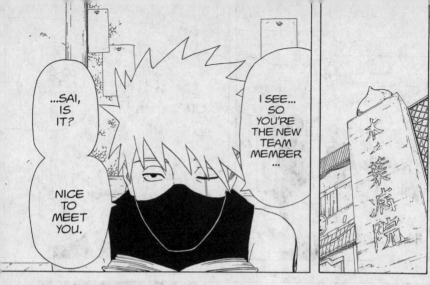

木ノ葉病院
I SEE... SO YOU'RE THE NEW TEAM MEMBER...
...SAI, IS IT?
NICE TO MEET YOU.
...YES, SIR.
HEY, SAKURA, COME HERE A SECOND...
?
FWP FWP
TEP
THOSE BRUISES ON THE BOYS' FACES... DID THEY GET INTO A FIGHT?
KNOWING NARUTO'S TEMPER, I CAN GUESS WHAT HAPPENED, BUT...
Make-Out

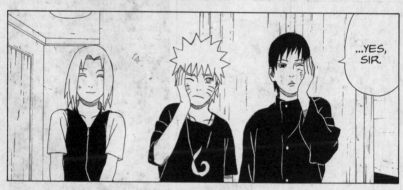

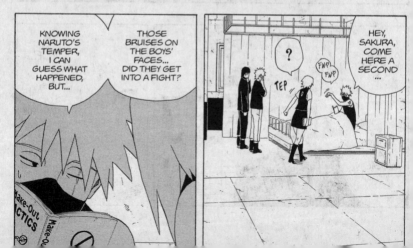

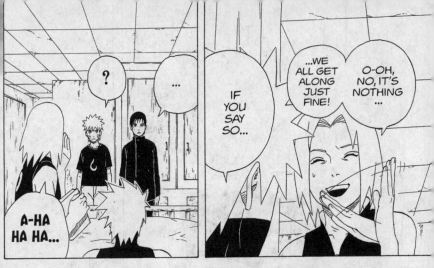

O-OH, NO, IT'S NOTHING ...
...WE ALL GET ALONG JUST FINE!
IF YOU SAY SO...
...
?
A-HA HA HA...
SO THIS IS HATAKE KAKASHI, FAMED EVEN AMONG THOSE OF THE FOUNDATION...
...I BET HE'S LOOKED ME UP TOO.
...
NARUTO ...
YUP...
...
MASTER KAKASHI ...
...ON OUR LAST MISSION, WE...

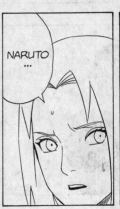

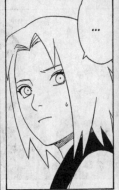

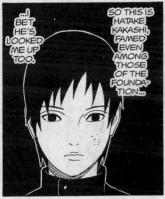

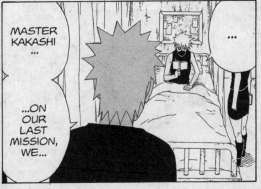

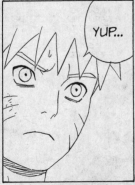

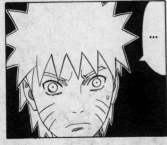

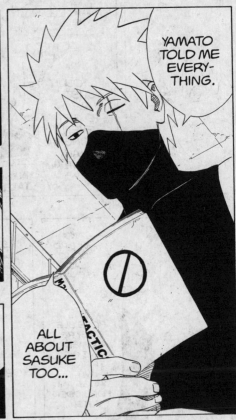

READ THIS WAY
YAMATO TOLD ME EVERY-THING.
ALL ABOUT SASUKE TOO...
...
...
...
AND WHERE I'M AT NOW, I'M NOT STRONG ENOUGH TO BRING SASUKE BACK...
...HE'S BECOME TOO STRONG...
WE'RE RUNNING OUT OF TIME...
AT THIS RATE, HE'LL SOON BE...

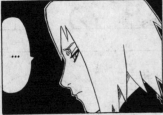

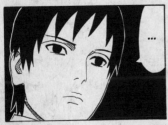

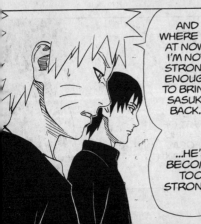

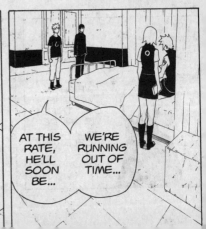

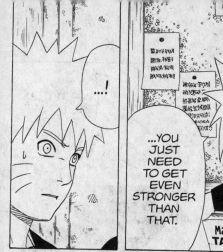

...!
WELL ...IN THAT CASE...
...YOU JUST NEED TO GET EVEN STRONGER THAN THAT.
Make-Out TACTICS
AS I SEE IT, SASUKE'S RATE OF MATURATION ...
...ISN'T ORDINARY...
AND ACCORDING TO LADY TSUNADE ...
...IT'S POSSIBLE THEY'RE AUGMENTING HIS TRAINING WITH DRUGS AND FORBIDDEN JUTSU...
... COURTESY OF KABUTO...
I REALIZE THERE ARE NO BOOKS THAT CAN HELP US UNDERSTAND...
...THE MINDSET OF THOSE WHO PERFORM LIVE HUMAN EXPERIMENTS ...
The Effects of Medicinals
WHICH IS WHY THE ONLY THING WE *CAN* DO IS SUPER-ACCELERATE OUR OWN GROWTH.

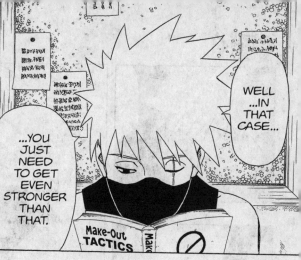

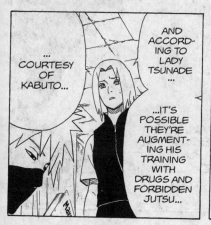

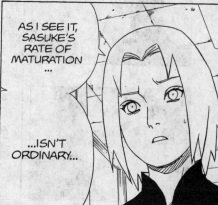

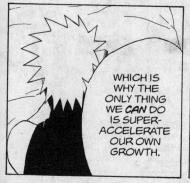

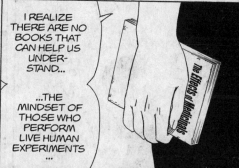

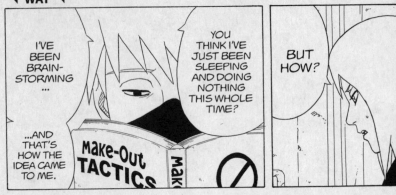

READ THIS WAY

BUT HOW?
YOU THINK I'VE JUST BEEN SLEEPING AND DOING NOTHING THIS WHOLE TIME?
I'VE BEEN BRAIN-STORMING ...
...AND THAT'S HOW THE IDEA CAME TO ME.
Make-Out TACTICS
BUT THIS METHOD IS MORE SUITED TO NARUTO...
...OR RATHER, IT WILL *ONLY* WORK WITH NARUTO.
...
HM...
AND IF IT DOES PAN OUT...
...NARUTO, YOU MAY EVEN SURPASS ME.

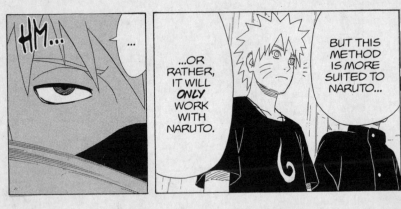

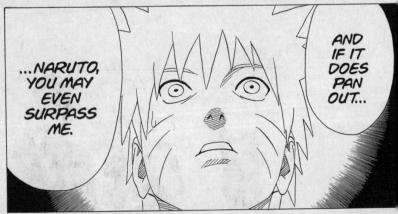

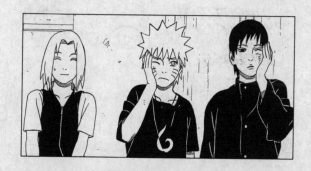

Number 312: The Impending Menace!!

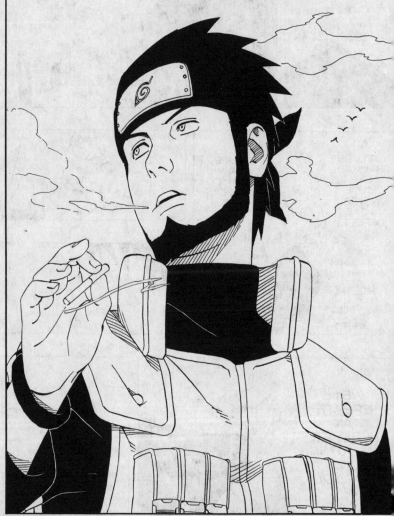

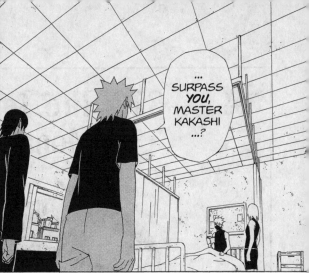

... SURPASS YOU, MASTER KAKASHI ...?
THAT'S RIGHT.
...
...
I'LL BE WORKING WITH YOU ONE-ON-ONE...
...IT'LL BE TRAINING LIKE YOU'VE NEVER DONE BEFORE.
...
NEVER ...? HOW ...?
WE'LL CREATE AN ULTIMATE NINJUTSU, ONLY FOR YOU.

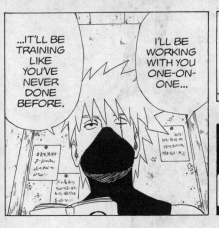

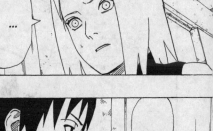

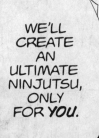

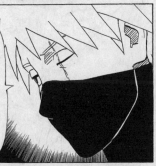

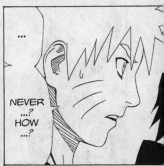

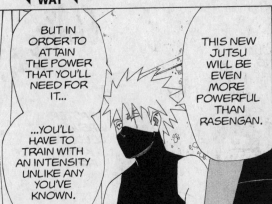

READ THIS WAY

THIS NEW JUTSU WILL BE EVEN MORE POWERFUL THAN RASENGAN.
BUT IN ORDER TO ATTAIN THE POWER THAT YOU'LL NEED FOR IT...
...YOU'LL HAVE TO TRAIN WITH AN INTENSITY UNLIKE ANY YOU'VE KNOWN.
IT'S NOT LIKE SOME CHARACTER IN A NOVEL. YOU CAN'T GET STRONGER IN JUST A FEW DAYS.
AND IT WON'T BE LIKE A PRE-EXISTING JUTSU SUCH AS THE RASENGAN...
...THAT WE CAN BREAK DOWN AND WORK ON IN SIMPLER STAGES.
... MASSIVE AMOUNT OF TIME ...?
BUT I JUST TOLD YOU, WE'RE OUT OF TIME! SASUKE'S ALMOST...
...!
THAT'S WHY I FIGURED OUT A WAY TO DO IT IN A SHORT PERIOD.
H-HOW ...?
WELL ...

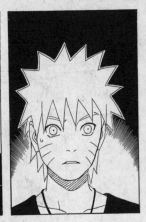

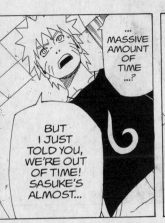

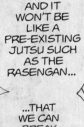

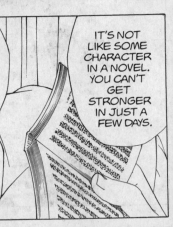

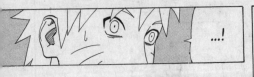

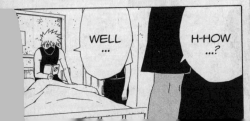

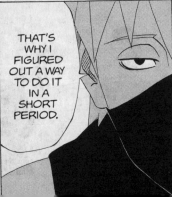

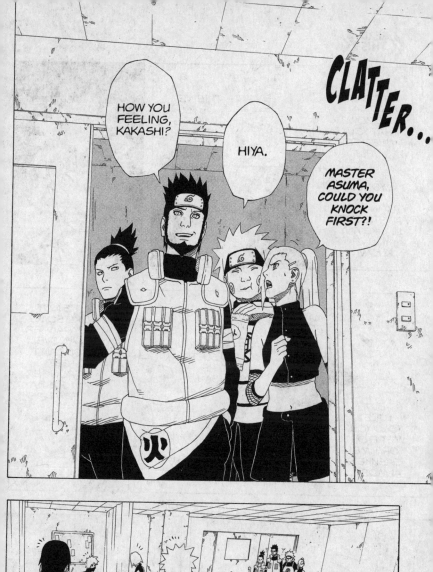

CLATTER...
MASTER ASUMA, COULD YOU KNOCK FIRST?!
HIYA.
HOW YOU FEELING, KAKASHI?
SHUFF SHUFF

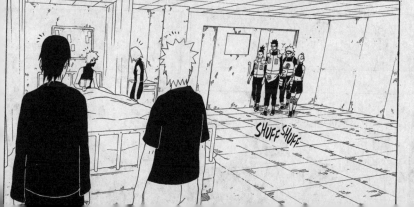

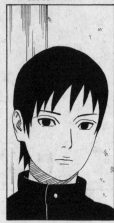

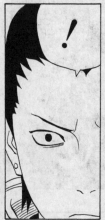

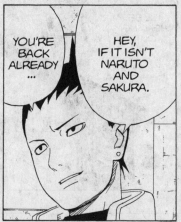

READ THIS WAY

HEY, IF IT ISN'T NARUTO AND SAKURA.
YOU'RE BACK ALREADY ...
!
YOU'RE THAT KID FROM...
!
OH!
?
HI.

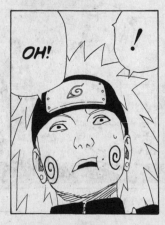

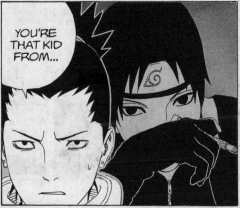

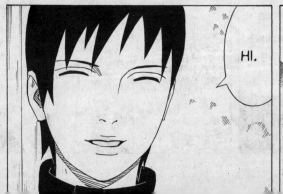

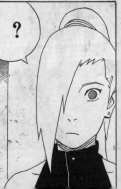

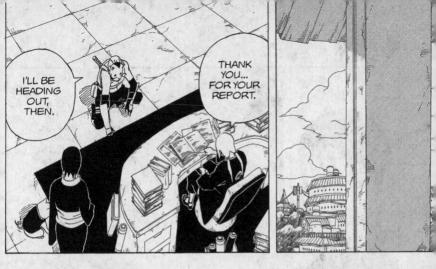

THANK YOU... FOR YOUR REPORT.
I'LL BE HEADING OUT, THEN.
FWUSH
IT SEEMS THE AKATSUKI IS STARTING TO REALLY MAKE THEIR MOVE.
WHICH MEANS IT'S ONLY A MATTER OF TIME BEFORE THEIR NEXT FORAY INTO KONOHA TERRITORY.
IT'S DANGEROUS ...BUT ALSO THE BEST OPPORTUNITY TO SMASH THEM.
WE'VE GOT NO TIME LEFT TO LOSE.

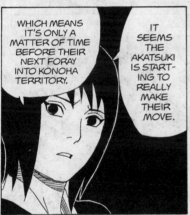

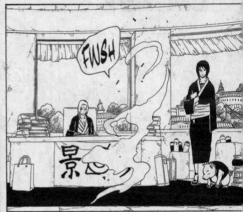

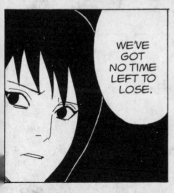

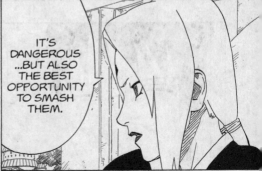

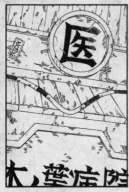

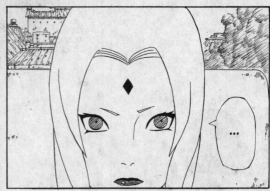

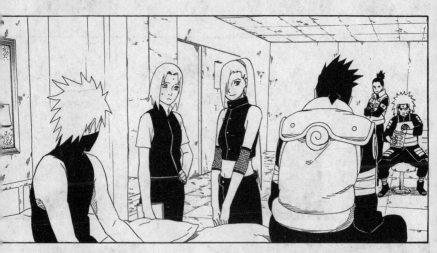

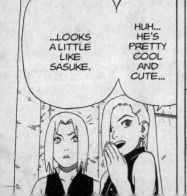

READ THIS WAY
...
医
OHH, SO THAT'S WHAT THAT WAS ABOUT.
MY NAME IS SAI.
AND YOU MAY ADDRESS ME ACCORDINGLY.
HUH... HE'S PRETTY COOL AND CUTE...
...LOOKS A LITTLE LIKE SASUKE.

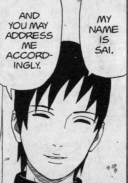

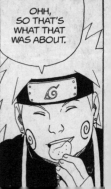

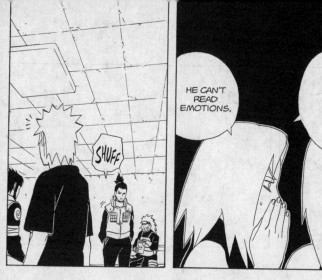

UH, MAYBE IN LOOKS, BUT INSIDE HE'S QUITE DIFFERENT.
HE CAN'T READ EMOTIONS.
SHUFF
LADY TSUNADE TOLD ME WHAT HAPPENED WITH SASUKE.
NEXT TIME SOMETHING COMES UP, I'LL HELP TOO.
ESPECIALLY NOW THAT THAT BOTHERSOME CHŪNIN SELECTION EXAM IS OVER.
...
THANKS ...
...

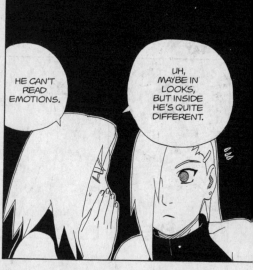

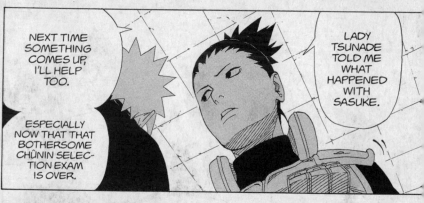

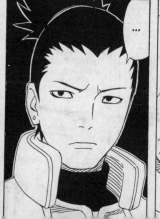

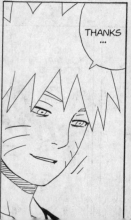

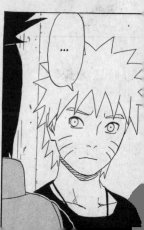

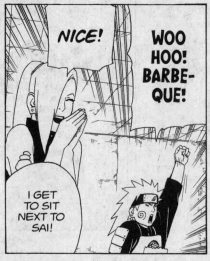

READ THIS WAY

WHY DON'T YOU ALL GO ON AHEAD TO YAKINIKU Q, THE BBQ HOUSE.
TEAM KAKASHI, YOU'RE WELCOME TO JOIN US.
WOO HOO! BARBE-QUE!
NICE!
I GET TO SIT NEXT TO SAI!
I'M BUYING. BUT IN THE MEAN-TIME...
...KAKASHI AND I HAVE SOME BUSINESS TO DISCUSS.
...HEY, WAIT A SEC!!
MASTER KAKASHI, WHAT ABOUT THAT TRAINING YOU WERE TELLING ME ABOUT?!
...RIGHT. HMM...
WELL! WE'LL GET BACK TO THAT LATER.
WHAT?!
AW, MAN! JUST WHEN I WAS GETTING ALL EXCITED!

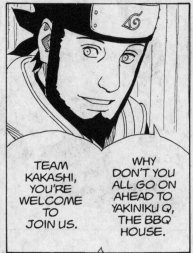

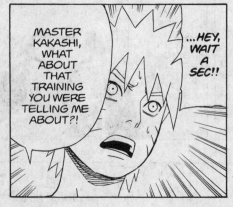

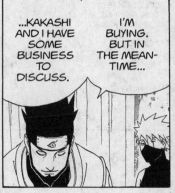

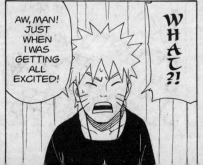

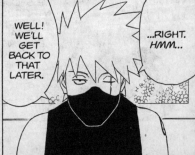

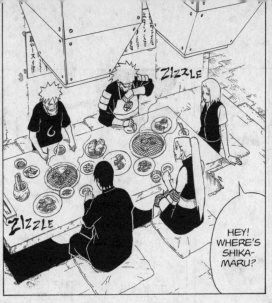

焼肉Q
(YAKINIKU Q)
ZIZZLE
ZIZZLE
HEY! WHERE'S SHIKA-MARU?
HOME. HE'S GOTTA GO COLLECT MEDICINAL ANTLERS WITH HIS DAD OR SOME-THING.
HUH.
BUT HE'S ALWAYS CELEBRATED MISSION COMPLETIONS WITH US BEFORE...
HOW ODD...
FAP
WELL, SINCE HE'S NOT HERE... I GET SHIKA-MARU'S!
HEY, CHOJI! WE SHOULD INTRODUCE OURSELVES TO SAI BEFORE WE START EATING.
OH, RIGHT...

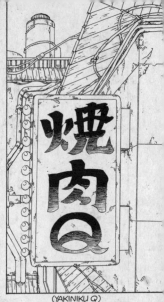

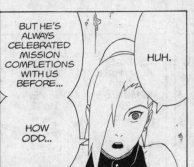

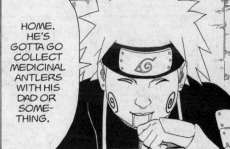

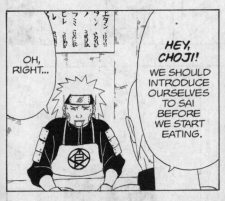

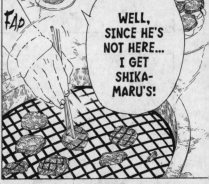

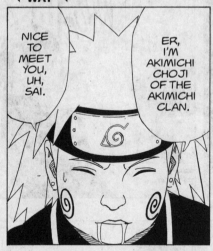

READ THIS WAY
... THANKS ...
FIRST IMPRESSIONS ARE EVERYTHING, SO I'VE GOT TO COME UP WITH A NICKNAME OR PET NAME RIGHT AWAY...
ER, I'M AKIMICHI CHOJI OF THE AKIMICHI CLAN.
NICE TO MEET YOU, UH, SAI.
NICE TO MEET YOU TOO... UH...
PERSON-ALITY TRAIT... TRAIT...
...!
DON'T TELL ME...!
...!
HE'S GOING TO SAY THE FOR-BIDDEN WORD!
... CHUB-
GRRR

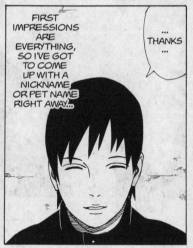

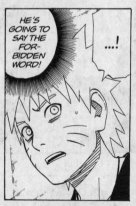

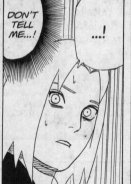

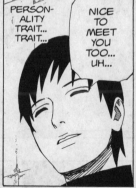

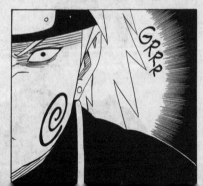

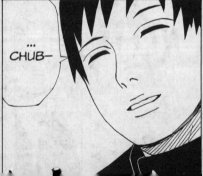

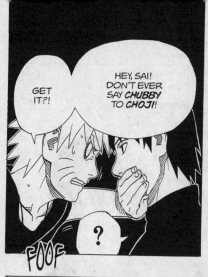

WHUP
!
HEY, SAI! DON'T EVER SAY CHUBBY TO CHOJI!
GET IT?!
?
FOOF
...WERE YOU ABOUT TO SAY SOME-THING?
A-HA HA... NO, NO...
NICK-NAMES ARE HARD...
I'M YAMANAKA INO. MY PARENTS OWN YAMANAKA FLOWERS.
NICE TO MEET YOU!
IN THE CASE OF WOMEN, IF YOU STATE THEIR PER-SONALITY TRAITS TOO BLUNTLY, YOU WILL ANGER THEM...
...WHICH MEANS I SHOULD SAY SOME-THING OPPOSITE ...
NICE TO MEET YOU... UM...

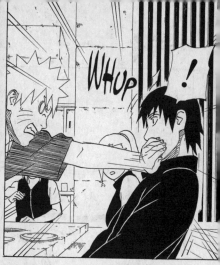

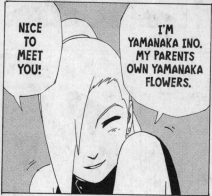

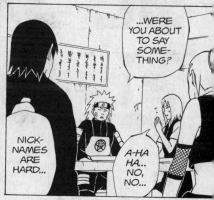

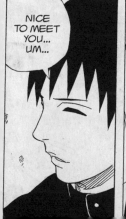

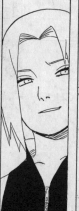

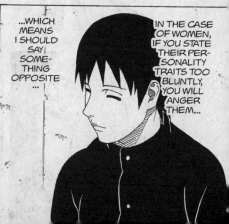

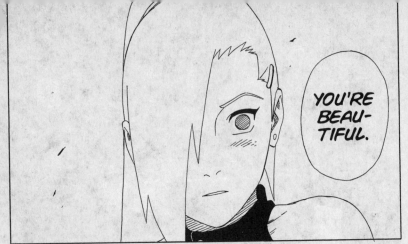

YOU'RE BEAU-TIFUL.

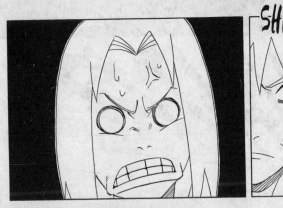

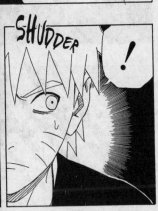

SHUDDER

!

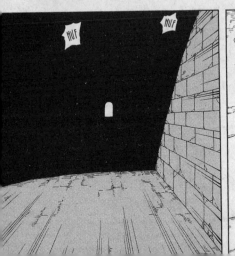

HUF

HUF

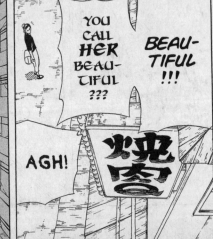

YOU CALL HER BEAU-TIFUL ???

BEAU-TIFUL !!!

AGH!

焼肉

HUF
HUF
WHIP
SPLASH
HNH ...
SPLISH
SPLISH
SPLISH

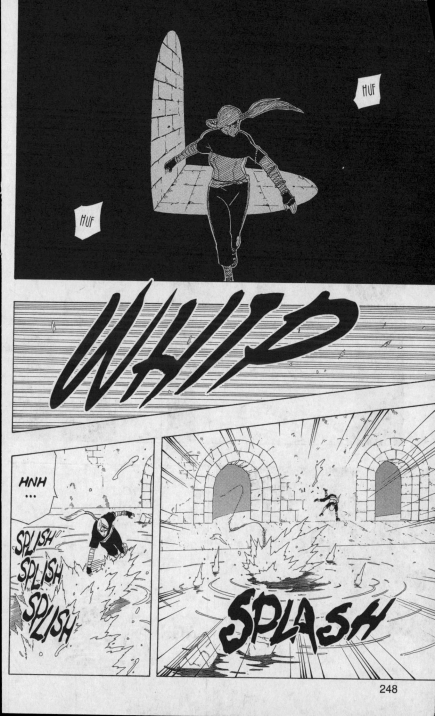

READ THIS WAY

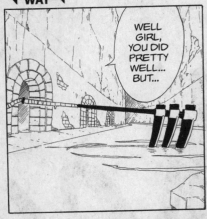

WELL GIRL, YOU DID PRETTY WELL... BUT...
HMM... THEN AGAIN, MY ATTACK SPEED IS THE SLOWEST AND MY AIM WORST AMONG THE AKATSUKI...
...SO I PROBABLY CAN'T HIT YOU ANYWAY, BUT...
SHUP...
SHUP...
JUST AS I SUS-PECTED ...YOU ARE FROM THE AKATSUKI ...
SHE'S ALL YOURS.

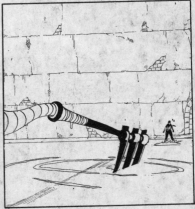

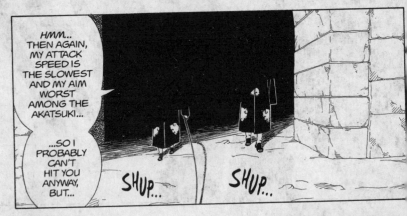

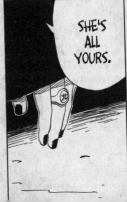

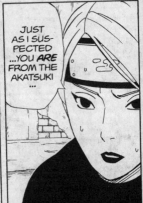

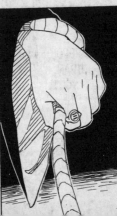

SHE'S THE JINCHŪRIKI HOST OF TWO TAILS.
BE CAREFUL, HIDAN, OR YOU'LL DIE.

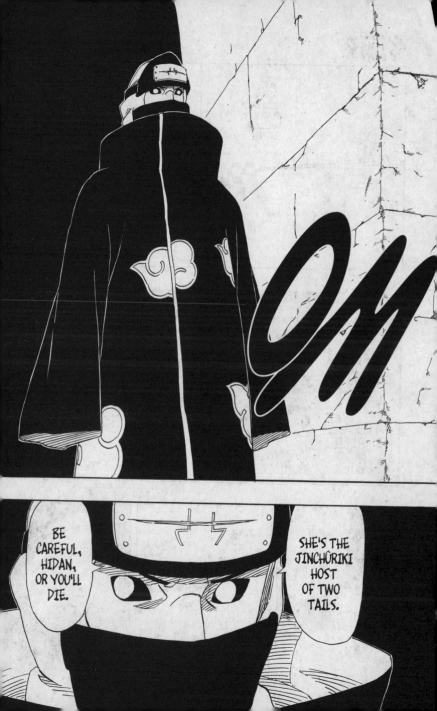

ME? YOU'RE USUALLY THE DOER.
OH COME ON, KAKUZU.
I'D LIKE NOTHING BETTER THAN TO BE KILLED.

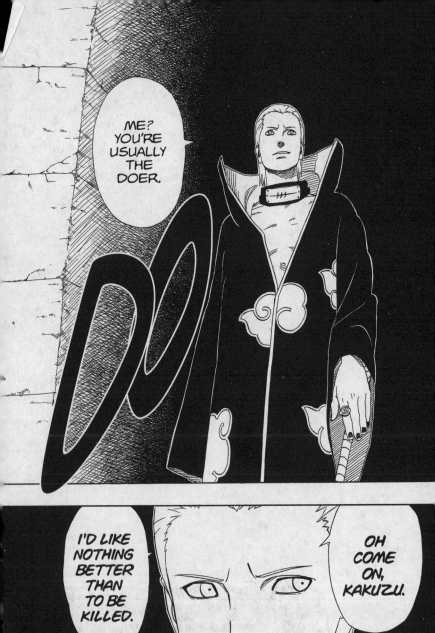

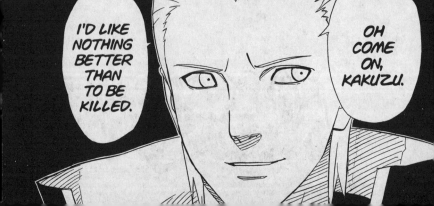

NARUTO

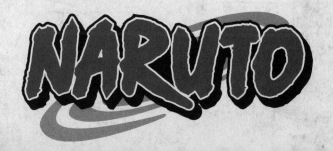

Number 313: The New Two!!

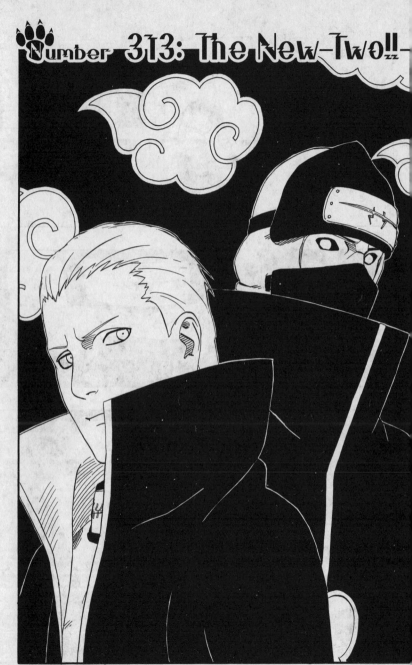

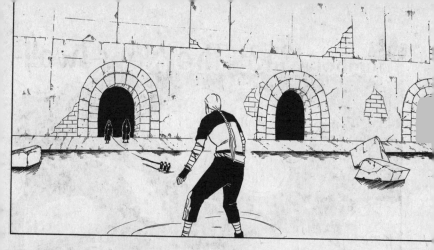

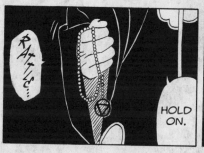

RATTLE...

HOLD ON.

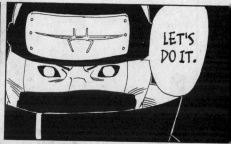

LET'S DO IT.

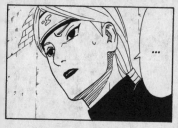

...

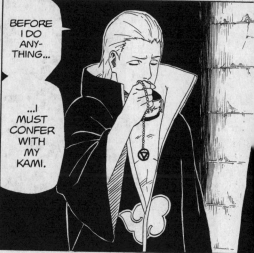

BEFORE I DO ANY-THING...

...I MUST CONFER WITH MY KAMI.

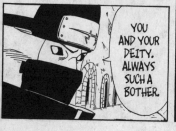

YOU AND YOUR DEITY. ALWAYS SUCH A BOTHER.

IT'S BOTHER-SOME TO ME TOO, BUT...
...THE COMMANDMENTS ARE STRICT, SO I HAVE NO CHOICE!
...
HEH... YOU THINK YOU CHASED ME IN HERE?
ACTUALLY...
FWP
I LURED YOU HERE!
SSSSS
BOOOM

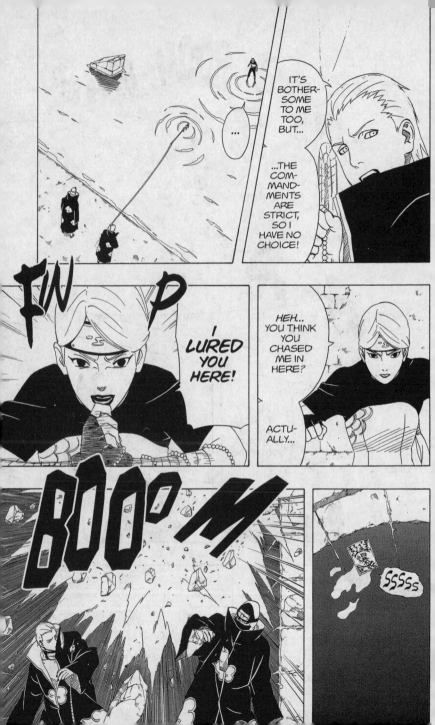

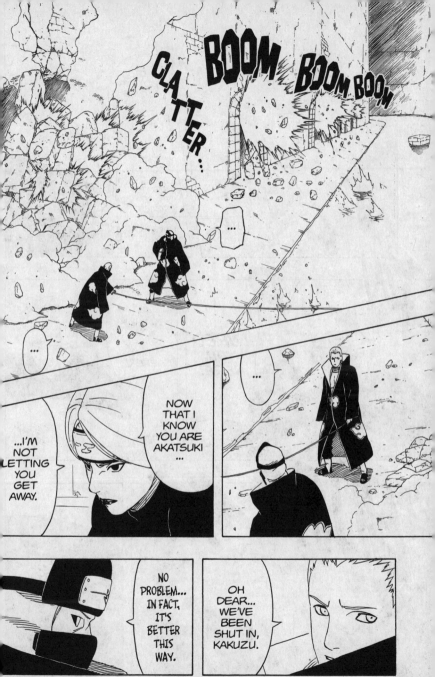

BOOM BOOM
BOOM
CLATTER...
...
...
...
NOW THAT I KNOW YOU ARE AKATSUKI ...
...I'M NOT LETTING YOU GET AWAY.
OH DEAR... WE'VE BEEN SHUT IN, KAKUZU.
NO PROBLEM... IN FACT, IT'S BETTER THIS WAY.

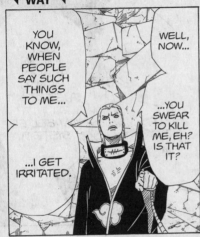

READ THIS WAY

UPON MY NAME, NI'I YUGITO OF KUMO-GAKURE...
...I SWEAR I WILL KILL YOU!!
WELL, NOW...
...YOU SWEAR TO KILL ME, EH? IS THAT IT?
YOU KNOW, WHEN PEOPLE SAY SUCH THINGS TO ME...
...I GET IRRITATED.
AND...
...WHEN I GET IRRITATED, I LOSE MY TEMPER.
AND WHEN I LOSE MY TEMPER...
SHUT UP, HIDAN.
YES, YES.
BUT YOU KNOW, WHEN I LOSE MY TEMPER, I START THINKING, WHO CARES ABOUT THE MISSION, IT'S TIME TO ATTACK.
ENOUGH, HIDAN.
THE MISSION IS ABSOLUTE.

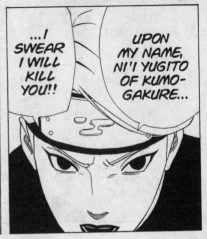

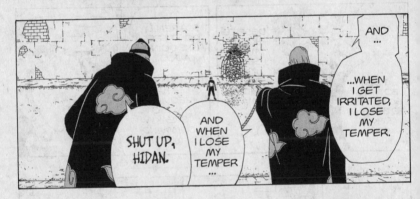

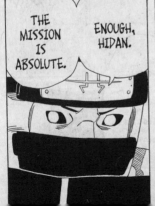

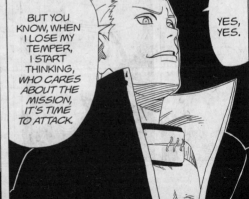

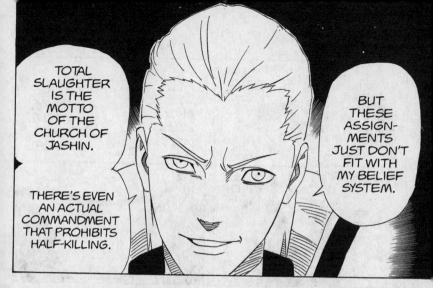

TOTAL SLAUGHTER IS THE MOTTO OF THE CHURCH OF JASHIN.

THERE'S EVEN AN ACTUAL COMMANDMENT THAT PROHIBITS HALF-KILLING.

BUT THESE ASSIGN-MENTS JUST DON'T FIT WITH MY BELIEF SYSTEM.

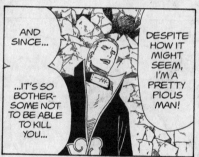

AND SINCE...

...IT'S SO BOTHER-SOME NOT TO BE ABLE TO KILL YOU...

DESPITE HOW IT MIGHT SEEM, I'M A PRETTY PIOUS MAN!

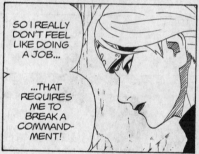

SO I REALLY DON'T FEEL LIKE DOING A JOB...

...THAT REQUIRES ME TO BREAK A COMMAND-MENT!

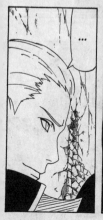

...

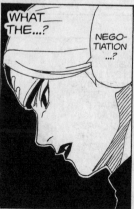

WHAT THE...?

NEGO-TIATION ...?

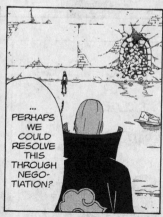

...PERHAPS WE COULD RESOLVE THIS THROUGH NEGO-TIATION?

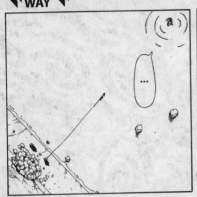

...

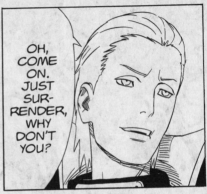

OH, COME ON. JUST SURRENDER, WHY DON'T YOU?

YOU MUST BE JOKING!!

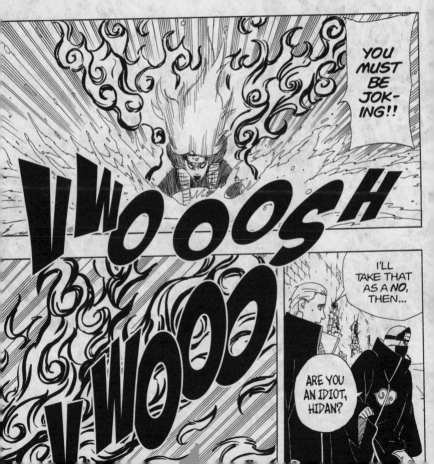

WOOOSH

WOOO

I'LL TAKE THAT AS A *NO*, THEN...

ARE YOU AN IDIOT, HIDAN?

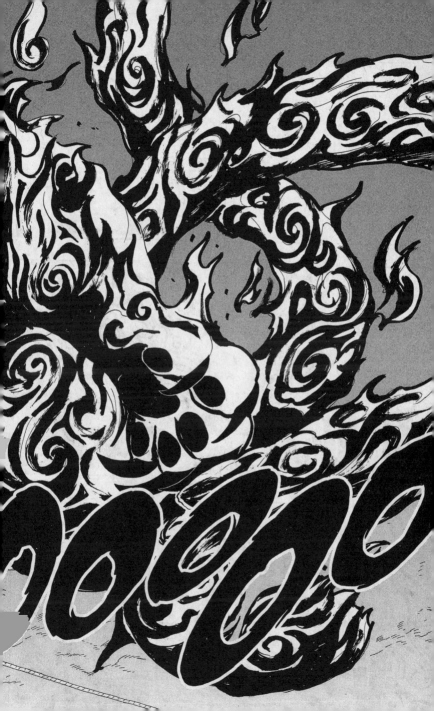

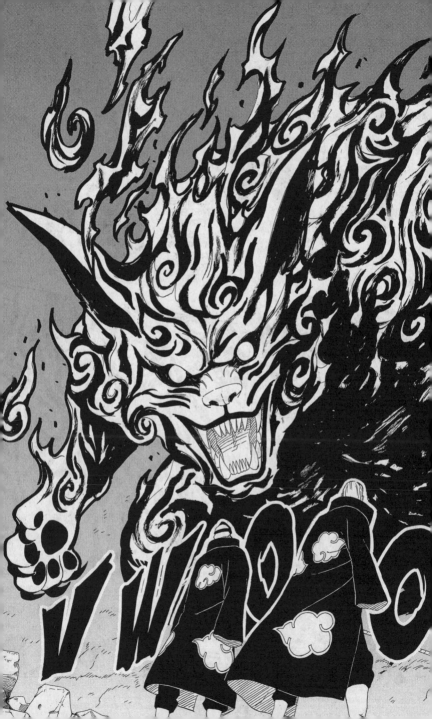

WHAT THE...? THIS JINCHÛ-RIKI HOST...
...SHE'S COMPLETELY TURNED HERSELF OVER TO HER TAILED BEAST SPIRIT!
FAP
GLOM
SWOOSH

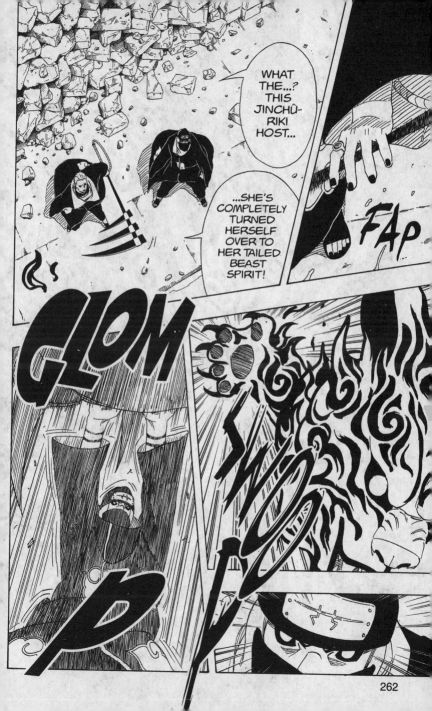

SLAM
OH NO!
FWOOOOO
AGH!
BLAAAZE
TAK

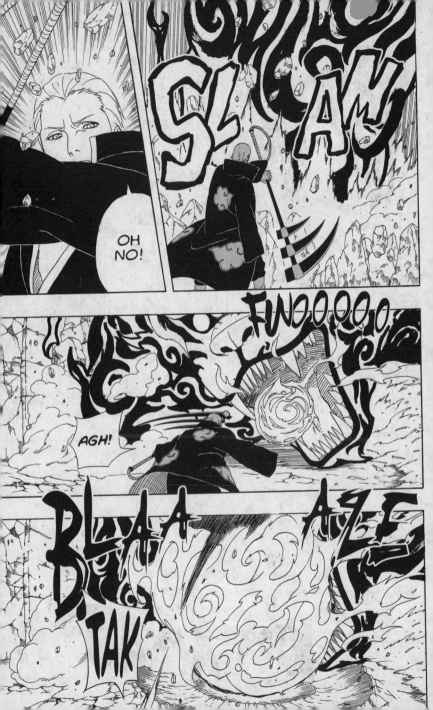

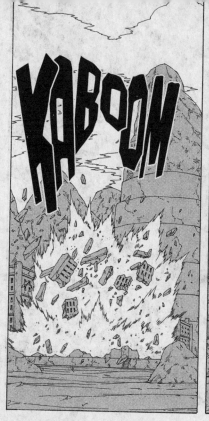

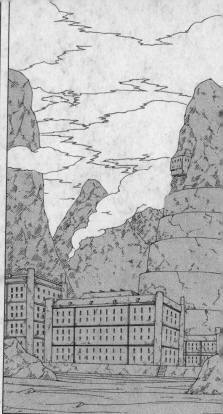

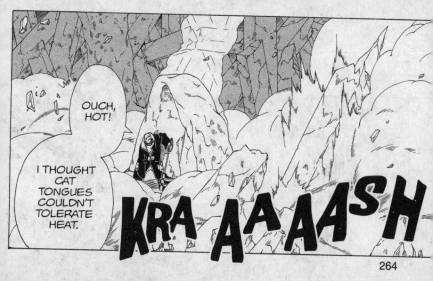

OUCH, HOT!

I THOUGHT CAT TONGUES COULDN'T TOLERATE HEAT.

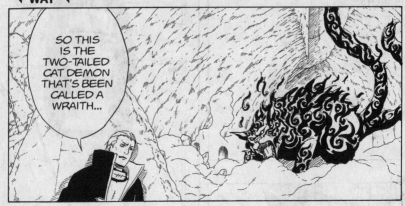

SO THIS IS THE TWO-TAILED CAT DEMON THAT'S BEEN CALLED A WRAITH...

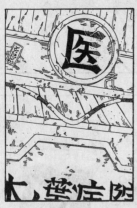

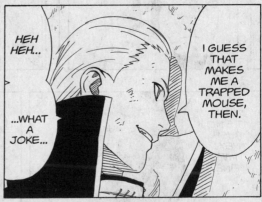

HEH HEH...

...WHAT A JOKE...

I GUESS THAT MAKES ME A TRAPPED MOUSE, THEN.

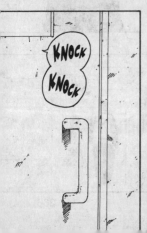

KNOCK

KNOCK

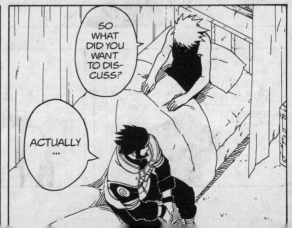

SO WHAT DID YOU WANT TO DIS-CUSS?

ACTUALLY...

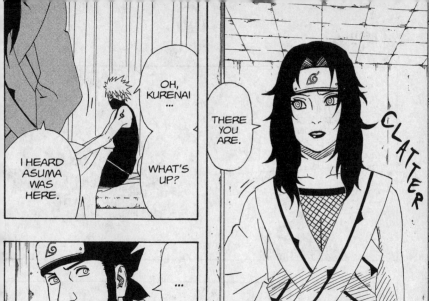

CLATTER
THERE YOU ARE.
OH, KURENAI...
WHAT'S UP?
I HEARD ASUMA WAS HERE.
...
I SEE...
SO WHERE WERE WE, ASUMA?
...
NAH, IT'S NO RUSH. NEXT TIME'S FINE.
LATER.
SHUP
...
NOW IT'S REALLY GOING TO BOTHER ME...

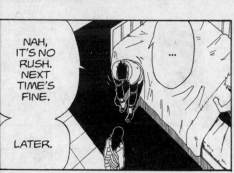

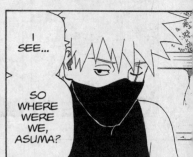

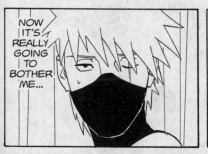

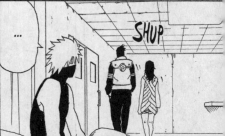

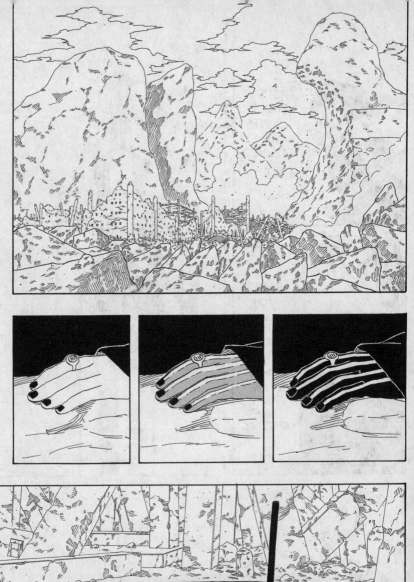
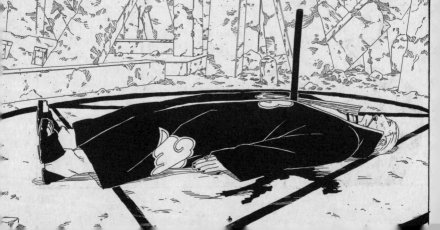

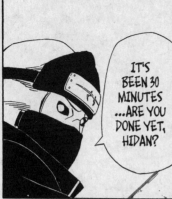

IT'S BEEN 30 MINUTES ...ARE YOU DONE YET, HIDAN?

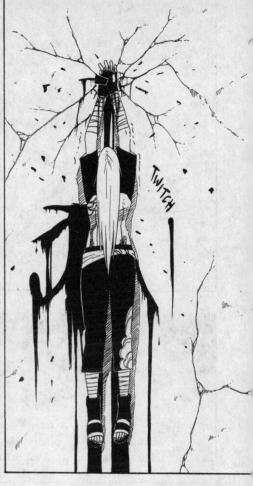

TWITCH

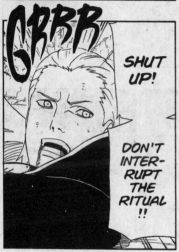

GRRR

SHUT UP!

DON'T INTER-RUPT THE RITUAL!!

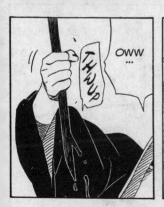

THWUP

OWW...

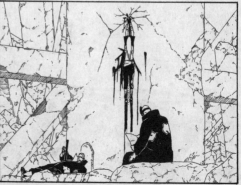

READ THIS WAY

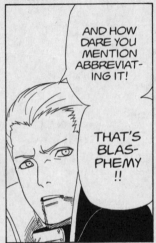

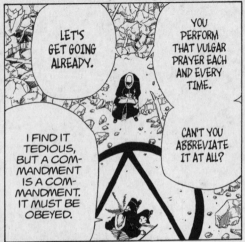

YOU PERFORM THAT VULGAR PRAYER EACH AND EVERY TIME.
CAN'T YOU ABBREVIATE IT AT ALL?
LET'S GET GOING ALREADY.
I FIND IT TEDIOUS, BUT A COMMANDMENT IS A COMMANDMENT. IT MUST BE OBEYED.
AND HOW DARE YOU MENTION ABBREVIATING IT!
THAT'S BLASPHEMY !!
...
WE STILL HAVE ONE ASSIGNMENT LEFT...
IT'S LIKE FINDING A NEEDLE IN A HAYSTACK...
THE LAND OF FIRE'S NEXT.

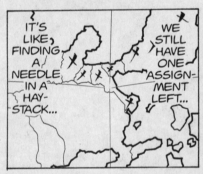

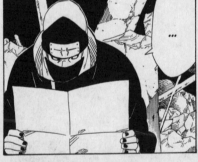

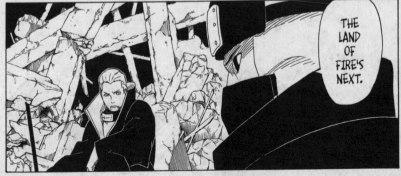

NARUTO

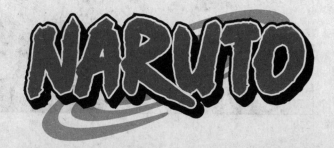

Number 314: The Akatsuki Strikes...!!

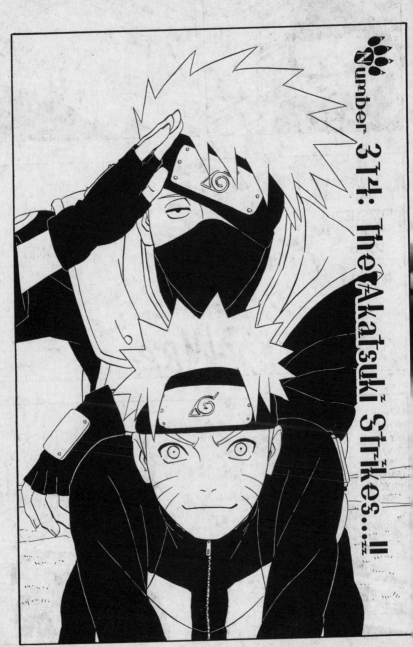

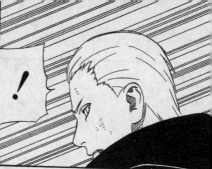

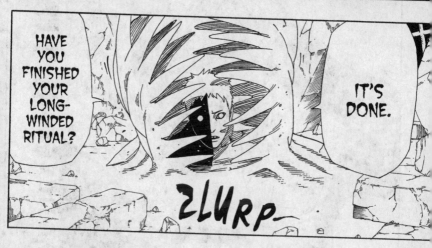

!
!
IT'S DONE.
HAVE YOU FINISHED YOUR LONG-WINDED RITUAL?
ZLURP
YOU AS WELL?
IGNORANT HEATHENS, THE LOT OF YOU.
SORROW BEGETS SOLI-TUDE.
THE ONLY THING YOU CAN HAVE FAITH IN IS YOUR-SELF.

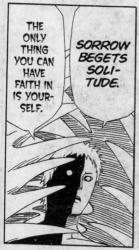

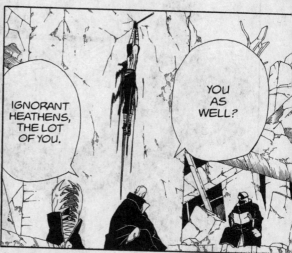

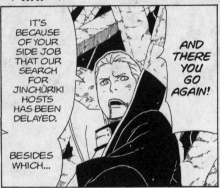

READ THIS WAY

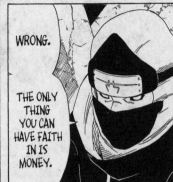

WRONG.
THE ONLY THING YOU CAN HAVE FAITH IN IS MONEY.
AND THERE YOU GO AGAIN!
IT'S BECAUSE OF YOUR SIDE JOB THAT OUR SEARCH FOR JINCHÛRIKI HOSTS HAS BEEN DELAYED.
BESIDES WHICH...
LOOK, I ONLY TEAMED UP WITH YOU BECAUSE YOU SAID RELIGION IS PROFIT-ABLE.
IF ANYONE HAS THE RIGHT TO COMPLAIN, IT'S ME, THE AKATSUKI'S PURSE-HOLDER.
MONEY IS IMPOR-TANT...
ENOUGH. YOU TWO, HEAD OUT TO YOUR NEXT HUNT RIGHT AWAY.
LEAVE THE TWO TAILS TO ME...
(FIRE TEMPLE)
火寺

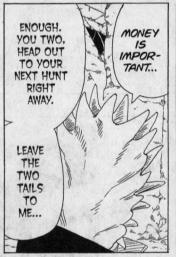

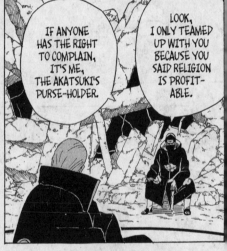

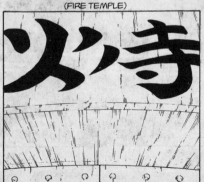

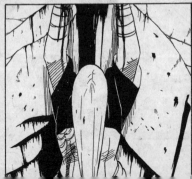

A TEMPLE? YOU SURE THIS IS THE PLACE?
WE'LL SEE.
THIS IS NO ORDINARY TEMPLE...
...SO THE ODDS ARE GOOD.
FWSSH...
SMASH

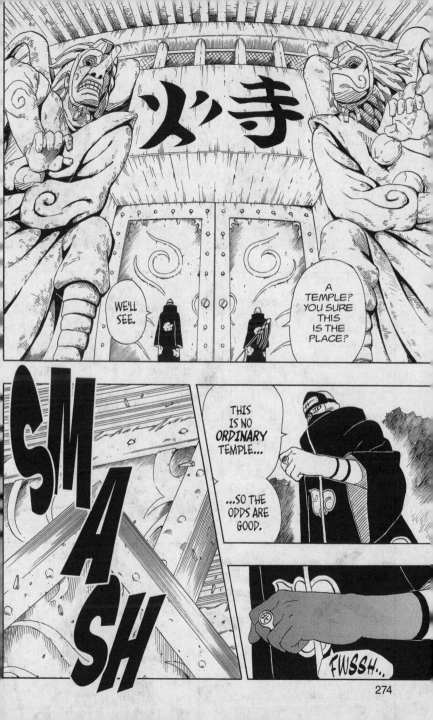

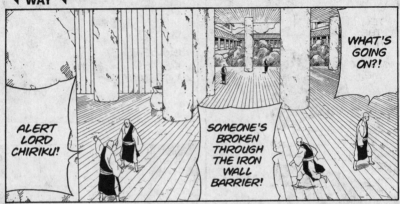

READ THIS WAY

WHAT'S GOING ON?!
SOMEONE'S BROKEN THROUGH THE IRON WALL BARRIER!
ALERT LORD CHIRIKU!
THEY DON'T LOOK VERY WILLING TO CONVERT TO THE CHURCH OF JASHIN...
HUP
THOSE ROBES... THEY LOOK LIKE...
THERE'S NO MISTAKE. THEY'RE FROM THE AKATSUKI!
STOMP STOMP
!
INTRUD-ERS!
WHO ARE THEY?
SHFF

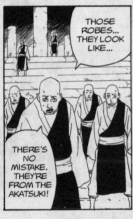

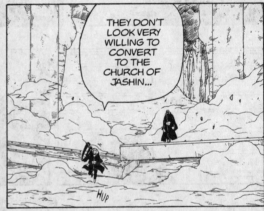

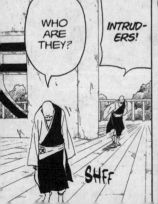

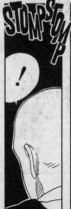

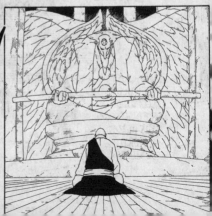

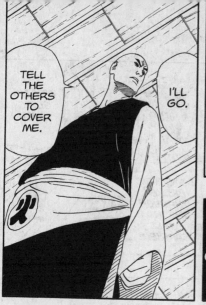

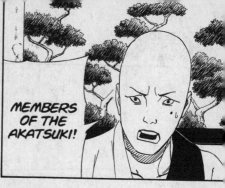

MEMBERS OF THE AKATSUKI!
I'LL GO.
TELL THE OTHERS TO COVER ME.
...
I KNEW THEY WOULD COME CALLING SOME-DAY, BUT...
!
AH, ANOTHER HIGHLY VIRTUOUS SORT...
NOT JUST VIRTUOUS. ACCORDING TO OUR BINGO BOOK, HIS HEAD'S WORTH 30 MILLION!

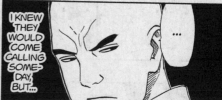

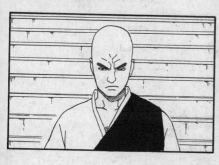

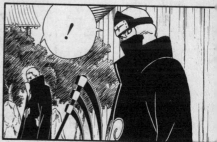

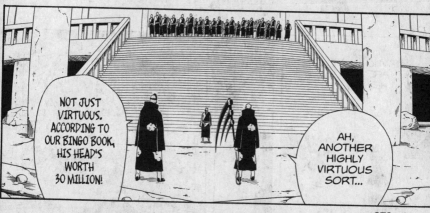

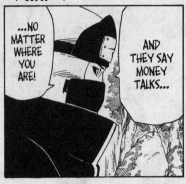

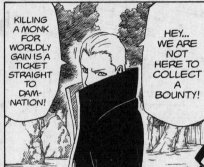

READ THIS WAY

HEY... WE ARE NOT HERE TO COLLECT A BOUNTY!
KILLING A MONK FOR WORLDLY GAIN IS A TICKET STRAIGHT TO DAM-NATION!
AND THEY SAY MONEY TALKS...
...NO MATTER WHERE YOU ARE!
I DO NOT KNOW WHAT BUSINESS BRINGS YOU HERE...
...BUT TURN AROUND AND GO HOME!
NOT GOING TO KILL US WITHOUT A CAUSE, EH?
THAT'S NOT ONE OF MY BELIEFS, THOUGH.
THIS FIRE TEMPLE IS A FAMED SHINOBI TEMPLE LOCATED IN THE LAND OF FIRE.
IT'S SAID THAT ALL THE MONKS WIELD A SPECIAL POWER KNOWN AS THE GIFT OF THE HOLY FOLK.

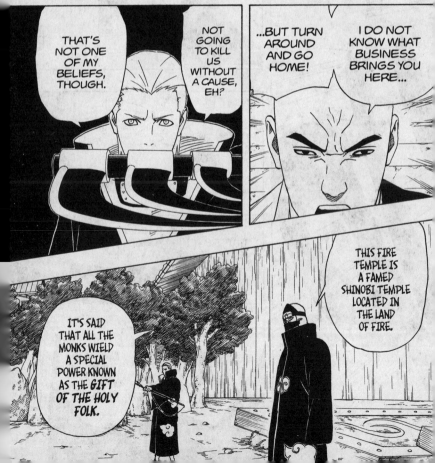

ESPECIALLY THIS MAN WORTH 30 MILLION. HE'S AN ELITE NINJA THAT WAS ONCE APPOINTED TO THE GUARDIAN SHINOBI TWELVE THAT PROTECT THE RULER OF THE LAND OF FIRE.
GUARDIAN SHINOBI TWELVE?
IMPRESSIVE...
THAT FIRE EMBLEM WAISTCLOTH IS PROOF...
SO BE CAREFUL, HIDAN, OR YOU'LL DIE.
ENOUGH, KAKUZU!

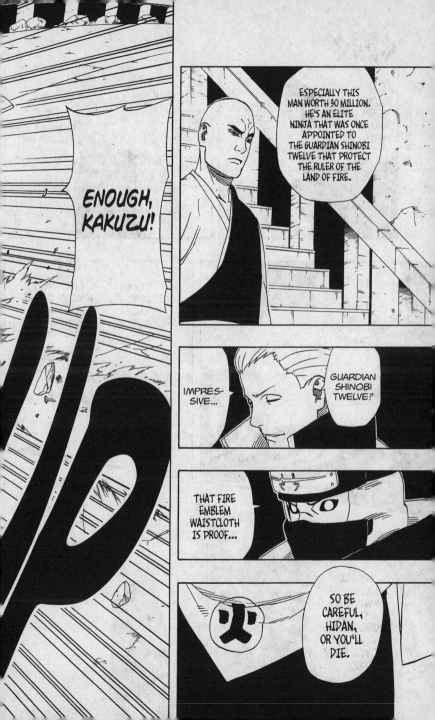

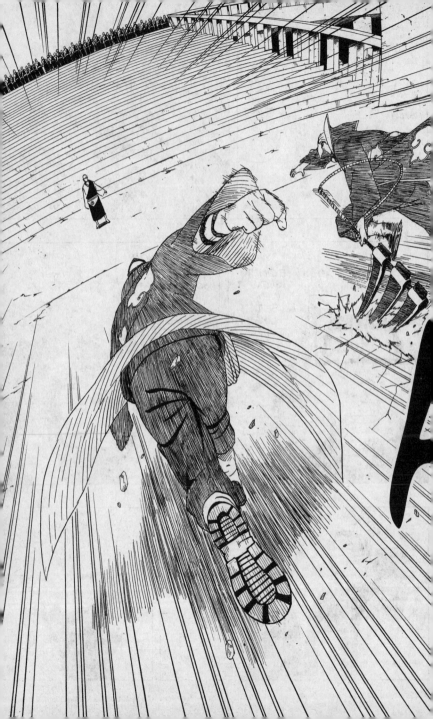

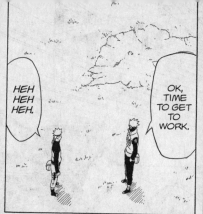

HEH HEH HEH.

OK, TIME TO GET TO WORK.

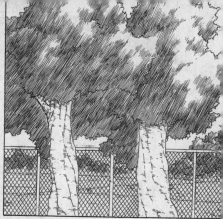

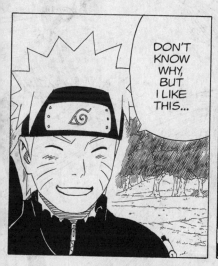

DON'T KNOW WHY, BUT I LIKE THIS...

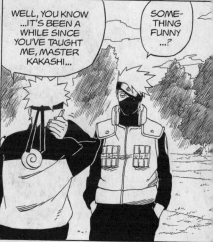

WELL, YOU KNOW ...IT'S BEEN A WHILE SINCE YOU'VE TAUGHT ME, MASTER KAKASHI...

SOME-THING FUNNY ...?

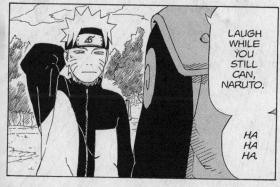

LAUGH WHILE YOU STILL CAN, NARUTO.

HA HA HA.

...

HEH...

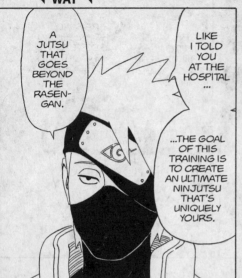

READ THIS WAY

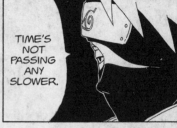

TIME'S NOT PASSING ANY SLOWER.
LIKE I TOLD YOU AT THE HOSPITAL...
...THE GOAL OF THIS TRAINING IS TO CREATE AN ULTIMATE NINJUTSU THAT'S UNIQUELY YOURS.
A JUTSU THAT GOES BEYOND THE RASEN-GAN.
...
IN ORDER TO DO THAT, YOU'LL NEED TO ACQUIRE TWO TECHNIQUES...
...THAT OF CHANGE IN CHAKRA NATURE AND CHANGE IN CHAKRA FORM.
CHANGE IN FORM... AND CHANGE IN NATURE?
THAT'S RIGHT... FOR EXAMPLE, TAKE THE CHIDORI.
FIRST, I CHANGE MY CHAKRA'S NATURE SO IT'S LIKE AN ELECTRICAL CURRENT.
AND THEN I CHANGE ITS FORM SO IT'LL DISCHARGE...
...AND SET ITS RANGE OF ACTION AND POWER LEVEL.

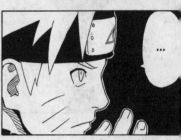

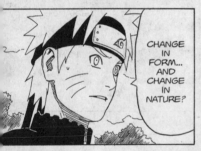

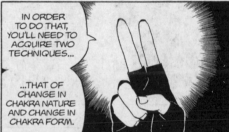

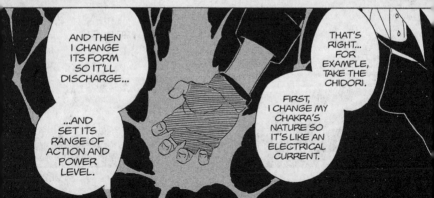

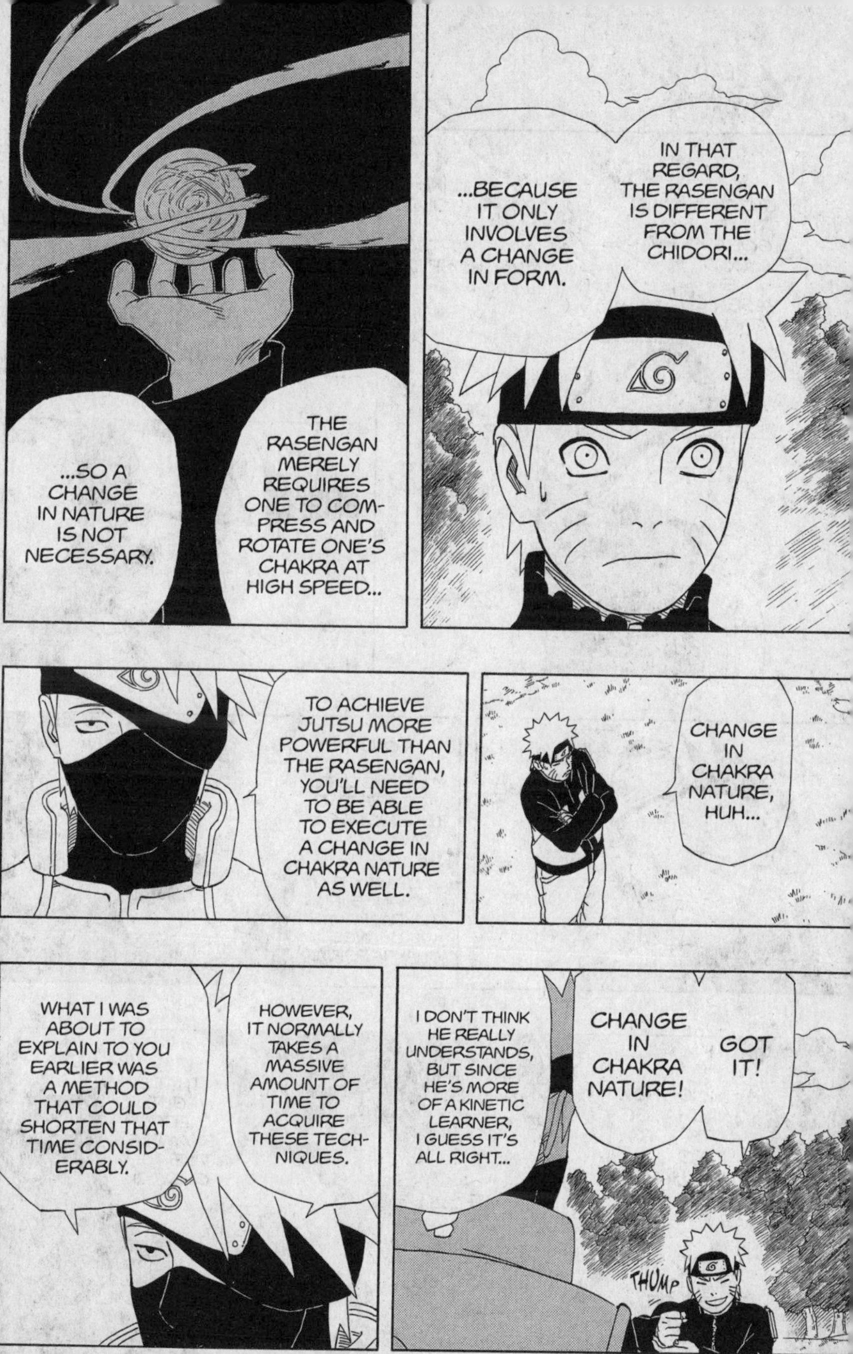
IN THAT REGARD, THE RASENGAN IS DIFFERENT FROM THE CHIDORI...
...BECAUSE IT ONLY INVOLVES A CHANGE IN FORM.
THE RASENGAN MERELY REQUIRES ONE TO COMPRESS AND ROTATE ONE'S CHAKRA AT HIGH SPEED...
...SO A CHANGE IN NATURE IS NOT NECESSARY.
CHANGE IN CHAKRA NATURE, HUH...
TO ACHIEVE JUTSU MORE POWERFUL THAN THE RASENGAN, YOU'LL NEED TO BE ABLE TO EXECUTE A CHANGE IN CHAKRA NATURE AS WELL.
GOT IT!
CHANGE IN CHAKRA NATURE!
THUMP
I DON'T THINK HE REALLY UNDERSTANDS, BUT SINCE HE'S MORE OF A KINETIC LEARNER, I GUESS IT'S ALL RIGHT...
HOWEVER, IT NORMALLY TAKES A MASSIVE AMOUNT OF TIME TO ACQUIRE THESE TECHNIQUES.
WHAT I WAS ABOUT TO EXPLAIN TO YOU EARLIER WAS A METHOD THAT COULD SHORTEN THAT TIME CONSIDERABLY.

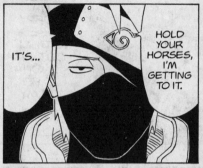

IT'S...

HOLD YOUR HORSES, I'M GETTING TO IT.

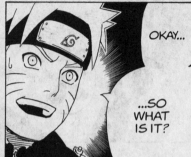

OKAY...

...SO WHAT IS IT?

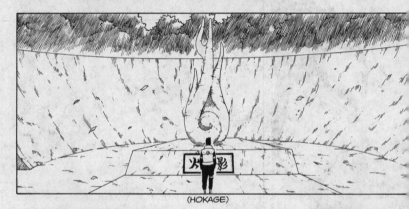

(HOKAGE)

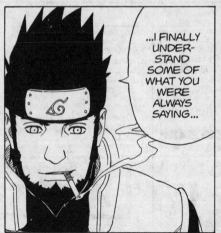

...I FINALLY UNDER-STAND SOME OF WHAT YOU WERE ALWAYS SAYING...

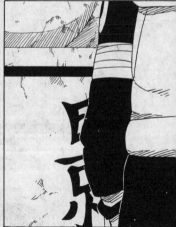

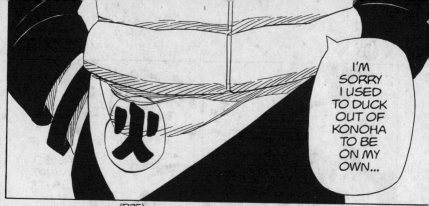

I'M SORRY I USED TO DUCK OUT OF KONOHA TO BE ON MY OWN...
(FIRE)
NOT THAT I REGRET ANY OF IT.
...
...MAYBE IT WASN'T SO BAD BEING BORN INTO THE SARUTOBI CLAN AFTER ALL.
YOU FULFILLED YOUR DUTY AS OUR VILLAGE LEADER...
TWITCH
火影

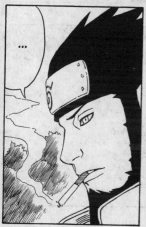

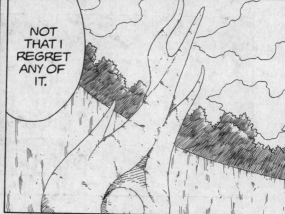

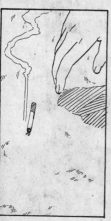

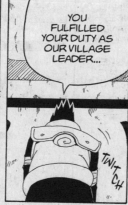

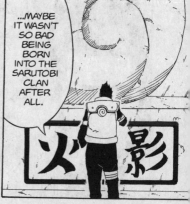

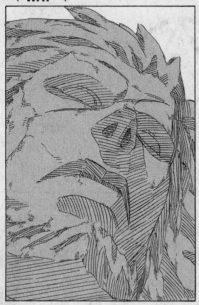

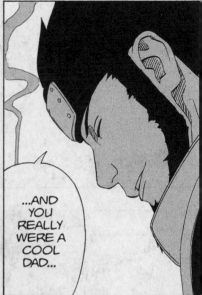

...AND YOU REALLY WERE A COOL DAD...

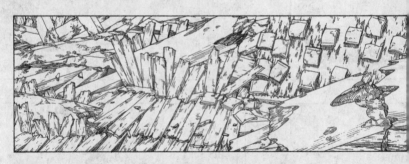

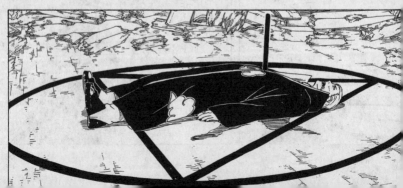

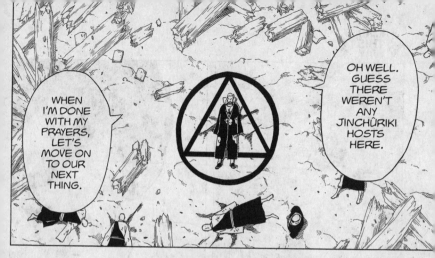

OH WELL. GUESS THERE WEREN'T ANY JINCHÛRIKI HOSTS HERE.
WHEN I'M DONE WITH MY PRAYERS, LET'S MOVE ON TO OUR NEXT THING.
FSH...
NO...
OOF
?
FLUMP
WE'RE TAKING HIS BODY TO THE COLLECTION OFFICE.
MONEY FIRST.
YOU KNOW SOME-THING...
...YOU ARE REALLY STARTING TO IRRITATE ME...

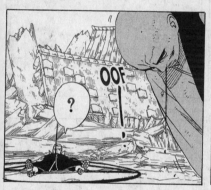

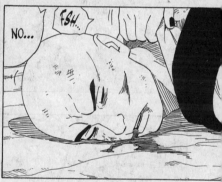

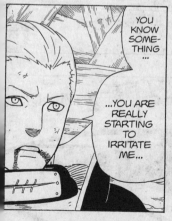

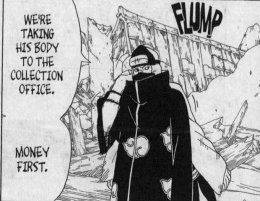

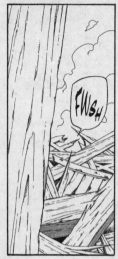

READ THIS WAY
I'VE GOT TO LET KONOHA KNOW...
FWSH
THE LAND OF FIRE IS VAST... WE'RE GOING TO TAKE OUR TIME HERE.
GREAT! MORE DELAYS!
OWW!!

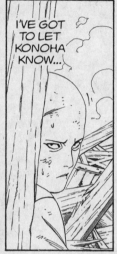

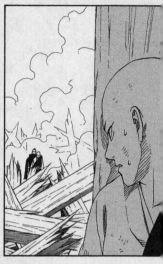

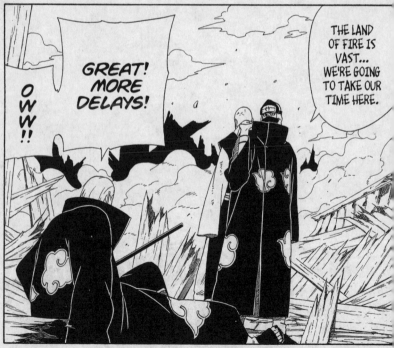

NARUTO

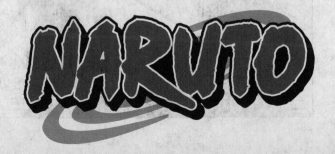

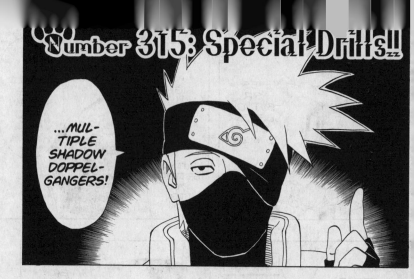

...MULTIPLE SHADOW DOPPELGANGERS!

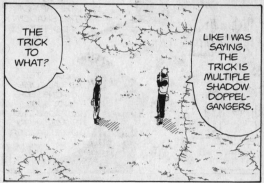

THE TRICK TO WHAT?

LIKE I WAS SAYING, THE TRICK IS MULTIPLE SHADOW DOPPELGANGERS.

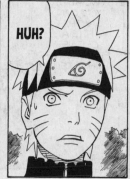

HUH?

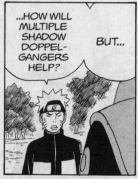

...HOW WILL MULTIPLE SHADOW DOPPELGANGERS HELP?

BUT...

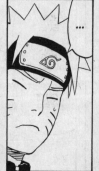

...

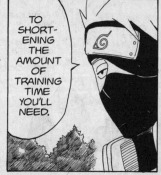

TO SHORTENING THE AMOUNT OF TRAINING TIME YOU'LL NEED.

289

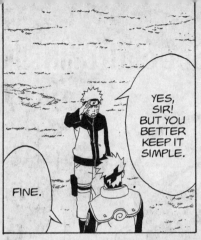

I SHOULD HAVE KNOWN YOU'D ASK.
ALL RIGHT, I'LL EXPLAIN...
...BUT YOU BETTER PAY ATTEN-TION.
YES, SIR! BUT YOU BETTER KEEP IT SIMPLE.
FINE.
AS YOU ALREADY KNOW, THE ART OF THE SHADOW DOPPEL-GANGER...
...CREATES ACTUAL COPIES OF ONESELF, NOT JUST ILLUSIONS LIKE THE ORDINARY DOPPELGANGER JUTSU.
Ordinary Doppelganger
Shadow Doppelganger
IN OTHER WORDS, YOU CAN SAY THAT IT IS A CLONE-PRODUCING NINJUTSU.
I KNOW THIS BECAUSE I TOO CAN MAKE SHADOW DOPPEL-GANGERS, THOUGH NOT QUITE AS MANY AS YOU...
HOW-EVER, THIS JUTSU ALSO IMPARTS A SPECIAL EFFECT TO ITS USER.
AS SOMEONE WHO USES SHADOW DOPPEL-GANGERS A LOT, YOU MAY HAVE PICKED UP ON THIS ALREADY...
ON WHAT?

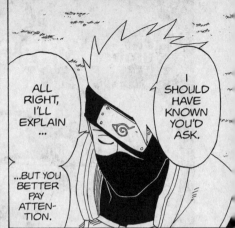

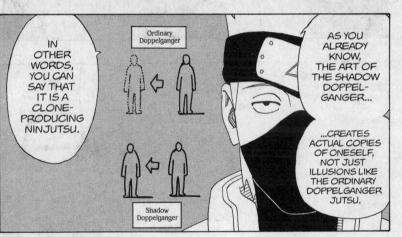

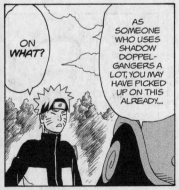

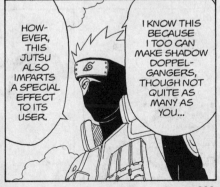

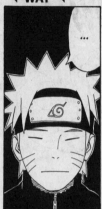

READ THIS WAY
WHEN YOU RELEASE THE JUTSU AND YOU'RE BACK TO JUST YOU...
...WHATEVER ALL YOUR CLONES HAVE EXPERI-ENCED...
...IS DEPOSITED IN YOUR OWN MEMORY BANK.
...
I TOLD YOU TO KEEP IT SIMPLE.
OKAY, SO YOU HAVEN'T NOTICED.
I DON'T EVEN UNDERSTAND WHAT YOU'RE TALKING ABOUT.
SIGH...
ALL RIGHT... LET'S BOTH JUST MAKE SHADOW DOPPEL-GANGERS, OK?
FWP
ART OF THE SHADOW DOPPEL-GANGER!
BOOF

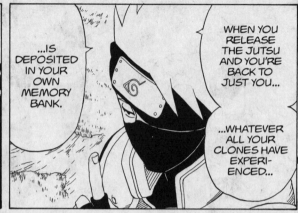

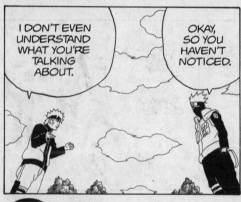

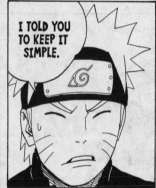

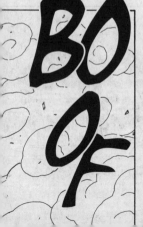

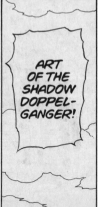

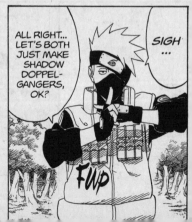

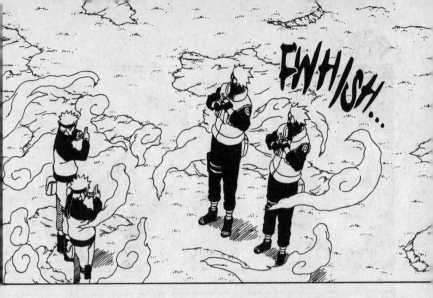

FWHISH...
GOOD! NOW, SPLIT UP INTO A TEAM OF ORIGINALS AND A TEAM OF CLONES...
SHUP
THE CLONE TEAM WILL GO HIDE IN THOSE WOODS OVER THERE...
...CLONE NARUTO, FOLLOW ME.

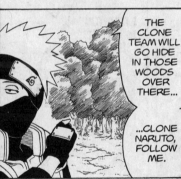

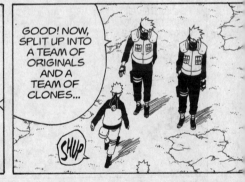

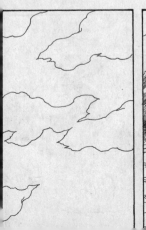

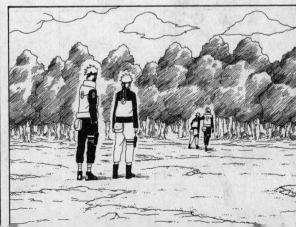

READ THIS WAY

NOW, WHILE THE ORIGINALS CAN'T SEE...
...US CLONES HERE IN THE WOODS...
...LET'S PLAY *ROSHAMBO.*
WHY?
JUST DO IT.
ROCK, PAPER, SCISSORS!
TA-
DAA
...
WHAT ARE OUR CLONES DOING?
DON'T WORRY, YOU'LL SEE SOON ENOUGH.

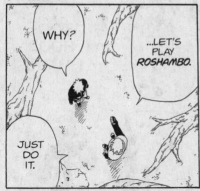

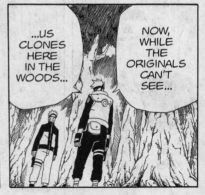

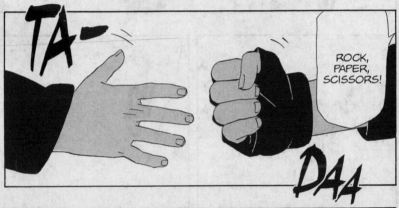

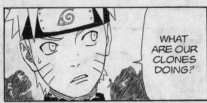

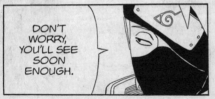

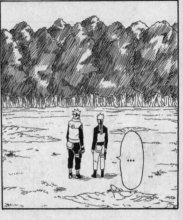

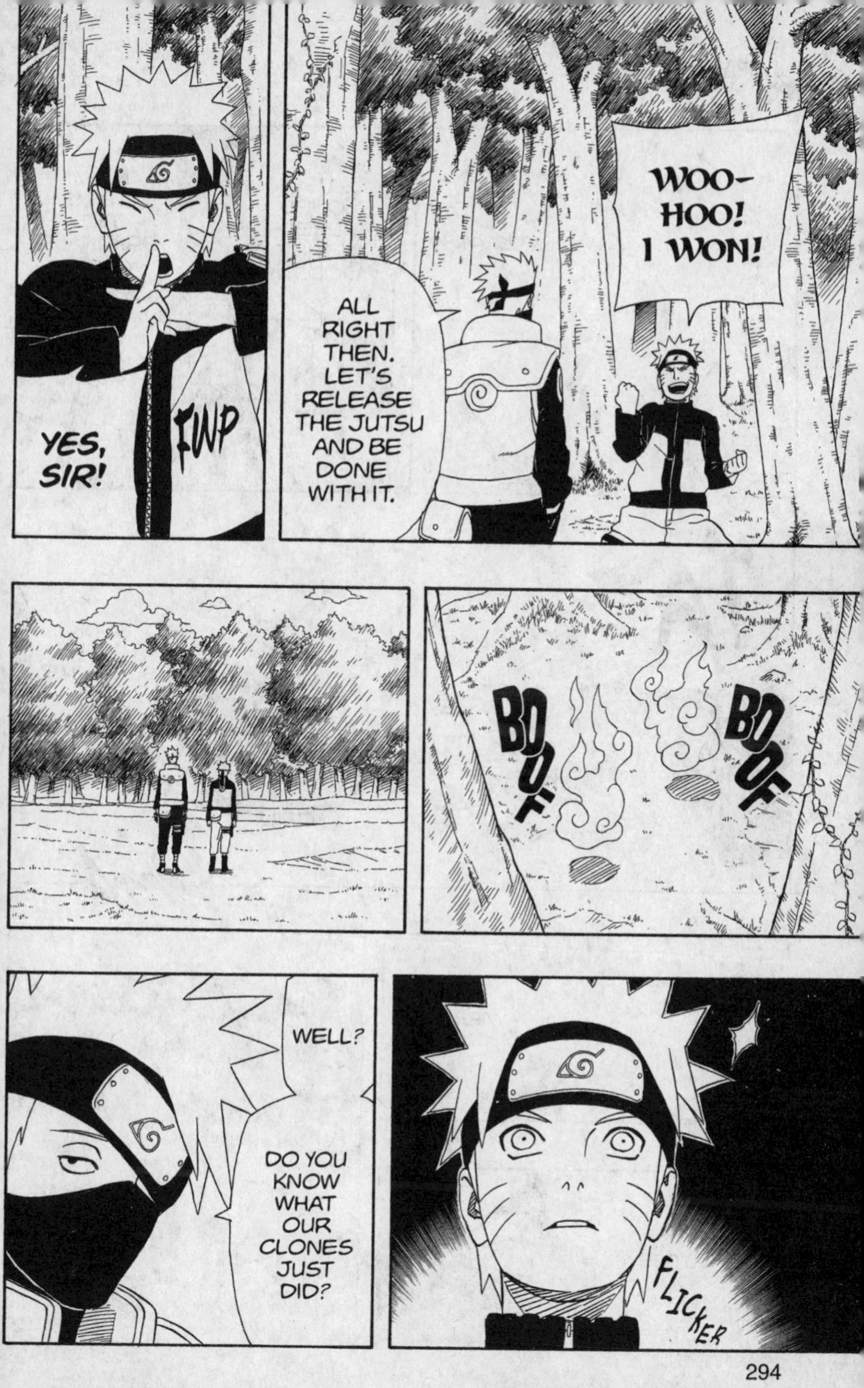
WOO-HOO! I WON!
ALL RIGHT THEN. LET'S RELEASE THE JUTSU AND BE DONE WITH IT.
FWP
YES, SIR!
BOOF
BOOF
FLICKER
WELL?
DO YOU KNOW WHAT OUR CLONES JUST DID?

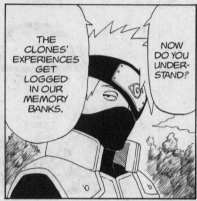

READ THIS WAY

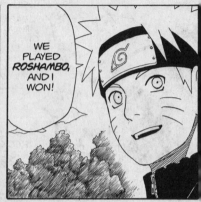

WE PLAYED *ROSHAMBO*, AND I WON!
NOW DO YOU UNDER-STAND?
THE CLONES' EXPERIENCES GET LOGGED IN OUR MEMORY BANKS.
WOW...
GUESS I JUST KINDA RANDOMLY MADE SHADOW DOPPELGANGERS IN THE PAST, SO I NEVER EVEN NOTICED.
ORIGINALLY, THIS JUTSU WAS USED FOR PARTICULARLY TRICKY INTELLIGENCE GATHERING...
...LIKE TRAVERSING DANGEROUS TERRAIN OR INFILTRATING ENEMY STRONG-HOLDS.
...
BUT HOW DOES ALL THIS RELATE...
...TO SHORTENING MY TRAINING PERIOD?
YES, YES, I'M STILL GETTING TO THAT.
HOW LORD JIRAIYA FOUND THE PATIENCE TO TEACH THIS KID THE RASENGAN IS COMPLETELY BEYOND ME...

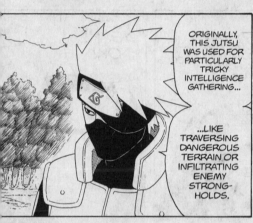

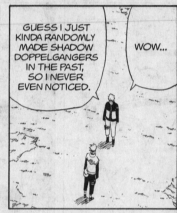

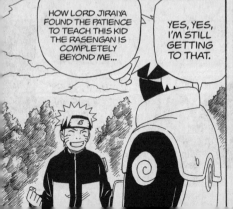

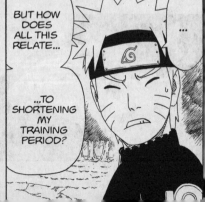

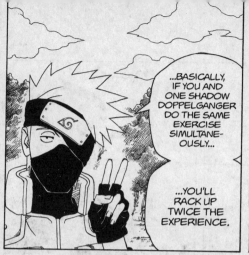

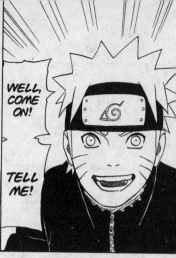

WELL, COME ON!
TELL ME!
...BASICALLY, IF YOU AND ONE SHADOW DOPPELGANGER DO THE SAME EXERCISE SIMULTANE-OUSLY...
...YOU'LL RACK UP TWICE THE EXPERIENCE.
YEAH! OK!
IN OTHER WORDS ...
...IF TWO OF YOU TRAIN TOGETHER, WE CUT THE TOTAL AMOUNT OF TRAINING TIME IN HALF.
THREE OF YOU WOULD ONLY TAKE A THIRD OF THE TIME.
ONE THOUSAND OF YOU WOULD GET IT DONE IN 1/1000TH OF THE TIME.

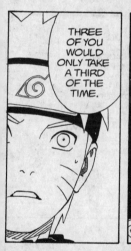

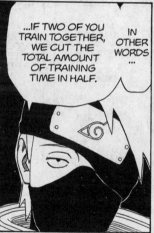

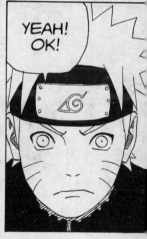

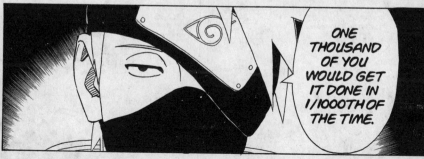

READ THIS WAY

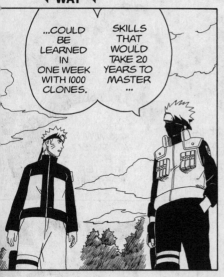

WOW... THAT'S A LOT...
JUST IMAGINE IT... ACCOMPLISHING IN ONE DAY WHAT WOULD NORMALLY TAKE TWO.
SKILLS THAT WOULD TAKE 20 YEARS TO MASTER ...
...COULD BE LEARNED IN ONE WEEK WITH 1000 CLONES.
WOW!!
THAT'S GENIUS!
...
THIS TRAINING TO ACHIEVE CHANGE IN CHAKRA NATURE THAT WE'RE ABOUT TO START...
...IT MEANS WE'RE GOING TO USE MULTIPLE SHADOW DOPPELGANGERS THE WHOLE TIME.
AYE, SIR!

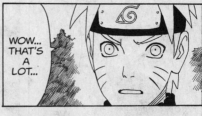

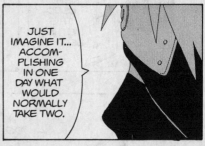

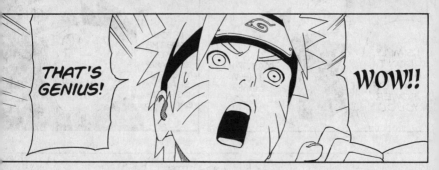

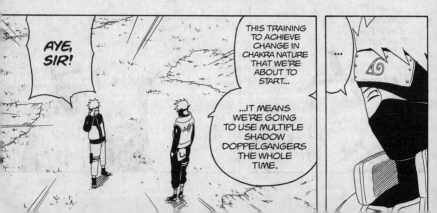

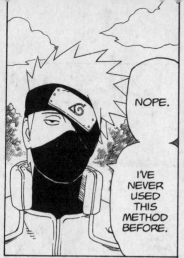

NOW I KNOW WHY YOU'RE SO STRONG, MASTER KAKASHI!
THIS IS HOW YOU'VE BEEN TRAINING, HUH?
NOPE.
I'VE NEVER USED THIS METHOD BEFORE.
HUH??? WHY NOT?
IF YOU HAVE THE POWER TO MAKE MULTIPLE SHADOW DOPPEL-GANGERS...
I DO...
...BUT I CAN'T MAINTAIN THEM LONG ENOUGH.
I SIMPLY DON'T HAVE THE KIND OF POWER YOU DO.
AND A JUTSU THAT FORCES ME TO DIVIDE AND DISPERSE MY CHAKRA INTO EQUAL PORTIONS...
...ISN'T GOOD FOR ME, NOT HAVING A LOT OF CHAKRA TO BEGIN WITH.
WAIT A SEC...
...I HAVE MORE CHAKRA THAN YOU DO??

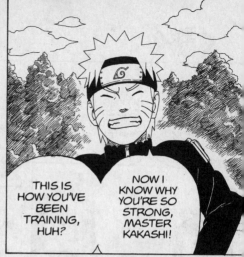

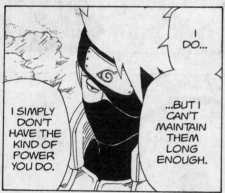

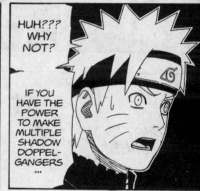

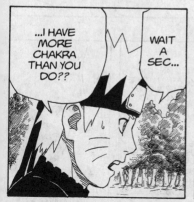

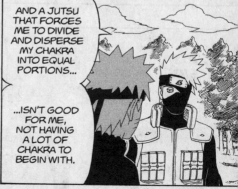

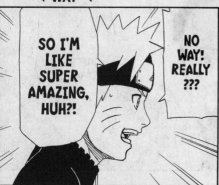

READ THIS WAY

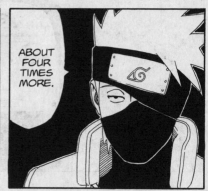

ABOUT FOUR TIMES MORE.
NO WAY! REALLY ???
SO I'M LIKE SUPER AMAZING, HUH?!
IF YAMATO WASN'T SUP-PRESSING THE NINE-TAILS' CHAKRA ...
...IT WOULD BE 100 TIMES MORE.
!
AND THAT'S WHY THIS TRAINING TECHNIQUE ALSO ONLY WORKS FOR YOU...
...NARUTO.
CRUNCH
!

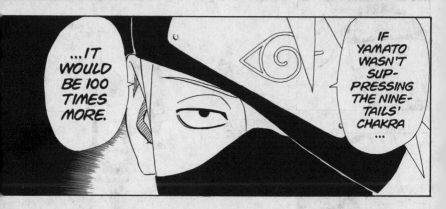

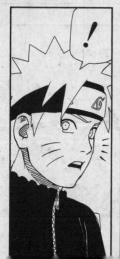

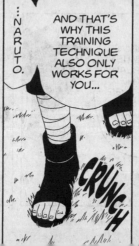

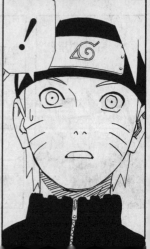

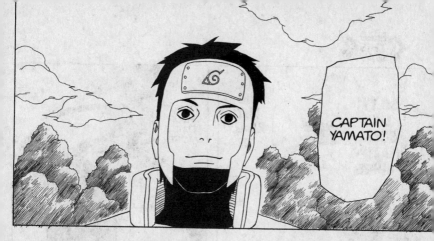

CAPTAIN YAMATO!

...

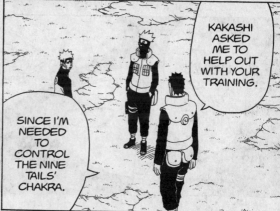

KAKASHI ASKED ME TO HELP OUT WITH YOUR TRAINING.

SINCE I'M NEEDED TO CONTROL THE NINE TAILS' CHAKRA.

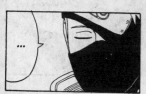

...

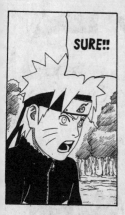

SURE!!

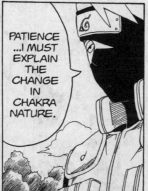

PATIENCE ...I MUST EXPLAIN THE CHANGE IN CHAKRA NATURE.

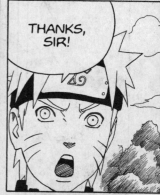

THANKS, SIR!

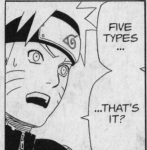

READ THIS WAY

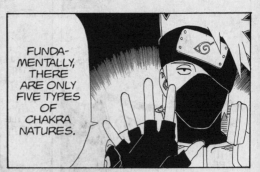

FUNDAMENTALLY, THERE ARE ONLY FIVE TYPES OF CHAKRA NATURES.
FIVE TYPES ...
...THAT'S IT?
FIRE, WIND, WATER, LIGHTNING, AND EARTH.
THESE FIVE NATURES ARE ALSO THE ORIGIN OF THE FIVE PRINCIPAL SHINOBI TERRITORIES' NAMES... AND THE FOUNDATION FOR ALL NINJUTSU.
火
風
雷
土
水
WOW... I HAD NO IDEA...
MOST EVERYONE'S CHAKRA FITS ONE OF THESE NATURES.
FOR EXAMPLE, MEMBERS OF THE UCHIHA CLAN ALL POSSESS A FIERY NATURE...
...WHICH IS WHY THEY EXCEL AT FIRE STYLE JUTSU.

(DIAGRAM CLOCKWISE FROM TOP: FIRE, WIND, LIGHTNING, EARTH, WATER)

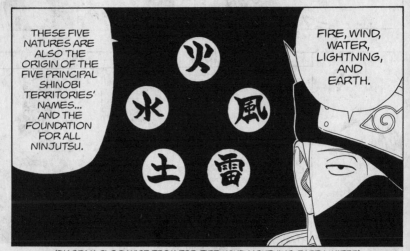

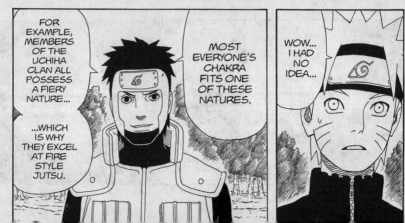

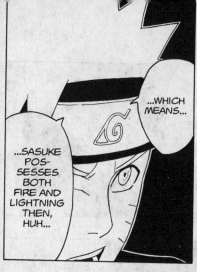

WIND NATURE LEADS TO WIND STYLE JUTSU...
...AND LIGHTNING NATURE TO LIGHTNING STYLE JUTSU.
FOR EXAMPLE, THE CHIDORI IS A TYPE OF LIGHTNING STYLE JUTSU.
...WHICH MEANS...
...SASUKE POSSESSES BOTH FIRE AND LIGHTNING THEN, HUH...
...AND YOU SEEM TO HAVE NONE.
NOT ONLY THAT, WE STILL DON'T EVEN KNOW WHICH NATURE YOU'RE PREDISPOSED TO.
SHFF SHFF
SWISH...
?
FFWT
SO WE'RE GOING TO FIND OUT USING THESE SLIPS OF PAPER.

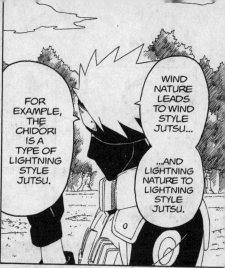

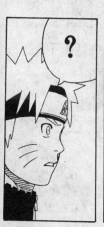

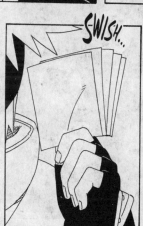

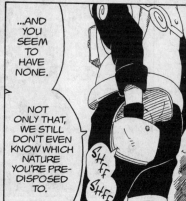

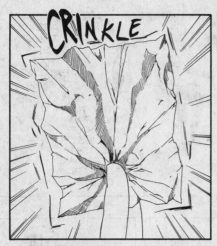

HOW?
...
CRINKLE
?
IF YOU HAVE LIGHTNING NATURE, THE PAPER WILL WRINKLE.
WITH WIND NATURE, THE PAPER TEARS.
FIRE NATURE, THE PAPER BURNS.
WATER NATURE, THE PAPER BECOMES WET.
AND EARTH NATURE, THE PAPER CRUM-BLES.

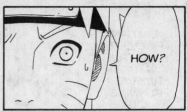

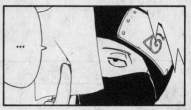

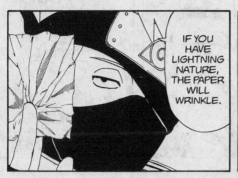

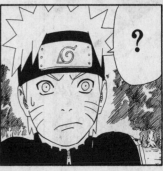

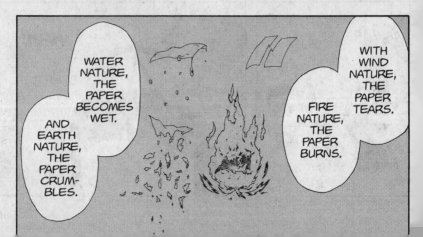

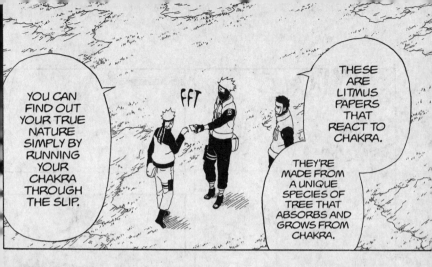

THESE ARE LITMUS PAPERS THAT REACT TO CHAKRA.
THEY'RE MADE FROM A UNIQUE SPECIES OF TREE THAT ABSORBS AND GROWS FROM CHAKRA.
FFT
YOU CAN FIND OUT YOUR TRUE NATURE SIMPLY BY RUNNING YOUR CHAKRA THROUGH THE SLIP.
THIP
...
ALL RIGHT ...
HMM
HAH!
...
AAH!

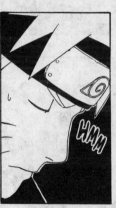

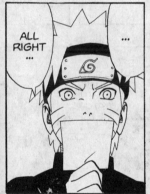

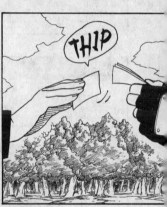

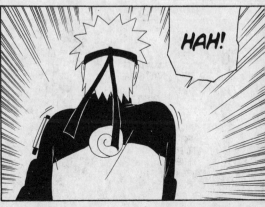

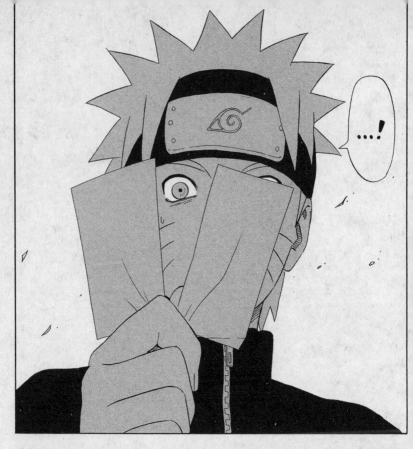

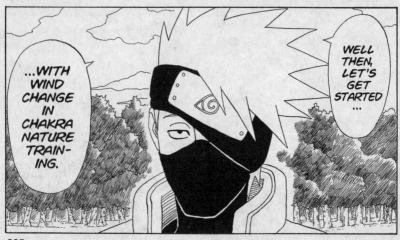

...!
WELL THEN, LET'S GET STARTED ...
...WITH WIND CHANGE IN CHAKRA NATURE TRAIN-ING.

NARUTO

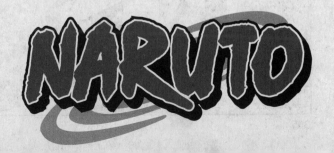

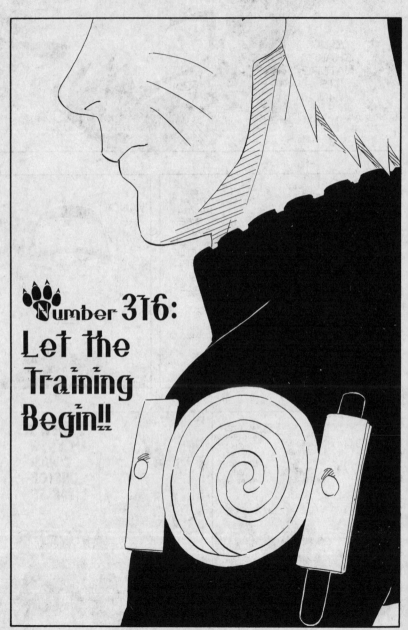

Number 316:
Let the
Training
Begin!!

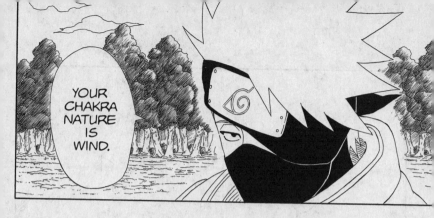

YOUR CHAKRA NATURE IS WIND.
WIND ...
IT'S A CHAKRA NATURE THAT'S UNRIVALED IN BATTLE POWER...
...ABLE TO CUT, TEAR, AND SEVER ANYTHING AND EVERYTHING IN ITS PATH.
I KNEW IT! I KNEW I WAS UNSTOP-PABLE!
WHOA, NARUTO. HOLD YOUR HORSES. WE'VE ONLY JUST FIGURED THIS OUT.
MASTER KAKASHI'S RIGHT. FIRST YOU MUST BE TRAINED ...
...SO YOU CAN PROPERLY USE AND CONTROL YOUR NATURE.
...HMM?

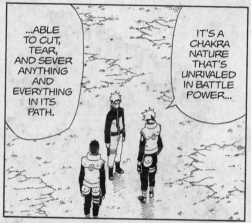

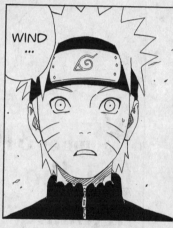

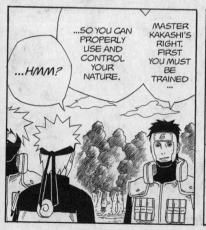

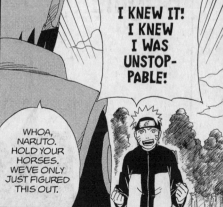

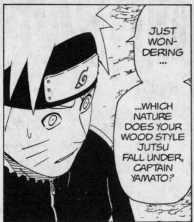

JUST WONDERING...

...WHICH NATURE DOES YOUR WOOD STYLE JUTSU FALL UNDER, CAPTAIN YAMATO?

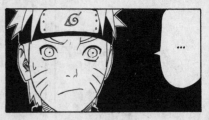

...

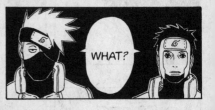

WHAT?

WHISPER

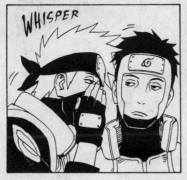

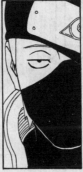

...

FWP FWP

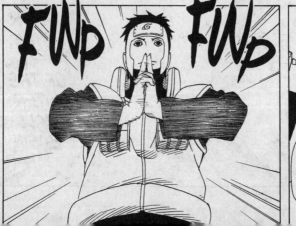

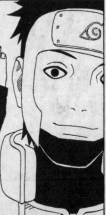

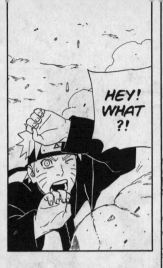

HEY! WHAT ?!

THUDTHUDTHU!

EARTH STYLE! RAMPART OF FLOWING SOIL !!

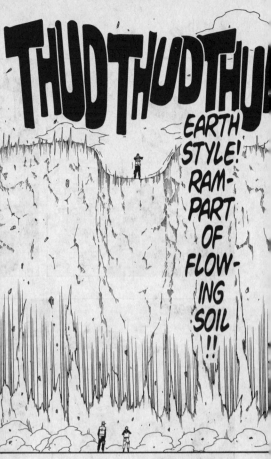

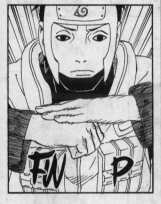

FN P

SPOUR

WATER STYLE! ART OF THE WATERFALL BASIN !!

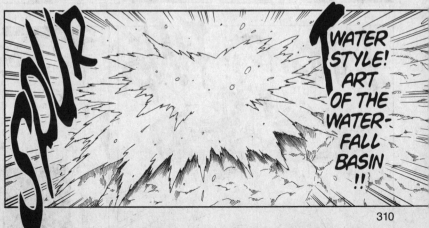

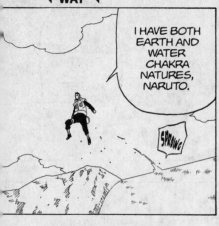

READ THIS WAY

THOOOOM!
WHOA! WATER-FALL! COOL!
I HAVE BOTH EARTH AND WATER CHAKRA NATURES, NARUTO.
SPRONG
YOU HAVE TWO TOO, CAPTAIN YAMATO?! AWE-SOME!
ONCE YOU HIT JONIN RANK, MOST EVERY-ONE HAS AT LEAST TWO NATURES.
I CAN USE NATURES OTHER THAN JUST LIGHTNING, Y'KNOW.
SO... INCLUDING HIS WOOD STYLE... CAPTAIN YAMATO HAS THREE?!
NO, NO, THAT'S NOT QUITE IT.
?

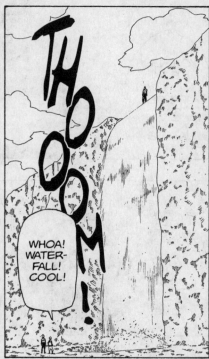

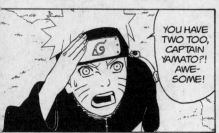

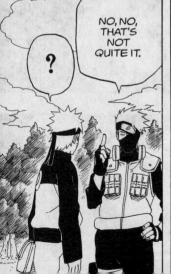

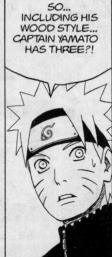

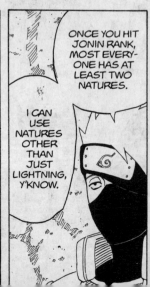

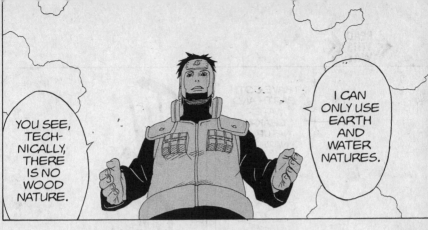

I CAN ONLY USE EARTH AND WATER NATURES.
YOU SEE, TECHNICALLY, THERE IS NO WOOD NATURE.
THEN HOW?
YOU USE THE TWO SIMULTANEOUSLY.
IF YOU ACTIVATE EARTH AND WATER NATURES TOGETHER...
...YOU CAN CREATE A WOOD NATURE.
EARTH WITH MY RIGHT HAND.
WATER WITH MY LEFT.
CLAP

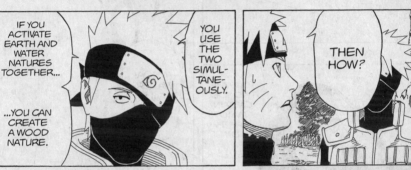

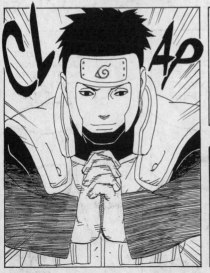

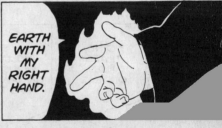

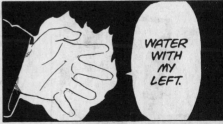

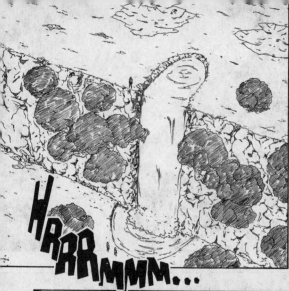

ZWOO...
ZWOO...
HRRRMMM...
SWEET...
WHEN ONE POSSESSES TWO CHAKRA NATURES...
...IT'S NOT THAT DIFFICULT TO USE EACH NATURE SEPARATELY.
SPURT
BUT TO ACTIVATE BOTH OF THEM SIMULTANEOUSLY...
土
水
THIS ABILITY TO ACTIVATE TWO NATURES AT THE SAME TIME...
...AND CREATE AN ENTIRELY NEW CHAKRA NATURE...
(EARTH) (WATER)

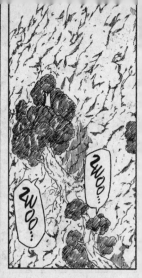

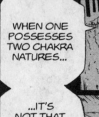

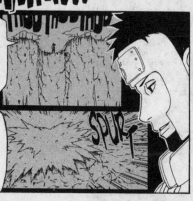

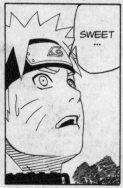

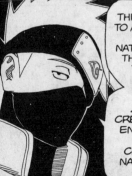

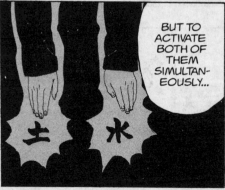

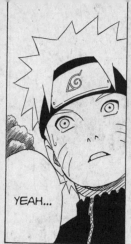

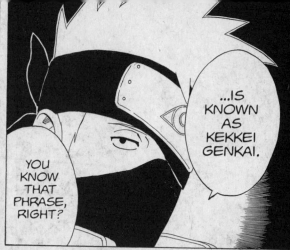

...IS KNOWN AS KEKKEI GENKAI.
YOU KNOW THAT PHRASE, RIGHT?
YEAH...
REMEMBER OUR FIGHT WITH HAKU?
HE HAD A KEKKEI GENKAI CALLED ***HYOTON***, OR ICE STYLE.
HE WAS ABLE TO MANIPULATE WIND AND WATER CHANGES IN CHAKRA NATURE SIMULTANEOUSLY TO CREATE ICE.
AND HE COULD PERFORM SUCH A SPECIAL JUTSU BECAUSE HE WAS OF A KEKKEI GENKAI-BEARING CLAN.
HAKU, TOO ...?
THAT'S WHY I COULDN'T COPY HIS JUTSU WITH MY SHARINGAN.

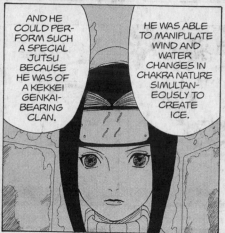

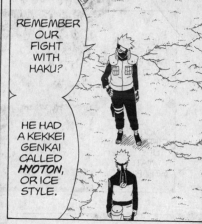

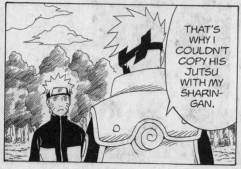

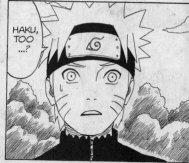

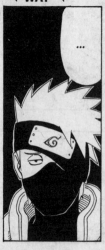

READ THIS WAY

...
ALL RIGHT, TIME TO START EXPLAIN-ING YOUR EXERCISE ...
THEN WHAT ABOUT SHIKAMARU'S SHADOW POSSESSION OR CHOJI'S ART OF EXPANSION?
...
AND HOW DO MEDICAL NINJUTSU AND GENJUTSU WORK?
MM... IT'S GOING TO TAKE TOO LONG TO EXPLAIN ...
...AND WILL ONLY END UP CON-FUSING YOU IN THE END...
WHY DON'T YOU LEAVE THE IMPLICIT AND EXPLICIT ASPECTS OF CHANGE IN CHAKRA NATURE UNTIL NEXT TIME, KAKASHI?
WE SHOULD START THE EXERCISE.

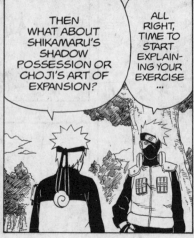

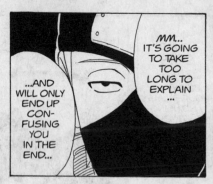

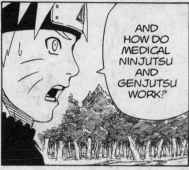

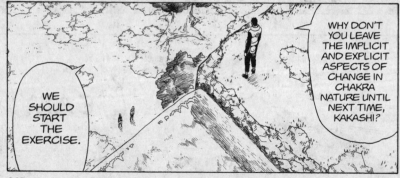

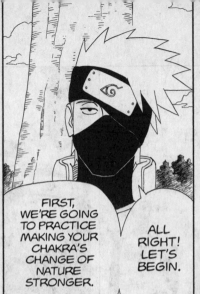

ALL RIGHT! LET'S BEGIN.
FIRST, WE'RE GOING TO PRACTICE MAKING YOUR CHAKRA'S CHANGE OF NATURE STRONGER.
YUP.
...
?
RIGHT! STRONGER! HOW...?
YOU'RE GOING TO HOLD A LEAF BETWEEN YOUR PALMS AND USING JUST YOUR CHAKRA...
...TEAR IT COM-PLETELY IN TWO.
EASY!

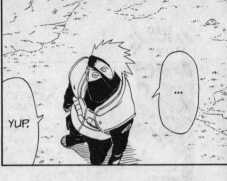

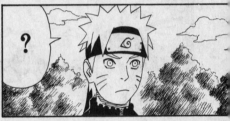

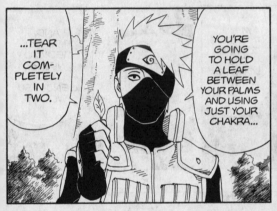

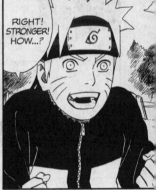

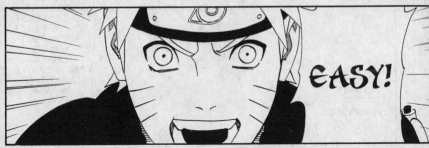

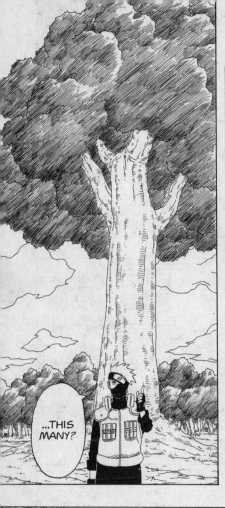

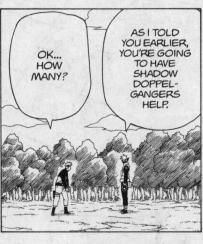

AS I TOLD YOU EARLIER, YOU'RE GOING TO HAVE SHADOW DOPPEL-GANGERS HELP.

OK... HOW MANY?

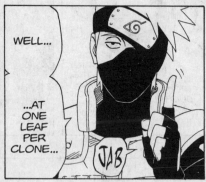

WELL...

...AT ONE LEAF PER CLONE...

...THIS MANY?

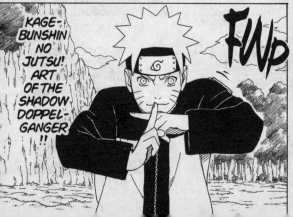

KAGE-BUNSHIN NO JUTSU! ART OF THE SHADOW DOPPEL-GANGER!!

FWP

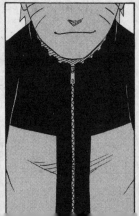

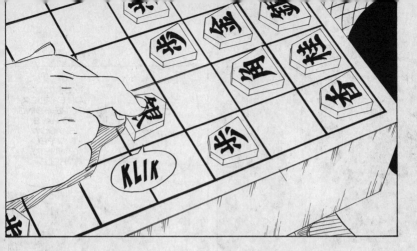

KLIK
IT'S UNUSUAL FOR YOU TO USE THE CLIMBING SILVER MOVE RIGHT AWAY.
LET'S TAKE OUR TIME AND NOT RUSH.
KLIK
IT'S ACTING AS THE INFIL-TRATION OF THE ENEMY CAMP.
YOU NEED TO BE ABLE TO MAKE SUCH PLAYS AT TIMES.
I THOUGHT YOU HATED MOVES LIKE THIS?
JUST LIKE ME...
AGAINST A SUPERIOR OPPONENT, ONE MUST MAKE SOME SACRIFICES ...
...IN ORDER TO PROTECT ONE'S KING.
...

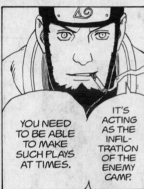

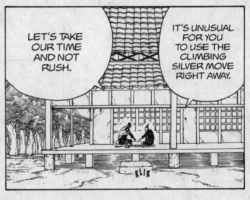

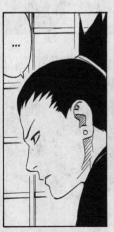

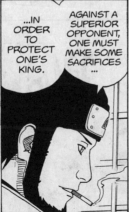

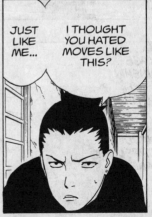

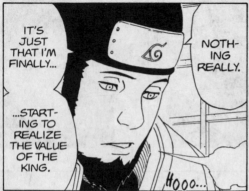

READ THIS WAY

WHAT'S GOING ON?
NOTHING REALLY.
HOOO...
IT'S JUST THAT I'M FINALLY...
...STARTING TO REALIZE THE VALUE OF THE KING.
WELL, ONE LOSES IF ONE'S KING IS TAKEN...
...SO...
IF KONOHA'S SHINOBI WERE LIKENED TO SHOGI PIECES...
...SHIKAMARU, RIGHT NOW YOU'D BE A KNIGHT.
...
HOW SO?
KNIGHTS MAY BE WEAK, BUT THEY CAN ADVANCE BY LEAPING OVER OTHER PIECES. SUCH UNIQUE MOVEMENT ...
...IS SIMILAR TO YOUR QUICK WIT AND UNPREDICTABLE MIND.

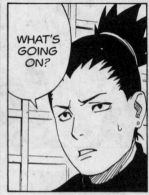

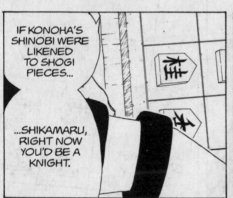

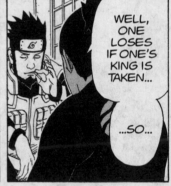

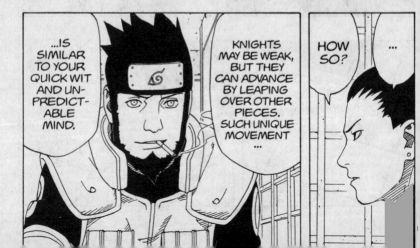

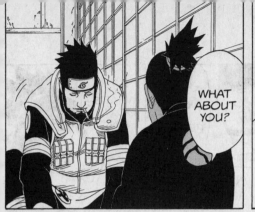

...
WHAT ABOUT YOU?
KLIK
I'M NOTHING SPECIAL, JUST...
A SACRIFICIAL PIECE, HUH...
KLIK
THEN...
...DO YOU KNOW WHO THE KING IS?

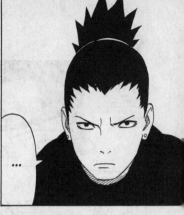

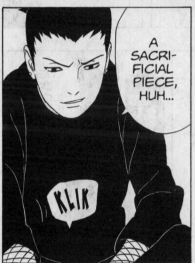

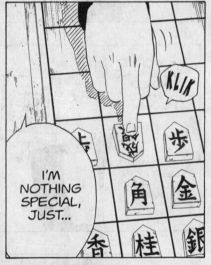

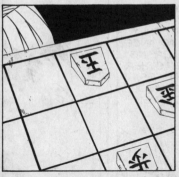

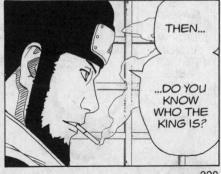

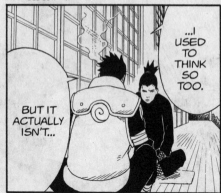

READ THIS WAY
...
ISN'T IT THE HOKAGE?
...I USED TO THINK SO TOO.
BUT IT ACTUALLY ISN'T...
THEN WHO ...?
KLIK
WHEN THE TIME COMES, YOU'LL KNOW.

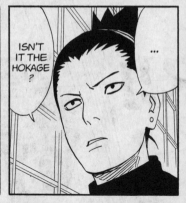

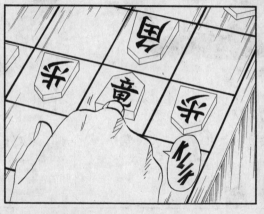

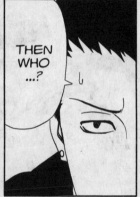

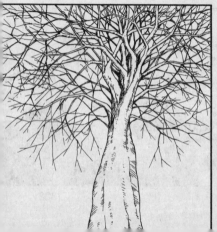

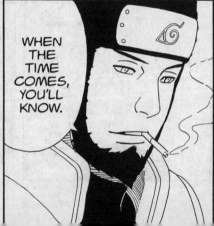

R!!
FFT
!

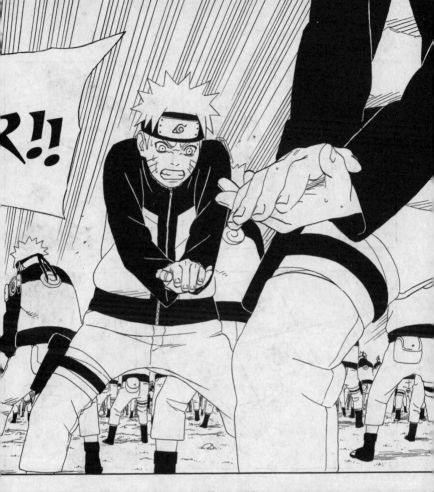

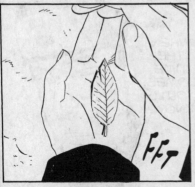

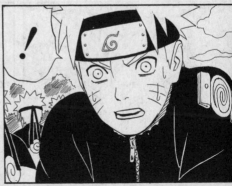

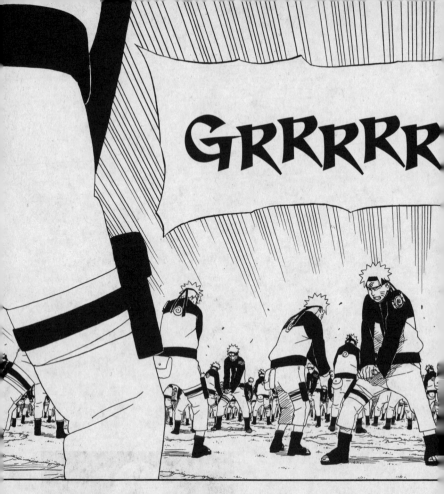

GRRRRRR
HE'S ALREADY STARTING TO GET TEARS...
...THIS MIGHT GO QUICKLY AFTER ALL.
Make-Out PARADISE
Make-

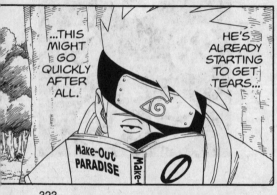

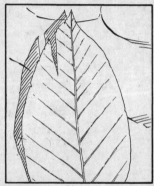

火
風
雷
土
水

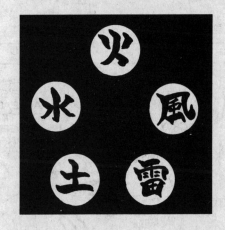

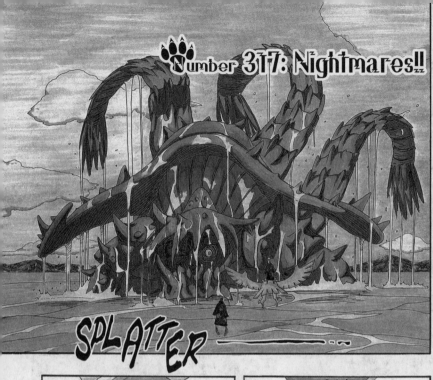

Number 317: Nightmares!!
SPLATTER
SO THIS IS THREE TAILS, HUH? LOOKS PRETTY STRONG...
...KINDA LIKE A GIANT TURTLE...
THINK I'LL LET YOU TAKE THE LEAD THIS TIME, DEIDARA.
YOU'RE AN OFFICIAL MEMBER OF THE AKATSUKI, HMMM, TOBI.
YOU DO IT!
!
BUT...
YAH!!
SPLASH

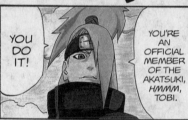

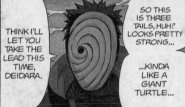

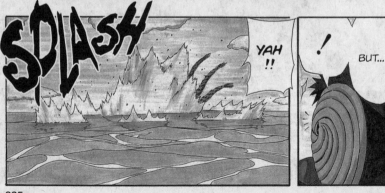

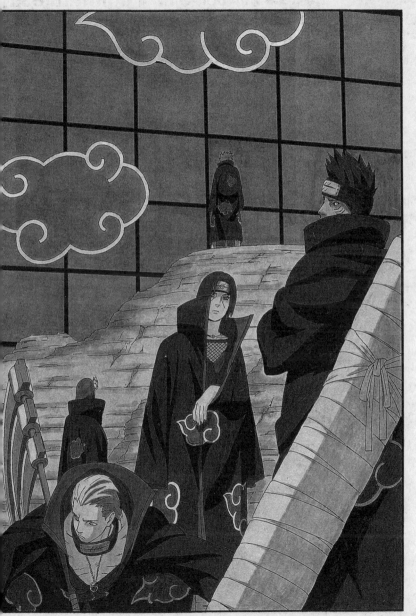

326

Number 317: Nightmares!!

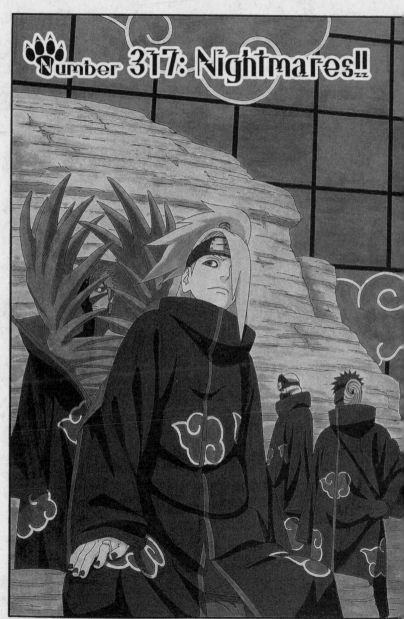

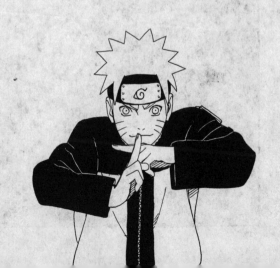

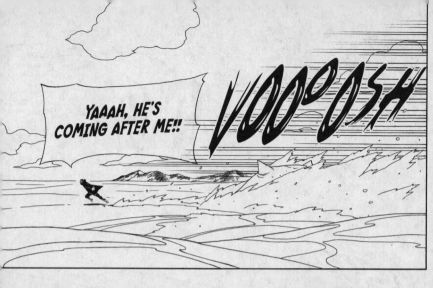

VOOOOOSH
YAAAH, HE'S COMING AFTER ME!!
DON'T YOU THINK THEY SHOULD HAVE ASSIGNED KISAME AGAINST A WATER TYPE?!
THIS IS A STUPID MISTAKE IN PERSONNEL SELECTION!
HMMM. YOU ARE RIDICULOUS...
YAAAAAH!!
FFT
HURL
FWD

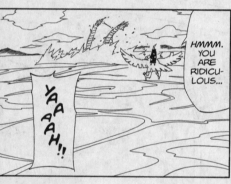

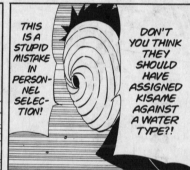

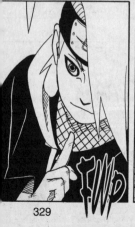

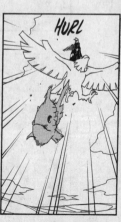

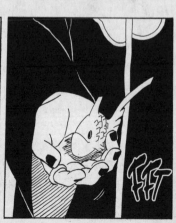

SPLASH
FWOOSH
SWISH
YEEAAGH!
SPLOOSH
YAAH!

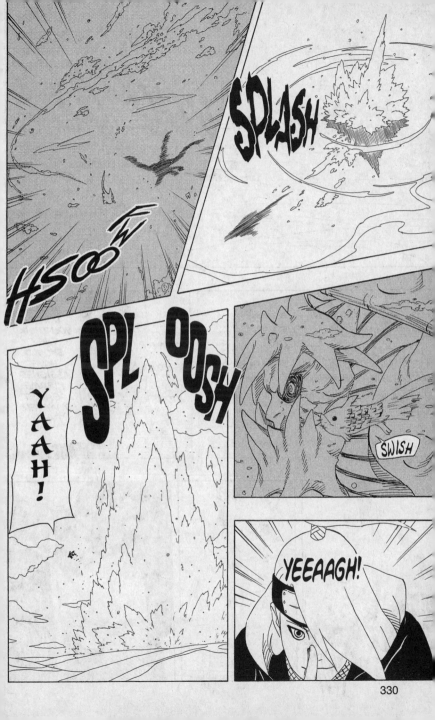

THOOOM
座
(SIT)

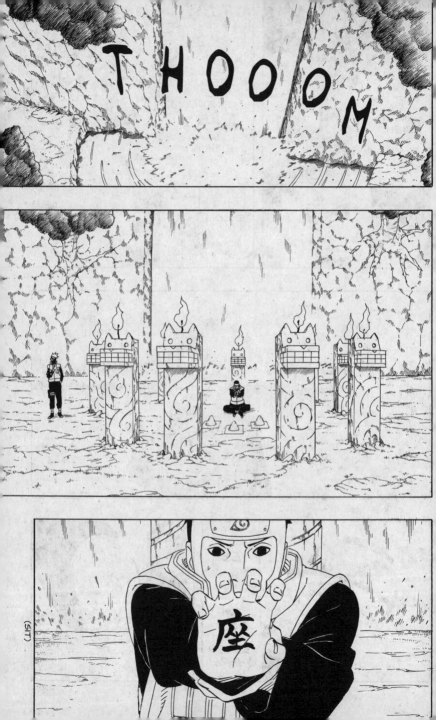

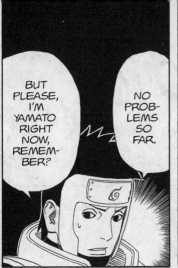

NO PROBLEMS SO FAR.
BUT PLEASE, I'M YAMATO RIGHT NOW, REMEMBER?
WELL? ARE YOU ABLE TO CONTROL THE NINE TAILS' CHAKRA EASILY...
... TENZO?
RIGHT, RIGHT.
YES!
I'M GETTING SOMEWHERE!
HUF
HUF

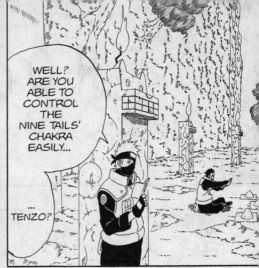

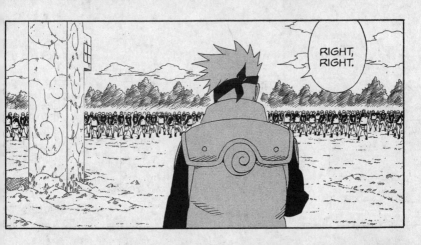

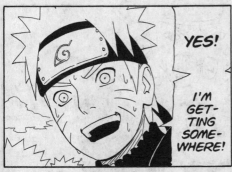

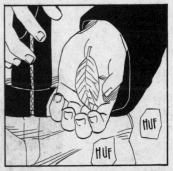

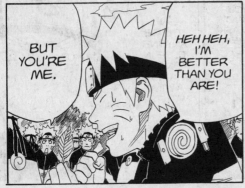

READ THIS WAY

GAH!
I'M NOT GETTING ANYWHERE YET!
HEH HEH, I'M BETTER THAN YOU ARE!
BUT YOU'RE ME.
YES!
HEH HEH HEH ...
GAH...
...THAT ONE OF ME IS PRETTY GOOD.
!
Make-Out
HOLD ON, MASTER KAKASHI. I HAVE A QUESTION ...

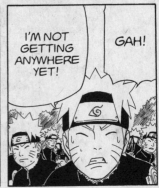

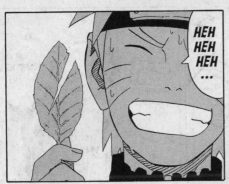

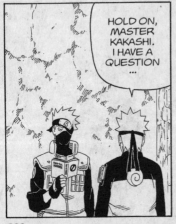

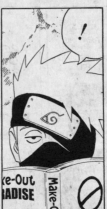

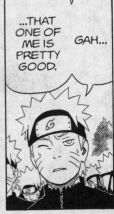

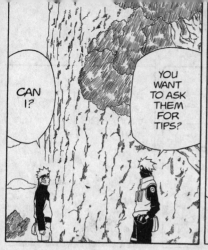

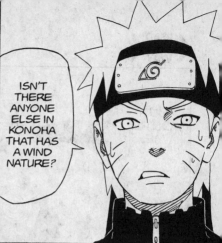

ISN'T THERE ANYONE ELSE IN KONOHA THAT HAS A WIND NATURE?
YOU WANT TO ASK THEM FOR TIPS?
CAN I?
...THERE IS ONE IN PARTICULAR.
HE'S PROBABLY PLAYING SHOGI RIGHT NOW...
CHECK-MATE.
ARGH! LOST AGAIN!
LOOKS LIKE YOU'RE TREATING US TO THE DINNER AND PARTY...
...AFTER OUR NEXT ASSIGNMENT, MASTER.

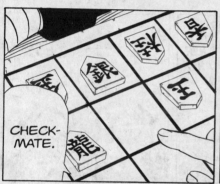

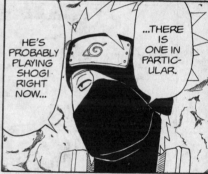

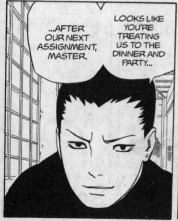

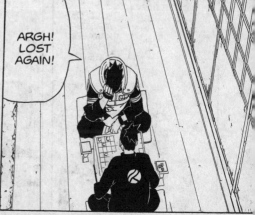

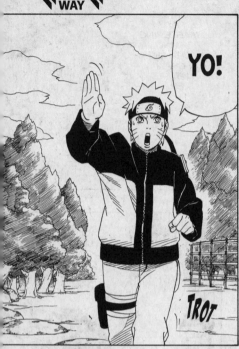

READ THIS WAY

OH, ALL RIGHT ...
MASTER ASUMA!
?!
YO!
TROT
OH... IT'S YOU, NARUTO.
WHAT'S UP?
ACTU-ALLY...
...I WANTED TO ASK YOU SOME-THING.
KLUNK

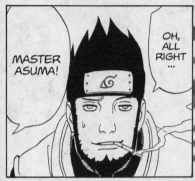

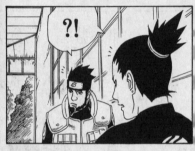

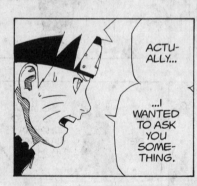

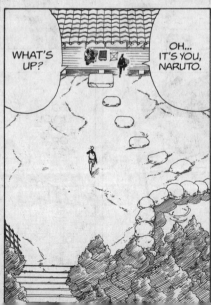

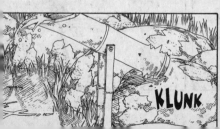

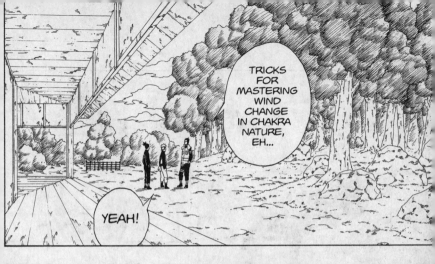

TRICKS FOR MASTERING WIND CHANGE IN CHAKRA NATURE, EH...
YEAH!
YOU'RE DOING CHANGE IN CHAKRA NATURE DRILLS?
YUP!
YOU CAN'T DO IT IF YOU AREN'T SHARP.
SURE YOU'RE UP TO THAT?
THAT'S WHY I CAME TO ASK MASTER ASUMA FOR TIPS.
...SO YOU HAVE WIND CHAKRA NATURE, HUH...
WELL, I'LL BE.
SO WILL YOU HELP ME OR NOT?
...

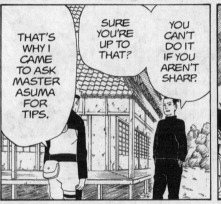

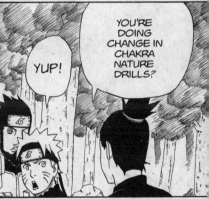

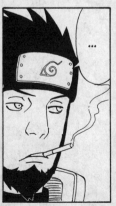

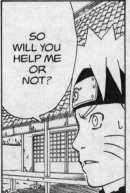

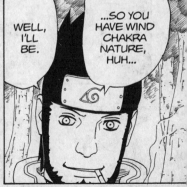

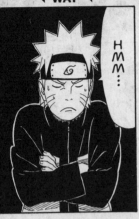

READ THIS WAY

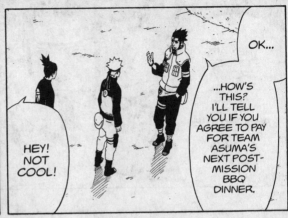

OK...
...HOW'S THIS? I'LL TELL YOU IF YOU AGREE TO PAY FOR TEAM ASUMA'S NEXT POST-MISSION BBQ DINNER.
HEY! NOT COOL!
HMM...
IF IT MEANS YOU'LL HELP ME? DEAL.
GOOD! NEGOTI-ATIONS CON-CLUDED.
KLATTA
KLATTA
FWSH...
!

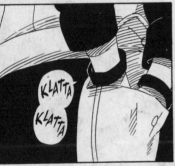

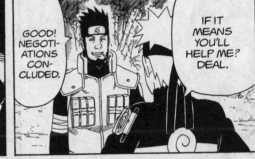

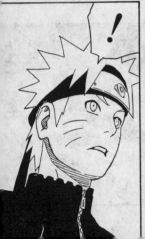

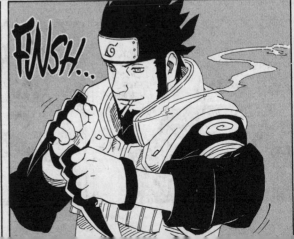

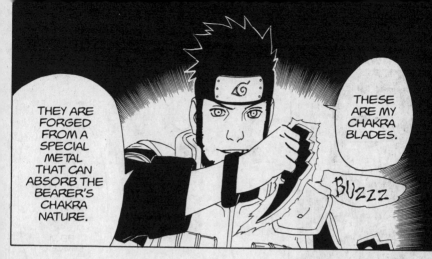

THESE ARE MY CHAKRA BLADES.
BUZZZ
THEY ARE FORGED FROM A SPECIAL METAL THAT CAN ABSORB THE BEARER'S CHAKRA NATURE.
TAKE ONE.
FFT
...
NOW TRY SENDING YOUR CHAKRA INTO THE BLADE.
NO PROB-LEM.
UNH!
CLENCH
BUZZZZ
MY CHAKRA LOOKS DIFFERENT FROM MASTER ASUMA'S.

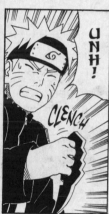

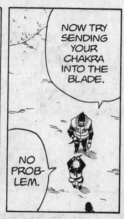

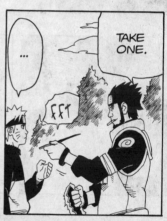

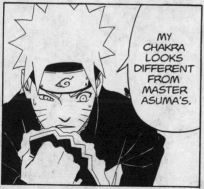

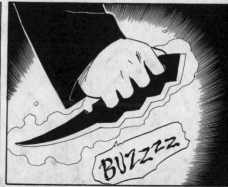

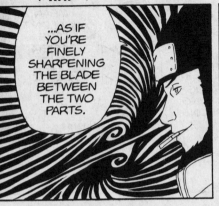

READ THIS WAY

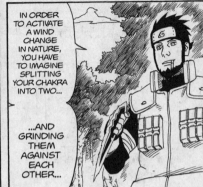

IN ORDER TO ACTIVATE A WIND CHANGE IN NATURE, YOU HAVE TO IMAGINE SPLITTING YOUR CHAKRA INTO TWO...
...AND GRINDING THEM AGAINST EACH OTHER...
...AS IF YOU'RE FINELY SHARPENING THE BLADE BETWEEN THE TWO PARTS.
... SHARP-ENING THE BLADE, HUH...
THAT'S RIGHT.
FINELY AND SHARPLY. THAT'S THE TRICK.
...
Y'KNOW...
...I WAS JUST THINK-ING...
YES...?
WHAT'S THE POINT OF USING THE WIND CHANGE IN NATURE ...
...WHEN WE ALREADY HAVE SHARP-EDGED NINJA TOOLS TO BEGIN WITH?

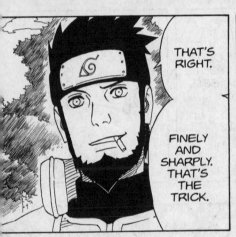

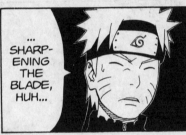

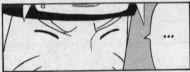

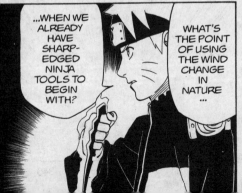

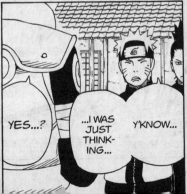

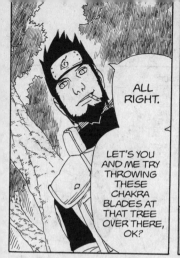

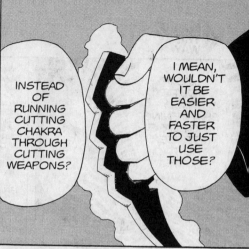

I MEAN, WOULDN'T IT BE EASIER AND FASTER TO JUST USE THOSE?
INSTEAD OF RUNNING CUTTING CHAKRA THROUGH CUTTING WEAPONS?
ALL RIGHT.
LET'S YOU AND ME TRY THROWING THESE CHAKRA BLADES AT THAT TREE OVER THERE, OK?
...
WHY ...?
JUST DO IT. YOU'LL SEE.
CROUCH
CROUCH
WHOOSH

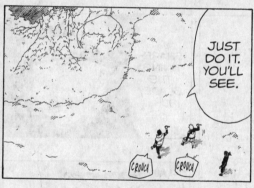

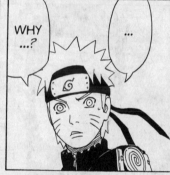

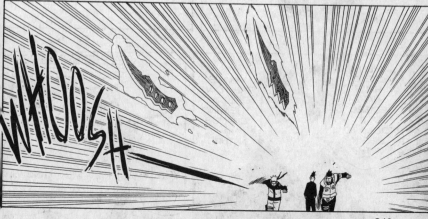

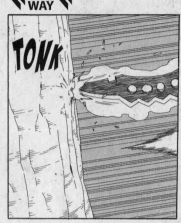

TONK

SWISH

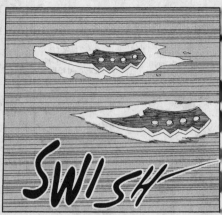

VOOSH

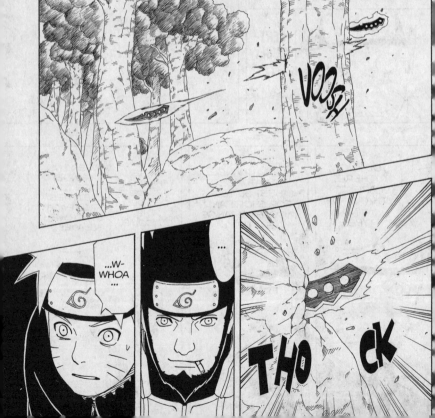

...W-WHOA...

...

THOCK

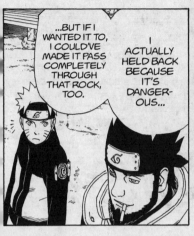

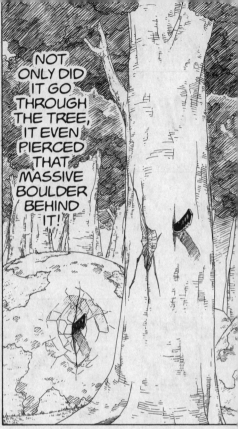

NOT ONLY DID IT GO THROUGH THE TREE, IT EVEN PIERCED THAT MASSIVE BOULDER BEHIND IT!
I ACTUALLY HELD BACK BECAUSE IT'S DANGER-OUS...
...BUT IF I WANTED IT TO, I COULD'VE MADE IT PASS COMPLETELY THROUGH THAT ROCK, TOO.
SERI-OUSLY ?!
WHEN TWO SHINOBI OF EQUAL ABILITIES FACE EACH OTHER WITH BLADES...
...THE SHARPER BLADE DECIDES THE OUTCOME.
WIND CHANGE IN NATURE IS BEST SUITED FOR SHORT AND MIDDLE DISTANCE BATTLES.
YOU KNOW, THERE AREN'T THAT MANY WIND TYPES.

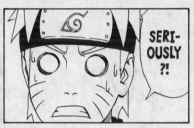

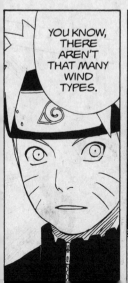

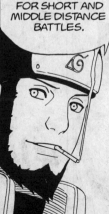

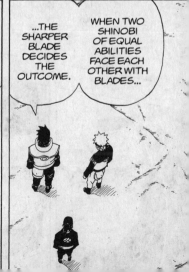

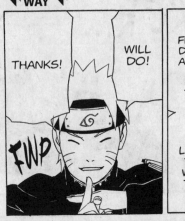

THANKS!

WILL DO!

FWP

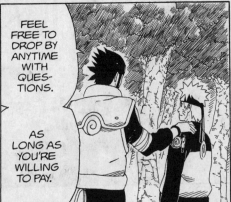

FEEL FREE TO DROP BY ANYTIME WITH QUESTIONS.

AS LONG AS YOU'RE WILLING TO PAY.

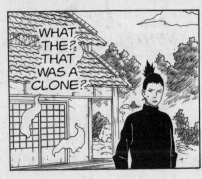

WHAT THE? THAT WAS A CLONE?

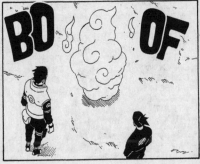

BO OF

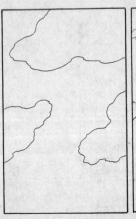

YOU'RE CRUEL...

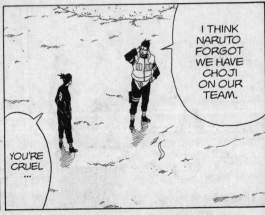

I THINK NARUTO FORGOT WE HAVE CHOJI ON OUR TEAM.

343

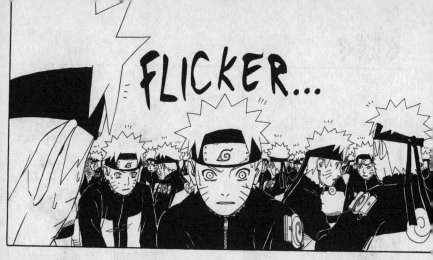

FLICKER...
OH, I SEE NOW!
ALL RIGHT!
IT SEEMS HE WAS ABLE TO GET SOME TIPS OUT OF ASUMA.
AND HE'S ALREADY MAKING GOOD USE OF THE ART OF THE SHADOW DOPPEL-GANGER'S SPECIAL TRAIT, TOO.
I SEE...
EVEN MIGHTY CHIRIKU.
(SHADOW)

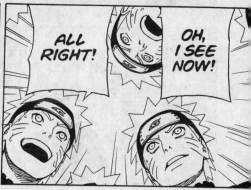

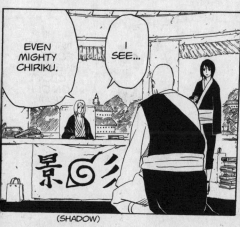

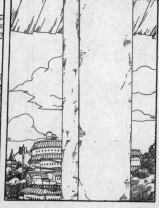

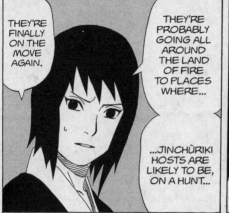

READ THIS WAY

I HAPPENED TO BE OUT ON PERIMETER PATROL...
...WHEN I RETURNED, IT WAS ALREADY TOO LATE...
THEY'RE FINALLY ON THE MOVE AGAIN.
THEY'RE PROBABLY GOING ALL AROUND THE LAND OF FIRE TO PLACES WHERE...
...JINCHÛRIKI HOSTS ARE LIKELY TO BE, ON A HUNT...
...
DON'T LET THEM LEAVE THE LAND OF FIRE.
ALERT THE 20 NEWLY FORMED...
...PLATOONS IMMEDI-ATELY.

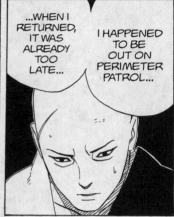

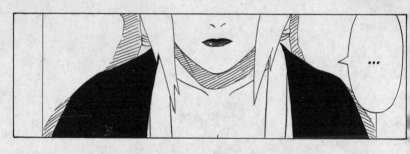

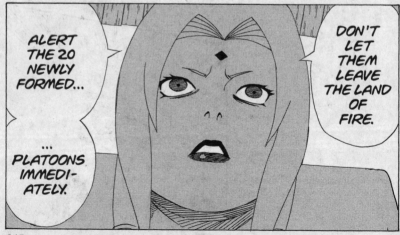

THO CK

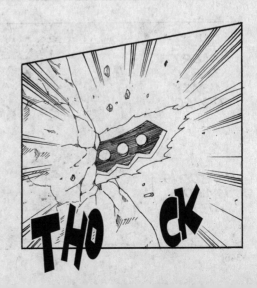

Number 318: Smooth Training

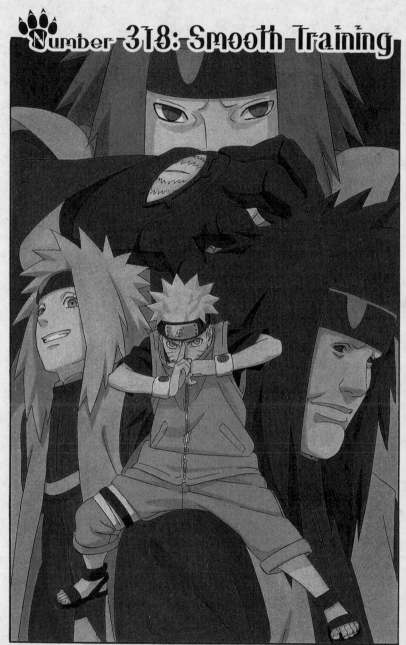

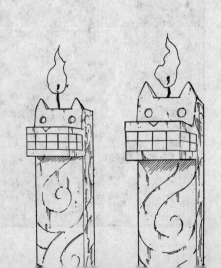

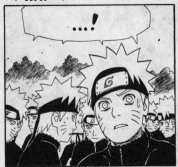

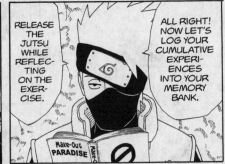

READ THIS WAY

ALL RIGHT! NOW LET'S LOG YOUR CUMULATIVE EXPERIENCES INTO YOUR MEMORY BANK.
RELEASE THE JUTSU WHILE REFLECTING ON THE EXERCISE.
Make-Out PARADISE
...!
YES, SIR!
BOOF BOOF BOOF
PHEW...

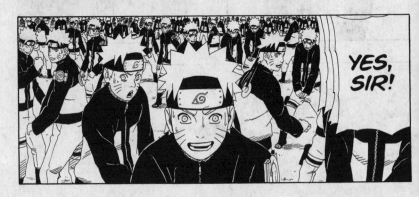

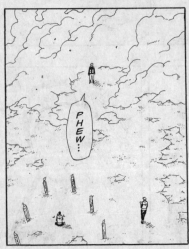

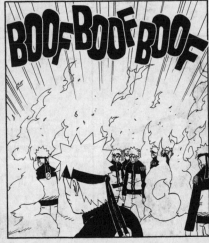

READ THIS WAY

FADE
FADE
PHEW ...
WOOSH
...
...
...

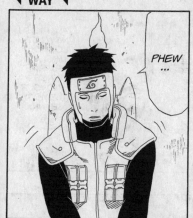

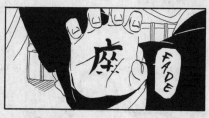

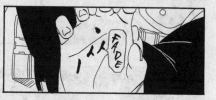

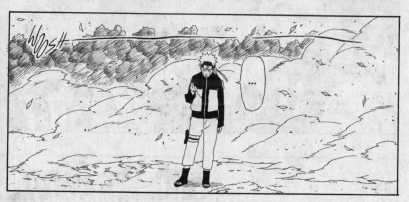

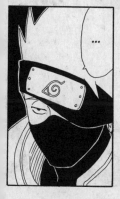

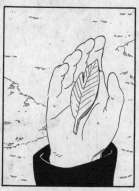

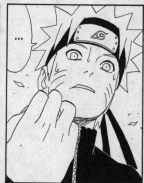

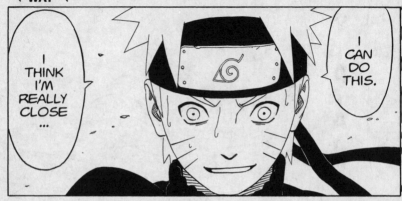

I THINK I'M REALLY CLOSE ...

I CAN DO THIS.

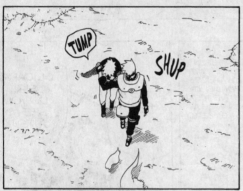

TUMP

SHUP

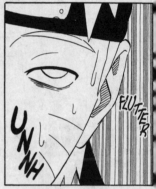

UNNH

FLUTTER

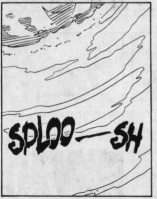

SPLOO—SH

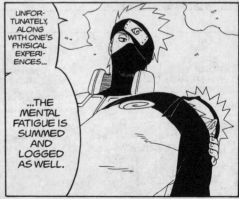

UNFORTUNATELY, ALONG WITH ONE'S PHYSICAL EXPERIENCES...

...THE MENTAL FATIGUE IS SUMMED AND LOGGED AS WELL.

351

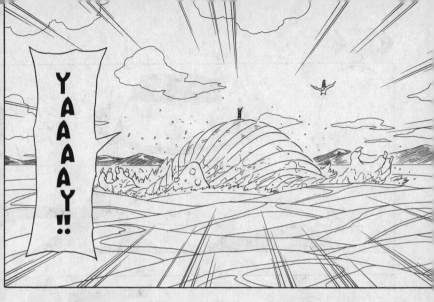

YAAAAY!!
DEIDARA, SIR! DO YOU SEE MY JUTSU?!
HE'S A GONER!
TO HAVE BEEN ENTRUSTED WITH SUCH A HUGE RESPONSIBILITY WHEN I'VE JUST BEEN MADE A FULL MEMBER...
I'M PRETTY AMAZING, AREN'T I?!
...IT MEANS YOU ALL APPROVE OF ME, RIGHT?!
...
ACTUALLY... MY ARTFUL DETONATING CLAY DID THE HEAVY LIFTING.
THE CREDIT FOR THIS MASTER-PIECE IS MINE ALONE, *HMMM?*

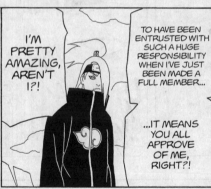

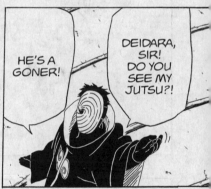

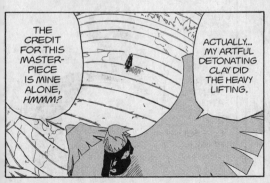

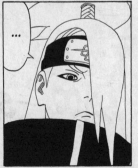

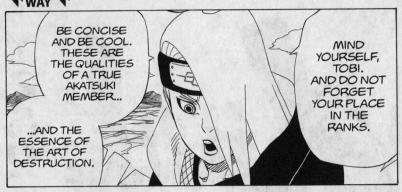

READ THIS WAY

MIND YOURSELF, TOBI. AND DO NOT FORGET YOUR PLACE IN THE RANKS.
BE CONCISE AND BE COOL. THESE ARE THE QUALITIES OF A TRUE AKATSUKI MEMBER...
...AND THE ESSENCE OF THE ART OF DESTRUCTION.
REMEMBER, TRUE ART RESULTS FROM A MOMENT OF PASSION ARISING OUT OF A SEA OF CALM...
NO OFFENSE, SIR, BUT YOU SURE DO LIKE TO HEAR YOURSELF TALK...
...HA HA HA...
GRRR
...
JUST KIDD...
KABOOM
...AAAARRRGH!
HUF
HUF

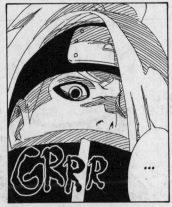

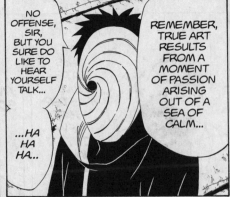

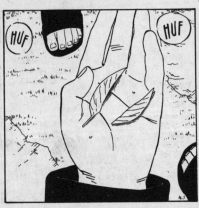

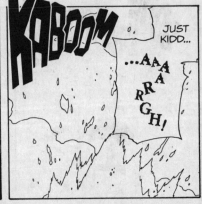

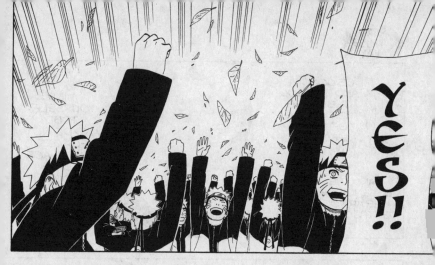

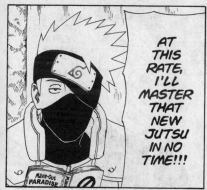

YES!!
I DID IT!
I AM AWE-SOME!
AT THIS RATE, I'LL MASTER THAT NEW JUTSU IN NO TIME!!!
Make-Out PARADISE
ACTUALLY... IT'S COMING QUICKLY BECAUSE OF THIS TRAINING METHOD.
WHICH, LET'S NOT FORGET, WAS MY GENIUS IDEA IN THE FIRST PLACE...
BOOF BOOF BOOF

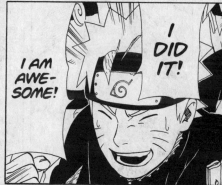

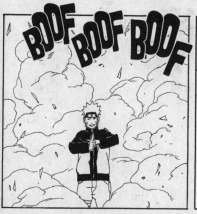

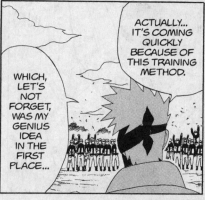

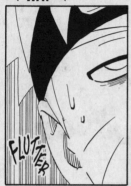

READ THIS WAY

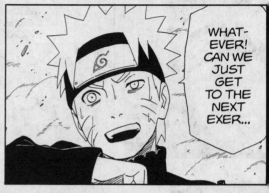

WHAT-EVER! CAN WE JUST GET TO THE NEXT EXER...
FLUTTER
TUMP
...AND YES, IT'S ONLY POSSIBLE BECAUSE YOU'RE **YOU**, NARUTO.
MAKE-OUT PARADISE
SHUP
YAMATO, LET'S TAKE A BREAK WHILE HE'S OUT.
THOOM
...
BLINK...

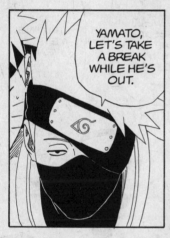

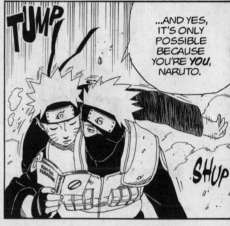

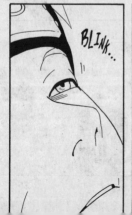

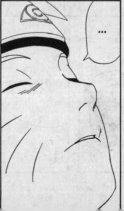

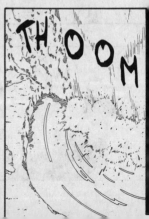

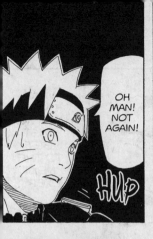

WEL-COME BACK.
OH MAN! NOT AGAIN!
HUP
THIS TRAINING METHOD WEARS YOU OUT...
...WE'LL RESUME AFTER YOU'VE RESTED...
...WITH THE NEXT STEP.
AND WHAT'S THAT?
DOINK

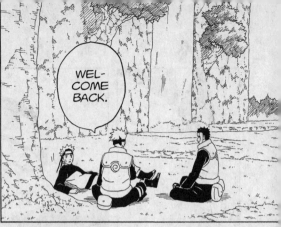

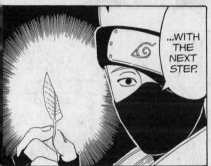

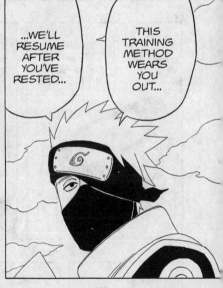

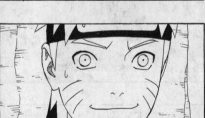

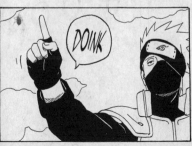

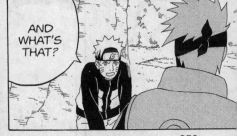

READ THIS WAY

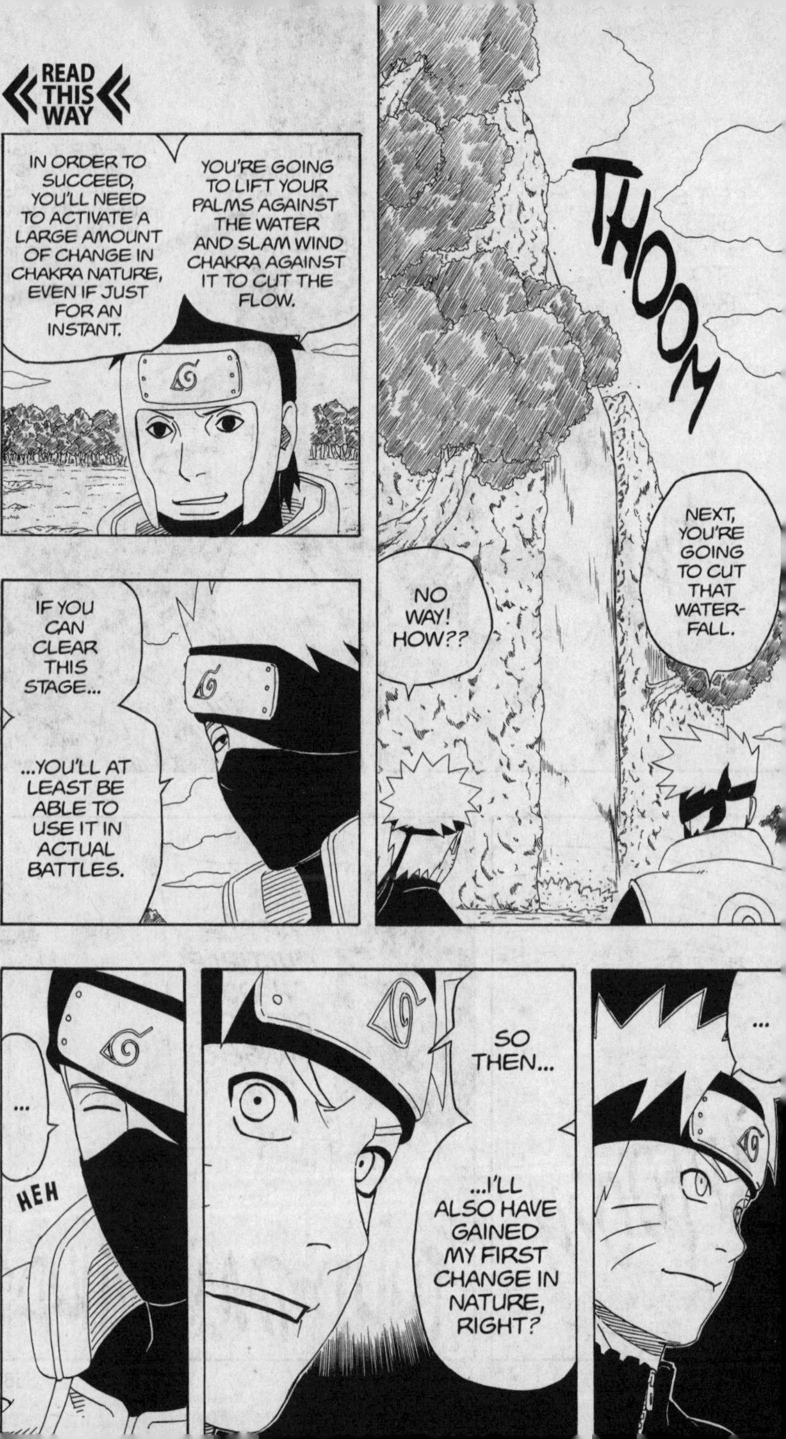
THOOM
NEXT, YOU'RE GOING TO CUT THAT WATER-FALL.
NO WAY! HOW??
YOU'RE GOING TO LIFT YOUR PALMS AGAINST THE WATER AND SLAM WIND CHAKRA AGAINST IT TO CUT THE FLOW.
IN ORDER TO SUCCEED, YOU'LL NEED TO ACTIVATE A LARGE AMOUNT OF CHANGE IN CHAKRA NATURE, EVEN IF JUST FOR AN INSTANT.
IF YOU CAN CLEAR THIS STAGE...
...YOU'LL AT LEAST BE ABLE TO USE IT IN ACTUAL BATTLES.
...
SO THEN...
...I'LL ALSO HAVE GAINED MY FIRST CHANGE IN NATURE, RIGHT?
...
HEH

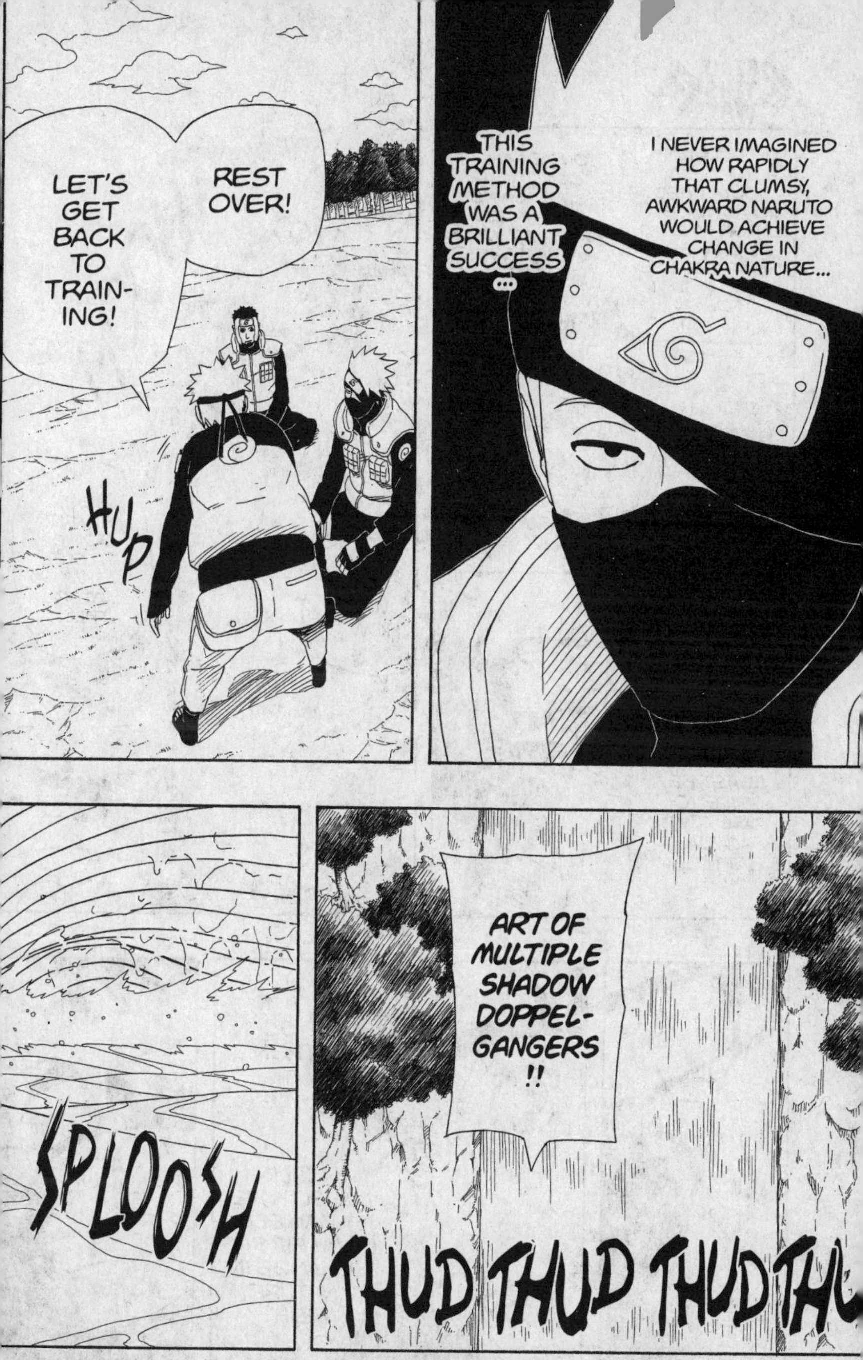
I NEVER IMAGINED HOW RAPIDLY THAT CLUMSY, AWKWARD NARUTO WOULD ACHIEVE CHANGE IN CHAKRA NATURE...
THIS TRAINING METHOD WAS A BRILLIANT SUCCESS...
REST OVER!
LET'S GET BACK TO TRAIN-ING!
HUP
ART OF MULTIPLE SHADOW DOPPEL-GANGERS!!
THUD THUD THUD THU
SPLOOSH

READ THIS WAY

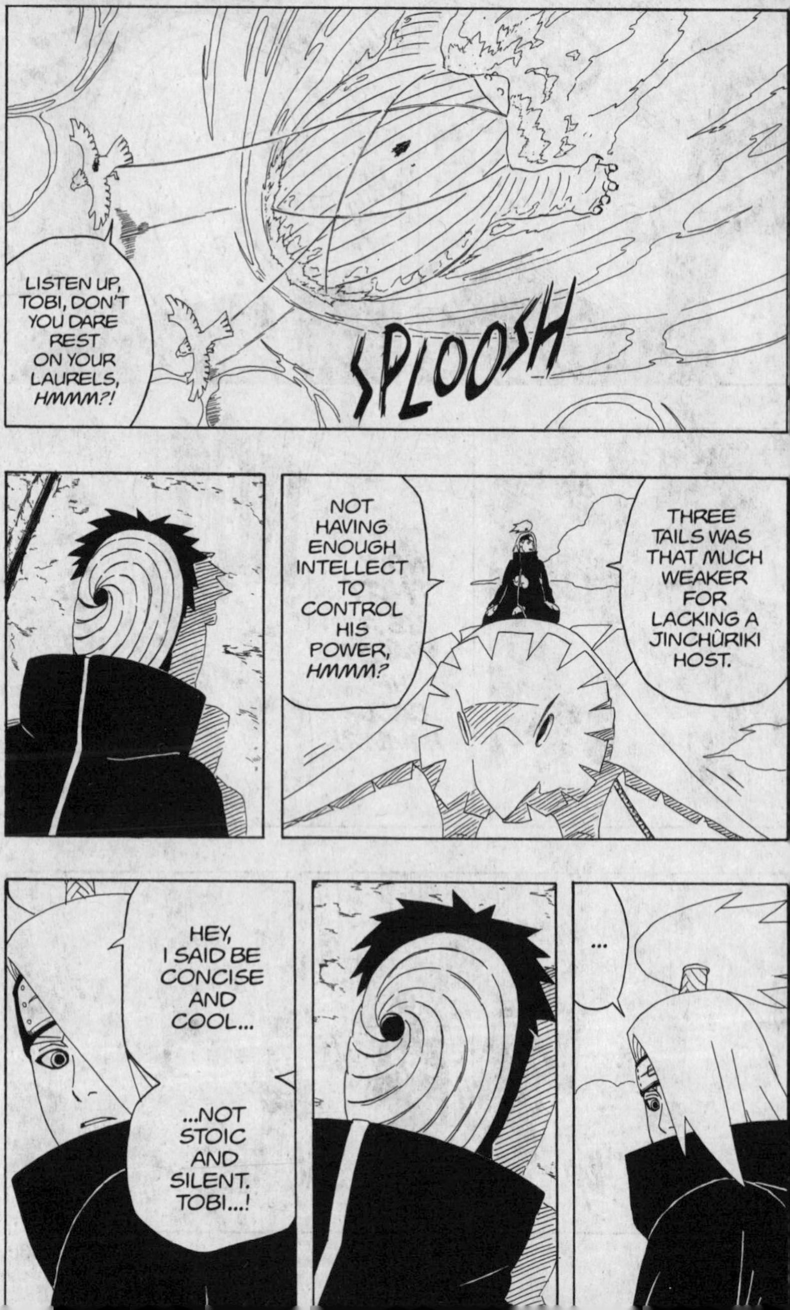
SPLOOSH
LISTEN UP, TOBI, DON'T YOU DARE REST ON YOUR LAURELS, HMMM?!
THREE TAILS WAS THAT MUCH WEAKER FOR LACKING A JINCHÛRIKI HOST.
NOT HAVING ENOUGH INTELLECT TO CONTROL HIS POWER, HMMM?
...
HEY, I SAID BE CONCISE AND COOL...
...NOT STOIC AND SILENT. TOBI...!

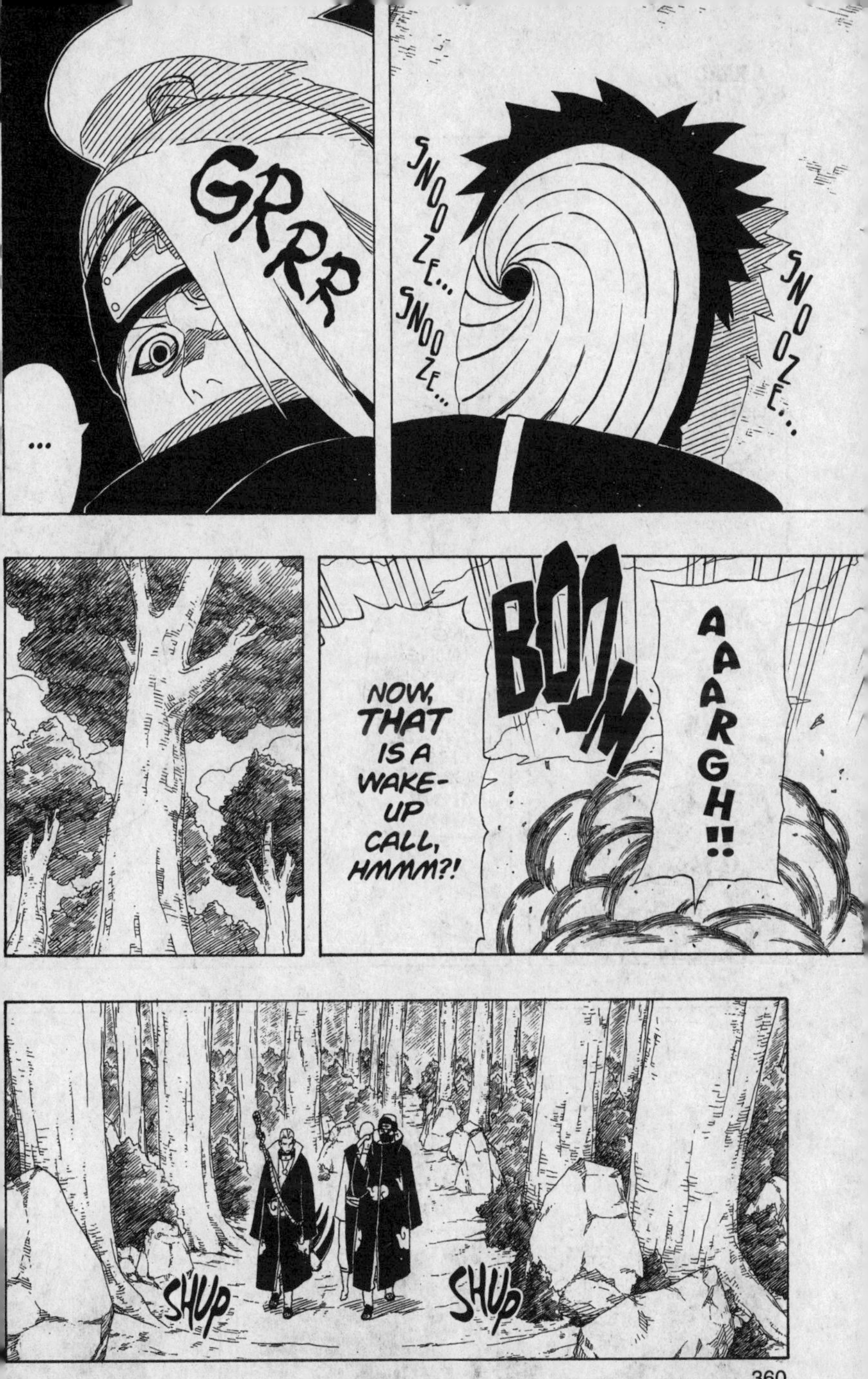
SNOOZE...
SNOOZE... SNOOZE...
GRRR
...
AAARGH!!
BOOM
NOW, THAT IS A WAKE-UP CALL, HMMM?!
SHUP
SHUP

READ THIS WAY

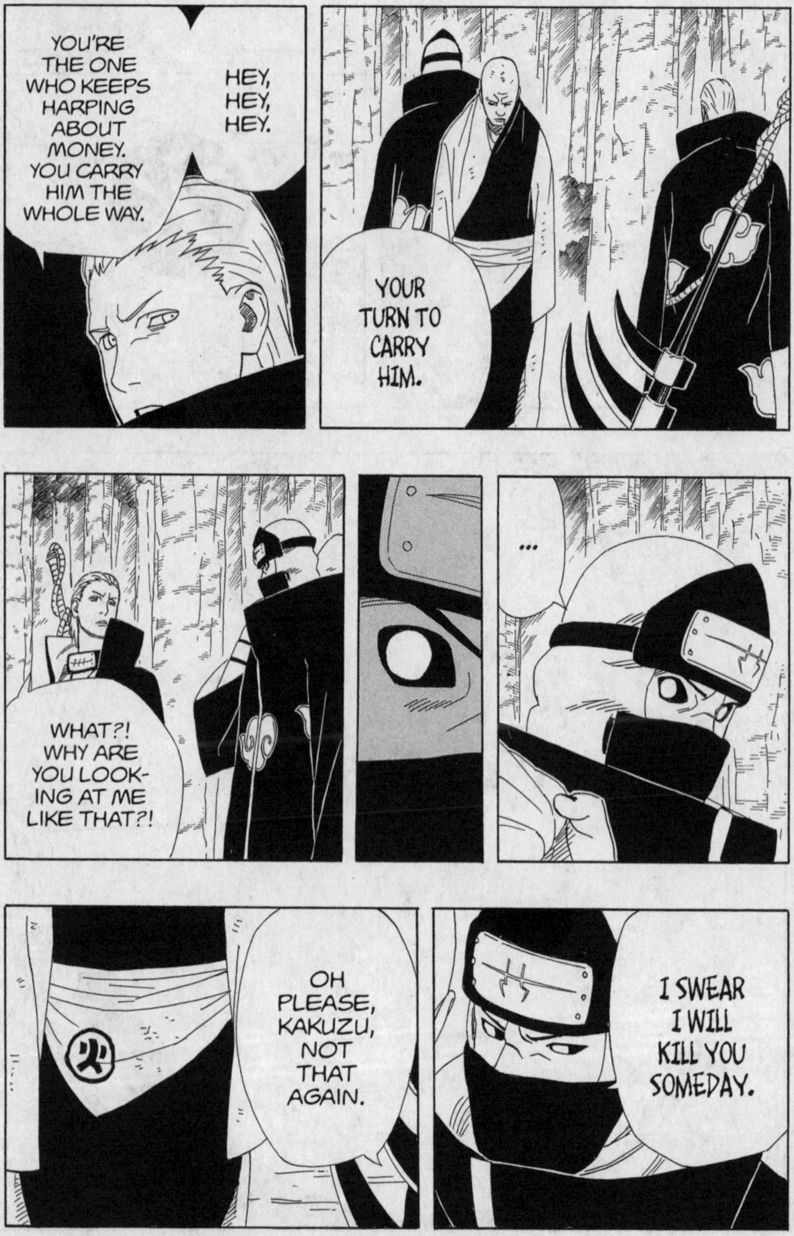
YOUR TURN TO CARRY HIM.
HEY, HEY, HEY.
YOU'RE THE ONE WHO KEEPS HARPING ABOUT MONEY. YOU CARRY HIM THE WHOLE WAY.
...
WHAT?! WHY ARE YOU LOOK-ING AT ME LIKE THAT?!
I SWEAR I WILL KILL YOU SOMEDAY.
OH PLEASE, KAKUZU, NOT THAT AGAIN.

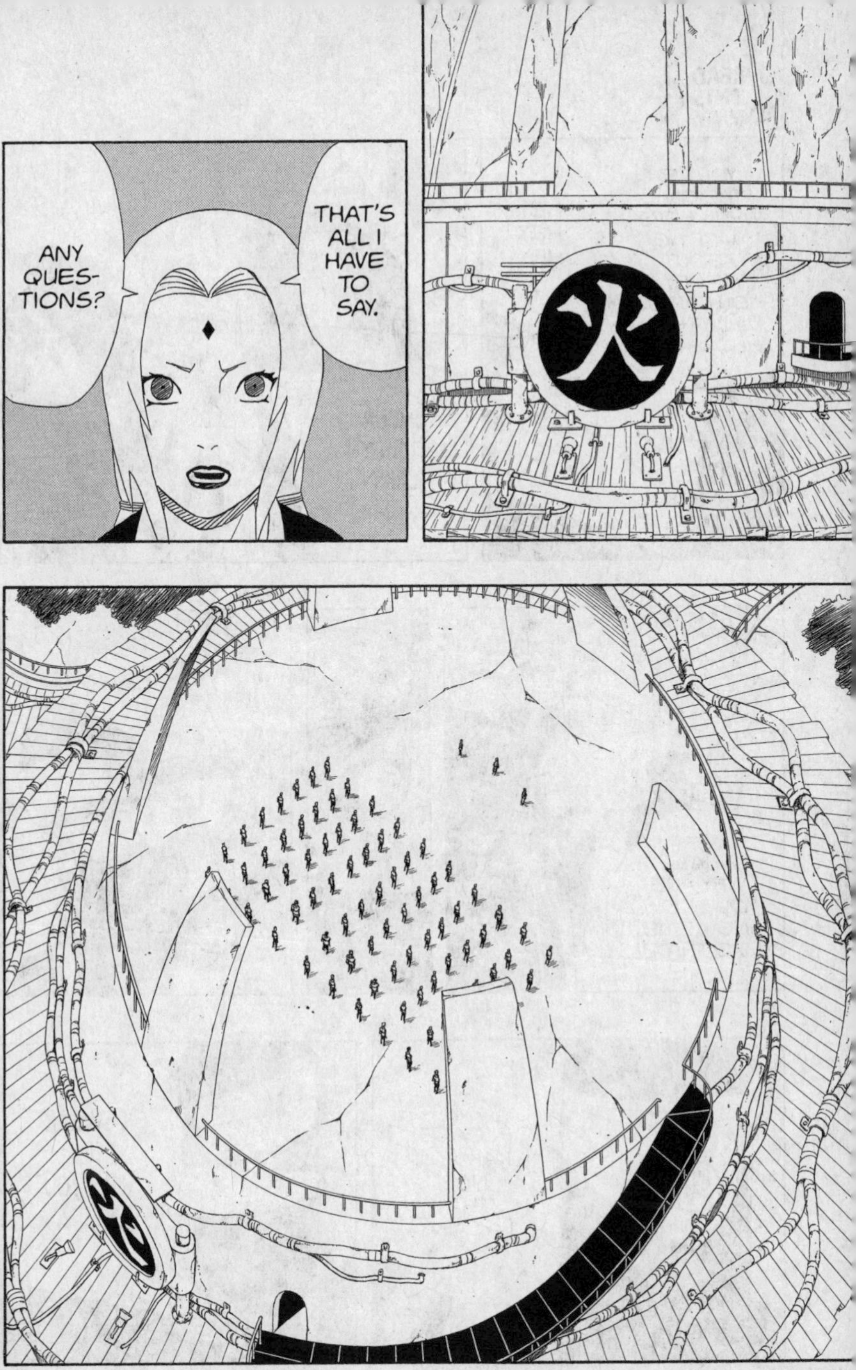
THAT'S ALL I HAVE TO SAY.
ANY QUES-TIONS?

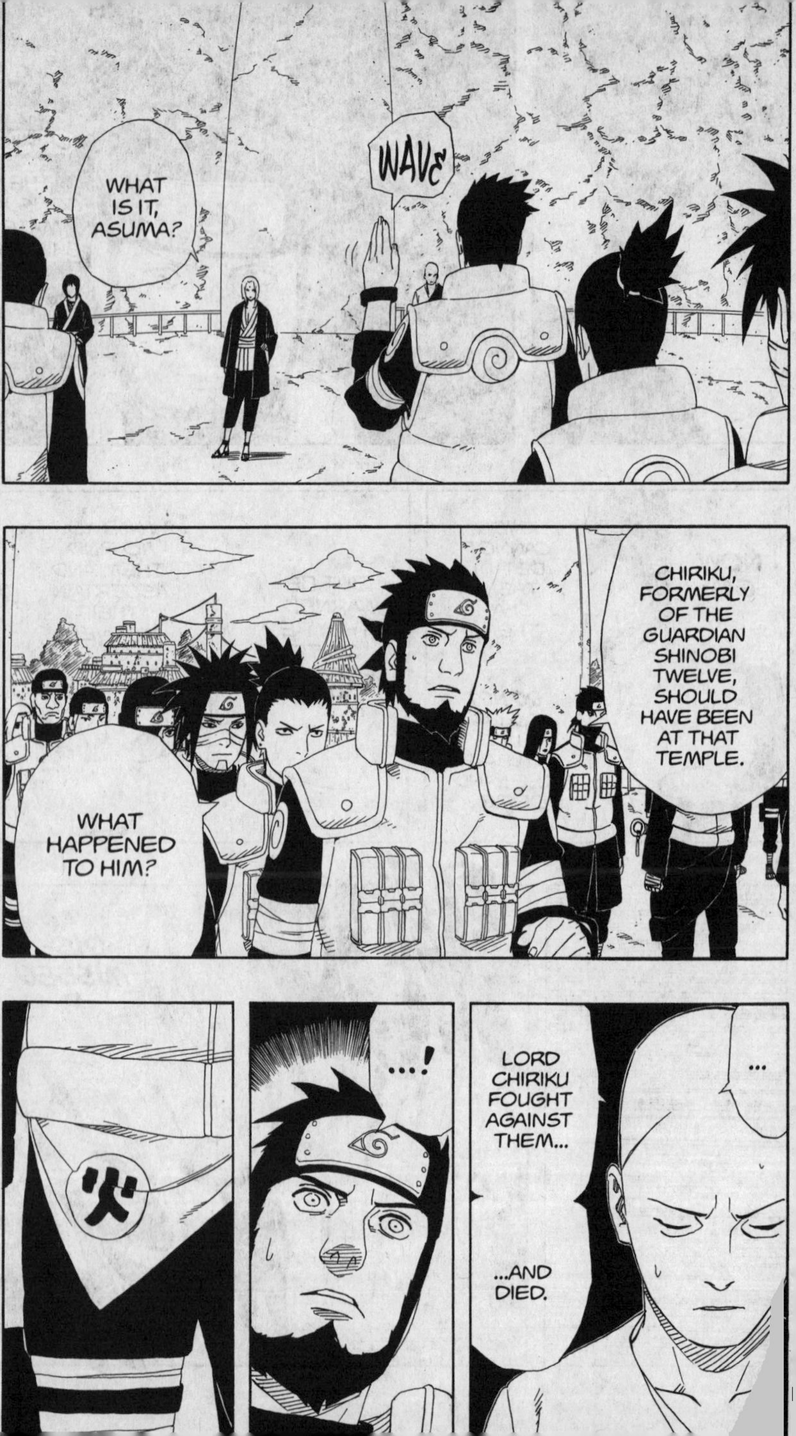
WAVE
WHAT IS IT, ASUMA?
CHIRIKU, FORMERLY OF THE GUARDIAN SHINOBI TWELVE, SHOULD HAVE BEEN AT THAT TEMPLE.
WHAT HAPPENED TO HIM?
...
LORD CHIRIKU FOUGHT AGAINST THEM...
...AND DIED.
...!

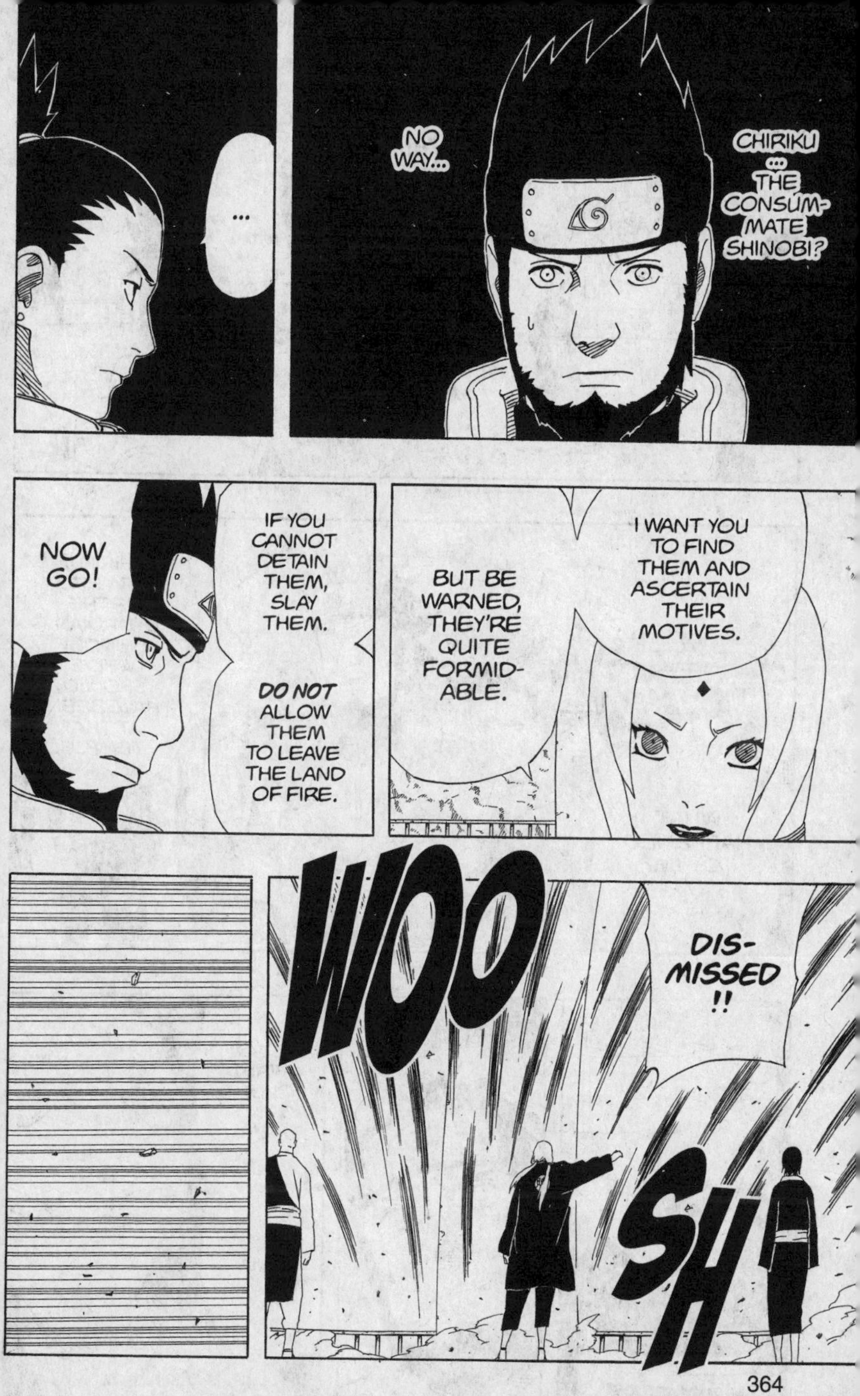
CHIRIKU ... THE CONSUM-MATE SHINOBI?
NO WAY...
...
I WANT YOU TO FIND THEM AND ASCERTAIN THEIR MOTIVES.
BUT BE WARNED, THEY'RE QUITE FORMID-ABLE.
IF YOU CANNOT DETAIN THEM, SLAY THEM.
DO NOT ALLOW THEM TO LEAVE THE LAND OF FIRE.
NOW GO!
DIS-MISSED !!
WOOSH

READ THIS WAY

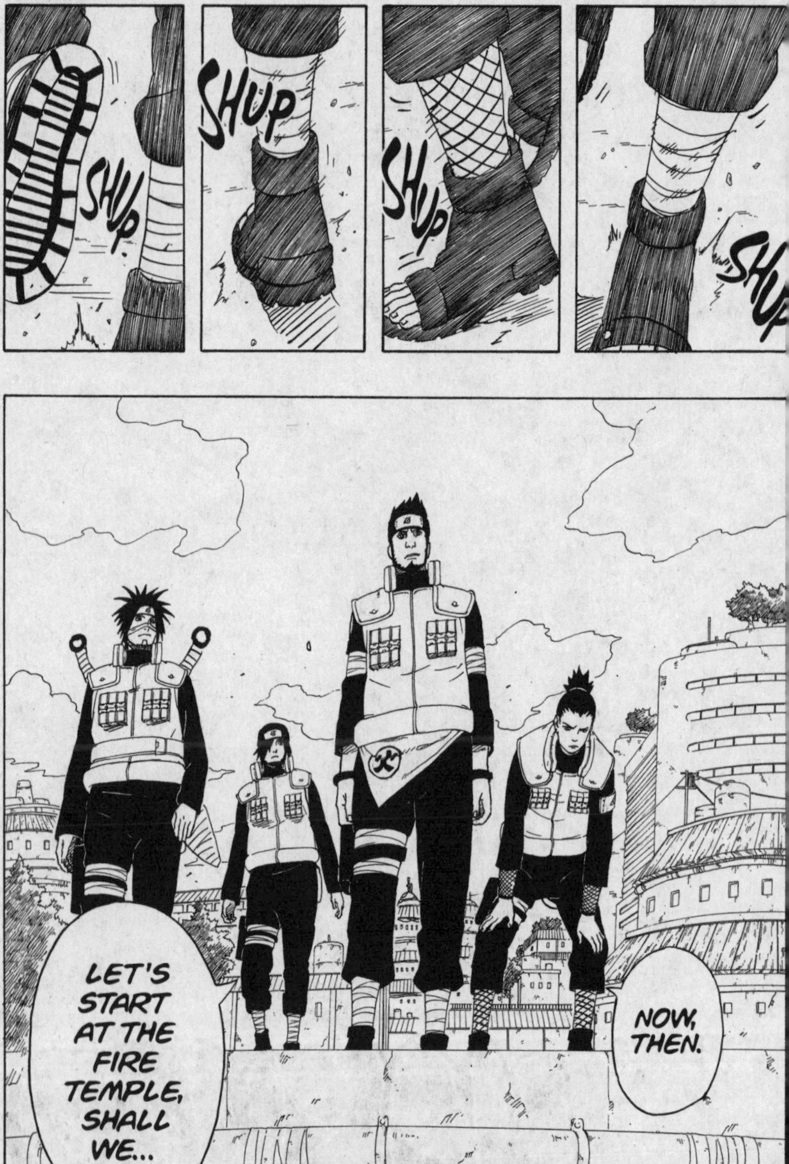
SHUP
SHUP
SHUP
SHUP
NOW, THEN.
LET'S START AT THE FIRE TEMPLE, SHALL WE...

NARUTO

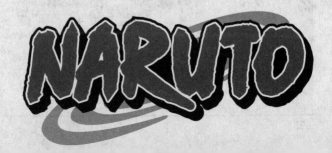

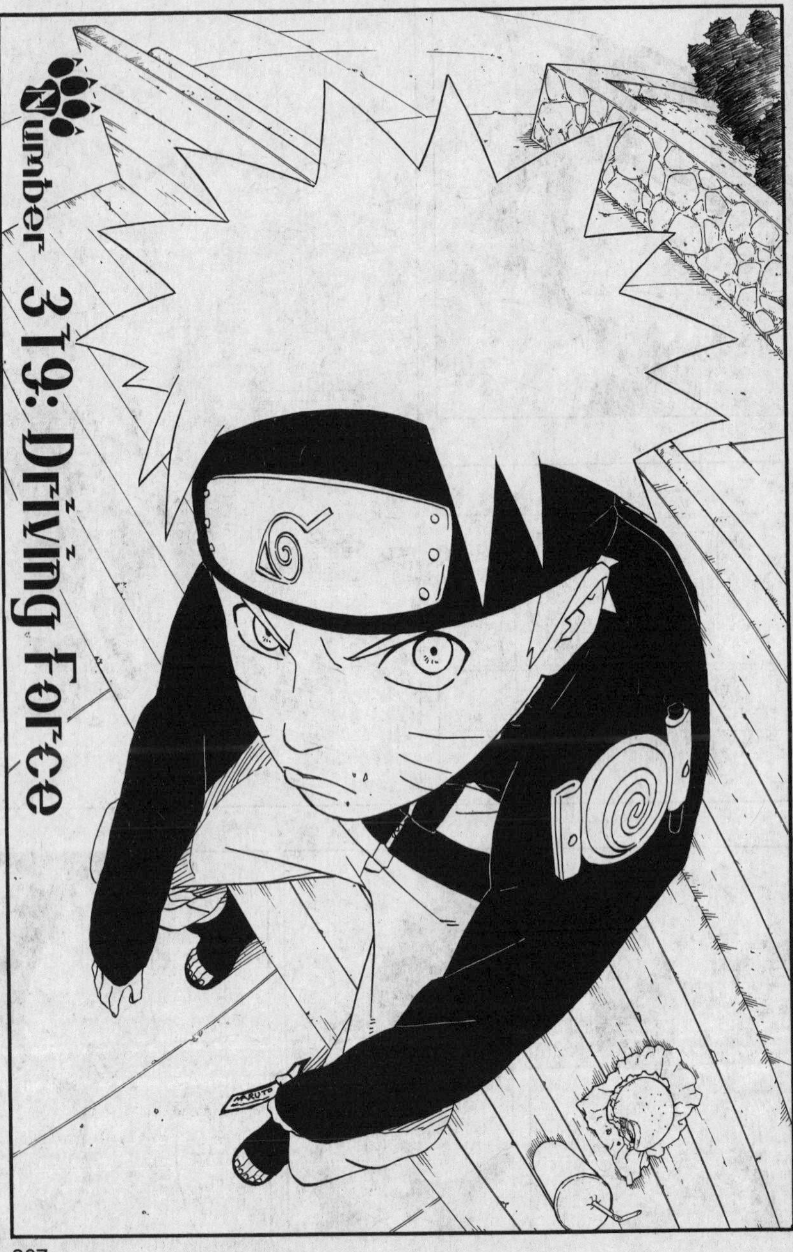
Number 319: Driving Force

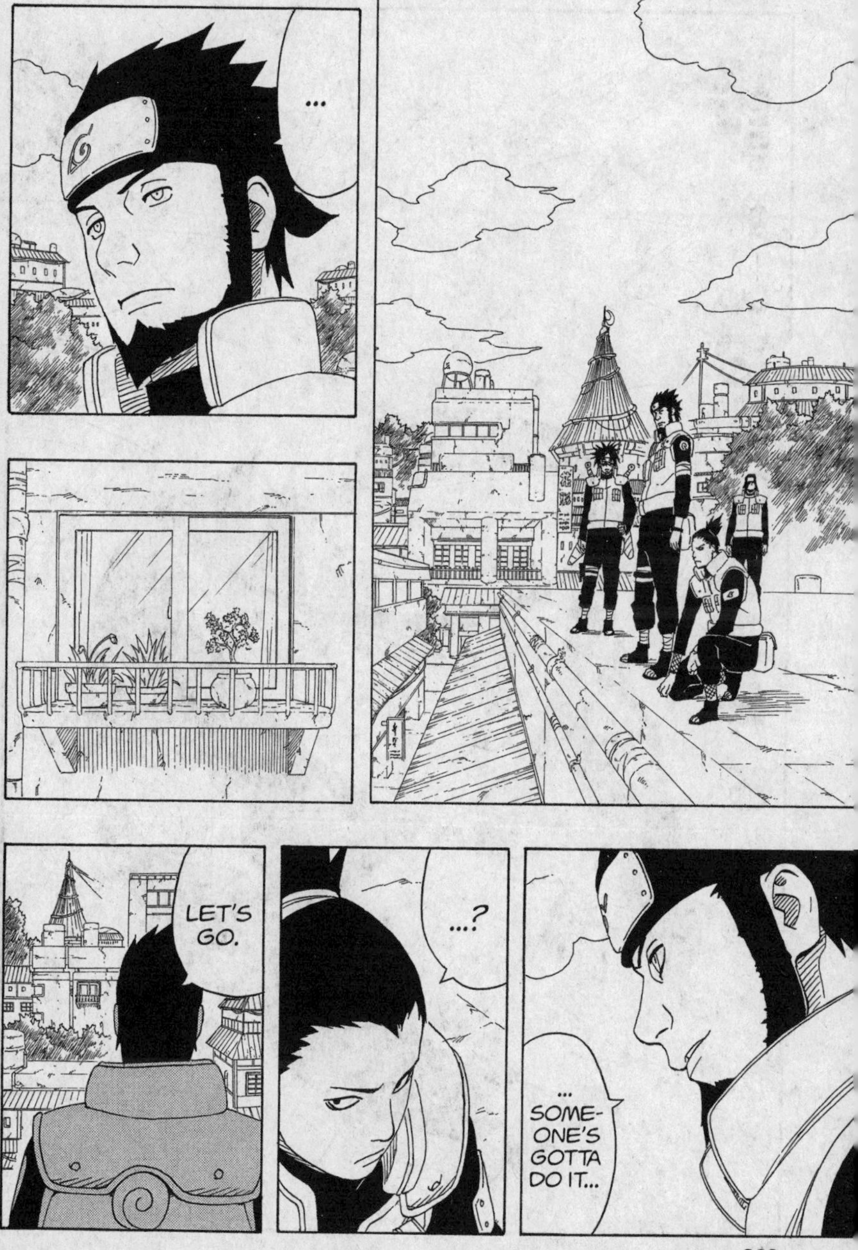
...
... SOME-ONE'S GOTTA DO IT...
...?
LET'S GO.

READ THIS WAY

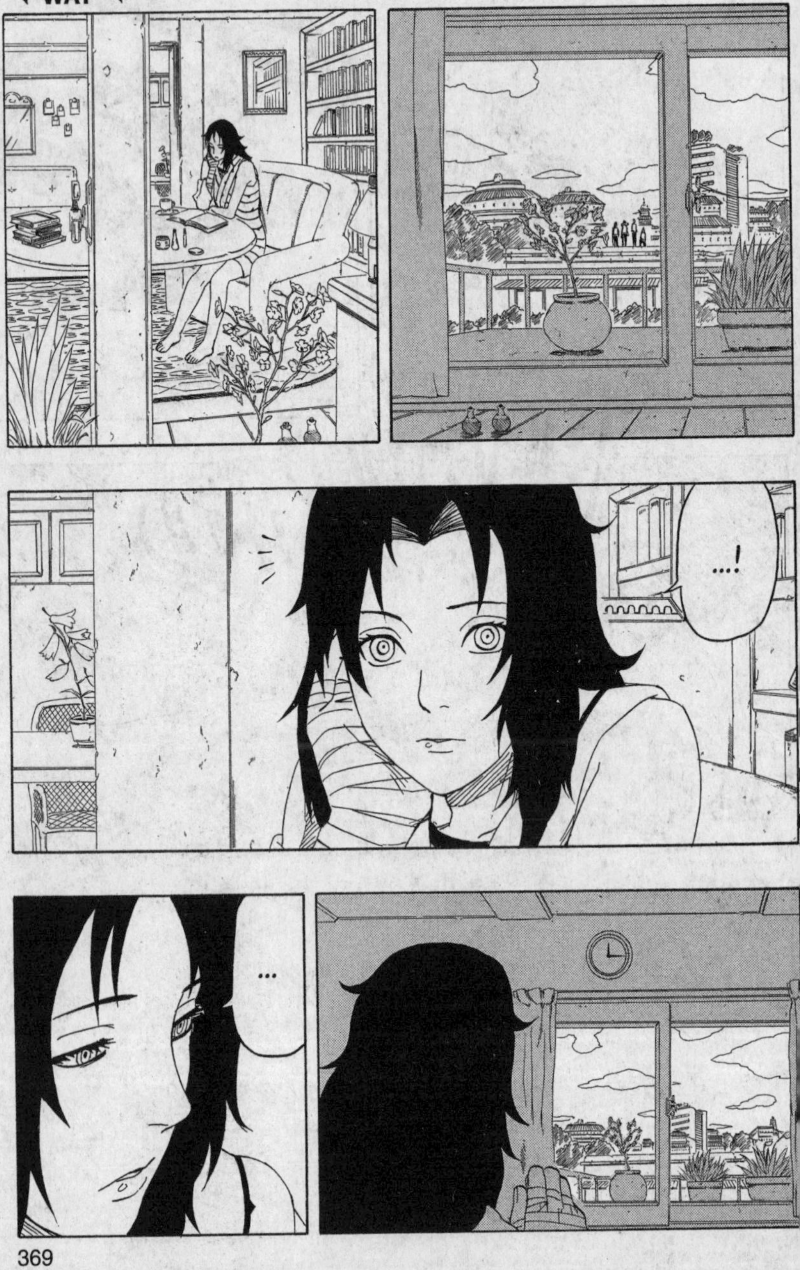
...!
...

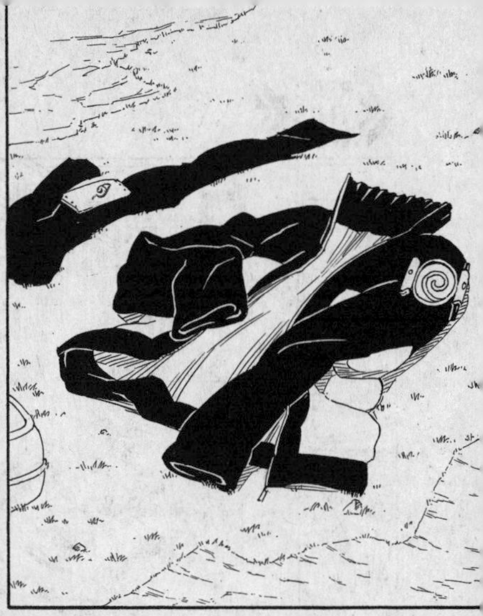

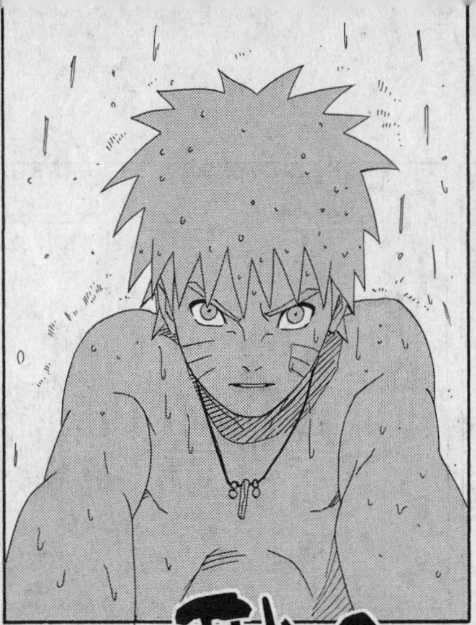

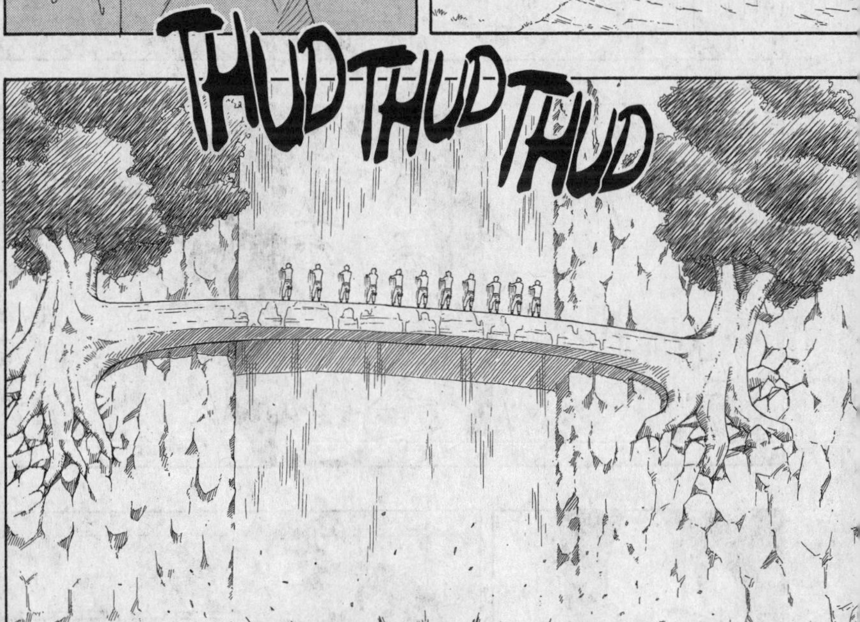
THUD THUD THUD

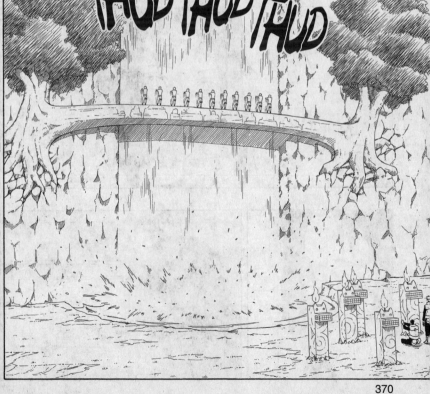

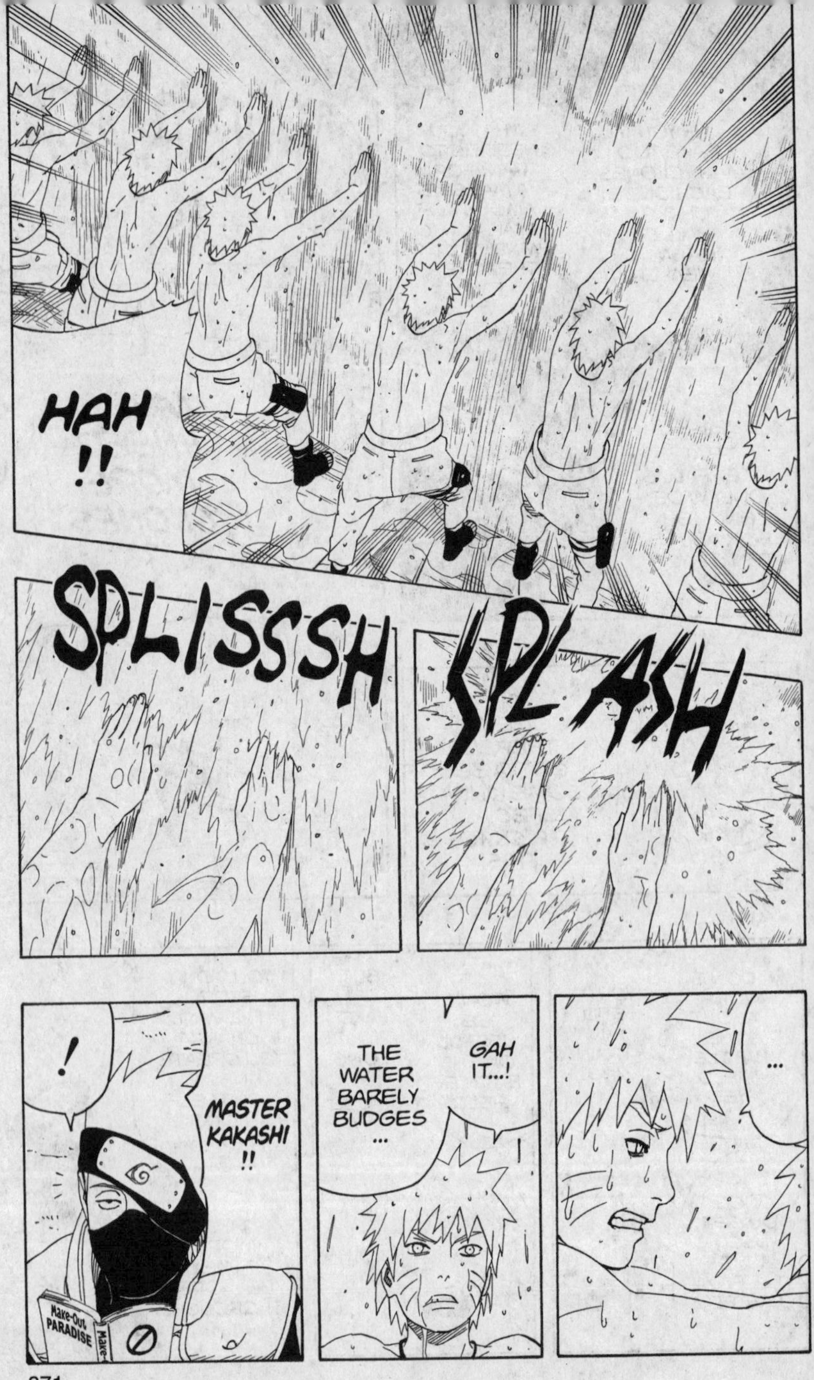
HAH!!
SPLASH
SPLISSSH
...
GAH IT...!
THE WATER BARELY BUDGES...
MASTER KAKASHI!!
!
Make-Out PARADISE

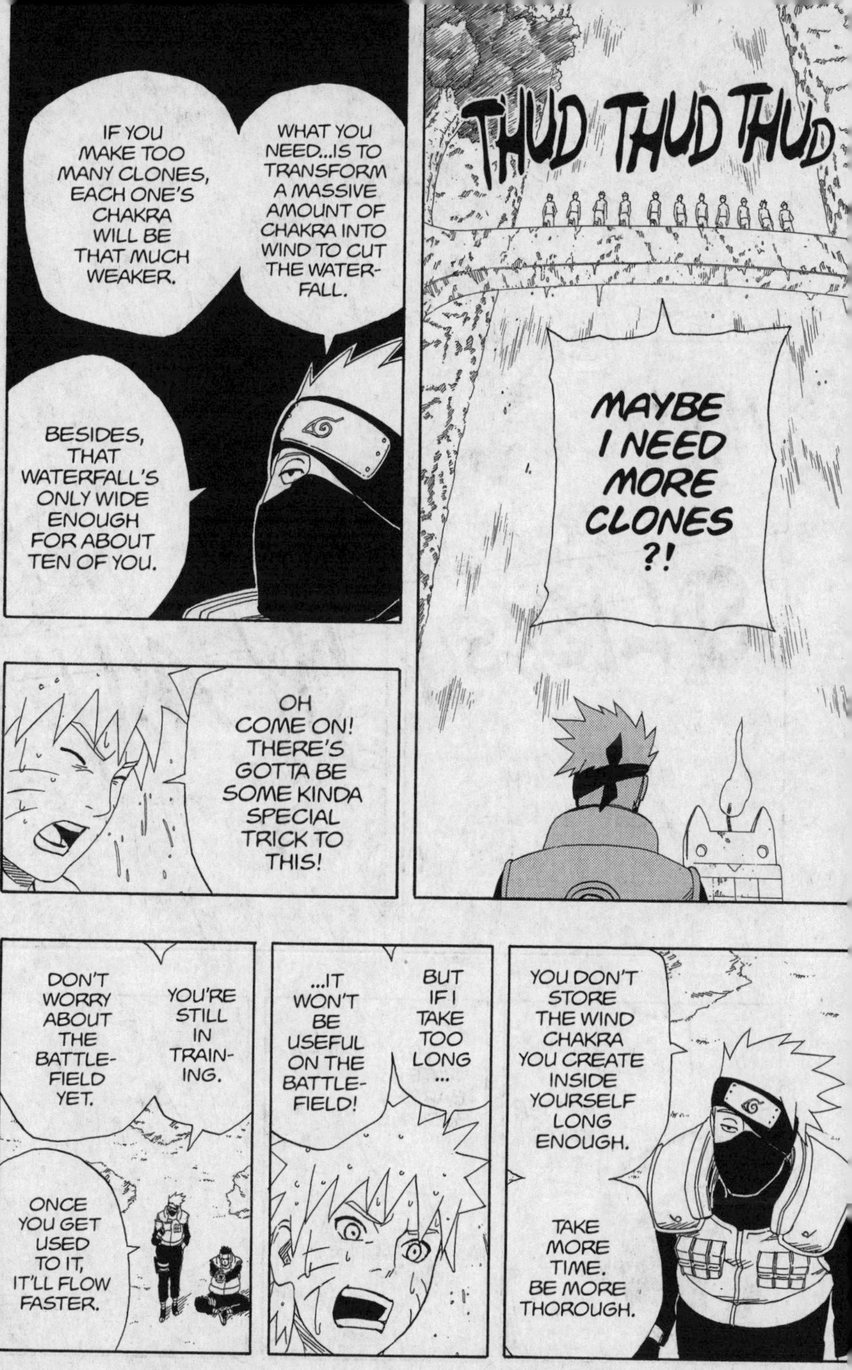
THUD THUD THUD
MAYBE I NEED MORE CLONES?!
WHAT YOU NEED...IS TO TRANSFORM A MASSIVE AMOUNT OF CHAKRA INTO WIND TO CUT THE WATER-FALL.
IF YOU MAKE TOO MANY CLONES, EACH ONE'S CHAKRA WILL BE THAT MUCH WEAKER.
BESIDES, THAT WATERFALL'S ONLY WIDE ENOUGH FOR ABOUT TEN OF YOU.
OH COME ON! THERE'S GOTTA BE SOME KINDA SPECIAL TRICK TO THIS!
YOU DON'T STORE THE WIND CHAKRA YOU CREATE INSIDE YOURSELF LONG ENOUGH.
TAKE MORE TIME. BE MORE THOROUGH.
BUT IF I TAKE TOO LONG...
...IT WON'T BE USEFUL ON THE BATTLE-FIELD!
YOU'RE STILL IN TRAIN-ING.
DON'T WORRY ABOUT THE BATTLE-FIELD YET.
ONCE YOU GET USED TO IT, IT'LL FLOW FASTER.

READ THIS WAY

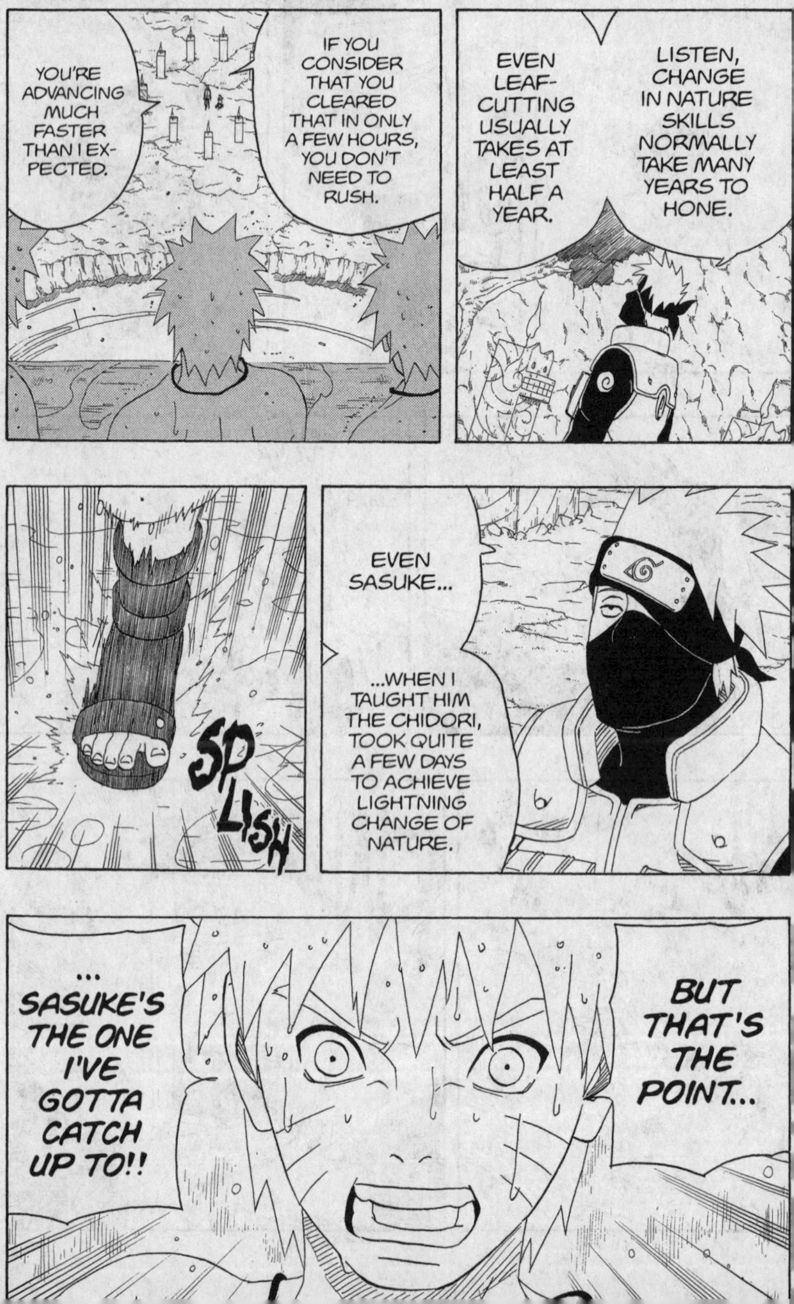

LISTEN, CHANGE IN NATURE SKILLS NORMALLY TAKE MANY YEARS TO HONE.
EVEN LEAF-CUTTING USUALLY TAKES AT LEAST HALF A YEAR.
IF YOU CONSIDER THAT YOU CLEARED THAT IN ONLY A FEW HOURS, YOU DON'T NEED TO RUSH.
YOU'RE ADVANCING MUCH FASTER THAN I EXPECTED.
EVEN SASUKE...
...WHEN I TAUGHT HIM THE CHIDORI, TOOK QUITE A FEW DAYS TO ACHIEVE LIGHTNING CHANGE OF NATURE.
SPLISH
BUT THAT'S THE POINT...
... SASUKE'S THE ONE I'VE GOTTA CATCH UP TO!!

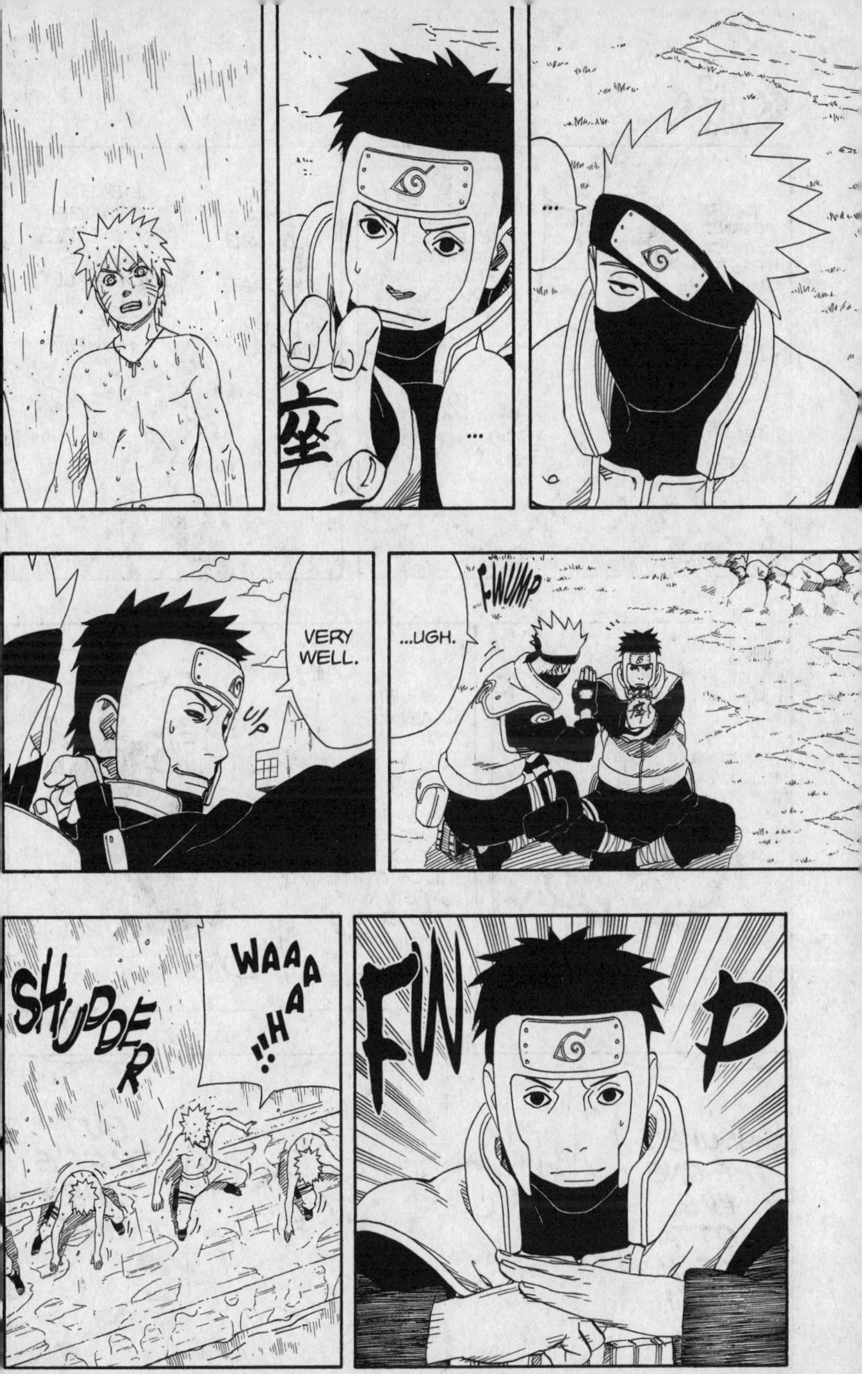
...
...
座
FWUMP
...UGH.
VERY WELL.
FW
P
WAAAHA!!
SHUDDER

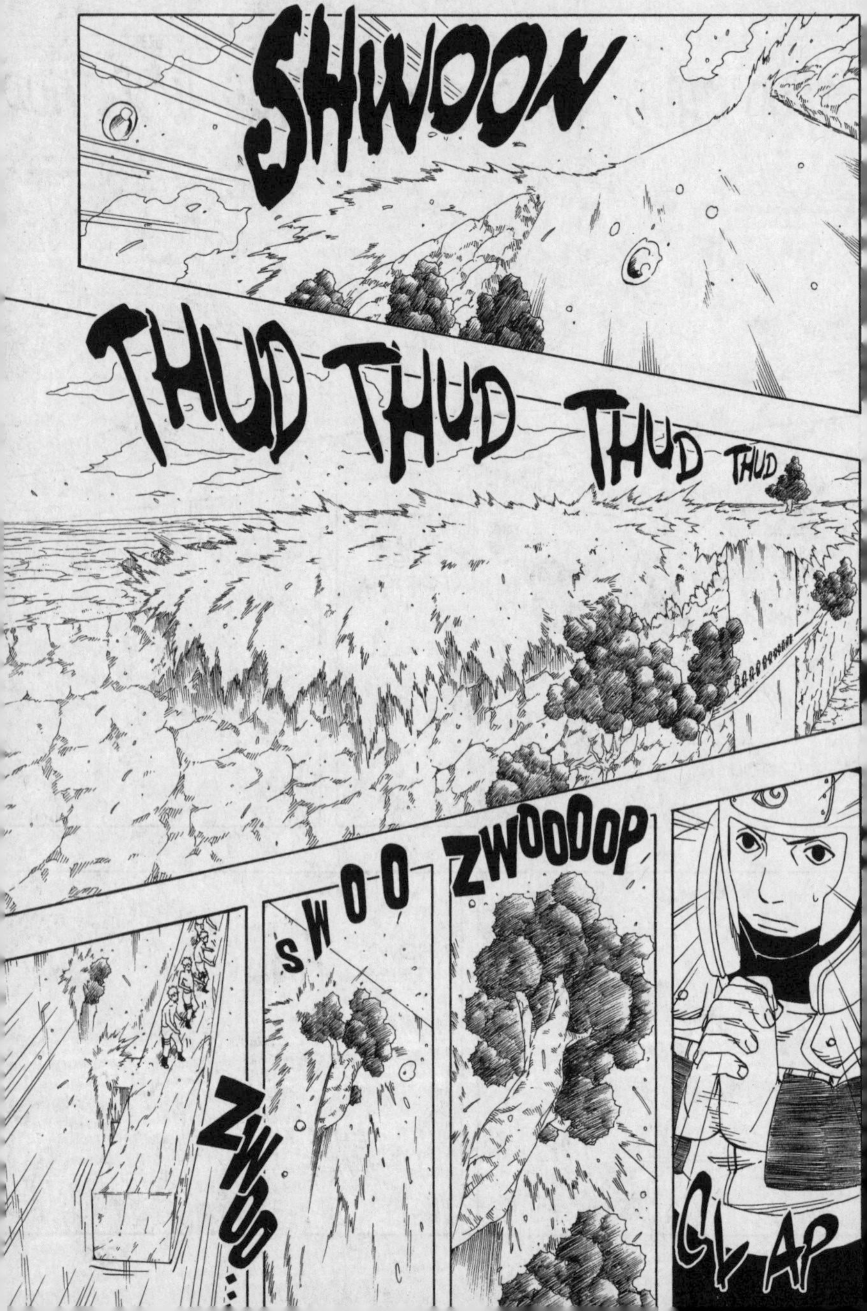
SHWOON
THUD THUD THUD THUD
CLAP
ZWOOOOP
SWOO
ZWOO...

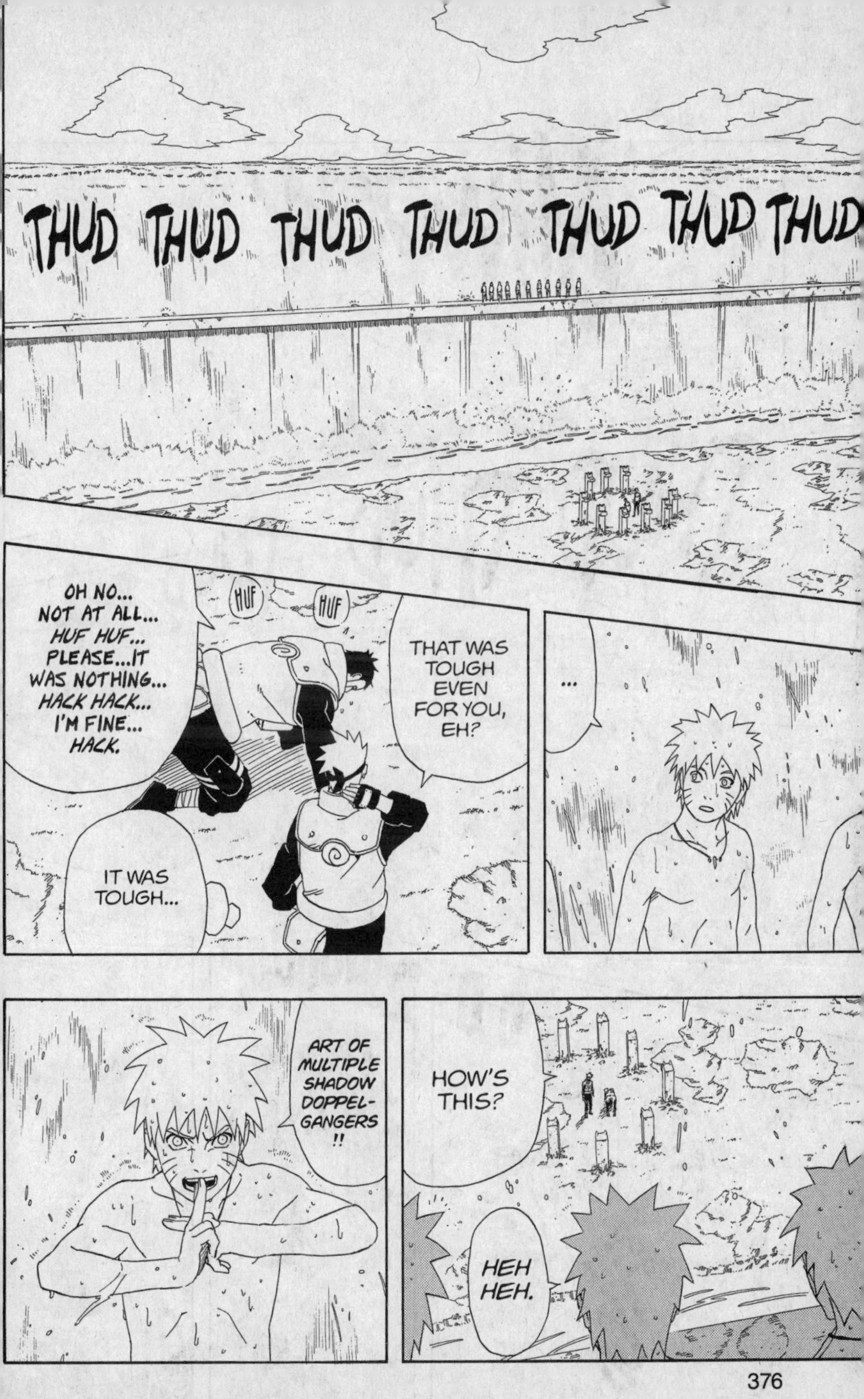
THUD THUD THUD THUD THUD THUD THUD
...
HUF
HUF
THAT WAS TOUGH EVEN FOR YOU, EH?
OH NO... NOT AT ALL... *HUF HUF*... PLEASE...IT WAS NOTHING... *HACK HACK*... I'M FINE... *HACK.*
IT WAS TOUGH...
HOW'S THIS?
HEH HEH.
ART OF MULTIPLE SHADOW DOPPEL-GANGERS !!

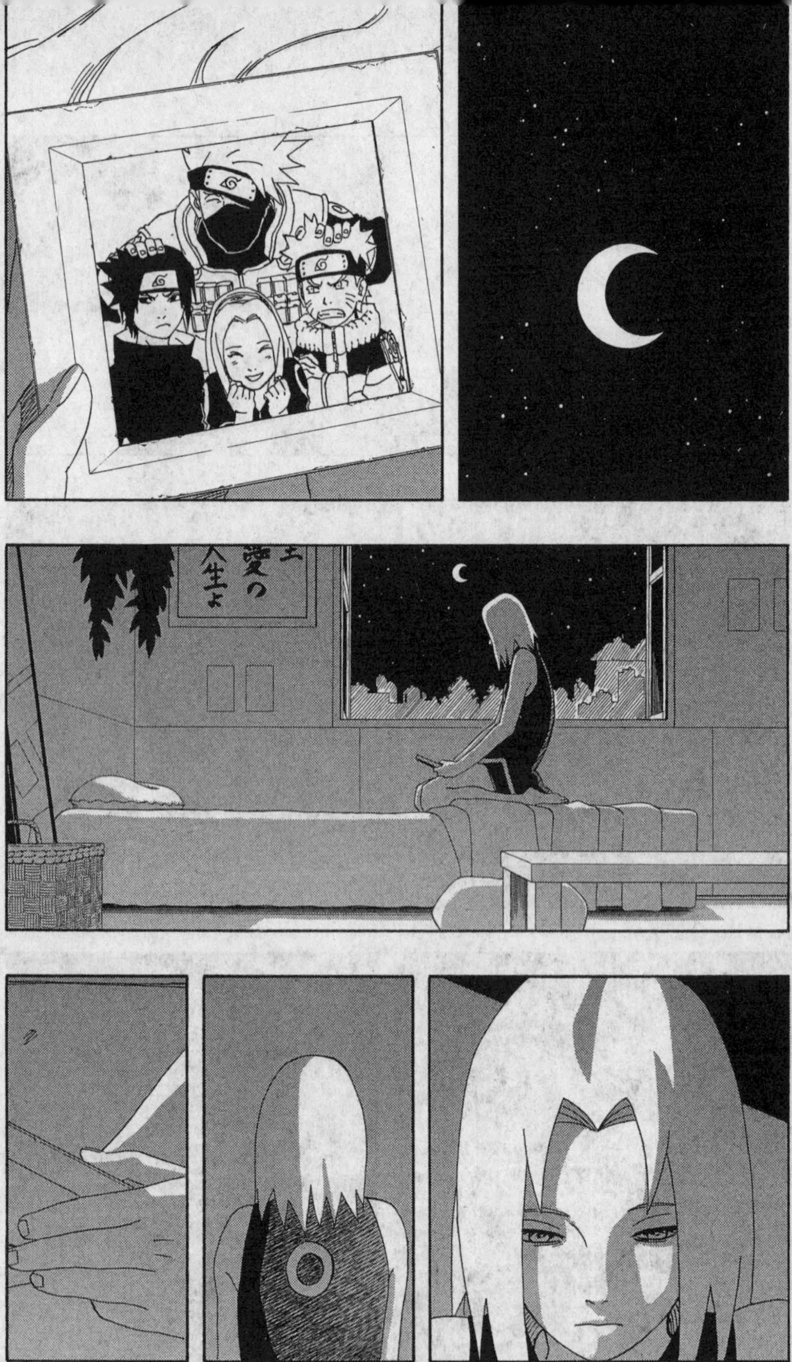
愛の人生よ

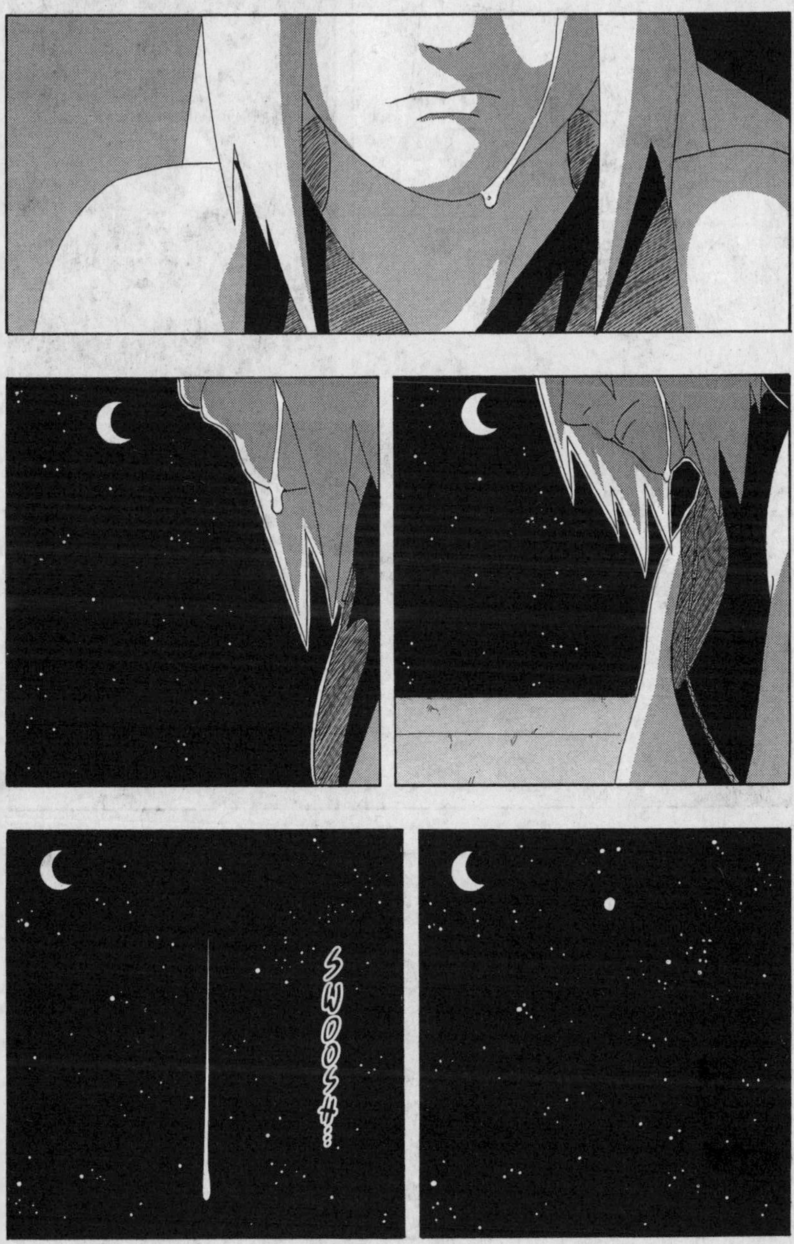
SWOOSH...

READ THIS WAY

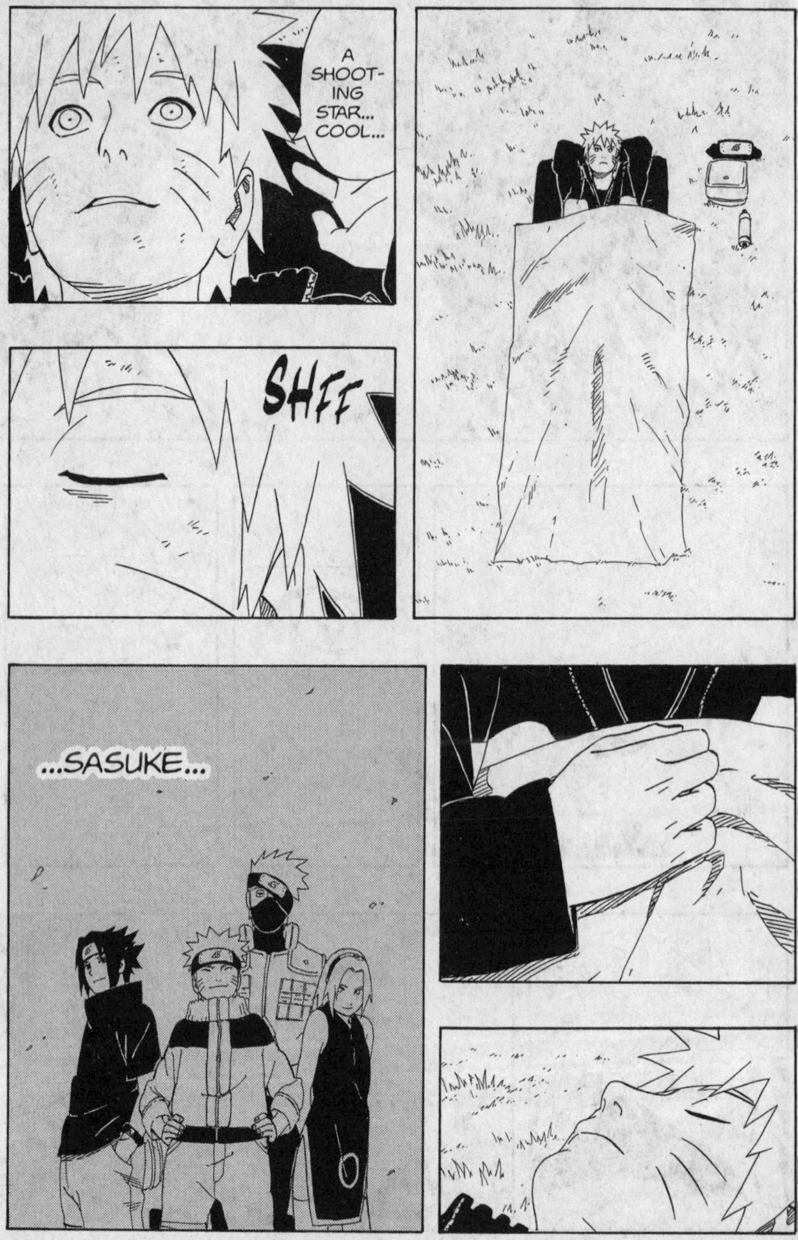
A SHOOTING STAR... COOL...
SHFF
...SASUKE...

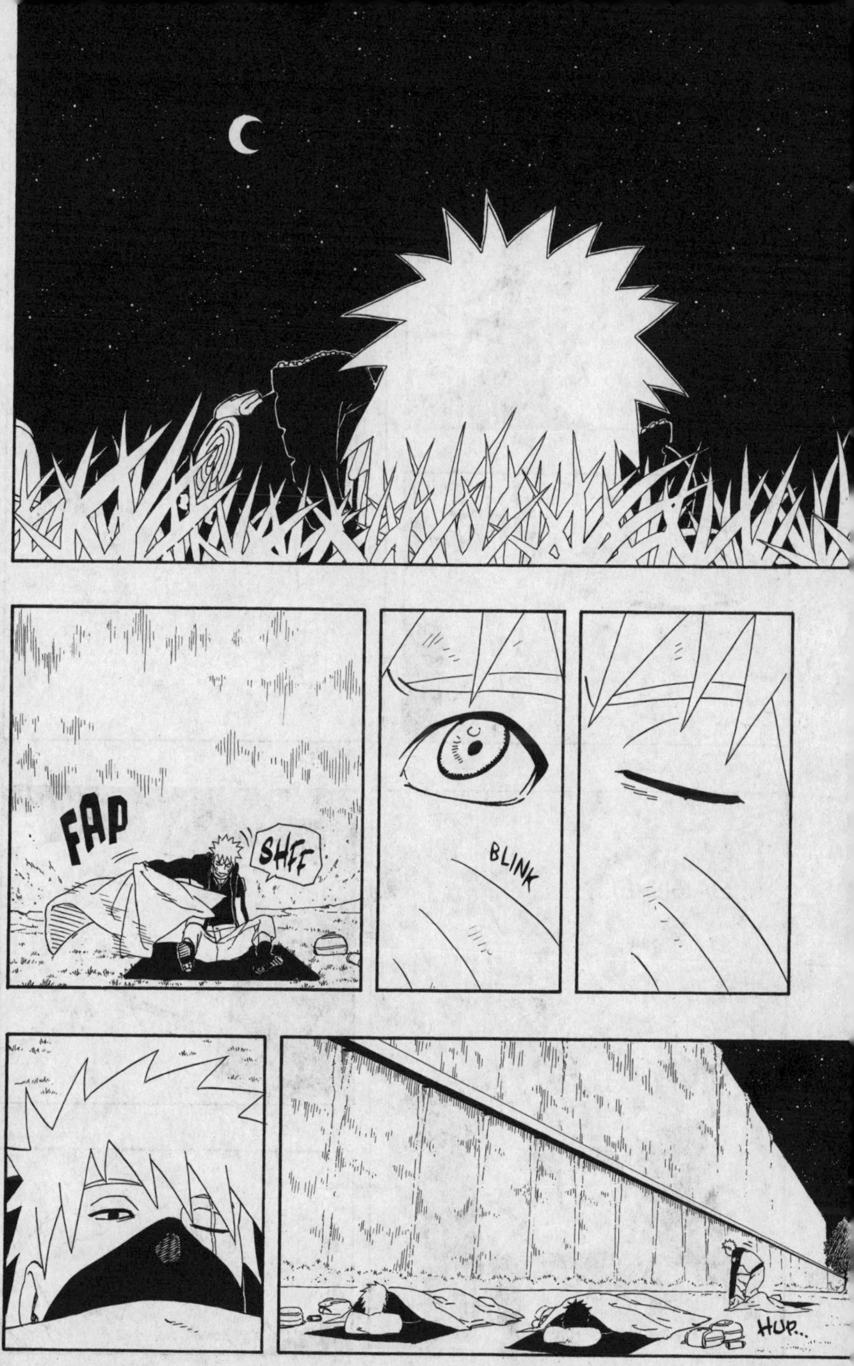
BLINK
FAP
SHFF
HUP..

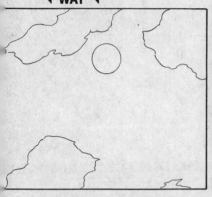

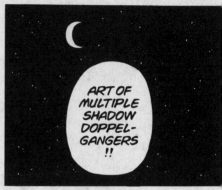

ART OF MULTIPLE SHADOW DOPPEL-GANGERS!!

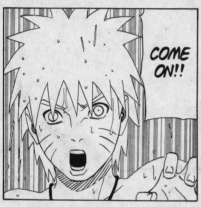

COME ON!!

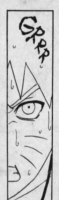

GRRR

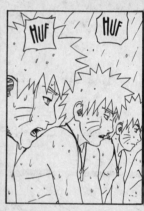

HUF HUF

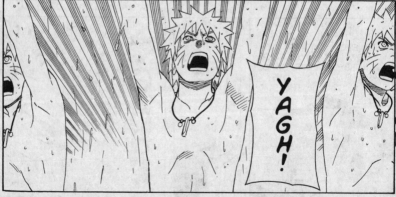

YAGH!

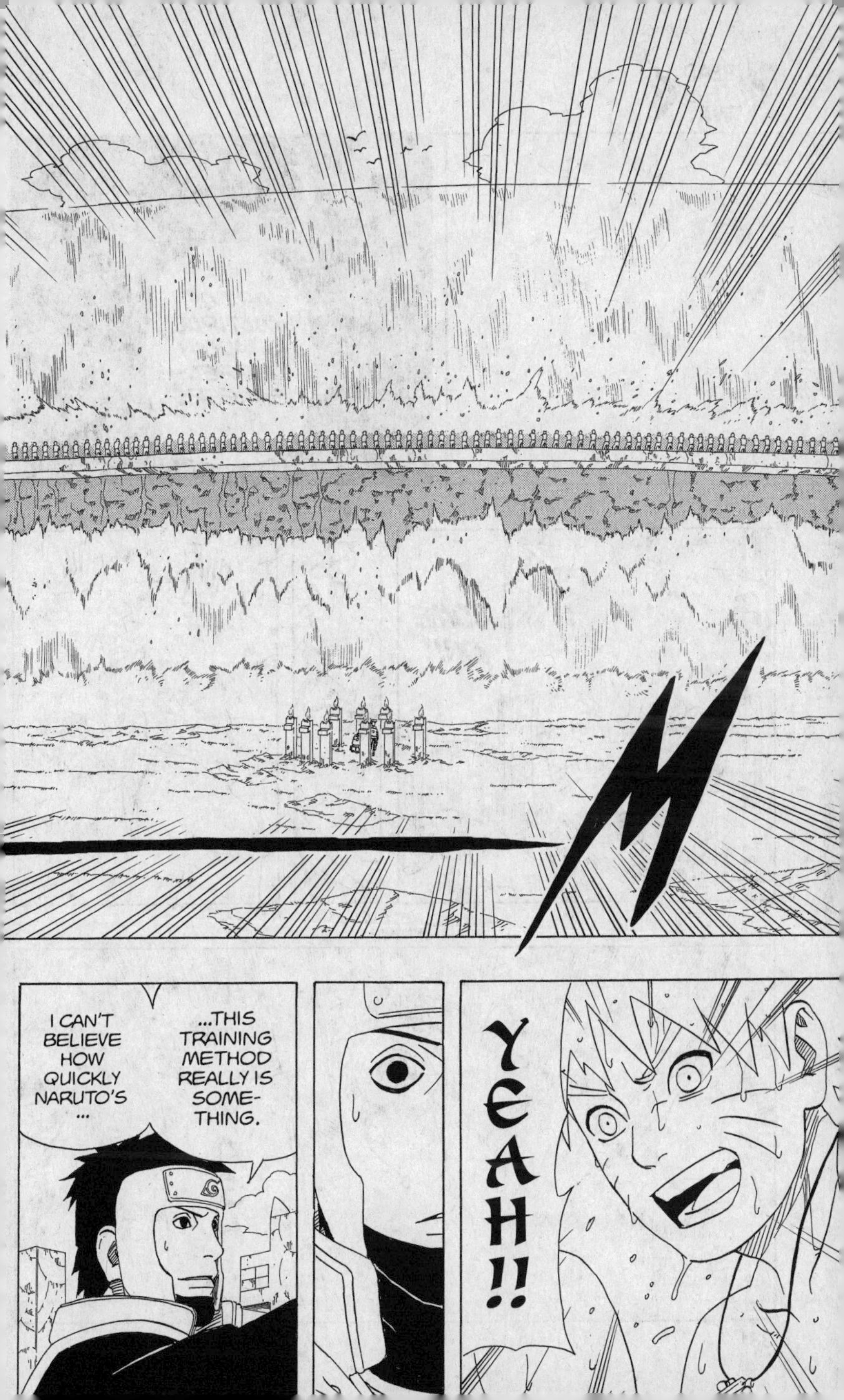
YEAH!!
...THIS TRAINING METHOD REALLY IS SOMETHING.
I CAN'T BELIEVE HOW QUICKLY NARUTO'S ...

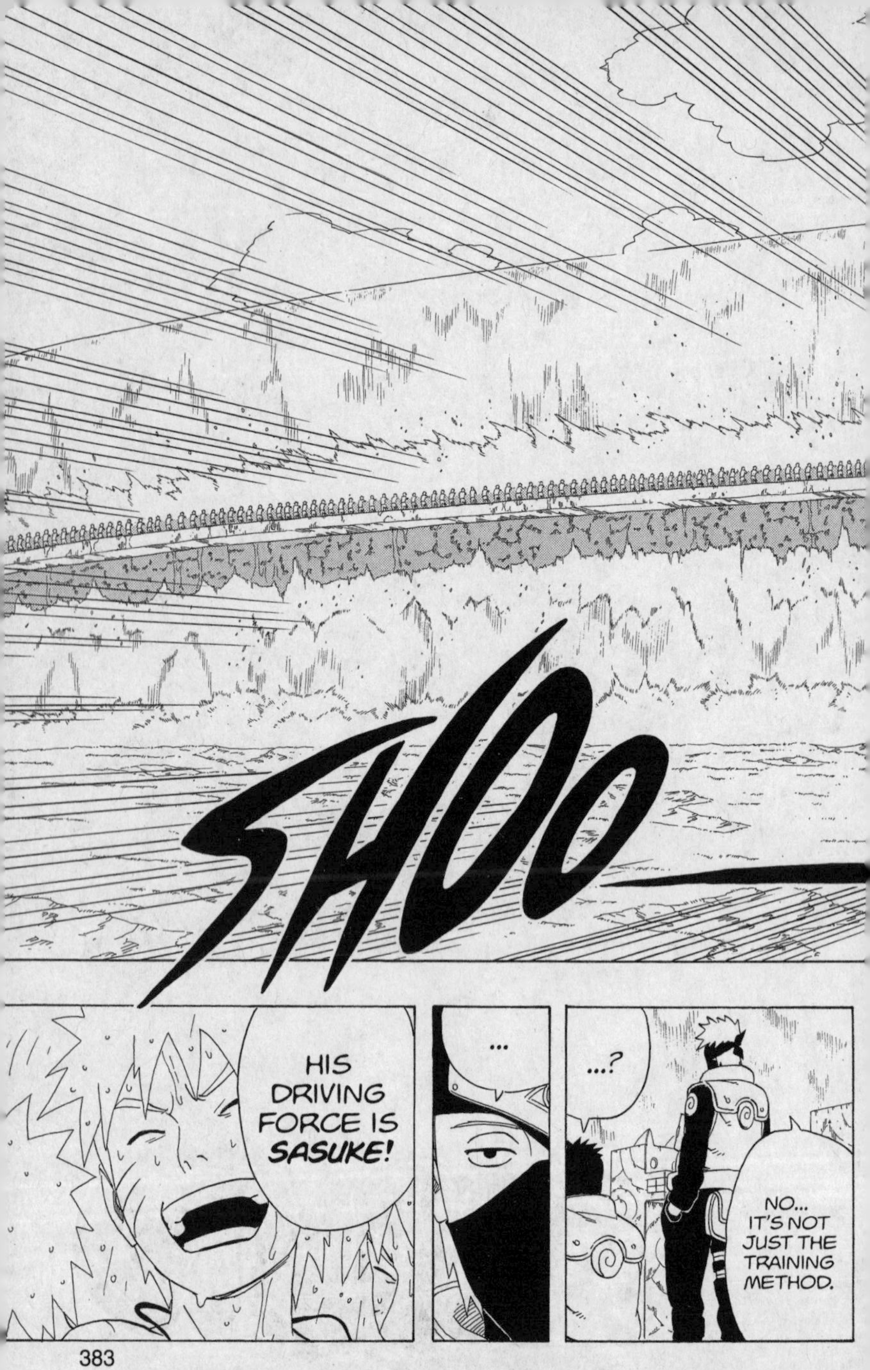
SHOO
...?
NO... IT'S NOT JUST THE TRAINING METHOD.
...
HIS DRIVING FORCE IS *SASUKE!*

NARUTO

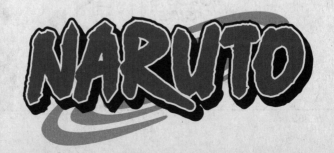

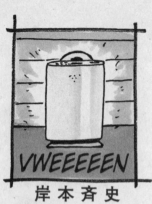

I recently bought an air purifier. My assistants are overjoyed, and I kinda feel good too.

—*Masashi Kishimoto, 2006*

岸本斉史

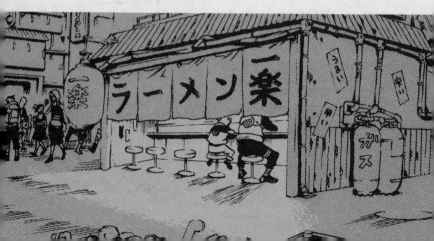

NARUTO

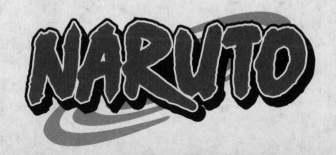

SH[redacted] EDITION

NARUTO

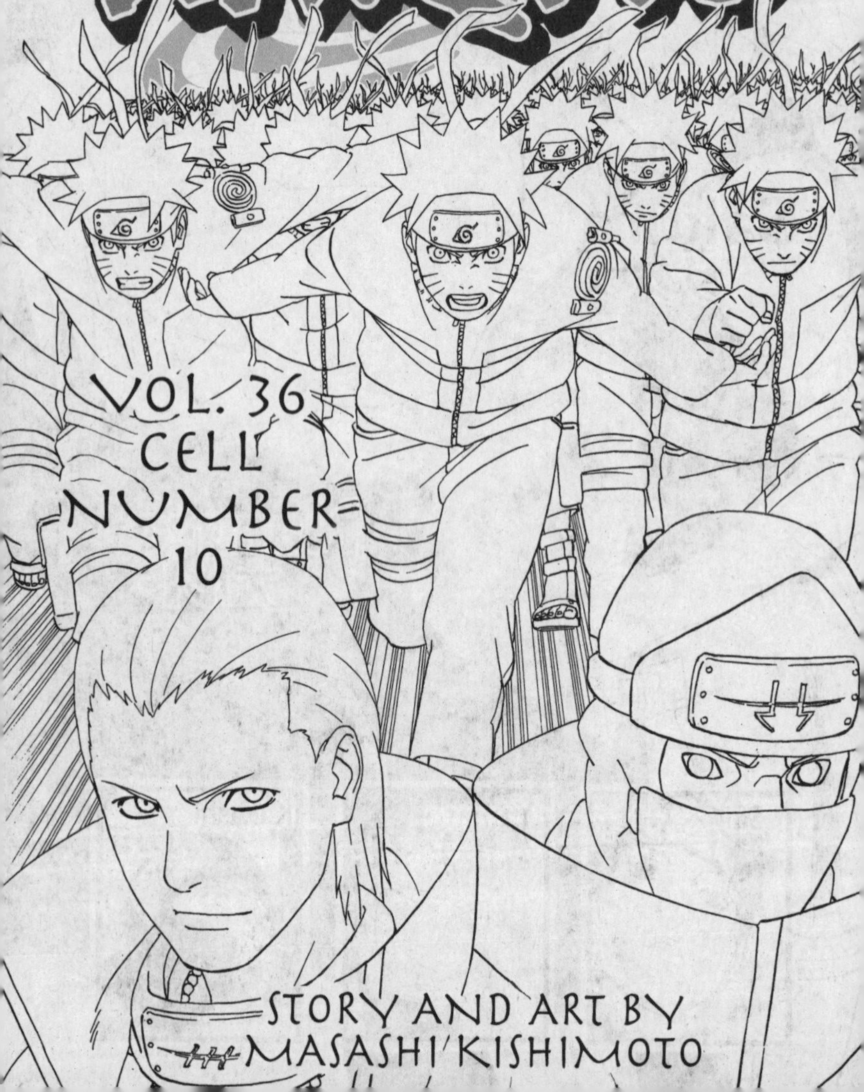

VOL. 36
CELL NUMBER 10

STORY AND ART BY
MASASHI KISHIMOTO

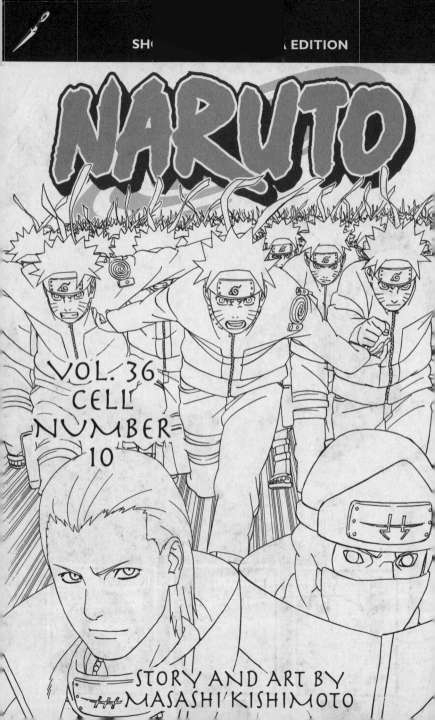

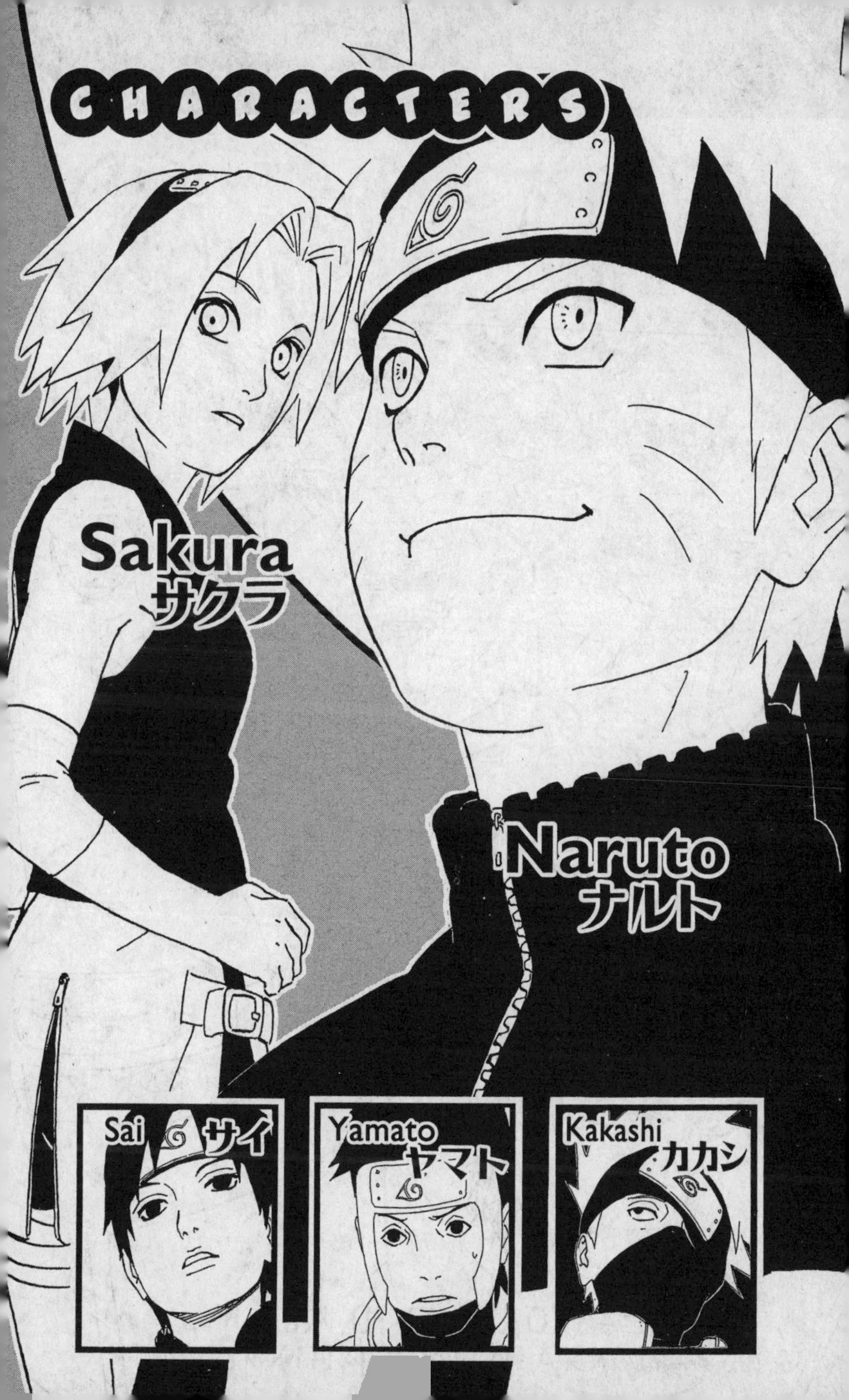
CHARACTERS
Sakura
サクラ
Naruto
ナルト
Sai
サイ
Yamato
ヤマト
Kakashi
カカシ

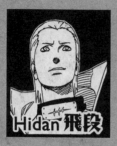

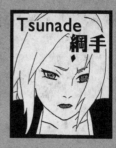

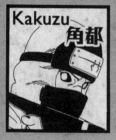

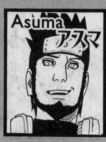

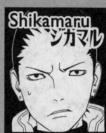

Hidan 飛段

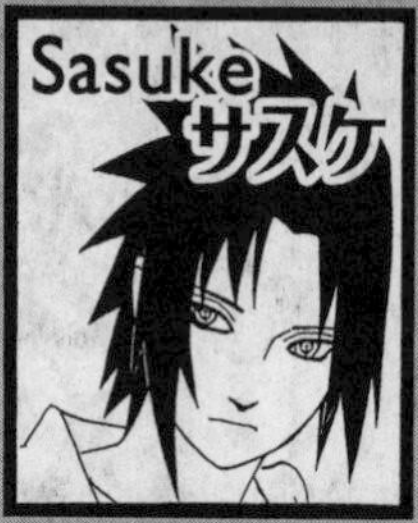

Sasuke サスケ

Tsunade 綱手

Kakuzu 角都

Asuma アスマ

Shikamaru シカマル

The Story So Far…

Naruto, the biggest troublemaker at the Ninja Academy in Konohagakure, finally becomes a ninja along with his classmates Sasuke and Sakura. During the Chûnin Selection Exams, Orochimaru and his henchmen launch *Operation: Destroy Konoha*. Naruto's mentor, the Third Hokage, sacrifices his own life to stop the attack, and Tsunade becomes Fifth Hokage. Lured by Orochimaru's promise of power, Sasuke leaves Konohagakure after defeating Naruto, who fights valiantly to stop his friend…

Two years pass and Naruto and his comrades grow up and track down Sasuke. However, they are left in the dust by Sasuke's immense power, and he escapes once more.

Meanwhile, Hidan and Kakuzu—members of the Akatsuki—seek to fulfill their organization's goal to possess all the jinchûriki hosts by confronting and capturing Yugito, the Two-Tailed Cat Demon. Though their plans for these immensely powerful beasts remain a mystery, it's a threat Konoha can ill afford to take lightly, especially after this deadly duo lays siege to a monastery in the Land of Fire and slaughters all the monks. Among them is Lord Chiriku—formerly of the Guardian Shinobi Twelve—whose body it now falls to Captain Asuma and Cell 10 to locate and retrieve…

NARUTO

VOL. 36
CELL NUMBER 10

CONTENTS

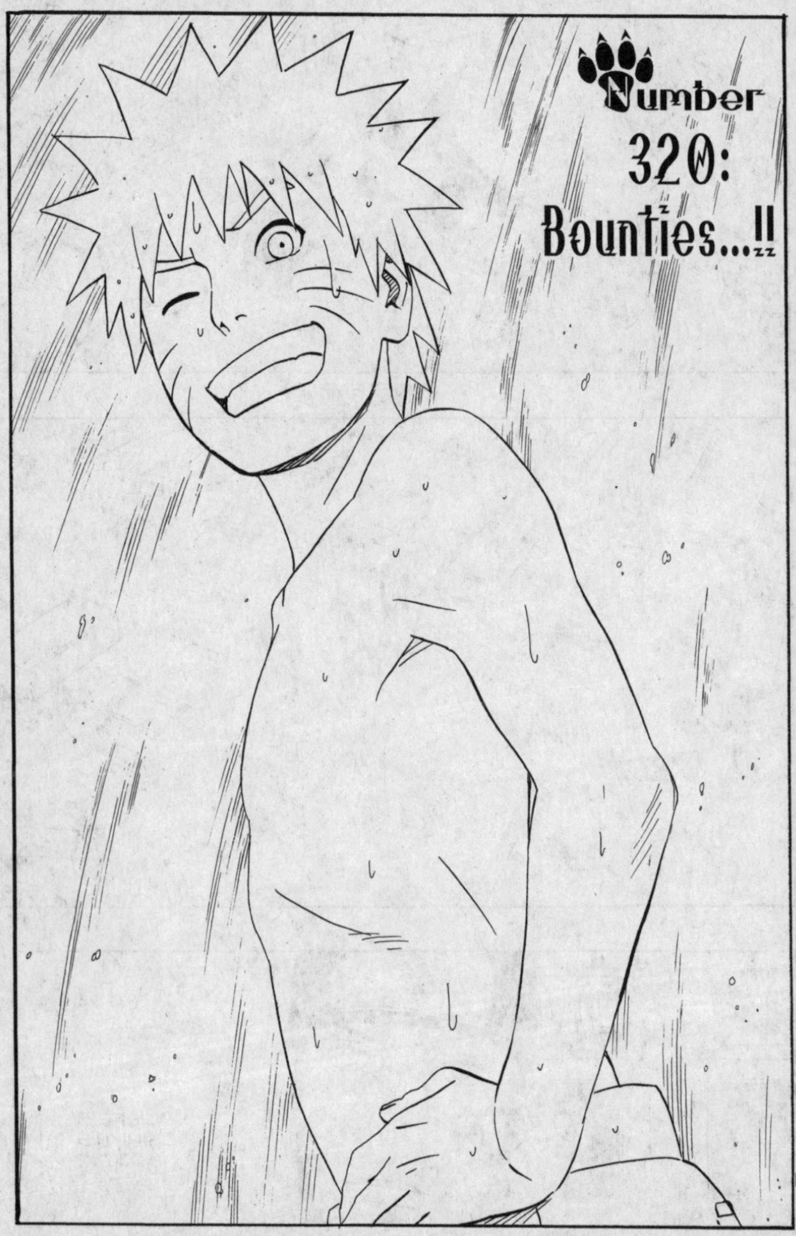
Number 320: Bounties...!!

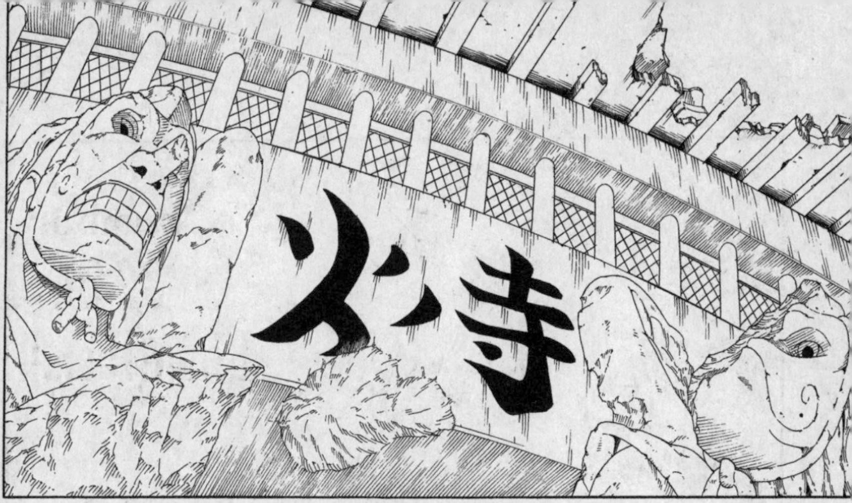
火寺

(FIRE TEMPLE)

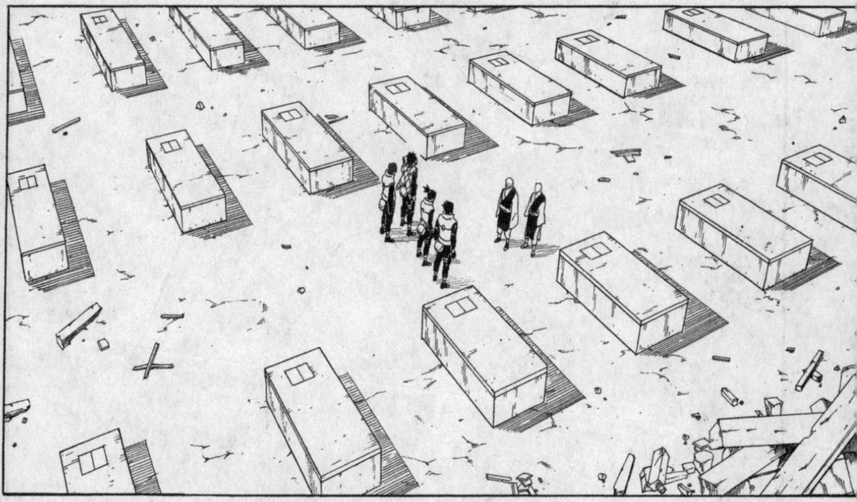

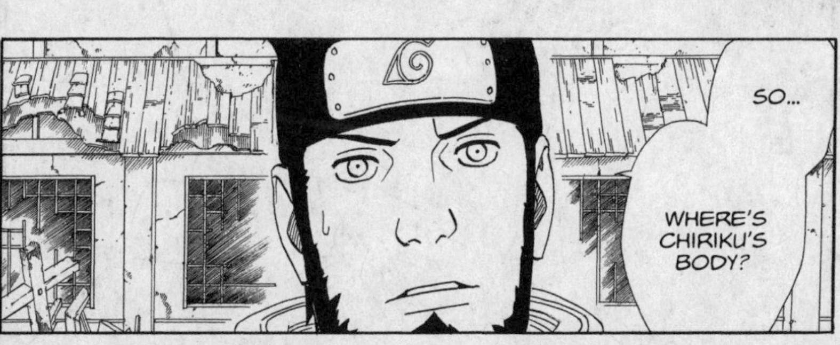
SO...
WHERE'S CHIRIKU'S BODY?

READ THIS WAY

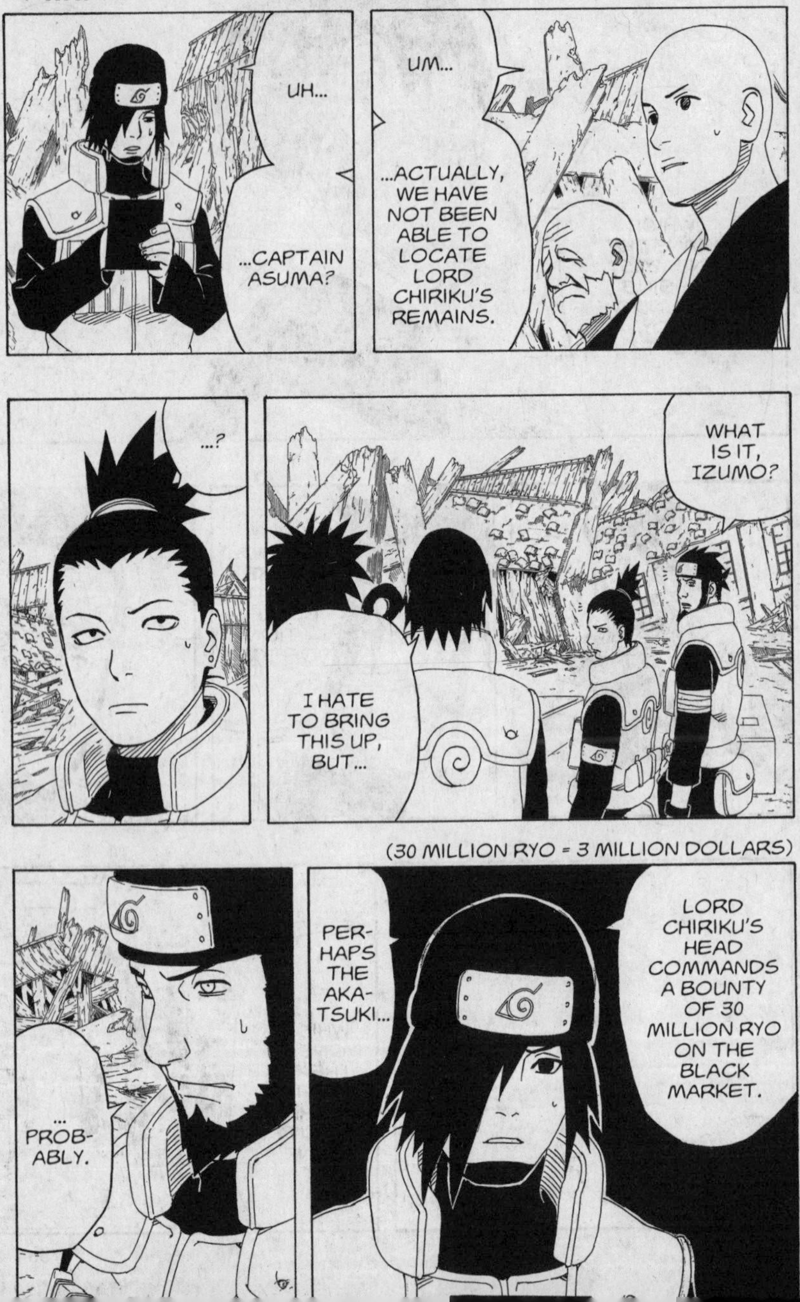
UM...
...ACTUALLY, WE HAVE NOT BEEN ABLE TO LOCATE LORD CHIRIKU'S REMAINS.
UH...
...CAPTAIN ASUMA?
WHAT IS IT, IZUMO?
I HATE TO BRING THIS UP, BUT...
...?
(30 MILLION RYO = 3 MILLION DOLLARS)
LORD CHIRIKU'S HEAD COMMANDS A BOUNTY OF 30 MILLION RYO ON THE BLACK MARKET.
PER-HAPS THE AKA-TSUKI...
... PROB-ABLY.

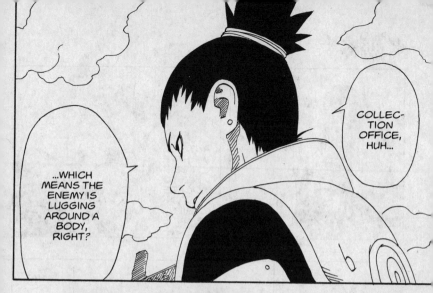

COLLECTION OFFICE, HUH...

...WHICH MEANS THE ENEMY IS LUGGING AROUND A BODY, RIGHT?

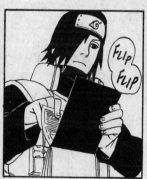

FLIP FLIP

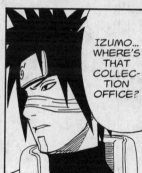

IZUMO... WHERE'S THAT COLLECTION OFFICE?

...

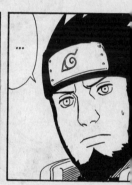

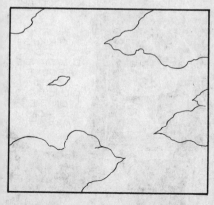

WHICH ONE? THERE ARE FIVE IN THIS VICINITY ALONE.

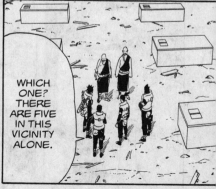

READ THIS WAY

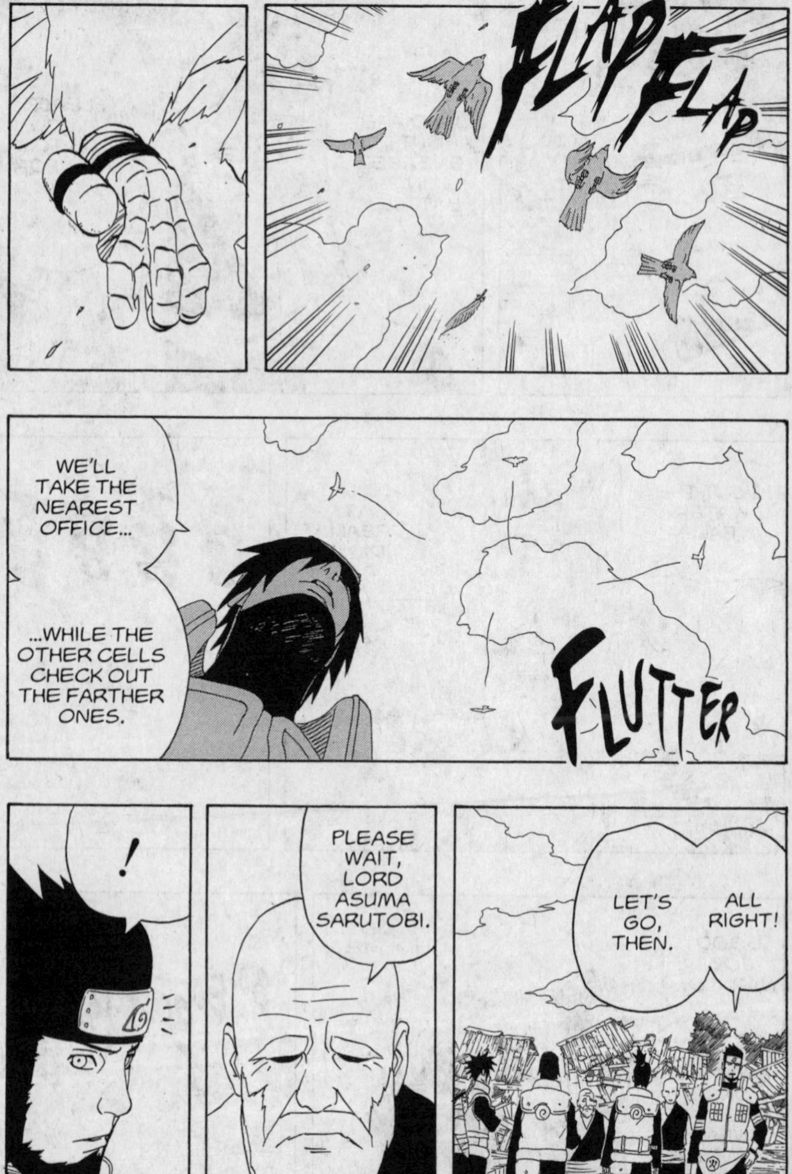
FLAP FLAP
WE'LL TAKE THE NEAREST OFFICE...
...WHILE THE OTHER CELLS CHECK OUT THE FARTHER ONES.
FLUTTER
ALL RIGHT!
LET'S GO, THEN.
PLEASE WAIT, LORD ASUMA SARUTOBI.
!

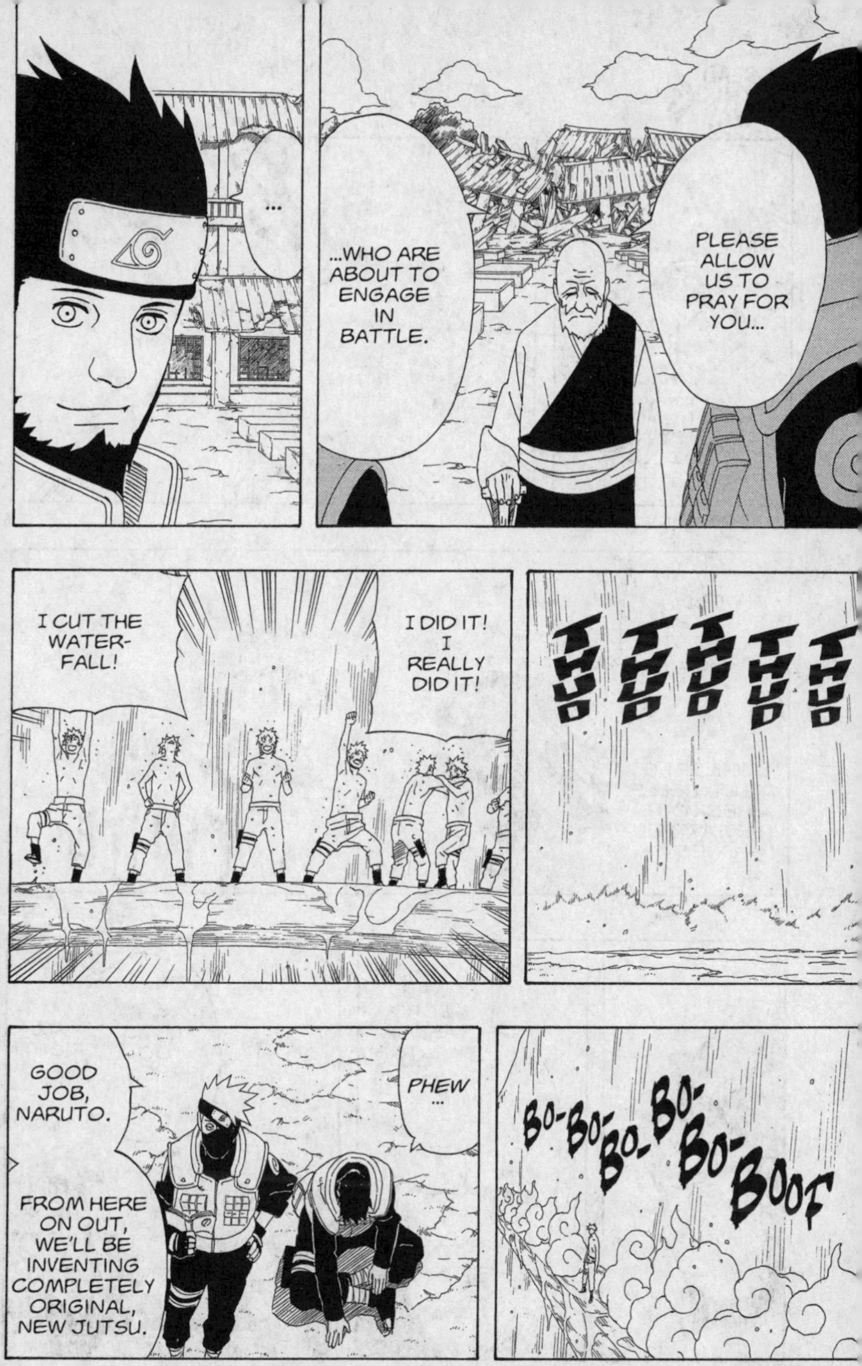
PLEASE ALLOW US TO PRAY FOR YOU...
...WHO ARE ABOUT TO ENGAGE IN BATTLE.
...
THUD THUD THUD THUD THUD
I DID IT! I REALLY DID IT!
I CUT THE WATER-FALL!
BO-BO-BO-BO-BO-BOOF
PHEW...
GOOD JOB, NARUTO.
FROM HERE ON OUT, WE'LL BE INVENTING COMPLETELY ORIGINAL, NEW JUTSU.

READ THIS WAY

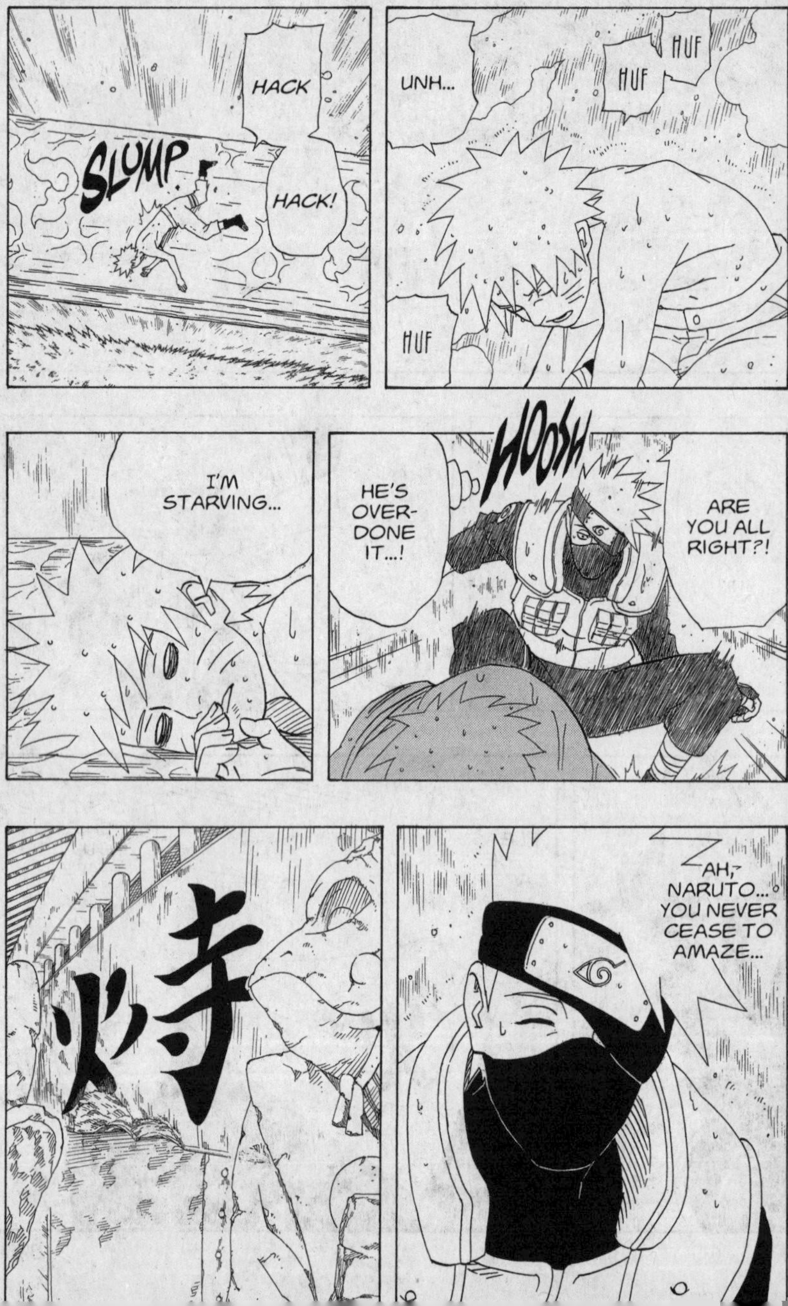
HUF
HUF
UNH...
HUF
HACK
HACK!
SLUMP
WHOOSH
ARE YOU ALL RIGHT?!
HE'S OVER-DONE IT...!
I'M STARVING...
AH, NARUTO... YOU NEVER CEASE TO AMAZE...

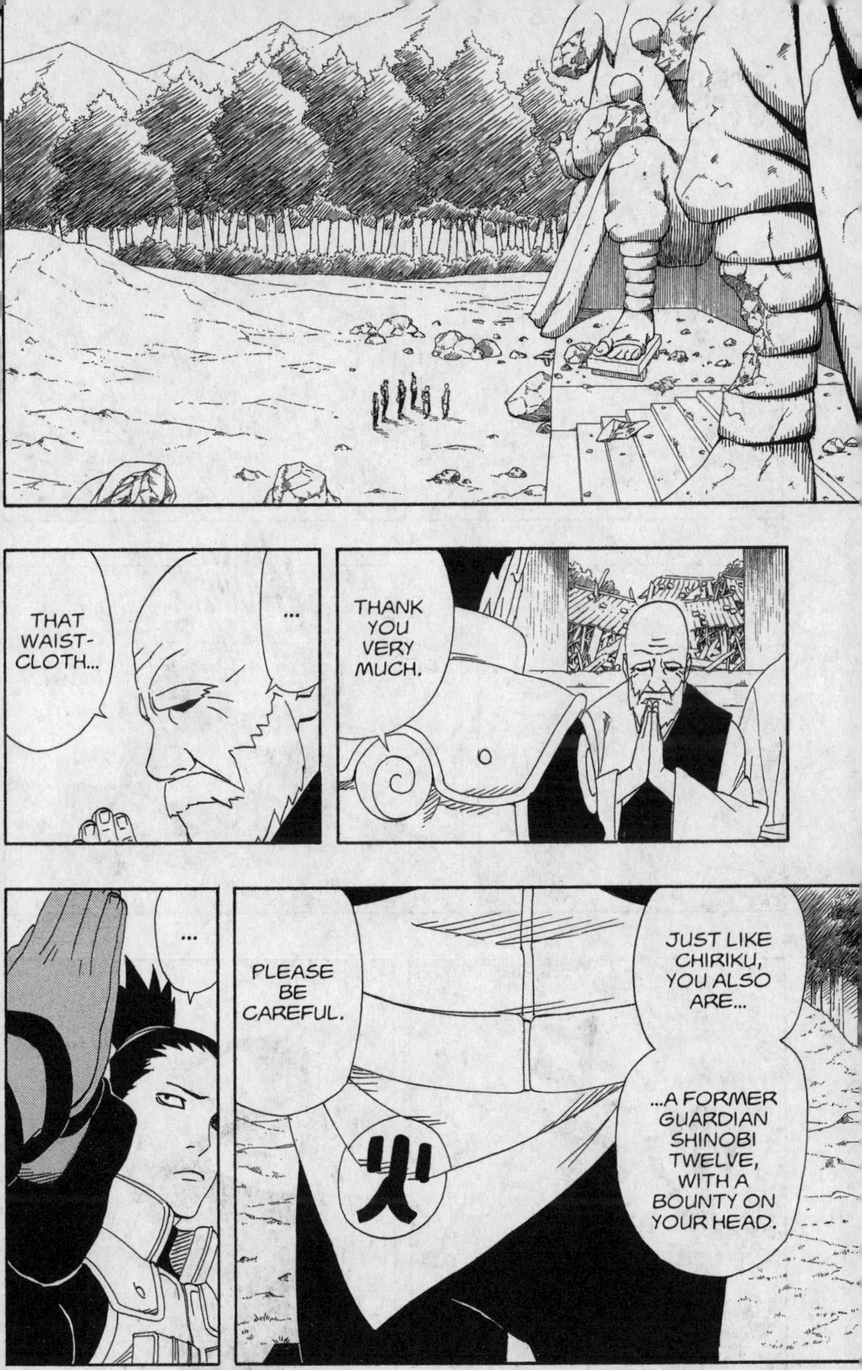
THANK YOU VERY MUCH.
...
THAT WAIST-CLOTH...
JUST LIKE CHIRIKU, YOU ALSO ARE...
...A FORMER GUARDIAN SHINOBI TWELVE, WITH A BOUNTY ON YOUR HEAD.
PLEASE BE CAREFUL.
...

READ THIS WAY

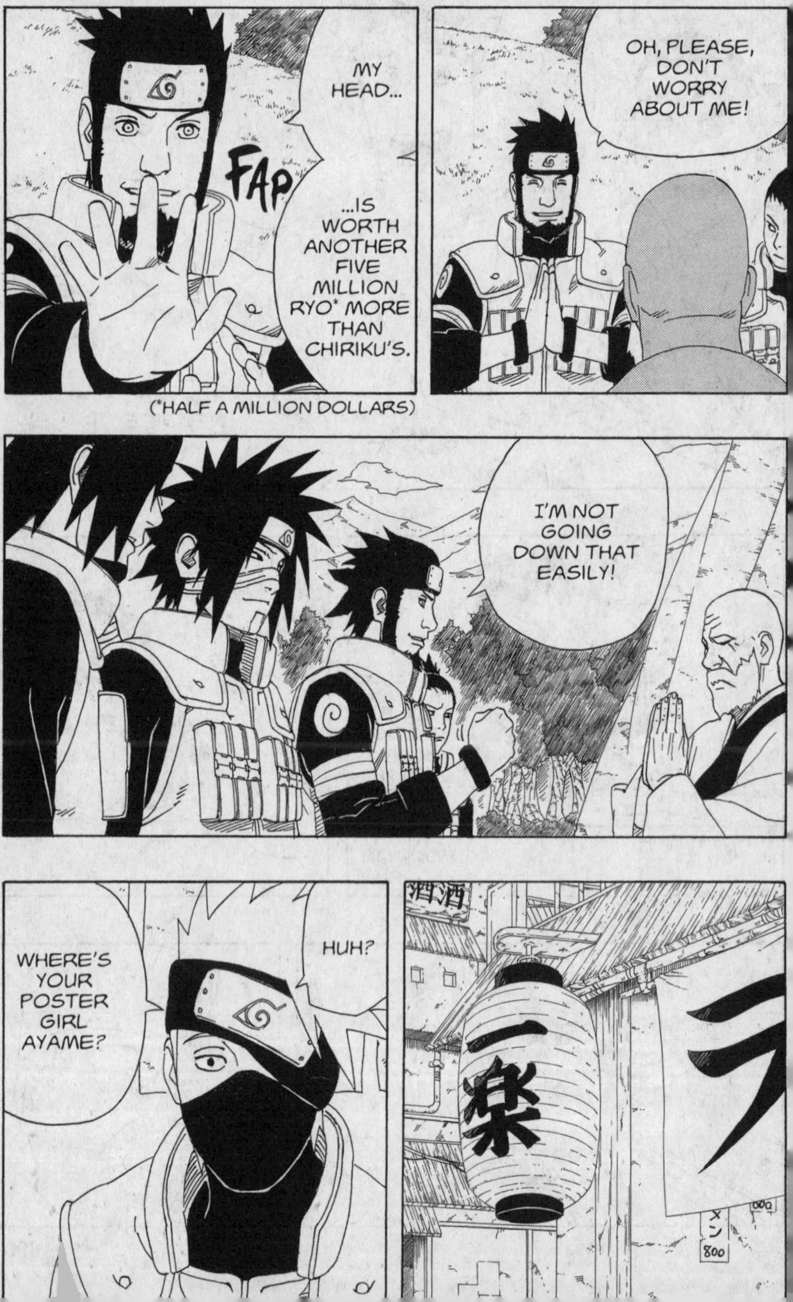
OH, PLEASE, DON'T WORRY ABOUT ME!
MY HEAD...
FAP
...IS WORTH ANOTHER FIVE MILLION RYO* MORE THAN CHIRIKU'S.
(*HALF A MILLION DOLLARS)
I'M NOT GOING DOWN THAT EASILY!
800
HUH?
WHERE'S YOUR POSTER GIRL AYAME?

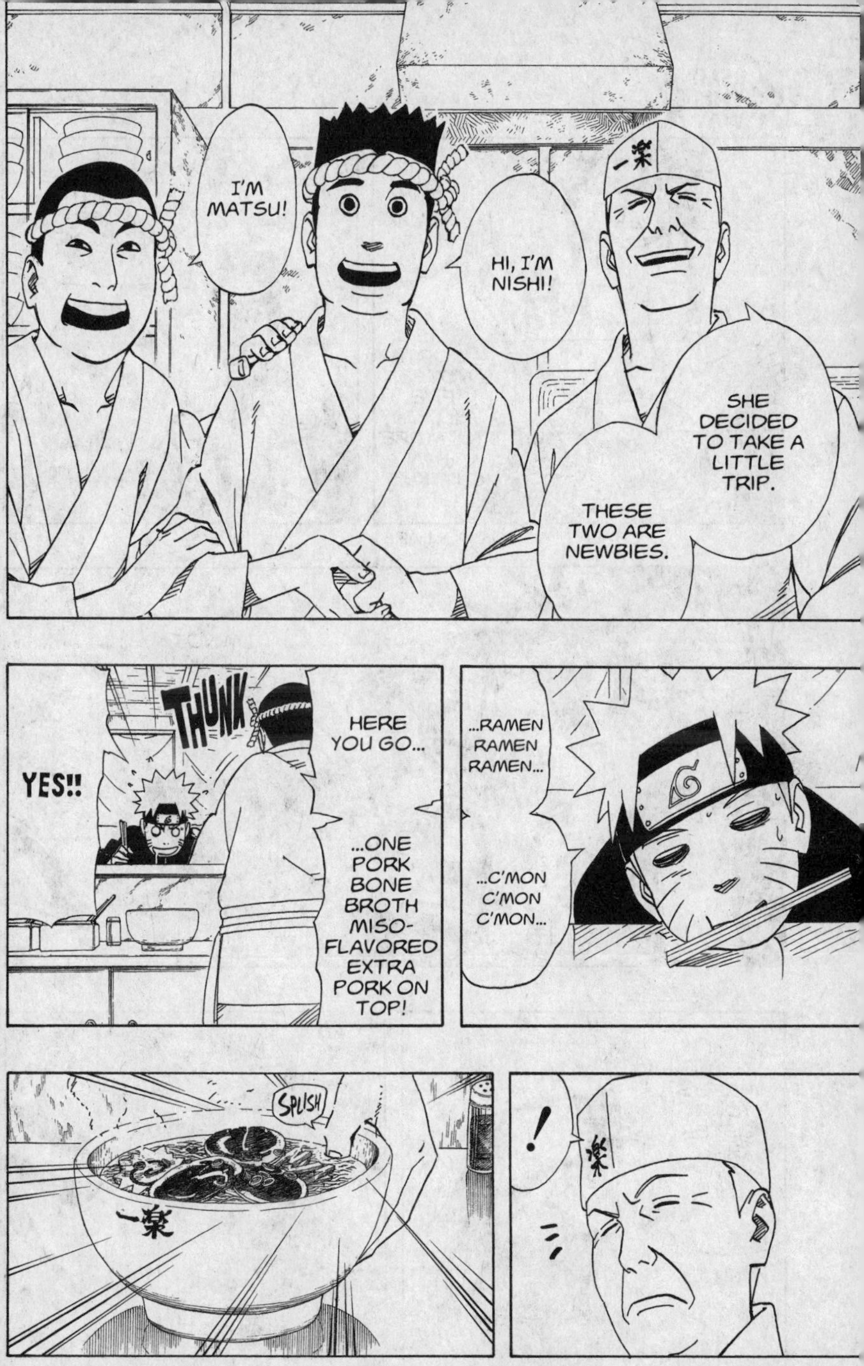
SHE DECIDED TO TAKE A LITTLE TRIP.
THESE TWO ARE NEWBIES.
HI, I'M NISHI!
I'M MATSU!
...RAMEN RAMEN RAMEN...
...C'MON C'MON C'MON...
HERE YOU GO...
...ONE PORK BONE BROTH MISO-FLAVORED EXTRA PORK ON TOP!
THUNK
YES!!
!
SPLISH

READ THIS WAY

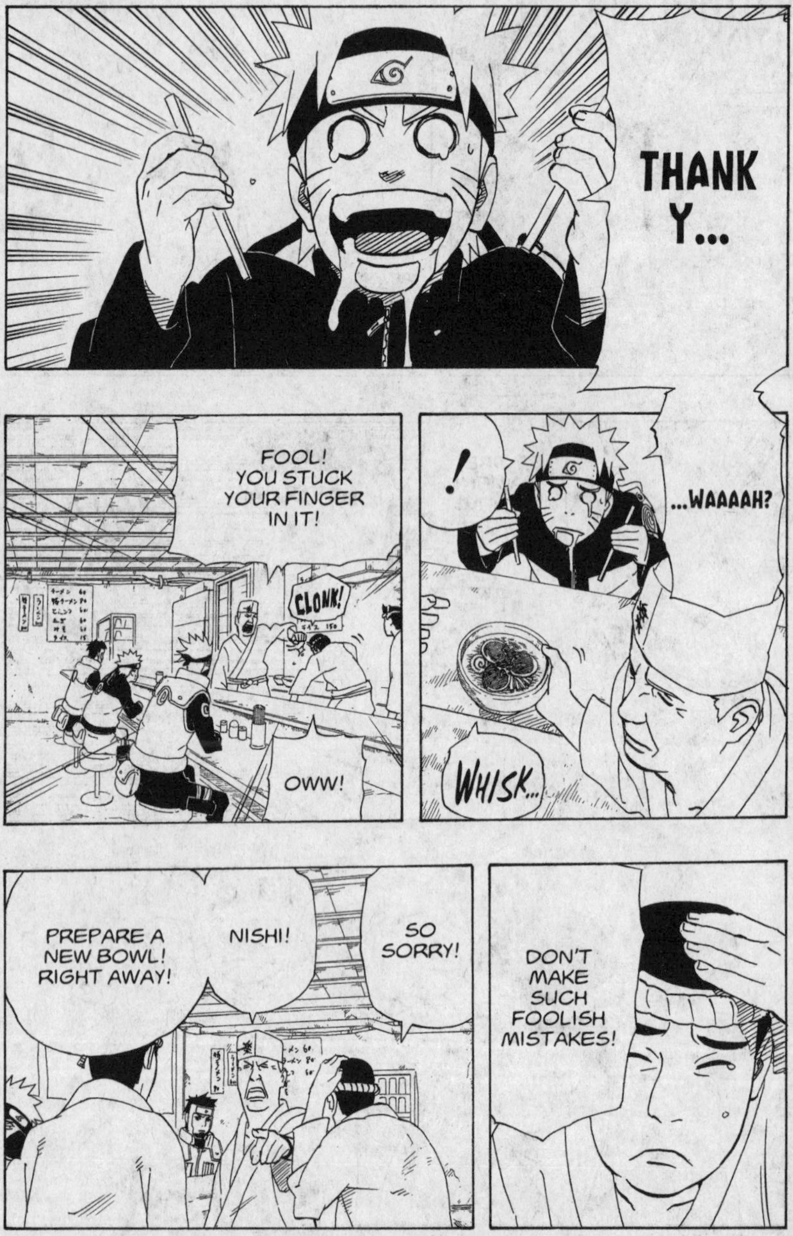

THANK Y...
!
...WAAAAH?
WHISK...
FOOL! YOU STUCK YOUR FINGER IN IT!
CLONK!
OWW!
DON'T MAKE SUCH FOOLISH MISTAKES!
SO SORRY!
NISHI!
PREPARE A NEW BOWL! RIGHT AWAY!

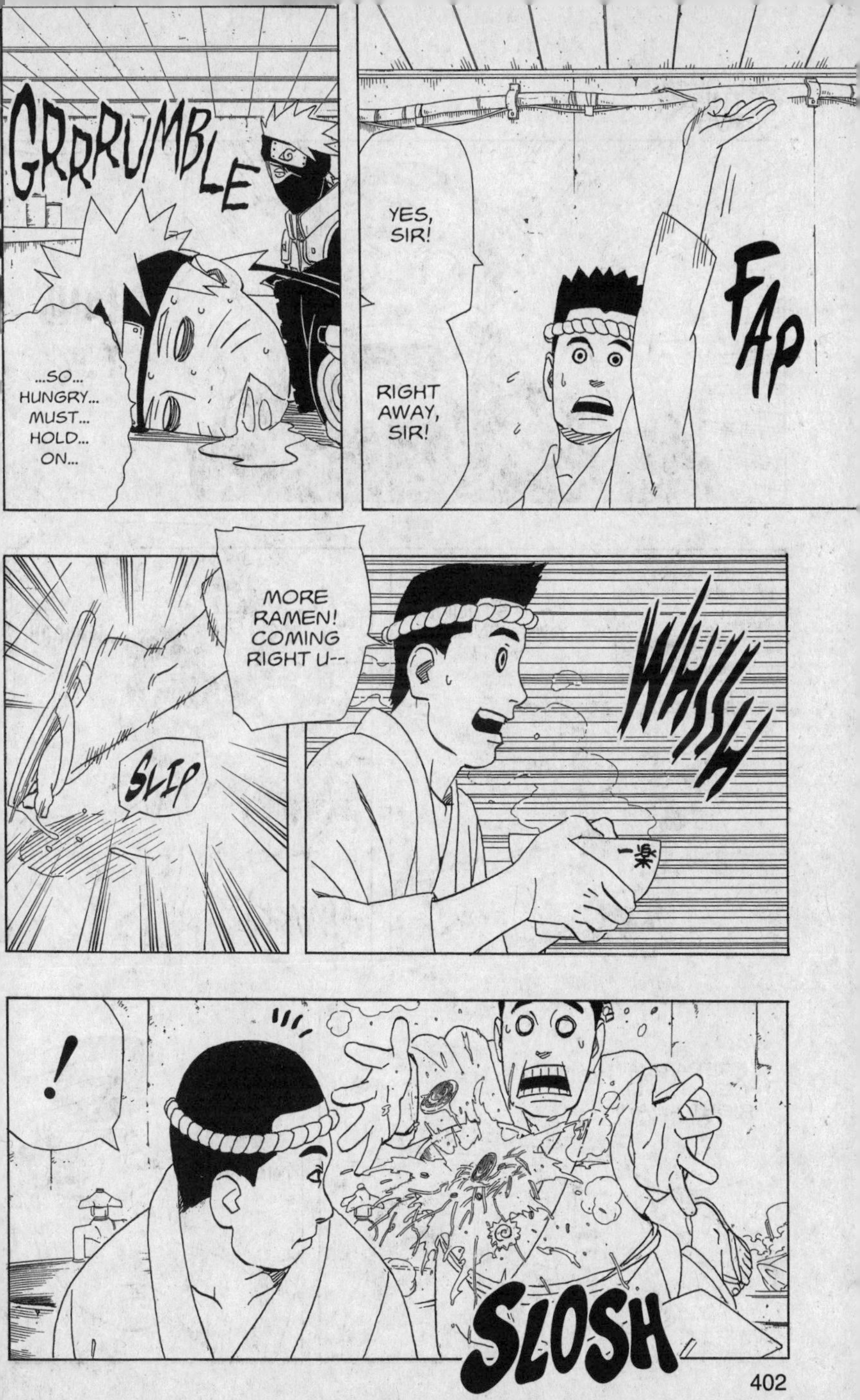
YES, SIR!
RIGHT AWAY, SIR!
FAP
GRRRUMBLE
...SO... HUNGRY... MUST... HOLD... ON...
MORE RAMEN! COMING RIGHT U--
WHSSH
一楽
SLIP
!
SLOSH

READ THIS WAY

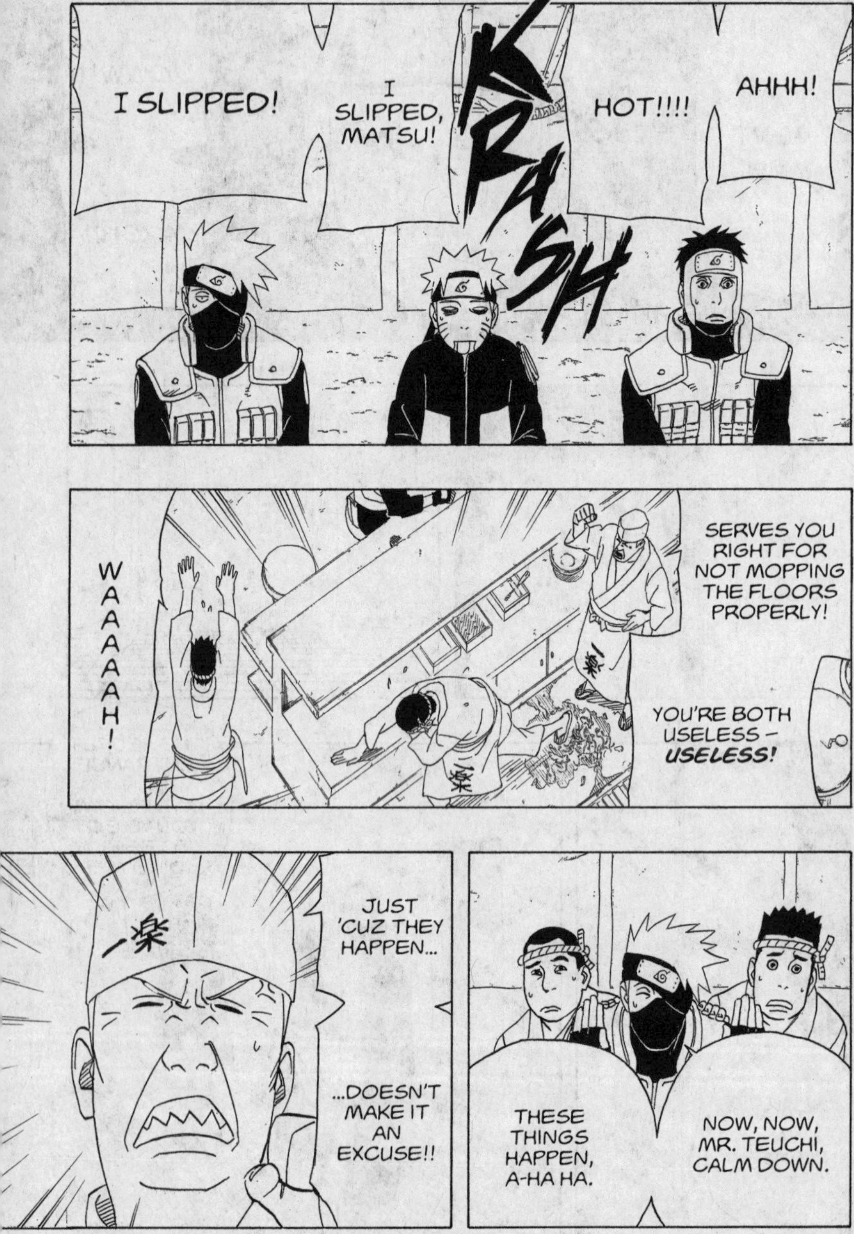

AHHH!
HOT!!!!
KRASH
I SLIPPED, MATSU!
I SLIPPED!
SERVES YOU RIGHT FOR NOT MOPPING THE FLOORS PROPERLY!
YOU'RE BOTH USELESS – *USELESS!*
WAAAAAAH!
NOW, NOW, MR. TEUCHI, CALM DOWN.
THESE THINGS HAPPEN, A-HA HA.
JUST 'CUZ THEY HAPPEN...
...DOESN'T MAKE IT AN EXCUSE!!

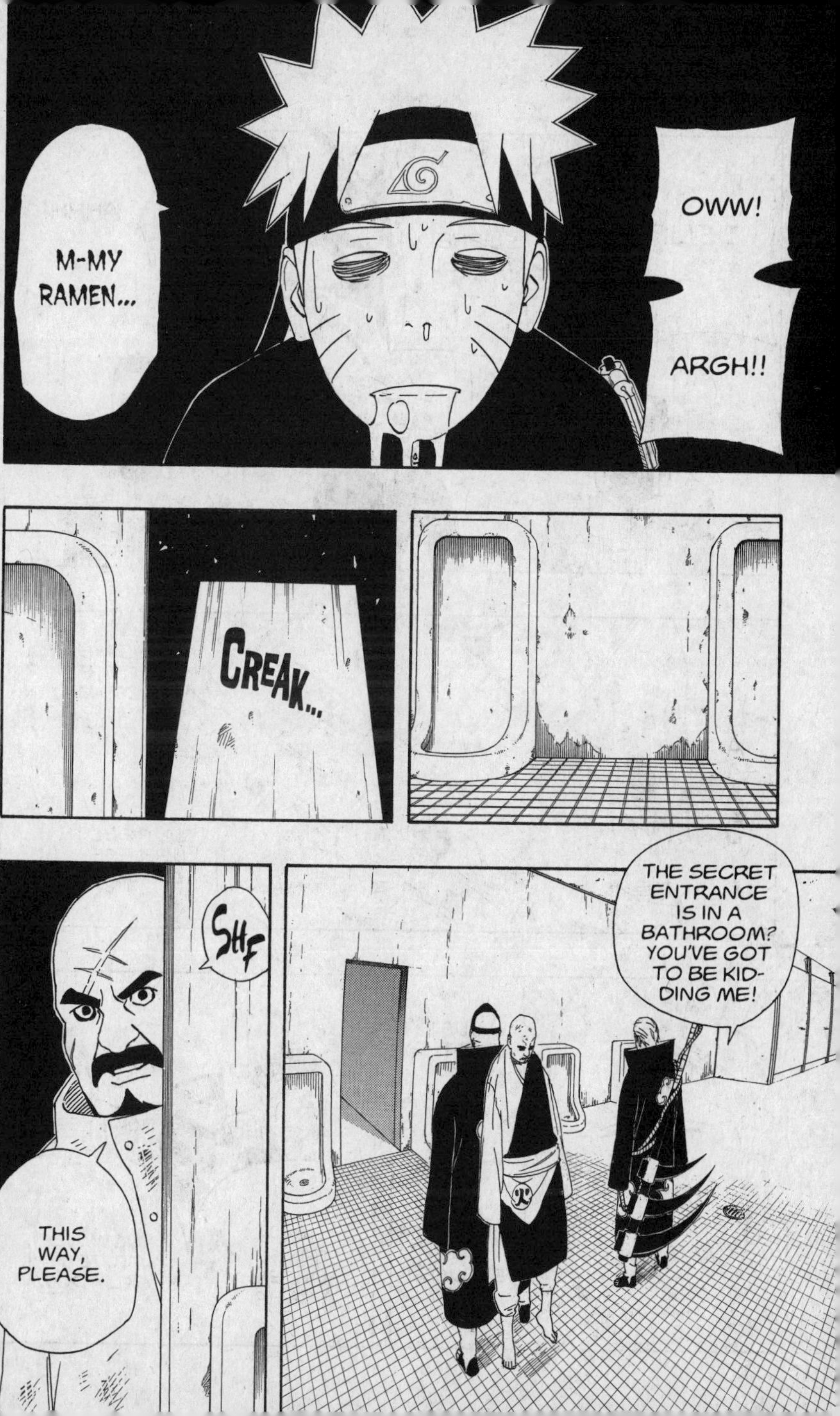
OWW!
ARGH!!
M-MY RAMEN...
CREAK...
THE SECRET ENTRANCE IS IN A BATHROOM? YOU'VE GOT TO BE KID-DING ME!
SHF
THIS WAY, PLEASE.

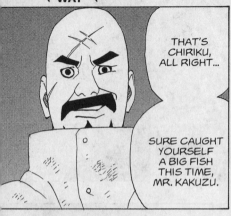

THAT'S CHIRIKU, ALL RIGHT...

SURE CAUGHT YOURSELF A BIG FISH THIS TIME, MR. KAKUZU.

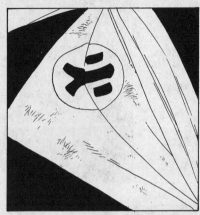

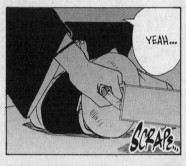

YEAH...

SCRAPE...

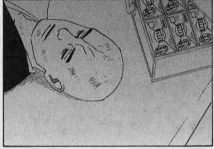

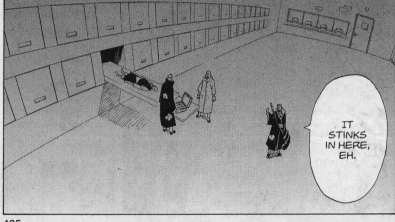

IT STINKS IN HERE, EH.

405

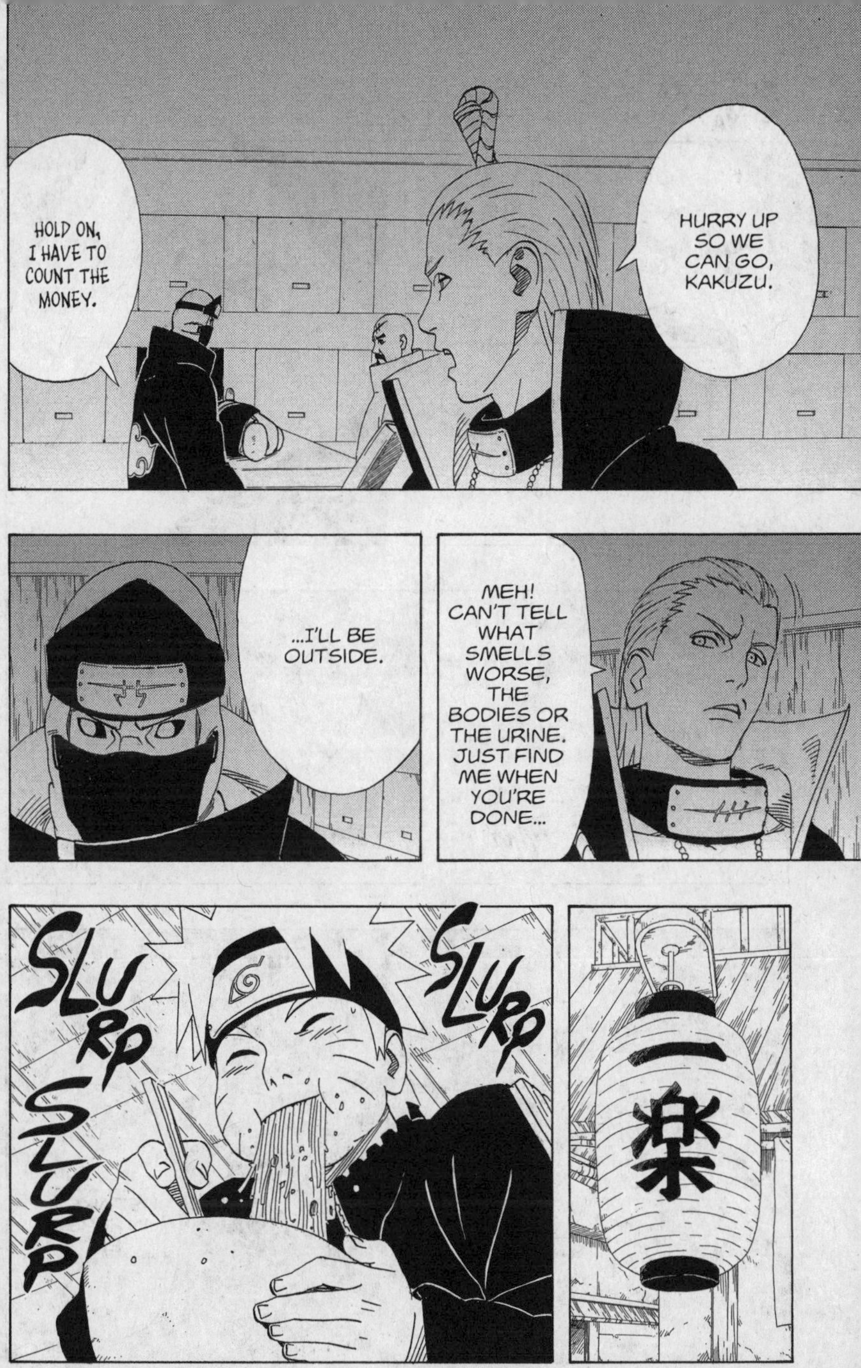
HURRY UP SO WE CAN GO, KAKUZU.
HOLD ON, I HAVE TO COUNT THE MONEY.
MEH! CAN'T TELL WHAT SMELLS WORSE, THE BODIES OR THE URINE. JUST FIND ME WHEN YOU'RE DONE...
...I'LL BE OUTSIDE.
一楽
SLURP
SLURP
SLURP

READ THIS WAY

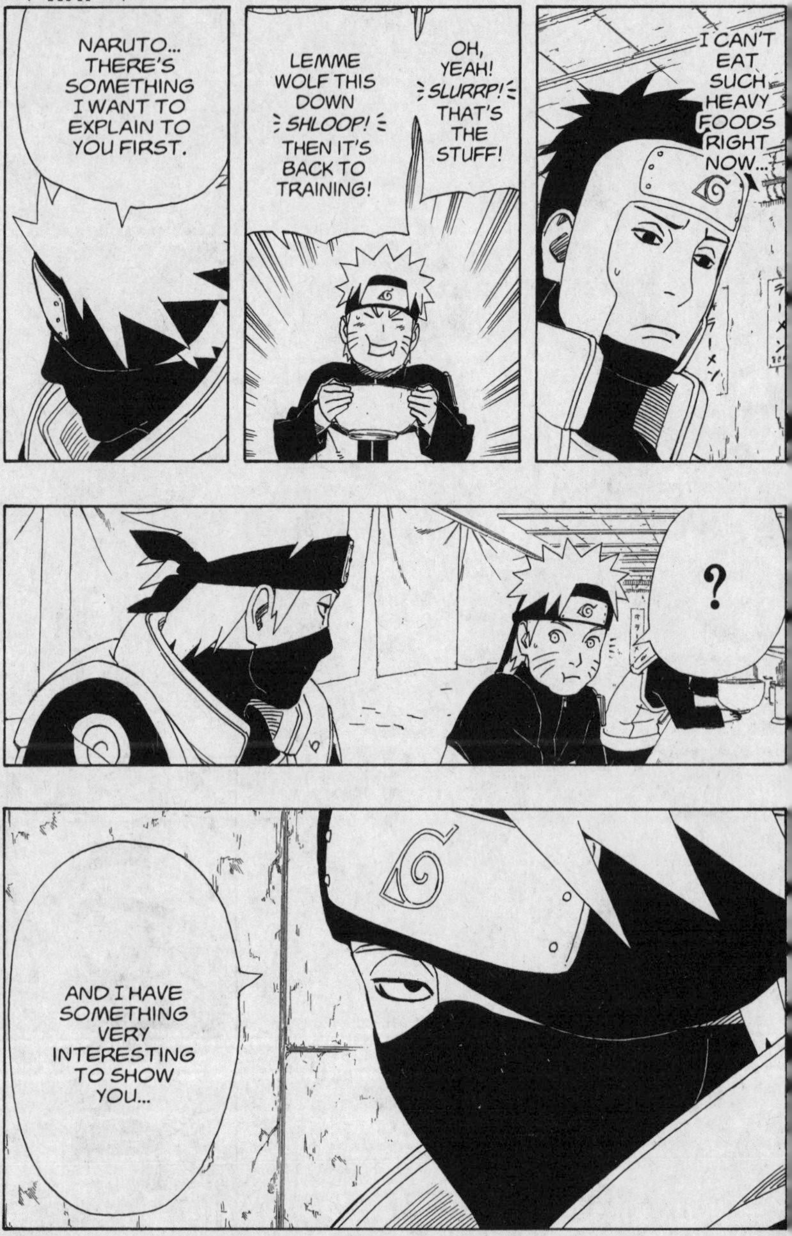

I CAN'T EAT SUCH HEAVY FOODS RIGHT NOW...
OH, YEAH! SLURRP! THAT'S THE STUFF!
LEMME WOLF THIS DOWN SHLOOP! THEN IT'S BACK TO TRAINING!
NARUTO... THERE'S SOMETHING I WANT TO EXPLAIN TO YOU FIRST.
?
AND I HAVE SOMETHING VERY INTERESTING TO SHOW YOU...

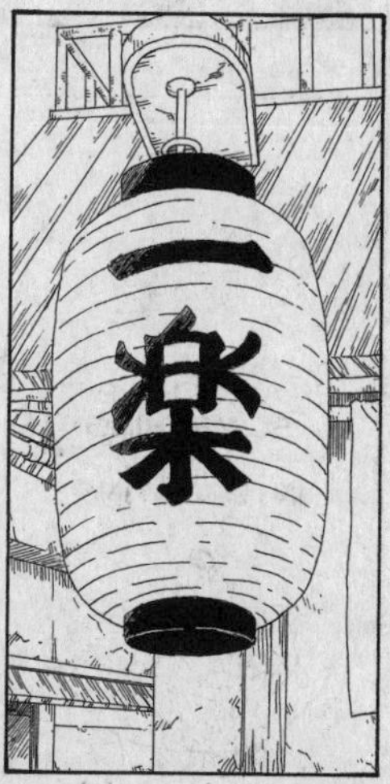
一楽

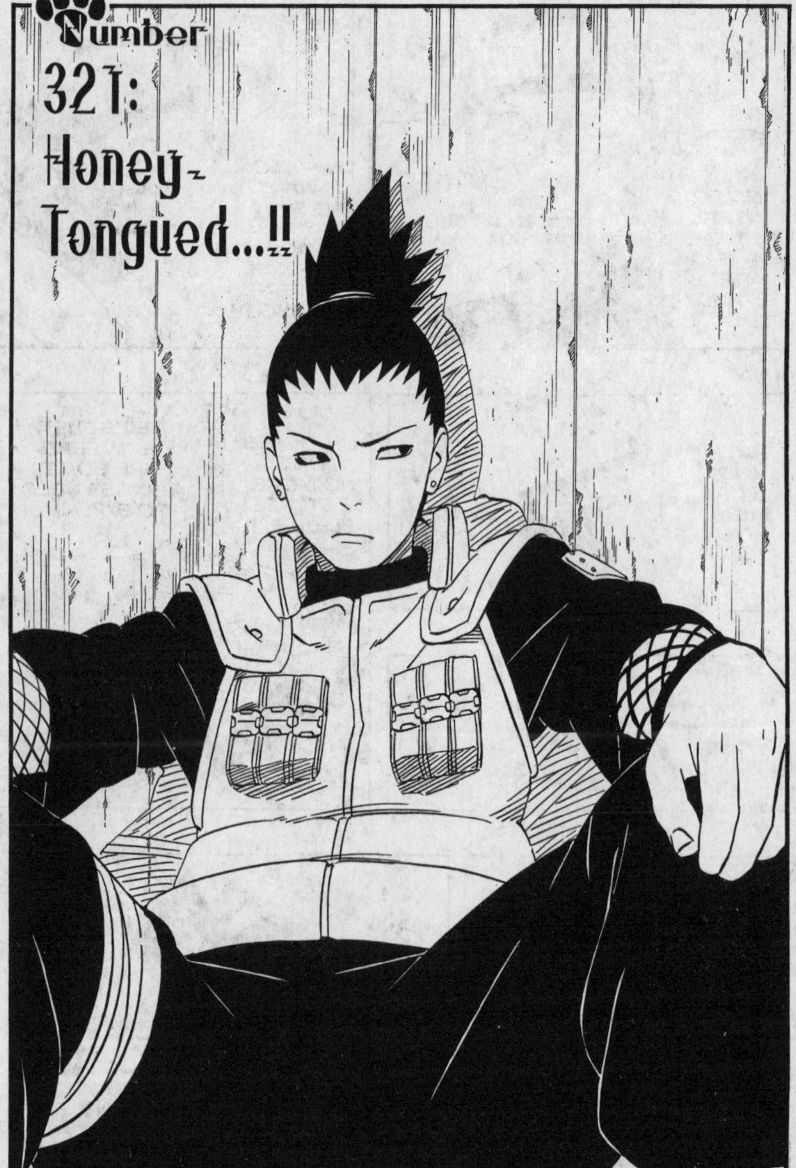
Number 321: Honey-Tongued...!!

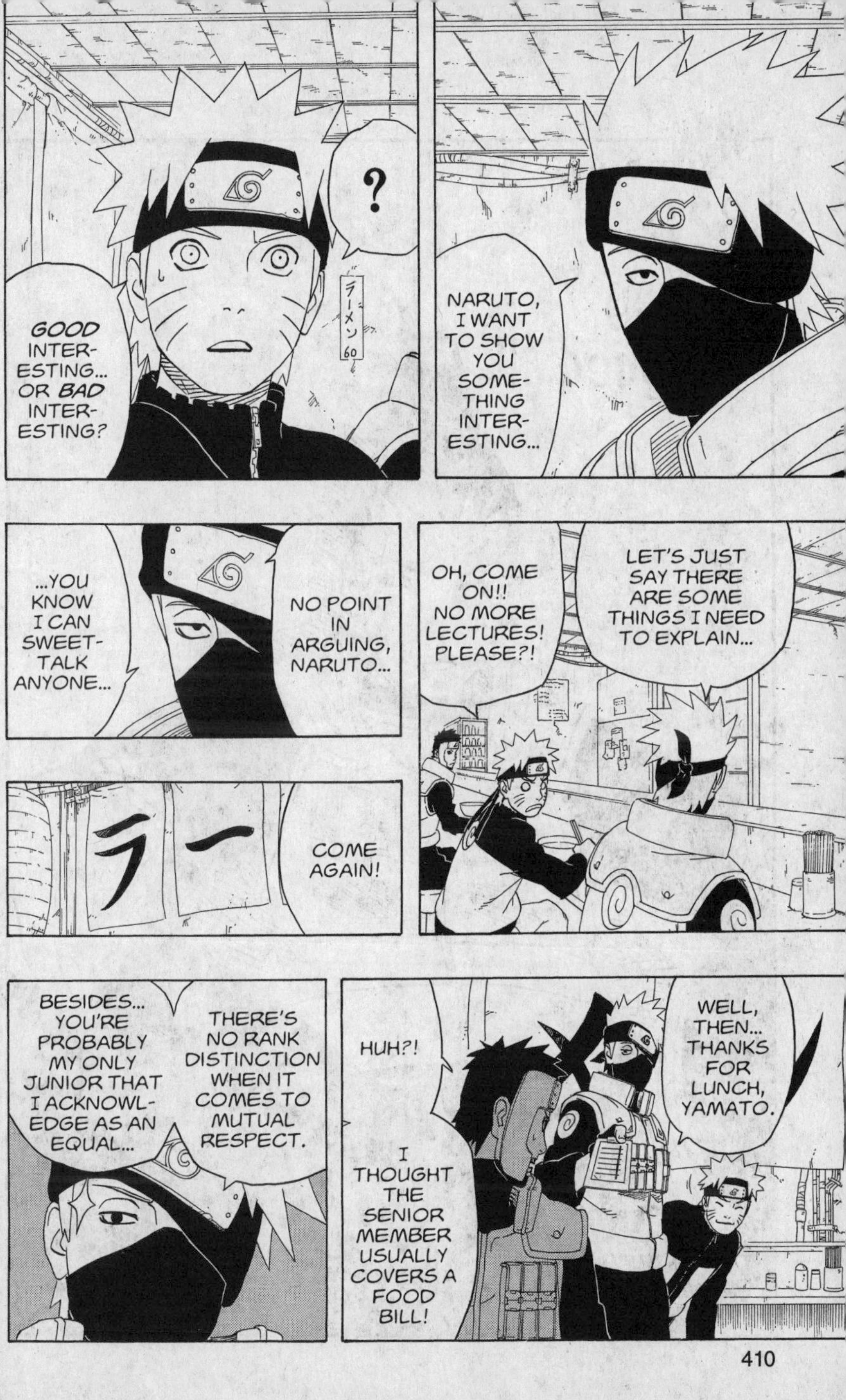
NARUTO, I WANT TO SHOW YOU SOMETHING INTERESTING...
?
ラーメン 60
GOOD INTERESTING... OR *BAD* INTERESTING?
LET'S JUST SAY THERE ARE SOME THINGS I NEED TO EXPLAIN...
OH, COME ON!! NO MORE LECTURES! PLEASE?!
NO POINT IN ARGUING, NARUTO...
...YOU KNOW I CAN SWEET-TALK ANYONE...
COME AGAIN!
ラー
WELL, THEN... THANKS FOR LUNCH, YAMATO.
HUH?!
I THOUGHT THE SENIOR MEMBER USUALLY COVERS A FOOD BILL!
THERE'S NO RANK DISTINCTION WHEN IT COMES TO MUTUAL RESPECT.
BESIDES... YOU'RE PROBABLY MY ONLY JUNIOR THAT I ACKNOWLEDGE AS AN EQUAL...

READ THIS WAY

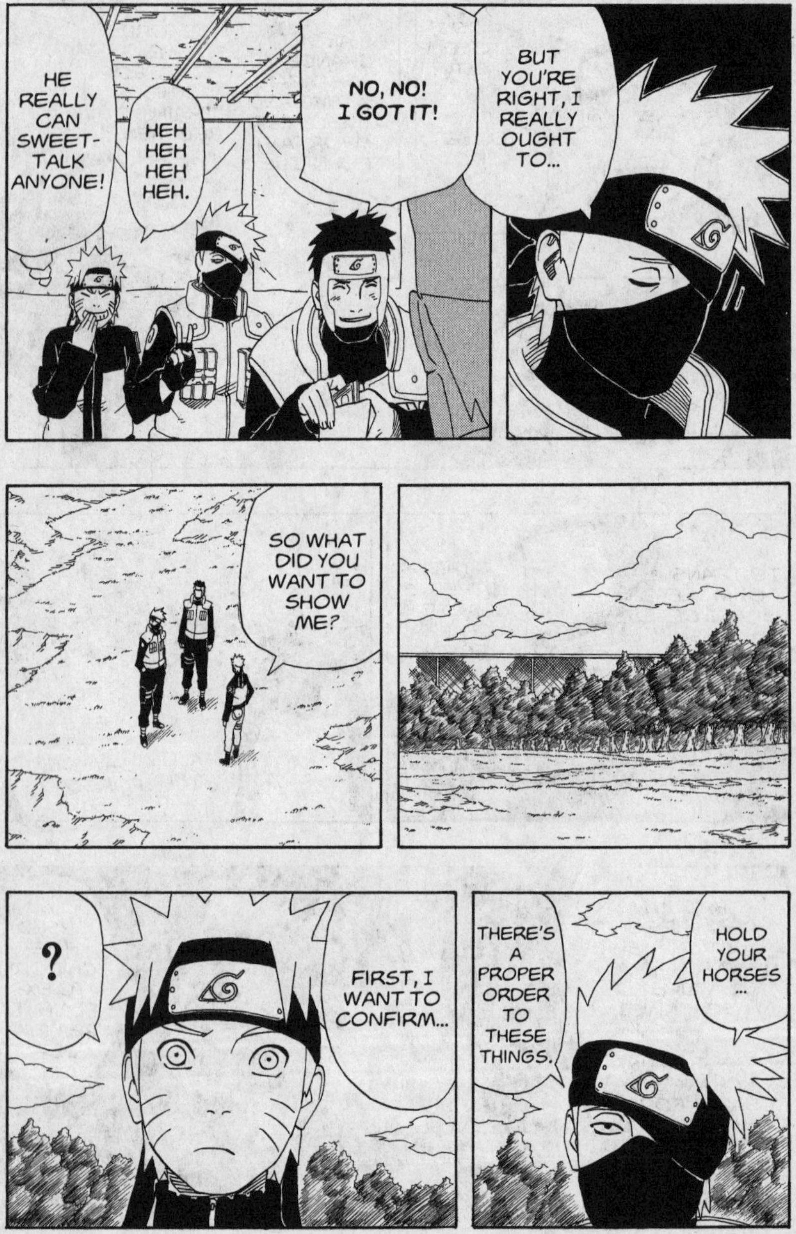
BUT YOU'RE RIGHT, I REALLY OUGHT TO...
NO, NO! I GOT IT!
HEH HEH HEH HEH.
HE REALLY CAN SWEET-TALK ANYONE!
SO WHAT DID YOU WANT TO SHOW ME?
HOLD YOUR HORSES ...
THERE'S A PROPER ORDER TO THESE THINGS.
FIRST, I WANT TO CONFIRM...
?

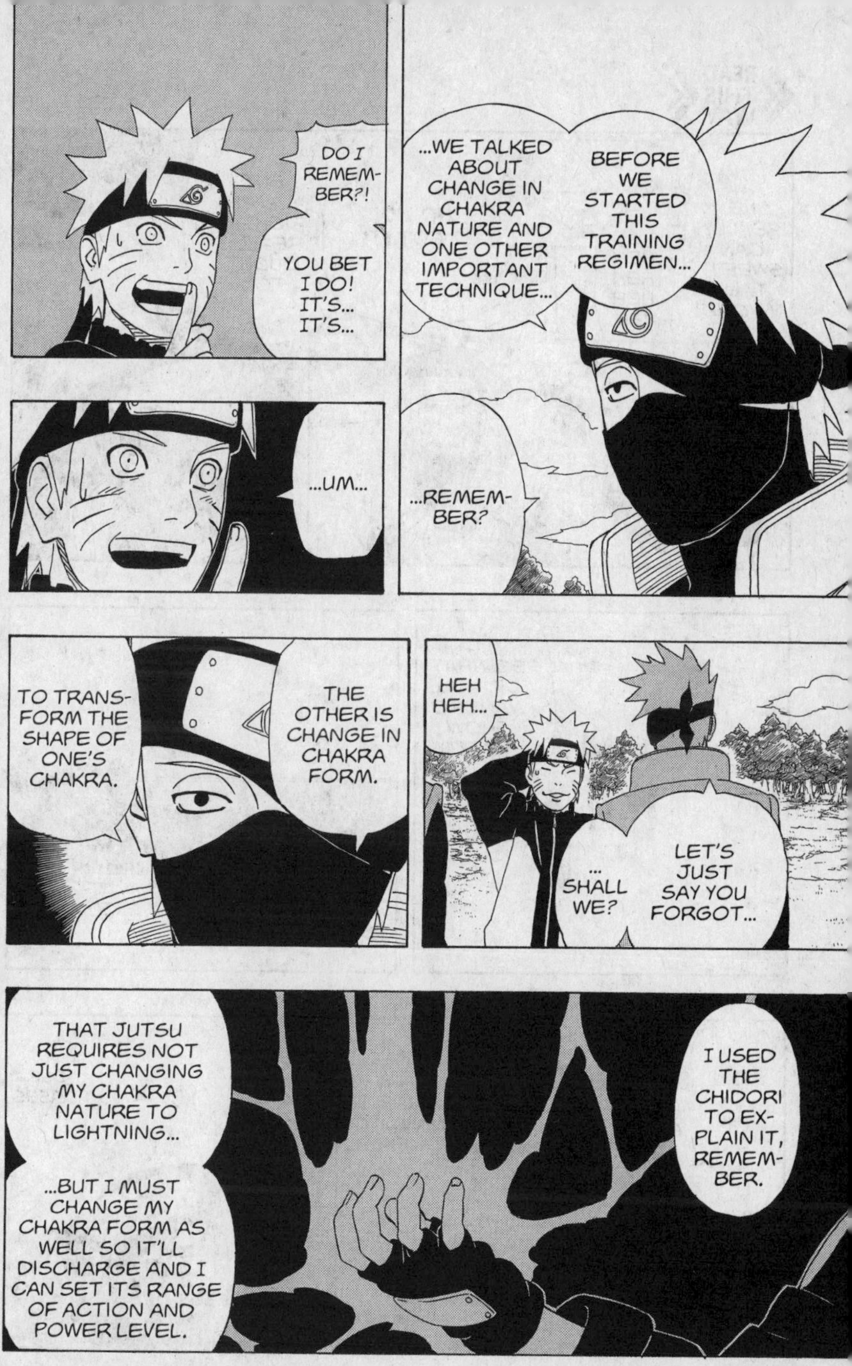
BEFORE WE STARTED THIS TRAINING REGIMEN...
...WE TALKED ABOUT CHANGE IN CHAKRA NATURE AND ONE OTHER IMPORTANT TECHNIQUE...
...REMEMBER?
DO I REMEMBER?!
YOU BET I DO! IT'S... IT'S...
...UM...
HEH HEH...
LET'S JUST SAY YOU FORGOT...
...SHALL WE?
THE OTHER IS CHANGE IN CHAKRA FORM.
TO TRANSFORM THE SHAPE OF ONE'S CHAKRA.
I USED THE CHIDORI TO EXPLAIN IT, REMEMBER.
THAT JUTSU REQUIRES NOT JUST CHANGING MY CHAKRA NATURE TO LIGHTNING...
...BUT I MUST CHANGE MY CHAKRA FORM AS WELL SO IT'LL DISCHARGE AND I CAN SET ITS RANGE OF ACTION AND POWER LEVEL.

READ THIS WAY

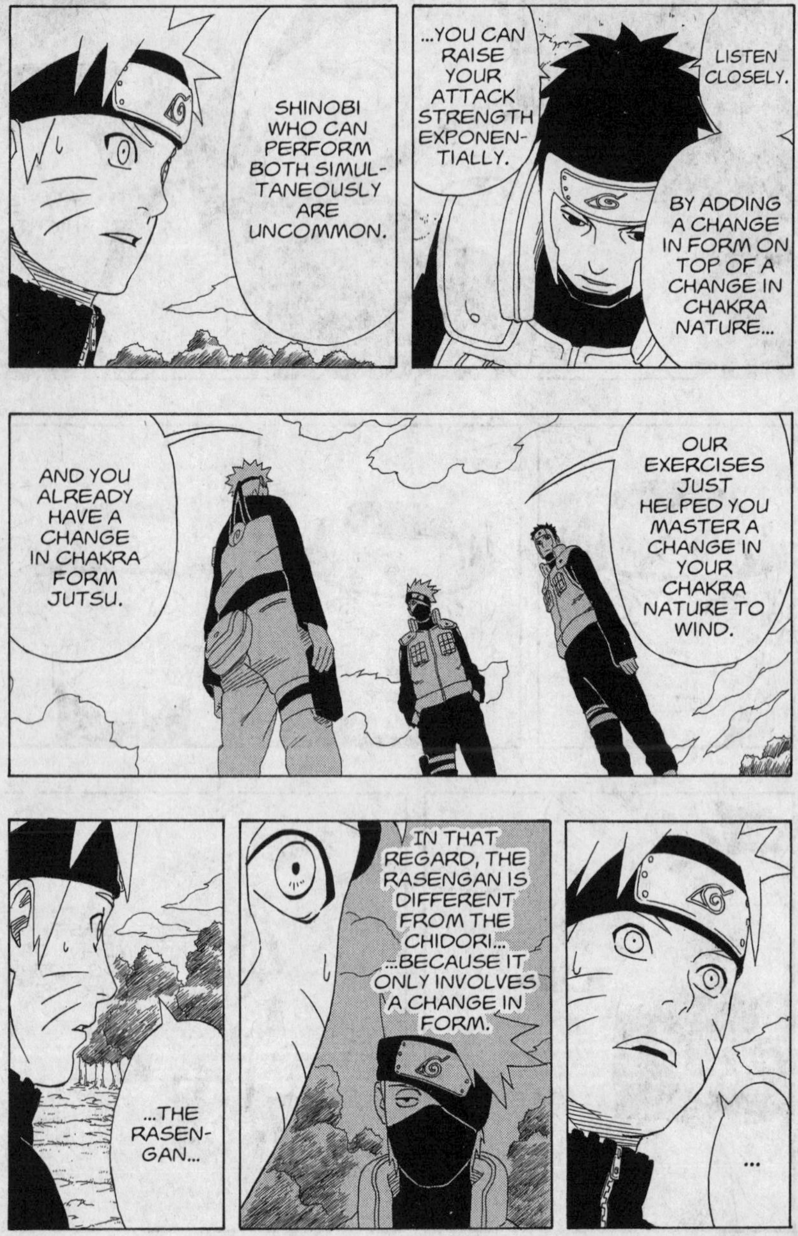
LISTEN CLOSELY.
BY ADDING A CHANGE IN FORM ON TOP OF A CHANGE IN CHAKRA NATURE...
...YOU CAN RAISE YOUR ATTACK STRENGTH EXPONEN-TIALLY.
SHINOBI WHO CAN PERFORM BOTH SIMUL-TANEOUSLY ARE UNCOMMON.
OUR EXERCISES JUST HELPED YOU MASTER A CHANGE IN YOUR CHAKRA NATURE TO WIND.
AND YOU ALREADY HAVE A CHANGE IN CHAKRA FORM JUTSU.
...
IN THAT REGARD, THE RASENGAN IS DIFFERENT FROM THE CHIDORI... ...BECAUSE IT ONLY INVOLVES A CHANGE IN FORM.
...THE RASEN-GAN...

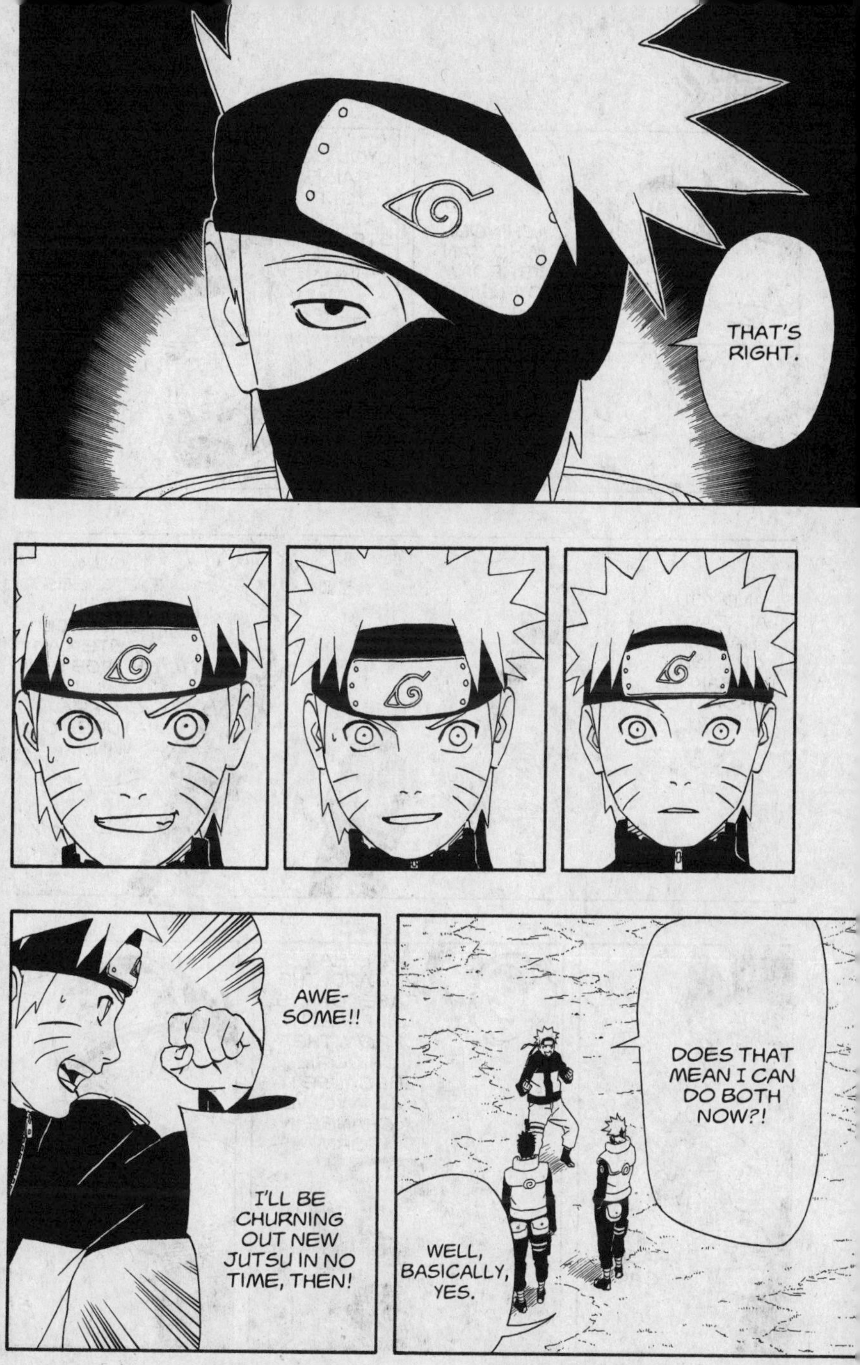
THAT'S RIGHT.
DOES THAT MEAN I CAN DO BOTH NOW?!
WELL, BASICALLY, YES.
AWE-SOME!!
I'LL BE CHURNING OUT NEW JUTSU IN NO TIME, THEN!

READ THIS WAY

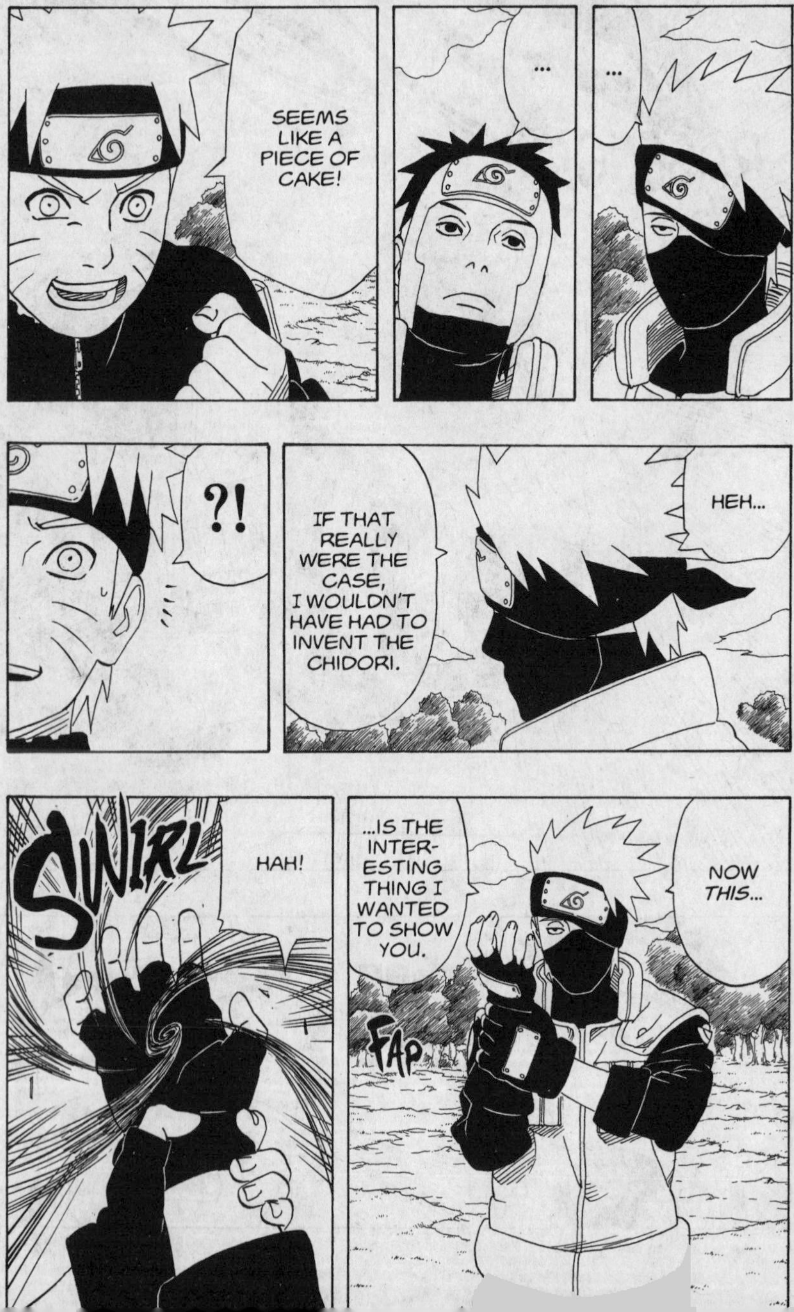
...
...
SEEMS LIKE A PIECE OF CAKE!
HEH...
IF THAT REALLY WERE THE CASE, I WOULDN'T HAVE HAD TO INVENT THE CHIDORI.
?!
NOW THIS...
...IS THE INTER-ESTING THING I WANTED TO SHOW YOU.
FAP
HAH!
SWIRL

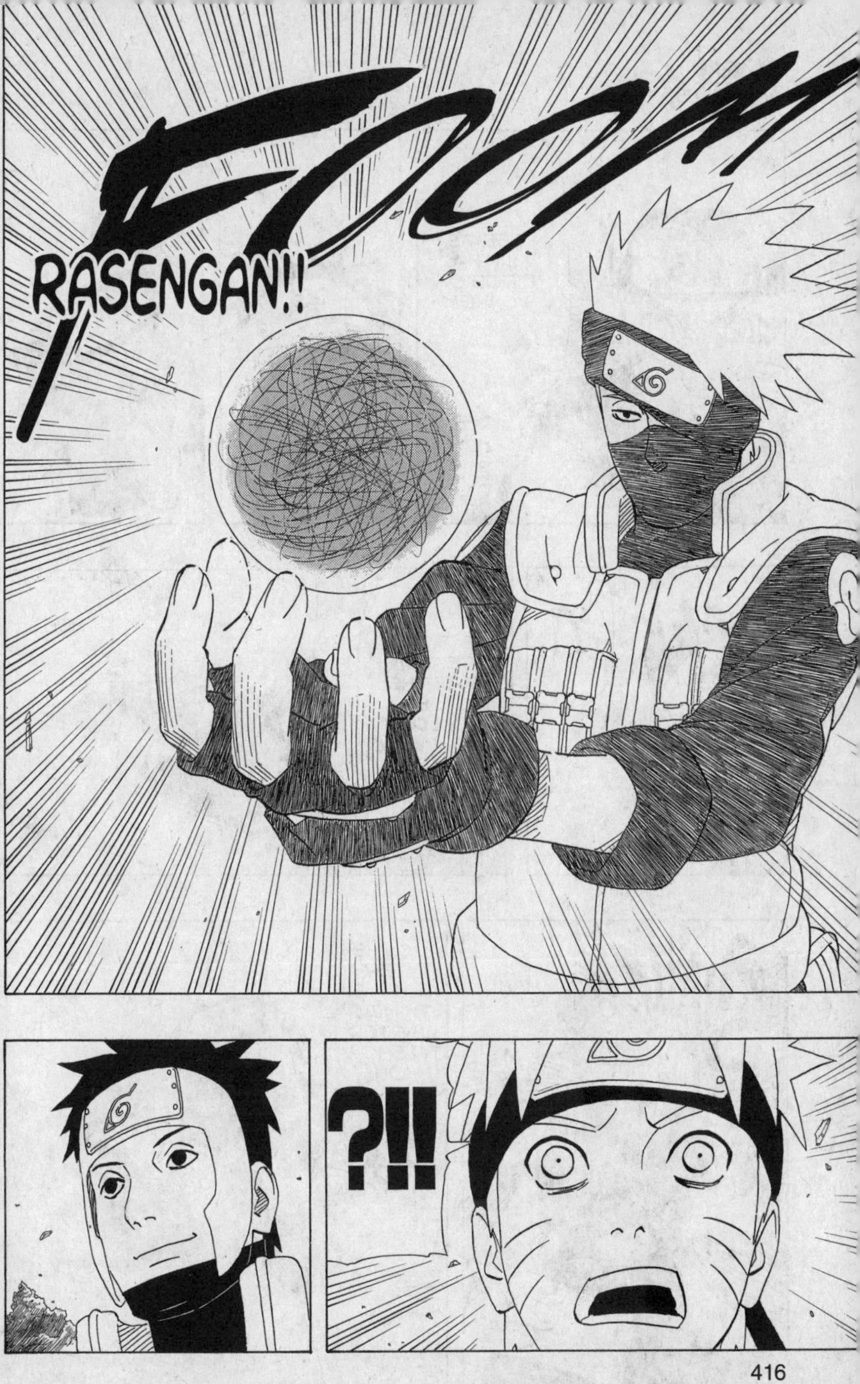
RASENGAN!!
?!!

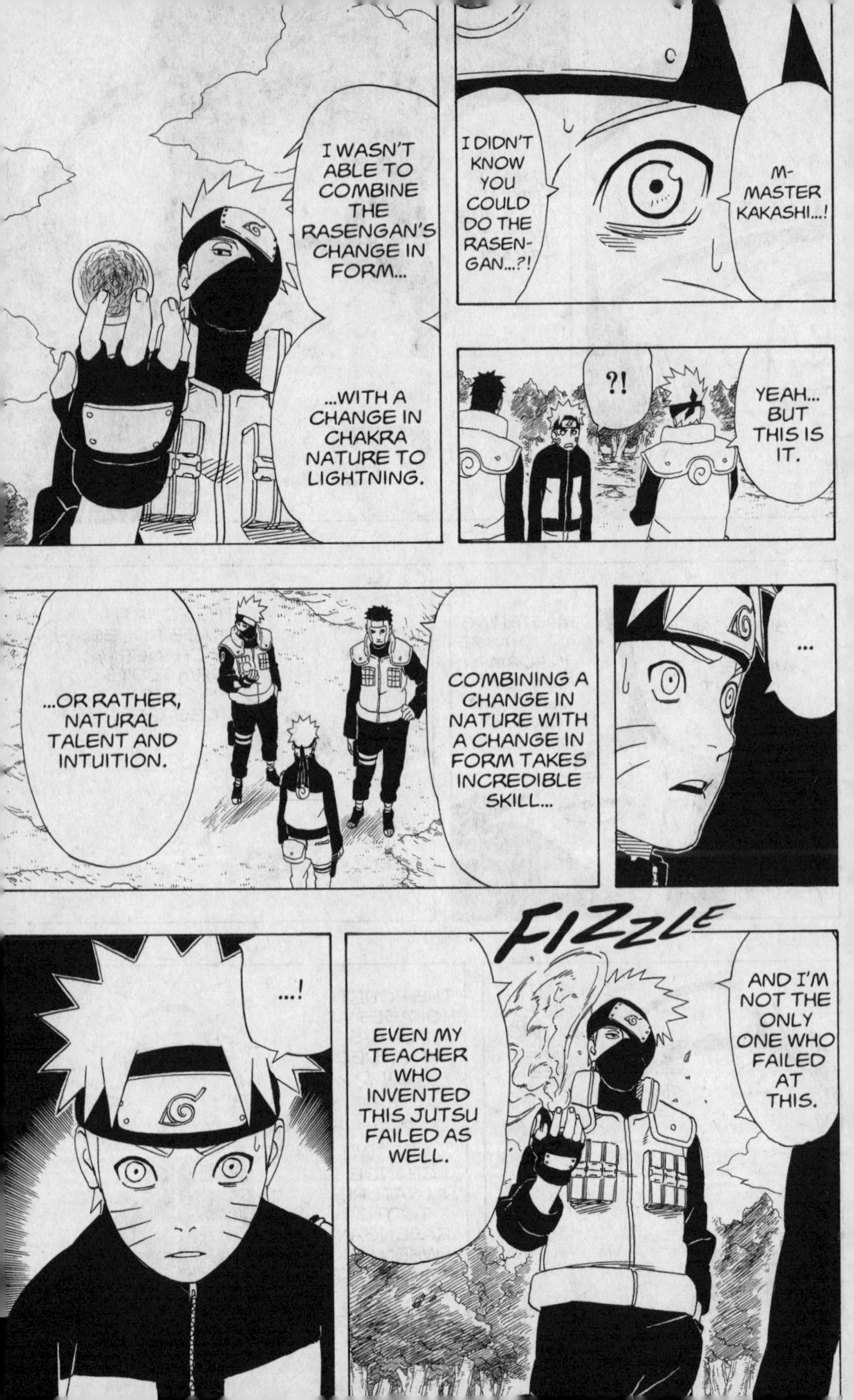
M-MASTER KAKASHI...!
I DIDN'T KNOW YOU COULD DO THE RASENGAN...?!
YEAH... BUT THIS IS IT.
?!
I WASN'T ABLE TO COMBINE THE RASENGAN'S CHANGE IN FORM...
...WITH A CHANGE IN CHAKRA NATURE TO LIGHTNING.
...
COMBINING A CHANGE IN NATURE WITH A CHANGE IN FORM TAKES INCREDIBLE SKILL...
...OR RATHER, NATURAL TALENT AND INTUITION.
FIZZLE
AND I'M NOT THE ONLY ONE WHO FAILED AT THIS.
EVEN MY TEACHER WHO INVENTED THIS JUTSU FAILED AS WELL.
...!

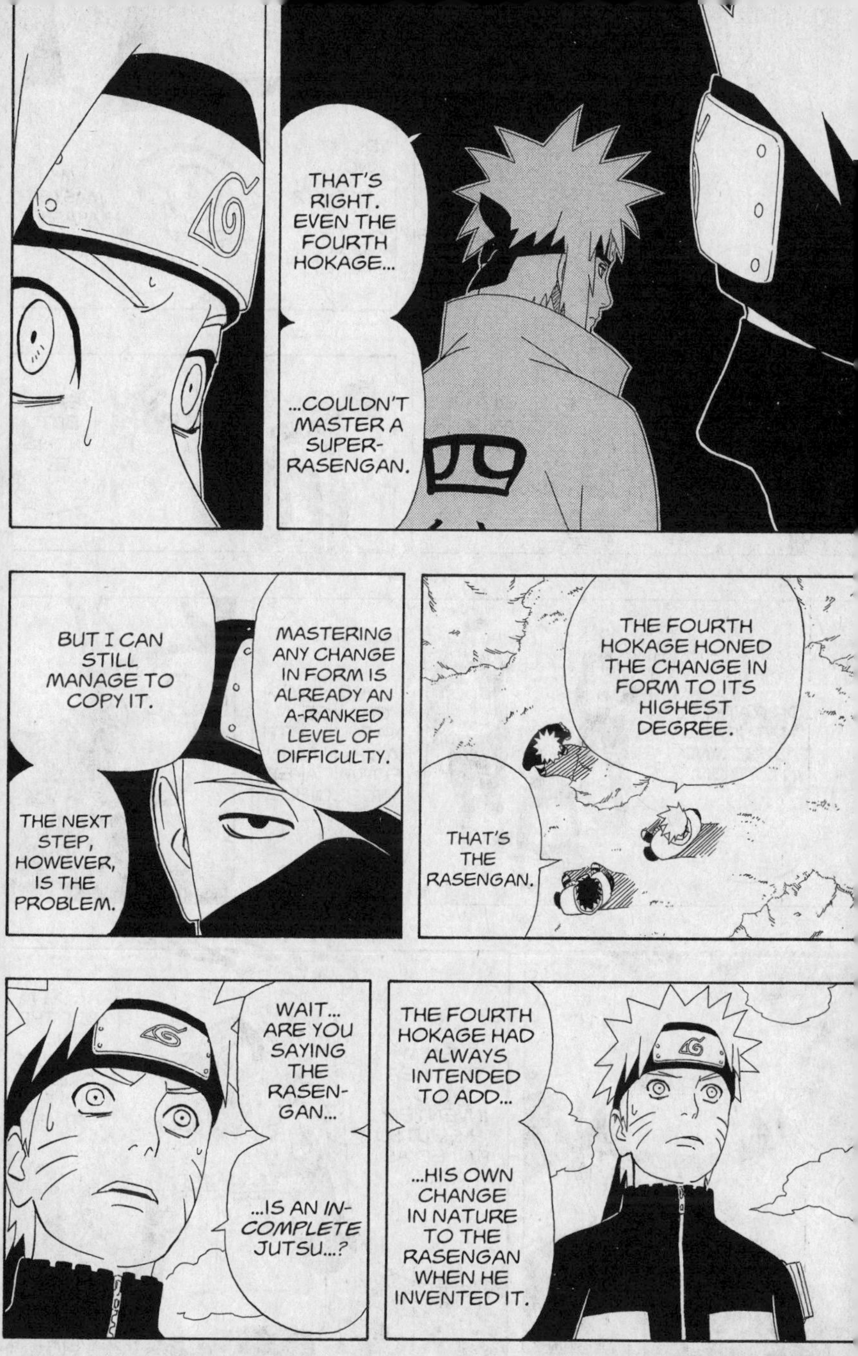
THAT'S RIGHT. EVEN THE FOURTH HOKAGE...
...COULDN'T MASTER A SUPER-RASENGAN.
THE FOURTH HOKAGE HONED THE CHANGE IN FORM TO ITS HIGHEST DEGREE.
THAT'S THE RASENGAN.
MASTERING ANY CHANGE IN FORM IS ALREADY AN A-RANKED LEVEL OF DIFFICULTY.
BUT I CAN STILL MANAGE TO COPY IT.
THE NEXT STEP, HOWEVER, IS THE PROBLEM.
THE FOURTH HOKAGE HAD ALWAYS INTENDED TO ADD...
...HIS OWN CHANGE IN NATURE TO THE RASENGAN WHEN HE INVENTED IT.
WAIT... ARE YOU SAYING THE RASENGAN...
...IS AN *INCOMPLETE* JUTSU...?

READ THIS WAY

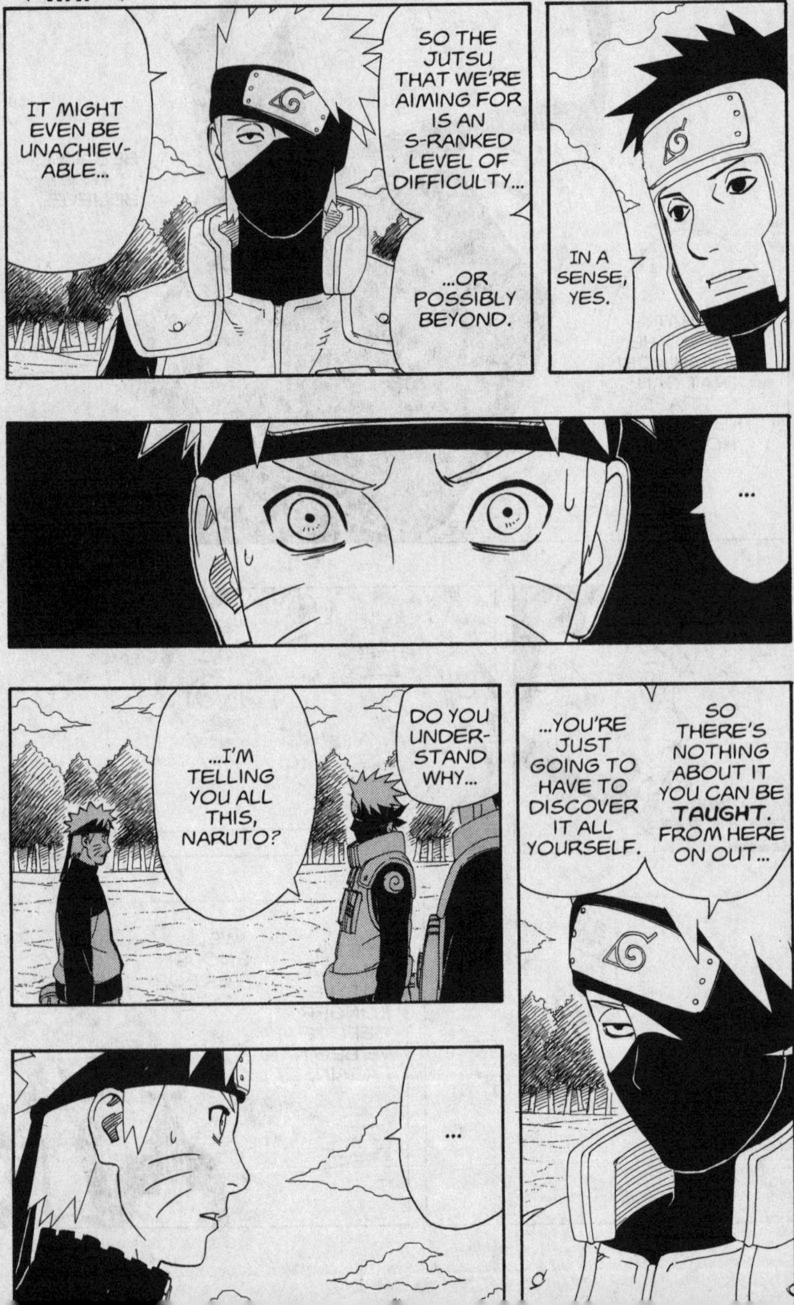
IN A SENSE, YES.
SO THE JUTSU THAT WE'RE AIMING FOR IS AN S-RANKED LEVEL OF DIFFICULTY...
...OR POSSIBLY BEYOND.
IT MIGHT EVEN BE UNACHIEVABLE...
...
SO THERE'S NOTHING ABOUT IT YOU CAN BE **TAUGHT**. FROM HERE ON OUT...
...YOU'RE JUST GOING TO HAVE TO DISCOVER IT ALL YOURSELF.
DO YOU UNDERSTAND WHY...
...I'M TELLING YOU ALL THIS, NARUTO?
...

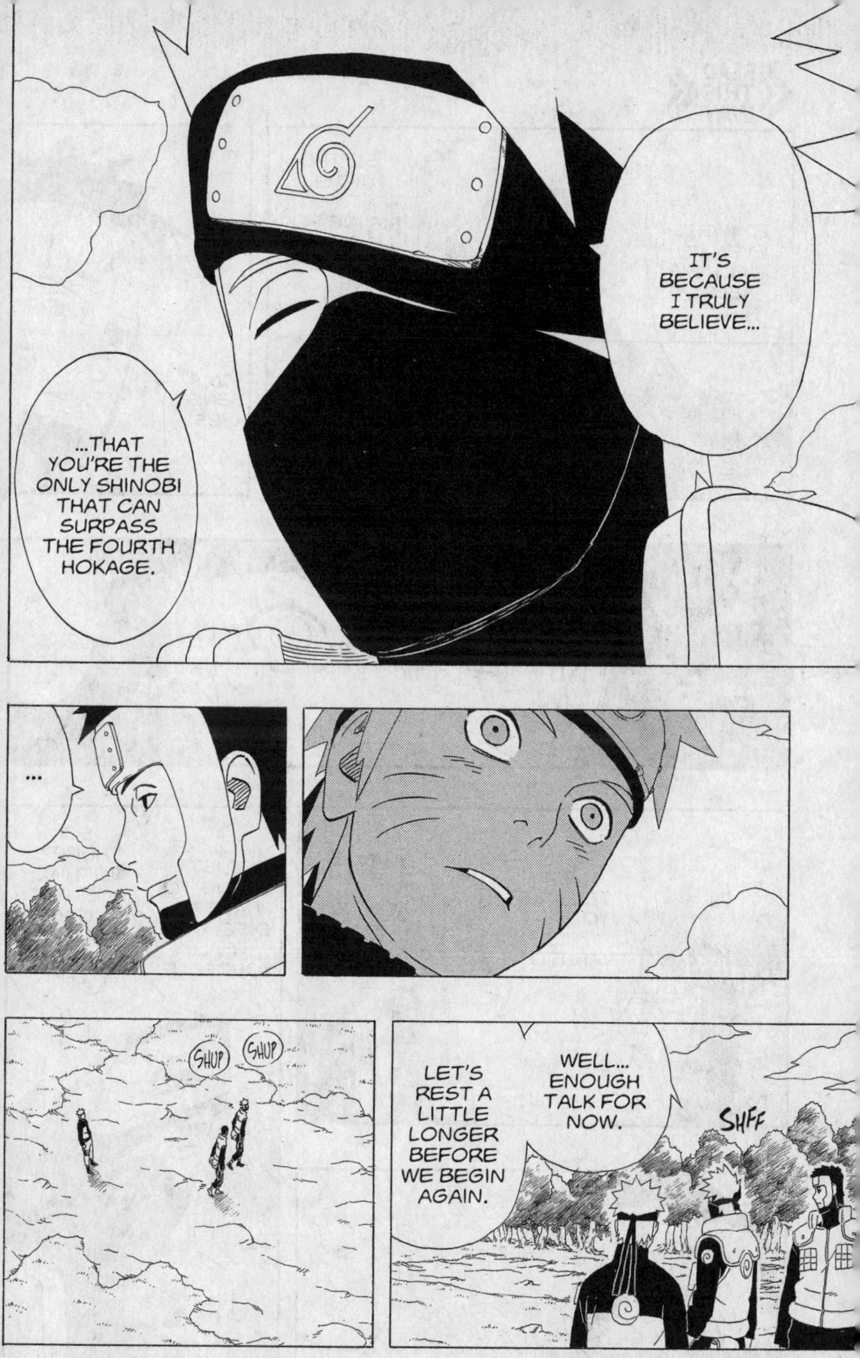
IT'S BECAUSE I TRULY BELIEVE...
...THAT YOU'RE THE ONLY SHINOBI THAT CAN SURPASS THE FOURTH HOKAGE.
...
WELL... ENOUGH TALK FOR NOW.
LET'S REST A LITTLE LONGER BEFORE WE BEGIN AGAIN.
SHFF
SHUP
SHUP

READ THIS WAY

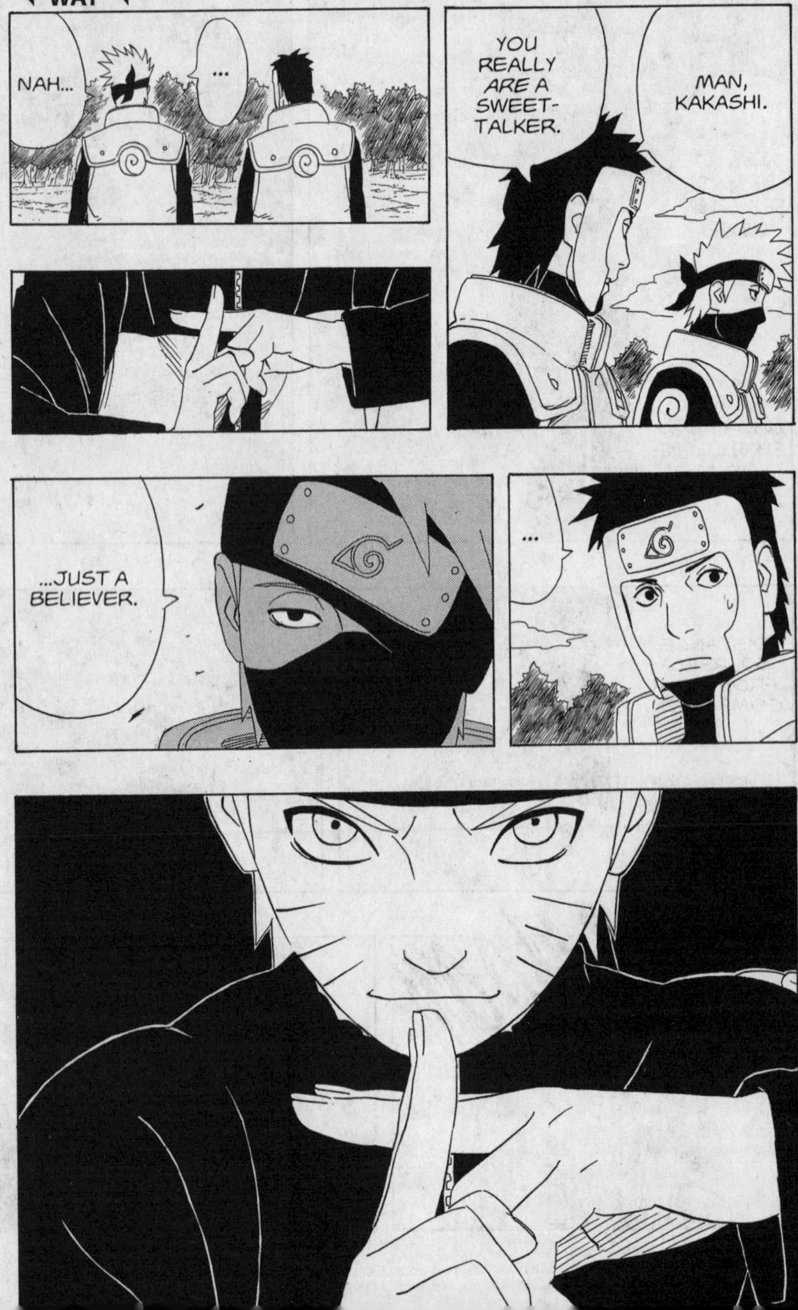
MAN, KAKASHI.
YOU REALLY ARE A SWEET-TALKER.
...
NAH...
...
...JUST A BELIEVER.

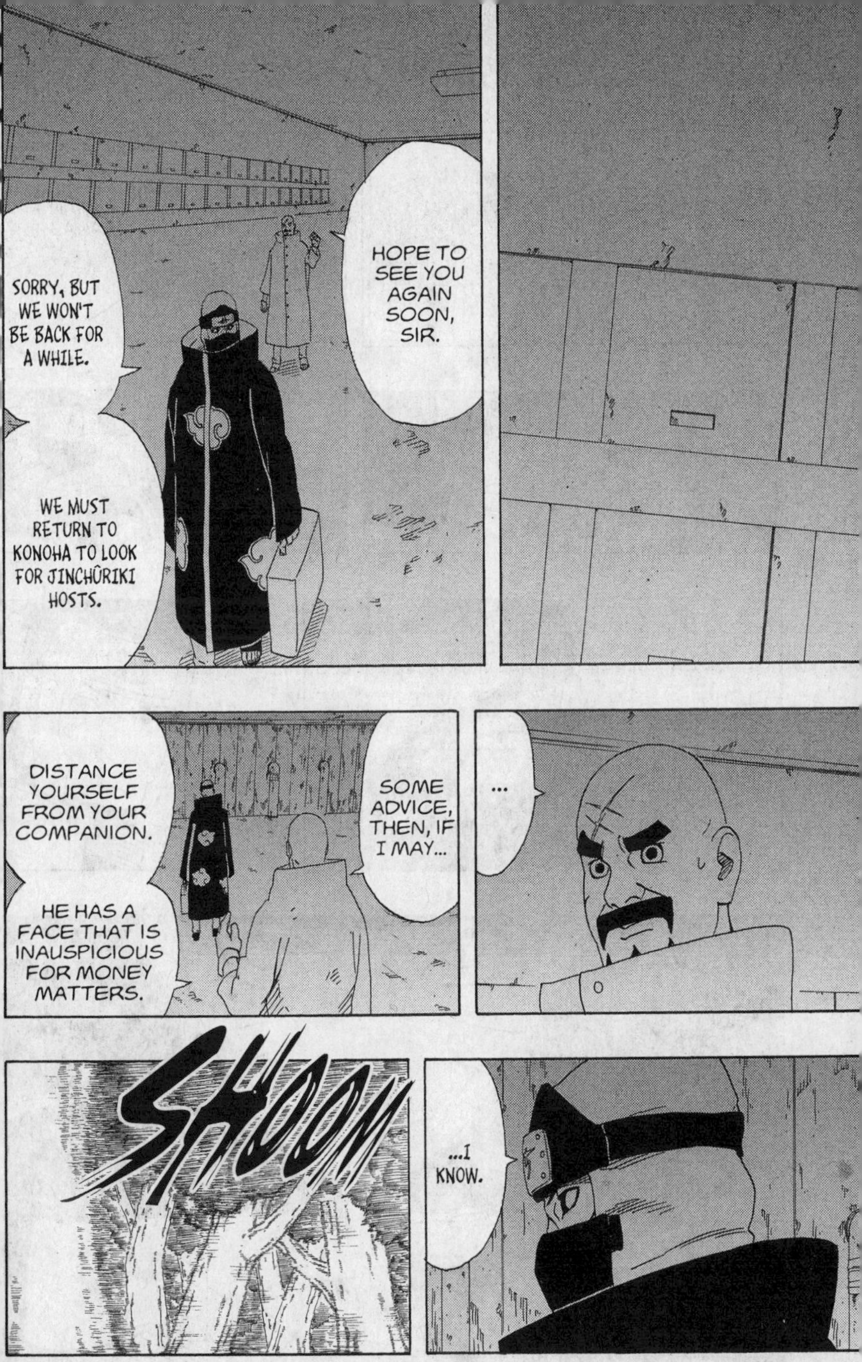
HOPE TO SEE YOU AGAIN SOON, SIR.
SORRY, BUT WE WON'T BE BACK FOR A WHILE.
WE MUST RETURN TO KONOHA TO LOOK FOR JINCHŪRIKI HOSTS.
...
SOME ADVICE, THEN, IF I MAY...
DISTANCE YOURSELF FROM YOUR COMPANION.
HE HAS A FACE THAT IS INAUSPICIOUS FOR MONEY MATTERS.
...I KNOW.
SHOOM

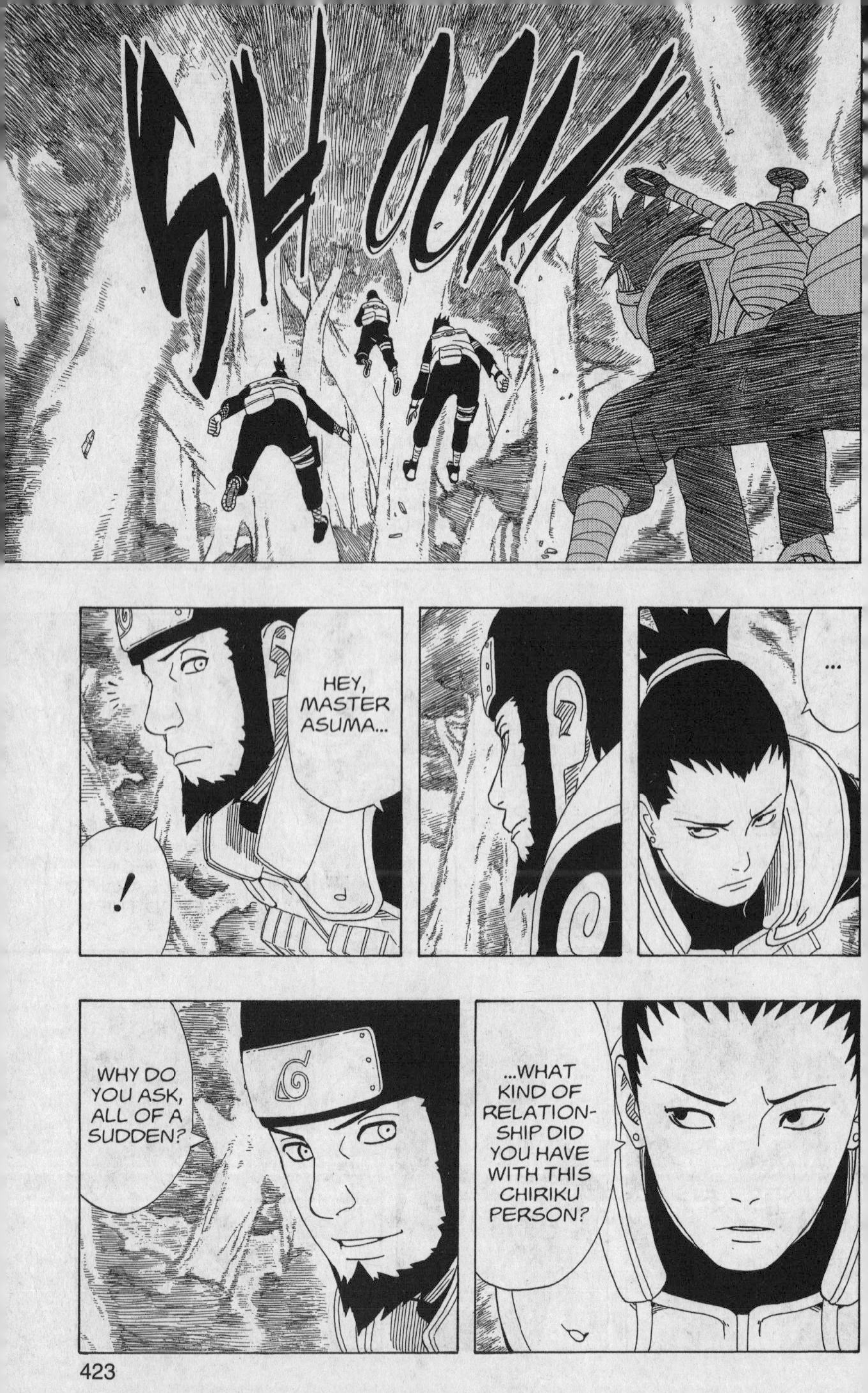
SHOOM
...
HEY, MASTER ASUMA...
!
...WHAT KIND OF RELATION-SHIP DID YOU HAVE WITH THIS CHIRIKU PERSON?
WHY DO YOU ASK, ALL OF A SUDDEN?

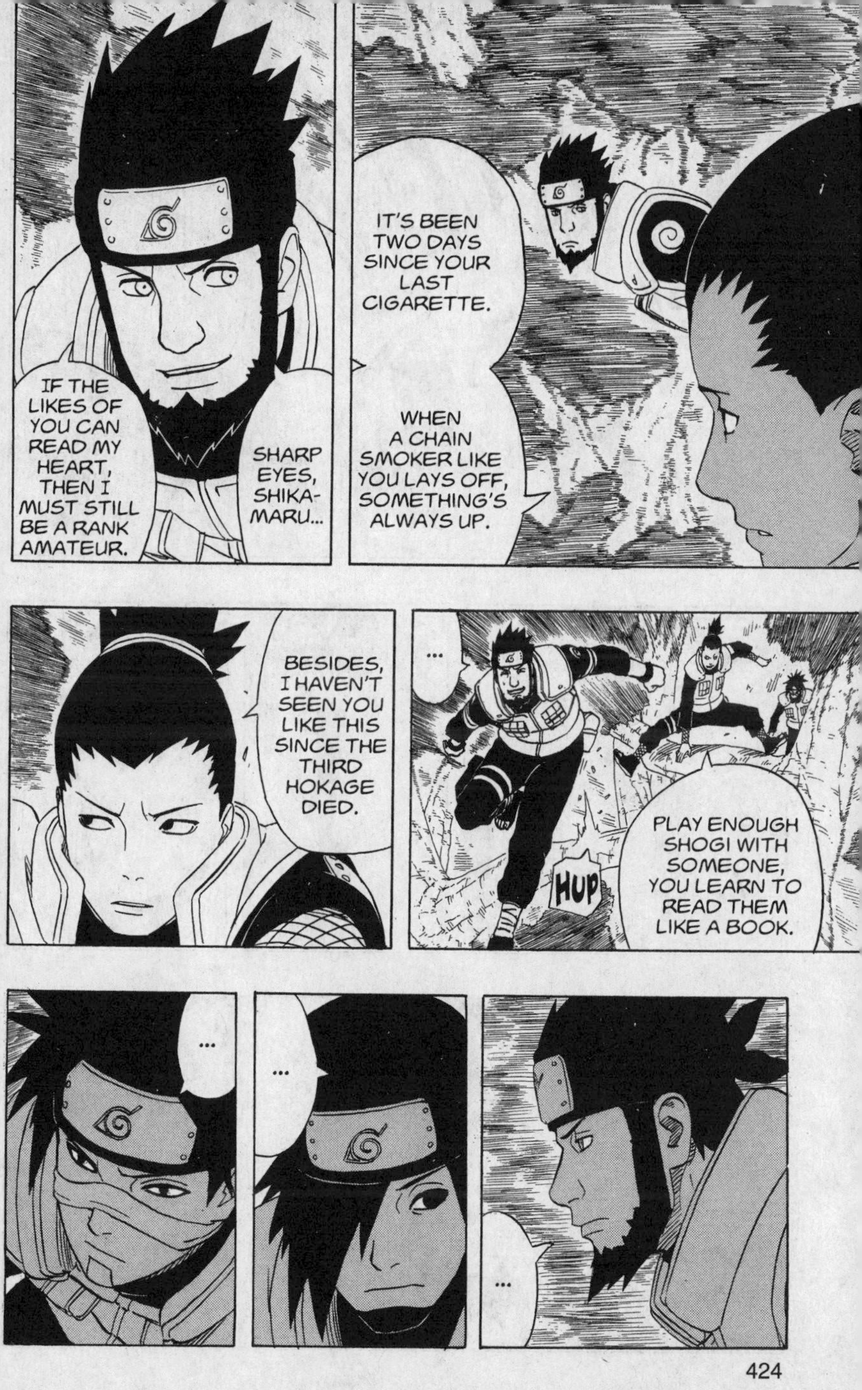
IT'S BEEN TWO DAYS SINCE YOUR LAST CIGARETTE.
WHEN A CHAIN SMOKER LIKE YOU LAYS OFF, SOMETHING'S ALWAYS UP.
SHARP EYES, SHIKAMARU...
IF THE LIKES OF YOU CAN READ MY HEART, THEN I MUST STILL BE A RANK AMATEUR.
...
PLAY ENOUGH SHOGI WITH SOMEONE, YOU LEARN TO READ THEM LIKE A BOOK.
HUP
BESIDES, I HAVEN'T SEEN YOU LIKE THIS SINCE THE THIRD HOKAGE DIED.
...
...
...

READ THIS WAY

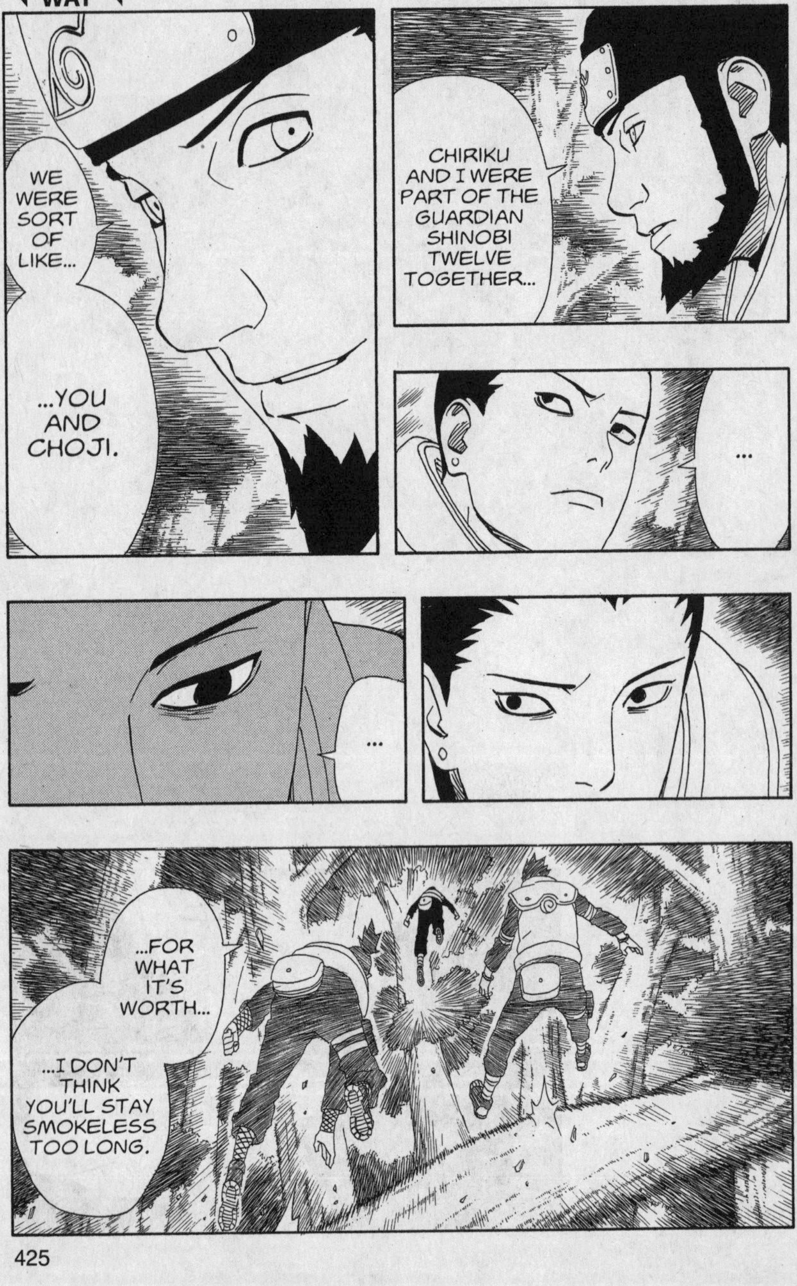
CHIRIKU AND I WERE PART OF THE GUARDIAN SHINOBI TWELVE TOGETHER...
...
WE WERE SORT OF LIKE...
...YOU AND CHOJI.
...
...FOR WHAT IT'S WORTH...
...I DON'T THINK YOU'LL STAY SMOKELESS TOO LONG.

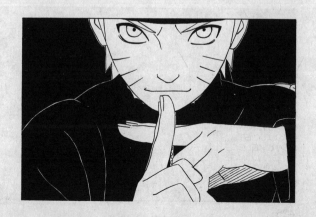

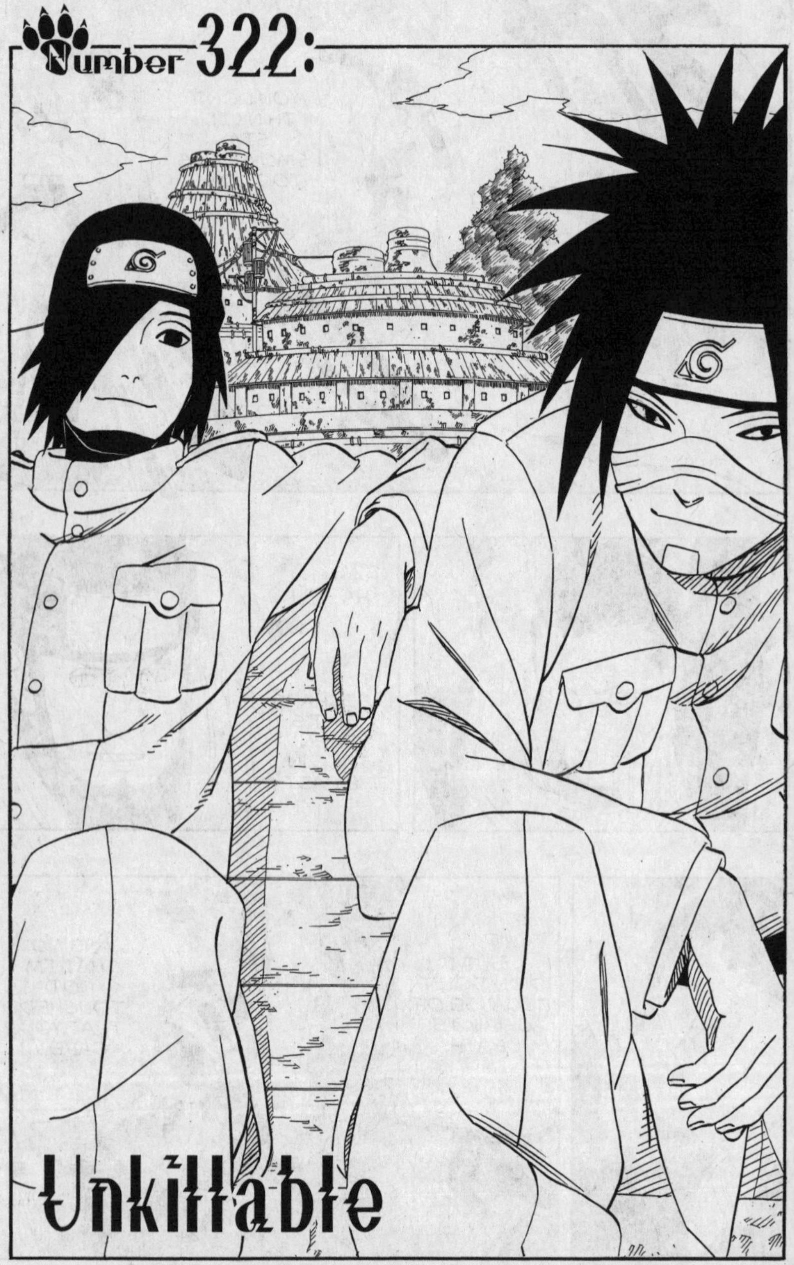
Number 322:
Unkillable

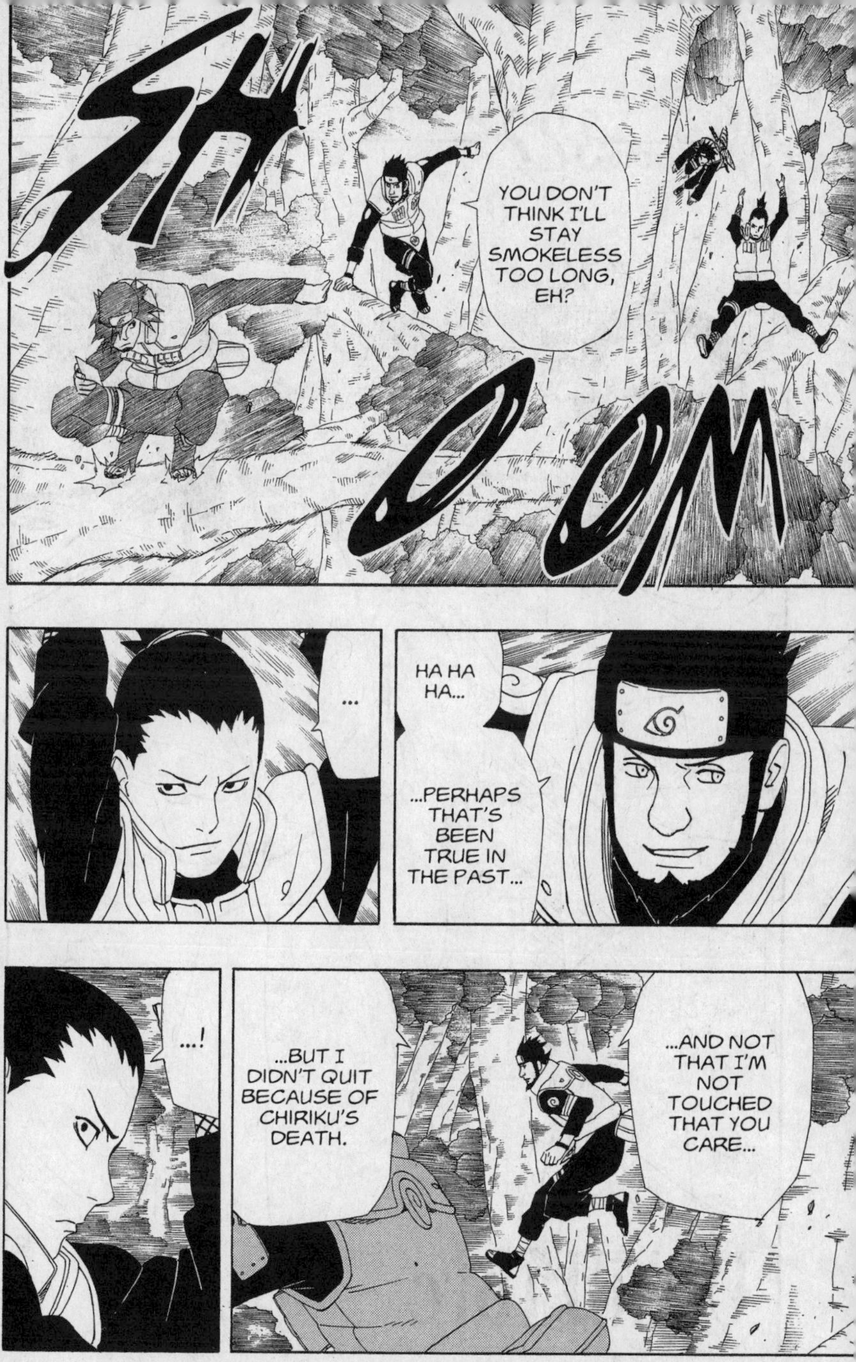
YOU DON'T THINK I'LL STAY SMOKELESS TOO LONG, EH?
SHH
OOM
HA HA HA...
...PERHAPS THAT'S BEEN TRUE IN THE PAST...
...
...AND NOT THAT I'M NOT TOUCHED THAT YOU CARE...
...BUT I DIDN'T QUIT BECAUSE OF CHIRIKU'S DEATH.
...!

READ THIS WAY

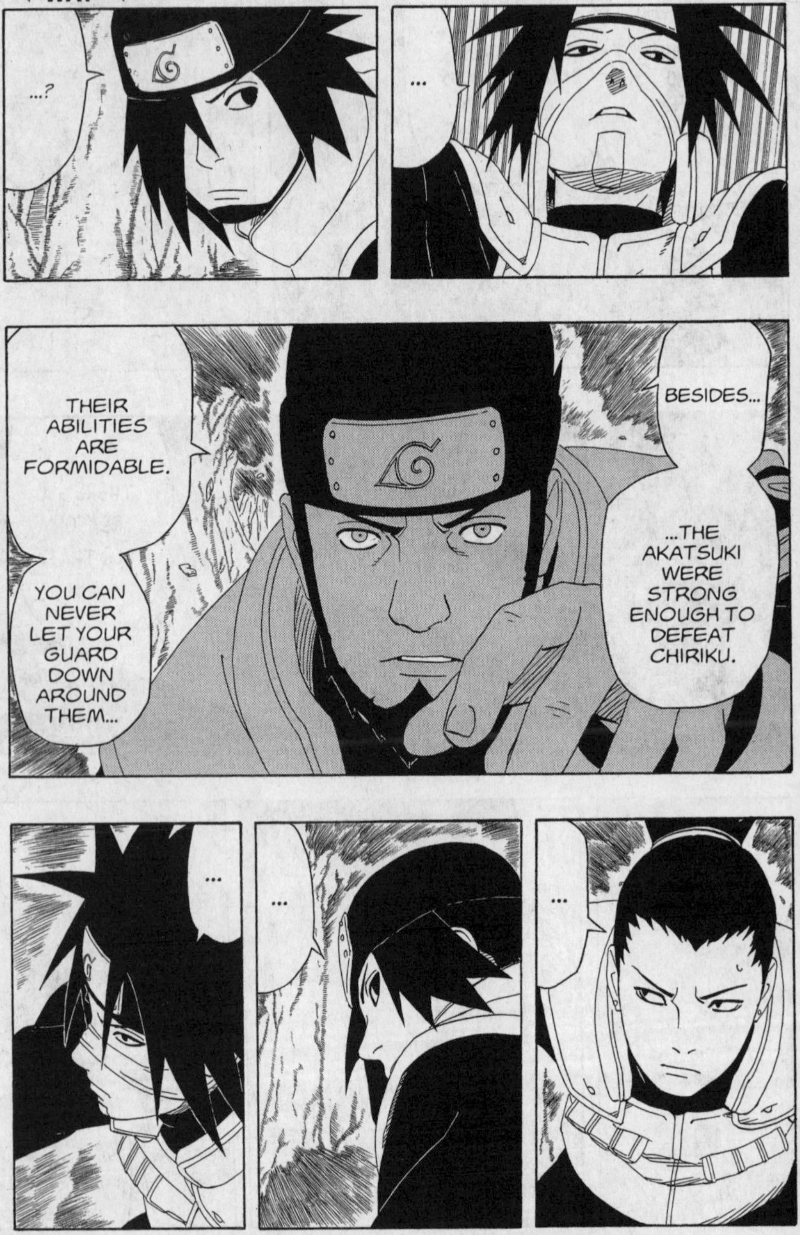
...
...?
BESIDES...
...THE AKATSUKI WERE STRONG ENOUGH TO DEFEAT CHIRIKU.
THEIR ABILITIES ARE FORMIDABLE.
YOU CAN NEVER LET YOUR GUARD DOWN AROUND THEM...
...
...
...

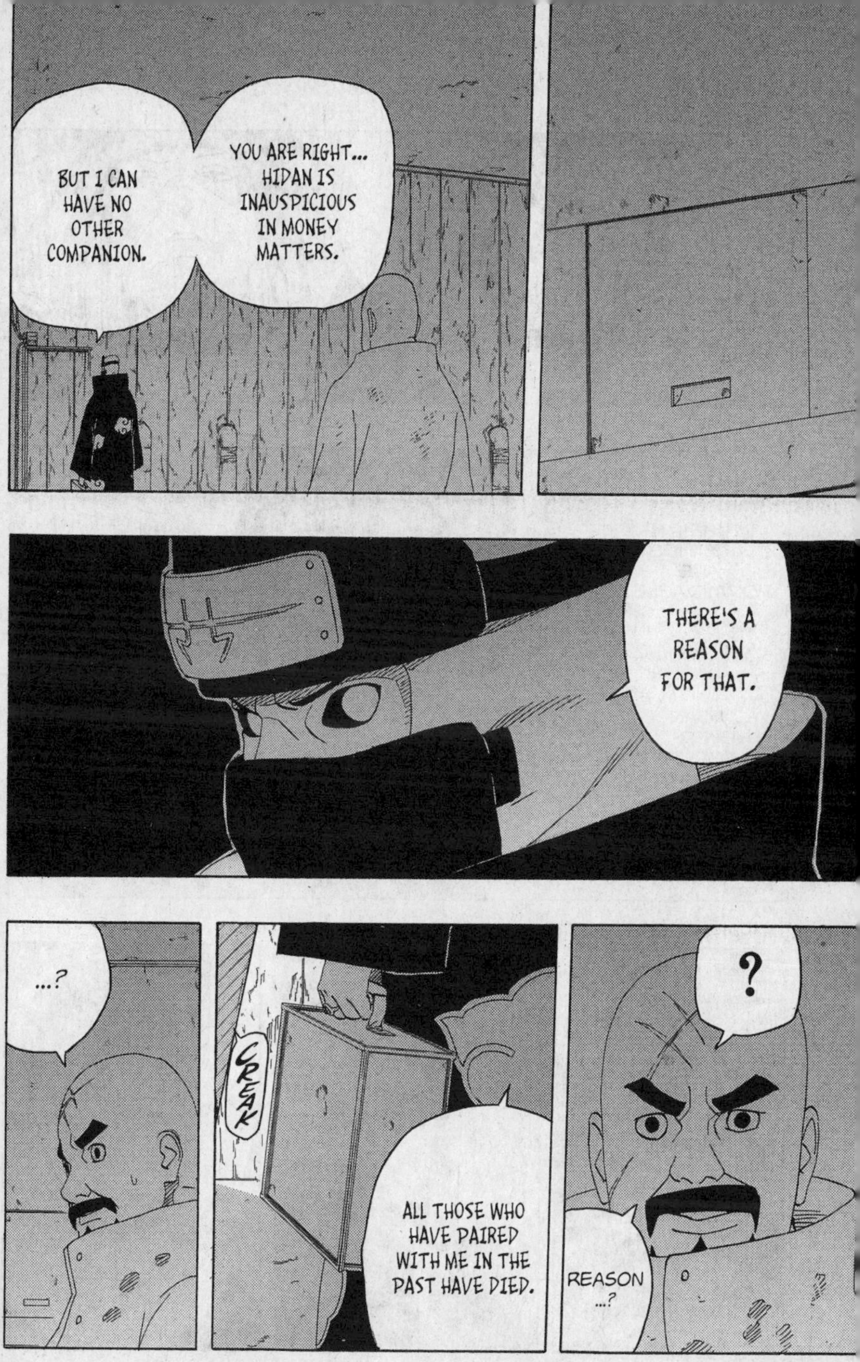
YOU ARE RIGHT... HIDAN IS INAUSPICIOUS IN MONEY MATTERS.
BUT I CAN HAVE NO OTHER COMPANION.
THERE'S A REASON FOR THAT.
?
REASON ...?
CREAK
ALL THOSE WHO HAVE PAIRED WITH ME IN THE PAST HAVE DIED.
...?

READ THIS WAY

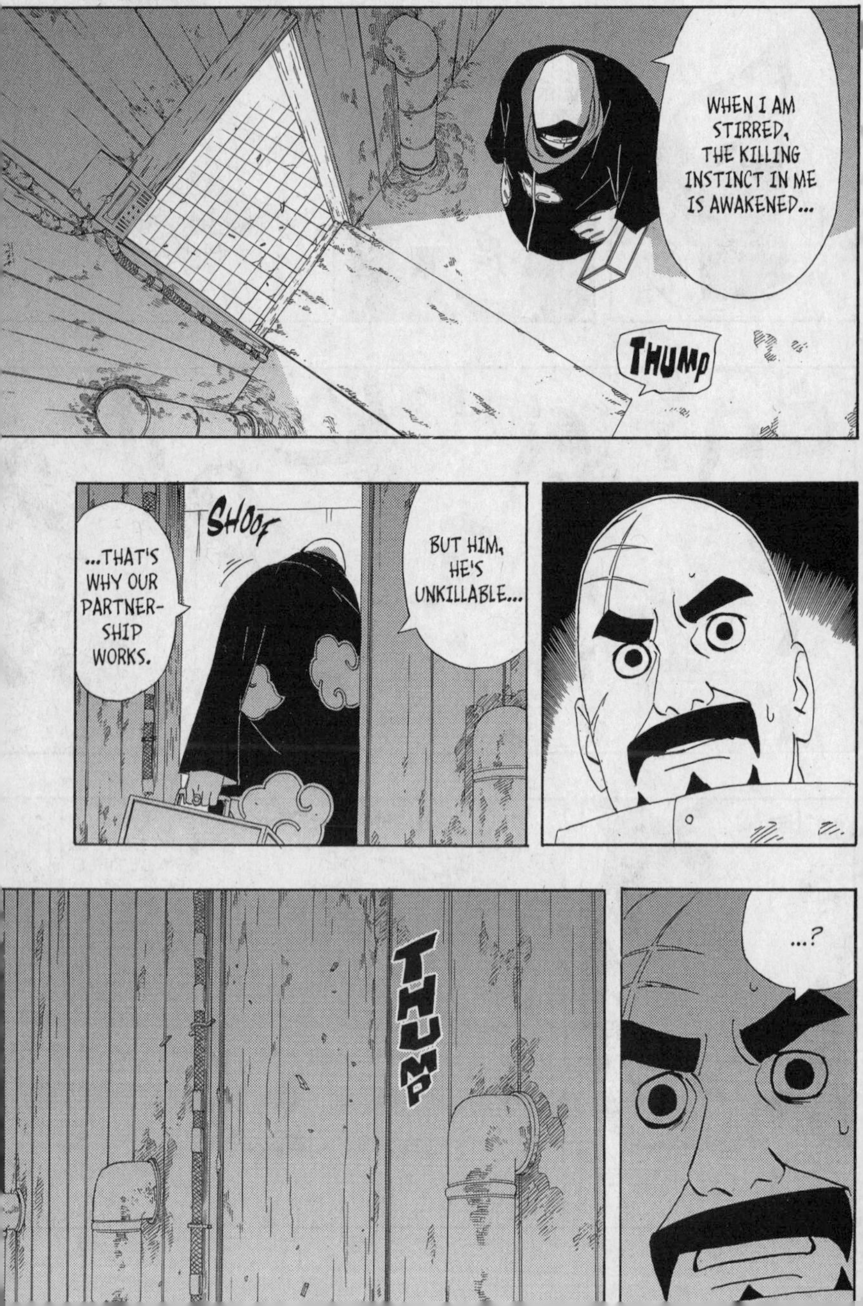
WHEN I AM STIRRED, THE KILLING INSTINCT IN ME IS AWAKENED...
THUMP
BUT HIM, HE'S UNKILLABLE...
SHOOF
...THAT'S WHY OUR PARTNER-SHIP WORKS.
...?
THUMP

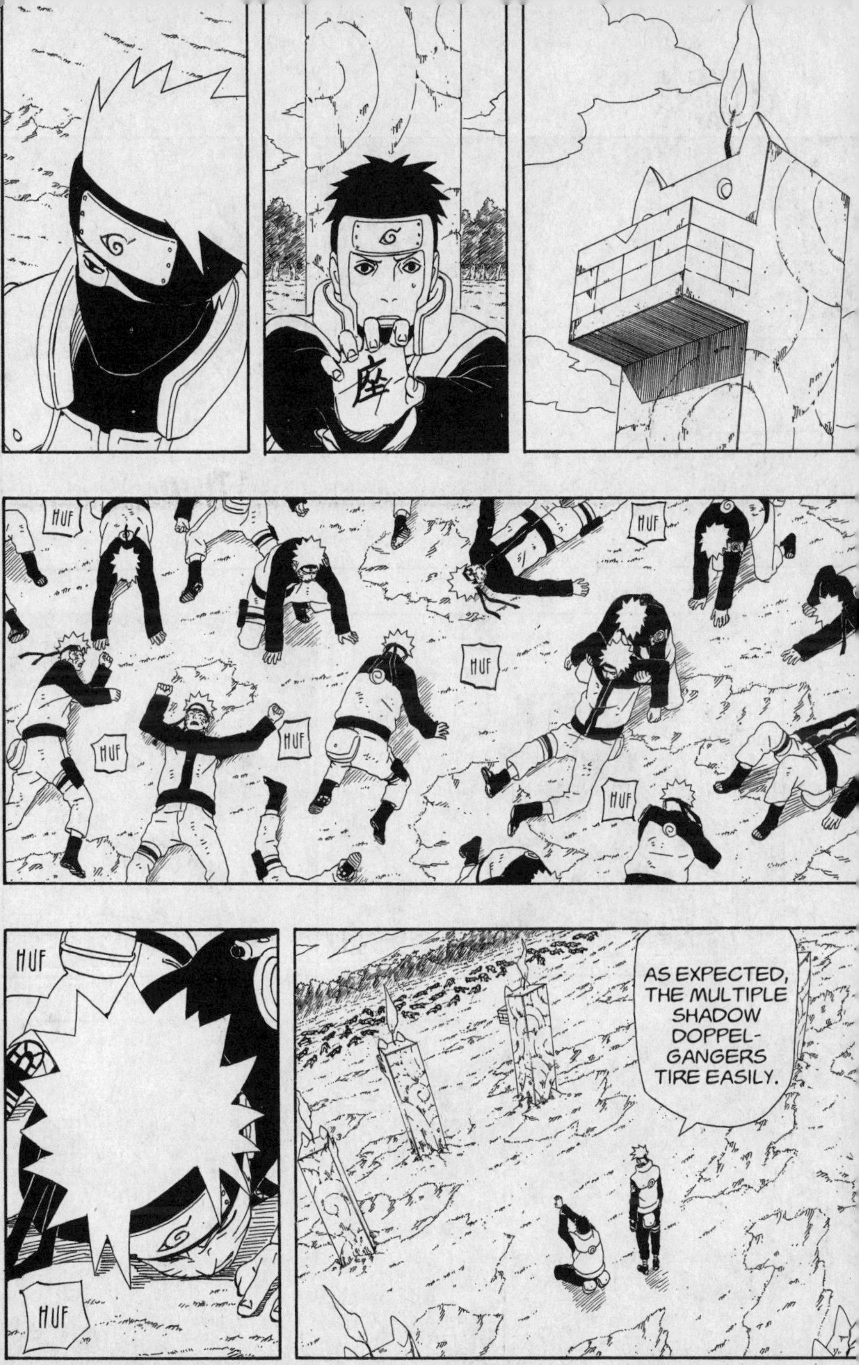
座
HUF
HUF
HUF
HUF
HUF
HUF
AS EXPECTED, THE MULTIPLE SHADOW DOPPEL-GANGERS TIRE EASILY.
HUF
HUF

READ THIS WAY

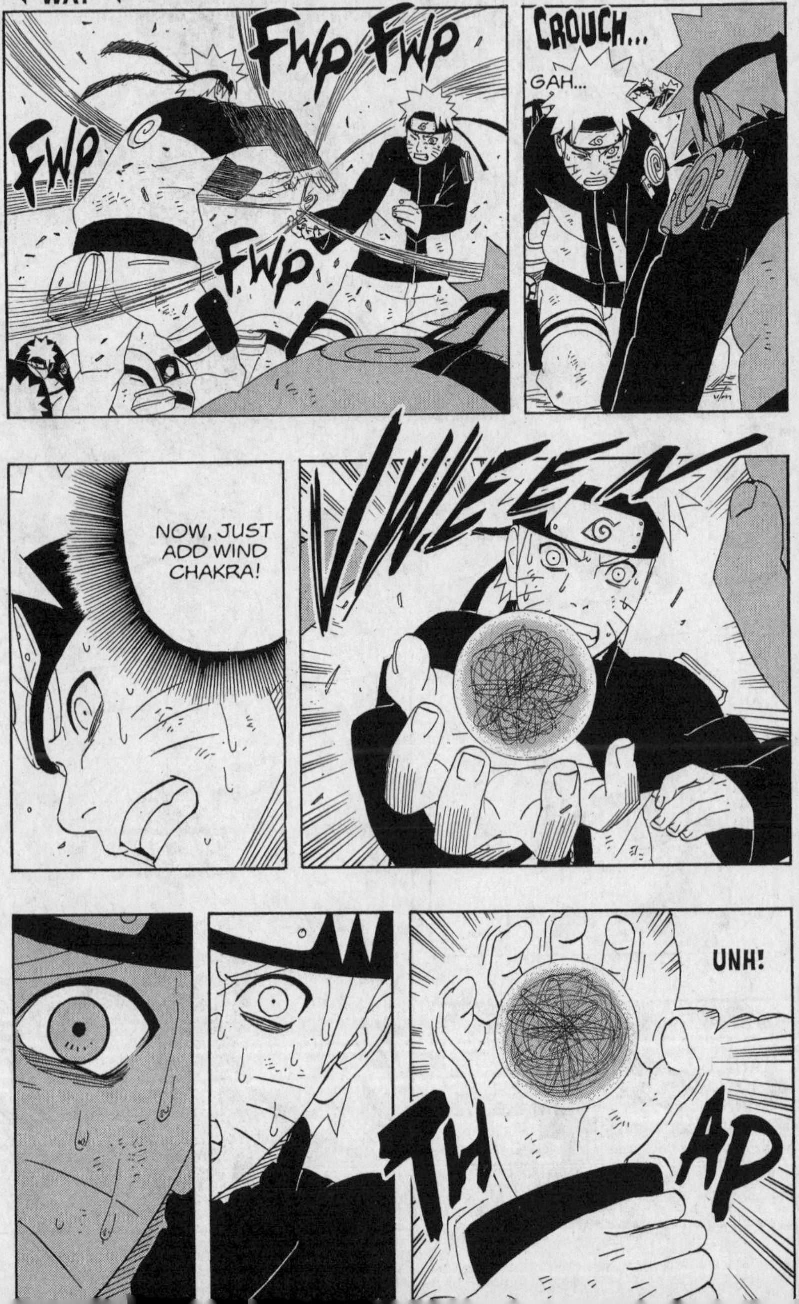
CROUCH...
GAH...
FWP FWP
FWP
FWP
VWEEN
NOW, JUST ADD WIND CHAKRA!
UNH!
THAP

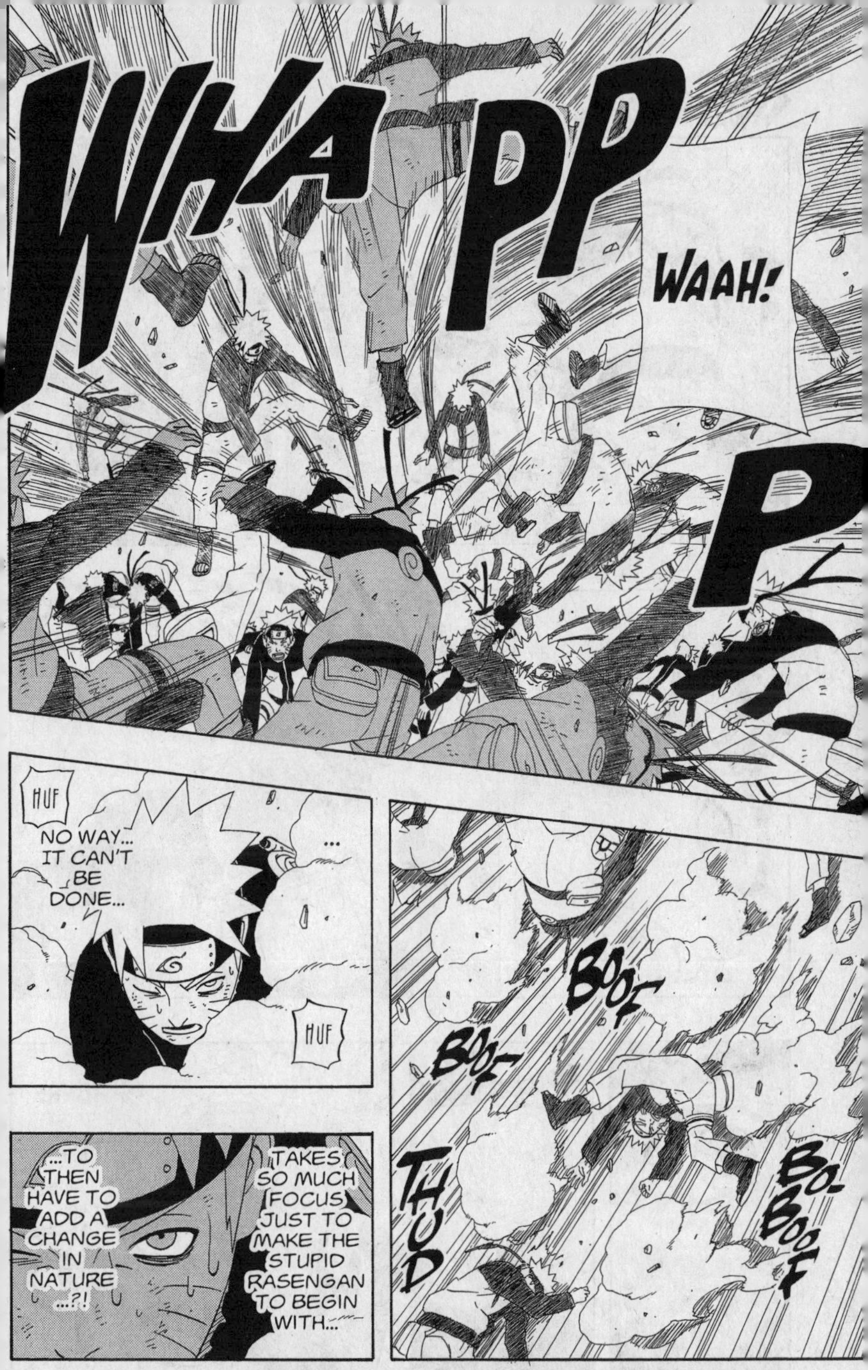
WHAPP
WAAH!
P
BOOF
BOOF
BO-BOOF
THUD
...
HUF
NO WAY... IT CAN'T BE DONE...
HUF
TAKES SO MUCH FOCUS JUST TO MAKE THE STUPID RASENGAN TO BEGIN WITH...
...TO THEN HAVE TO ADD A CHANGE IN NATURE ...?!

READ THIS WAY

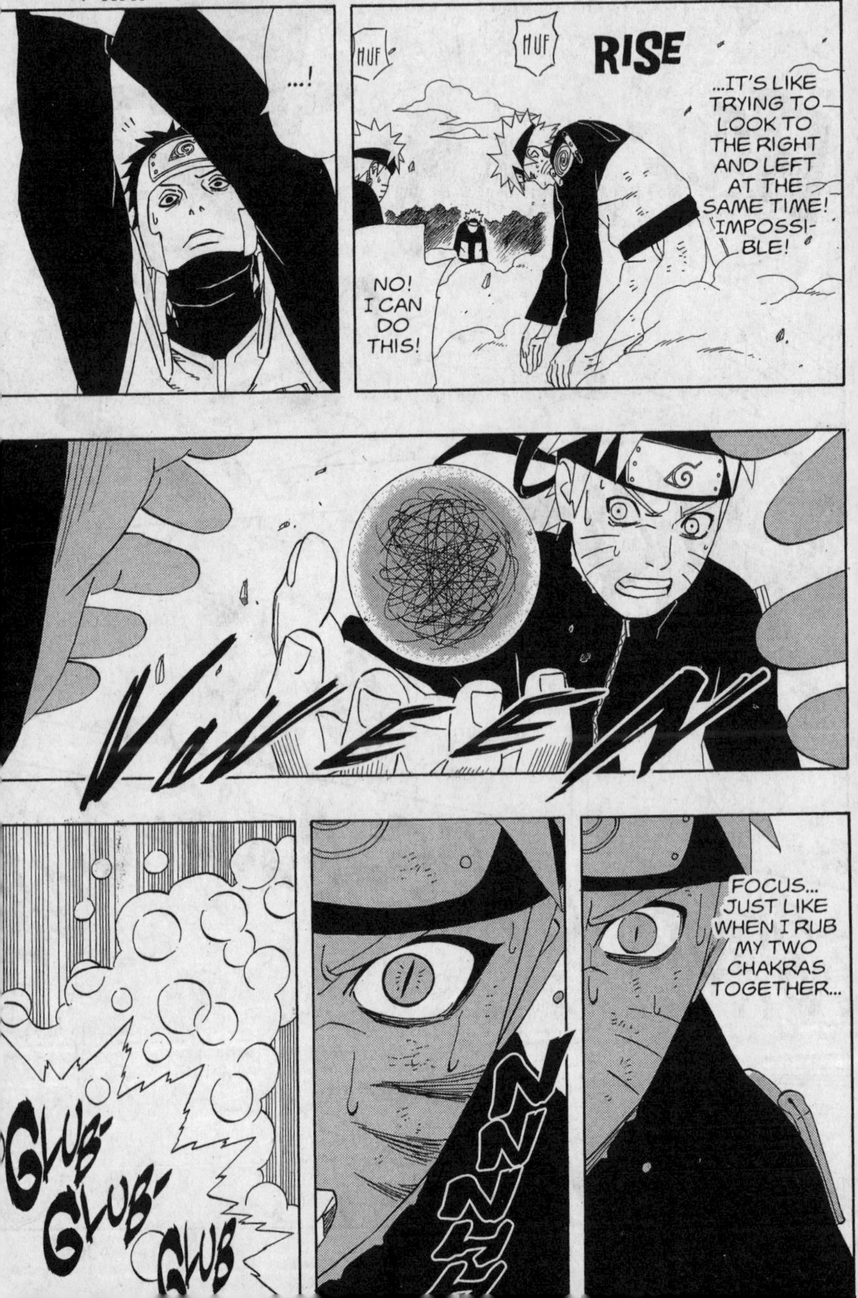

RISE
...IT'S LIKE TRYING TO LOOK TO THE RIGHT AND LEFT AT THE SAME TIME! IMPOSSIBLE!
HUF
HUF
NO! I CAN DO THIS!
...!
VWEEEN
FOCUS... JUST LIKE WHEN I RUB MY TWO CHAKRAS TOGETHER...
NNNHH
GLUB-GLUB-GLUB

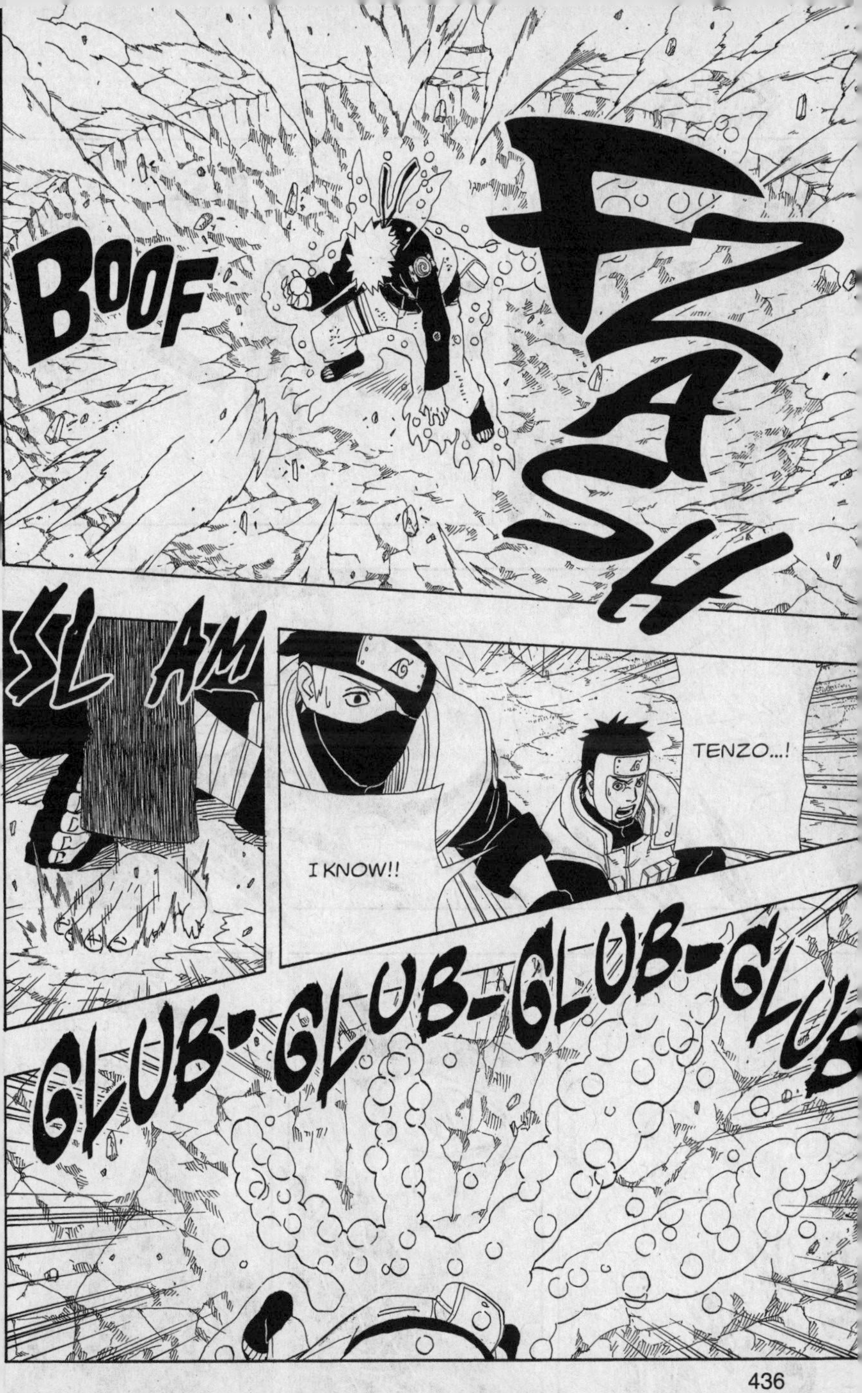
FZASH
BOOF
TENZO...!
I KNOW!!
SLAM
GLUB-GLUB-GLUB-GLUB-GLUB

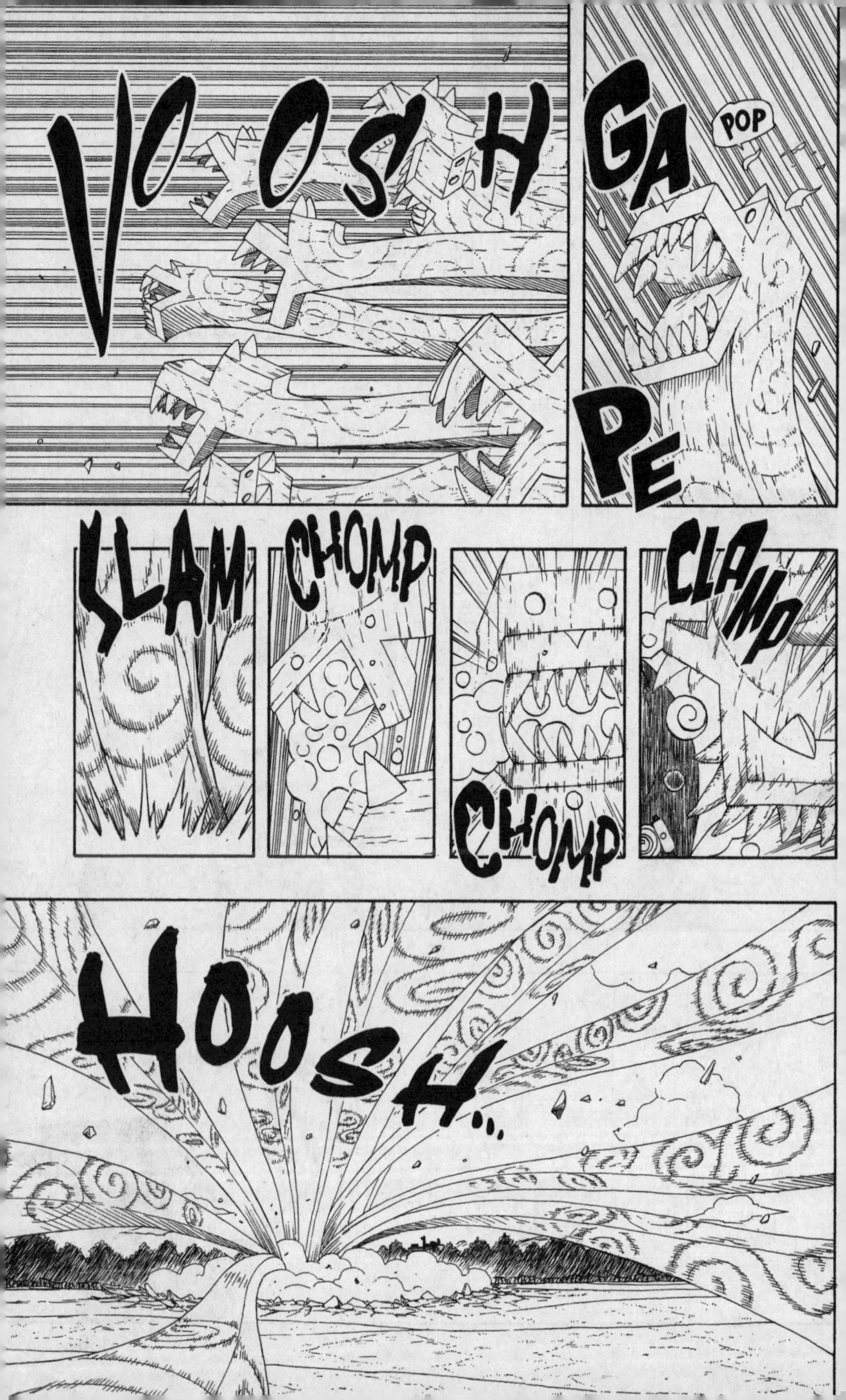
GA
POP
PE
VOOSH
CLAMP
CHOMP
CHOMP
SLAM
HOOSH...

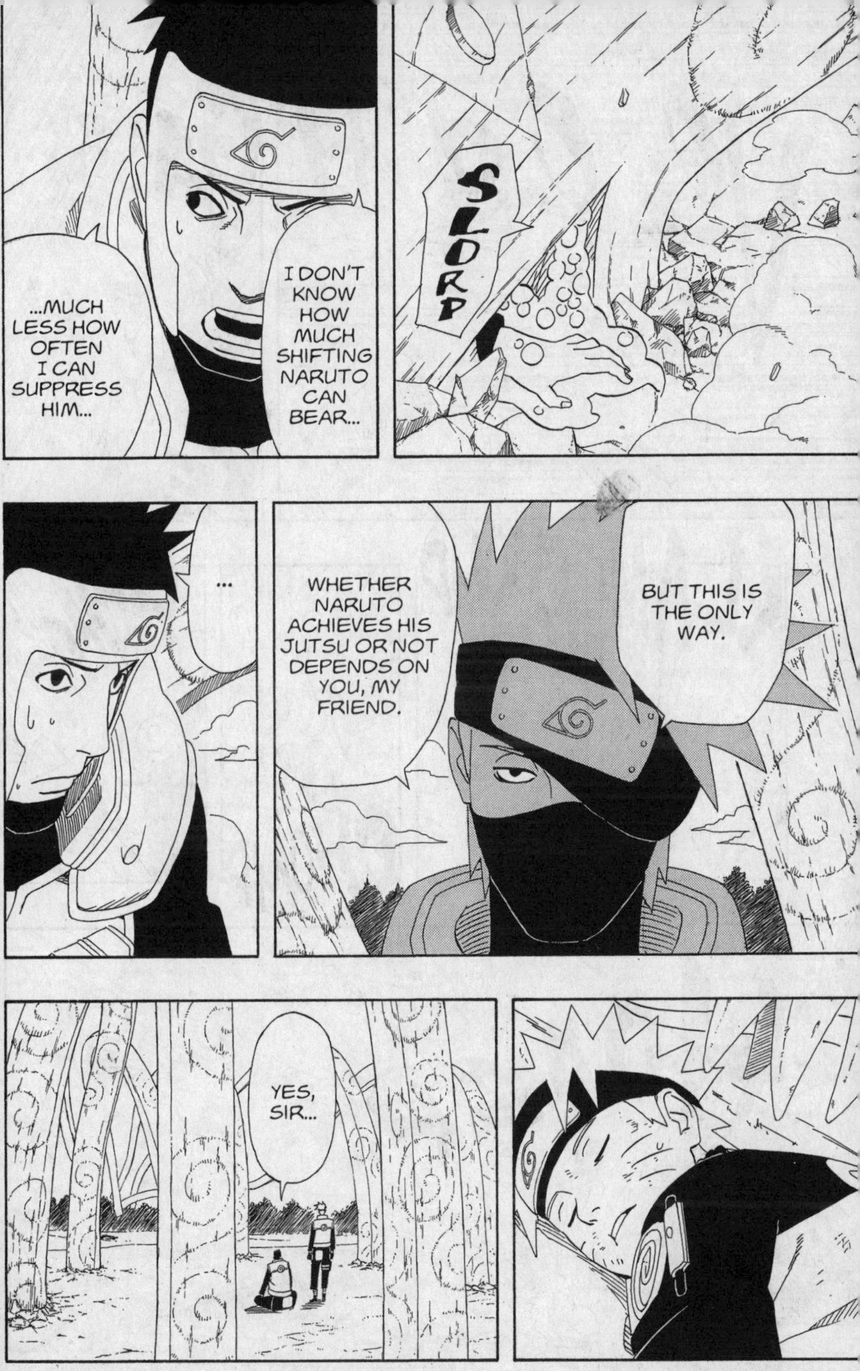
SLORP
I DON'T KNOW HOW MUCH SHIFTING NARUTO CAN BEAR...
...MUCH LESS HOW OFTEN I CAN SUPPRESS HIM...
WHETHER NARUTO ACHIEVES HIS JUTSU OR NOT DEPENDS ON YOU, MY FRIEND.
BUT THIS IS THE ONLY WAY.
...
YES, SIR...

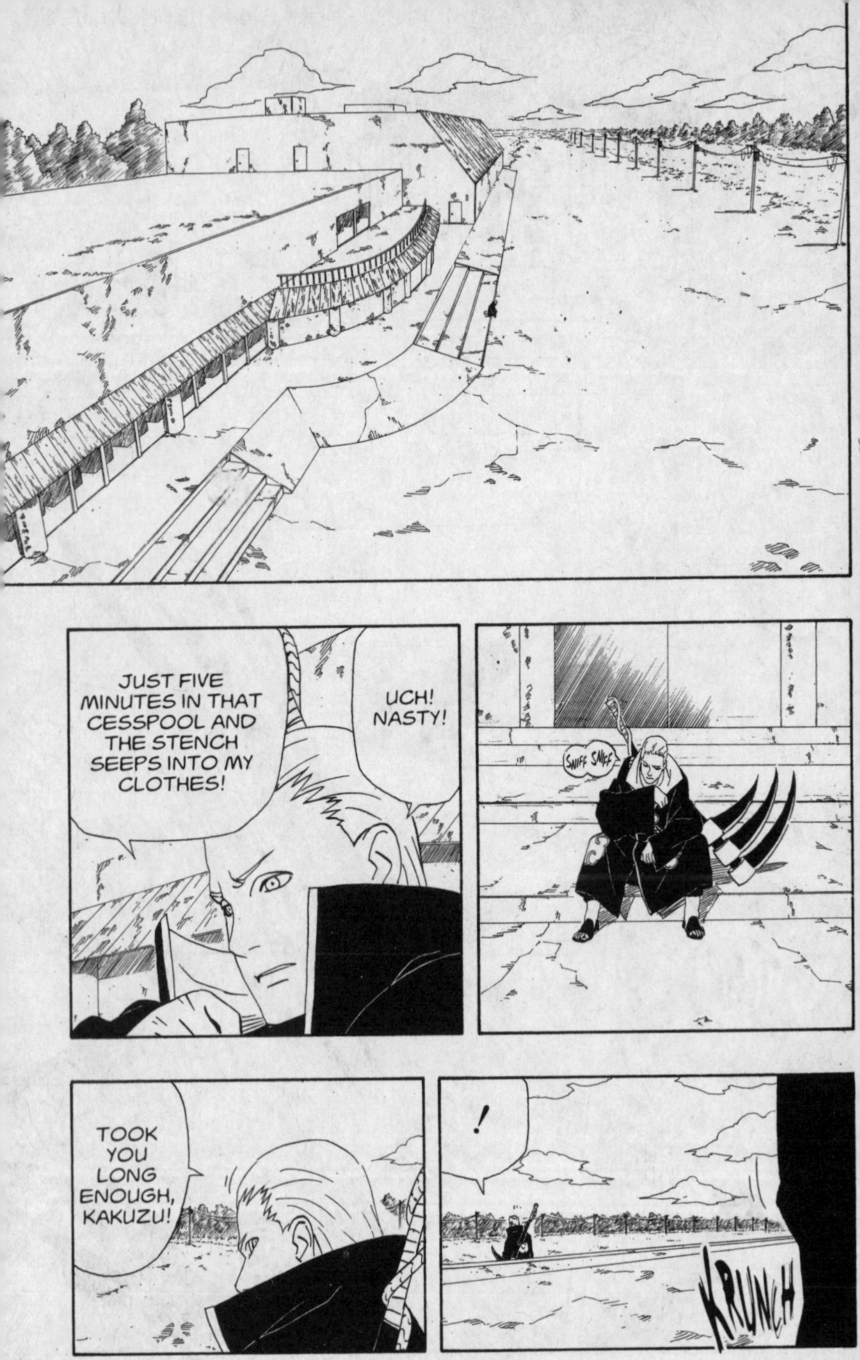
SNIFF SNIFF
UCH! NASTY!
JUST FIVE MINUTES IN THAT CESSPOOL AND THE STENCH SEEPS INTO MY CLOTHES!
!
KRUNCH
TOOK YOU LONG ENOUGH, KAKUZU!

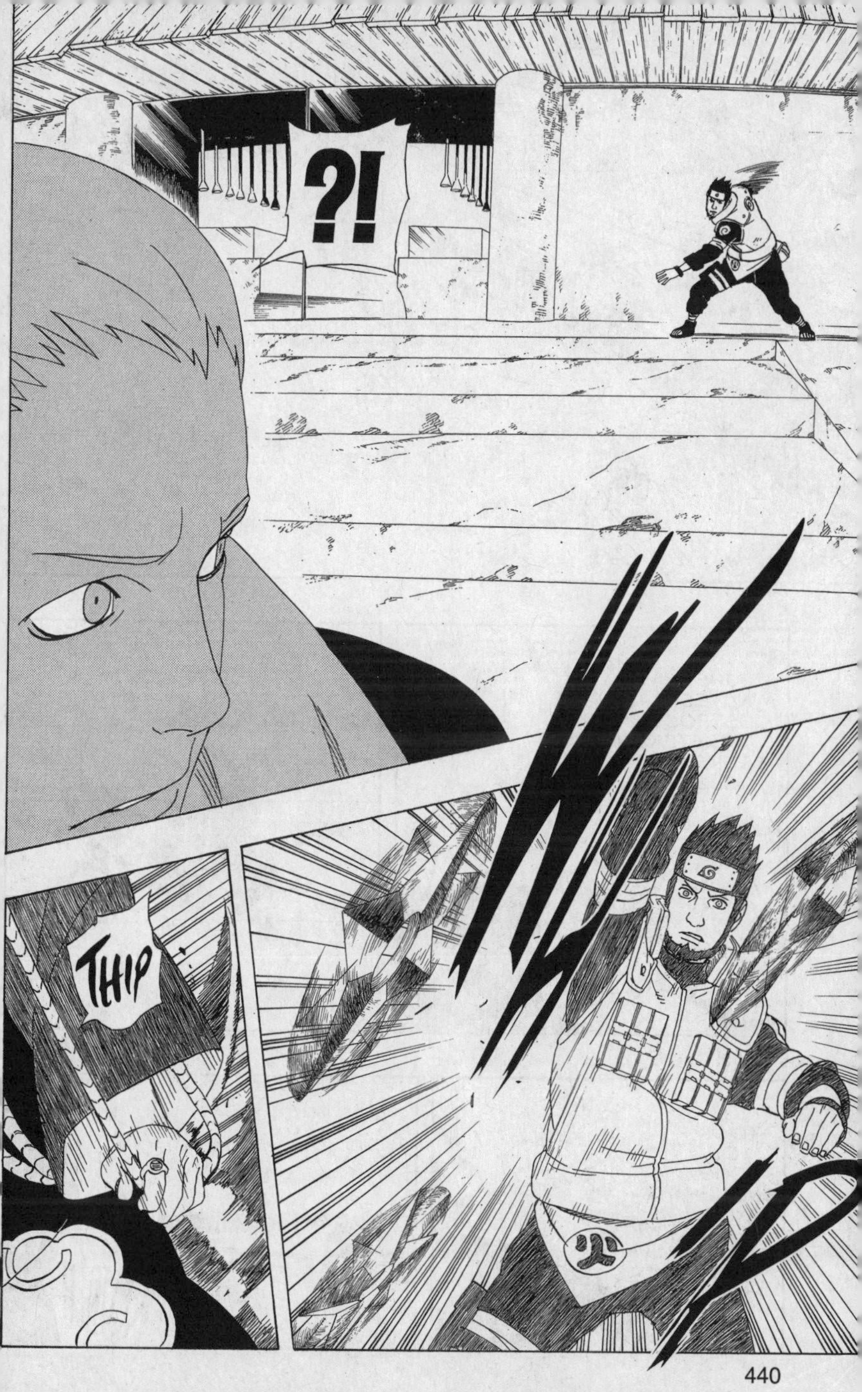
?!
THIP

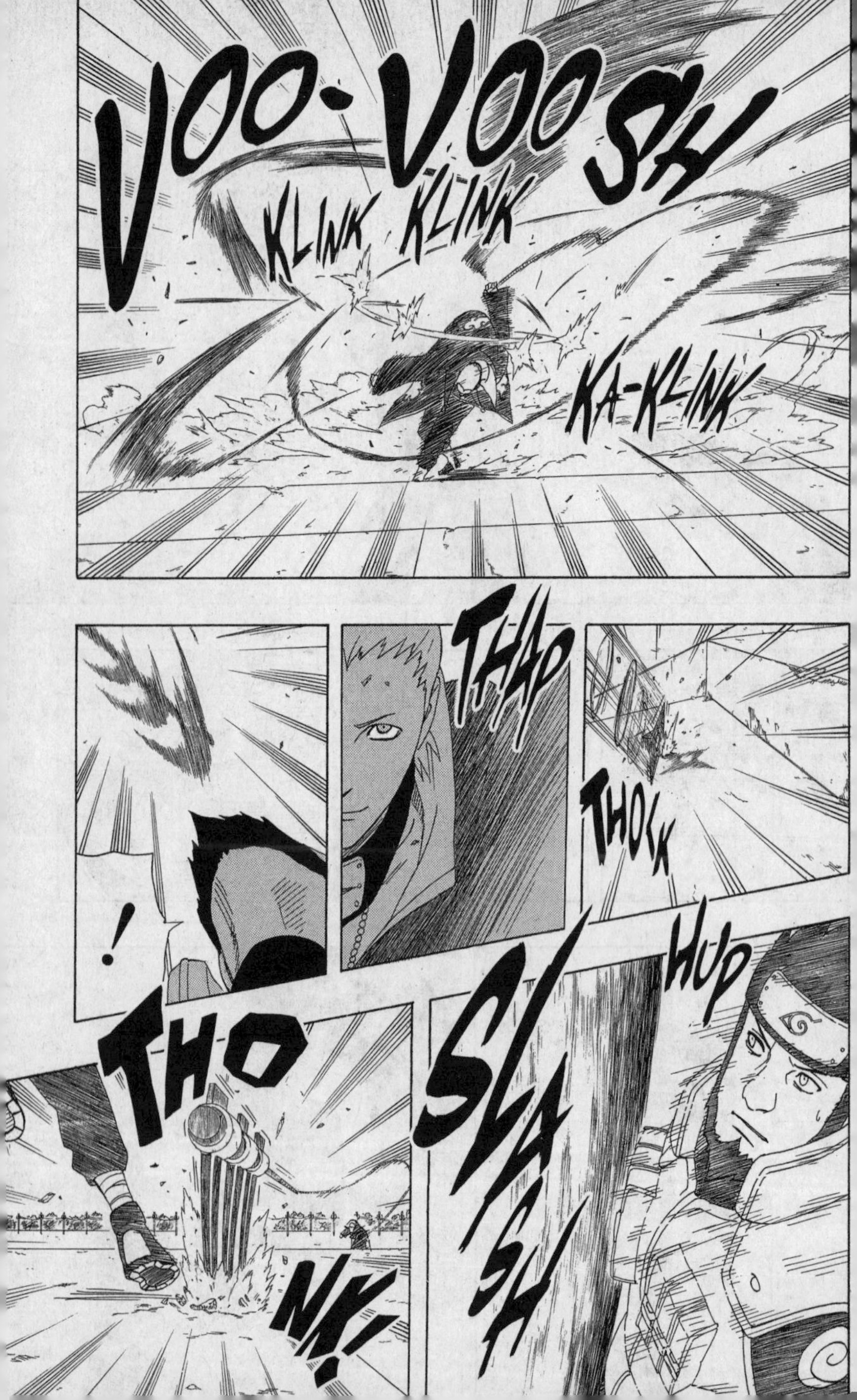
VOO-VOOSH
KLINK KLINK
KA-KLINK
THOCK
THAP
!
HUP
SLASH
THONK!

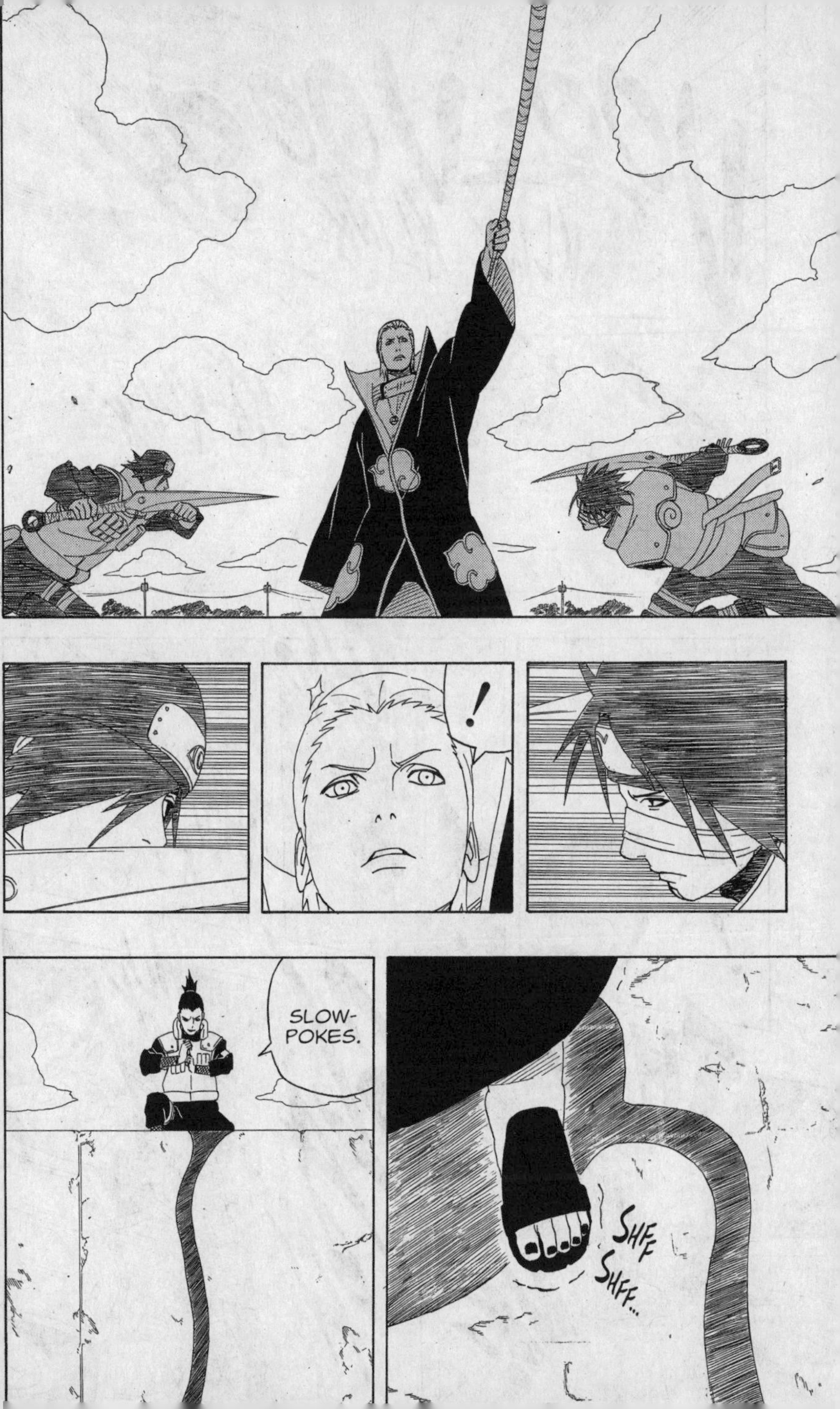
!
SLOW-POKES.
SHFF
SHFF...

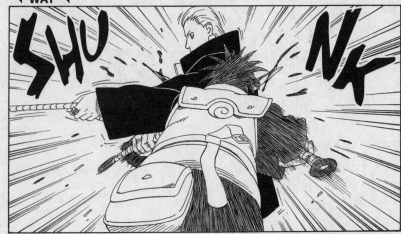

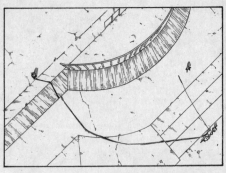

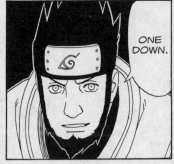

ONE DOWN.

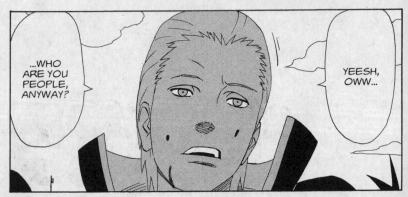

...WHO ARE YOU PEOPLE, ANYWAY?

YEESH, OWW...

443

NARUTO

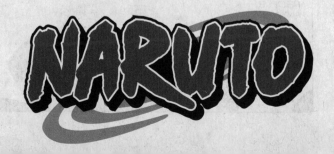

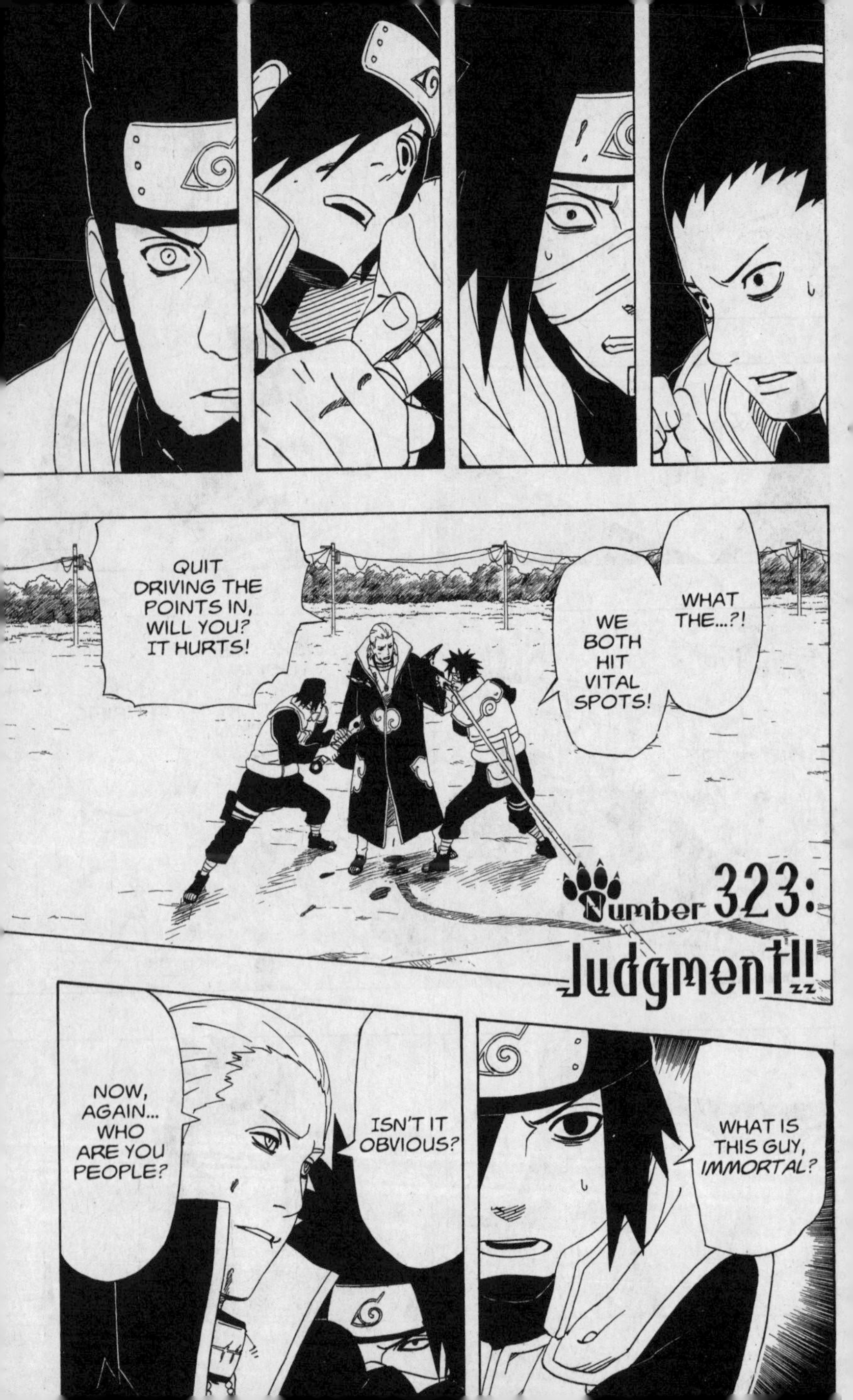
WHAT THE...?!
WE BOTH HIT VITAL SPOTS!
QUIT DRIVING THE POINTS IN, WILL YOU? IT HURTS!
Number 323: Judgment!!
WHAT IS THIS GUY, IMMORTAL?
NOW, AGAIN... WHO ARE YOU PEOPLE?
ISN'T IT OBVIOUS?

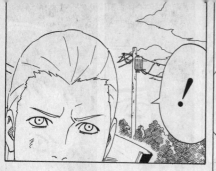

!

...

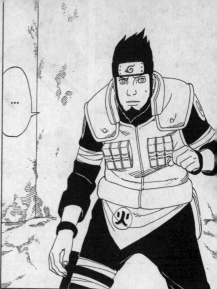

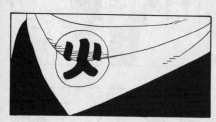

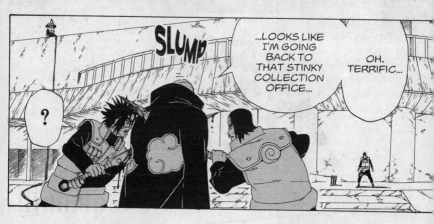

SLUMP

...LOOKS LIKE I'M GOING BACK TO THAT STINKY COLLECTION OFFICE...

OH. TERRIFIC...

?

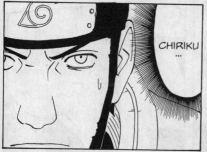

CHIRIKU ...

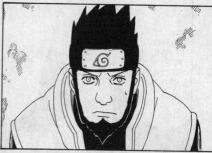

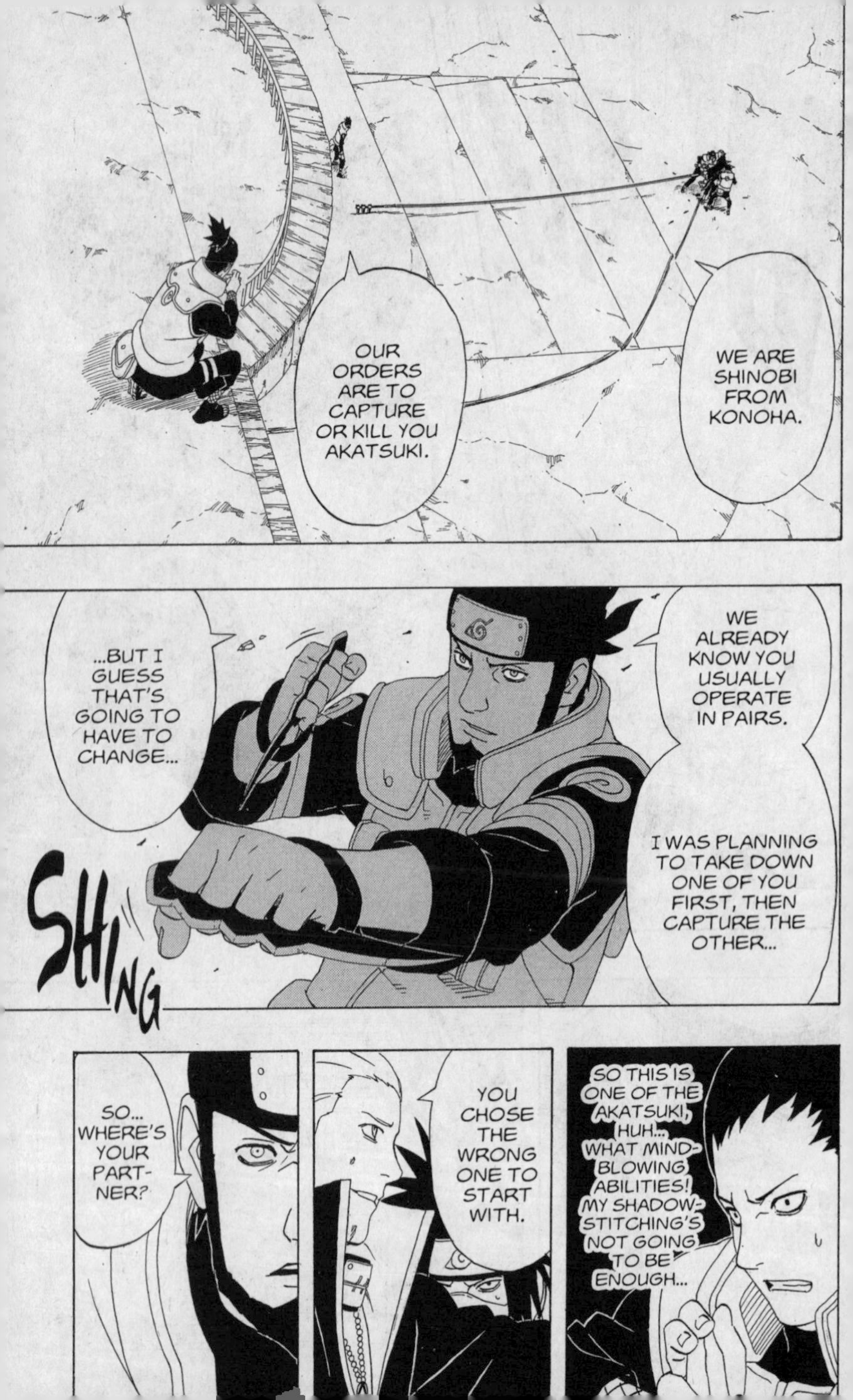
WE ARE SHINOBI FROM KONOHA.
OUR ORDERS ARE TO CAPTURE OR KILL YOU AKATSUKI.
WE ALREADY KNOW YOU USUALLY OPERATE IN PAIRS.
I WAS PLANNING TO TAKE DOWN ONE OF YOU FIRST, THEN CAPTURE THE OTHER...
...BUT I GUESS THAT'S GOING TO HAVE TO CHANGE...
SHING
SO THIS IS ONE OF THE AKATSUKI, HUH... WHAT MIND-BLOWING ABILITIES! MY SHADOW-STITCHING'S NOT GOING TO BE ENOUGH...
YOU CHOSE THE WRONG ONE TO START WITH.
SO... WHERE'S YOUR PART-NER?

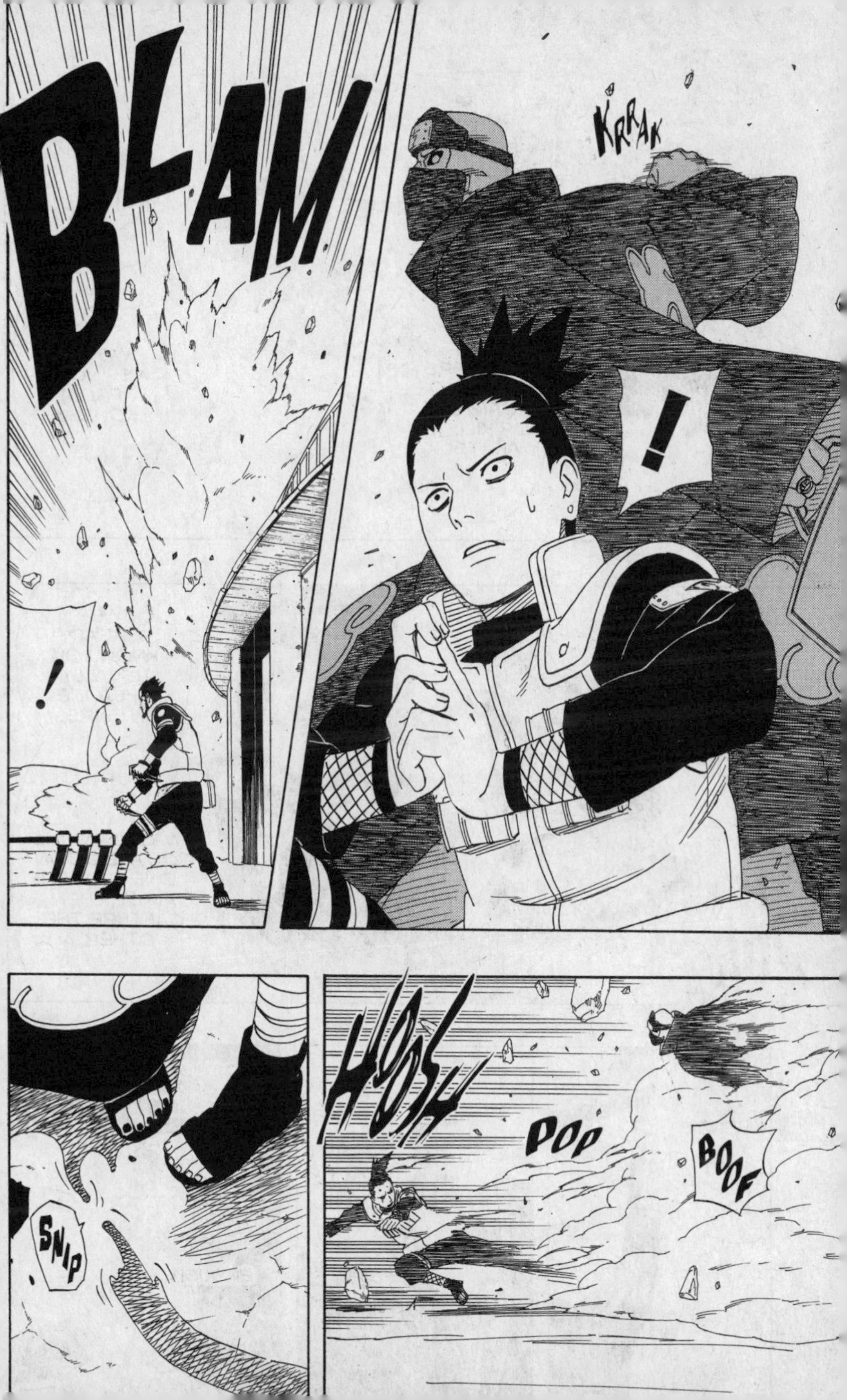
KRRAK
!
BLAM
!
HOSH
POP
BOOF
SNIP

READ THIS WAY

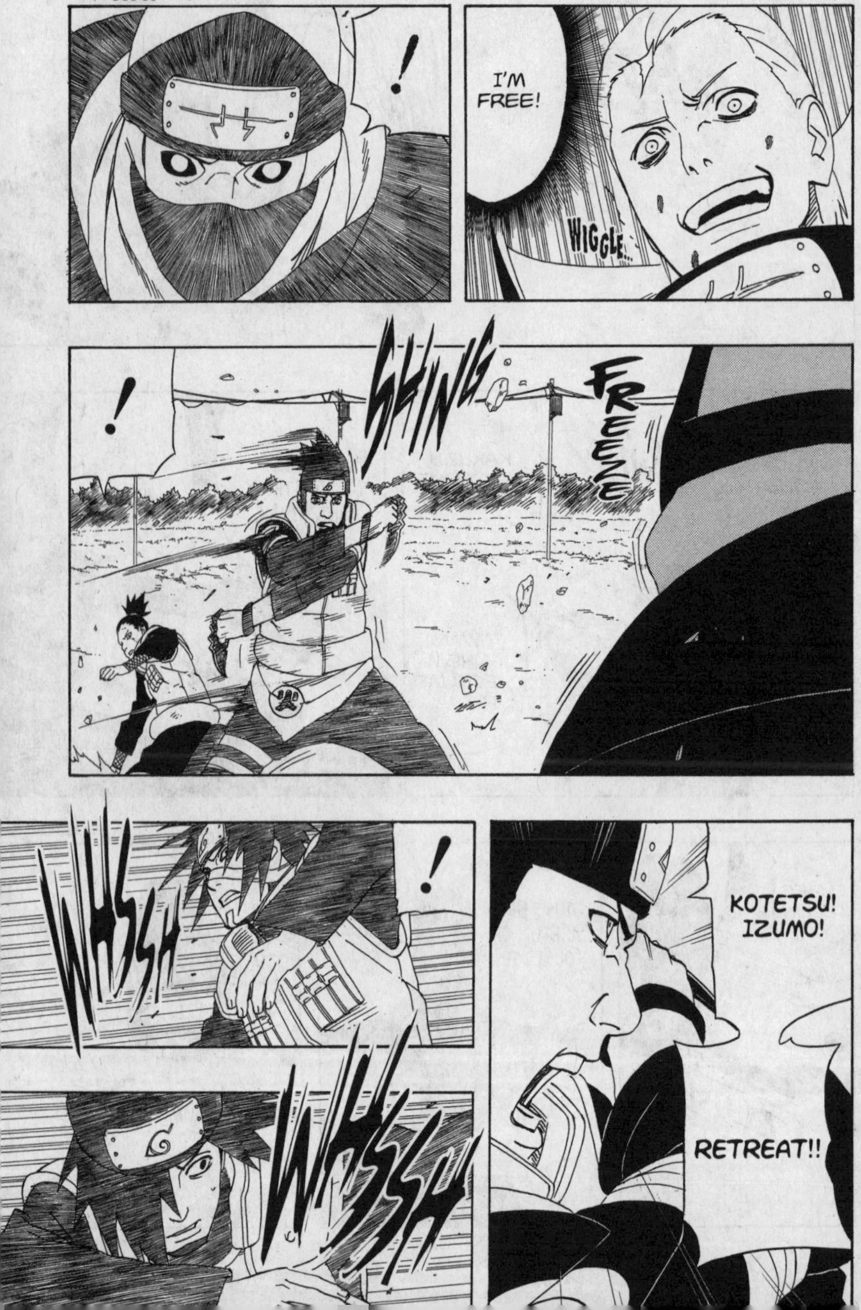
I'M FREE!
WIGGLE...
!
FREEZE
SKING
!
KOTETSU! IZUMO!
RETREAT!!
!
WHSH
WHSSH

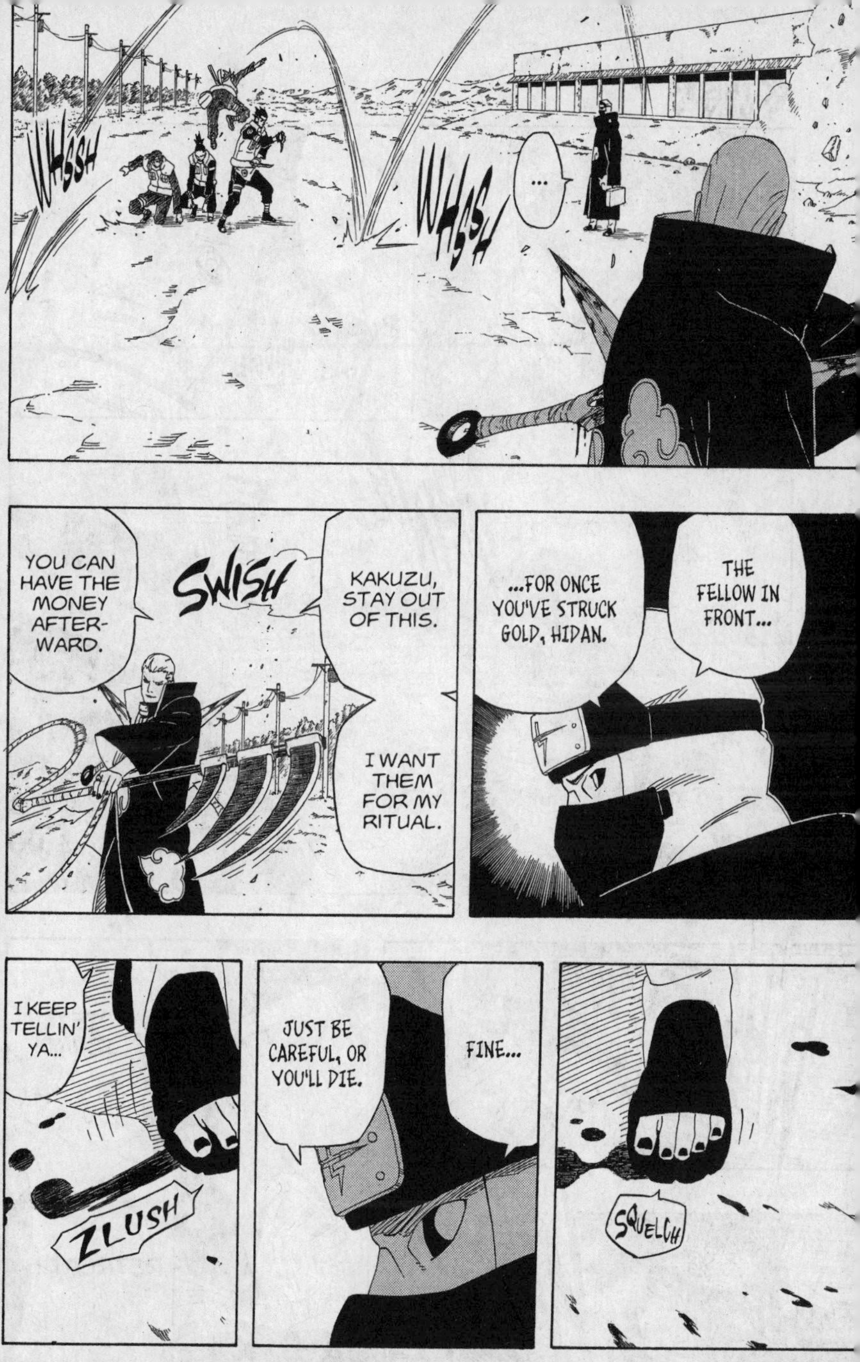
...
WHSSH
WHSSH
THE FELLOW IN FRONT...
...FOR ONCE YOU'VE STRUCK GOLD, HIDAN.
KAKUZU, STAY OUT OF THIS.
I WANT THEM FOR MY RITUAL.
SWISH
YOU CAN HAVE THE MONEY AFTER-WARD.
SQUELCH
FINE...
JUST BE CAREFUL, OR YOU'LL DIE.
I KEEP TELLIN' YA...
ZLUSH

READ THIS WAY

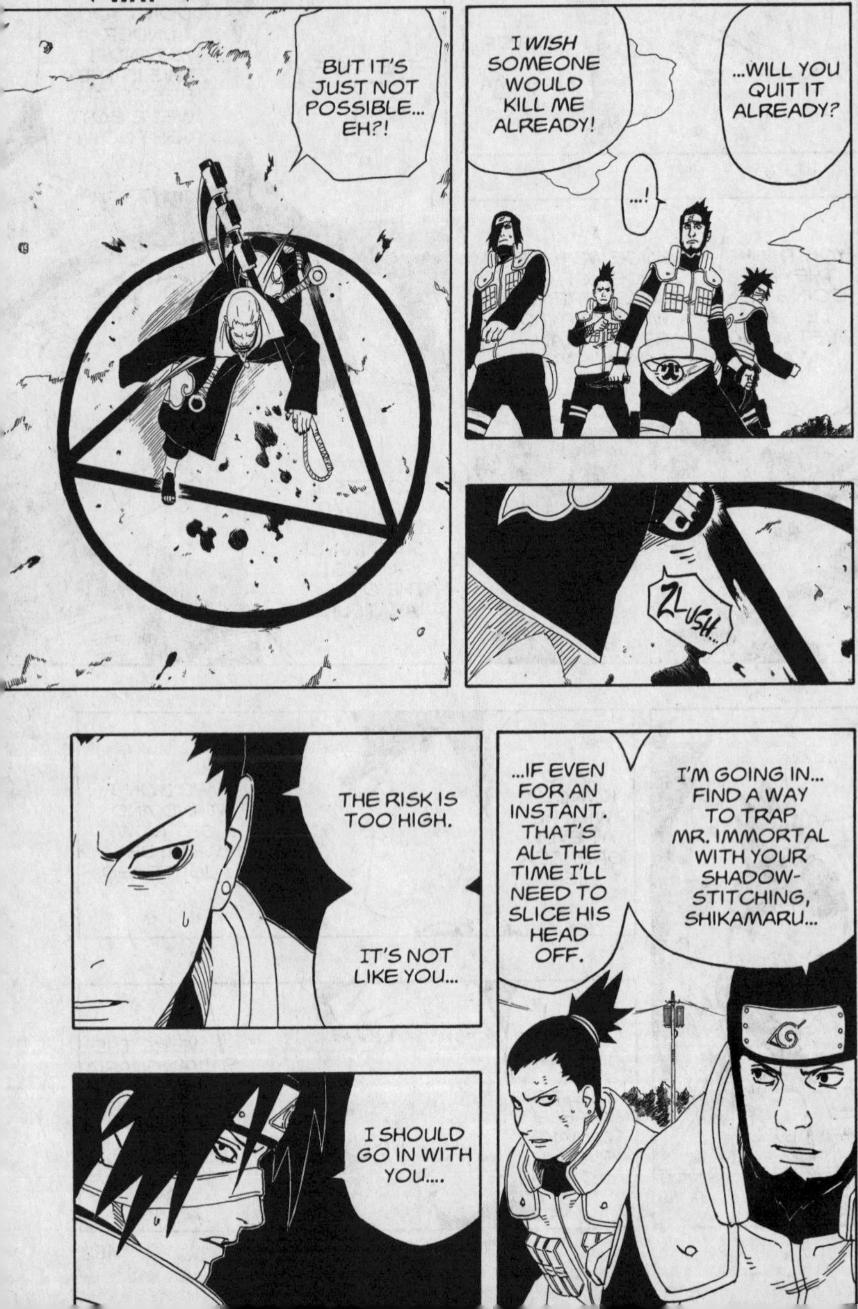
...WILL YOU QUIT IT ALREADY?
I WISH SOMEONE WOULD KILL ME ALREADY!
...!
ZLUSH...
BUT IT'S JUST NOT POSSIBLE... EH?!
I'M GOING IN... FIND A WAY TO TRAP MR. IMMORTAL WITH YOUR SHADOW-STITCHING, SHIKAMARU...
...IF EVEN FOR AN INSTANT. THAT'S ALL THE TIME I'LL NEED TO SLICE HIS HEAD OFF.
THE RISK IS TOO HIGH.
IT'S NOT LIKE YOU...
I SHOULD GO IN WITH YOU....

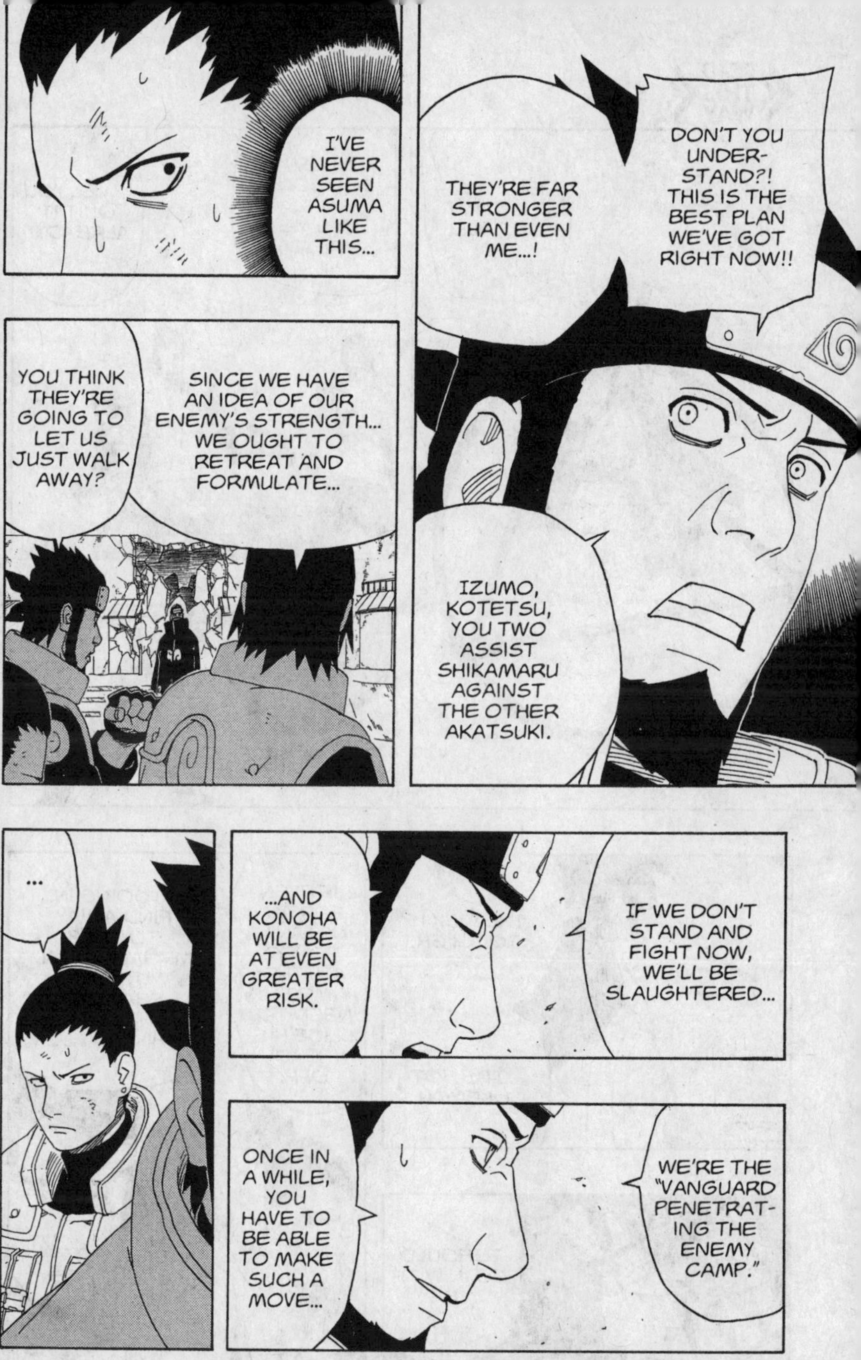
DON'T YOU UNDER-STAND?! THIS IS THE BEST PLAN WE'VE GOT RIGHT NOW!!
THEY'RE FAR STRONGER THAN EVEN ME...!
IZUMO, KOTETSU, YOU TWO ASSIST SHIKAMARU AGAINST THE OTHER AKATSUKI.
I'VE NEVER SEEN ASUMA LIKE THIS...
SINCE WE HAVE AN IDEA OF OUR ENEMY'S STRENGTH... WE OUGHT TO RETREAT AND FORMULATE...
YOU THINK THEY'RE GOING TO LET US JUST WALK AWAY?
IF WE DON'T STAND AND FIGHT NOW, WE'LL BE SLAUGHTERED...
...AND KONOHA WILL BE AT EVEN GREATER RISK.
WE'RE THE "VANGUARD PENETRAT-ING THE ENEMY CAMP."
ONCE IN A WHILE, YOU HAVE TO BE ABLE TO MAKE SUCH A MOVE...
...

READ THIS WAY

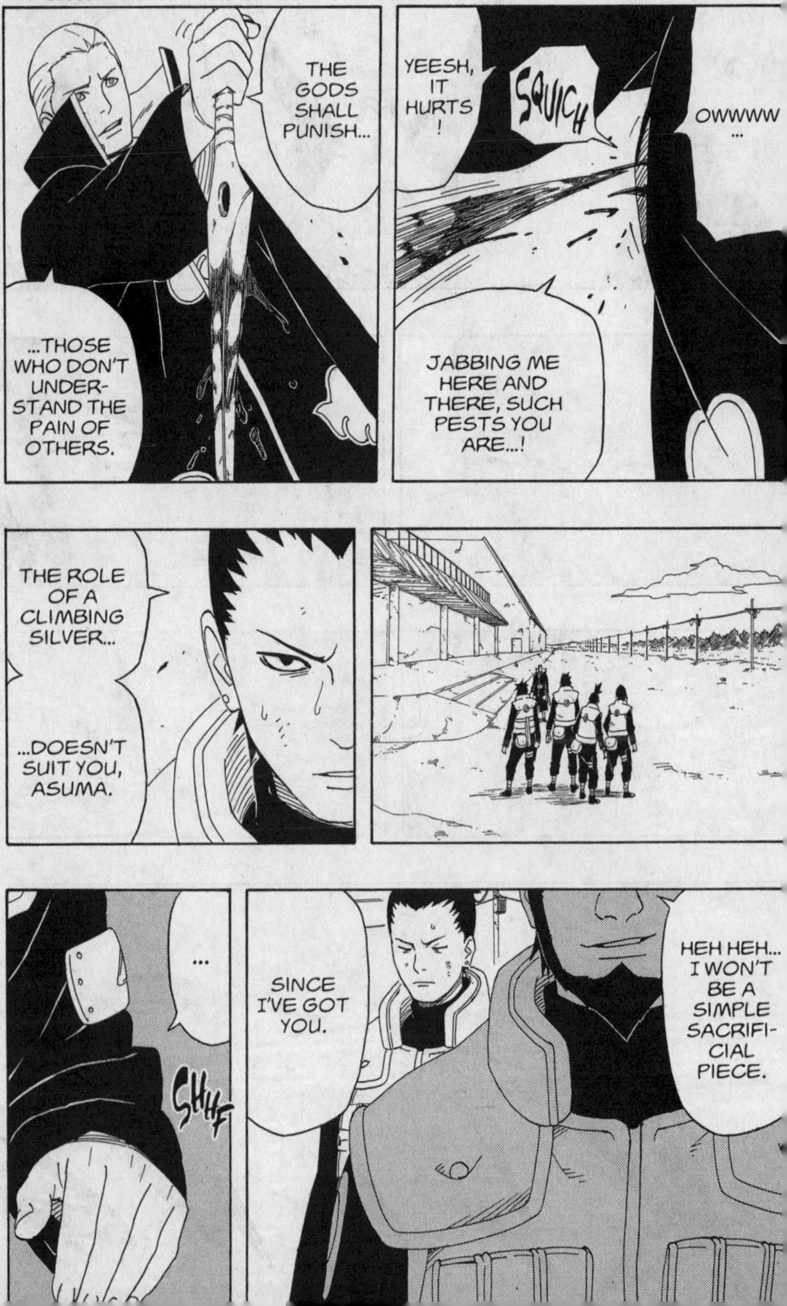
OWWWW...
SQUICH
YEESH, IT HURTS!
JABBING ME HERE AND THERE, SUCH PESTS YOU ARE...!
THE GODS SHALL PUNISH...
...THOSE WHO DON'T UNDER-STAND THE PAIN OF OTHERS.
THE ROLE OF A CLIMBING SILVER...
...DOESN'T SUIT YOU, ASUMA.
HEH HEH... I WON'T BE A SIMPLE SACRIFI-CIAL PIECE.
SINCE I'VE GOT YOU.
...
SHHF

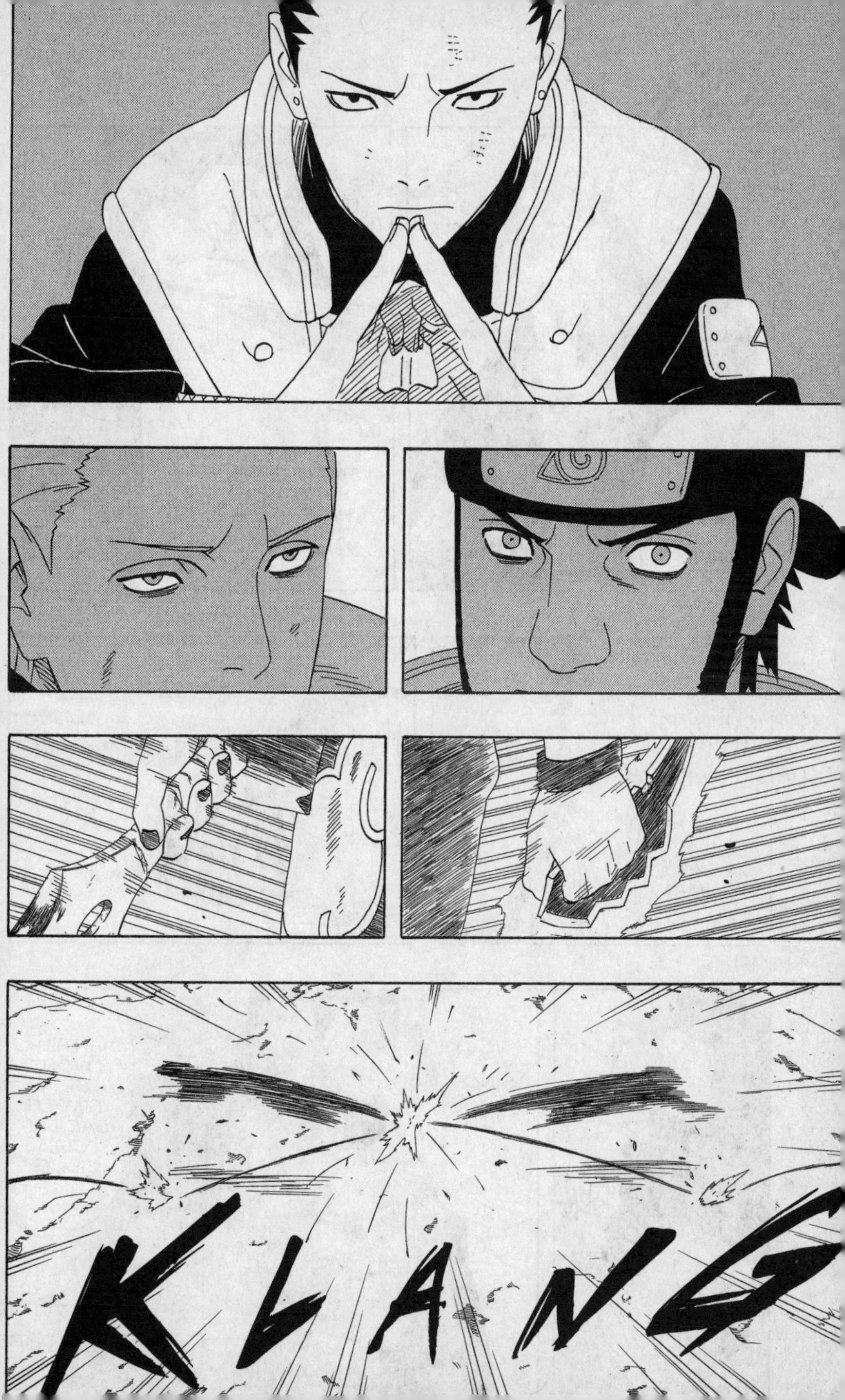
KLANG

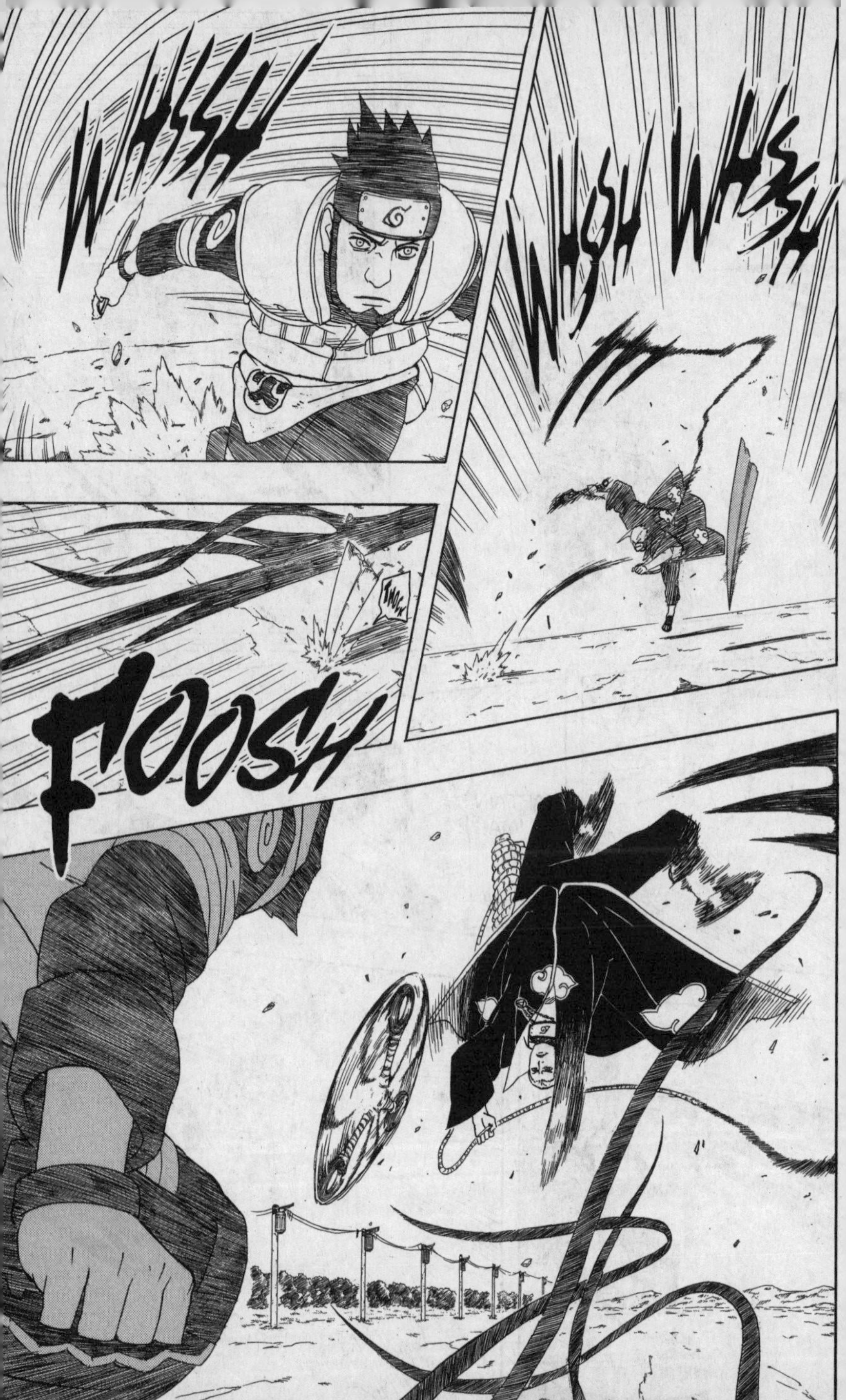
WHSH WHSH
WHSH
THOCK
FOOSH

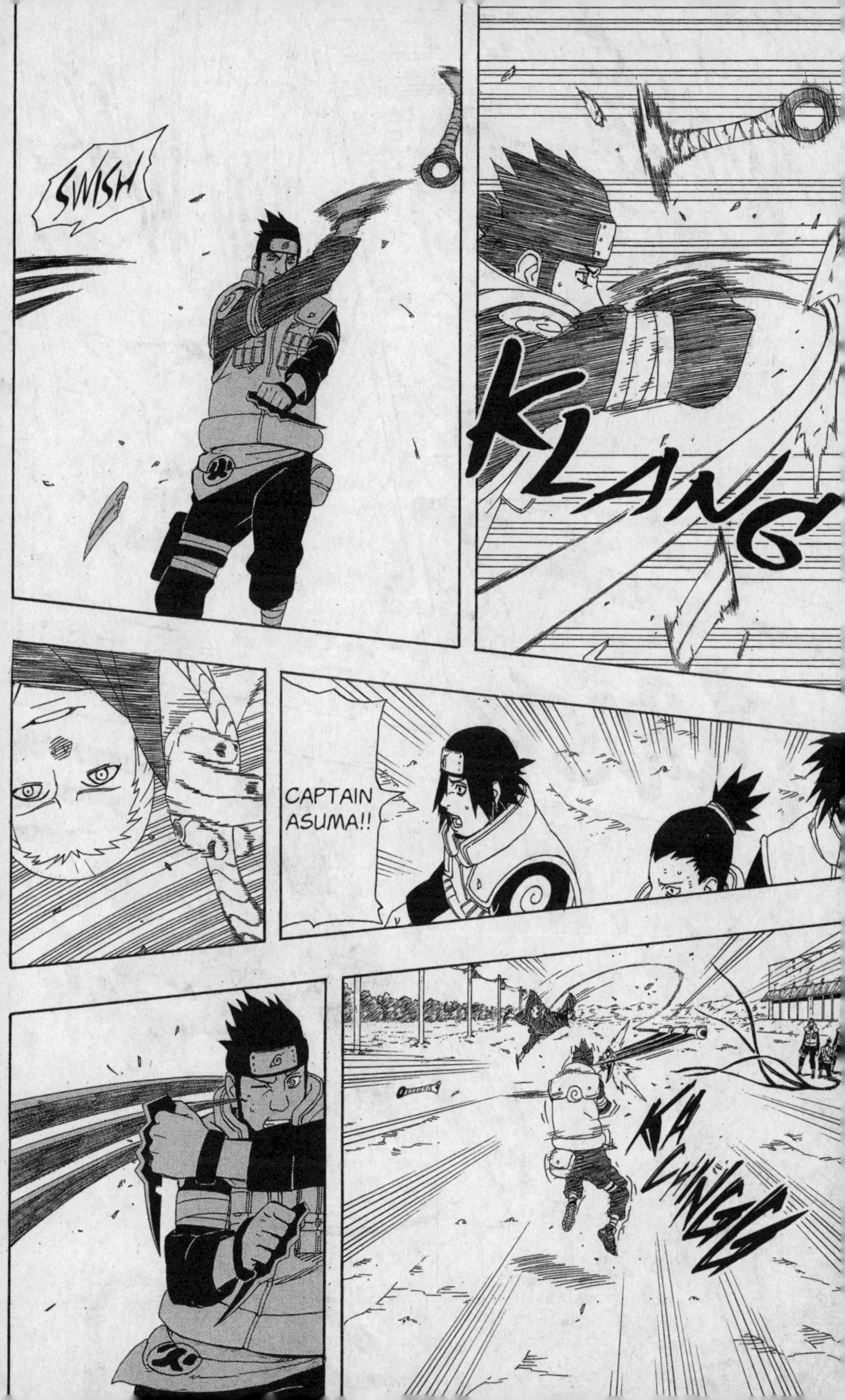
KLANG
SWISH
CAPTAIN ASUMA!!
KA CLINGG

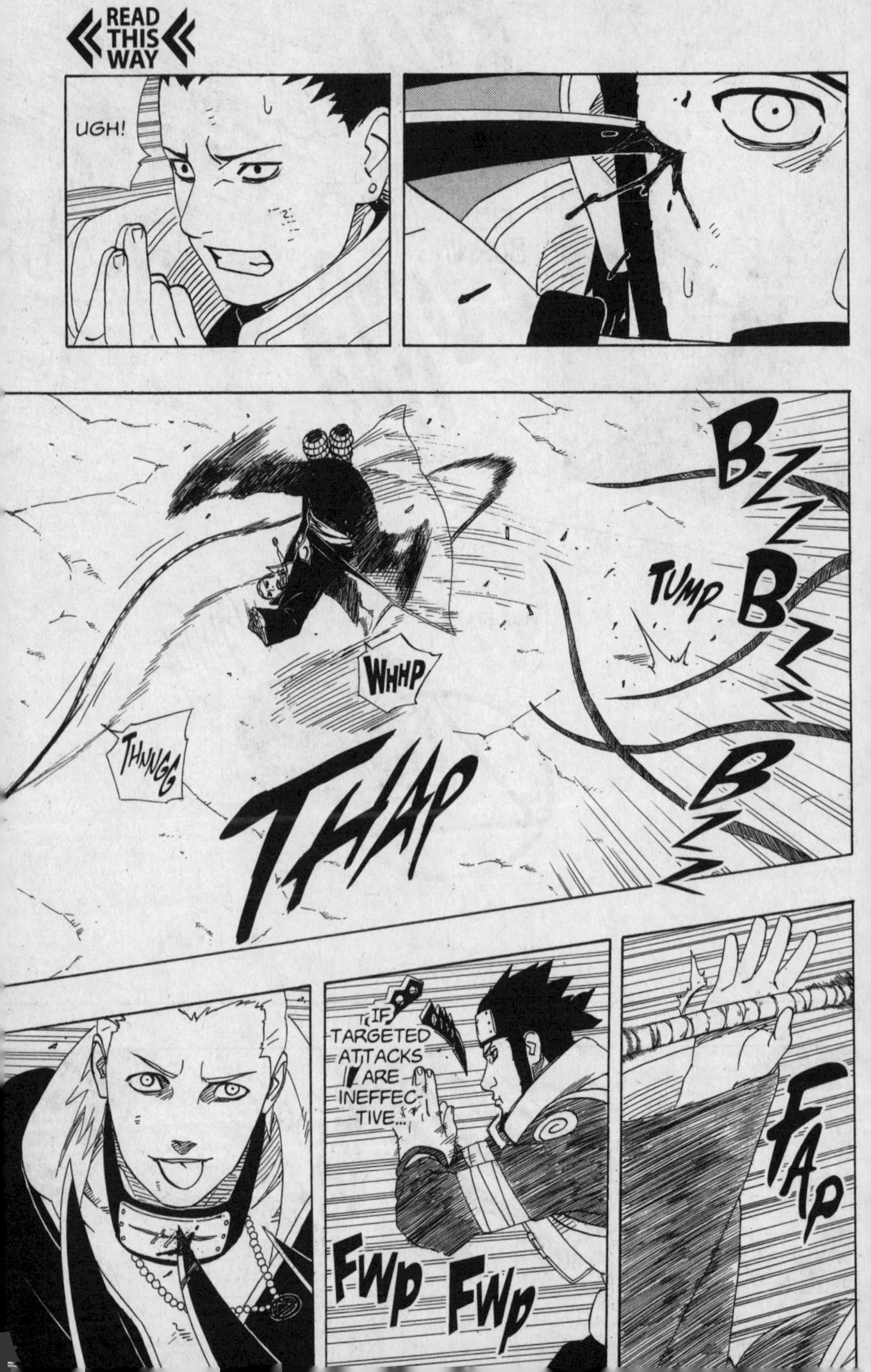
READ THIS WAY
UGH!
BZZZ
TUMP
BZZZ
BZZZ
WHHP
THAP
THNNGG
FAP
IF TARGETED ATTACKS ARE INEFFECTIVE...
FWP FWP

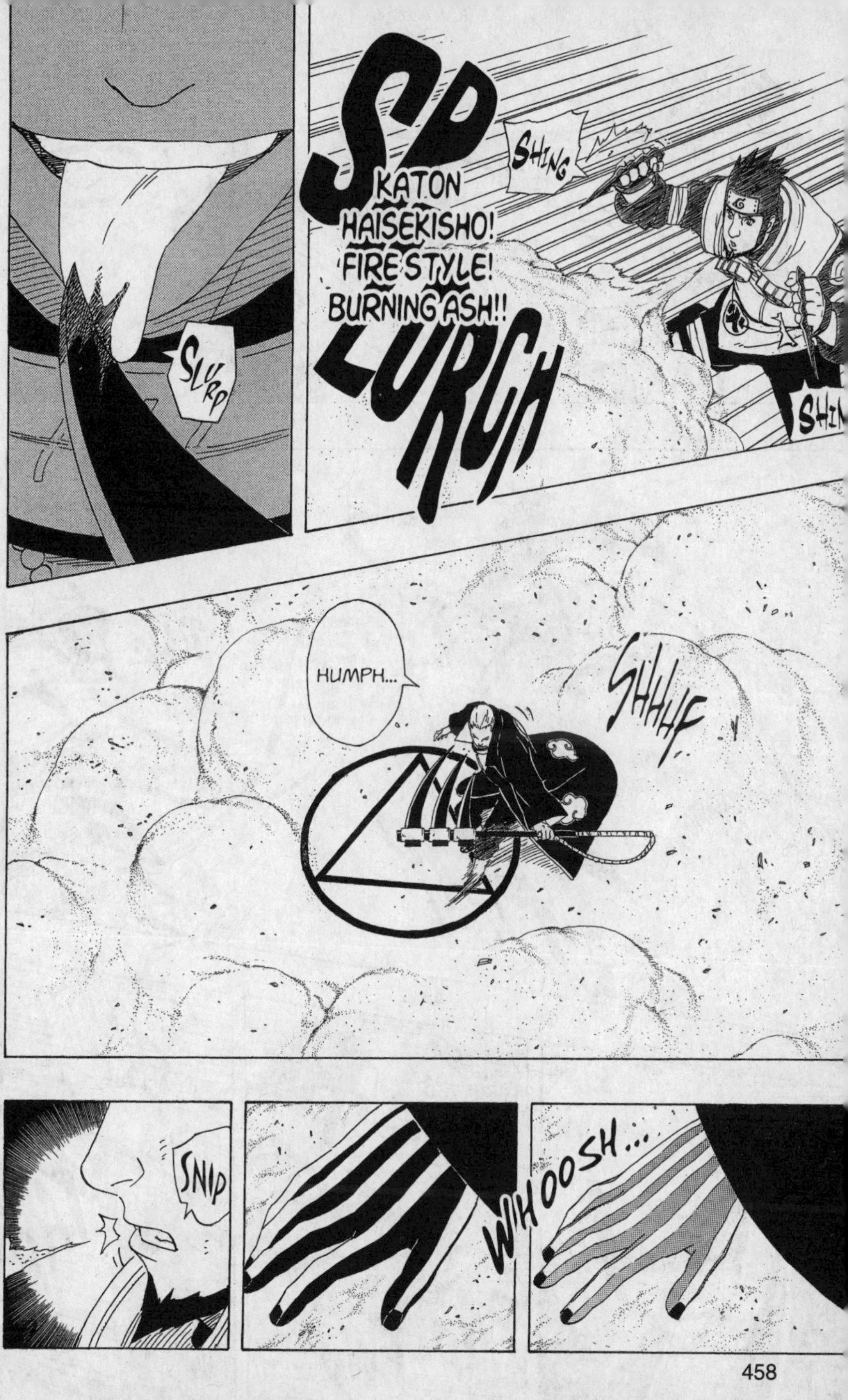
SHING
SHIN
KATON HAISEKISHO! FIRE STYLE! BURNING ASH!!
SP
LURCH
SLURP
HUMPH...
SHHHF
WHOOSH...
SNIP

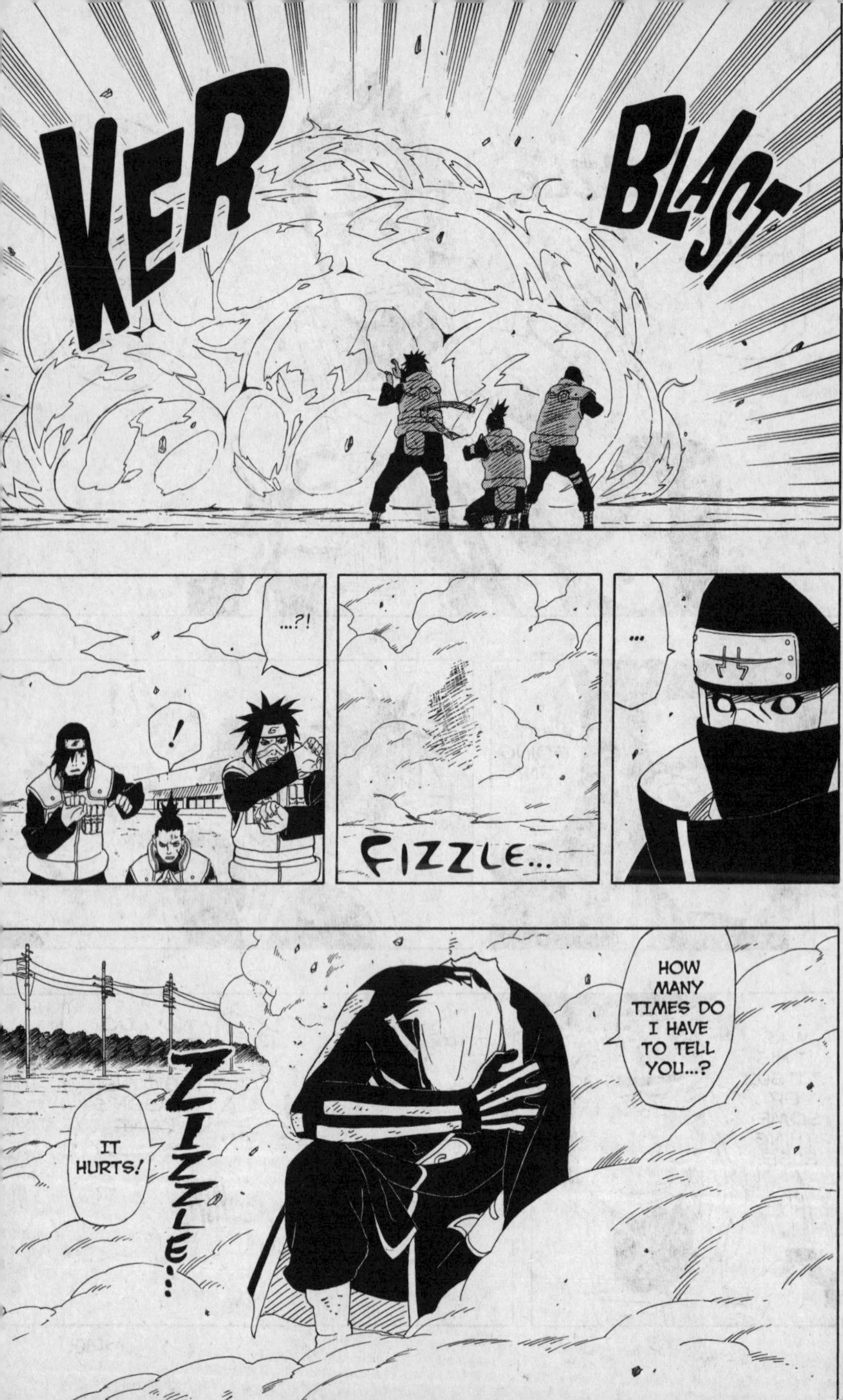
KER BLAST
...
FIZZLE...
...?!
!
HOW MANY TIMES DO I HAVE TO TELL YOU...?
ZIZZLE...
IT HURTS!

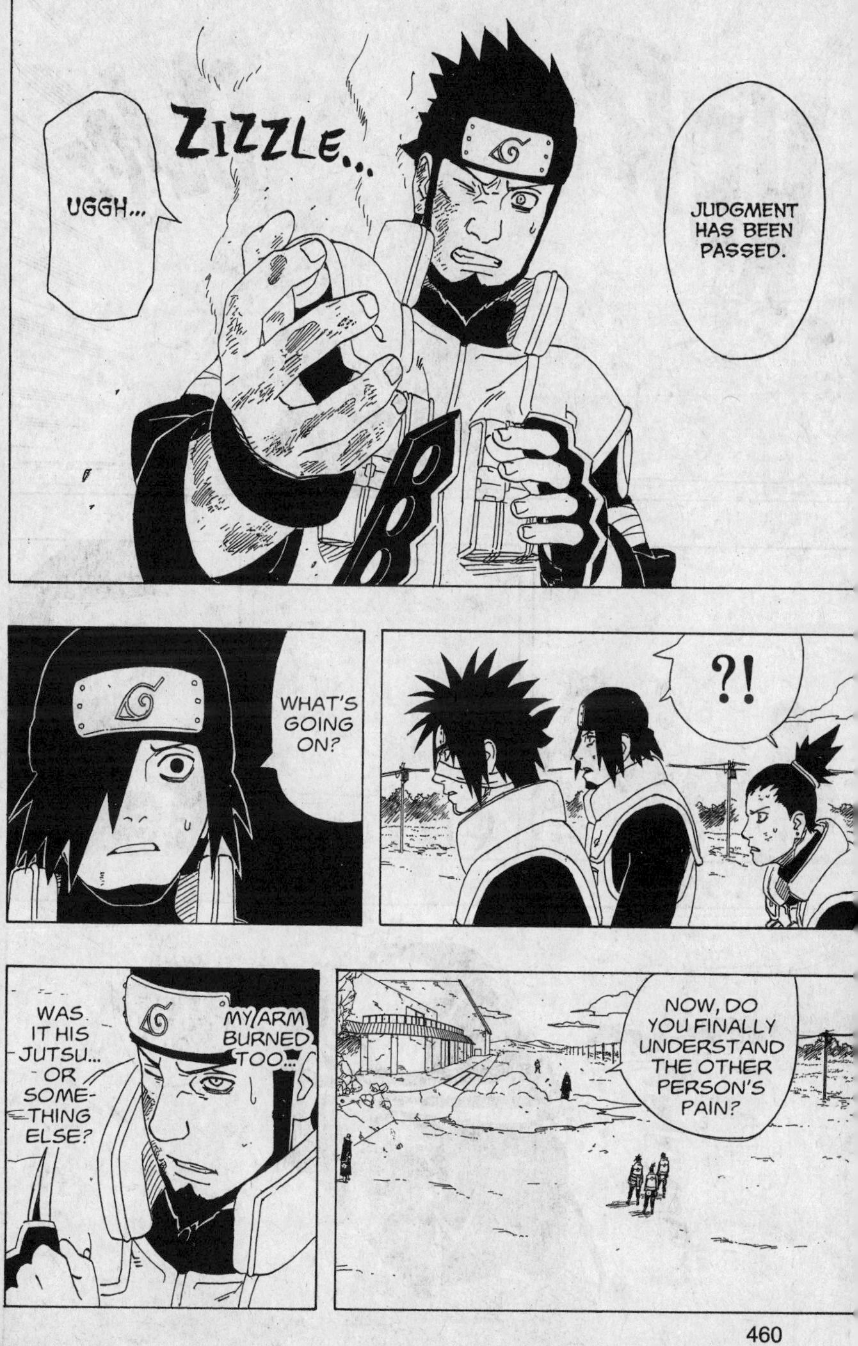
JUDGMENT HAS BEEN PASSED.
ZIZZLE...
UGGH...
?!
WHAT'S GOING ON?
NOW, DO YOU FINALLY UNDERSTAND THE OTHER PERSON'S PAIN?
MY ARM BURNED TOO...
WAS IT HIS JUTSU... OR SOMETHING ELSE?

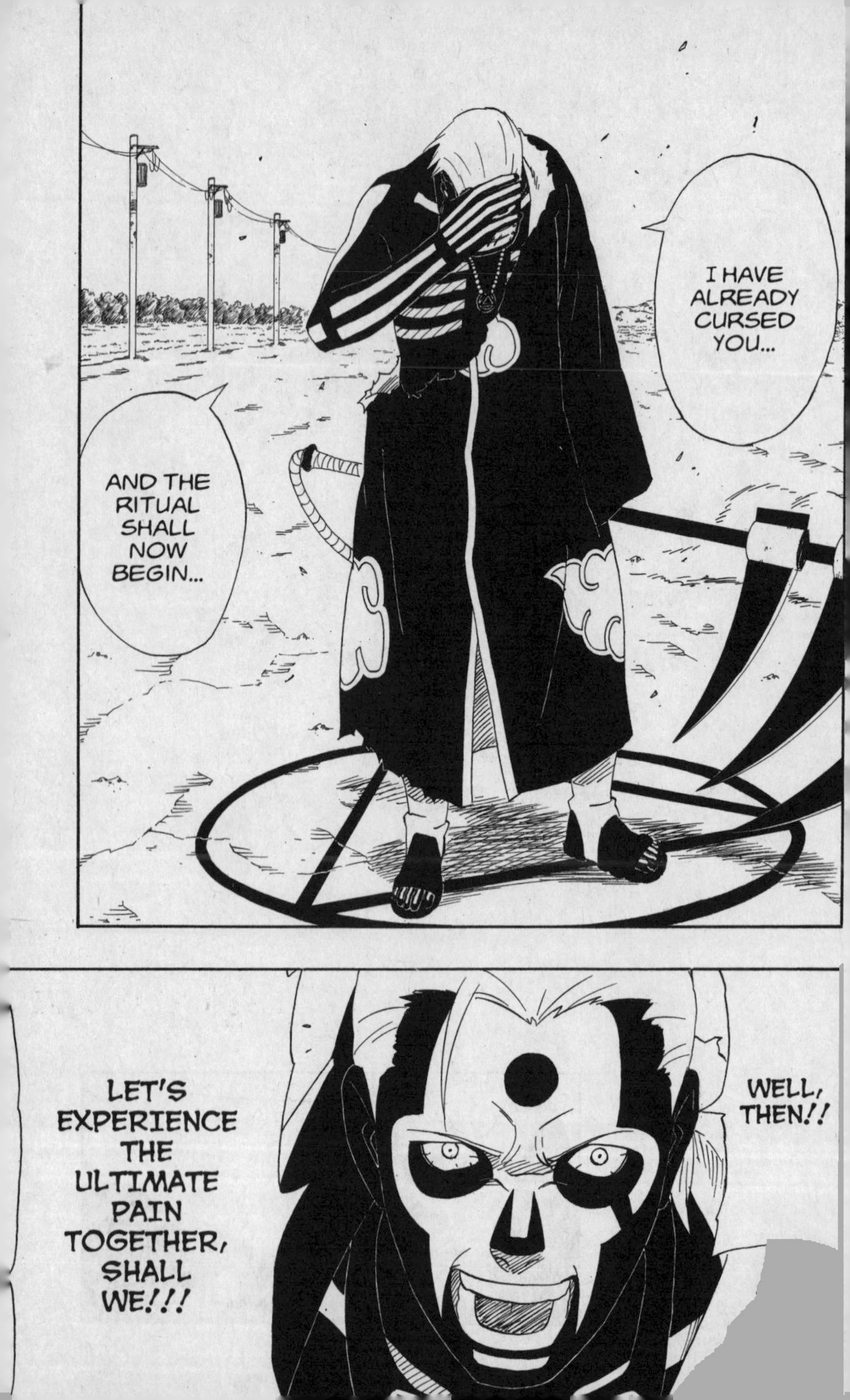
I HAVE ALREADY CURSED YOU...
AND THE RITUAL SHALL NOW BEGIN...
WELL, THEN!!
LET'S EXPERIENCE THE ULTIMATE PAIN TOGETHER, SHALL WE!!!

火

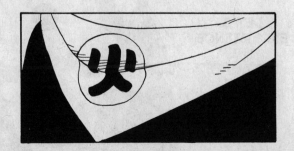

Number 324: Shikamaru's Analysis!!

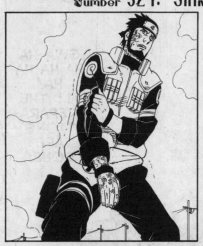

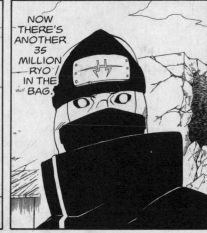

NOW THERE'S ANOTHER 35 MILLION RYO IN THE BAG.

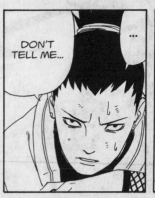

DON'T TELL ME...

...

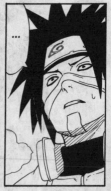

...

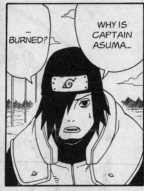

...BURNED?

WHY IS CAPTAIN ASUMA...

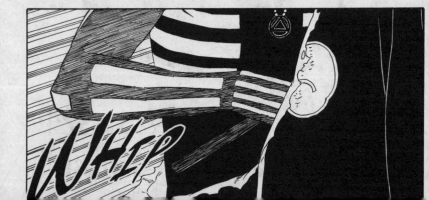

WHIP

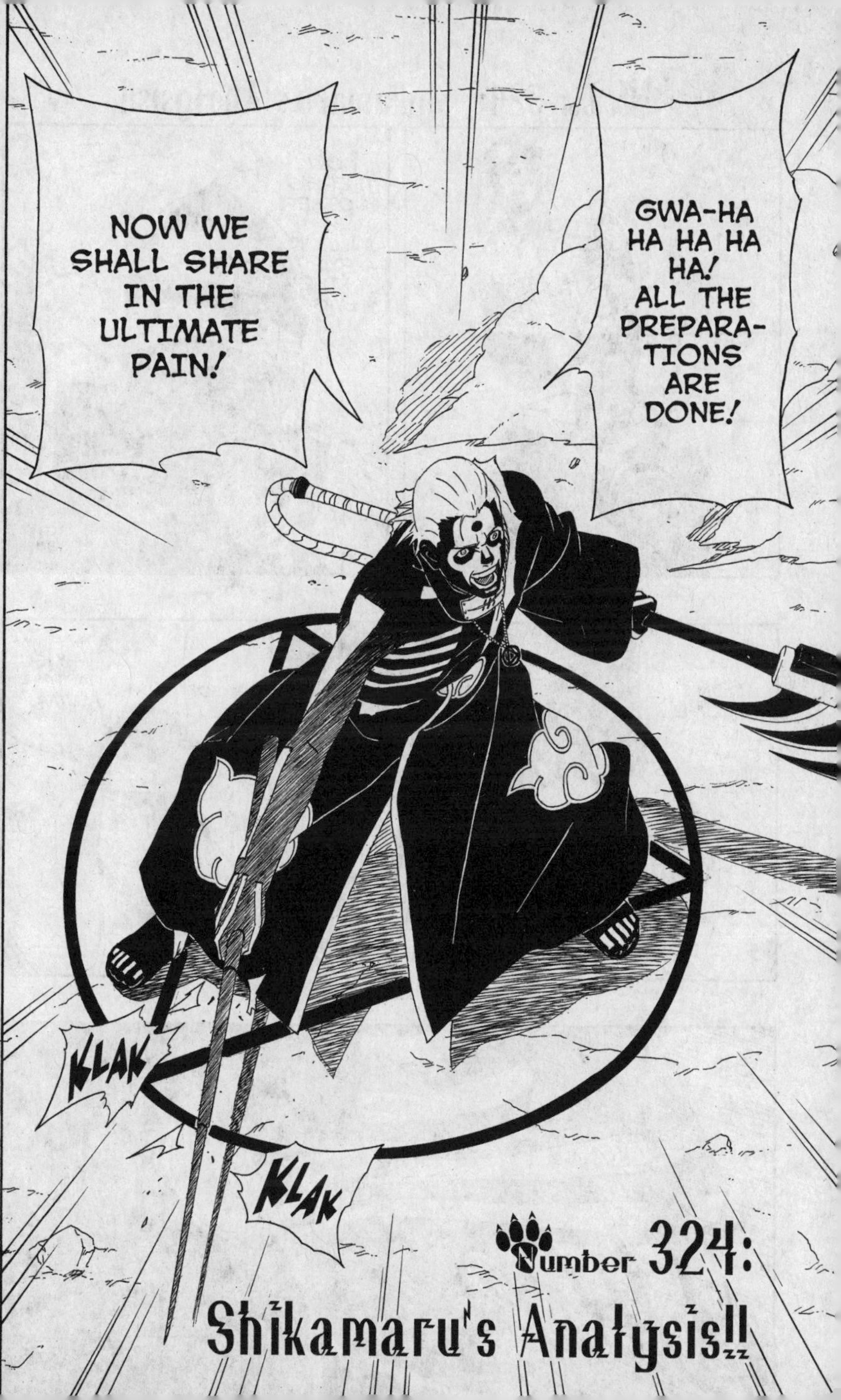
GWA-HA HA HA HA HA! ALL THE PREPARATIONS ARE DONE!
NOW WE SHALL SHARE IN THE ULTIMATE PAIN!
KLAK
KLAK
Number 324:
Shikamaru's Analysis!!

READ THIS WAY

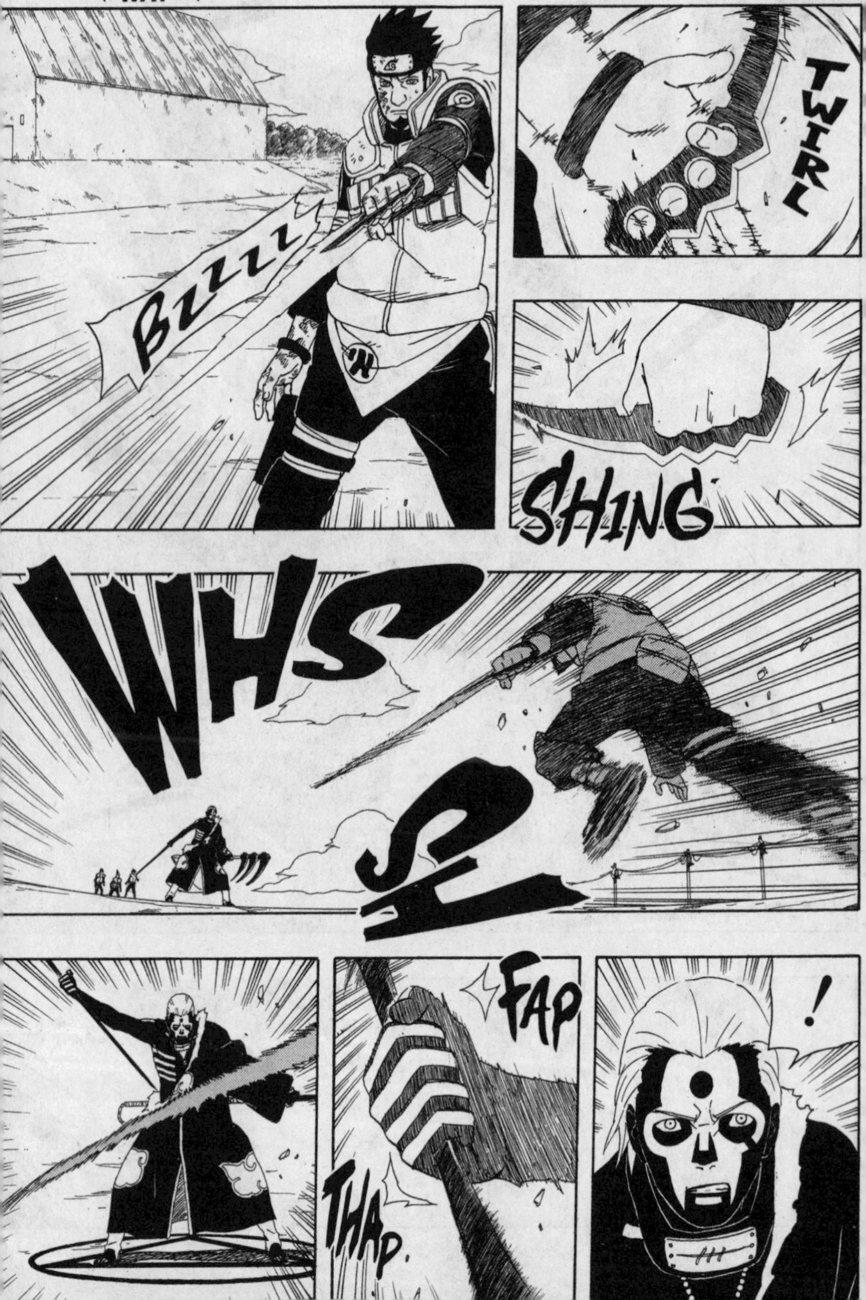
TWIRL
SHING
BZZZZ
WHSSH
!
FAP
THAP

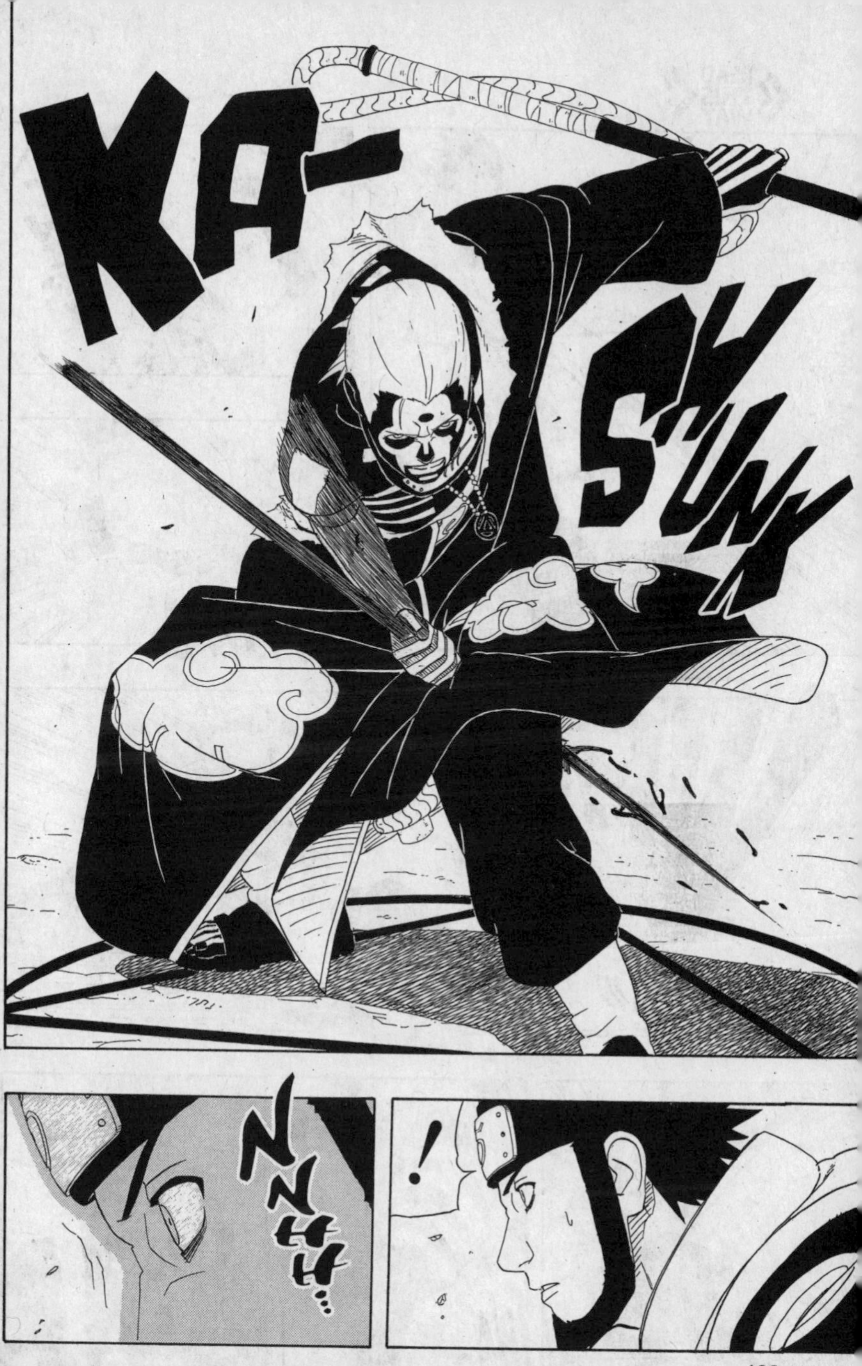
KA-
SHUNK
!
NNHH...

READ THIS WAY

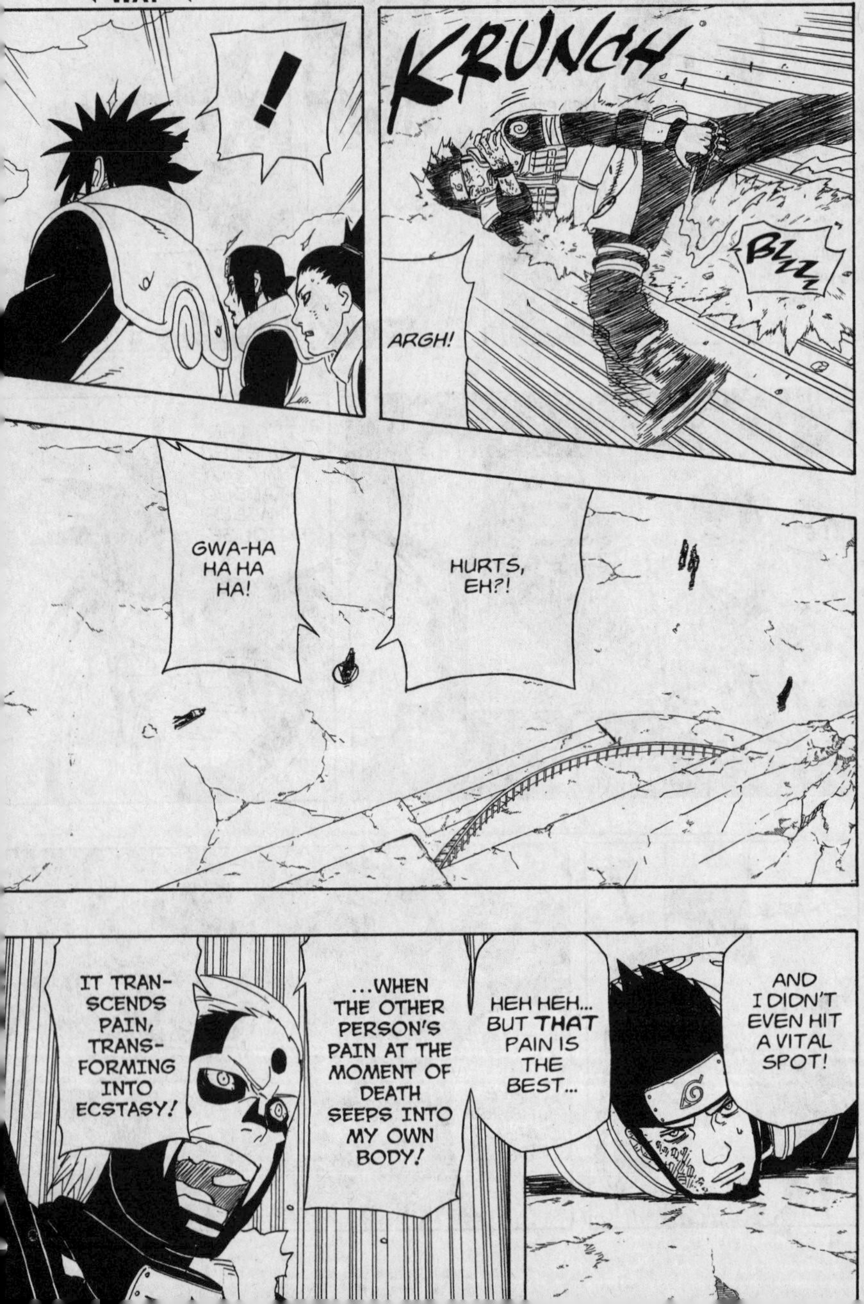
KRUNCH
BZZZ
ARGH!
!
HURTS, EH?!
GWA-HA HA HA HA!
AND I DIDN'T EVEN HIT A VITAL SPOT!
HEH HEH... BUT THAT PAIN IS THE BEST...
...WHEN THE OTHER PERSON'S PAIN AT THE MOMENT OF DEATH SEEPS INTO MY OWN BODY!
IT TRANSCENDS PAIN, TRANSFORMING INTO ECSTASY!

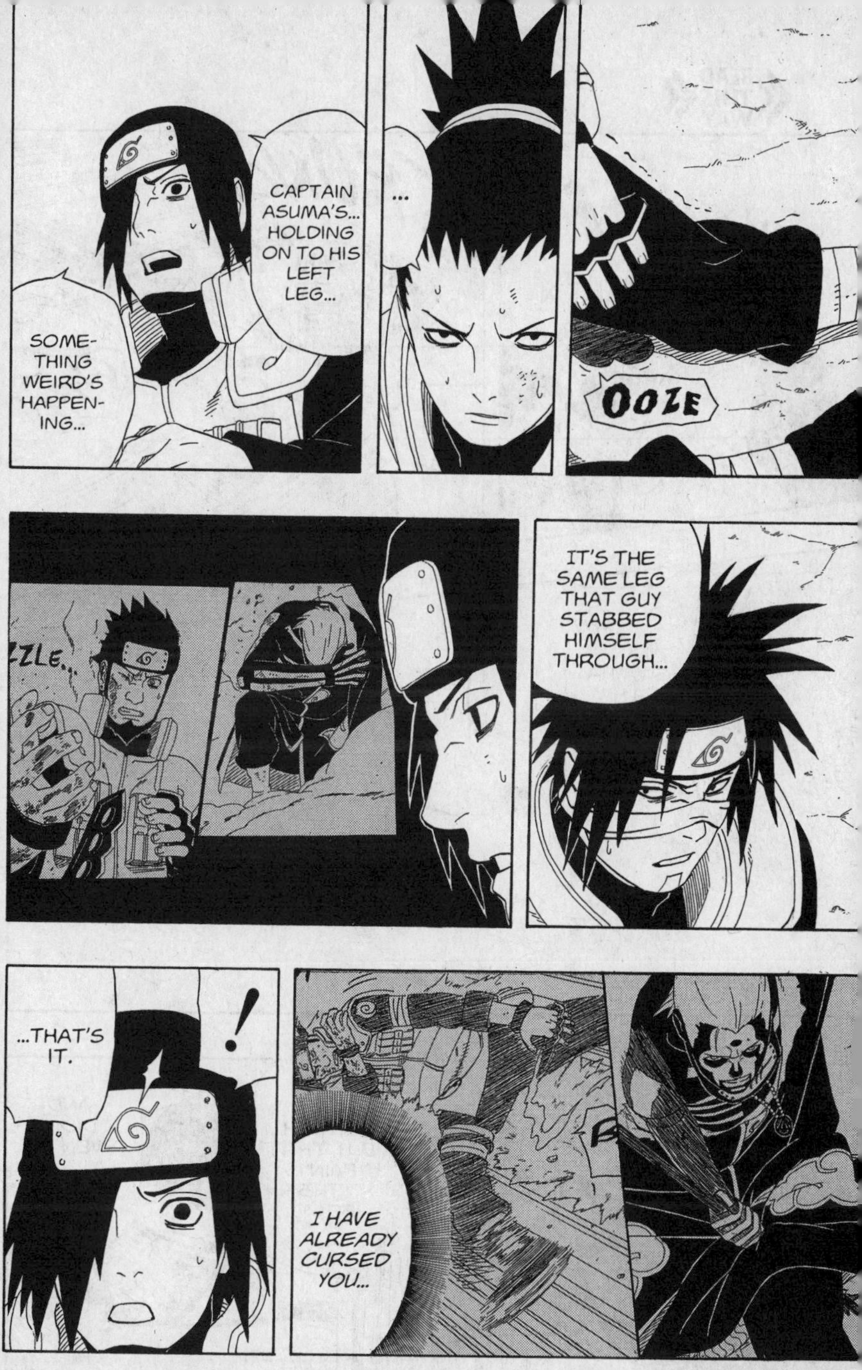
OOZE
...
CAPTAIN ASUMA'S... HOLDING ON TO HIS LEFT LEG...
SOME-THING WEIRD'S HAPPEN-ING...
IT'S THE SAME LEG THAT GUY STABBED HIMSELF THROUGH...
ZZLE...
I HAVE ALREADY CURSED YOU...
!
...THAT'S IT.

READ THIS WAY

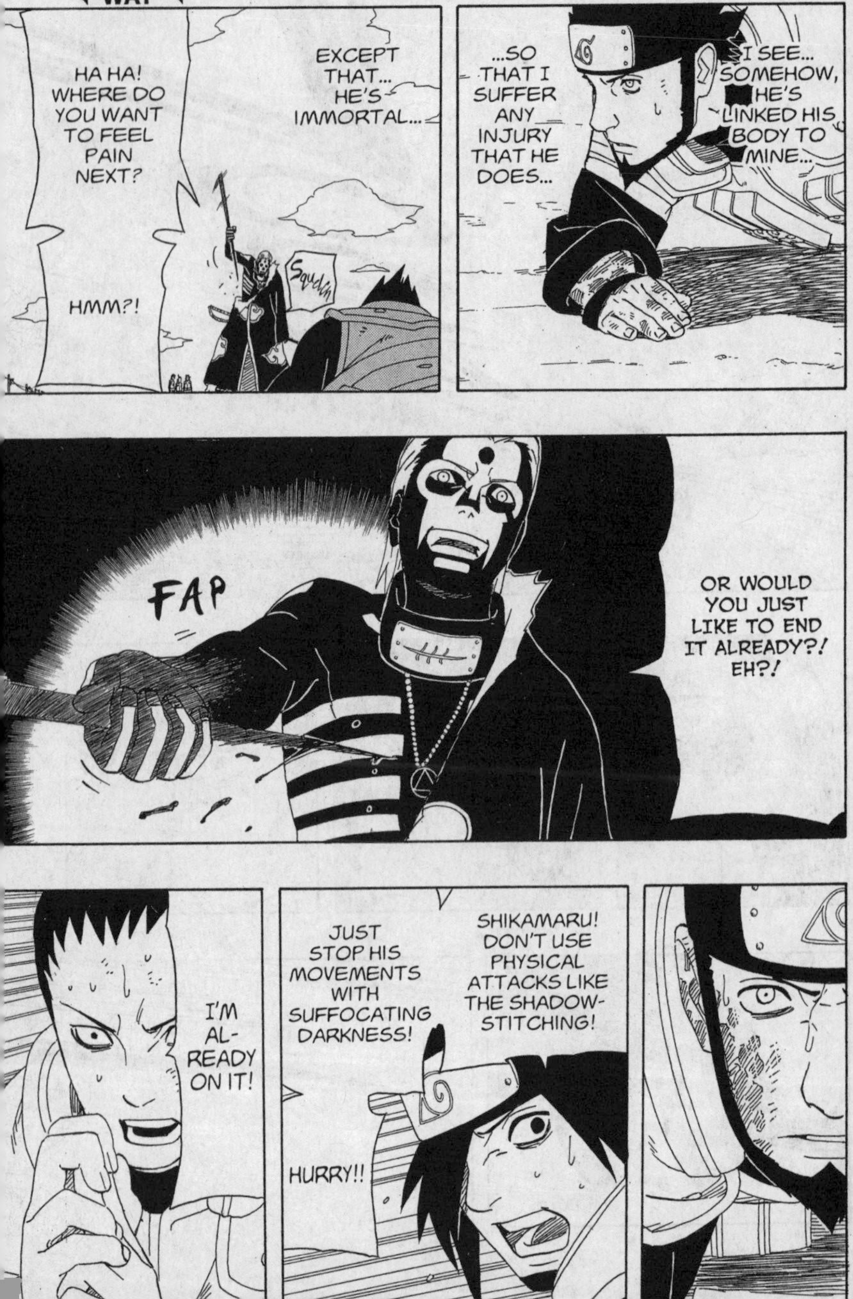
I SEE... SOMEHOW, HE'S LINKED HIS BODY TO MINE...
...SO THAT I SUFFER ANY INJURY THAT HE DOES...
EXCEPT THAT... HE'S IMMORTAL...
HA HA! WHERE DO YOU WANT TO FEEL PAIN NEXT?
HMM?!
OR WOULD YOU JUST LIKE TO END IT ALREADY?! EH?!
FAP
SHIKAMARU! DON'T USE PHYSICAL ATTACKS LIKE THE SHADOW-STITCHING!
JUST STOP HIS MOVEMENTS WITH SUFFOCATING DARKNESS!
HURRY!!
I'M AL-READY ON IT!

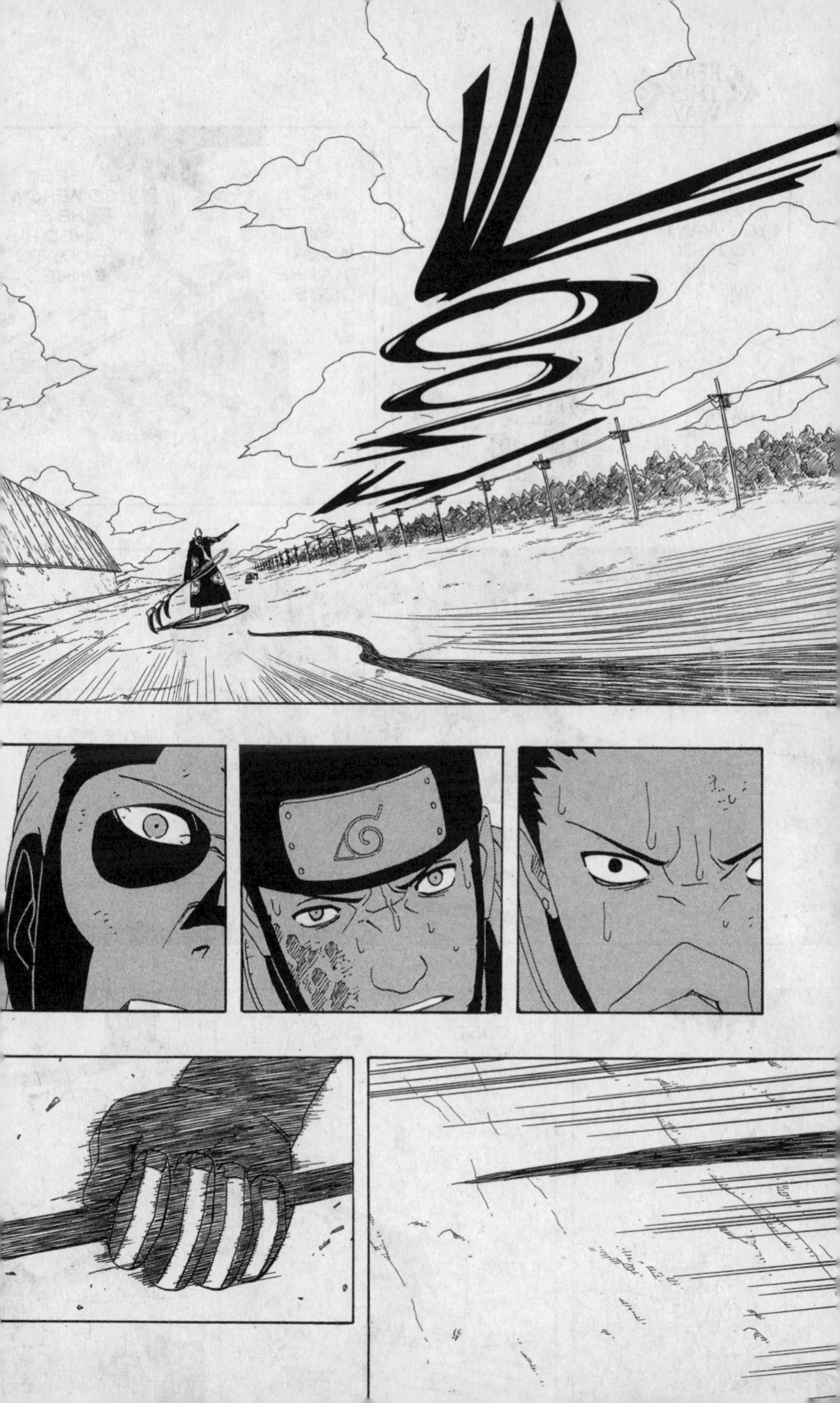

READ THIS WAY

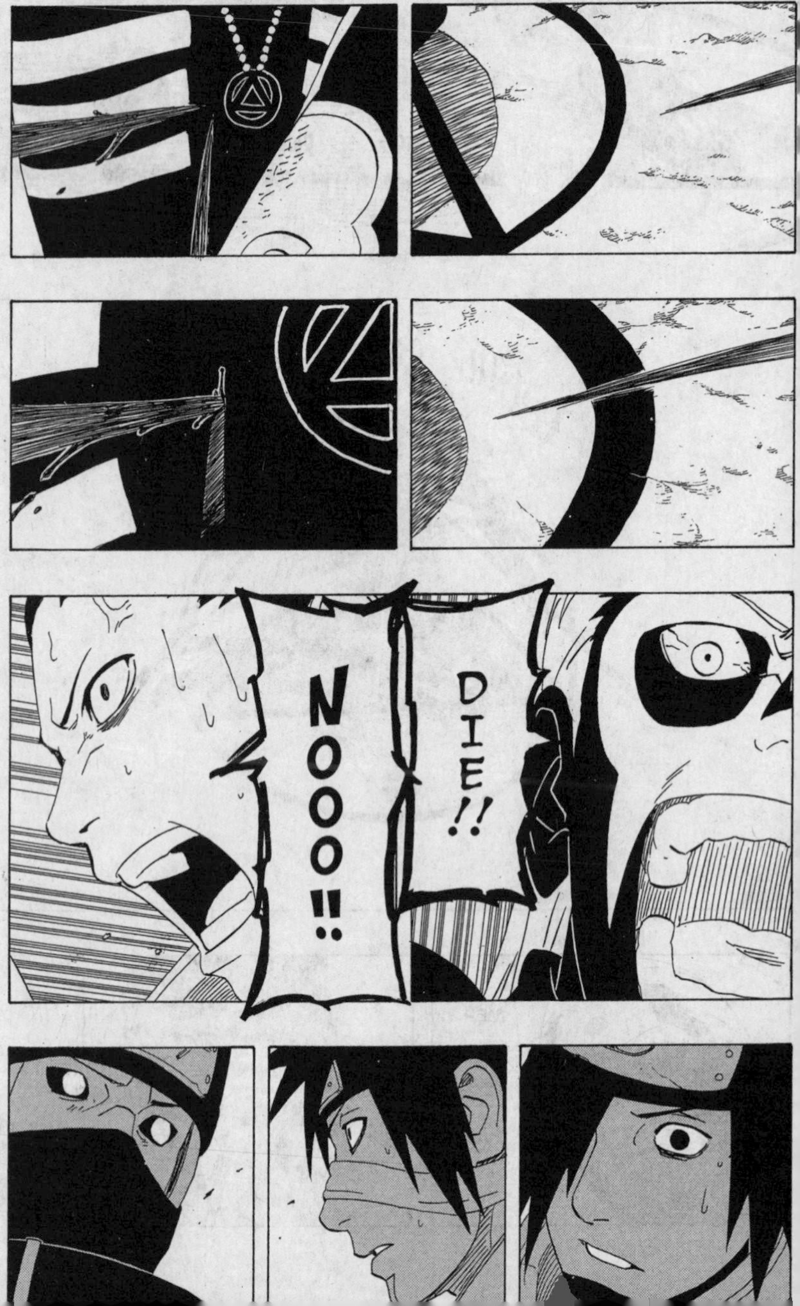
DIE!!
NOOOO!!

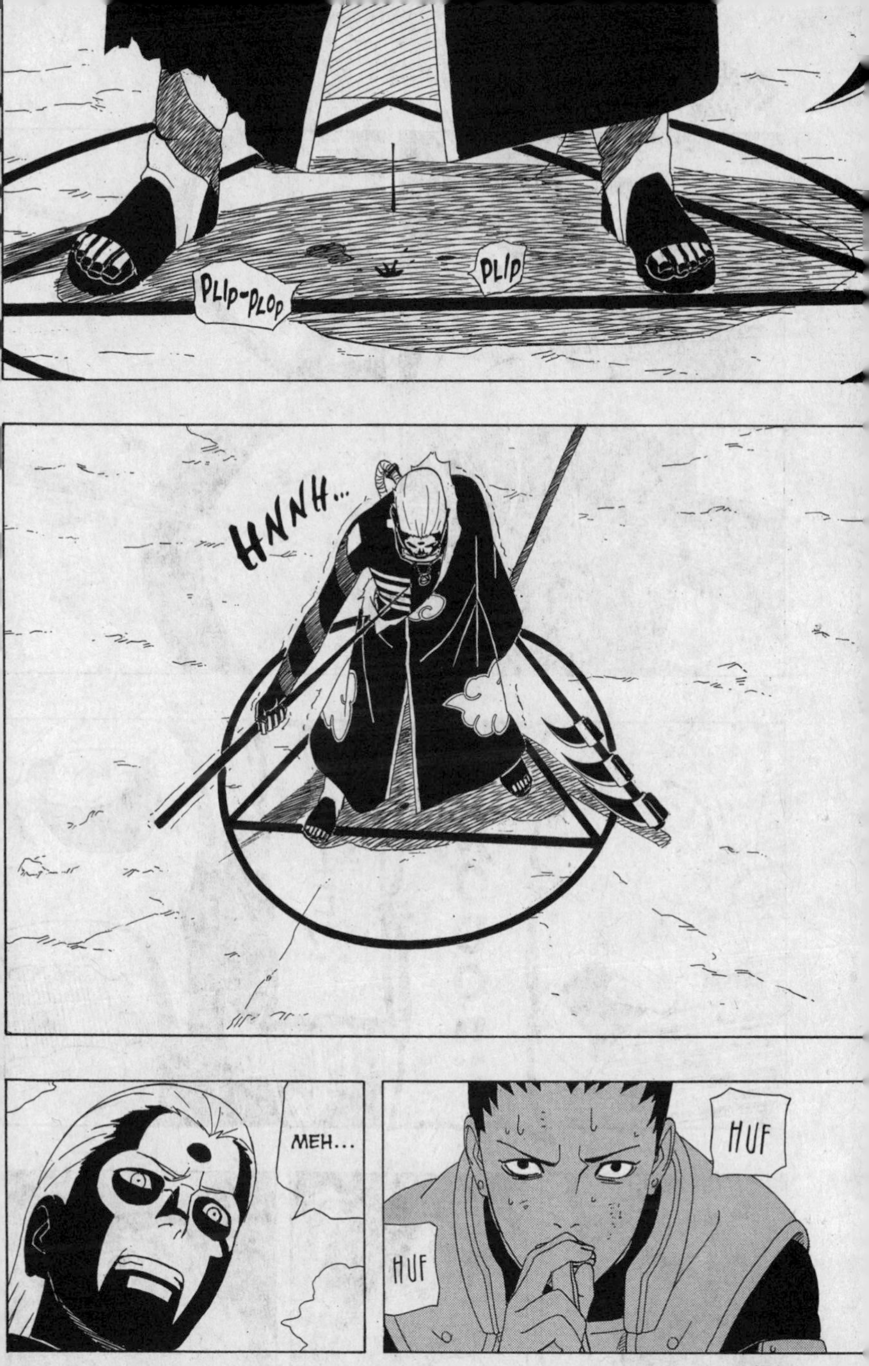
PLIP
PLIP-PLOP
HNNH...
HUF
HUF
MEH...

READ THIS WAY

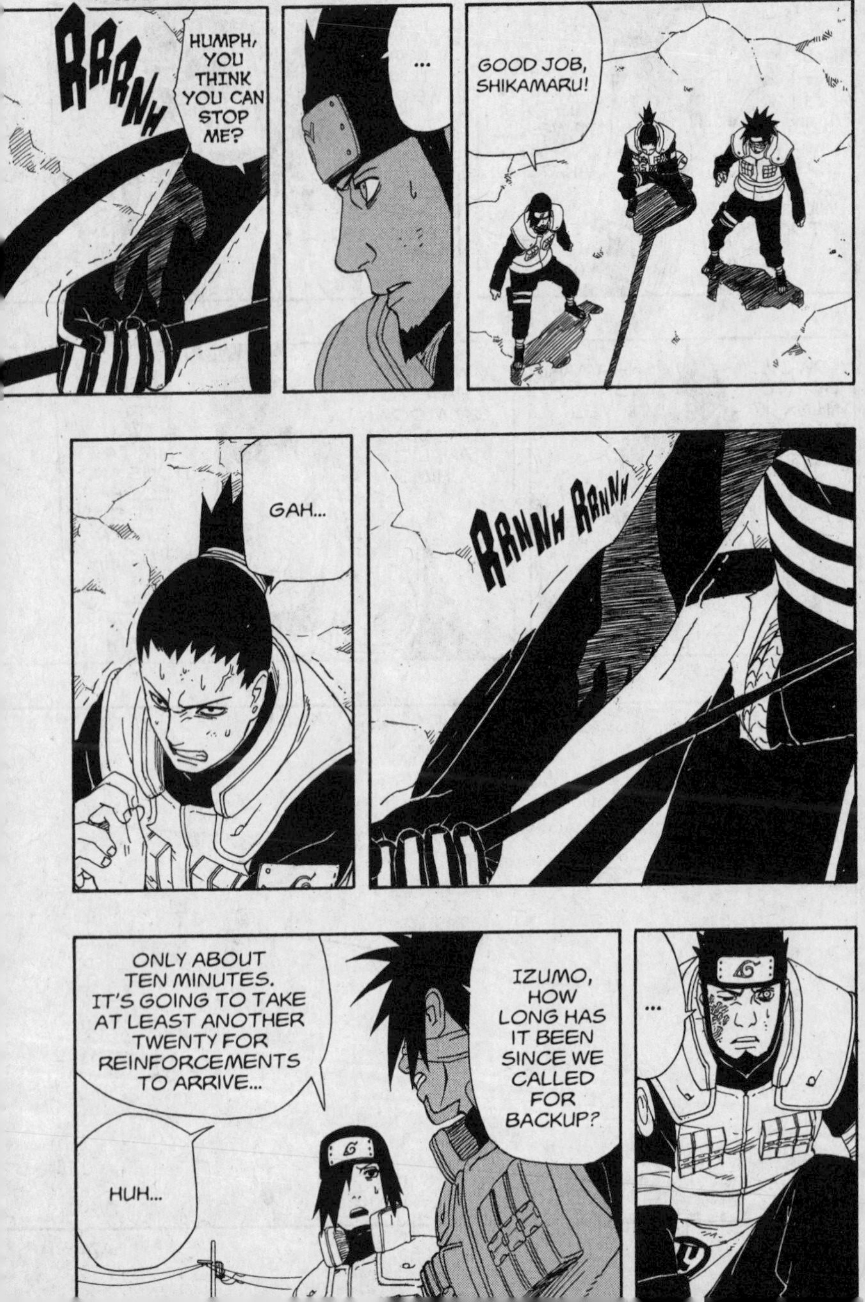
GOOD JOB, SHIKAMARU!
...
RRRNH
HUMPH, YOU THINK YOU CAN STOP ME?
RRNNH RRNNH
GAH...
...
IZUMO, HOW LONG HAS IT BEEN SINCE WE CALLED FOR BACKUP?
ONLY ABOUT TEN MINUTES. IT'S GOING TO TAKE AT LEAST ANOTHER TWENTY FOR REINFORCEMENTS TO ARRIVE...
HUH...

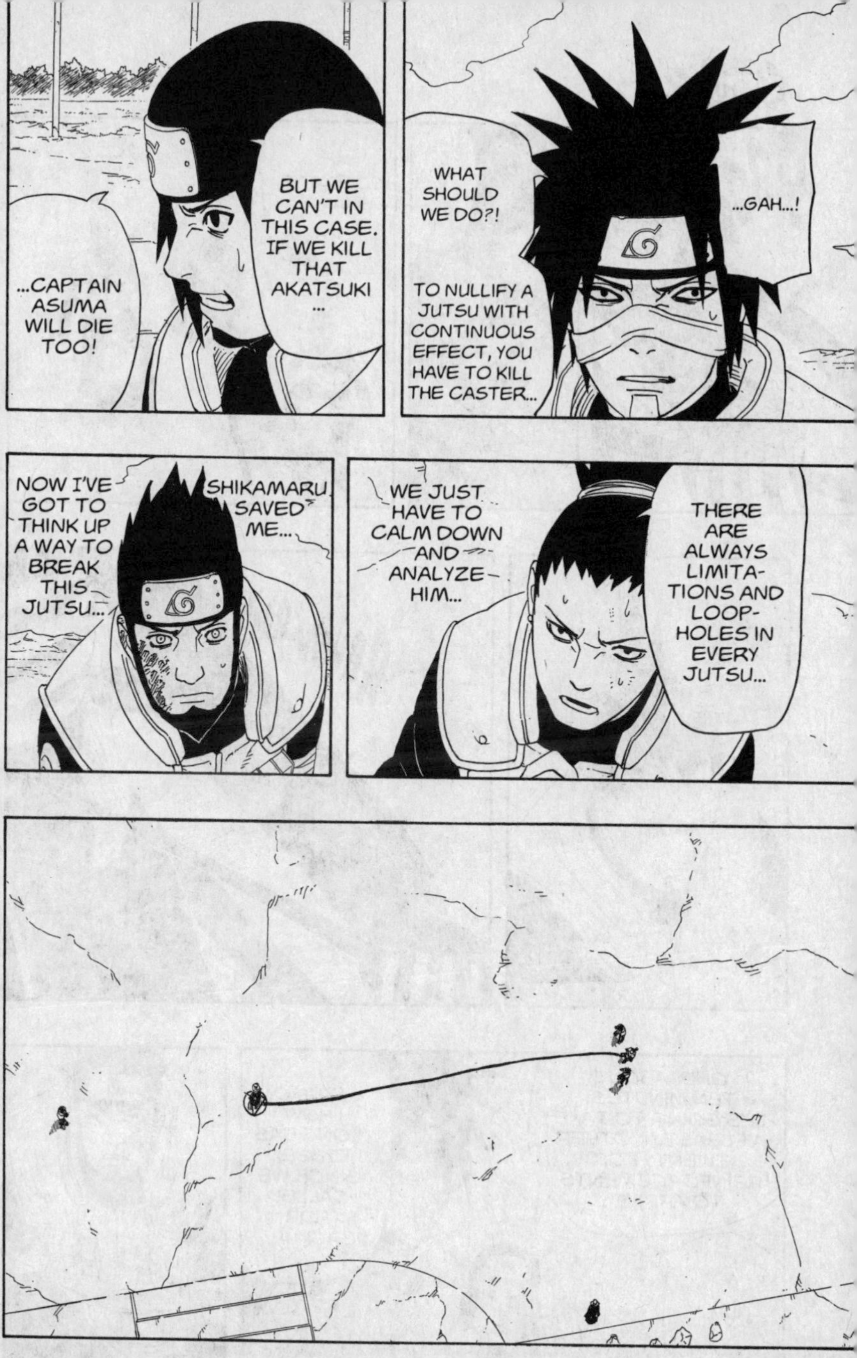
...GAH...!
WHAT SHOULD WE DO?!
TO NULLIFY A JUTSU WITH CONTINUOUS EFFECT, YOU HAVE TO KILL THE CASTER...
BUT WE CAN'T IN THIS CASE. IF WE KILL THAT AKATSUKI ...
...CAPTAIN ASUMA WILL DIE TOO!
THERE ARE ALWAYS LIMITATIONS AND LOOPHOLES IN EVERY JUTSU...
WE JUST HAVE TO CALM DOWN AND ANALYZE HIM...
SHIKAMARU SAVED ME...
NOW I'VE GOT TO THINK UP A WAY TO BREAK THIS JUTSU...

READ THIS WAY

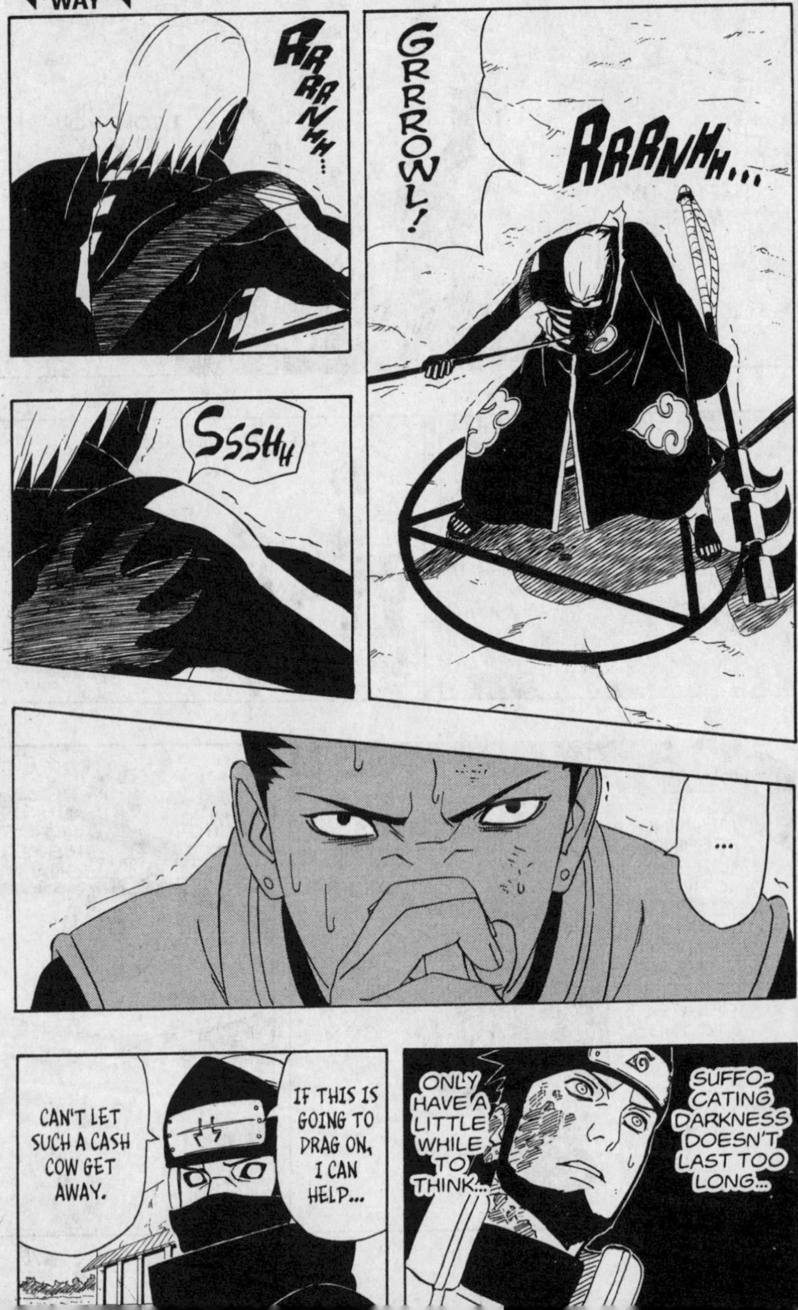

GRRROWL!
RRRNHH...
ARRRNHH...
SSSHH
...
SUFFO-CATING DARKNESS DOESN'T LAST TOO LONG...
ONLY HAVE A LITTLE WHILE TO THINK...
IF THIS IS GOING TO DRAG ON, I CAN HELP...
CAN'T LET SUCH A CASH COW GET AWAY.

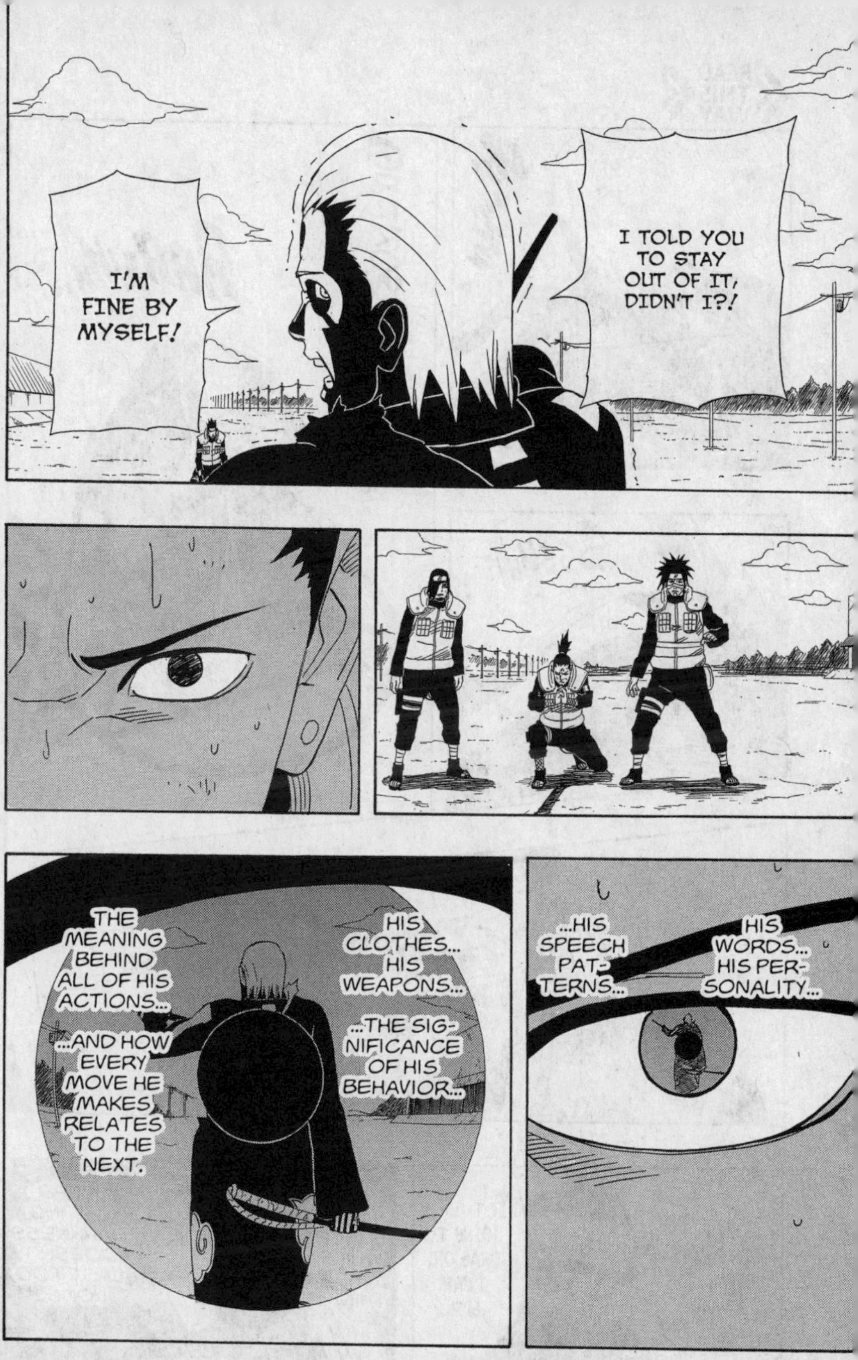
I TOLD YOU TO STAY OUT OF IT, DIDN'T I?!
I'M FINE BY MYSELF!
HIS WORDS... HIS PERSONALITY...
...HIS SPEECH PATTERNS...
HIS CLOTHES... HIS WEAPONS...
...THE SIGNIFICANCE OF HIS BEHAVIOR...
THE MEANING BEHIND ALL OF HIS ACTIONS...
...AND HOW EVERY MOVE HE MAKES RELATES TO THE NEXT.

READ THIS WAY

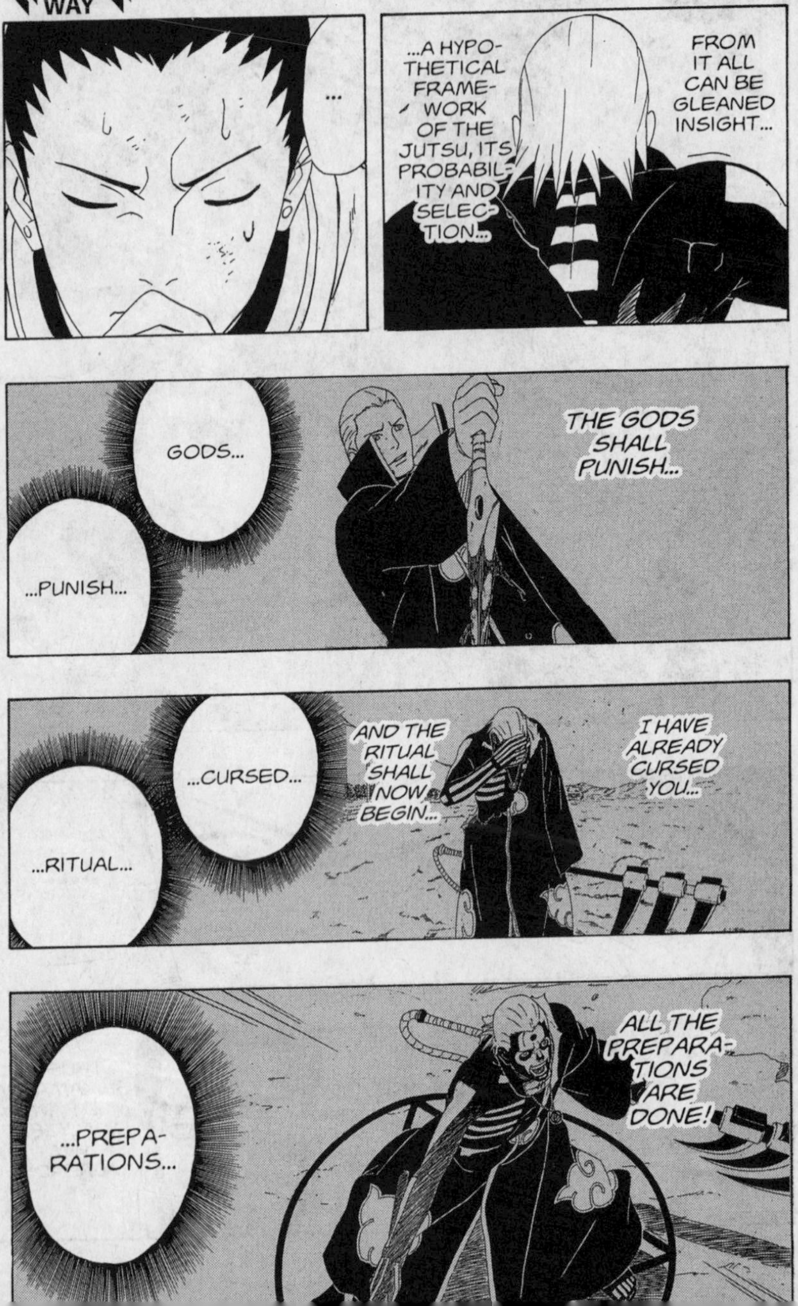
FROM IT ALL CAN BE GLEANED INSIGHT...
...A HYPO-THETICAL FRAME-WORK OF THE JUTSU, ITS PROBABIL-ITY AND SELEC-TION...
...
THE GODS SHALL PUNISH...
GODS...
...PUNISH...
I HAVE ALREADY CURSED YOU...
AND THE RITUAL SHALL NOW BEGIN...
...CURSED...
...RITUAL...
ALL THE PREPARA-TIONS ARE DONE!
...PREPA-RATIONS...

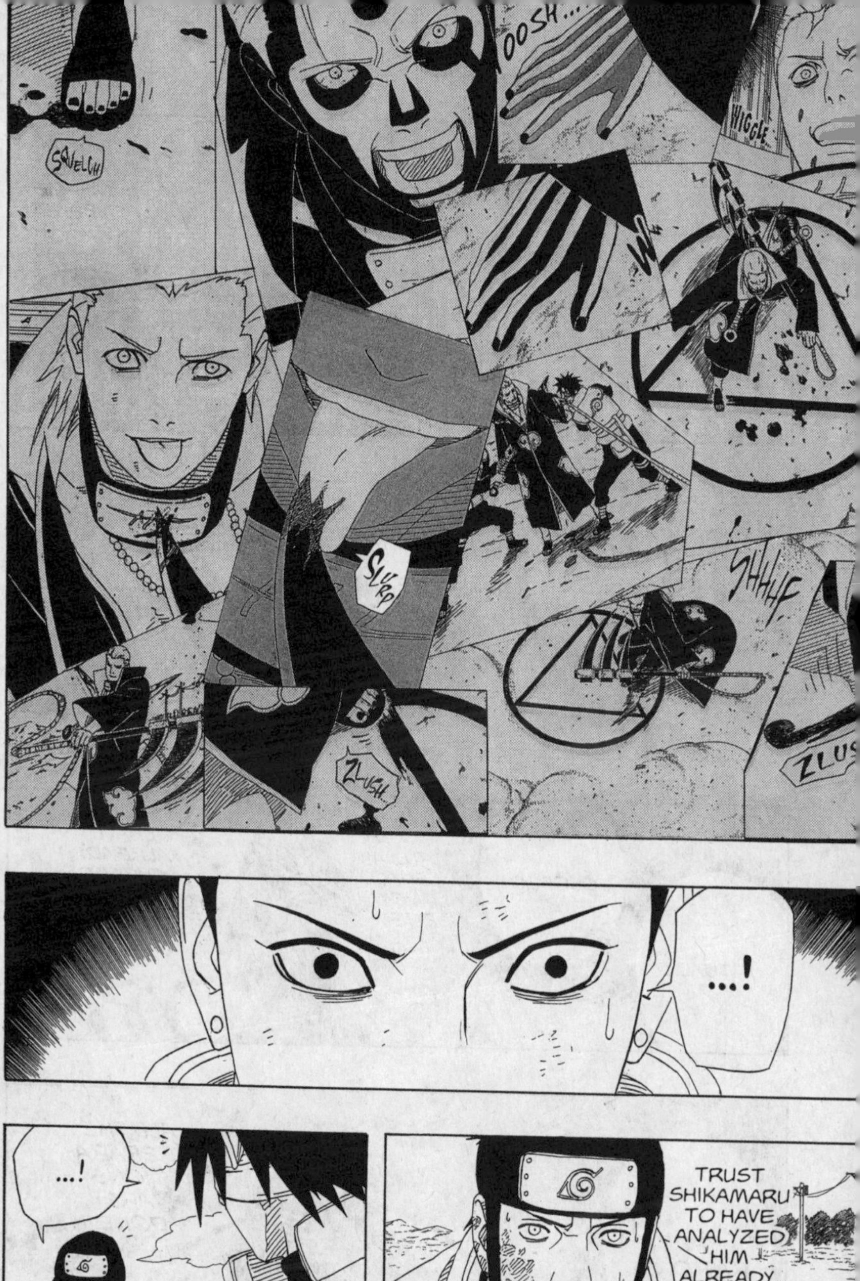
WIGGLE
OOSH...
SQUELCH
SHHUF
SLURP
ZLUS
ZLUSH
...!
TRUST SHIKAMARU TO HAVE ANALYZED HIM ALREADY.
...!

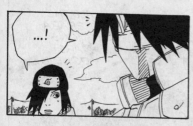

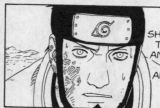

READ THIS WAY

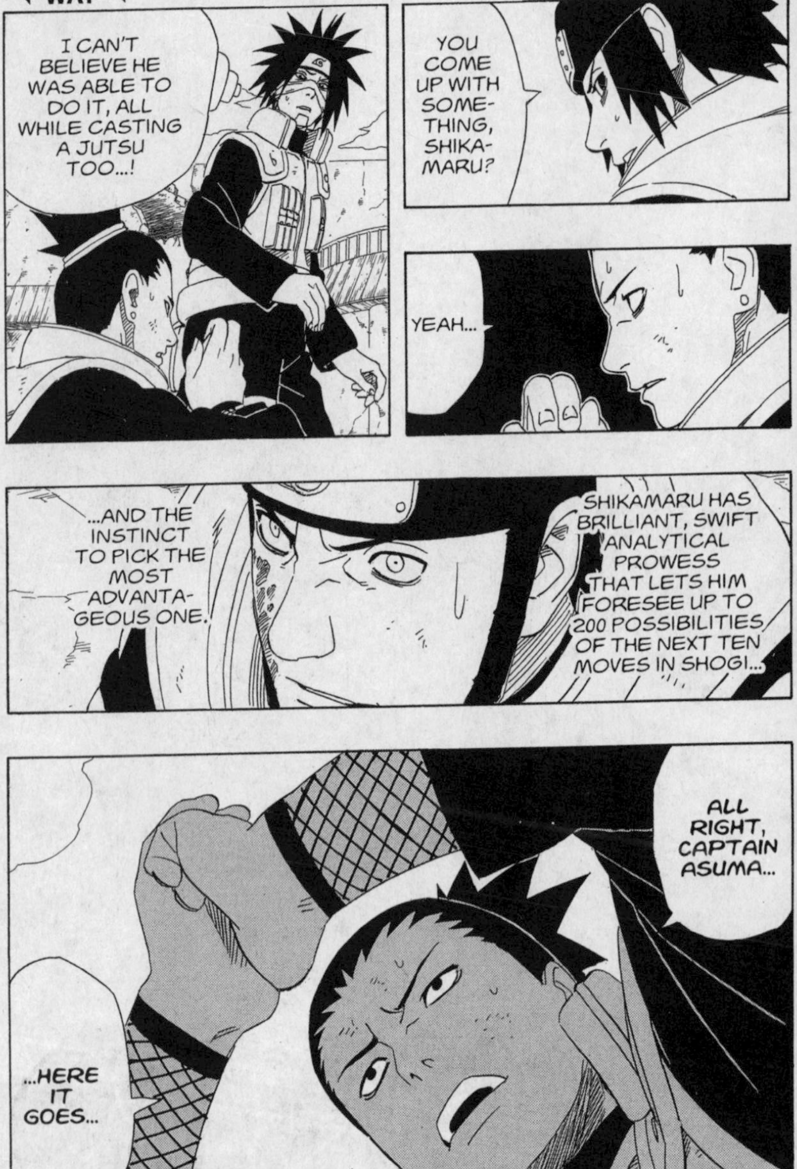
YOU COME UP WITH SOMETHING, SHIKAMARU?
YEAH...
I CAN'T BELIEVE HE WAS ABLE TO DO IT, ALL WHILE CASTING A JUTSU TOO...!
SHIKAMARU HAS BRILLIANT, SWIFT ANALYTICAL PROWESS THAT LETS HIM FORESEE UP TO 200 POSSIBILITIES OF THE NEXT TEN MOVES IN SHOGI...
...AND THE INSTINCT TO PICK THE MOST ADVANTAGEOUS ONE.
ALL RIGHT, CAPTAIN ASUMA...
...HERE IT GOES...

NARUTO

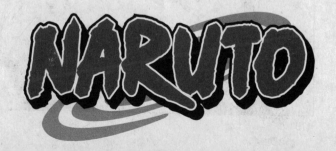

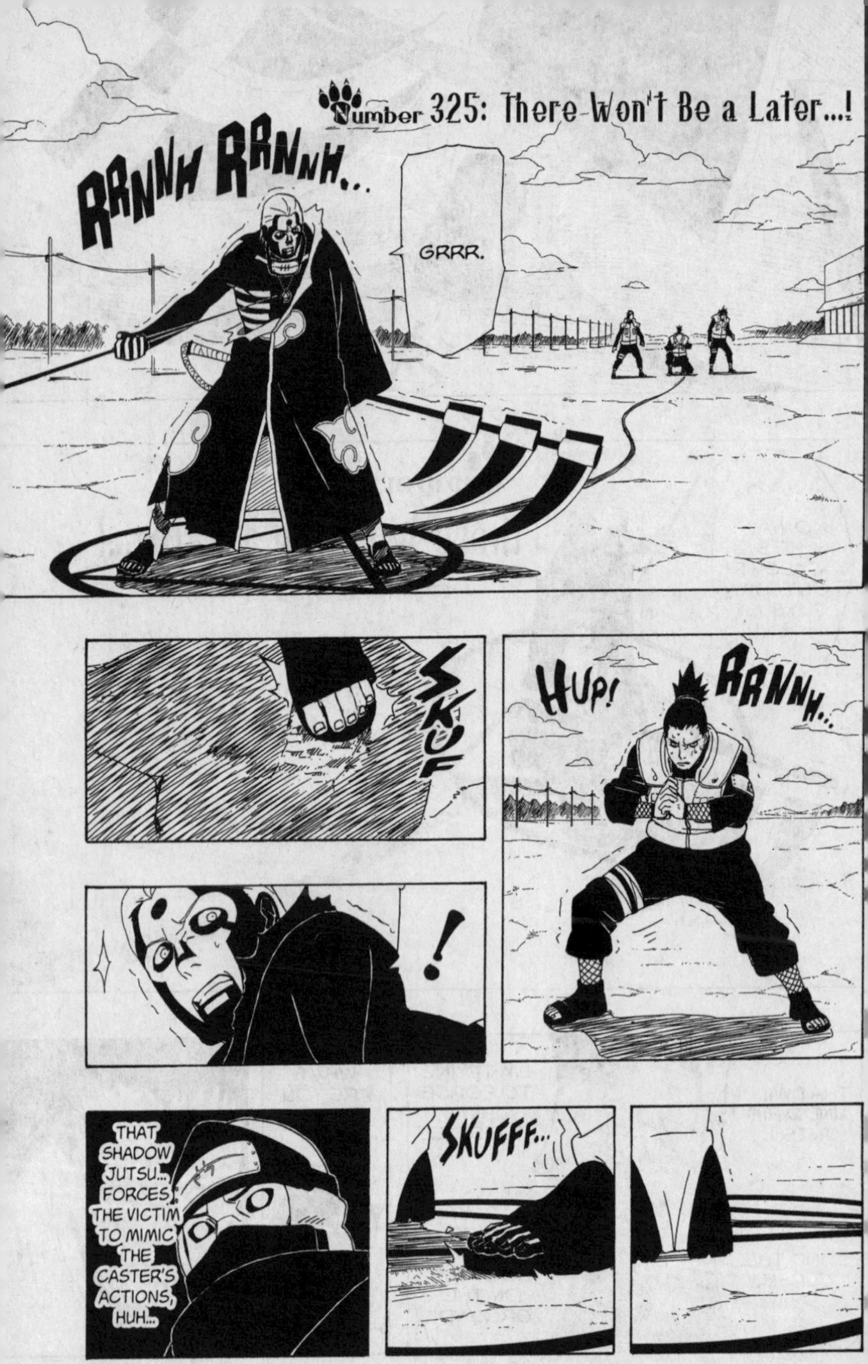
Number 325: There Won't Be a Later...!
RRNNH RRNNH...
GRRR.
HUP!
RRNNH...
SKUF
!
SKUFFF...
THAT SHADOW JUTSU... FORCES THE VICTIM TO MIMIC THE CASTER'S ACTIONS, HUH...

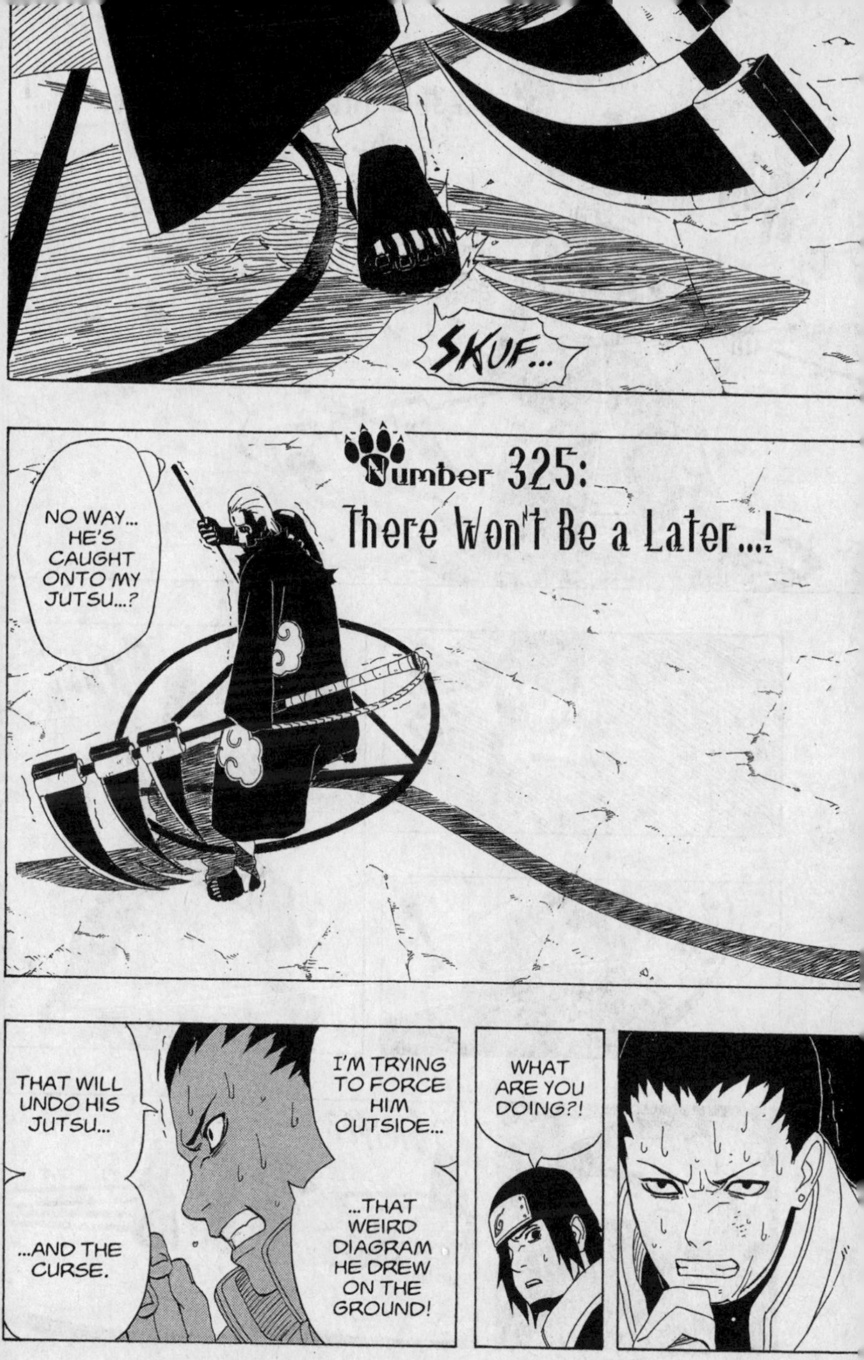
SKUF...
Number 325:
There Won't Be a Later...!
NO WAY... HE'S CAUGHT ONTO MY JUTSU...?
WHAT ARE YOU DOING?!
I'M TRYING TO FORCE HIM OUTSIDE...
...THAT WEIRD DIAGRAM HE DREW ON THE GROUND!
THAT WILL UNDO HIS JUTSU...
...AND THE CURSE.

READ THIS WAY

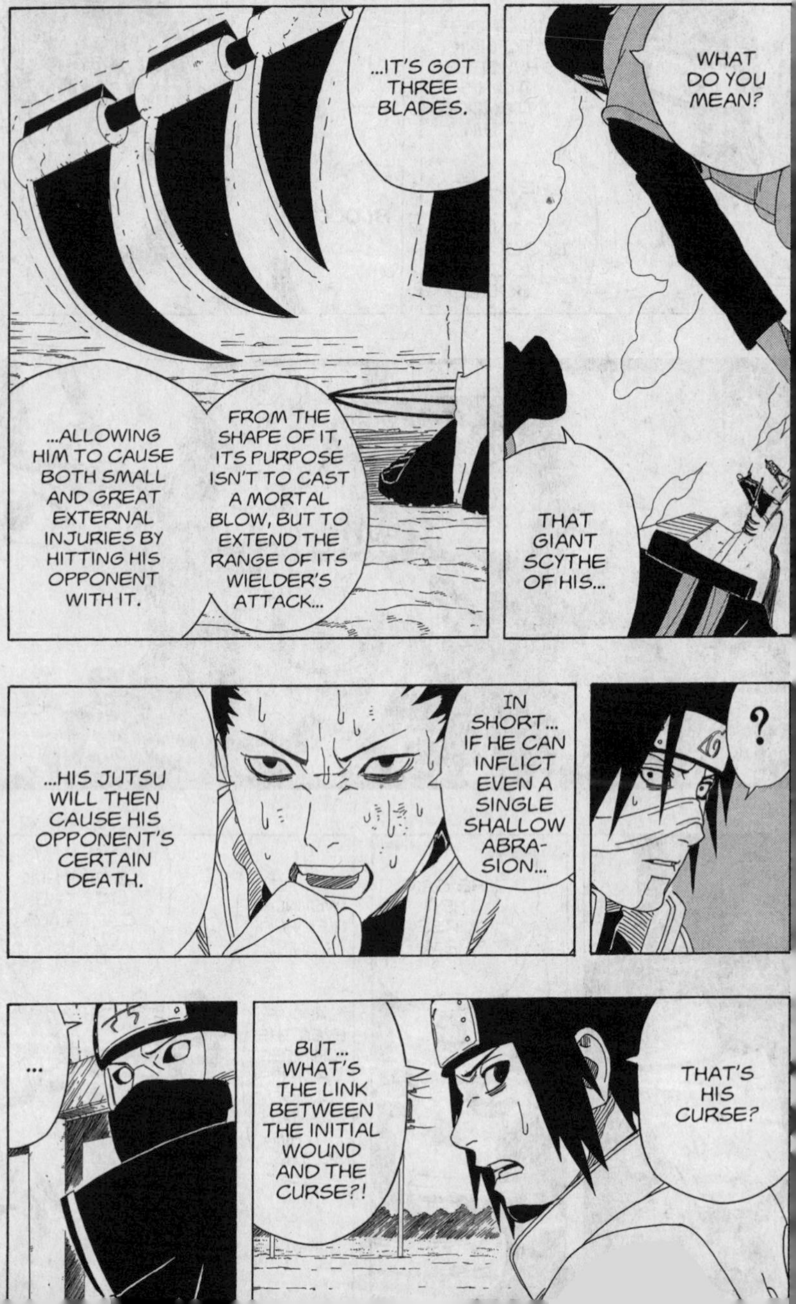
WHAT DO YOU MEAN?
THAT GIANT SCYTHE OF HIS...
...IT'S GOT THREE BLADES.
FROM THE SHAPE OF IT, ITS PURPOSE ISN'T TO CAST A MORTAL BLOW, BUT TO EXTEND THE RANGE OF ITS WIELDER'S ATTACK...
...ALLOWING HIM TO CAUSE BOTH SMALL AND GREAT EXTERNAL INJURIES BY HITTING HIS OPPONENT WITH IT.
?
IN SHORT... IF HE CAN INFLICT EVEN A SINGLE SHALLOW ABRASION...
...HIS JUTSU WILL THEN CAUSE HIS OPPONENT'S CERTAIN DEATH.
THAT'S HIS CURSE?
BUT... WHAT'S THE LINK BETWEEN THE INITIAL WOUND AND THE CURSE?!
...

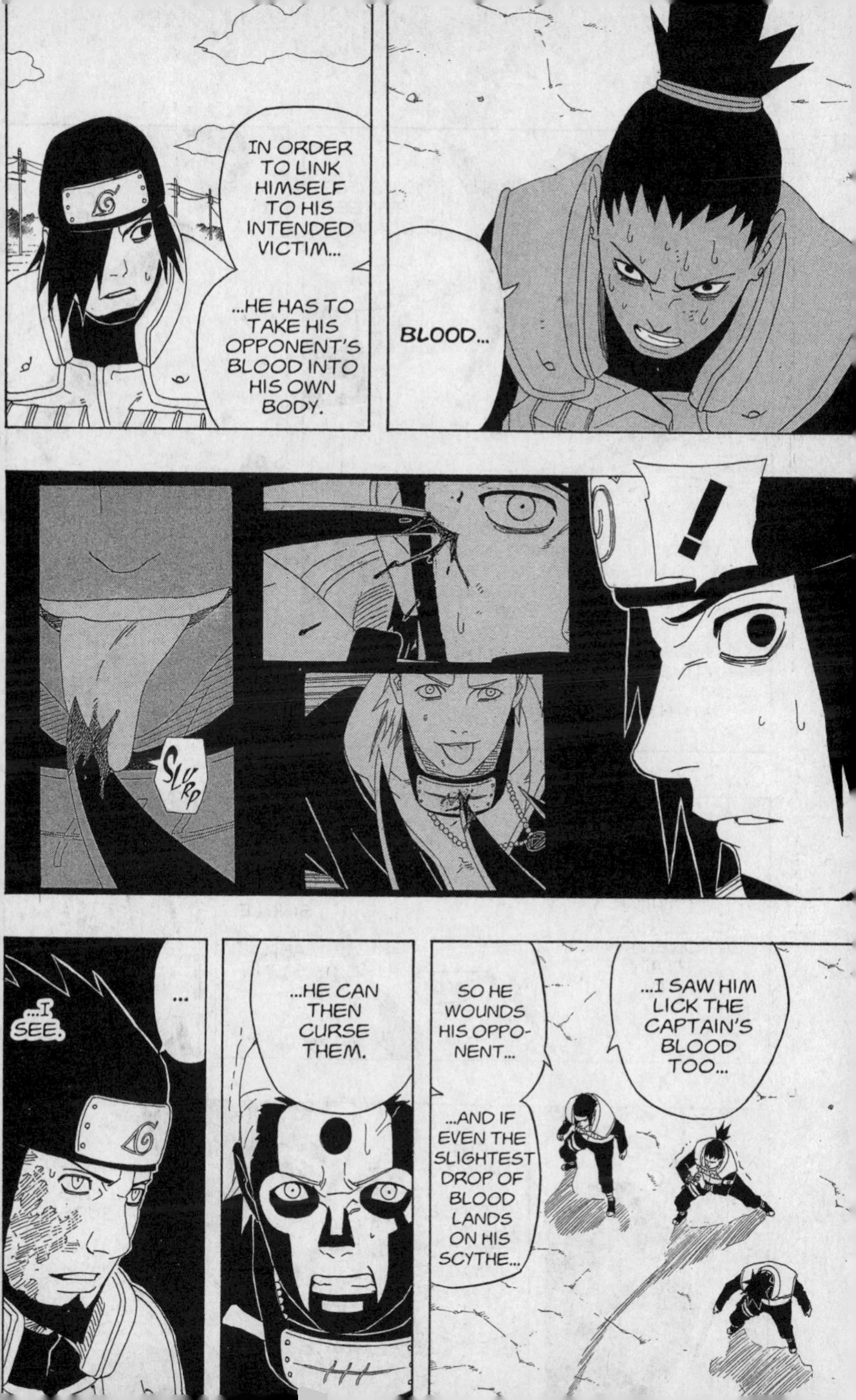
BLOOD...
IN ORDER TO LINK HIMSELF TO HIS INTENDED VICTIM...
...HE HAS TO TAKE HIS OPPONENT'S BLOOD INTO HIS OWN BODY.
!
SLURP
...I SAW HIM LICK THE CAPTAIN'S BLOOD TOO...
SO HE WOUNDS HIS OPPO-NENT...
...AND IF EVEN THE SLIGHTEST DROP OF BLOOD LANDS ON HIS SCYTHE...
...HE CAN THEN CURSE THEM.
...
...I SEE.

READ THIS WAY

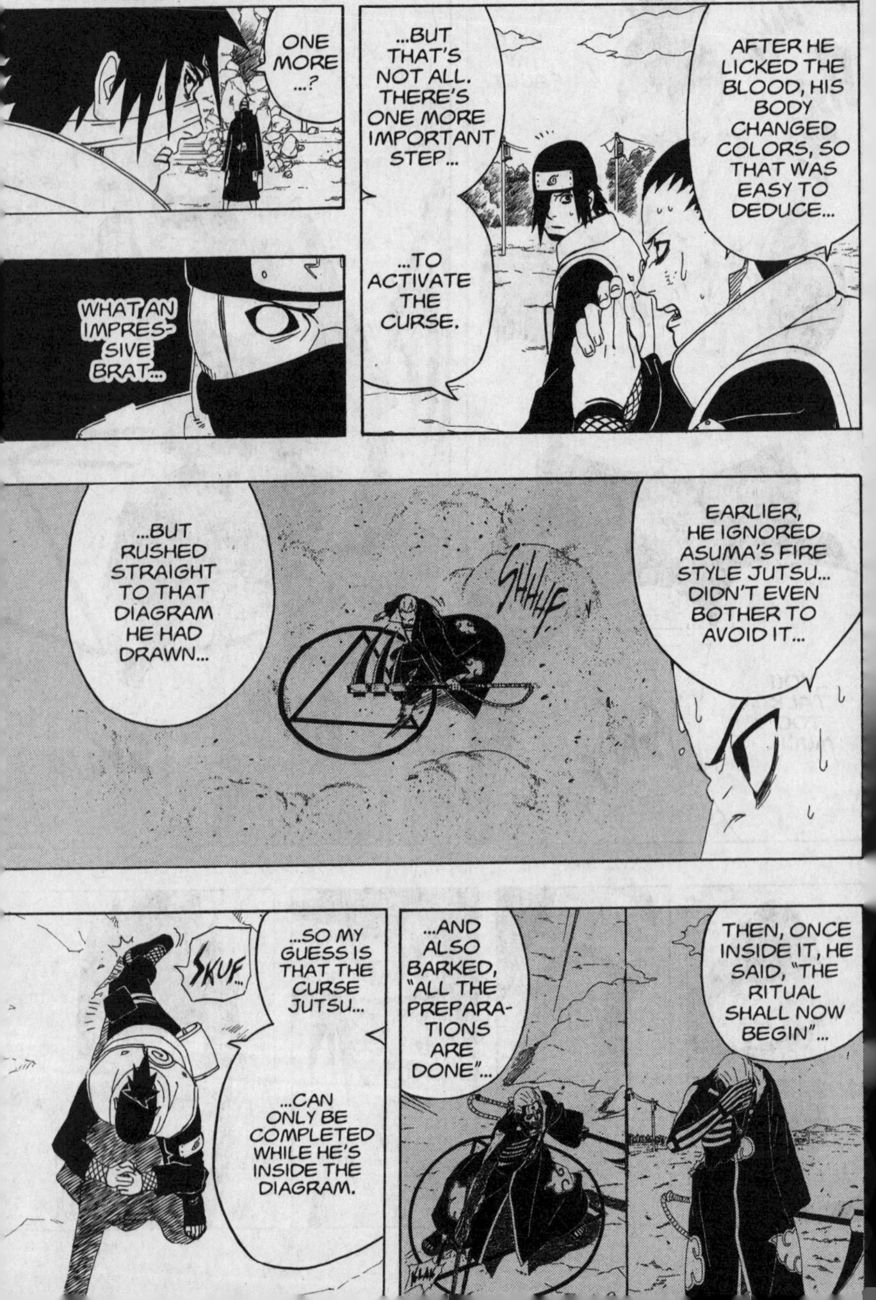
AFTER HE LICKED THE BLOOD, HIS BODY CHANGED COLORS, SO THAT WAS EASY TO DEDUCE...
...BUT THAT'S NOT ALL. THERE'S ONE MORE IMPORTANT STEP...
...TO ACTIVATE THE CURSE.
ONE MORE ...?
WHAT AN IMPRES-SIVE BRAT...
EARLIER, HE IGNORED ASUMA'S FIRE STYLE JUTSU... DIDN'T EVEN BOTHER TO AVOID IT...
SHHHF
...BUT RUSHED STRAIGHT TO THAT DIAGRAM HE HAD DRAWN...
THEN, ONCE INSIDE IT, HE SAID, "THE RITUAL SHALL NOW BEGIN"...
...AND ALSO BARKED, "ALL THE PREPARA-TIONS ARE DONE"...
...SO MY GUESS IS THAT THE CURSE JUTSU...
...CAN ONLY BE COMPLETED WHILE HE'S INSIDE THE DIAGRAM.
SKUF...

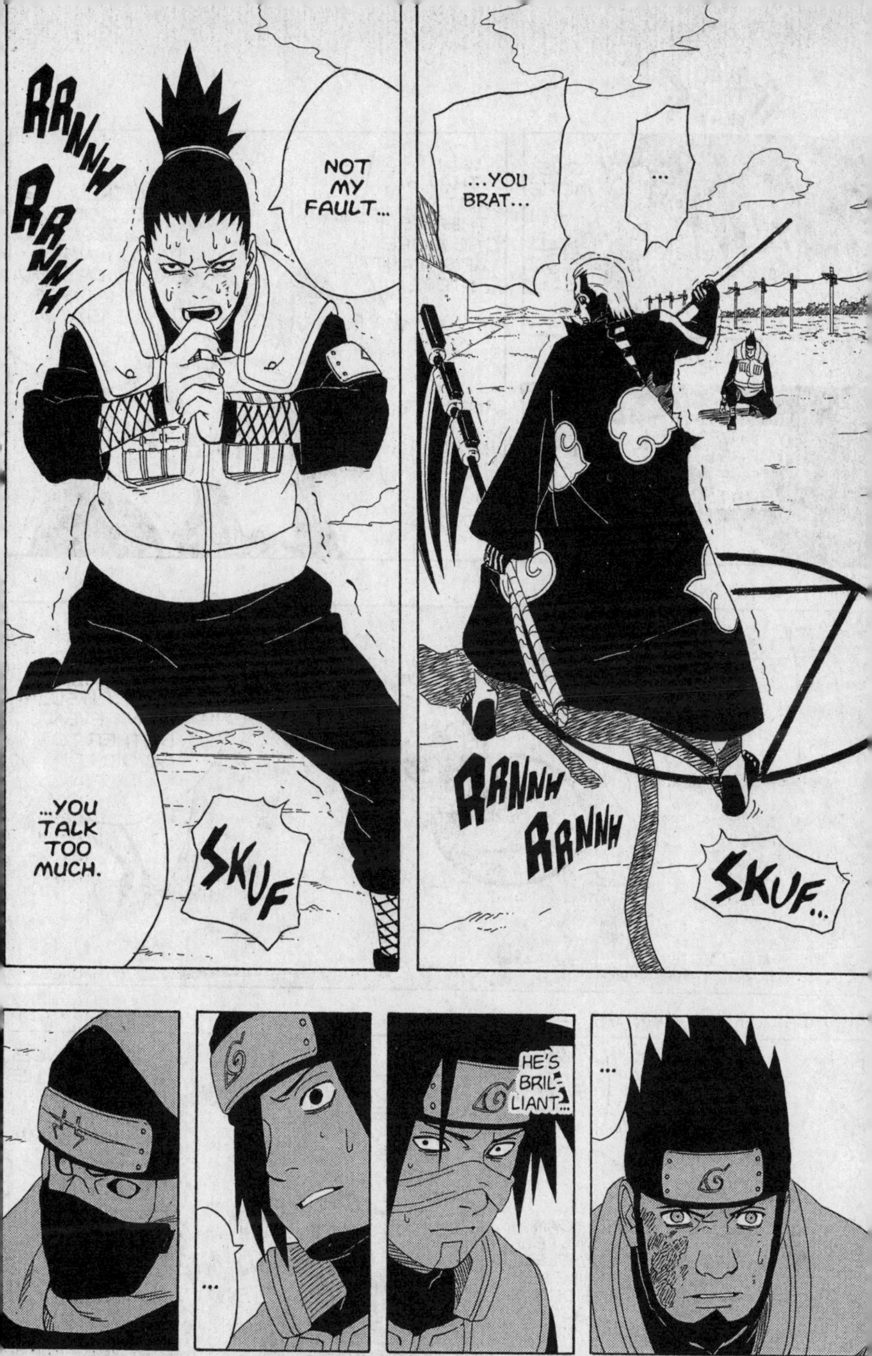
...
...YOU BRAT...
RRNNH RRNNH
SKUF...
NOT MY FAULT...
RRNNH RRNNH
...YOU TALK TOO MUCH.
SKUF
...
HE'S BRIL-LIANT...
...

READ THIS WAY

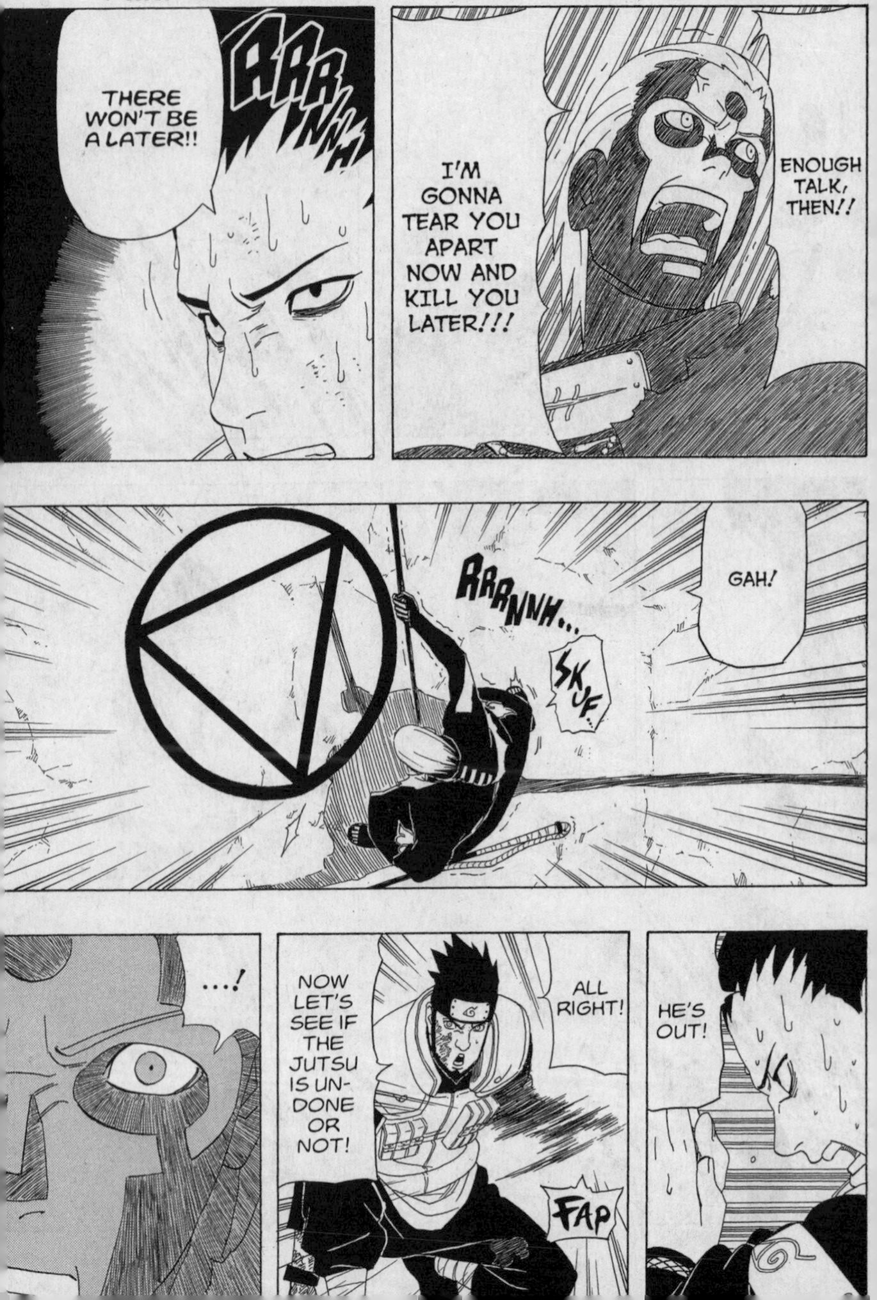

ENOUGH TALK, THEN!!
I'M GONNA TEAR YOU APART NOW AND KILL YOU LATER!!!
RRRNNH
THERE WON'T BE A LATER!!
GAH!
SKUF...
RRRNNH...
HE'S OUT!
ALL RIGHT!
NOW LET'S SEE IF THE JUTSU IS UN-DONE OR NOT!
FAP
...!

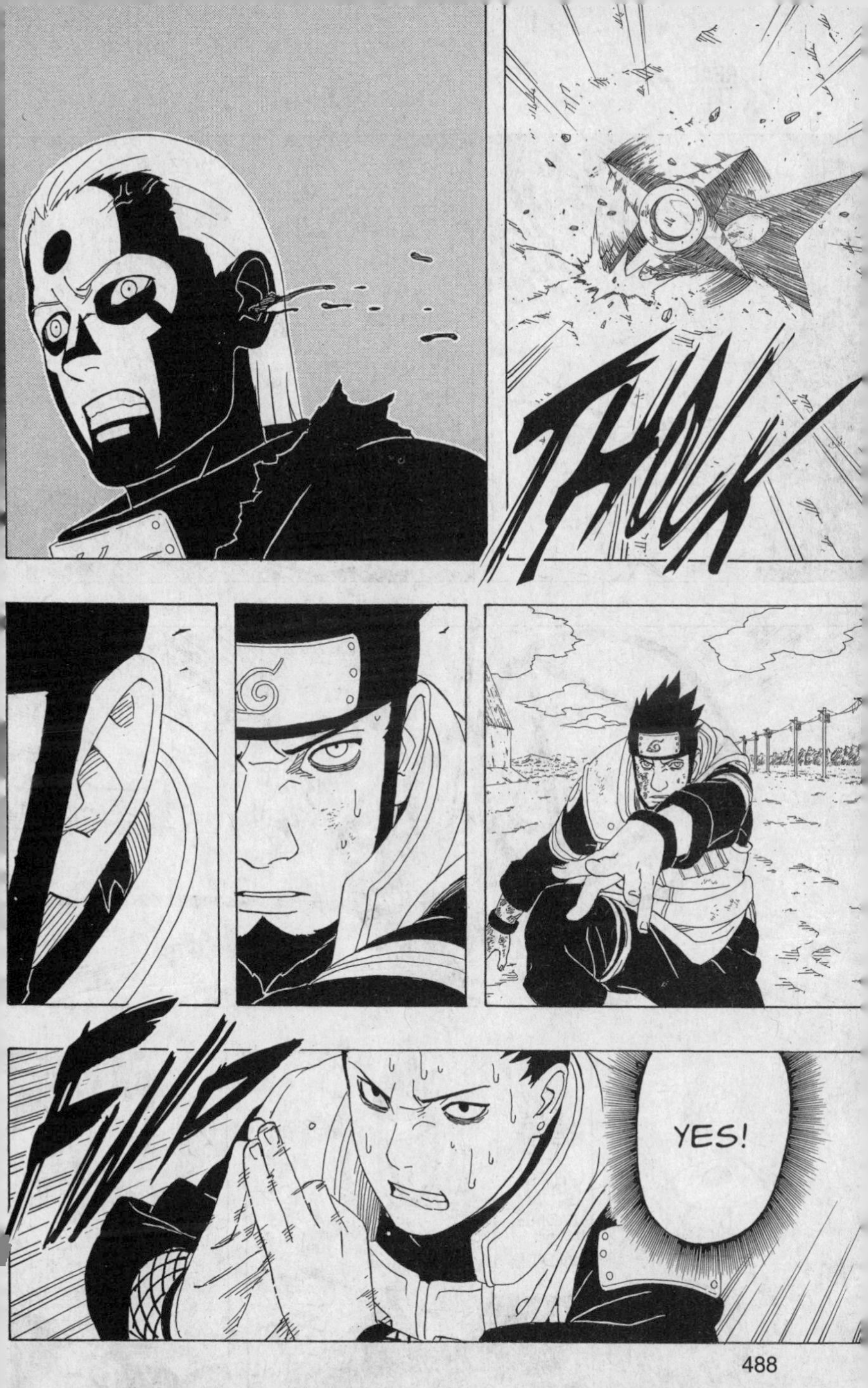
THUNK
YES!

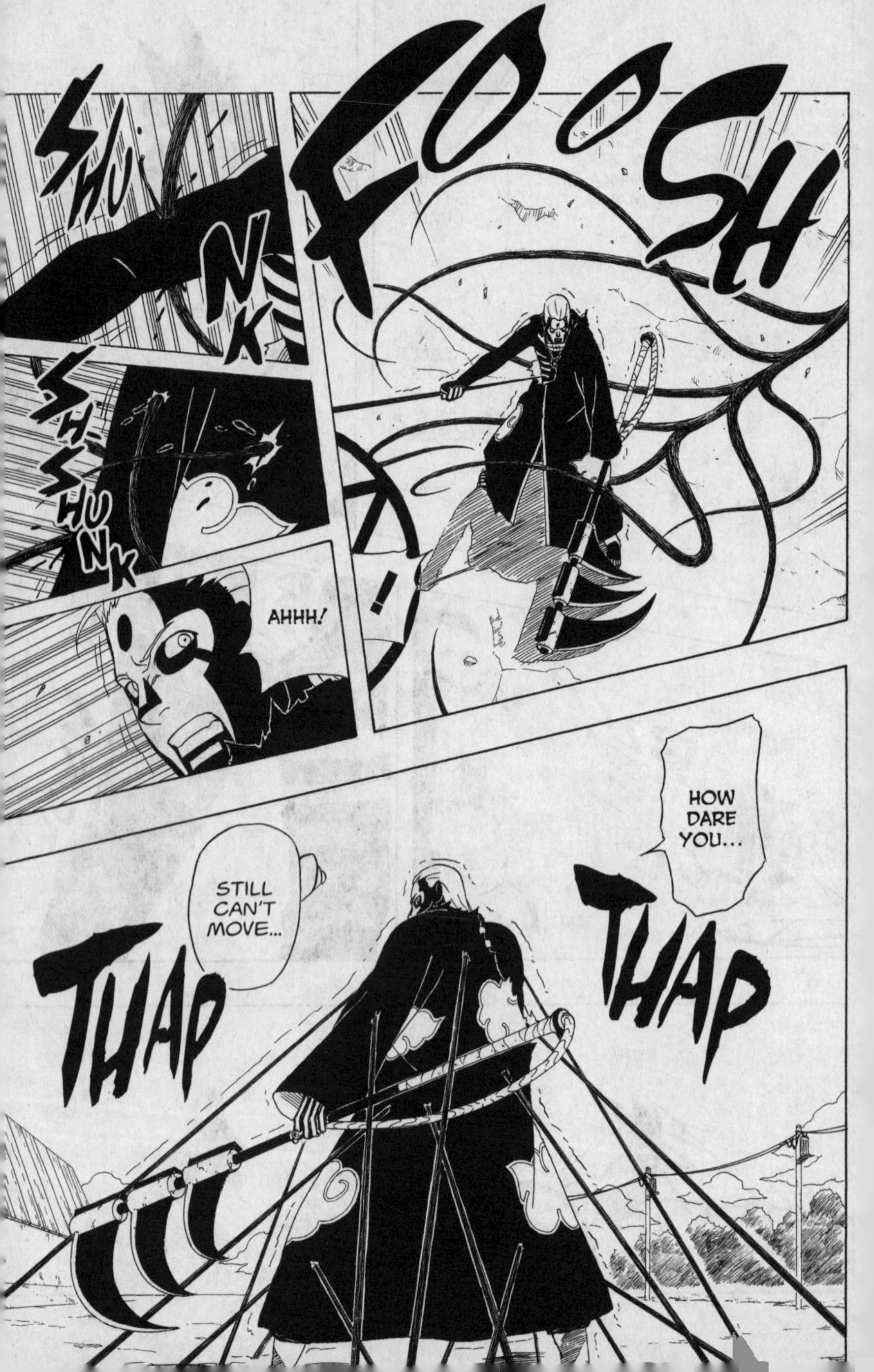
FOOSH
!
SHUNK
SHSHUNK
AHHH!
HOW DARE YOU...
THAP
STILL CAN'T MOVE...
THAP

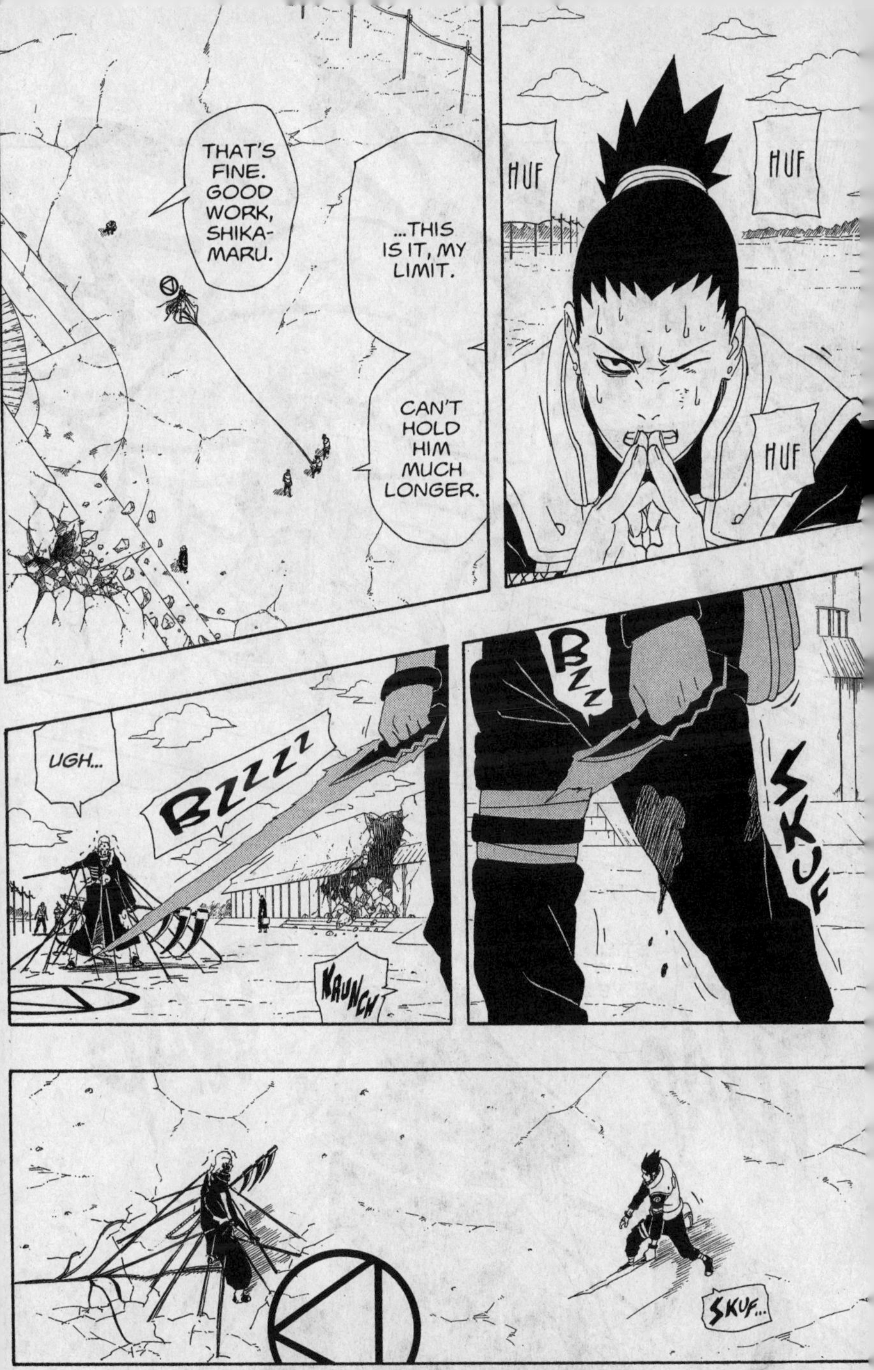
HUF
HUF
HUF
...THIS IS IT, MY LIMIT.
CAN'T HOLD HIM MUCH LONGER.
THAT'S FINE. GOOD WORK, SHIKAMARU.
BZZ
SKUF
BZZZZZ
UGH...
KRUNCH
SKUF...

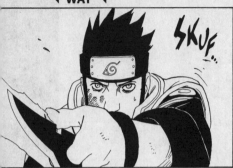

SKUF...

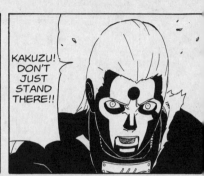

KAKUZU! DON'T JUST STAND THERE!!

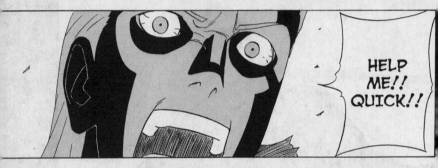

HELP ME!! QUICK!!

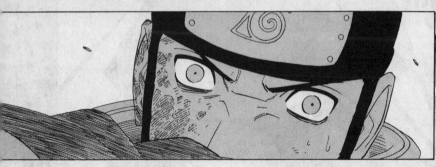

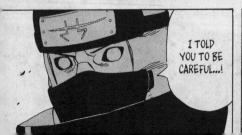

I TOLD YOU TO BE CAREFUL...!

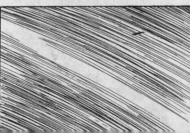

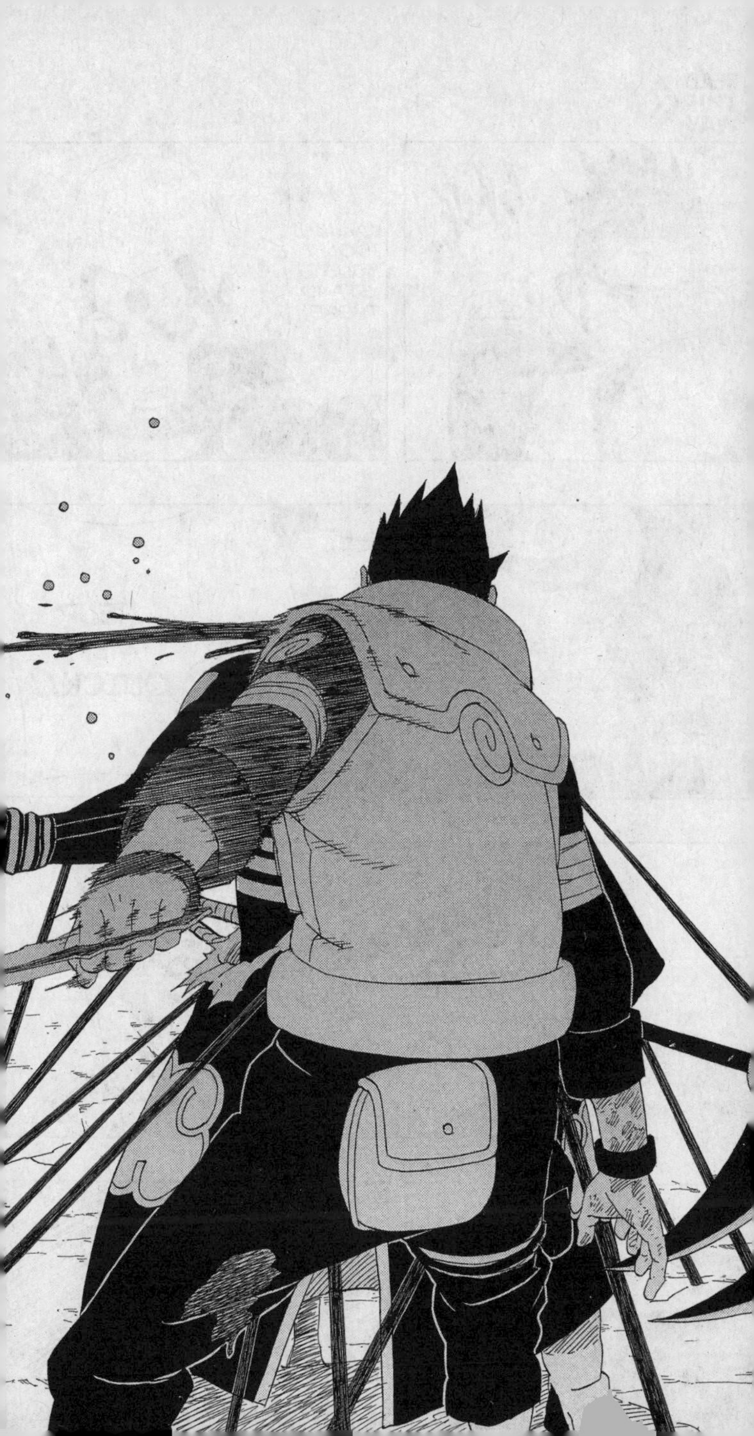

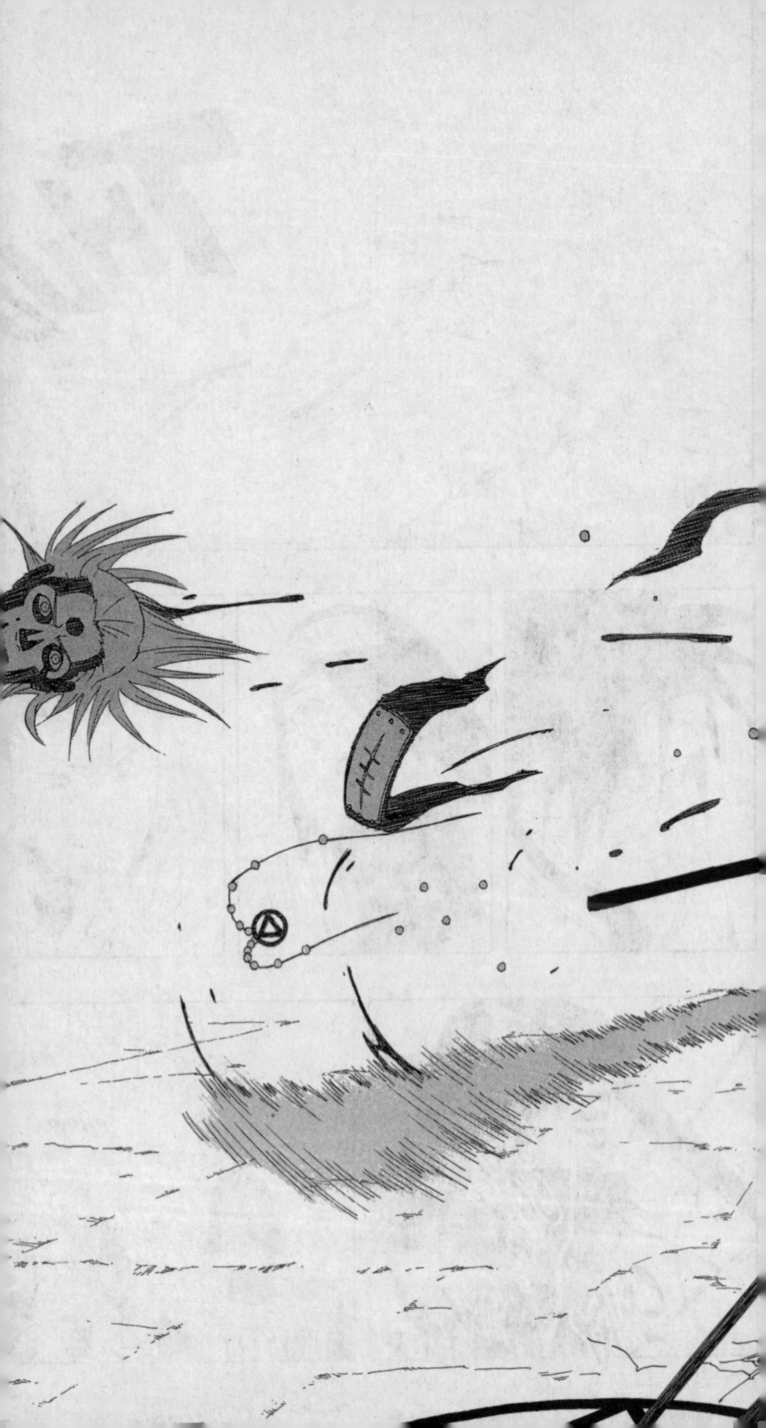

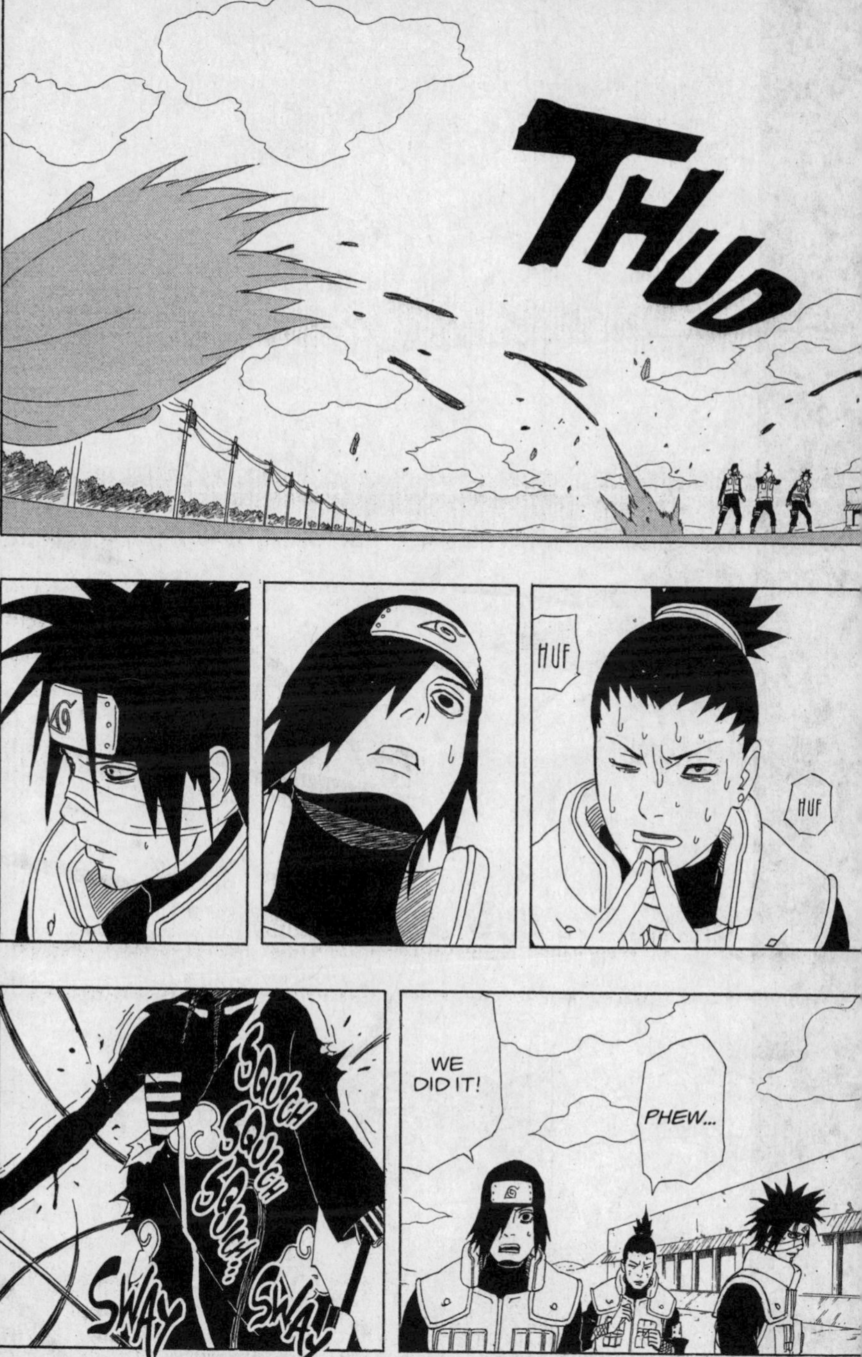
THUD
HUF
HUF
PHEW...
WE DID IT!
SQUICH
SQUICH
SQUICH
SQUICH...
SWAY
SWAY

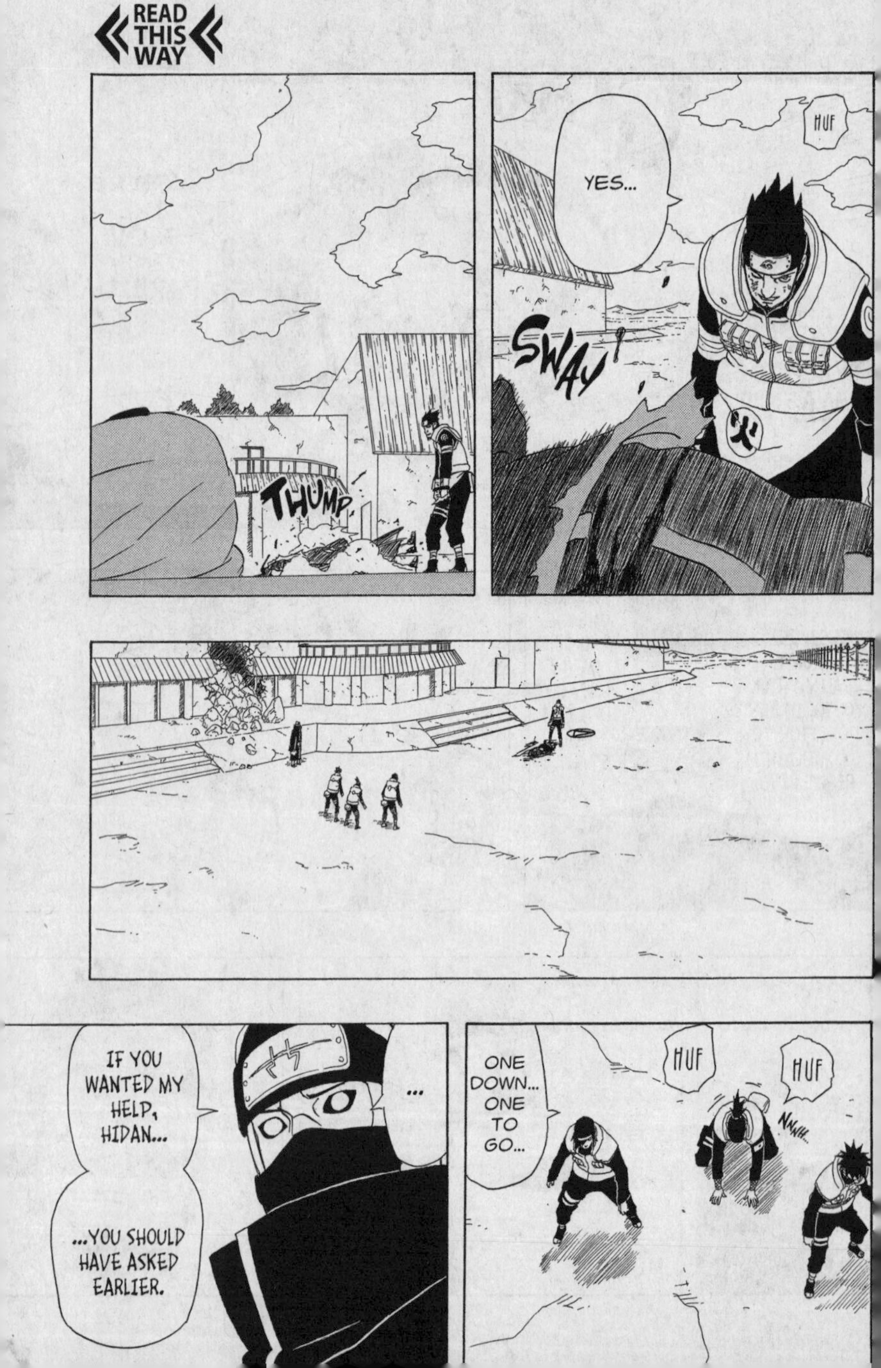
READ THIS WAY
HUF
YES...
SWAY
THUMP
HUF
HUF
NNNH...
ONE DOWN... ONE TO GO...
...
IF YOU WANTED MY HELP, HIDAN...
...YOU SHOULD HAVE ASKED EARLIER.

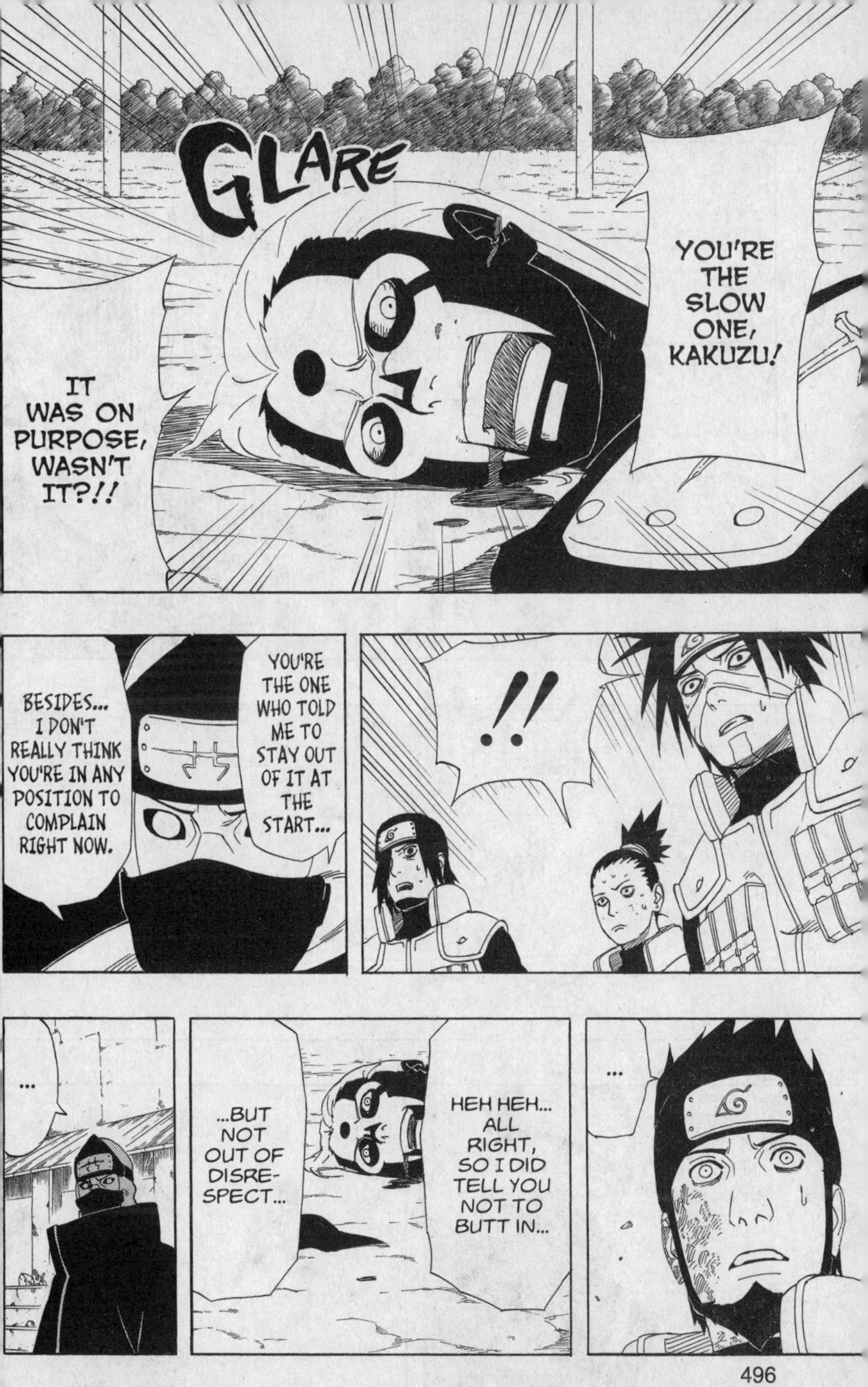
YOU'RE THE SLOW ONE, KAKUZU!
GLARE
IT WAS ON PURPOSE, WASN'T IT?!!
!!
YOU'RE THE ONE WHO TOLD ME TO STAY OUT OF IT AT THE START...
BESIDES... I DON'T REALLY THINK YOU'RE IN ANY POSITION TO COMPLAIN RIGHT NOW.
...
HEH HEH... ALL RIGHT, SO I DID TELL YOU NOT TO BUTT IN...
...BUT NOT OUT OF DISRESPECT...
...

READ THIS WAY

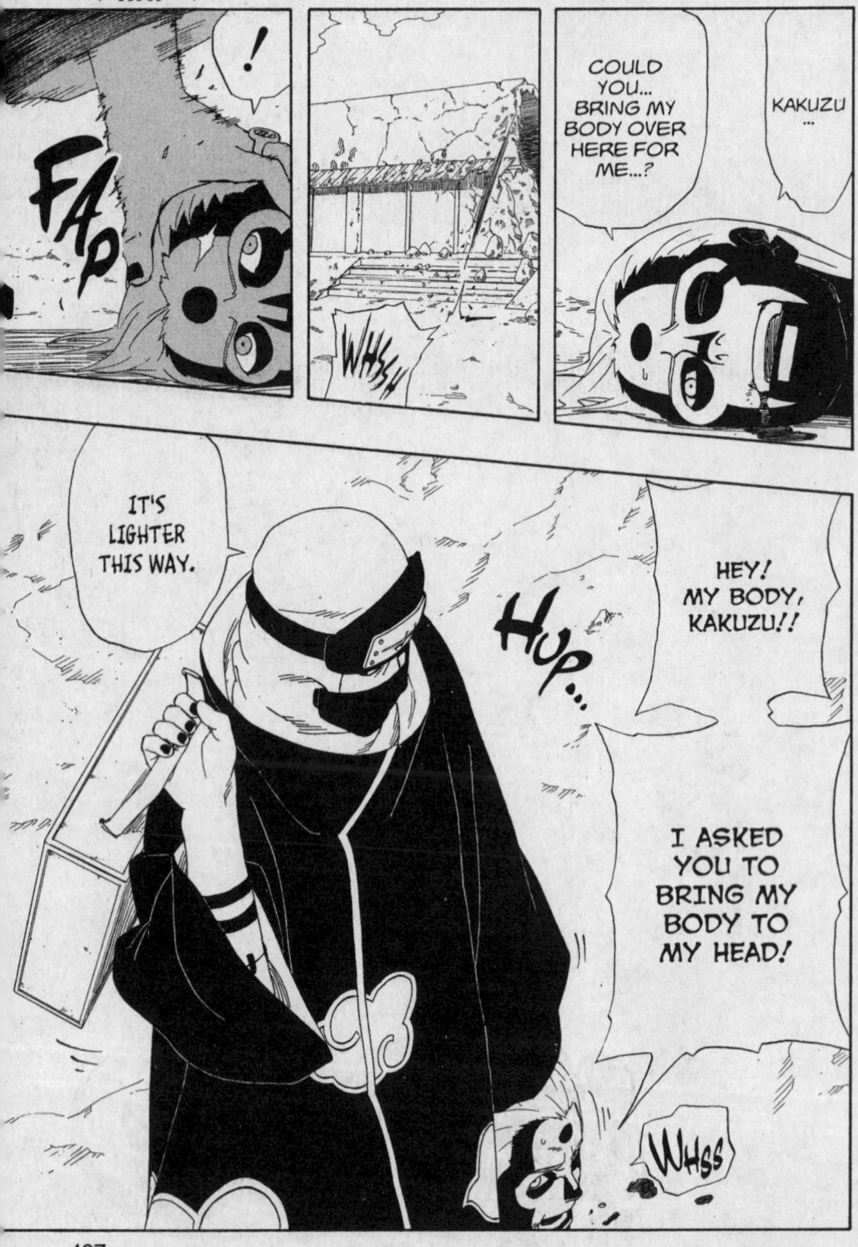
KAKUZU ...
COULD YOU... BRING MY BODY OVER HERE FOR ME...?
WHSSH
!
FAP
HEY! MY BODY, KAKUZU!!
I ASKED YOU TO BRING MY BODY TO MY HEAD!
HUP...
IT'S LIGHTER THIS WAY.
WHSS

NARUTO

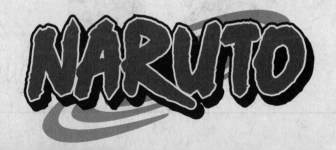

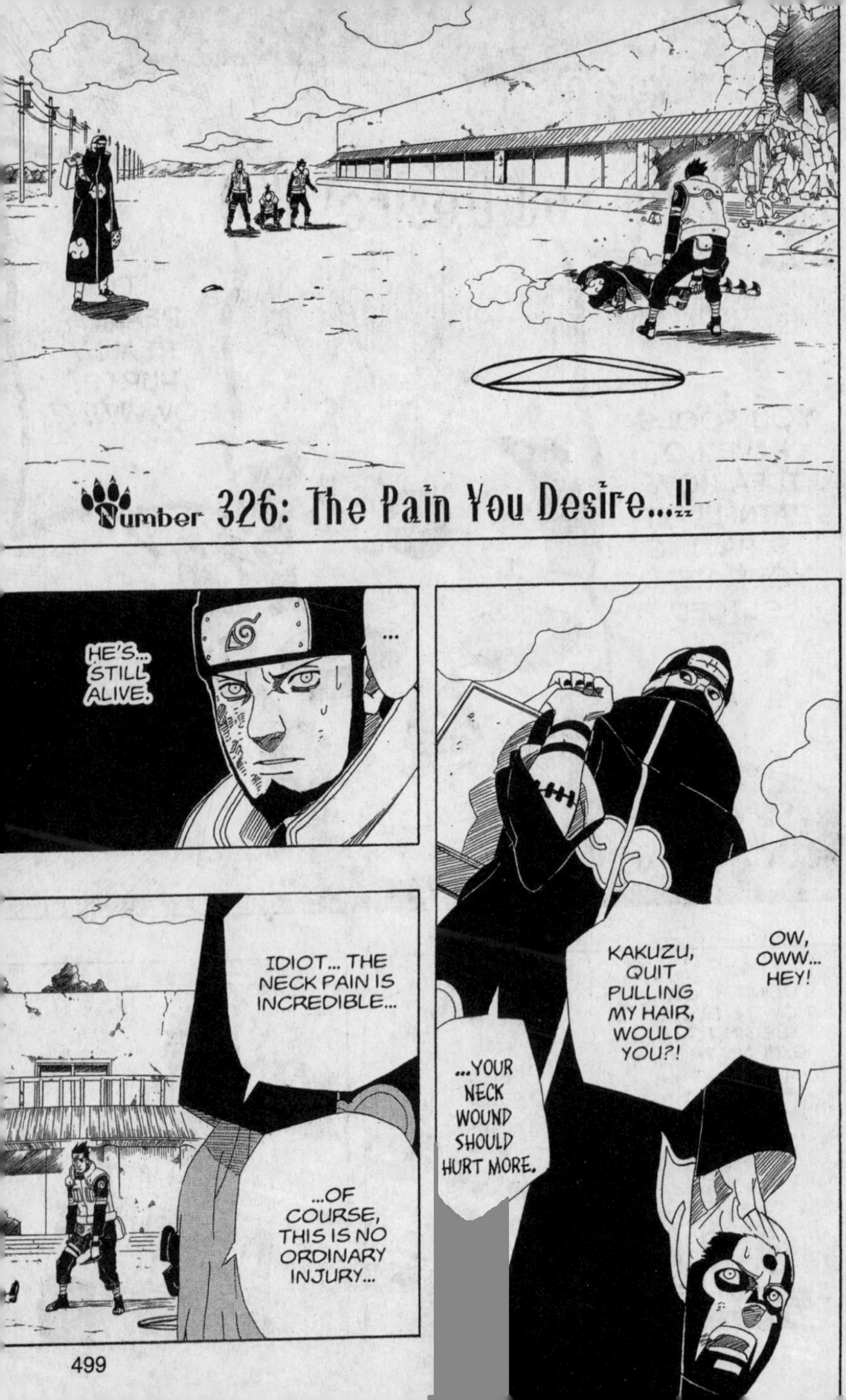
Number 326: The Pain You Desire...!!
OW, OWW... HEY!
KAKUZU, QUIT PULLING MY HAIR, WOULD YOU?!
...YOUR NECK WOUND SHOULD HURT MORE.
...
HE'S... STILL ALIVE.
IDIOT... THE NECK PAIN IS INCREDIBLE...
...OF COURSE, THIS IS NO ORDINARY INJURY...

Number 326: The Pain You Desire...!!

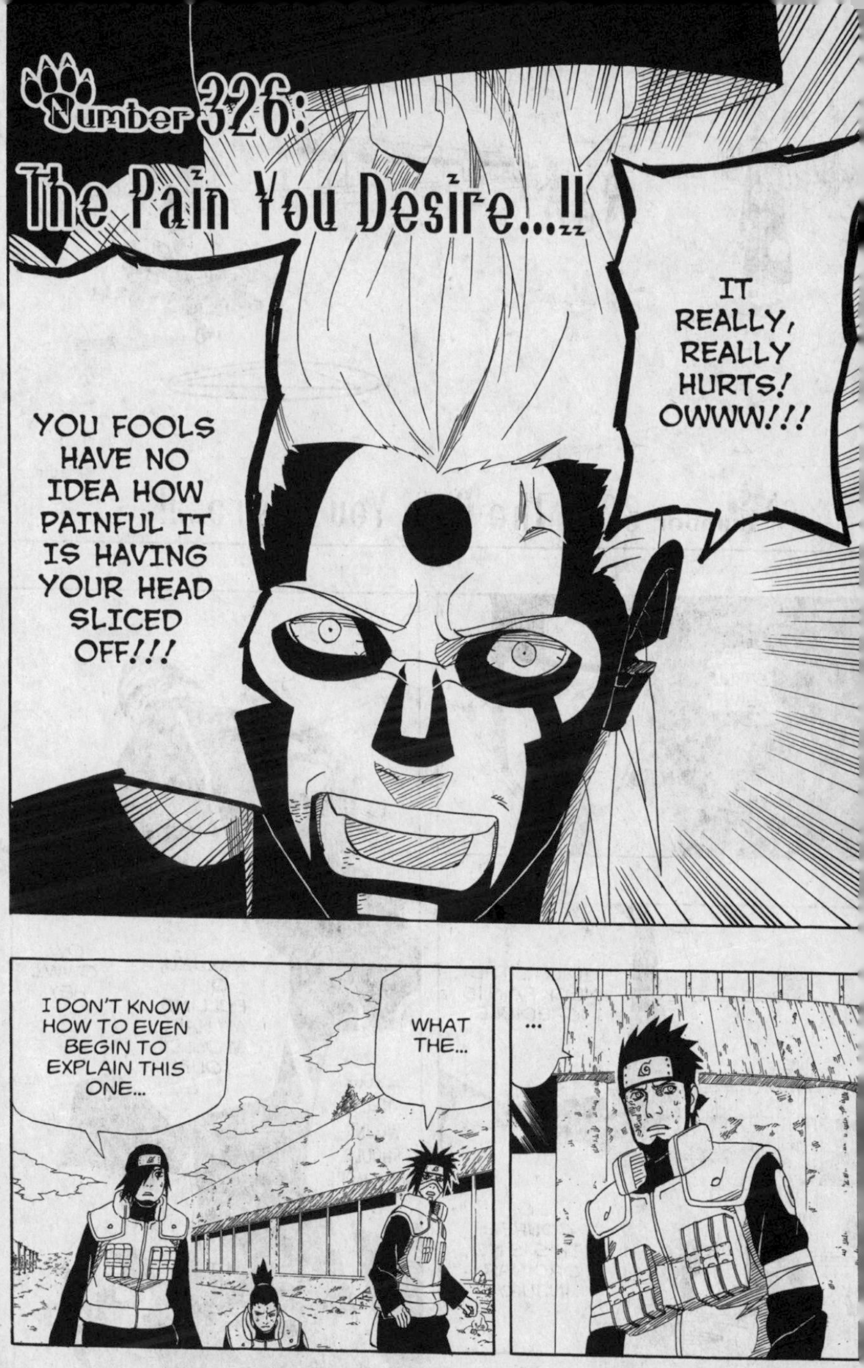

IT REALLY, REALLY HURTS! OWWW!!!
YOU FOOLS HAVE NO IDEA HOW PAINFUL IT IS HAVING YOUR HEAD SLICED OFF!!!
...
WHAT THE...
I DON'T KNOW HOW TO EVEN BEGIN TO EXPLAIN THIS ONE...

READ THIS WAY

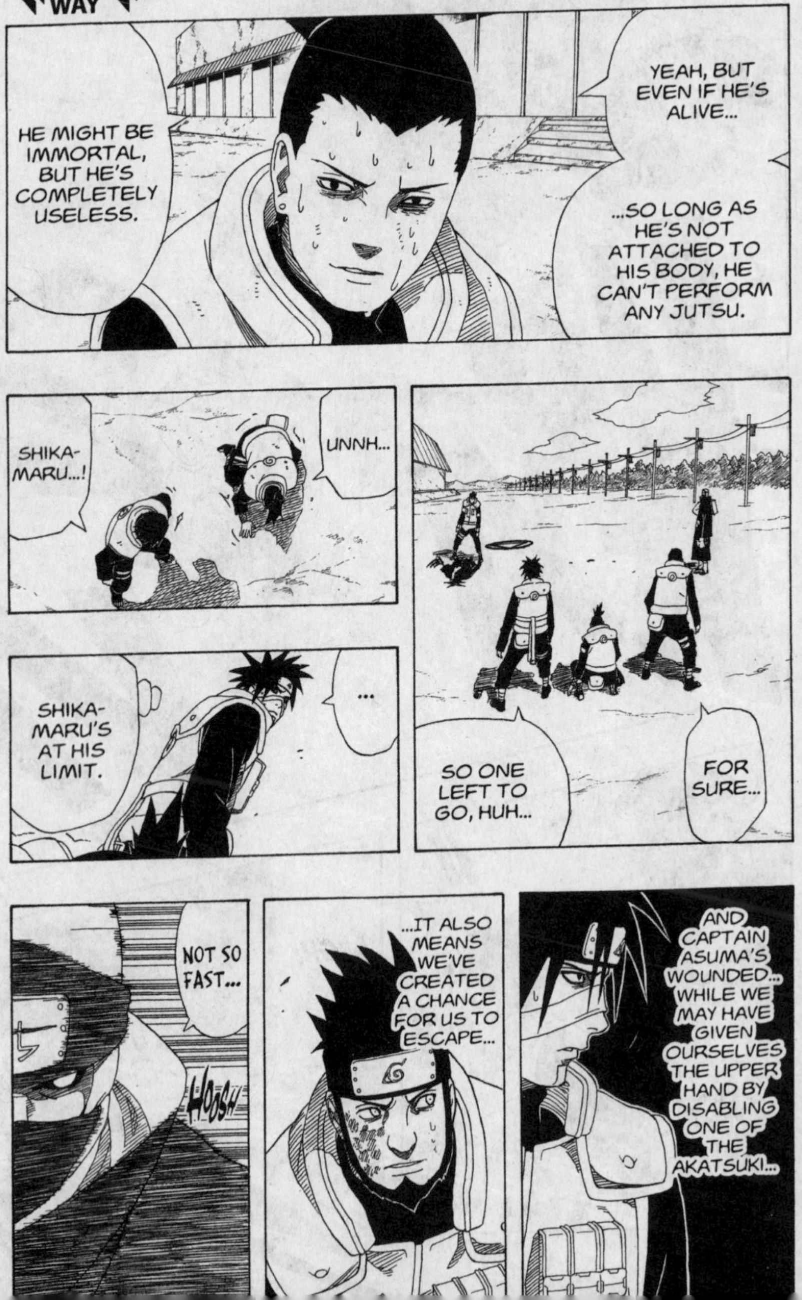
YEAH, BUT EVEN IF HE'S ALIVE...
...SO LONG AS HE'S NOT ATTACHED TO HIS BODY, HE CAN'T PERFORM ANY JUTSU.
HE MIGHT BE IMMORTAL, BUT HE'S COMPLETELY USELESS.
FOR SURE...
SO ONE LEFT TO GO, HUH...
UNNH...
SHIKA-MARU...!
...
SHIKA-MARU'S AT HIS LIMIT.
AND CAPTAIN ASUMA'S WOUNDED... WHILE WE MAY HAVE GIVEN OURSELVES THE UPPER HAND BY DISABLING ONE OF THE AKATSUKI...
...IT ALSO MEANS WE'VE CREATED A CHANCE FOR US TO ESCAPE...
NOT SO FAST...
WHOOSH

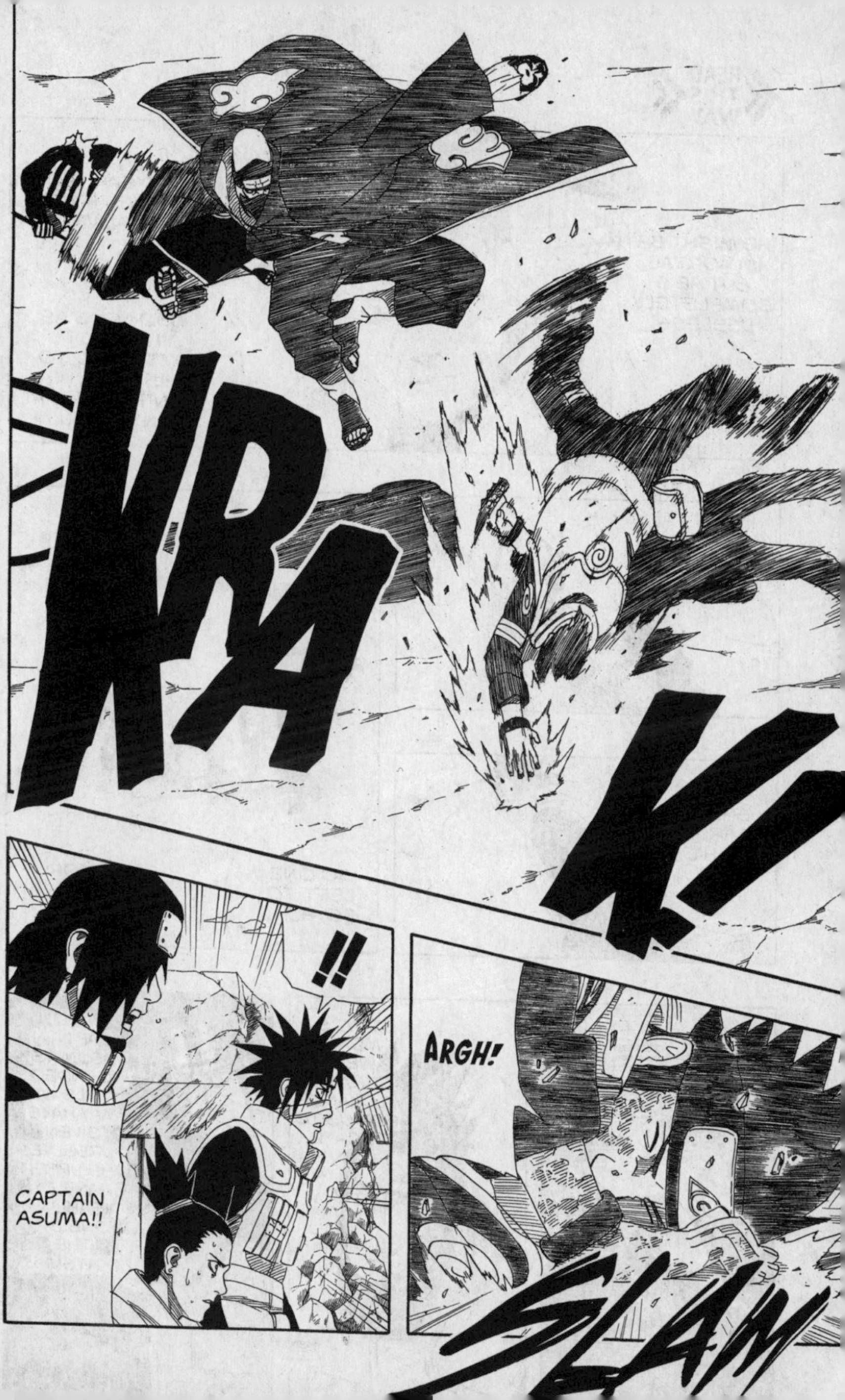
KRAK!
ARGH!
SLAM
!!
CAPTAIN ASUMA!!

READ THIS WAY

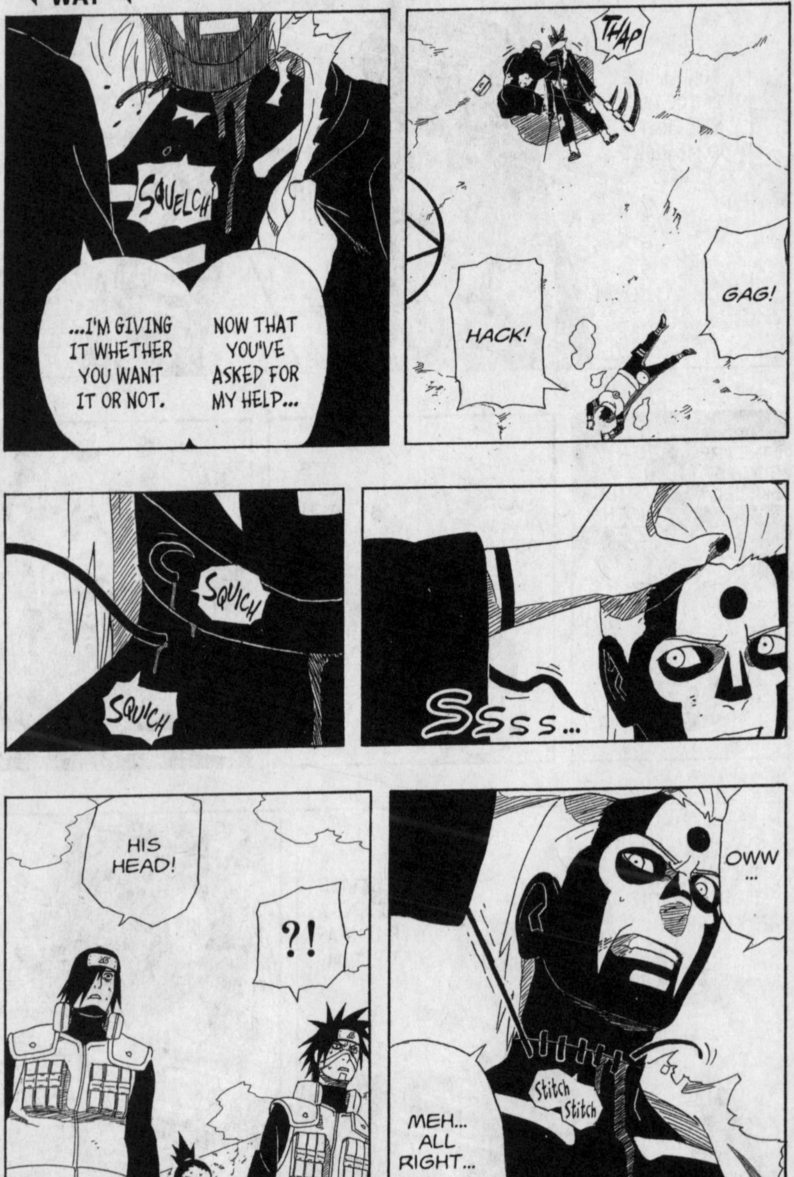
THAP
GAG!
HACK!
SQUELCH
NOW THAT YOU'VE ASKED FOR MY HELP...
...I'M GIVING IT WHETHER YOU WANT IT OR NOT.
SSSS...
SQUICH
SQUICH
OWW...
Stitch Stitch
MEH... ALL RIGHT...
HIS HEAD!
?!

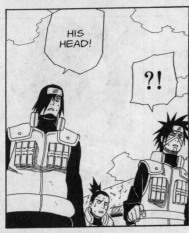

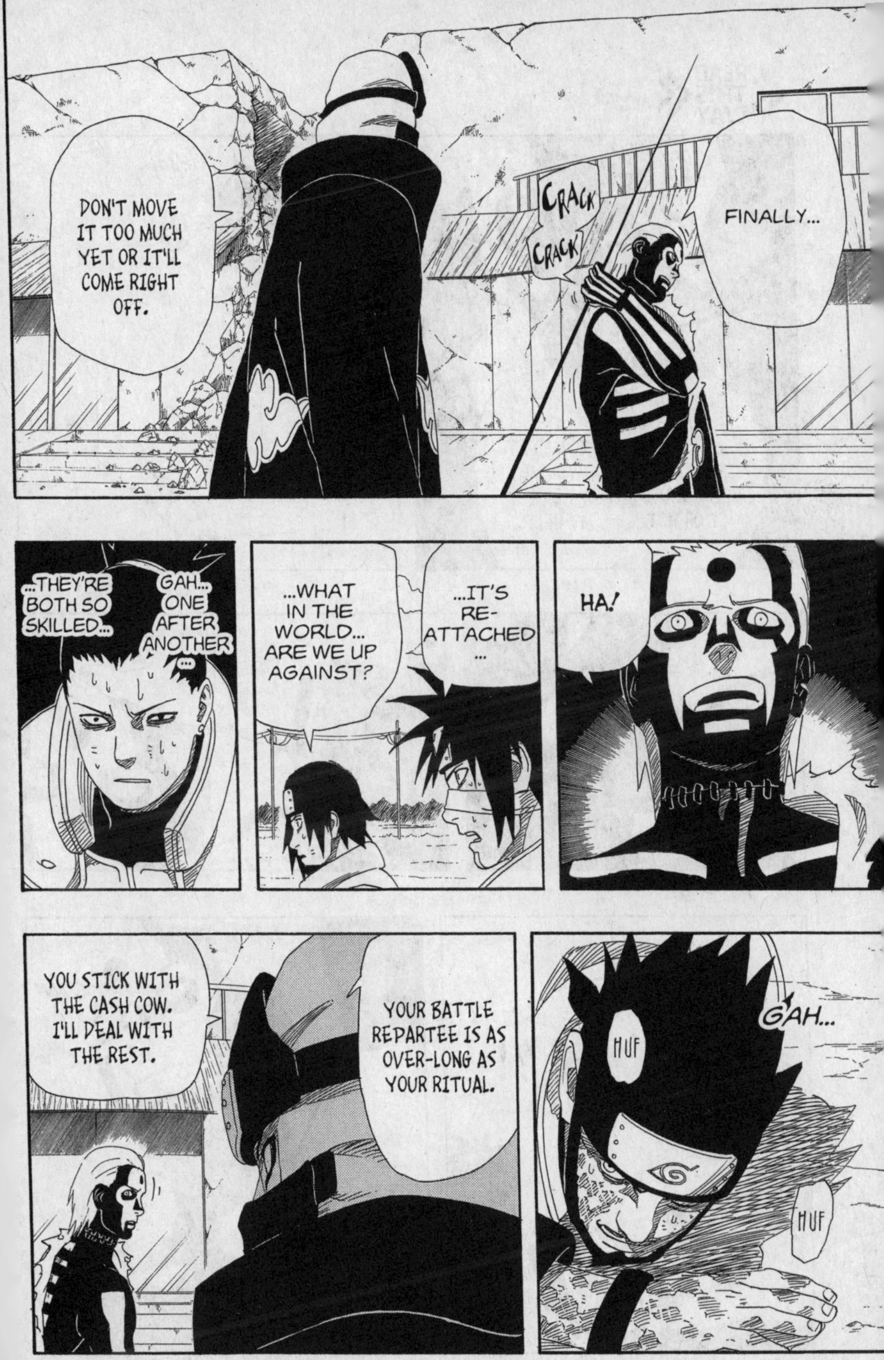
FINALLY...
CRACK
CRACK
DON'T MOVE IT TOO MUCH YET OR IT'LL COME RIGHT OFF.
HA!
...IT'S RE-ATTACHED ...
...WHAT IN THE WORLD... ARE WE UP AGAINST?
GAH... ONE AFTER ANOTHER ...
...THEY'RE BOTH SO SKILLED...
GAH...
HUF
HUF
YOUR BATTLE REPARTEE IS AS OVER-LONG AS YOUR RITUAL.
YOU STICK WITH THE CASH COW. I'LL DEAL WITH THE REST.

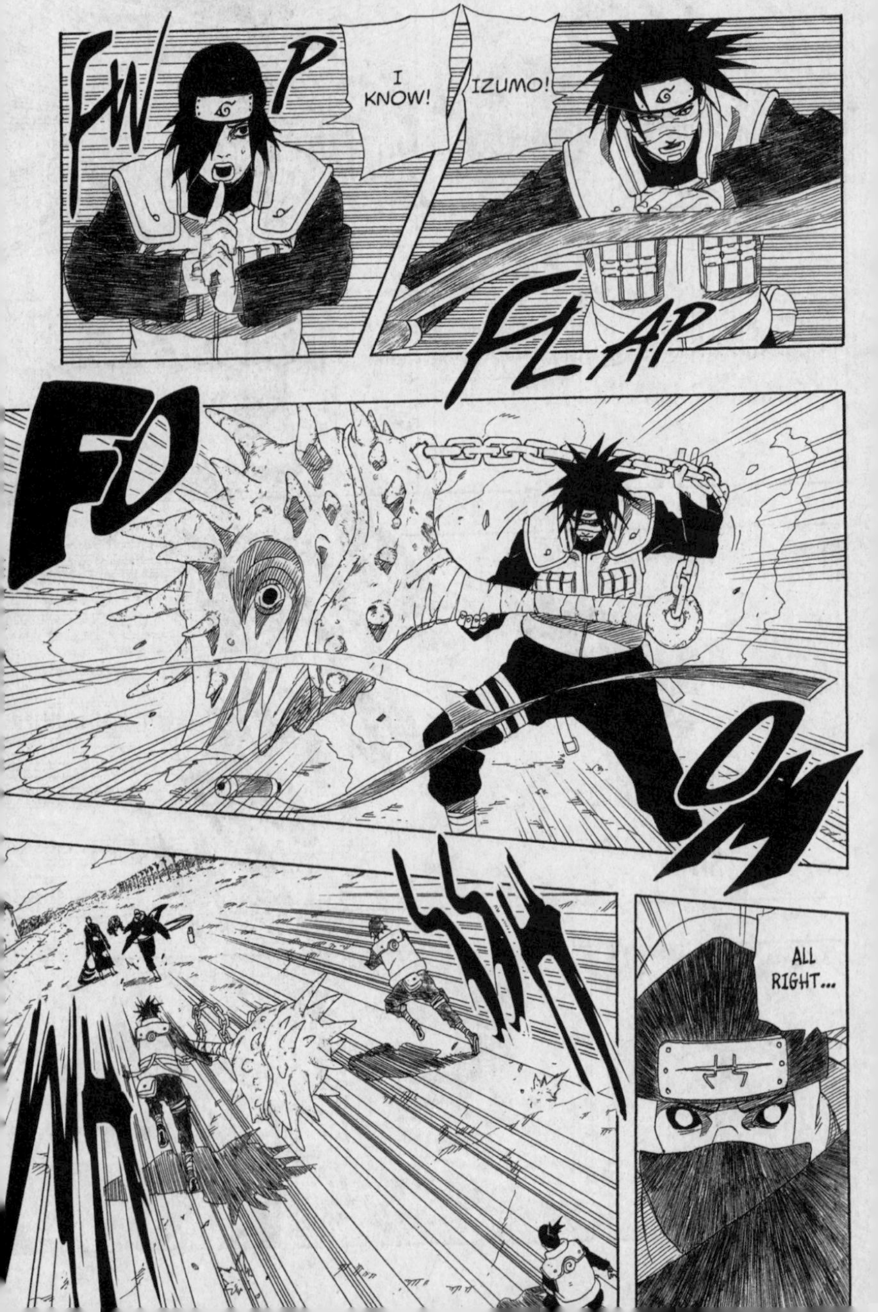
FLAP
IZUMO!
I KNOW!
FWP
FOOM
ALL RIGHT...
SSH
WHH

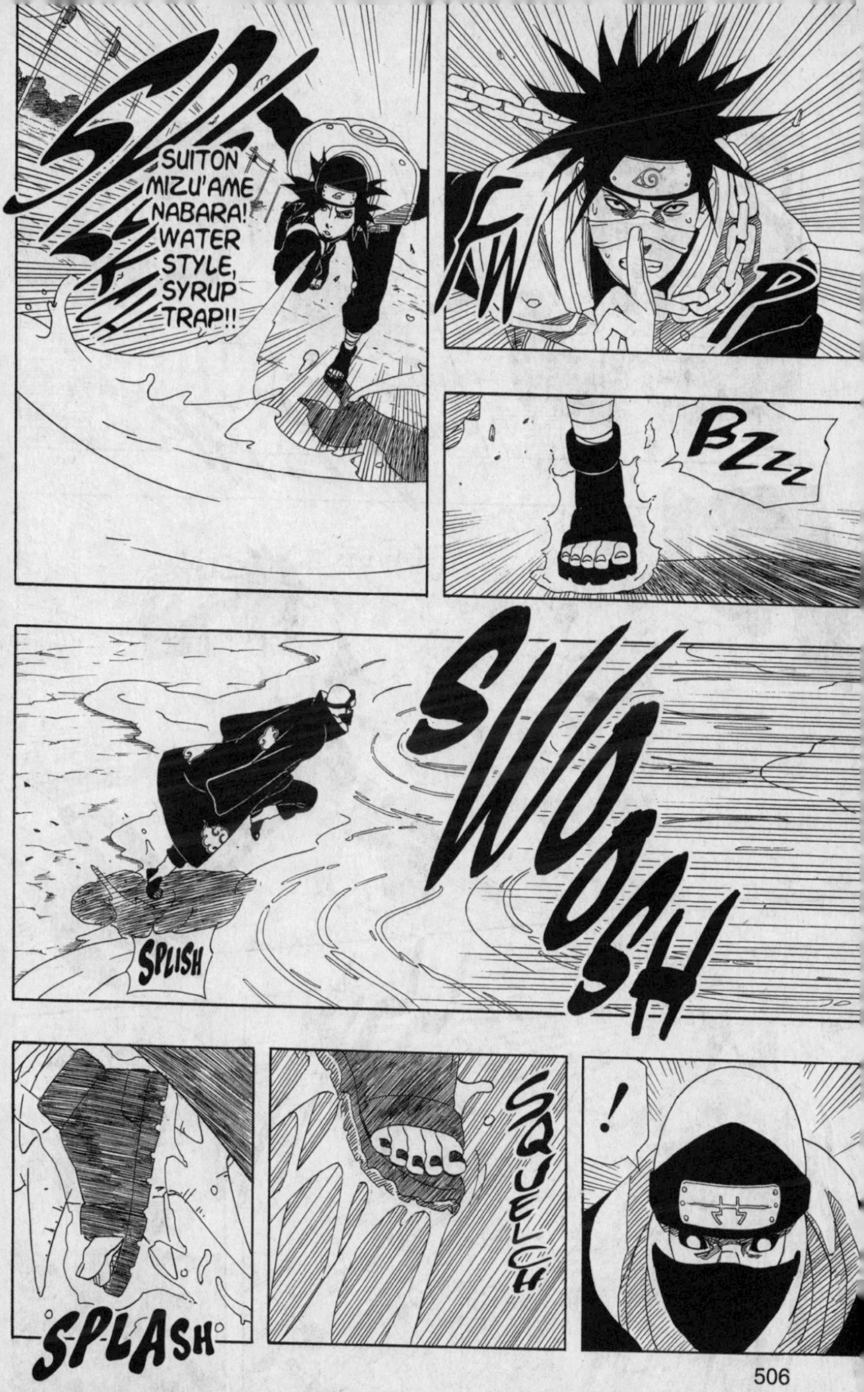
FWP
BZZZ
SUITON MIZU'AME NABARA! WATER STYLE, SYRUP TRAP!!
SWOOSH
SPLISH
!
SQUELCH
SPLASH

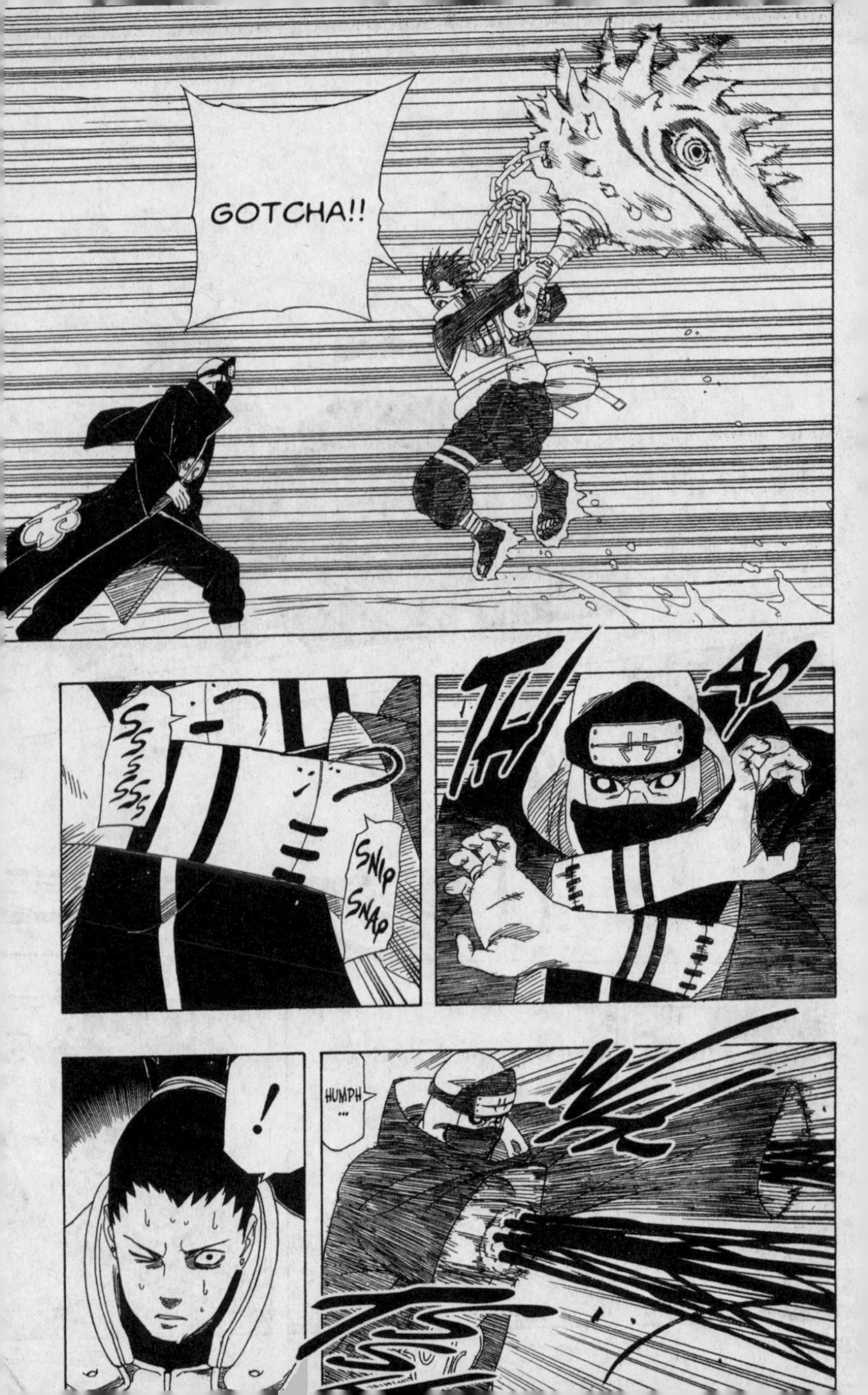
GOTCHA!!
THWAP
SSSSS
SNIP SNAP
HUMPH ...
!

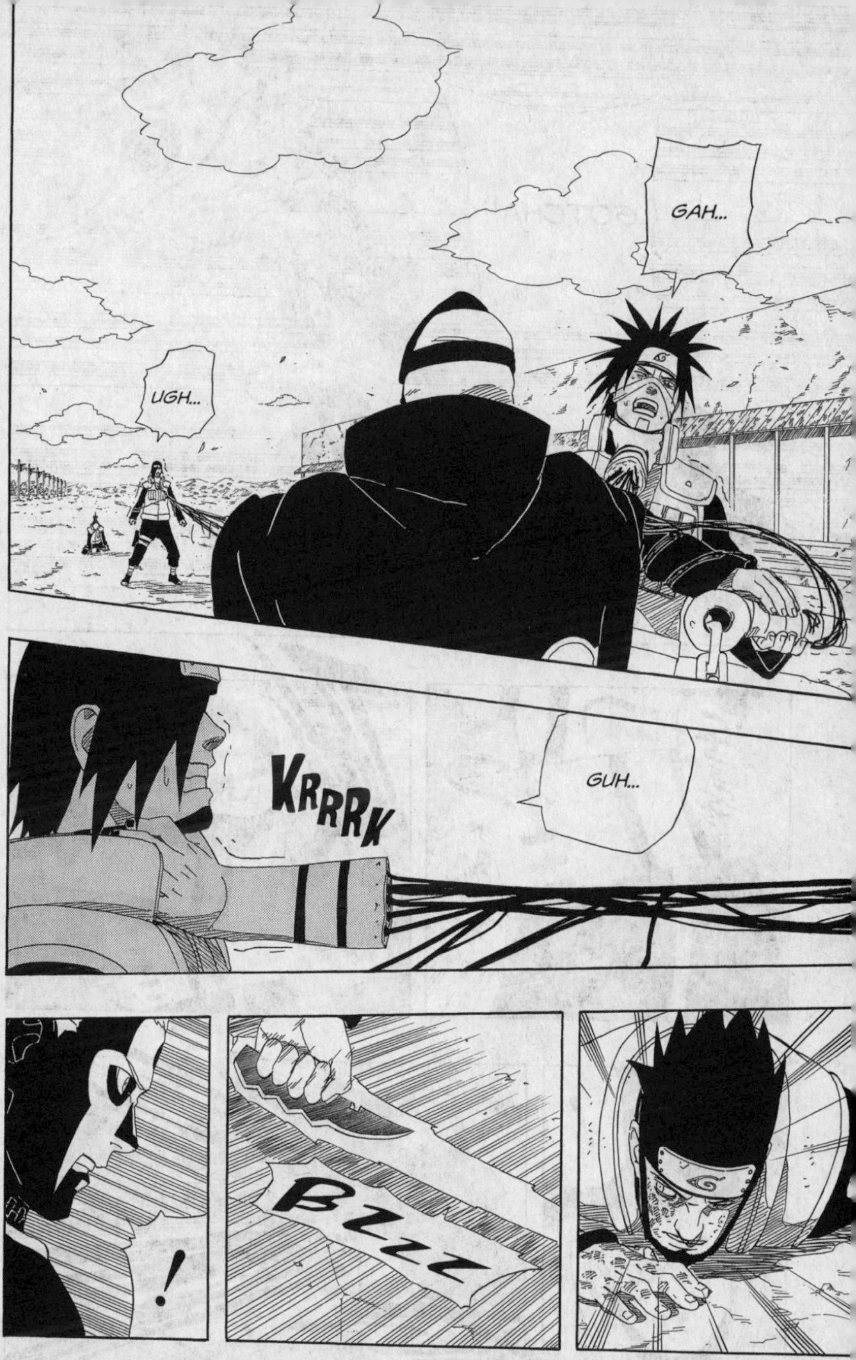
GAH...
UGH...
GUH...
KRRRK
BZZZ
!

READ THIS WAY

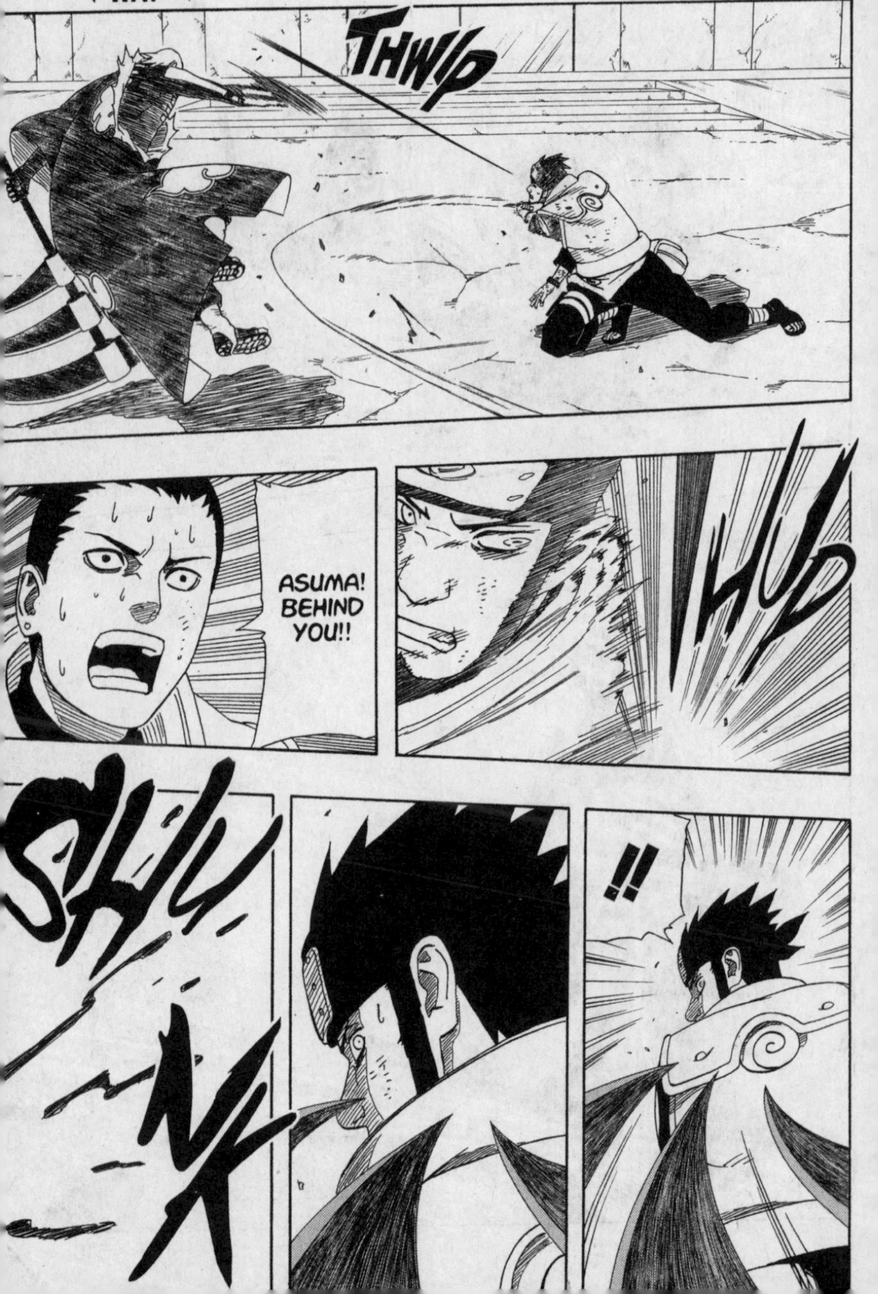
THWIP
WHUD
ASUMA! BEHIND YOU!!
!!
SHUNK

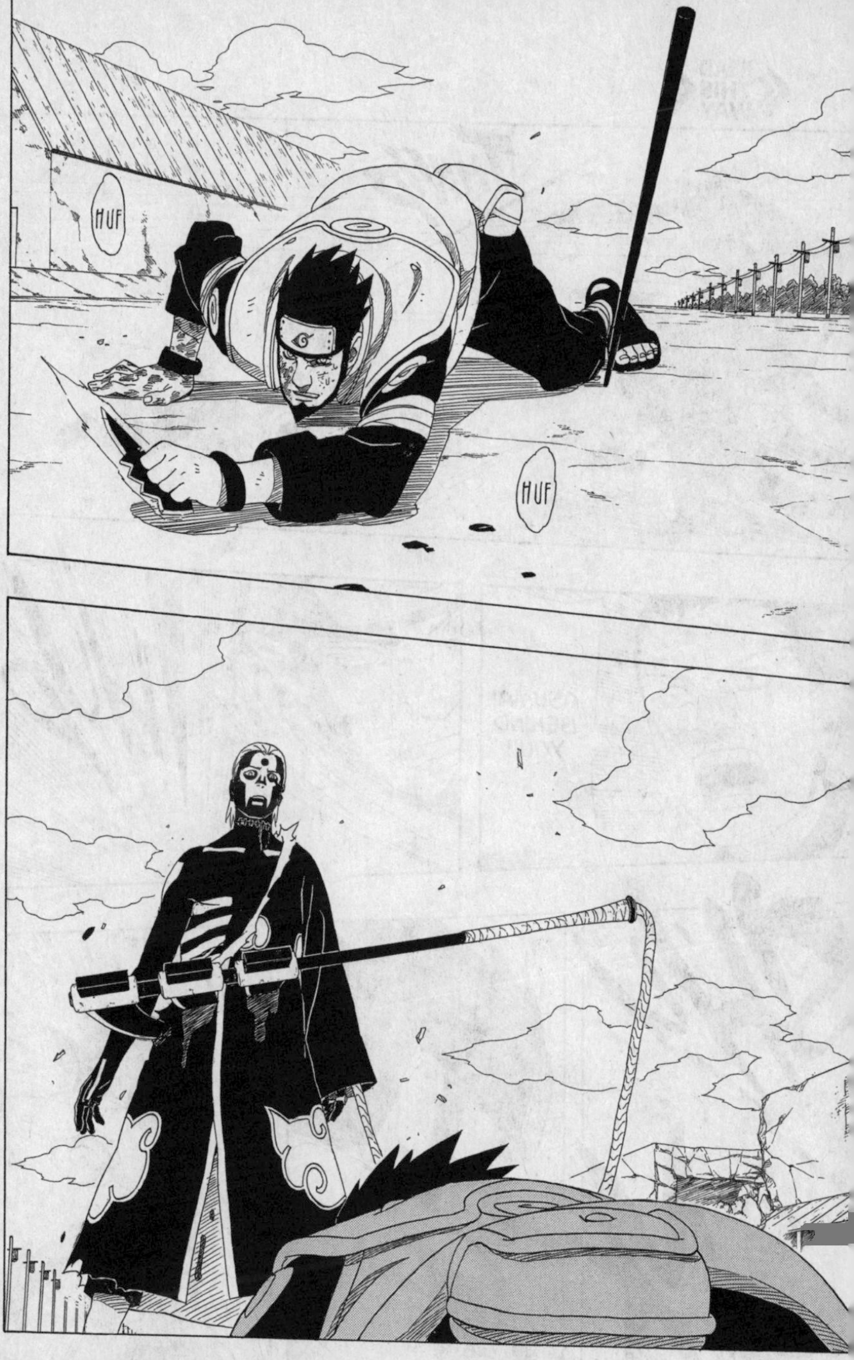
HUF
HUF

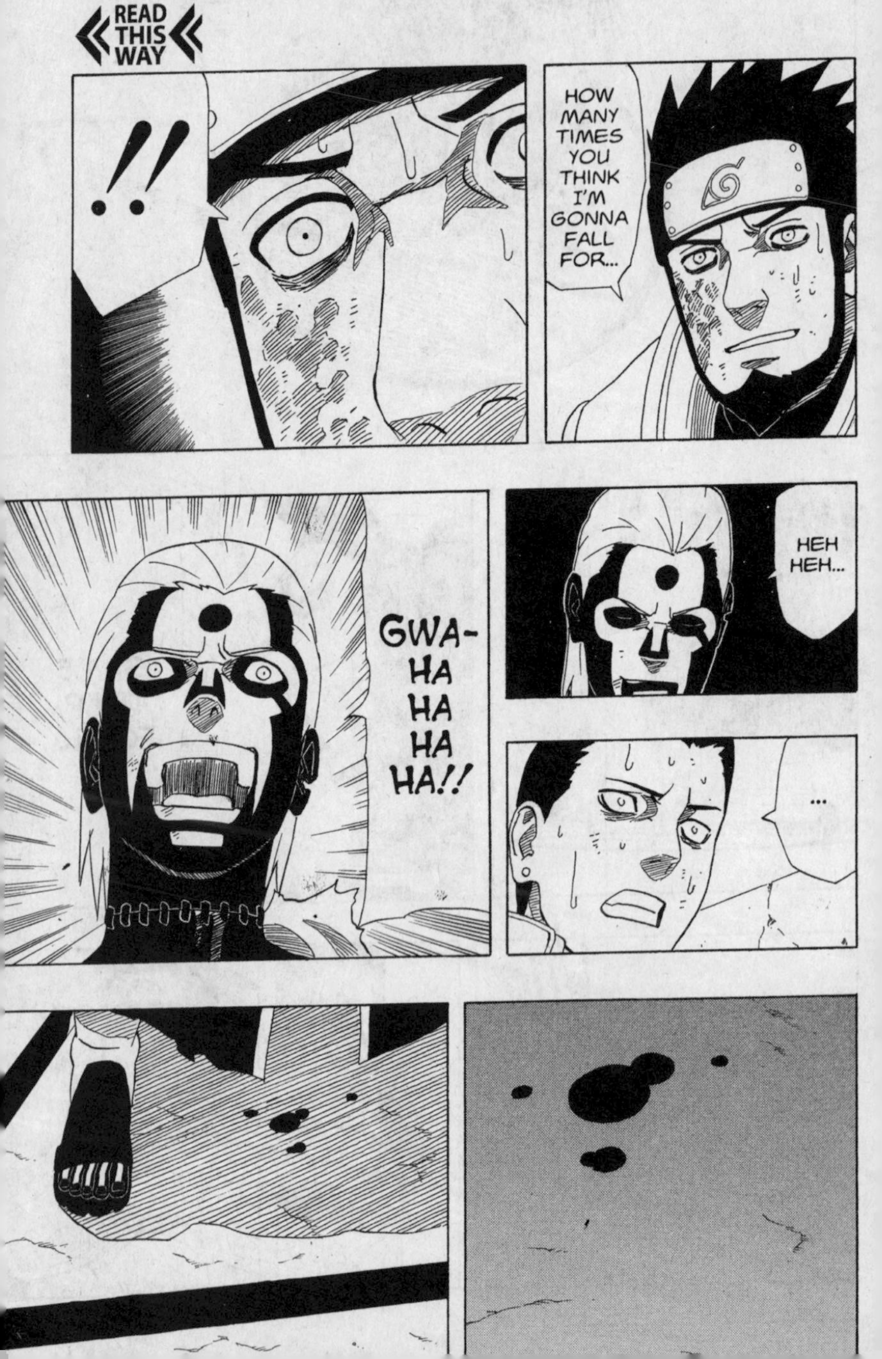
READ THIS WAY
HOW MANY TIMES YOU THINK I'M GONNA FALL FOR...
!!
HEH HEH...
GWA-HA HA HA HA!!
...

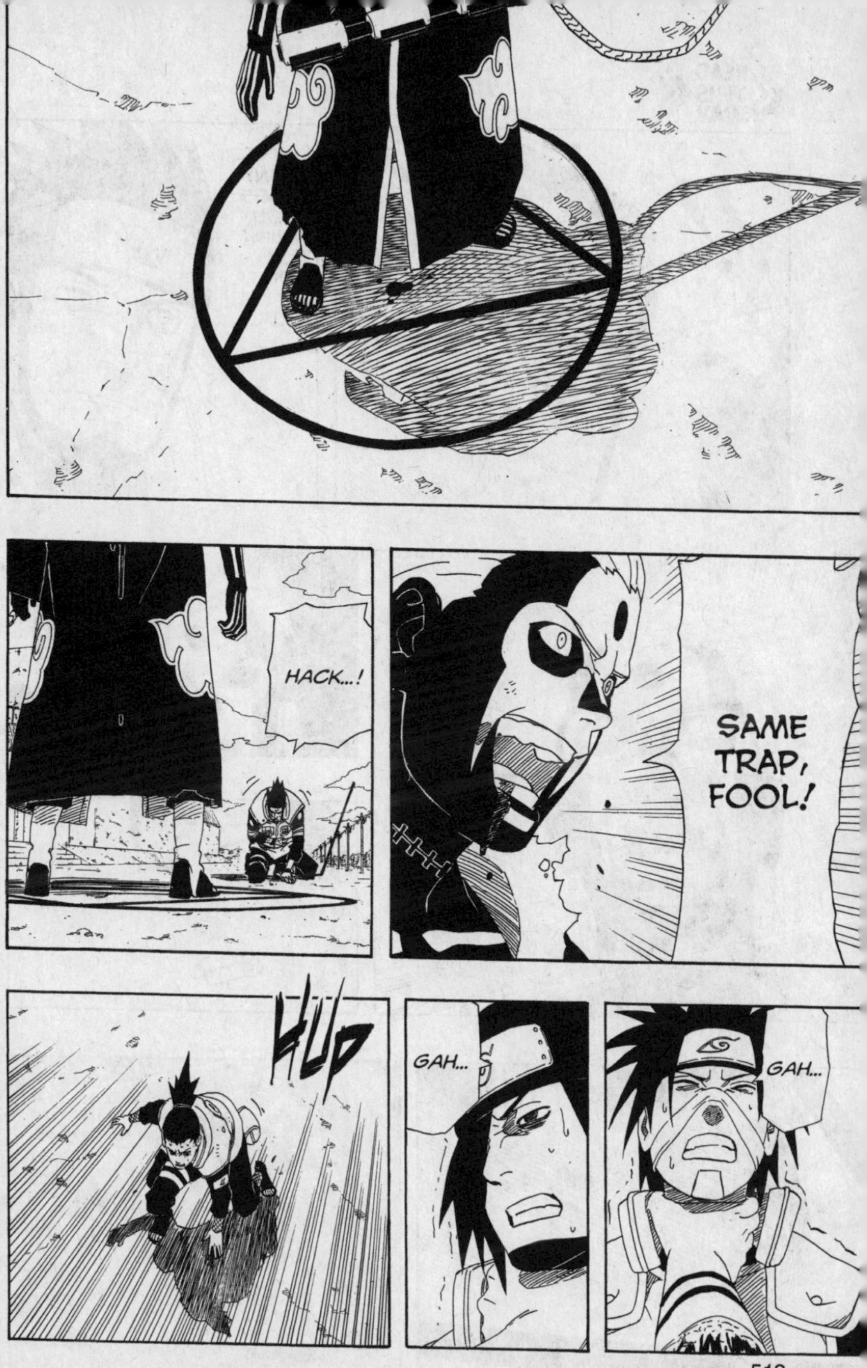
SAME TRAP, FOOL!
HACK...!
GAH...
GAH...
KUP

READ THIS WAY

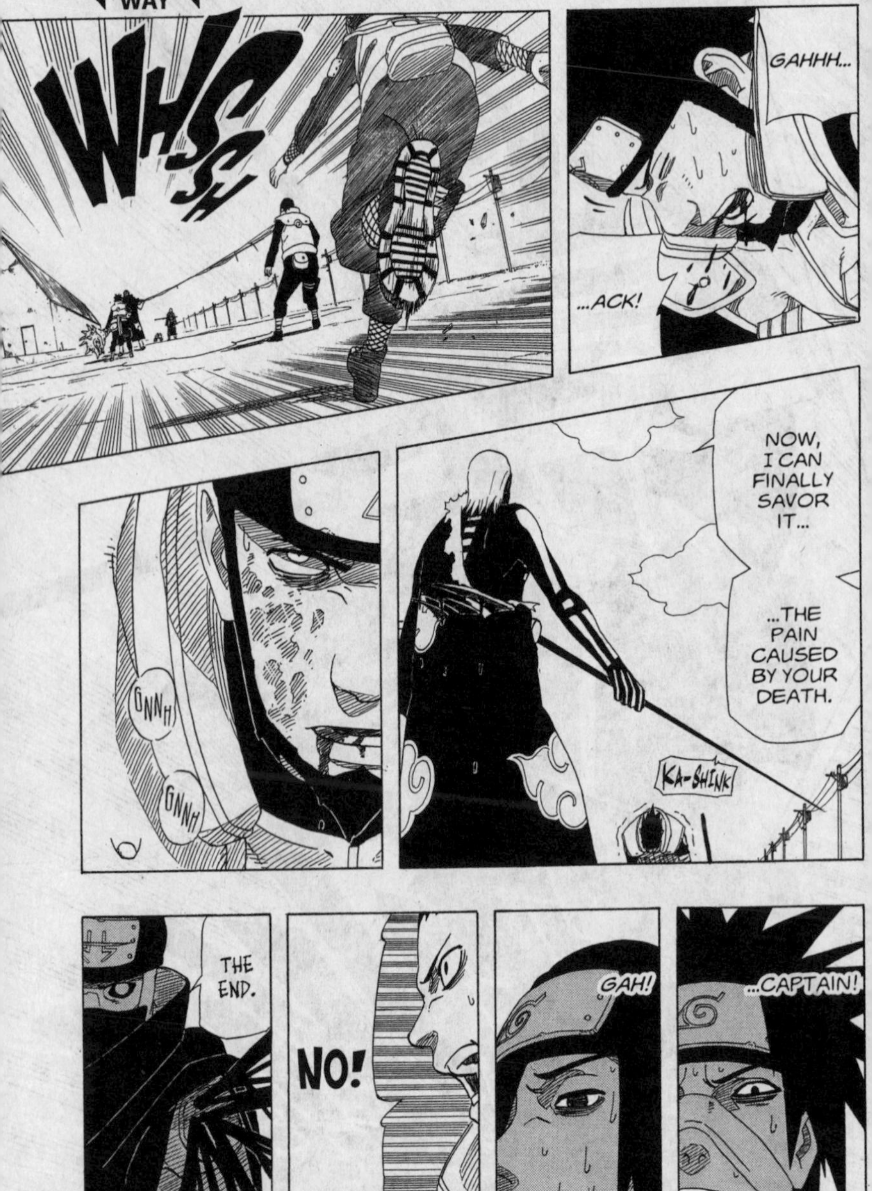
GAHHH...
...ACK!
WHSSH
NOW, I CAN FINALLY SAVOR IT...
...THE PAIN CAUSED BY YOUR DEATH.
KA-SHINK
GNNH
GNNH
...CAPTAIN!
GAH!
NO!
THE END.

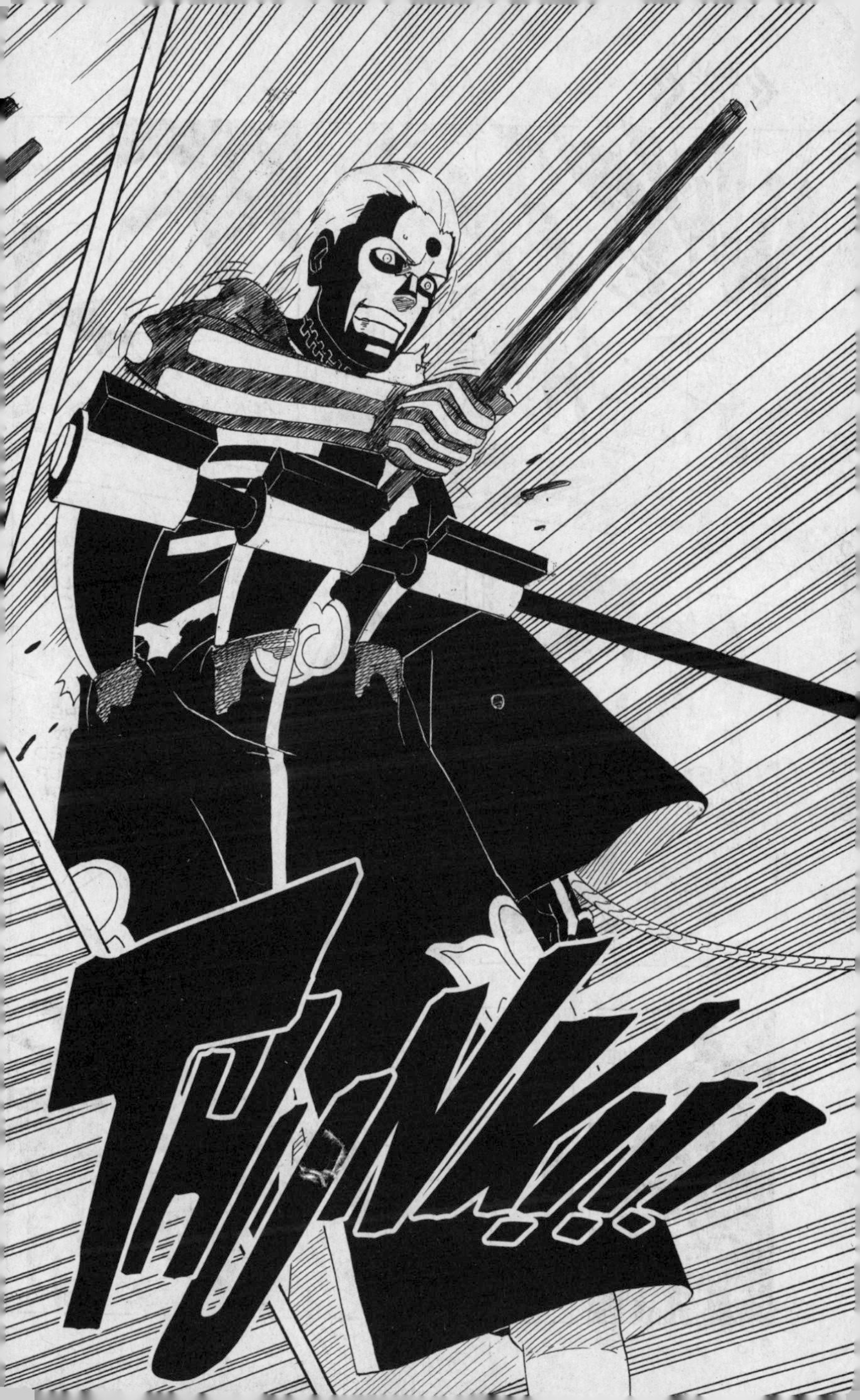
THUNK!!!

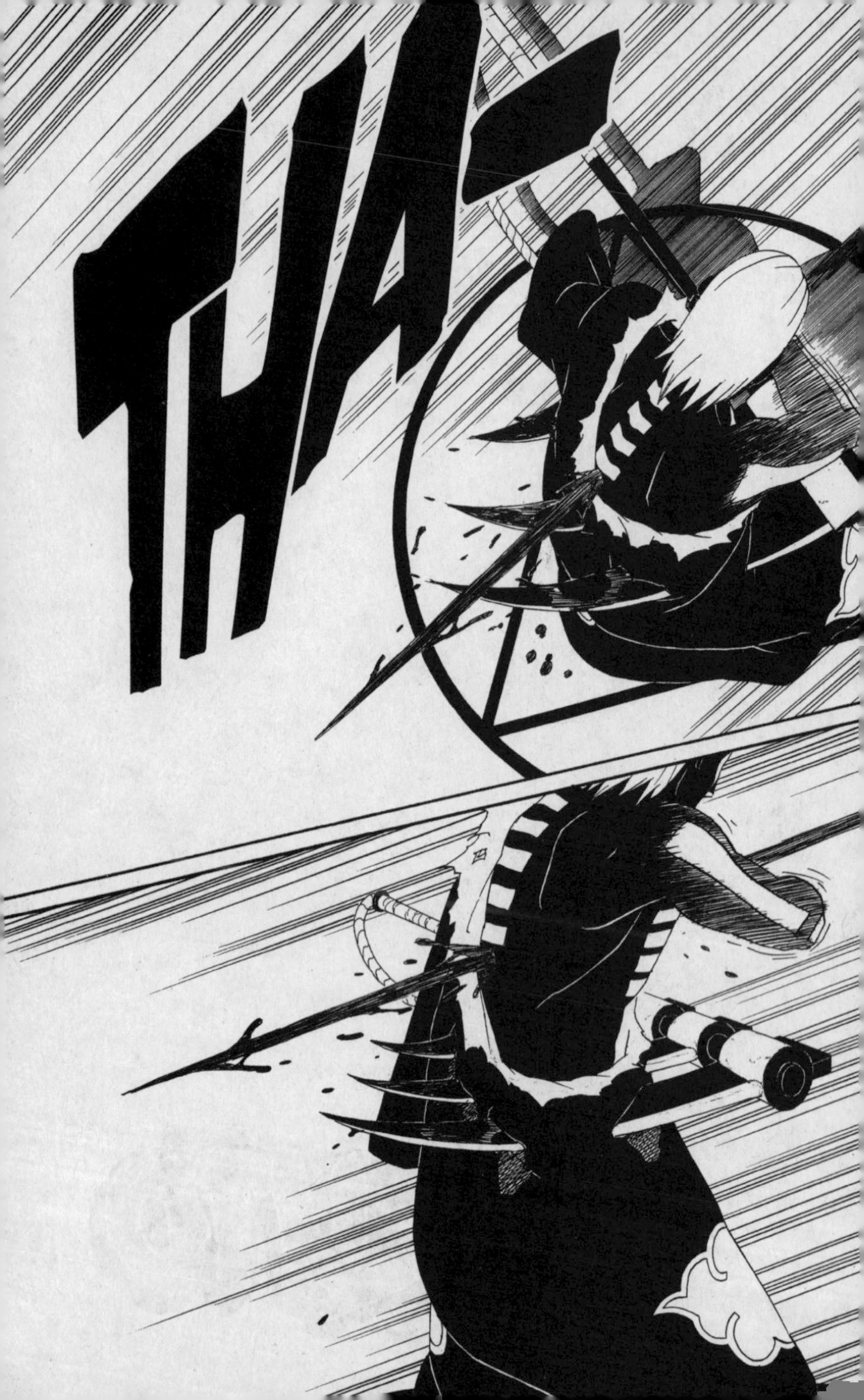
THA

NARUTO

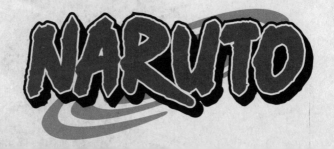

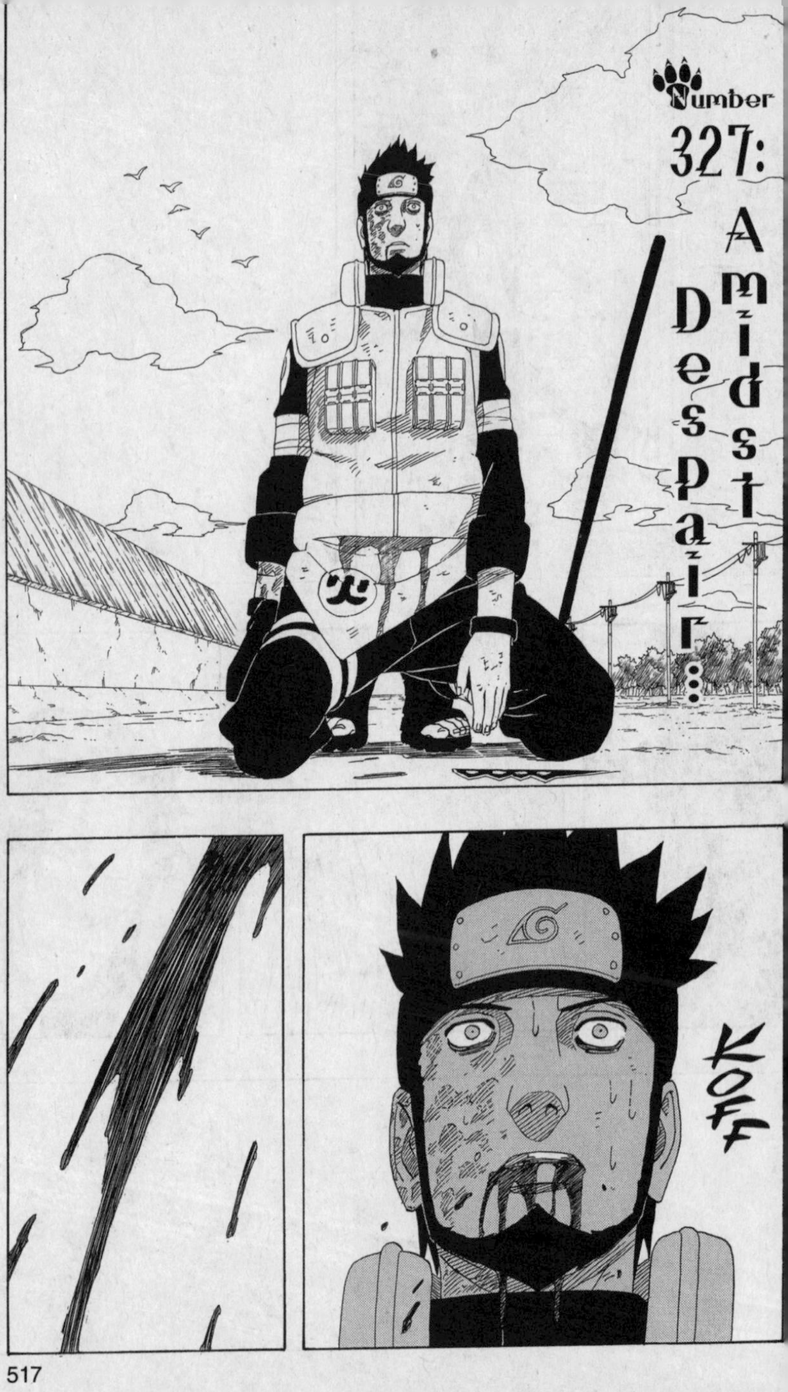
Number 327: Amidst Despair...
KOFF

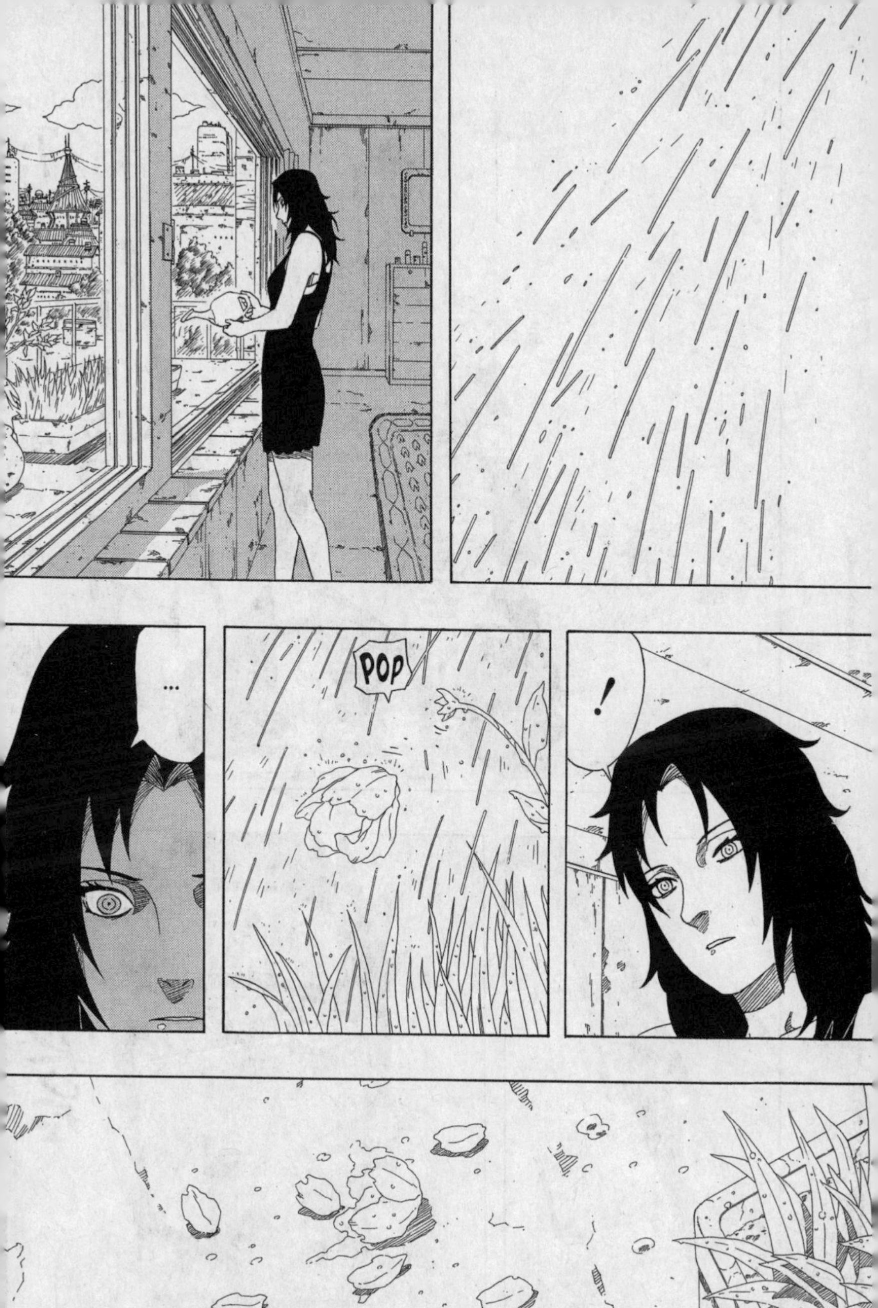
!
POP
...

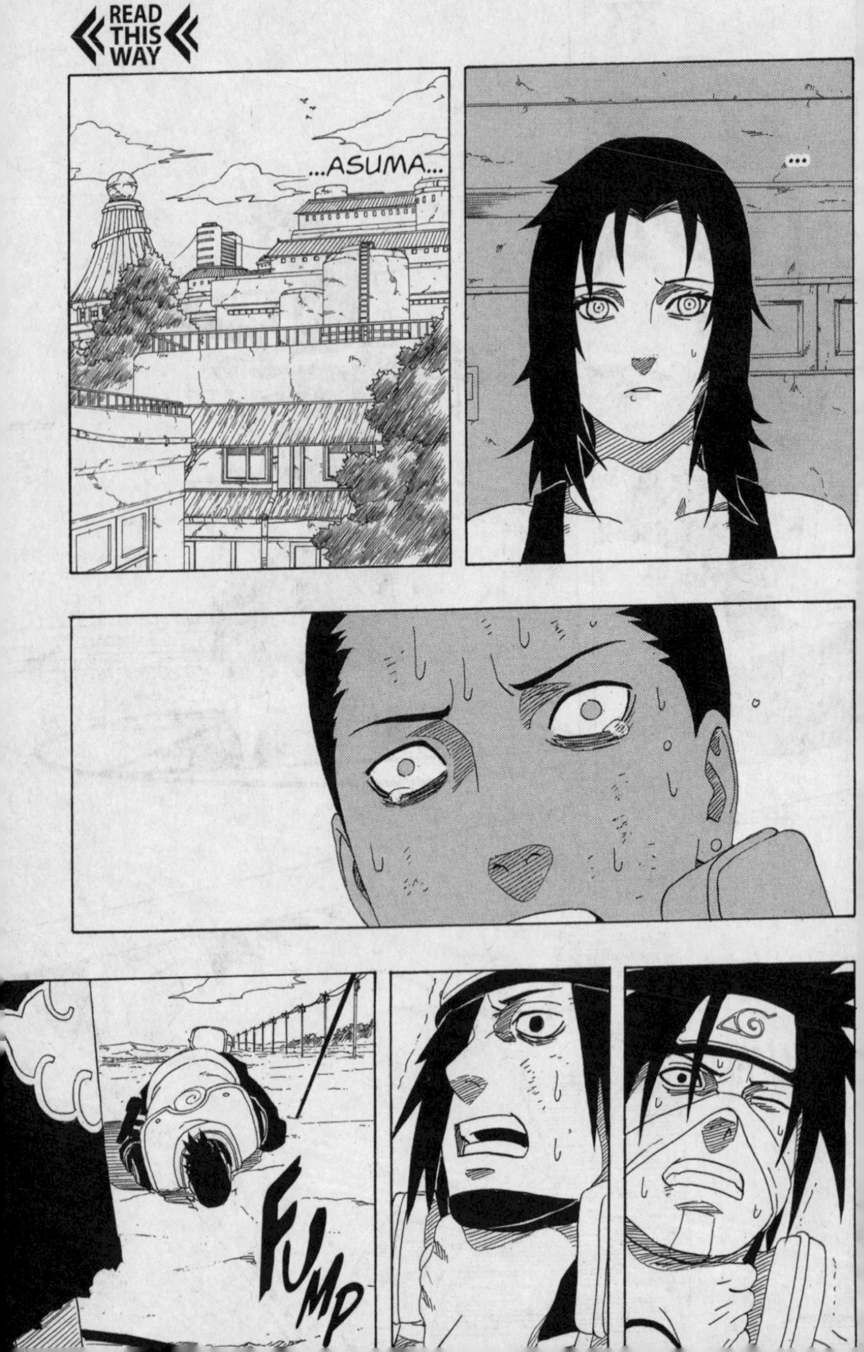
READ THIS WAY
...
...ASUMA...
FUMP

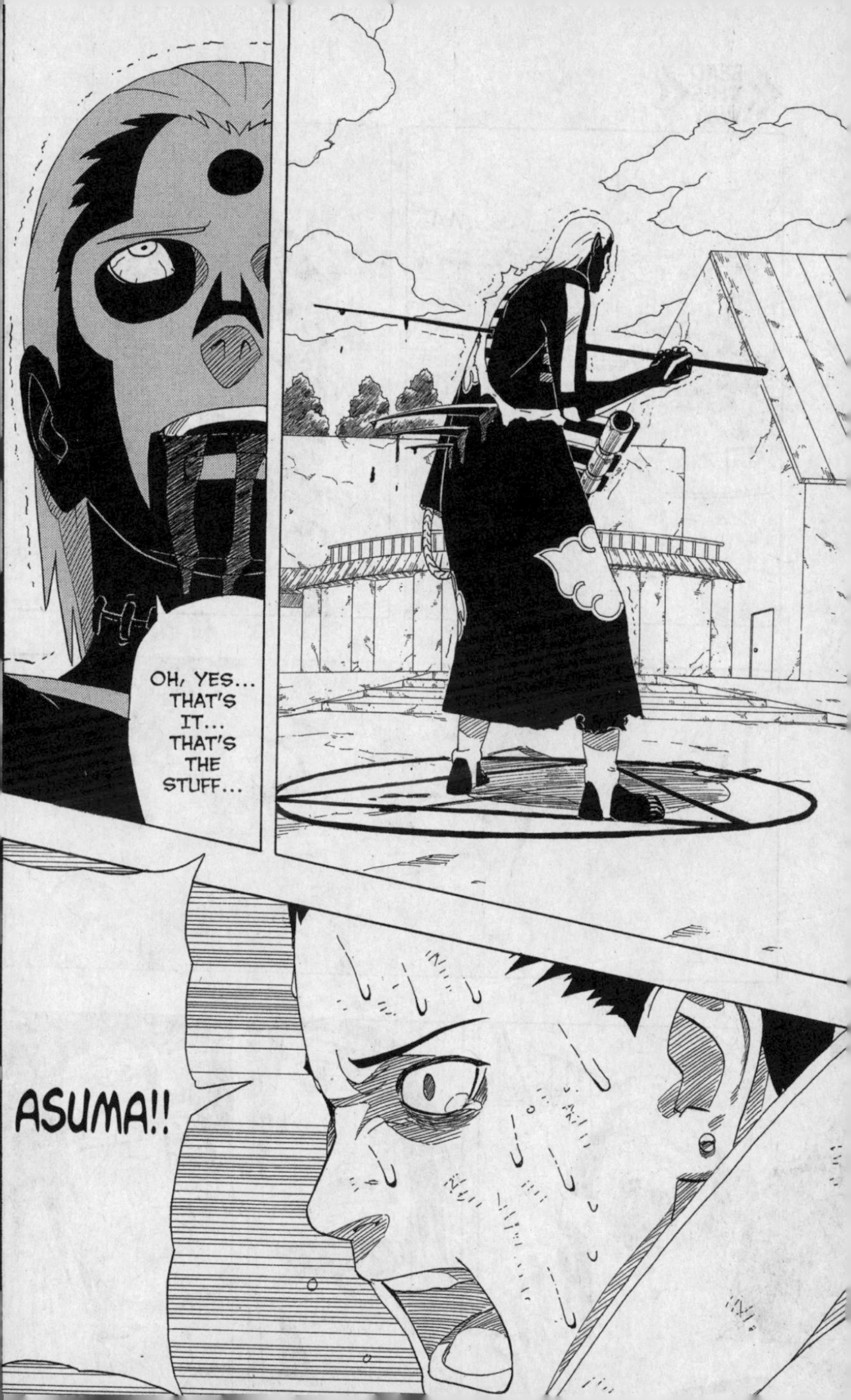
OH, YES... THAT'S IT... THAT'S THE STUFF...
ASUMA!!

READ THIS WAY

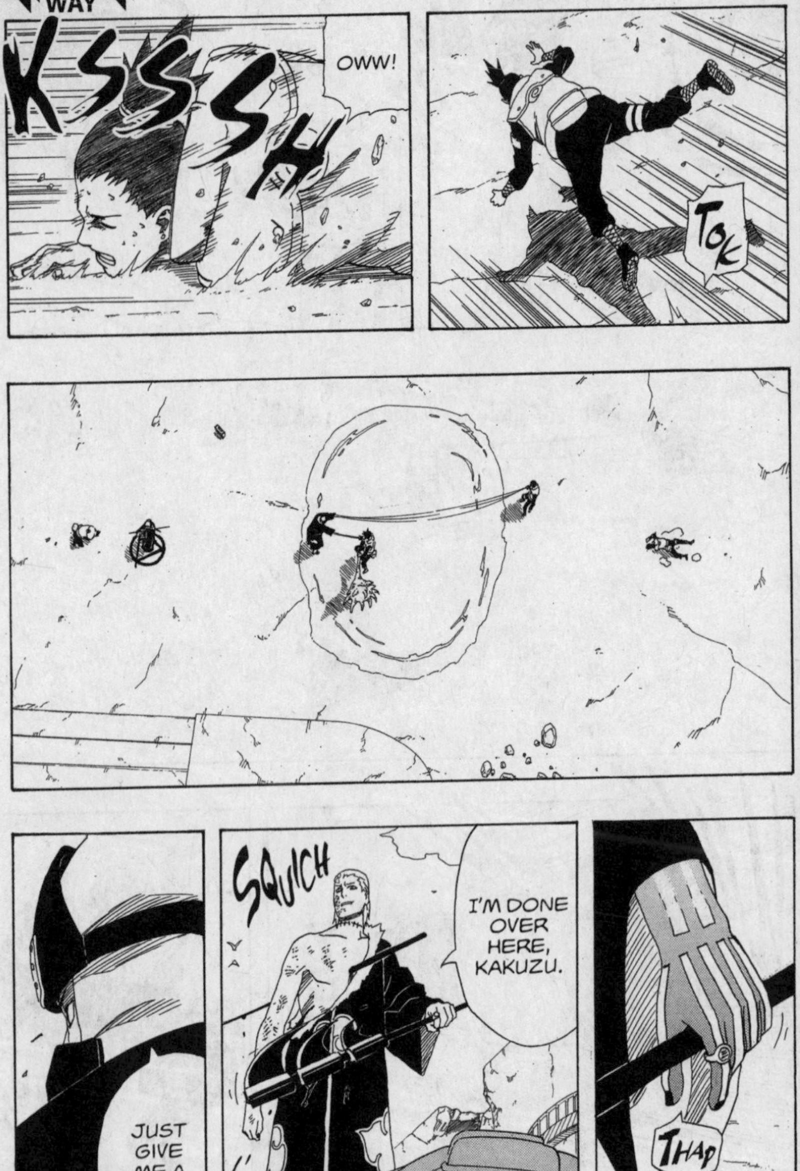
TOK
KSSSH
OWW!
THAP
SQUICH
I'M DONE OVER HERE, KAKUZU.
JUST GIVE ME A MINUTE.

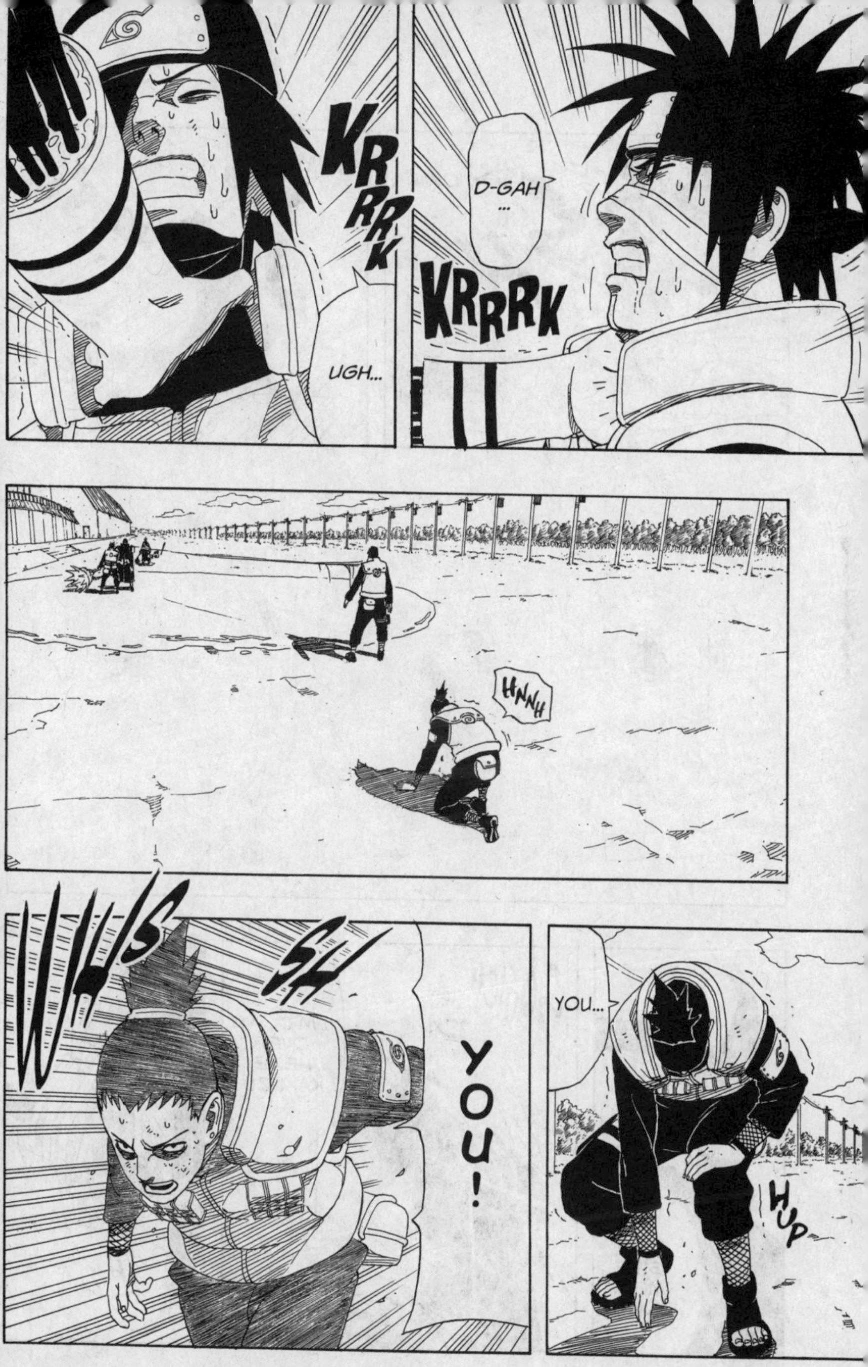
D-GAH ...
KRRRK
KRRRK
UGH...
HNNH
YOU...
HUP
WHSSH
YOU!

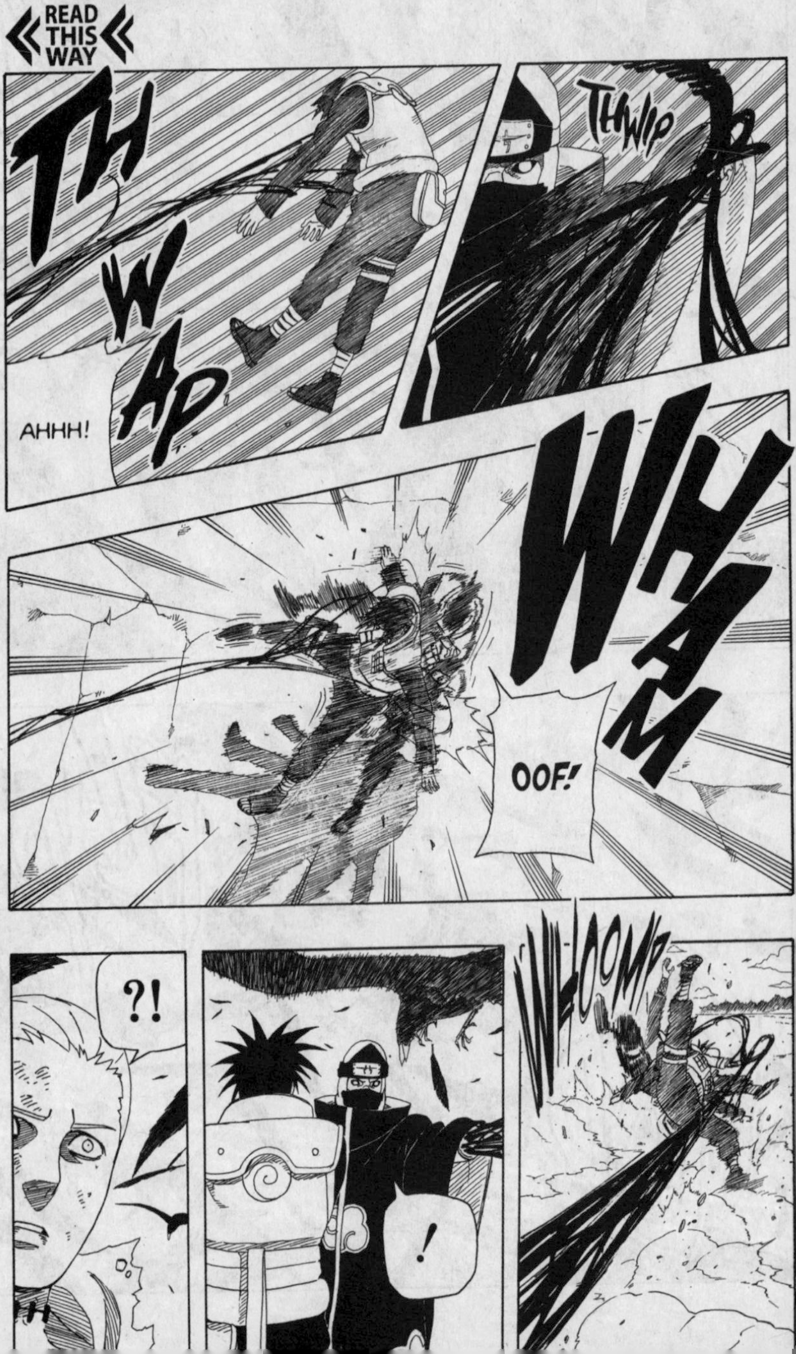

READ THIS WAY
THWIP
THWAP
AHHH!
WHAM
OOF!
WHOOMP
!
?!

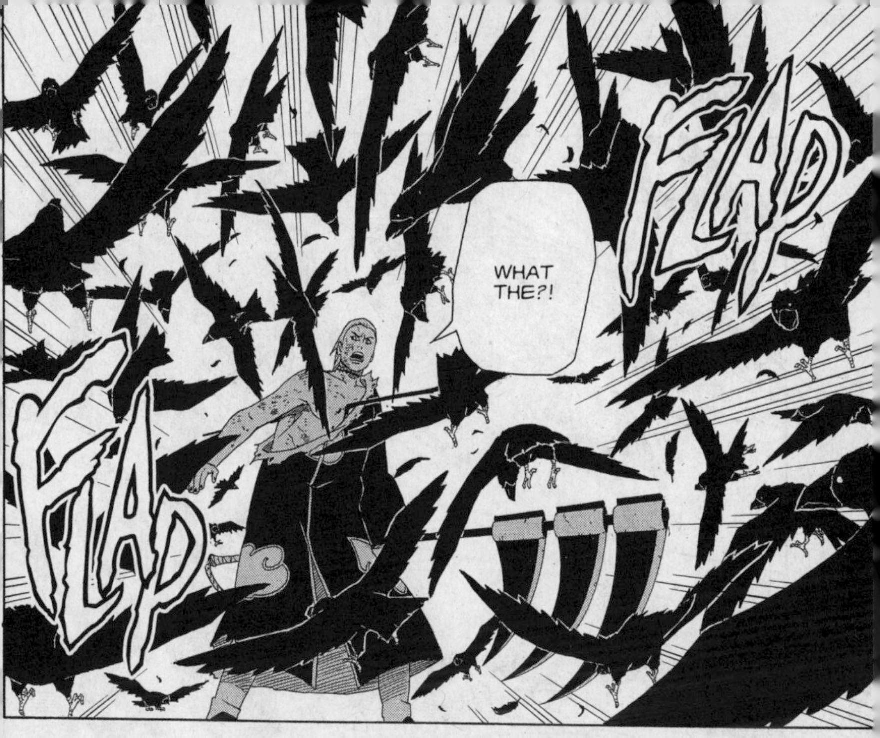
FLAP
WHAT THE?!
FLAP

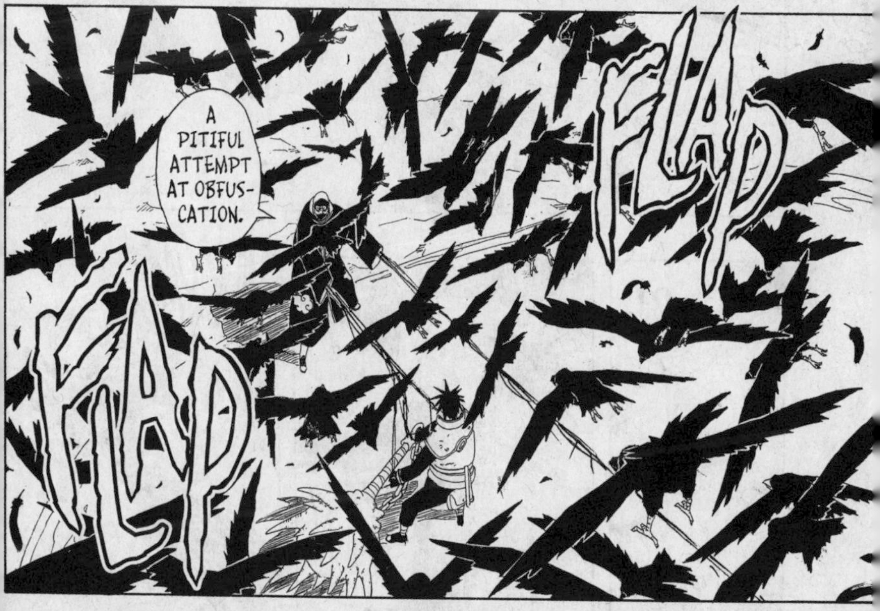
FLAP
A PITIFUL ATTEMPT AT OBFUS-CATION.
FLAP

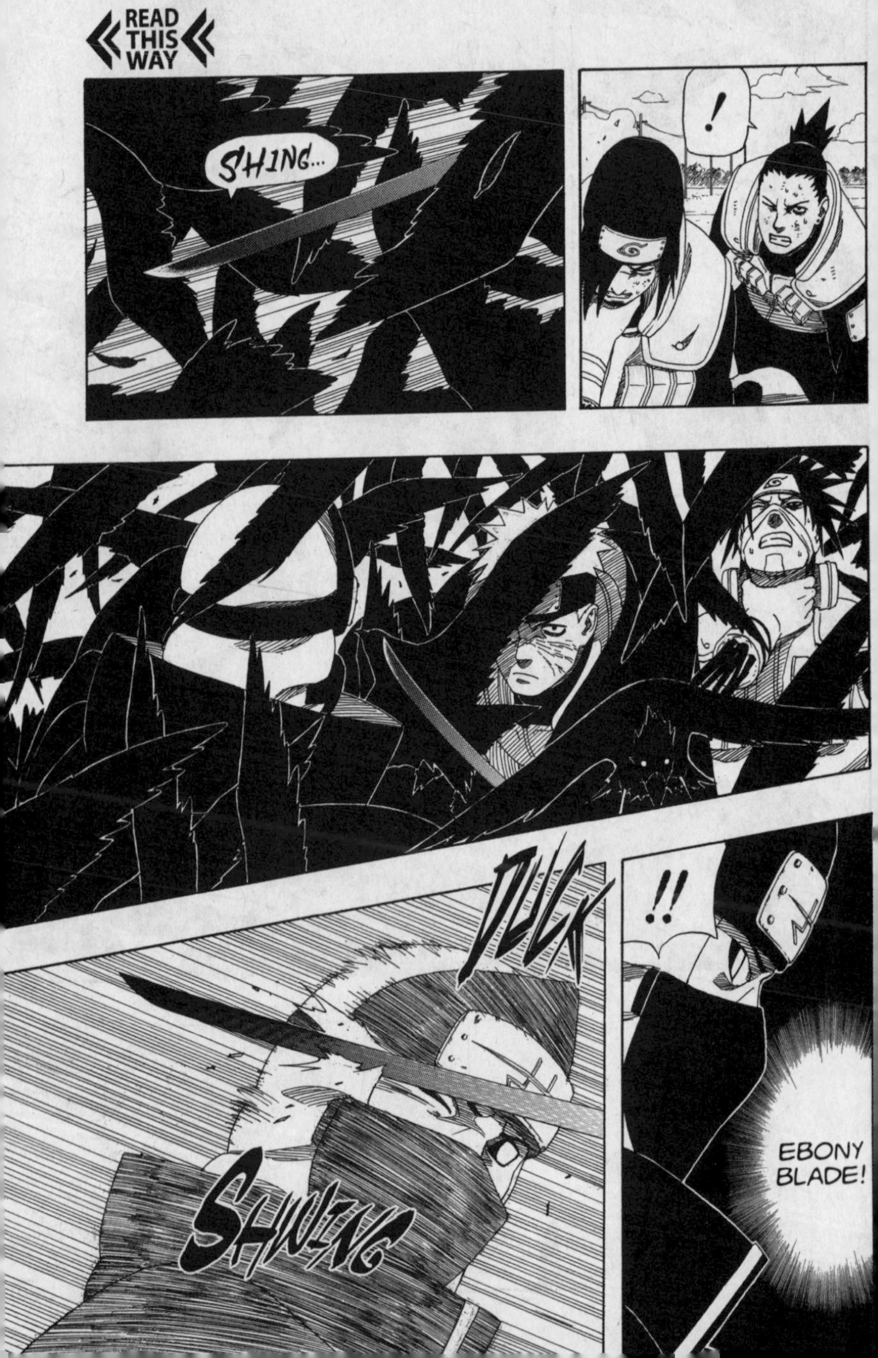
READ THIS WAY
!
SHING...
!!
EBONY BLADE!
DUCK
SHWING

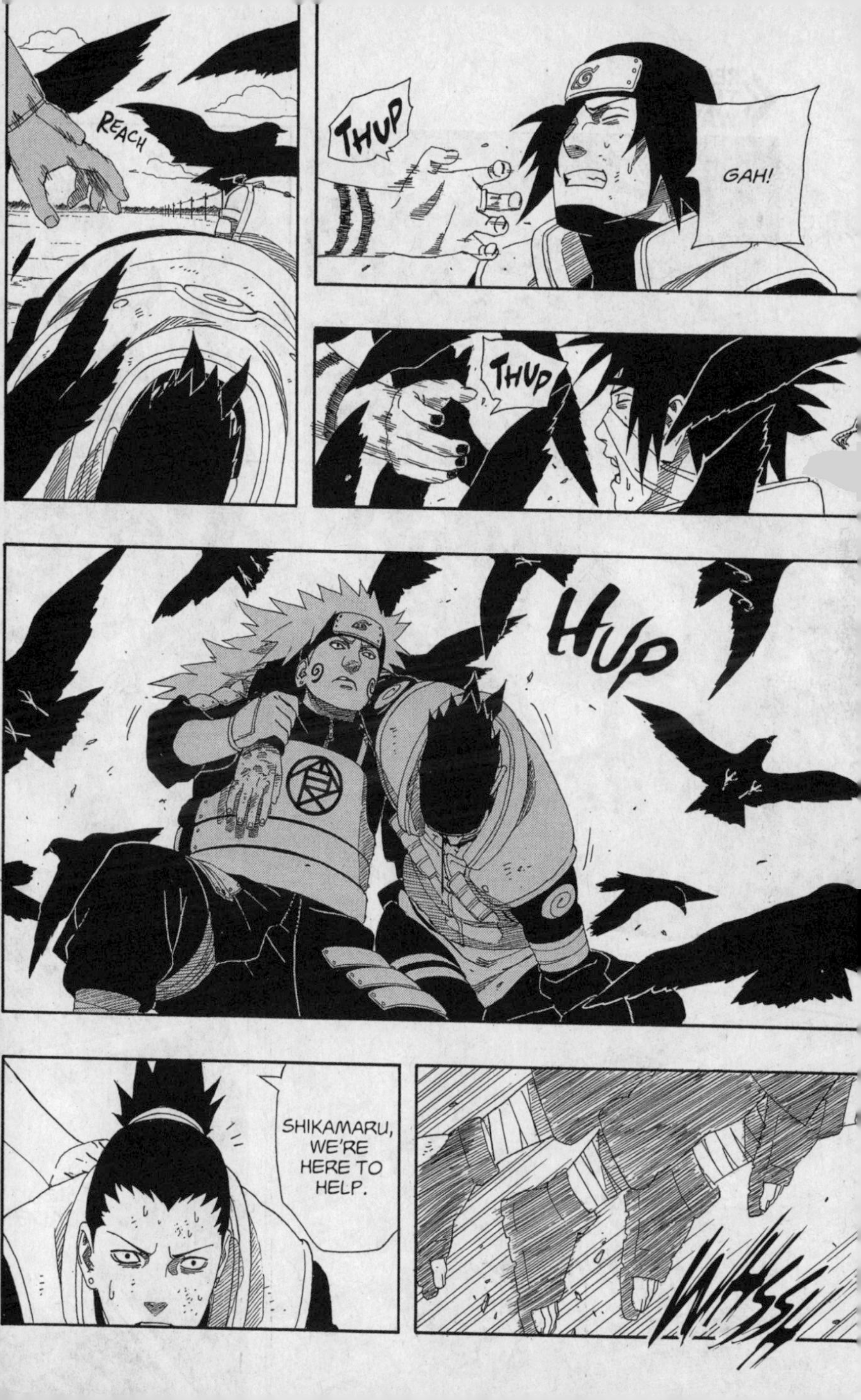
THUP
GAH!
THUP
REACH
HUP
WHSH
SHIKAMARU, WE'RE HERE TO HELP.

READ THIS WAY

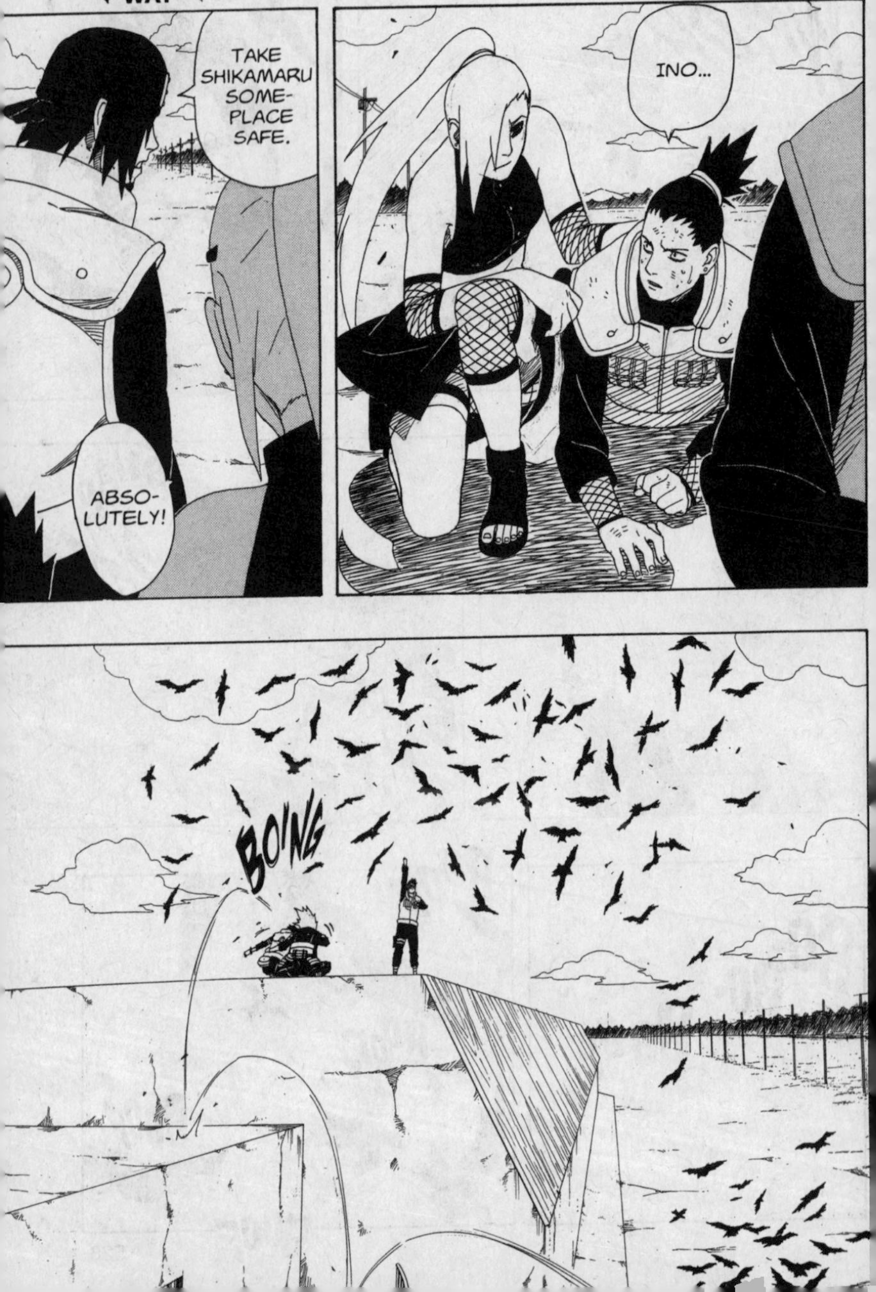
INO...
TAKE SHIKAMARU SOME-PLACE SAFE.
ABSO-LUTELY!
BOING

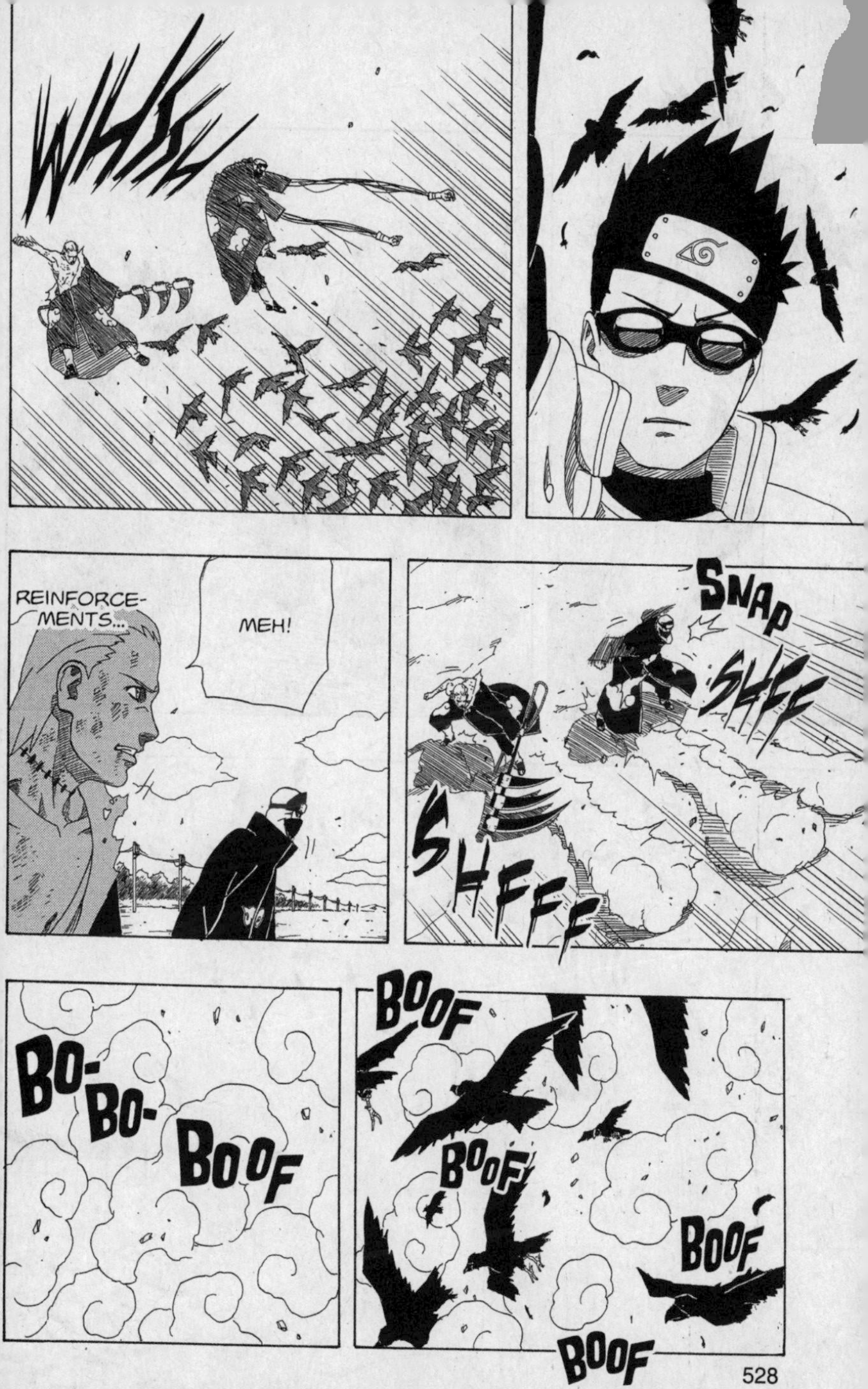
WHSSH
SNAP
SHFF
SHFFF
MEH!
REINFORCE-MENTS...
BOOF
BOOF
BOOF
BOOF
BO-BO-BOOF

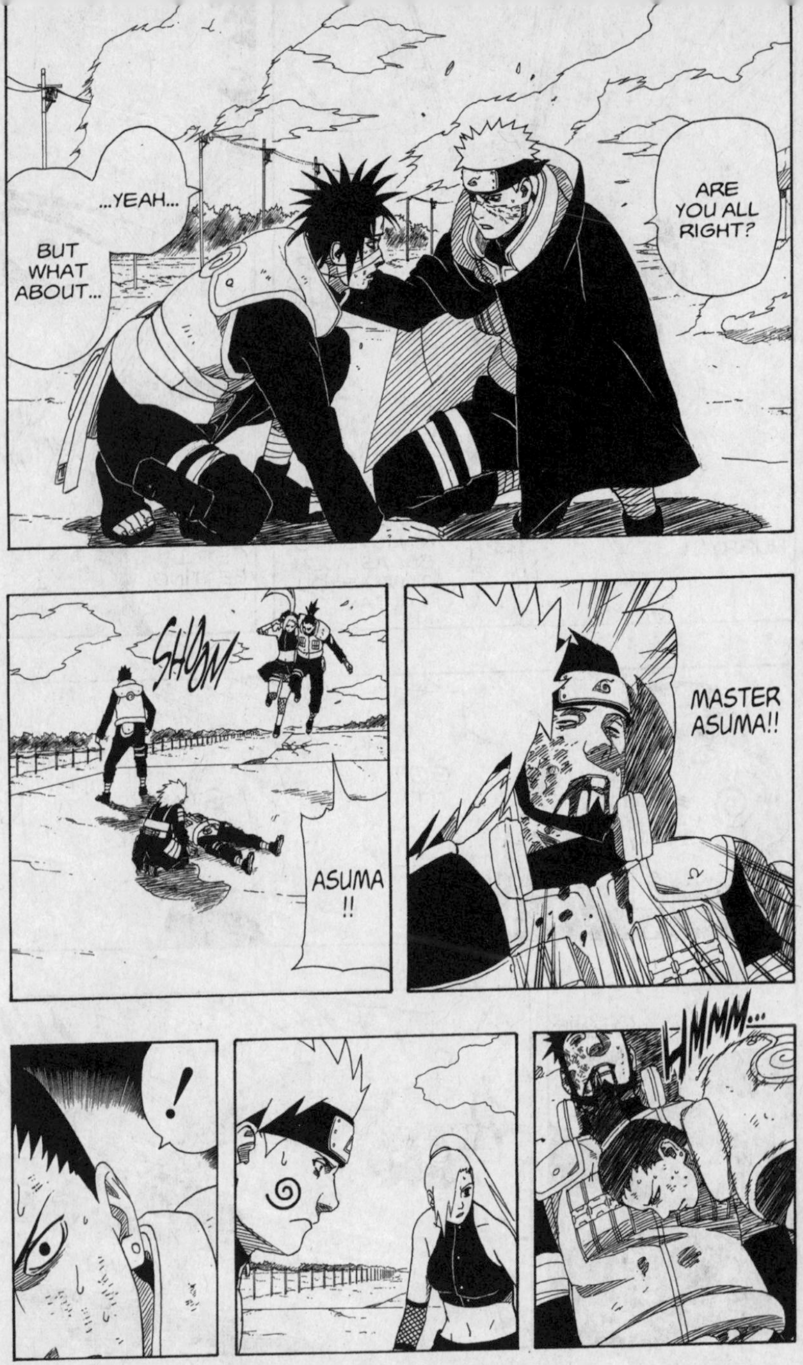

ARE YOU ALL RIGHT?
...YEAH...
BUT WHAT ABOUT...
MASTER ASUMA!!
SHOOM
ASUMA !!
HMMM...
!

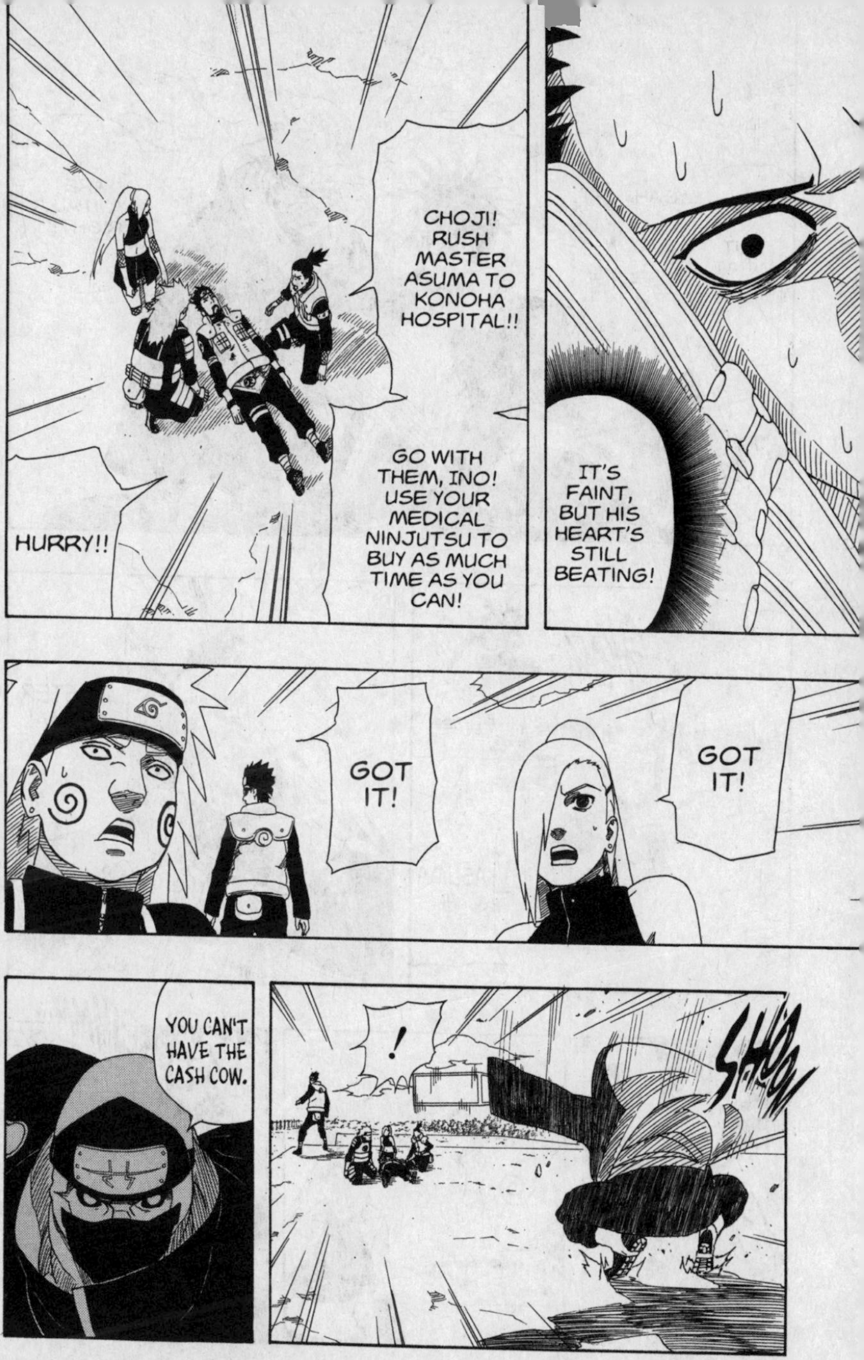
IT'S FAINT, BUT HIS HEART'S STILL BEATING!
CHOJI! RUSH MASTER ASUMA TO KONOHA HOSPITAL!!
GO WITH THEM, INO! USE YOUR MEDICAL NINJUTSU TO BUY AS MUCH TIME AS YOU CAN!
HURRY!!
GOT IT!
GOT IT!
!
SHOOM
YOU CAN'T HAVE THE CASH COW.

READ THIS WAY

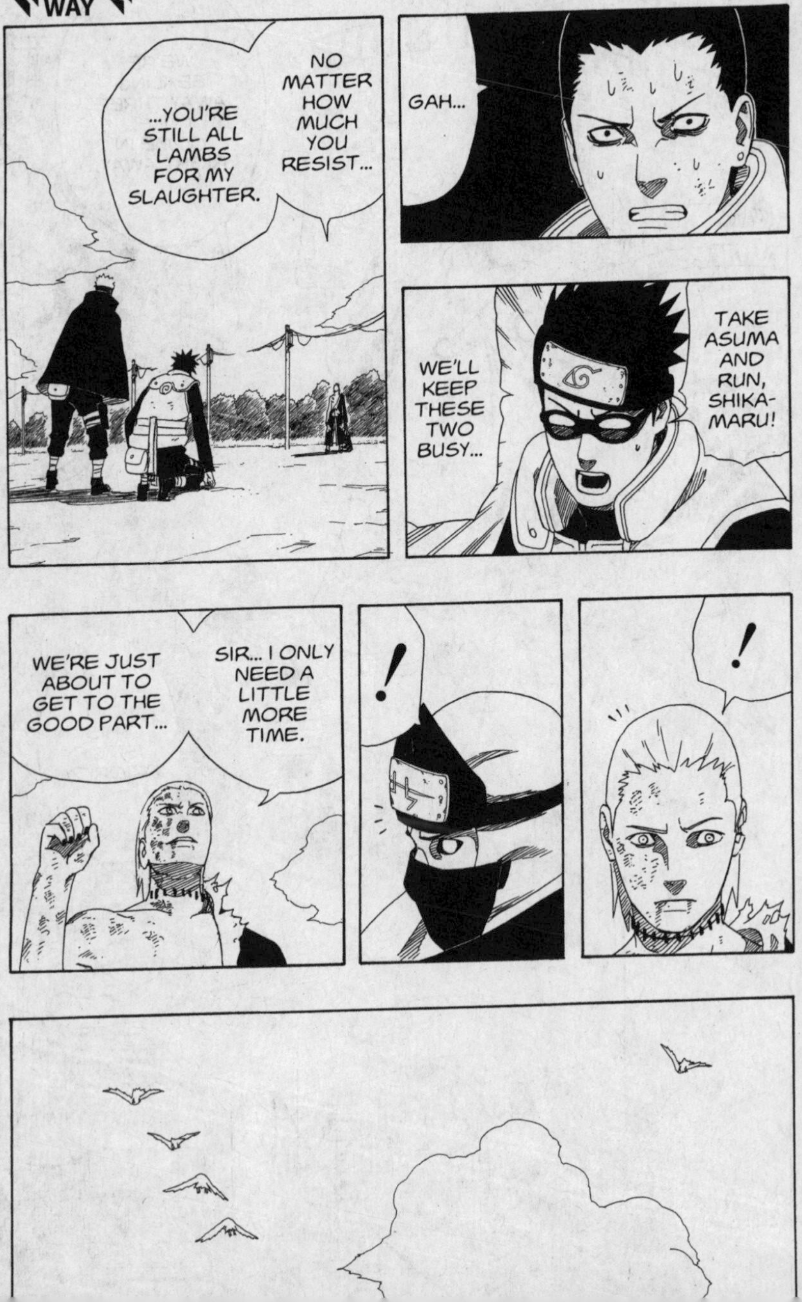
GAH...
TAKE ASUMA AND RUN, SHIKA-MARU!
WE'LL KEEP THESE TWO BUSY...
NO MATTER HOW MUCH YOU RESIST...
...YOU'RE STILL ALL LAMBS FOR MY SLAUGHTER.
!
!
SIR... I ONLY NEED A LITTLE MORE TIME.
WE'RE JUST ABOUT TO GET TO THE GOOD PART...

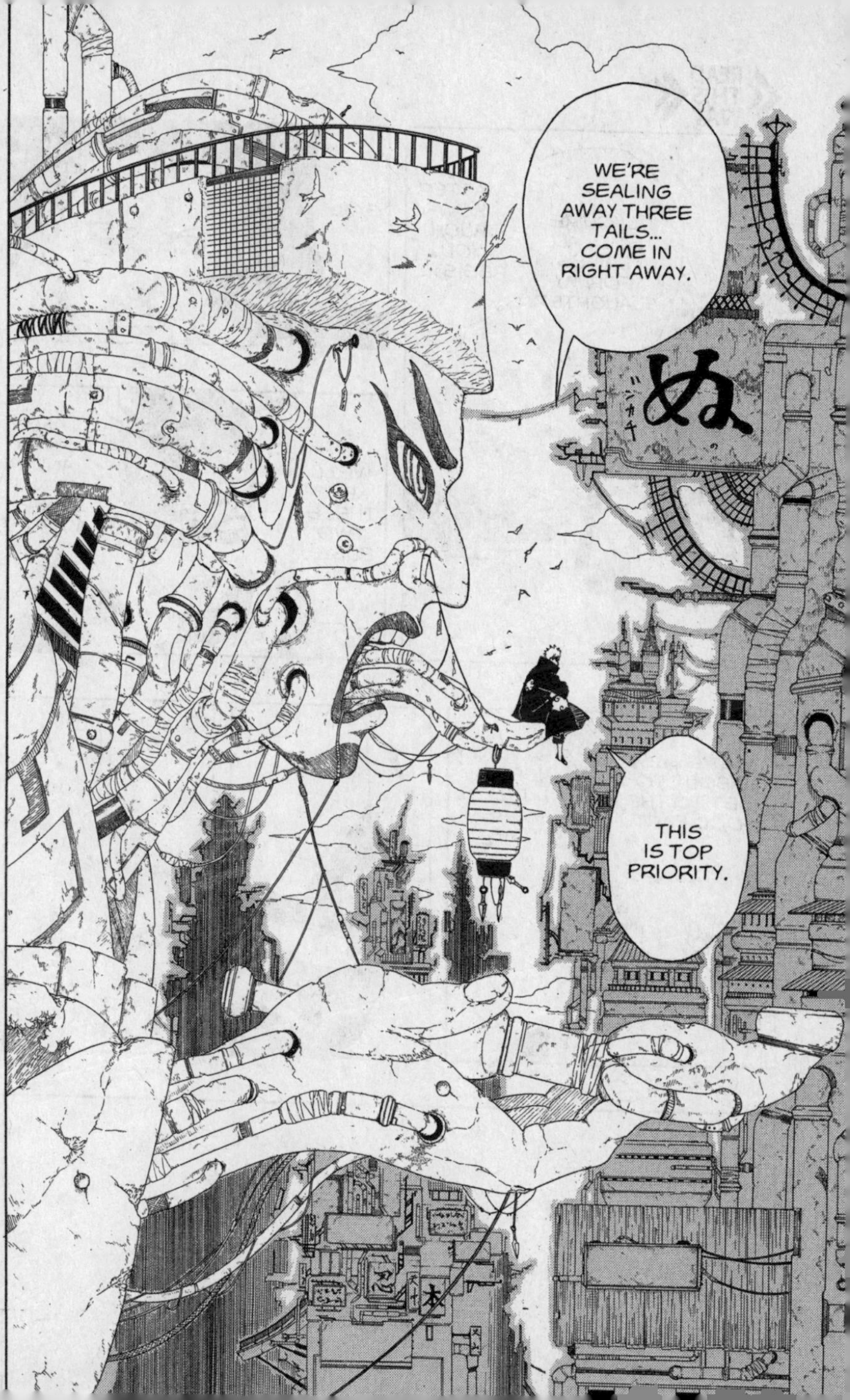
WE'RE SEALING AWAY THREE TAILS... COME IN RIGHT AWAY.
ぬ
THIS IS TOP PRIORITY.

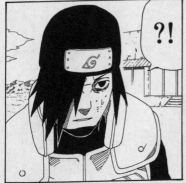

?!

ENOUGH, HIDAN.

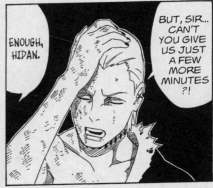

BUT, SIR... CAN'T YOU GIVE US JUST A FEW MORE MINUTES ?!

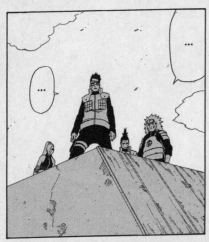

...

...

WE'LL BE BACK IN NO TIME, SO PREPARE YOURSELVES.

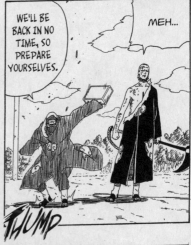

MEH...

THUMP

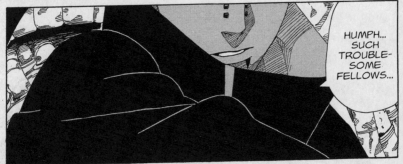

HUMPH... SUCH TROUBLE-SOME FELLOWS...

533

NARUTO

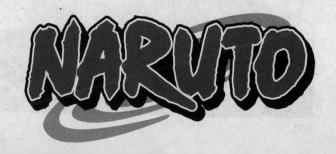

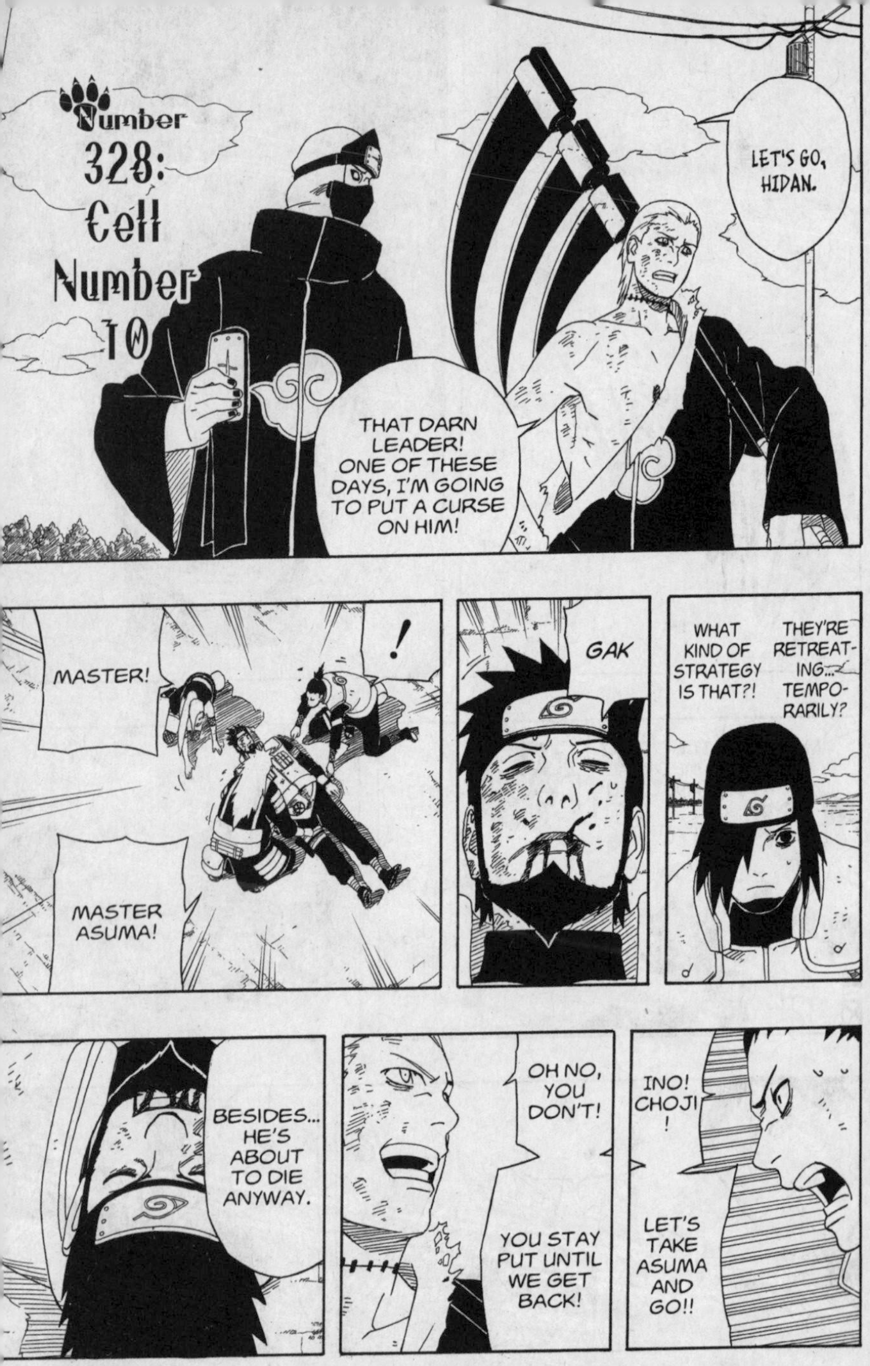
Number 328: Cell Number 10
LET'S GO, HIDAN.
THAT DARN LEADER! ONE OF THESE DAYS, I'M GOING TO PUT A CURSE ON HIM!
THEY'RE RETREATING... TEMPORARILY?
WHAT KIND OF STRATEGY IS THAT?!
GAK
!
MASTER!
MASTER ASUMA!
INO! CHOJI!
LET'S TAKE ASUMA AND GO!!
OH NO, YOU DON'T!
YOU STAY PUT UNTIL WE GET BACK!
BESIDES... HE'S ABOUT TO DIE ANYWAY.

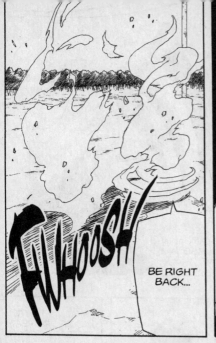

FWHOOSH!

BE RIGHT BACK...

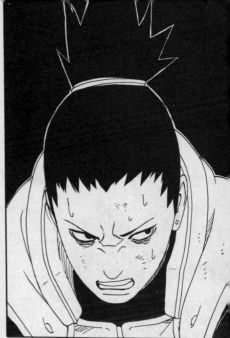

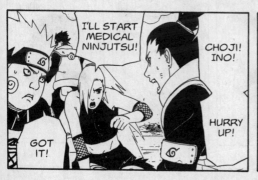

I'LL START MEDICAL NINJUTSU!

GOT IT!

CHOJI! INO!

HURRY UP!

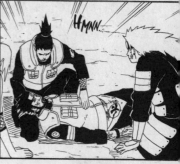

HMNN...

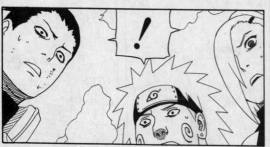

!

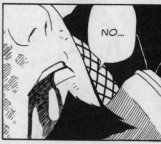

NO...

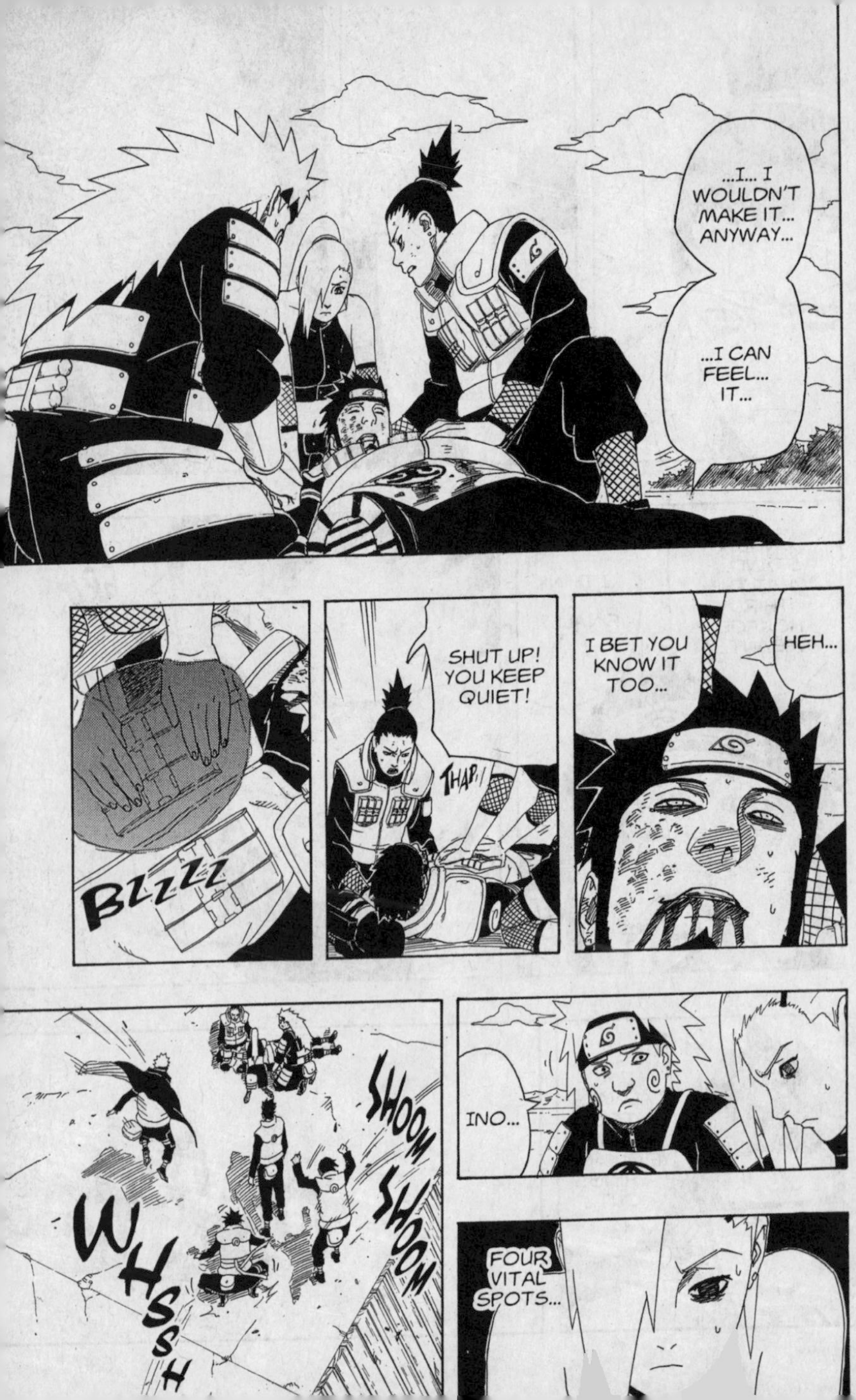
...I... I WOULDN'T MAKE IT... ANYWAY...
...I CAN FEEL... IT...
HEH...
I BET YOU KNOW IT TOO...
SHUT UP! YOU KEEP QUIET!
THAP
BZZZZ
INO...
SHOOM SHOOM SHOOM
WHSSH
FOUR VITAL SPOTS...

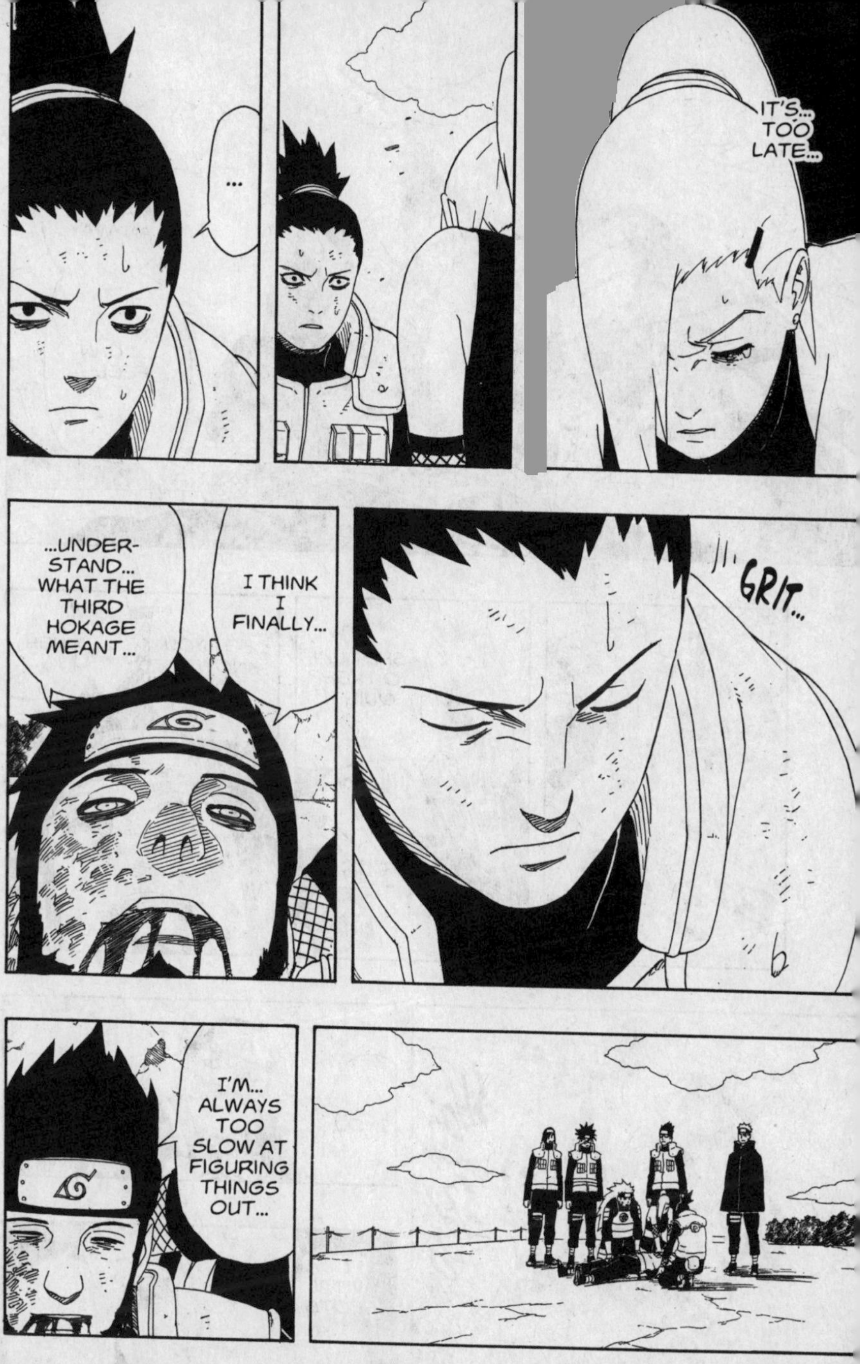
IT'S... TOO LATE...
...
GRIT...
I THINK I FINALLY...
...UNDERSTAND... WHAT THE THIRD HOKAGE MEANT...
I'M... ALWAYS TOO SLOW AT FIGURING THINGS OUT...

READ THIS WAY

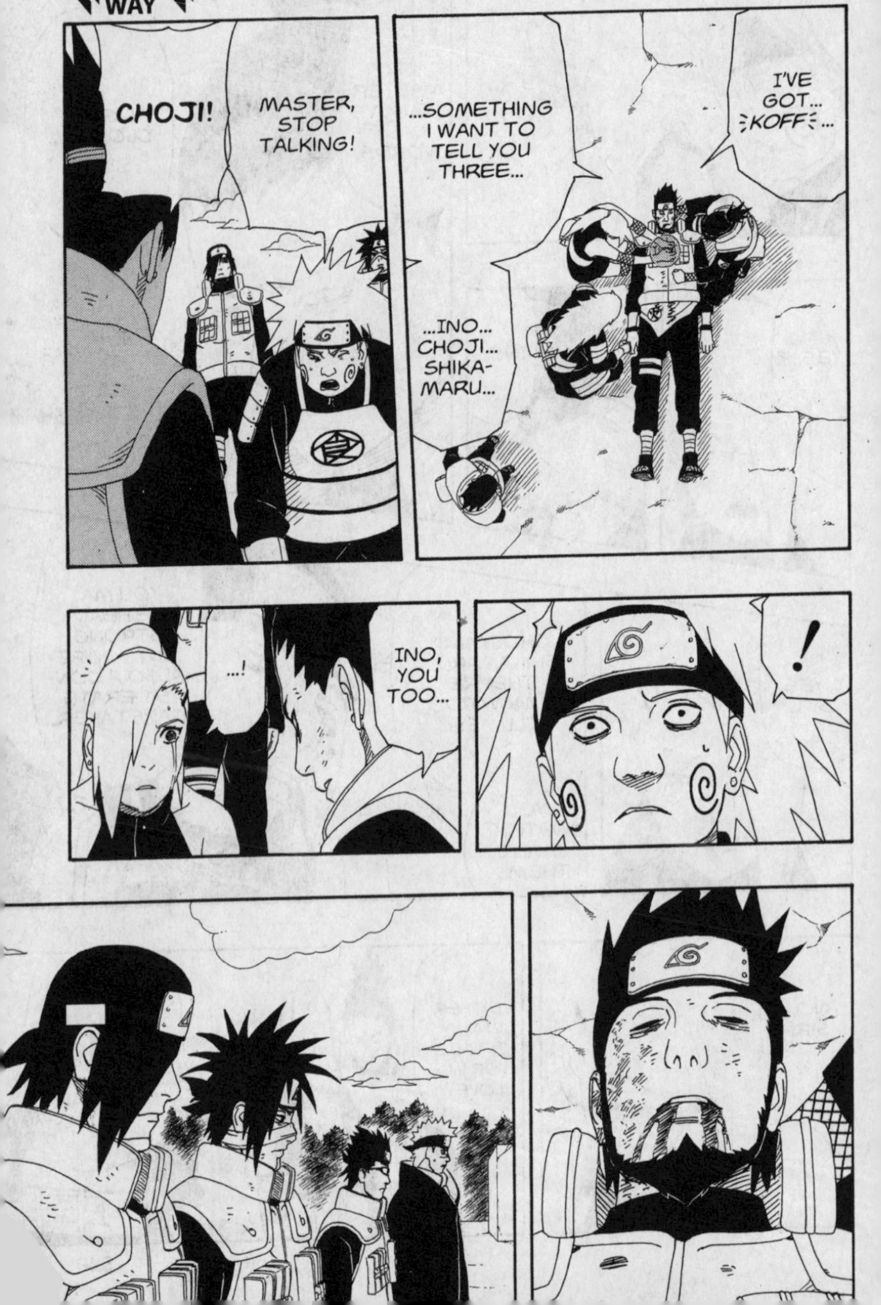
I'VE GOT... KOFF ...
...SOMETHING I WANT TO TELL YOU THREE...
...INO... CHOJI... SHIKA-MARU...
MASTER, STOP TALKING!
CHOJI!
!
INO, YOU TOO...
...!

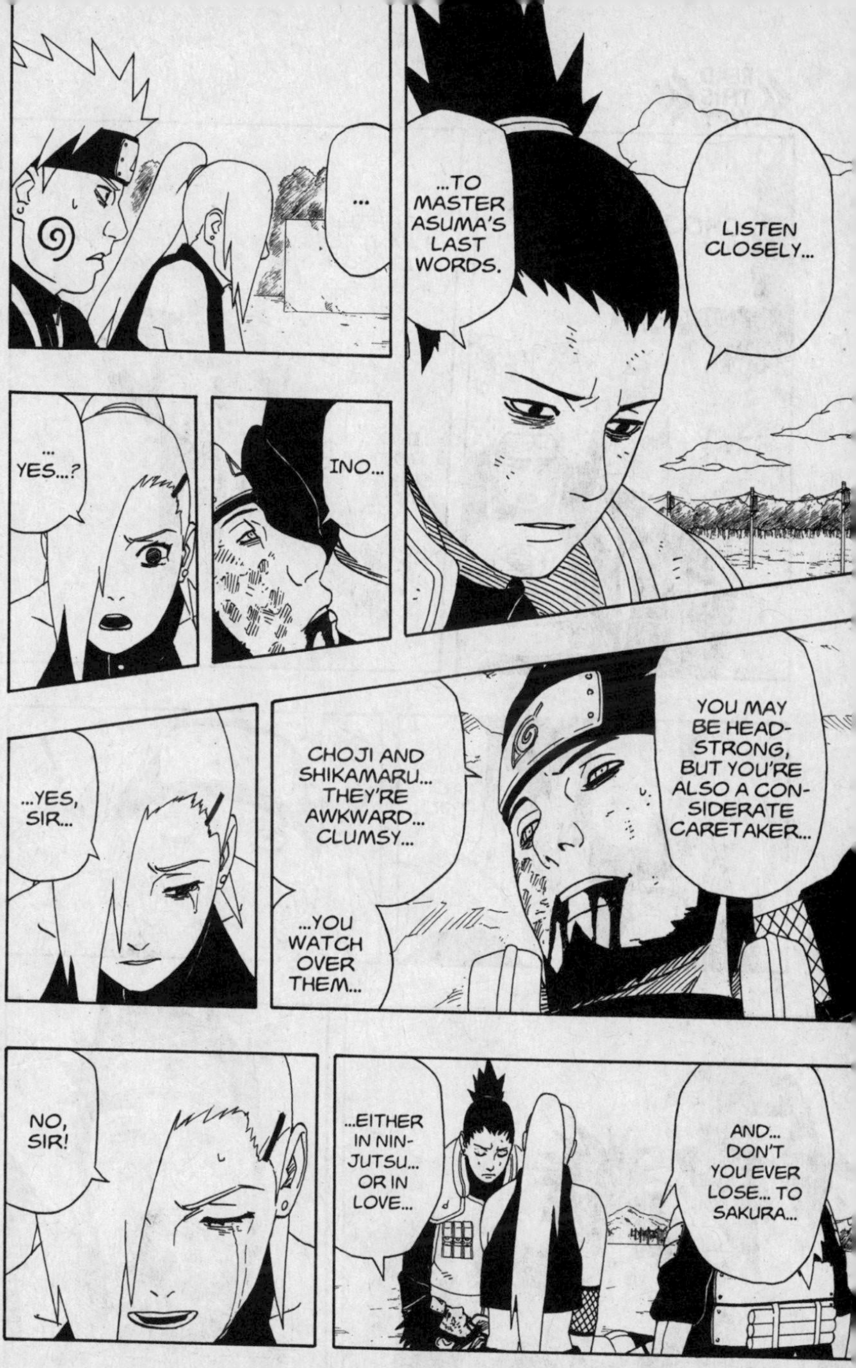
LISTEN CLOSELY...
...TO MASTER ASUMA'S LAST WORDS.
...
INO...
... YES...?
YOU MAY BE HEAD-STRONG, BUT YOU'RE ALSO A CON-SIDERATE CARETAKER...
CHOJI AND SHIKAMARU... THEY'RE AWKWARD... CLUMSY...
...YOU WATCH OVER THEM...
...YES, SIR...
AND... DON'T YOU EVER LOSE... TO SAKURA...
...EITHER IN NIN-JUTSU... OR IN LOVE...
NO, SIR!

READ THIS WAY

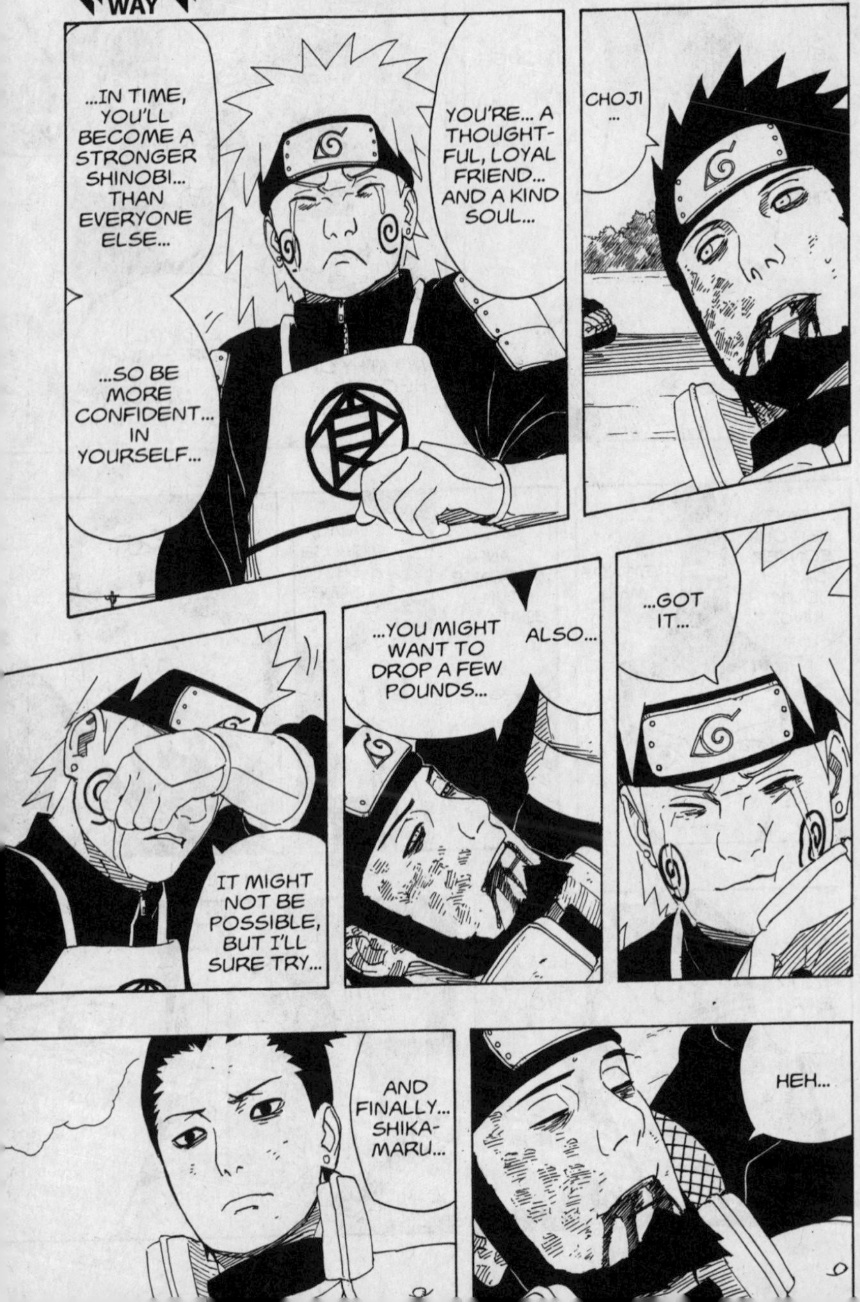
CHOJI ...
YOU'RE... A THOUGHTFUL, LOYAL FRIEND... AND A KIND SOUL...
...IN TIME, YOU'LL BECOME A STRONGER SHINOBI... THAN EVERYONE ELSE...
...SO BE MORE CONFIDENT... IN YOURSELF...
...GOT IT...
ALSO...
...YOU MIGHT WANT TO DROP A FEW POUNDS...
IT MIGHT NOT BE POSSIBLE, BUT I'LL SURE TRY...
HEH...
AND FINALLY... SHIKAMARU...

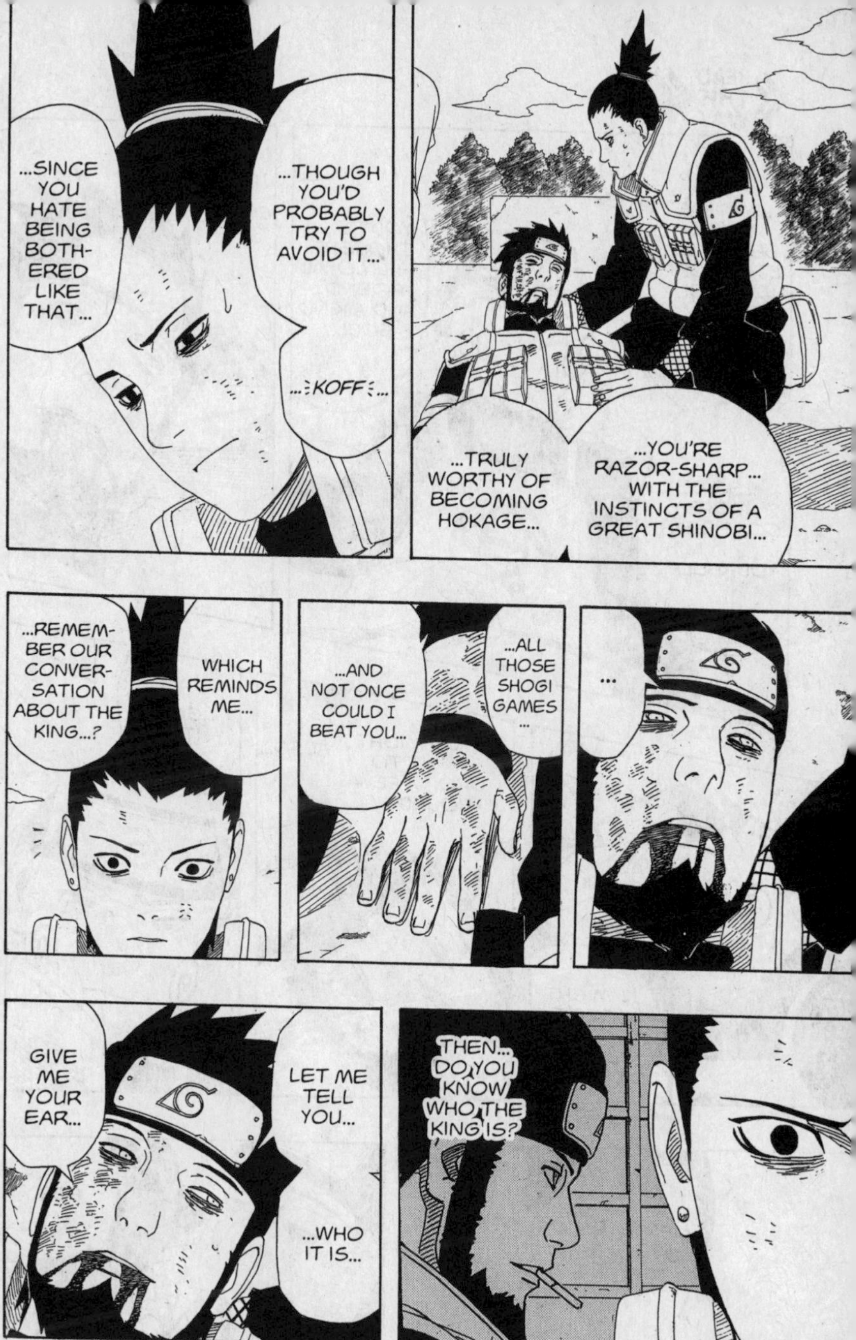
...YOU'RE RAZOR-SHARP... WITH THE INSTINCTS OF A GREAT SHINOBI...
...TRULY WORTHY OF BECOMING HOKAGE...
...THOUGH YOU'D PROBABLY TRY TO AVOID IT...
...KOFF...
...SINCE YOU HATE BEING BOTH-ERED LIKE THAT...
...
...ALL THOSE SHOGI GAMES...
...AND NOT ONCE COULD I BEAT YOU...
WHICH REMINDS ME...
...REMEM-BER OUR CONVER-SATION ABOUT THE KING...?
THEN... DO YOU KNOW WHO THE KING IS?
LET ME TELL YOU...
...WHO IT IS...
GIVE ME YOUR EAR...

READ THIS WAY

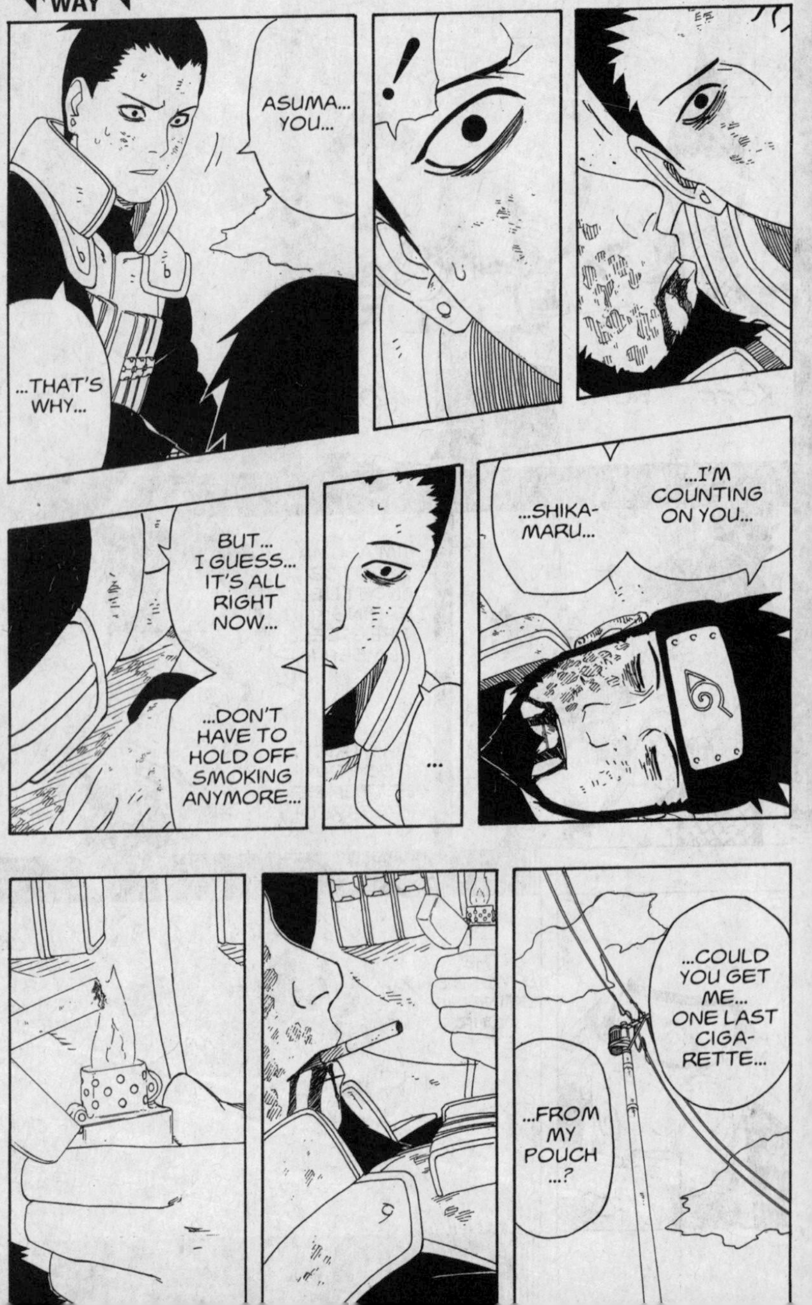
!
ASUMA... YOU...
...THAT'S WHY...
...SHIKA-MARU...
...I'M COUNTING ON YOU...
...
BUT... I GUESS... IT'S ALL RIGHT NOW...
...DON'T HAVE TO HOLD OFF SMOKING ANYMORE...
...COULD YOU GET ME... ONE LAST CIGA-RETTE...
...FROM MY POUCH ...?

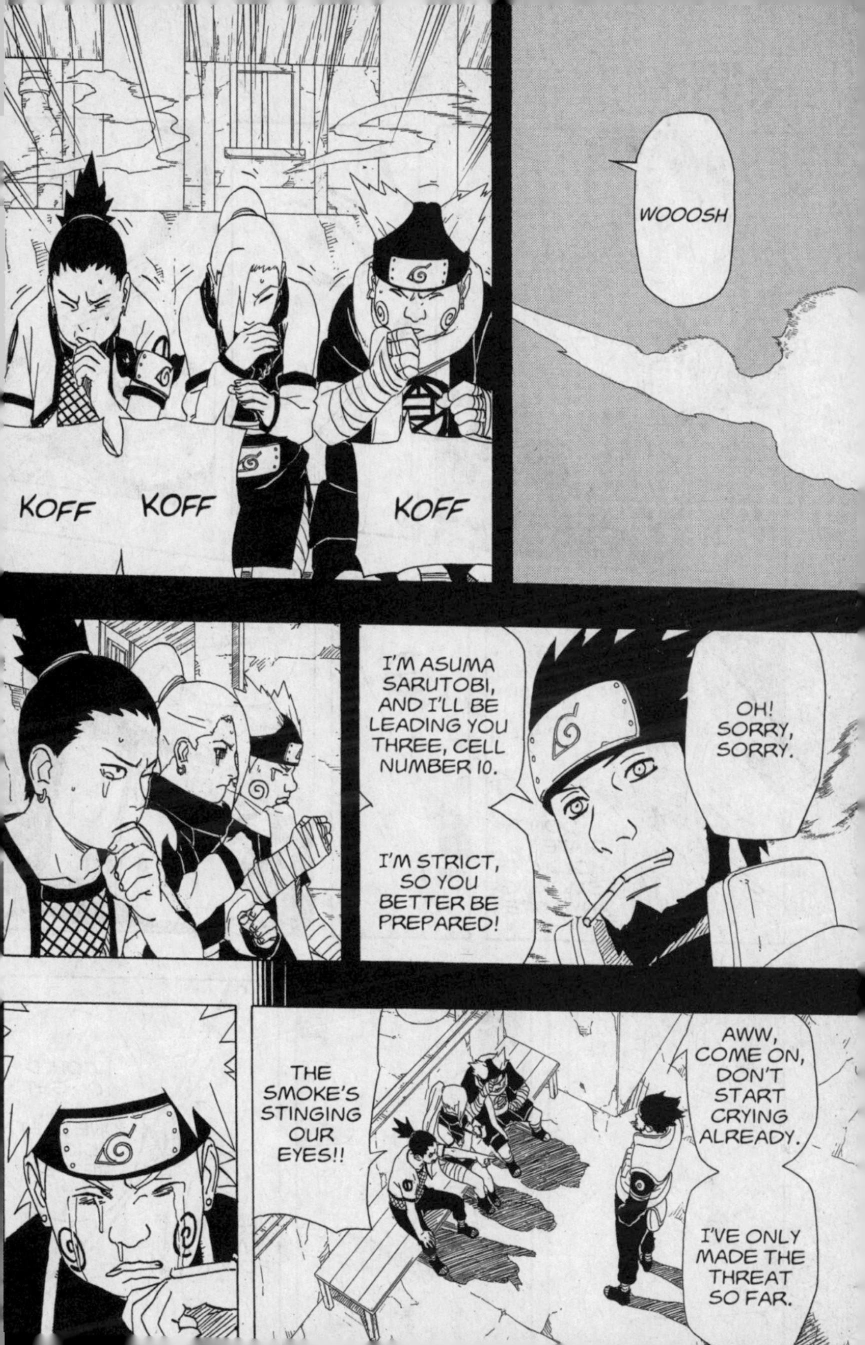
WOOOSH
KOFF
KOFF
KOFF
OH! SORRY, SORRY.
I'M ASUMA SARUTOBI, AND I'LL BE LEADING YOU THREE, CELL NUMBER 10.
I'M STRICT, SO YOU BETTER BE PREPARED!
AWW, COME ON, DON'T START CRYING ALREADY.
THE SMOKE'S STINGING OUR EYES!!
I'VE ONLY MADE THE THREAT SO FAR.

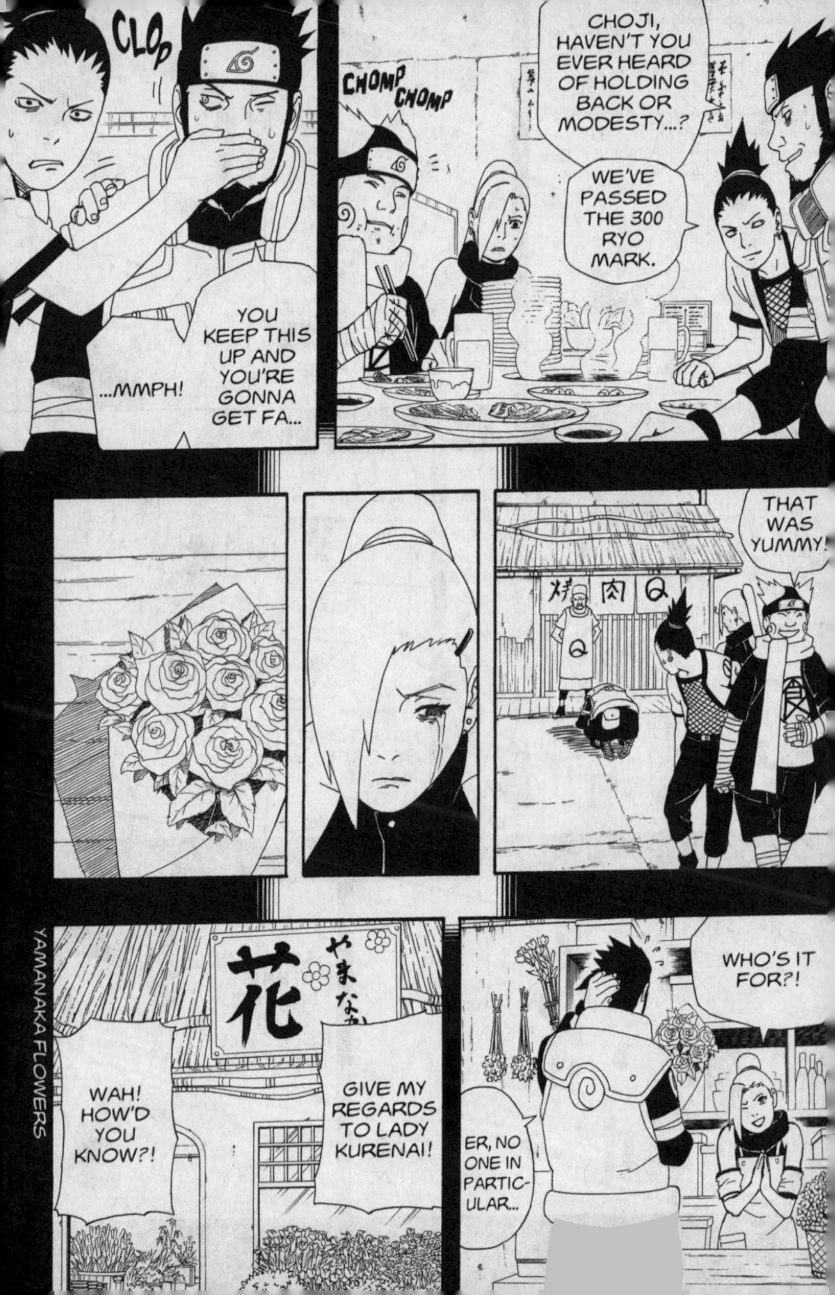
CHOMP CHOMP
CHOJI, HAVEN'T YOU EVER HEARD OF HOLDING BACK OR MODESTY...?
WE'VE PASSED THE 300 RYO MARK.
CLOP
YOU KEEP THIS UP AND YOU'RE GONNA GET FA...
...MMPH!
THAT WAS YUMMY!
焼肉Q
WHO'S IT FOR?!
ER, NO ONE IN PARTICULAR...
花
GIVE MY REGARDS TO LADY KURENAI!
WAH! HOW'D YOU KNOW?!
YAMANAKA FLOWERS

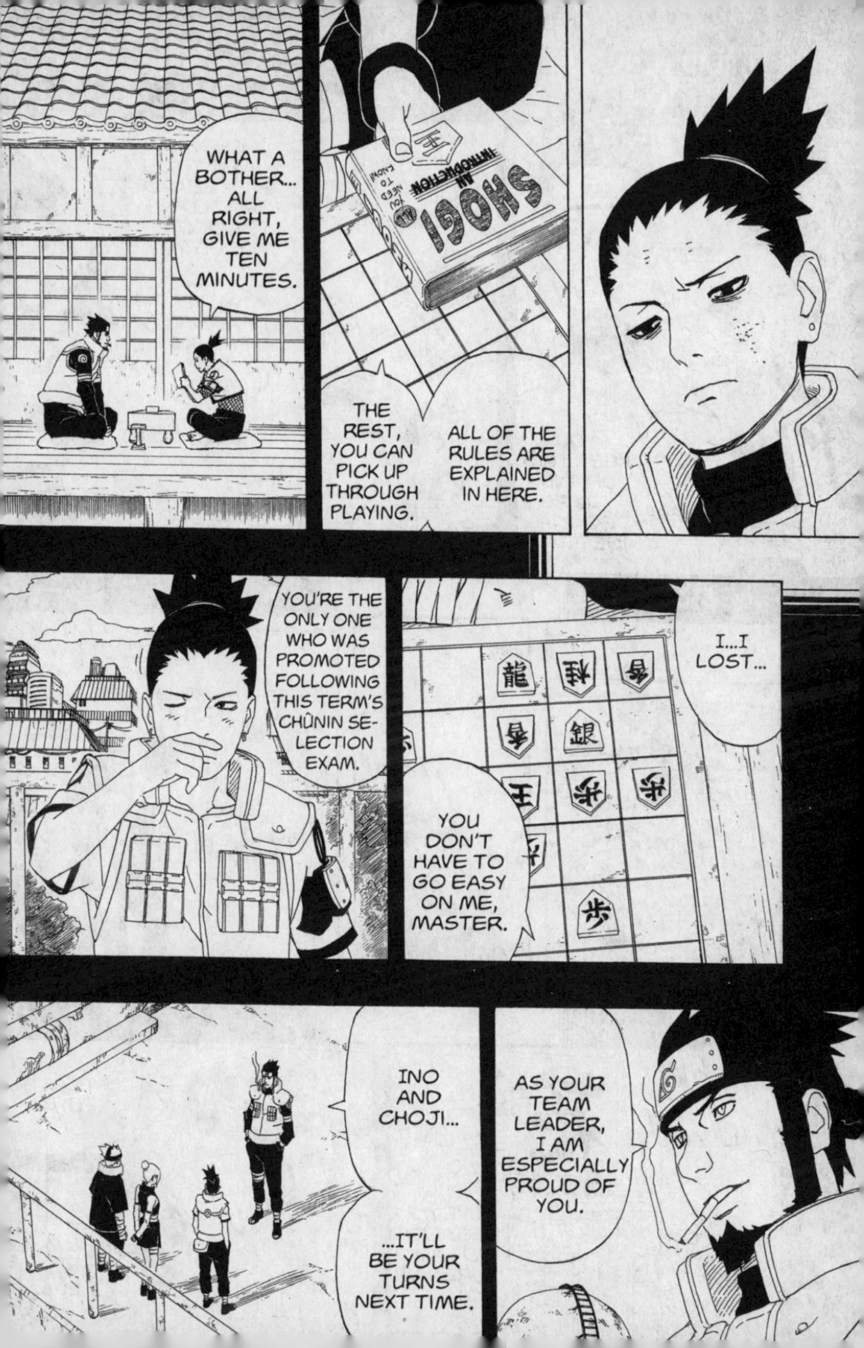
SHOGI
AN INTRODUCTION
ALL YOU NEED TO KNOW
ALL OF THE RULES ARE EXPLAINED IN HERE.
THE REST, YOU CAN PICK UP THROUGH PLAYING.
WHAT A BOTHER... ALL RIGHT, GIVE ME TEN MINUTES.
I...I LOST...
YOU DON'T HAVE TO GO EASY ON ME, MASTER.
YOU'RE THE ONLY ONE WHO WAS PROMOTED FOLLOWING THIS TERM'S CHÛNIN SELECTION EXAM.
AS YOUR TEAM LEADER, I AM ESPECIALLY PROUD OF YOU.
INO AND CHOJI...
...IT'LL BE YOUR TURNS NEXT TIME.

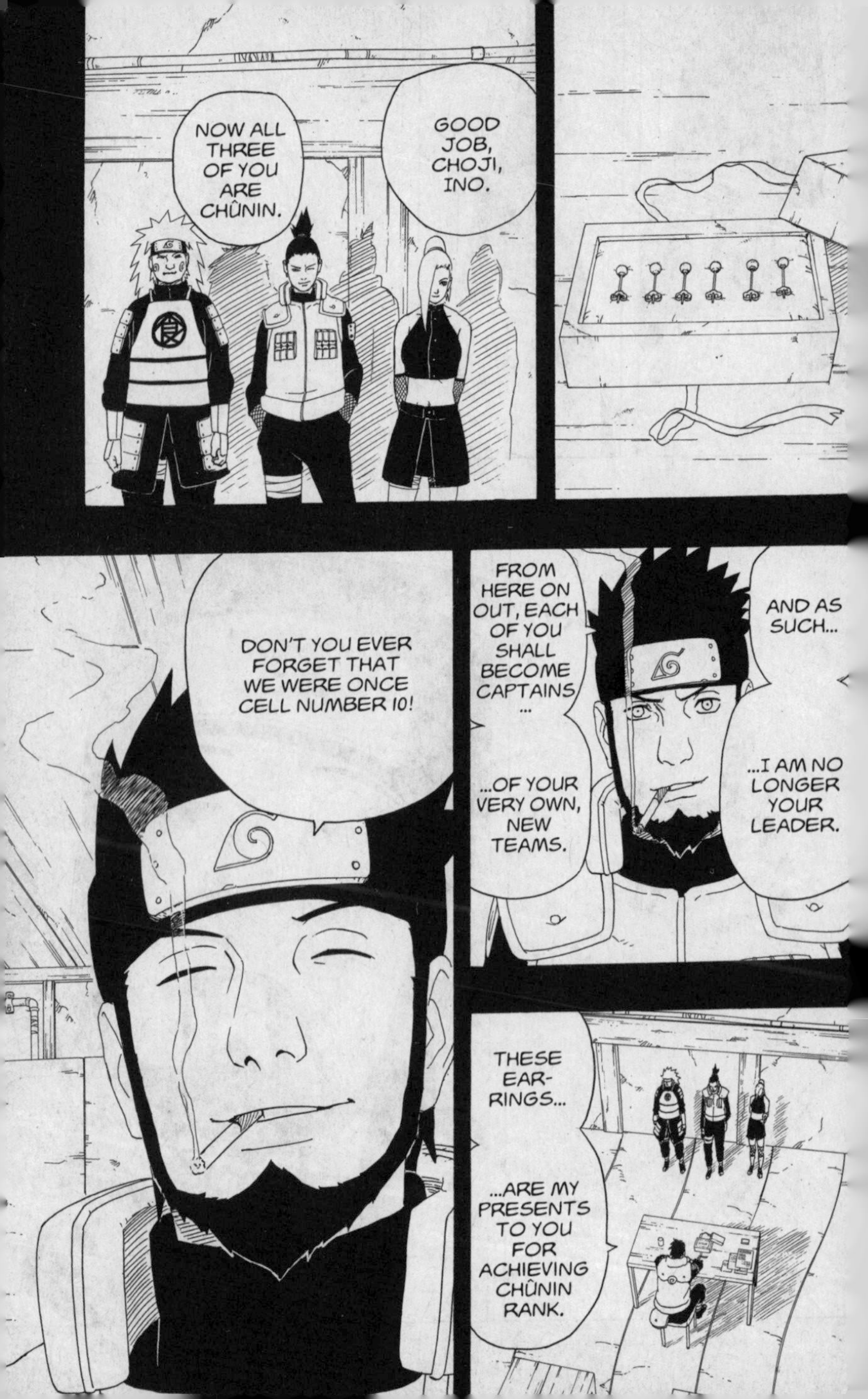
GOOD JOB, CHOJI, INO.
NOW ALL THREE OF YOU ARE CHÛNIN.
AND AS SUCH...
...I AM NO LONGER YOUR LEADER.
FROM HERE ON OUT, EACH OF YOU SHALL BECOME CAPTAINS ...
...OF YOUR VERY OWN, NEW TEAMS.
THESE EAR-RINGS...
...ARE MY PRESENTS TO YOU FOR ACHIEVING CHÛNIN RANK.
DON'T YOU EVER FORGET THAT WE WERE ONCE CELL NUMBER 10!

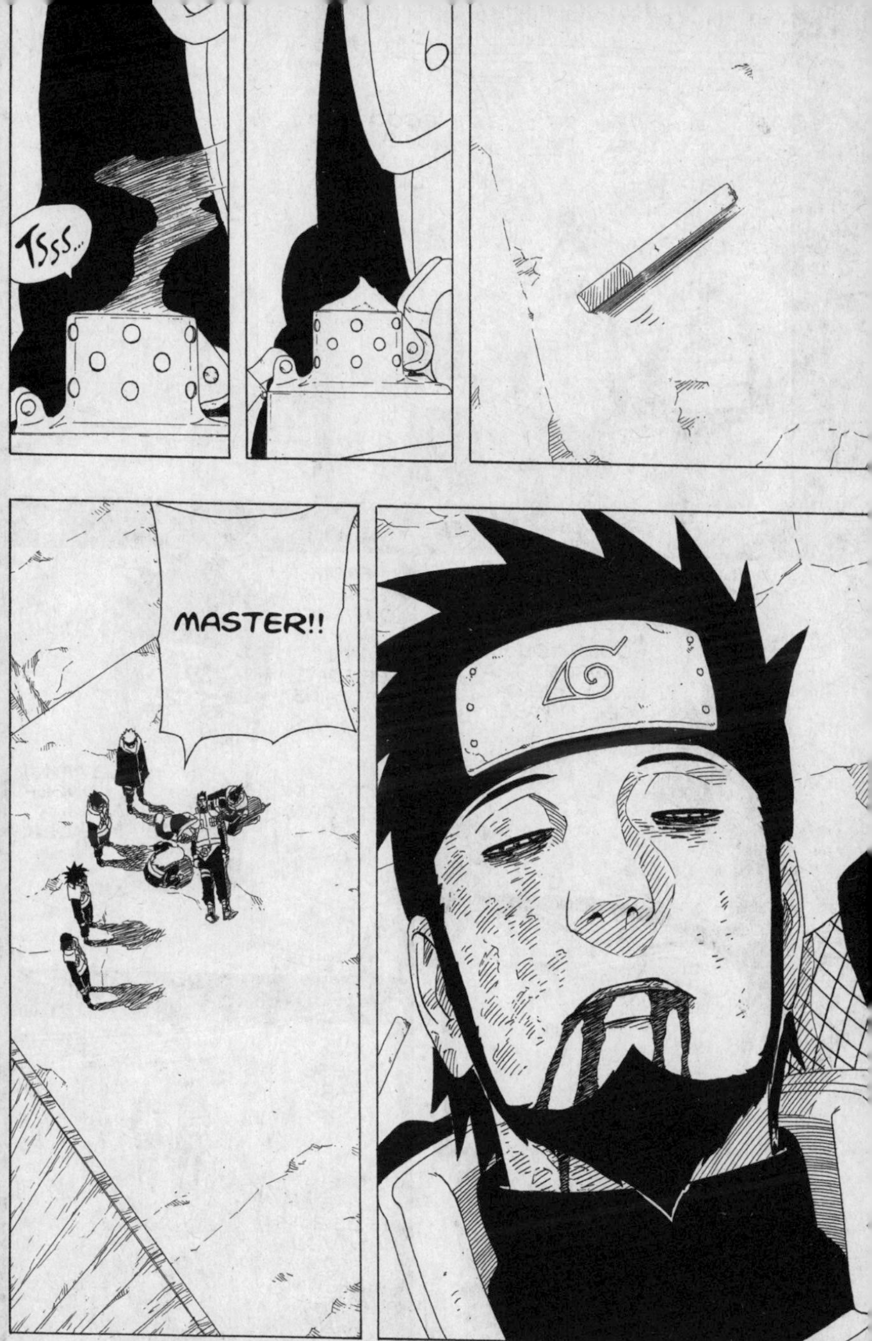
TSSS...
MASTER!!

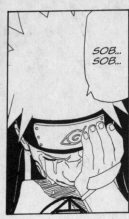

SOB... SOB...

...

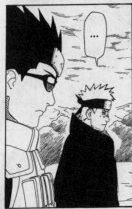

...

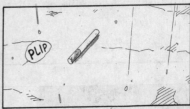

PLIP

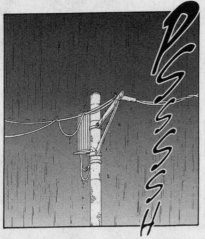

PSSSSSH

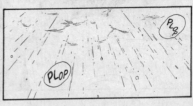

PLOP

PLOP

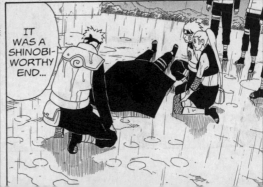

IT WAS A SHINOBI-WORTHY END...

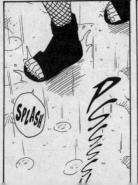

SPLASH

PSSSSSH

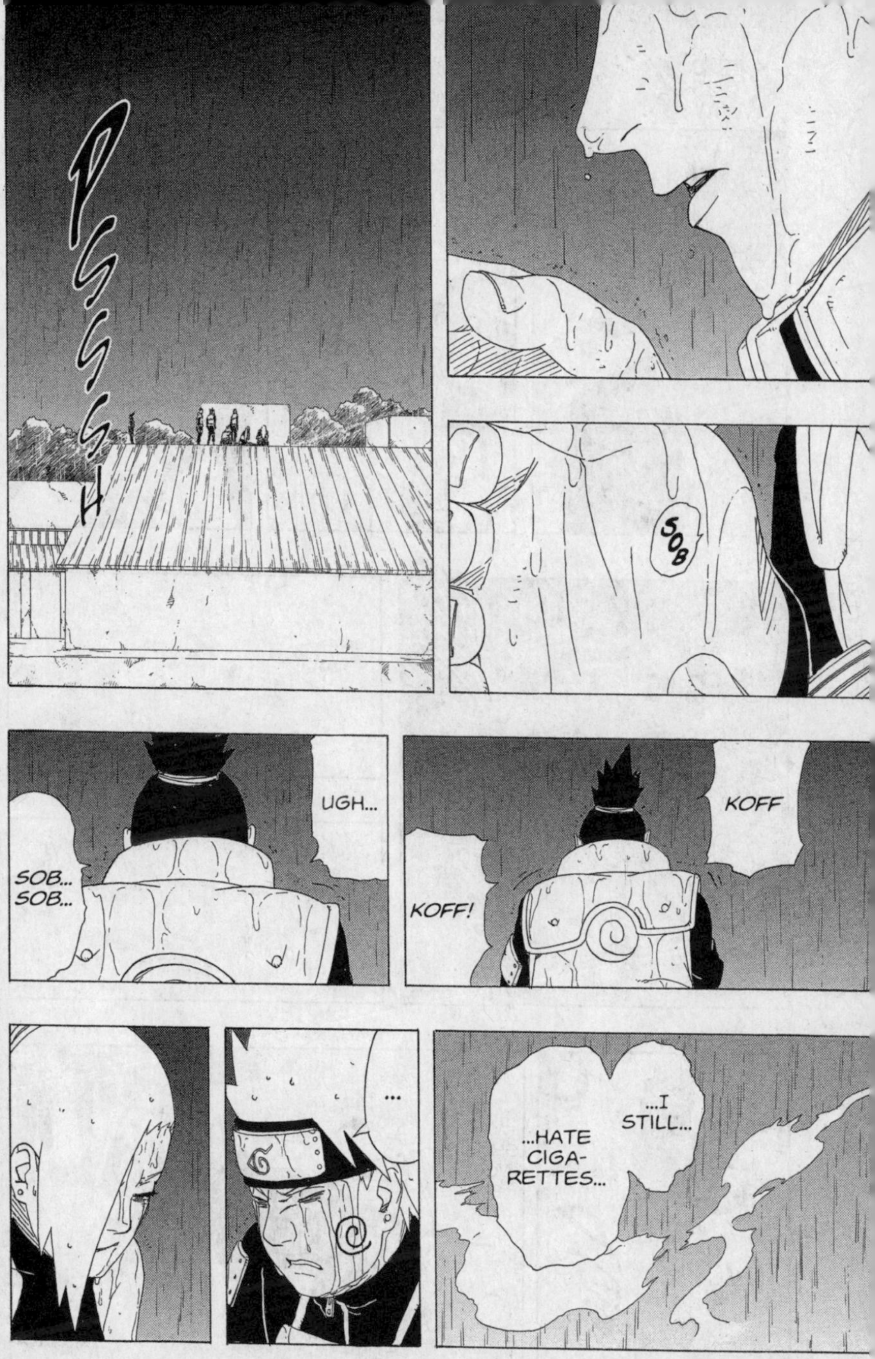
SOB
PSSSH
KOFF
KOFF!
UGH...
SOB... SOB...
...I STILL...
...HATE CIGA-RETTES...
...

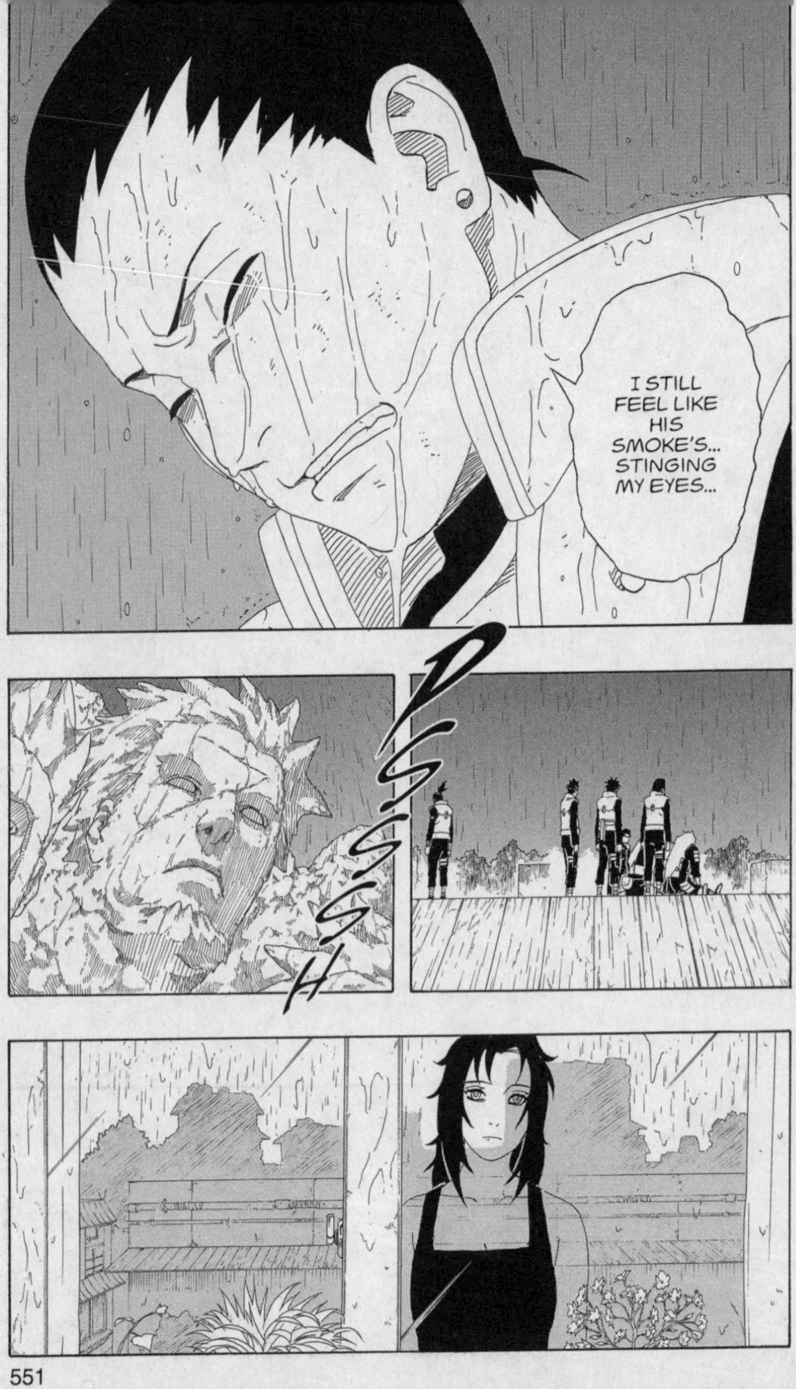
I STILL FEEL LIKE HIS SMOKE'S... STINGING MY EYES...
PSSSSH

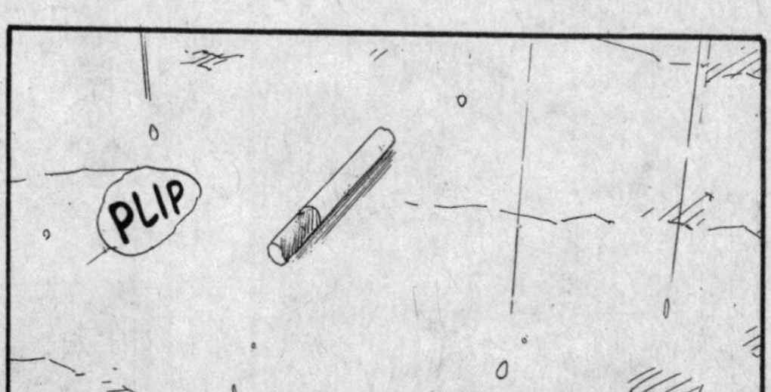
PLIP

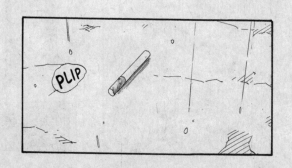

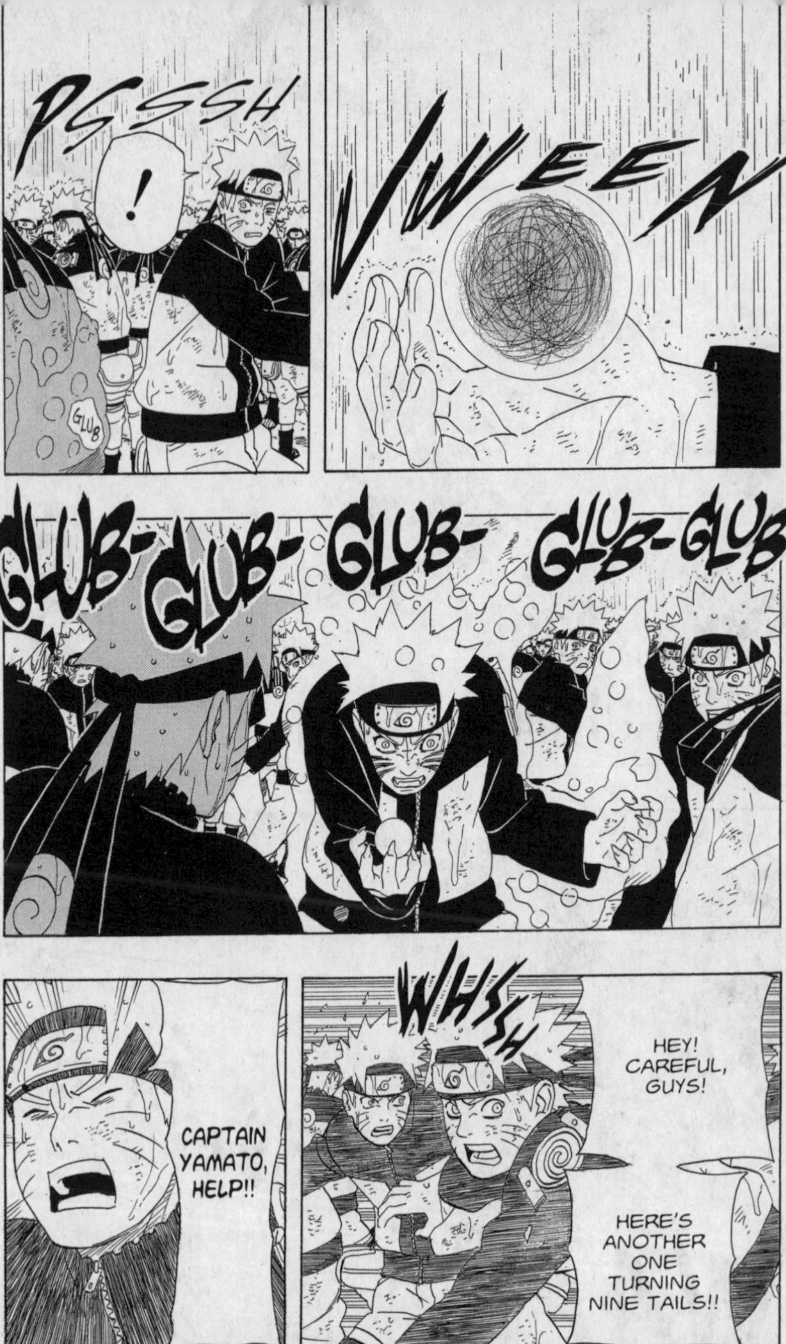
VWEEN
PSSSH
!
GLUB
GLUB-GLUB-GLUB-GLUB-GLUB
WHSSH
HEY! CAREFUL, GUYS!
HERE'S ANOTHER ONE TURNING NINE TAILS!!
CAPTAIN YAMATO, HELP!!

Number 329: The Ultimate Goal...!!

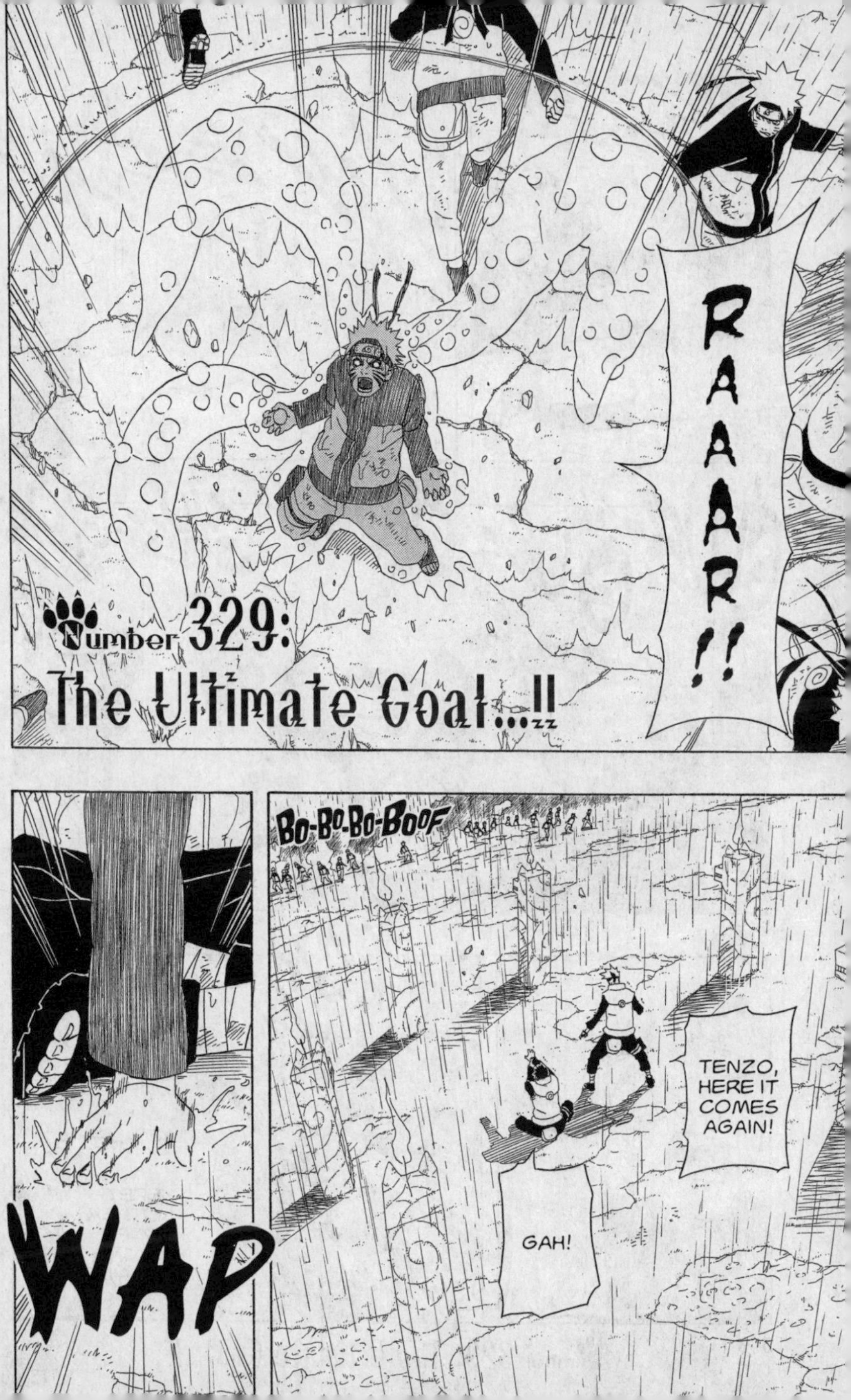
RAAAR!!
Number 329:
The Ultimate Goal...!!
BO-BO-BO-BOOF
TENZO, HERE IT COMES AGAIN!
GAH!
WAP

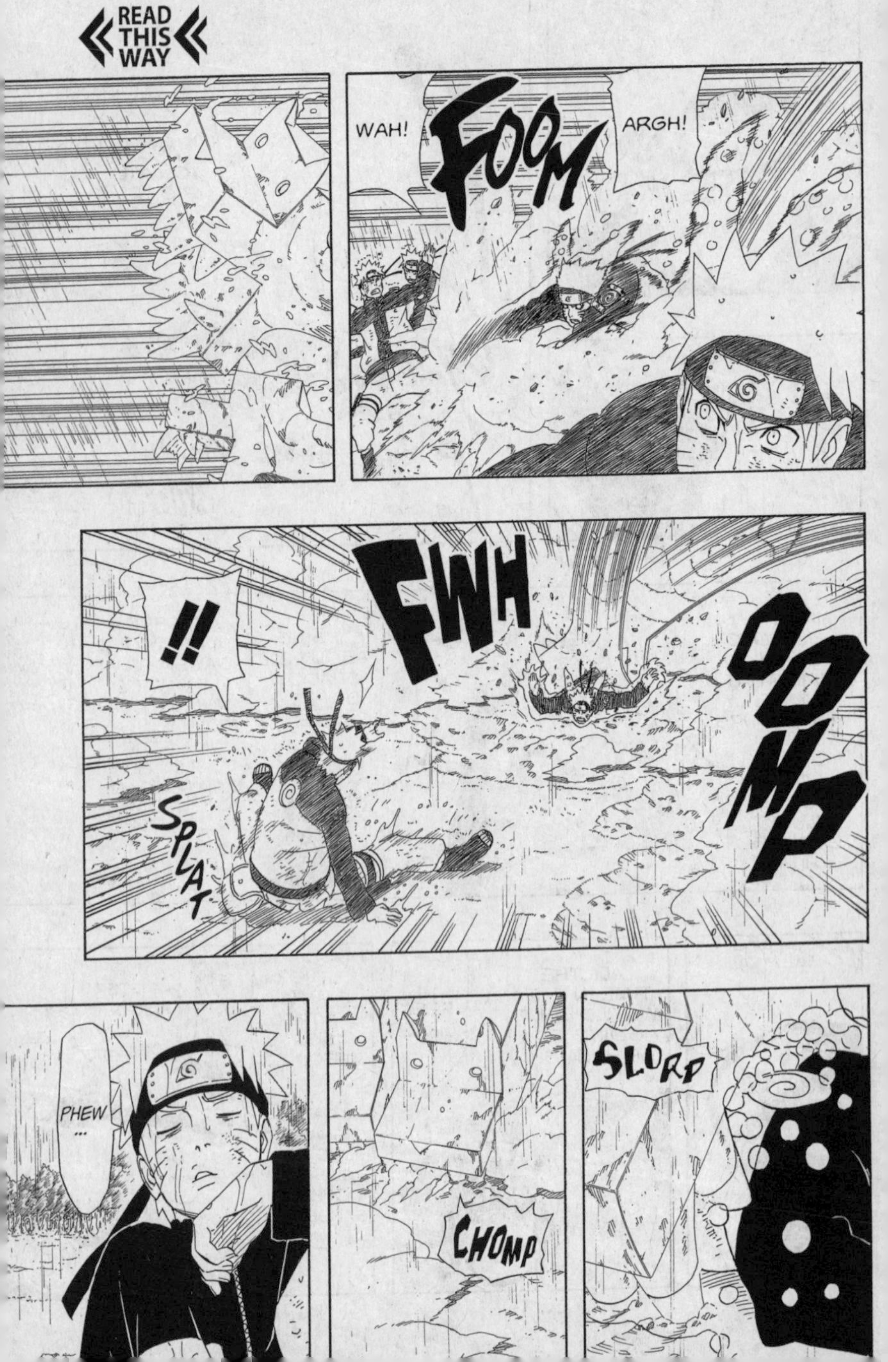
READ THIS WAY
ARGH!
FOOM
WAH!
OOMP
FWH
!!
SPLAT
SLORP
CHOMP
PHEW ...

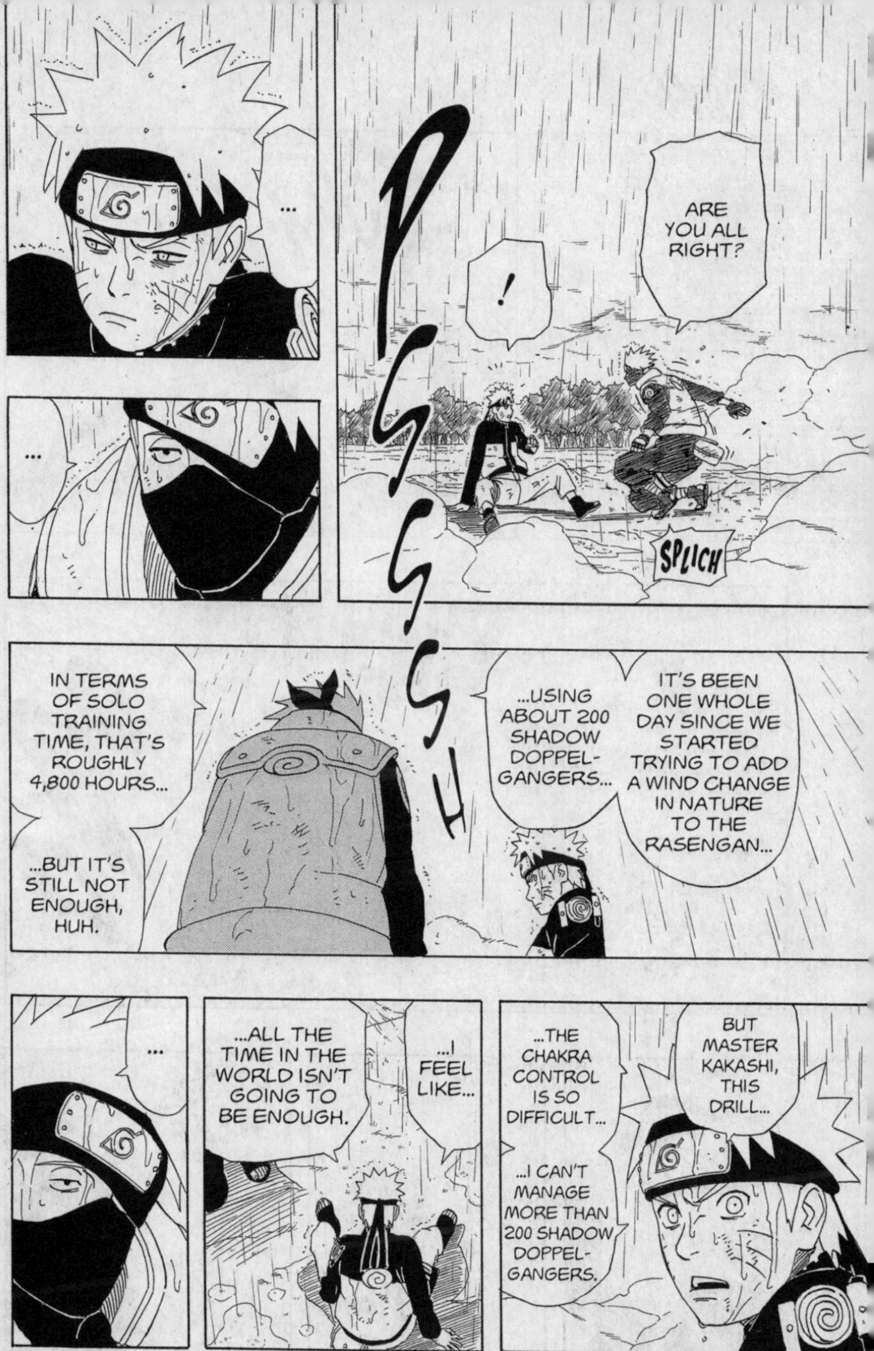
ARE YOU ALL RIGHT?
!
PSSSSH
SPLICH
...
...
IT'S BEEN ONE WHOLE DAY SINCE WE STARTED TRYING TO ADD A WIND CHANGE IN NATURE TO THE RASENGAN...
...USING ABOUT 200 SHADOW DOPPEL-GANGERS...
IN TERMS OF SOLO TRAINING TIME, THAT'S ROUGHLY 4,800 HOURS...
...BUT IT'S STILL NOT ENOUGH, HUH.
BUT MASTER KAKASHI, THIS DRILL...
...THE CHAKRA CONTROL IS SO DIFFICULT...
...I CAN'T MANAGE MORE THAN 200 SHADOW DOPPEL-GANGERS.
...I FEEL LIKE...
...ALL THE TIME IN THE WORLD ISN'T GOING TO BE ENOUGH.
...

READ THIS WAY

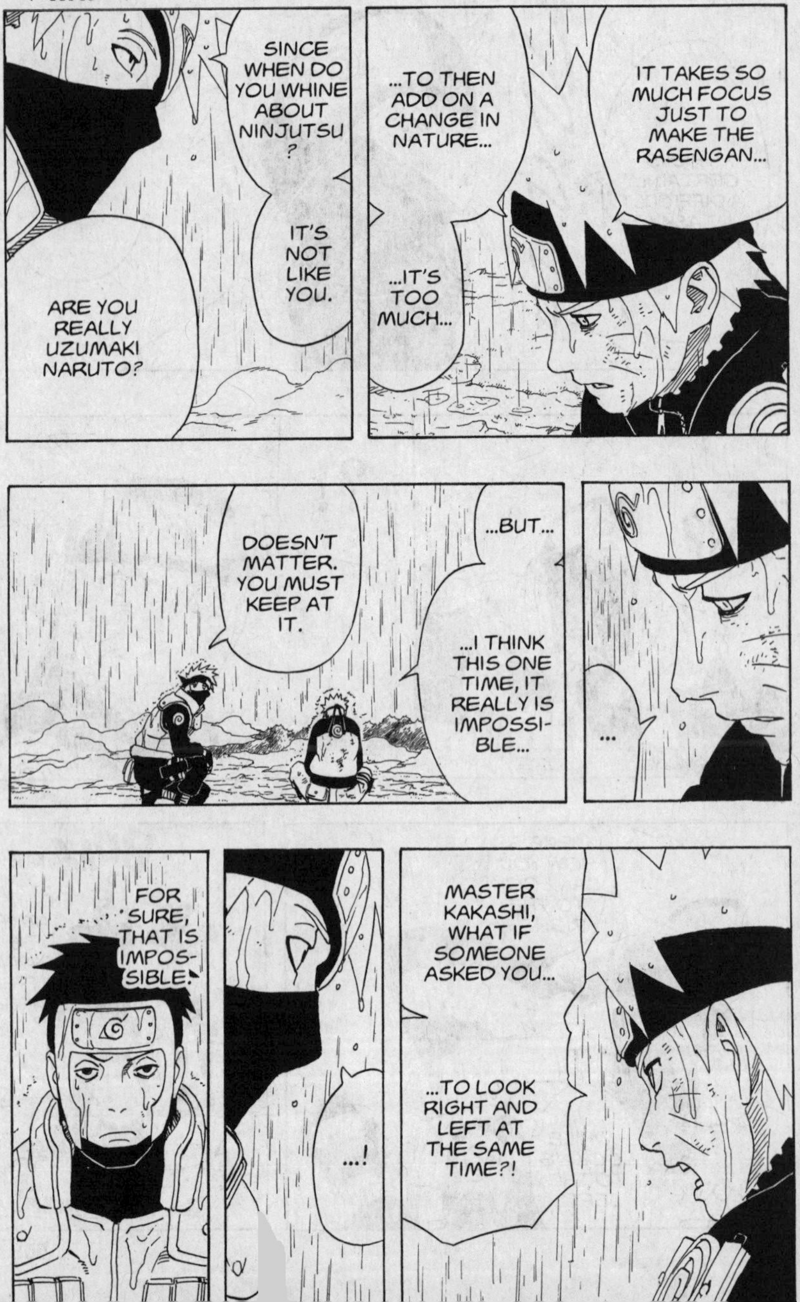

IT TAKES SO MUCH FOCUS JUST TO MAKE THE RASENGAN...
...TO THEN ADD ON A CHANGE IN NATURE...
...IT'S TOO MUCH...
SINCE WHEN DO YOU WHINE ABOUT NINJUTSU?
IT'S NOT LIKE YOU.
ARE YOU REALLY UZUMAKI NARUTO?
...
...BUT...
...I THINK THIS ONE TIME, IT REALLY IS IMPOSSIBLE...
DOESN'T MATTER. YOU MUST KEEP AT IT.
MASTER KAKASHI, WHAT IF SOMEONE ASKED YOU...
...TO LOOK RIGHT AND LEFT AT THE SAME TIME?!
...!
FOR SURE, THAT IS IMPOSSIBLE.

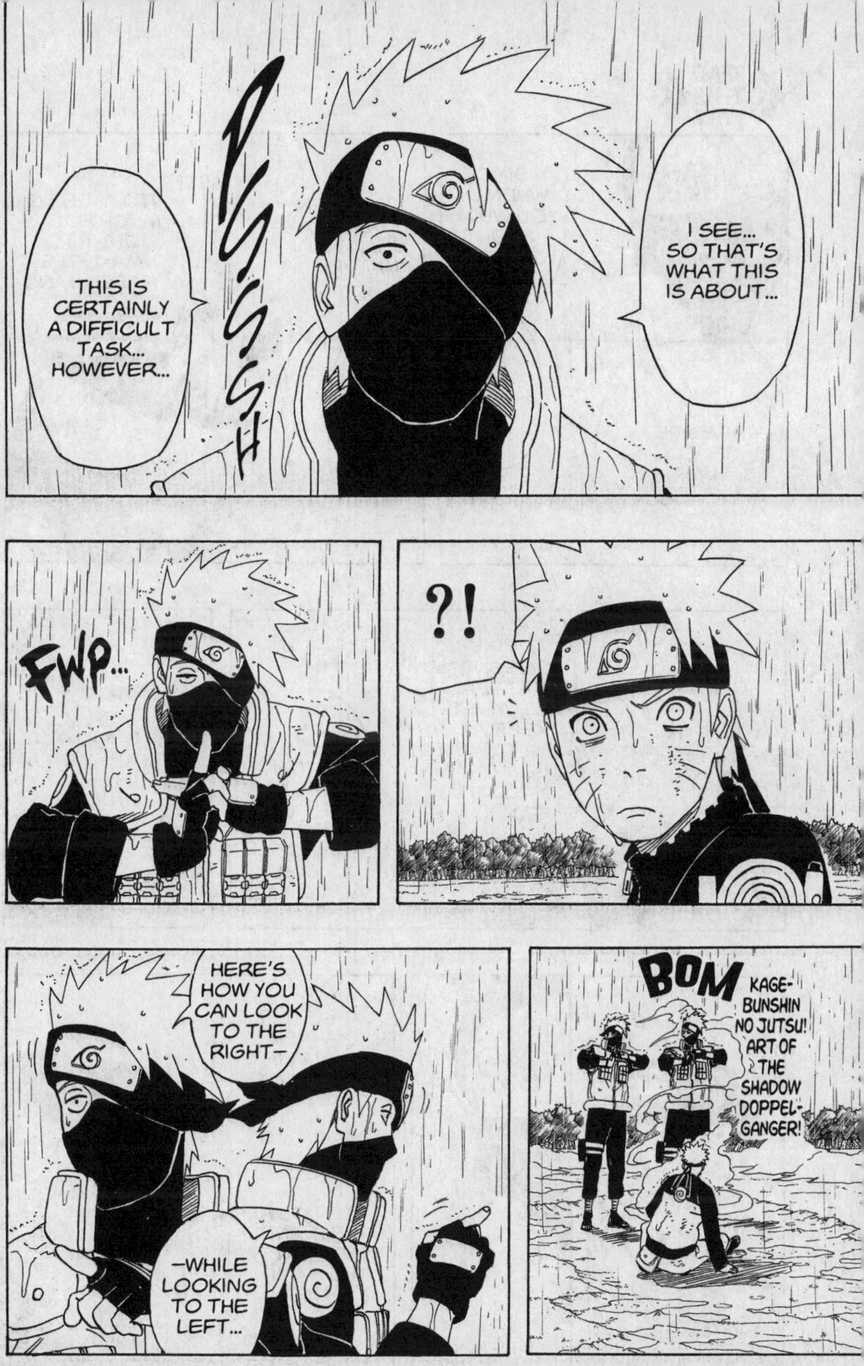
I SEE... SO THAT'S WHAT THIS IS ABOUT...
PSSSH
THIS IS CERTAINLY A DIFFICULT TASK... HOWEVER...
?!
FWP...
BOM
KAGE-BUNSHIN NO JUTSU! ART OF THE SHADOW DOPPEL-GANGER!
HERE'S HOW YOU CAN LOOK TO THE RIGHT—
—WHILE LOOKING TO THE LEFT...

READ THIS WAY

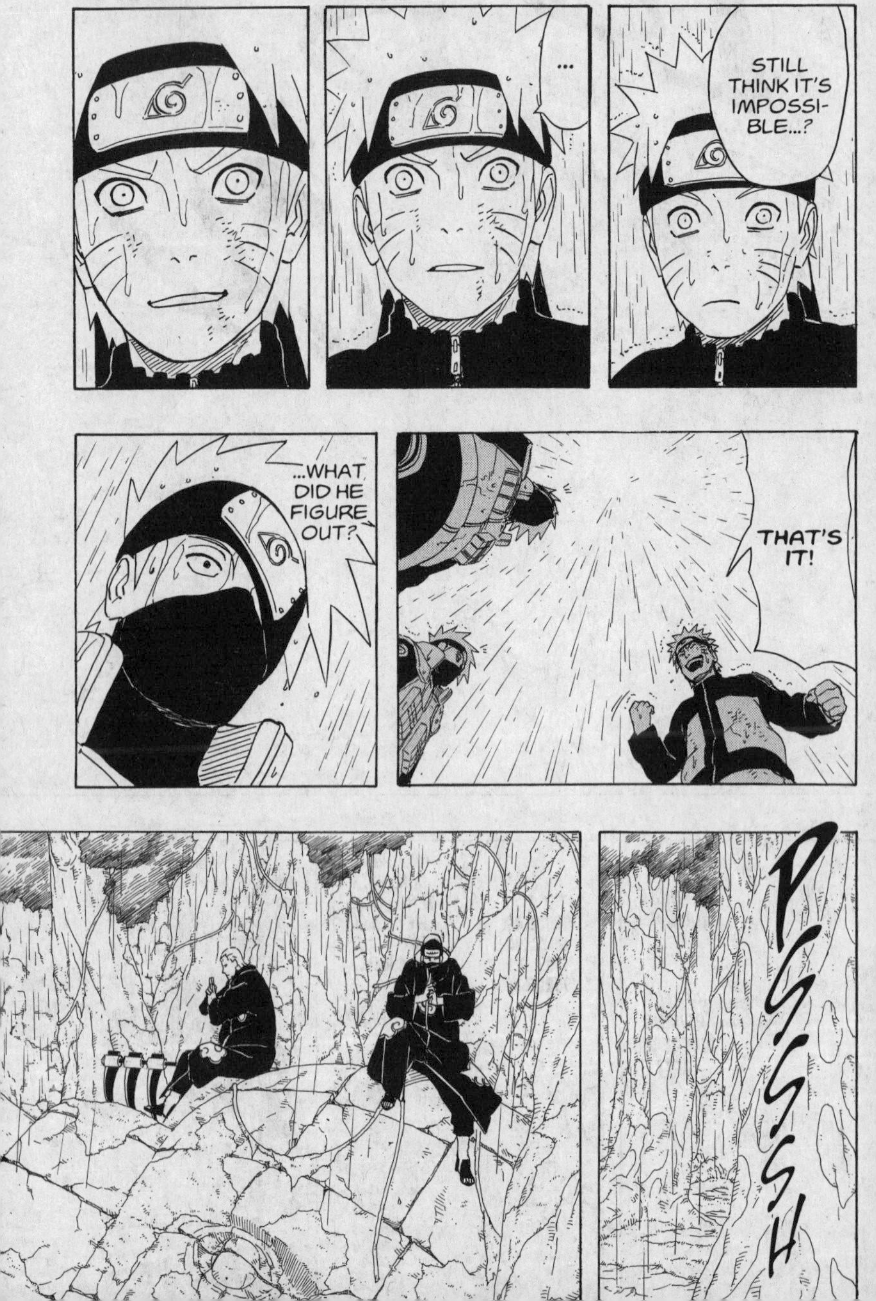
STILL THINK IT'S IMPOSSIBLE...?
...
THAT'S IT!
...WHAT DID HE FIGURE OUT?
PSSSH

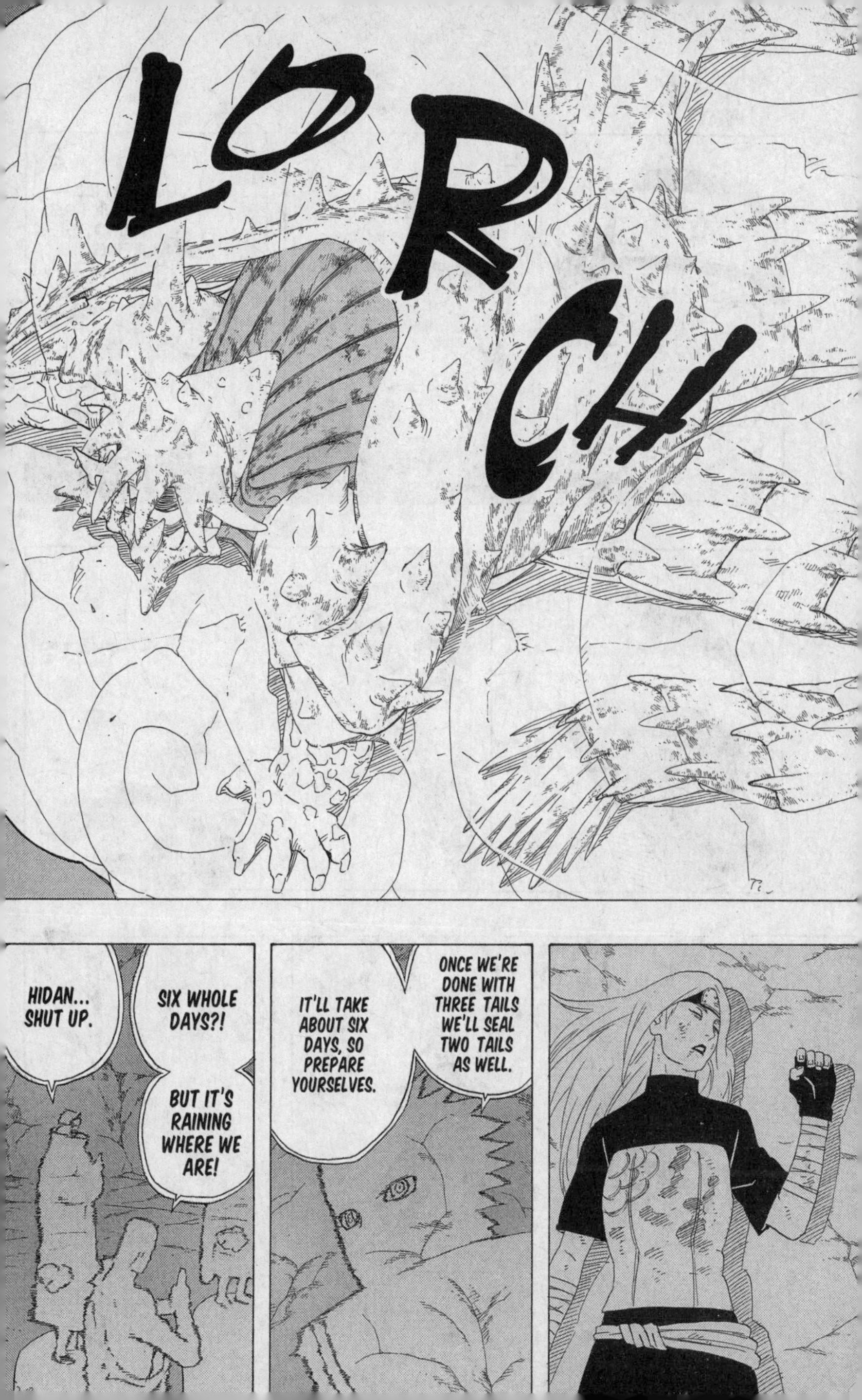
LORCH
ONCE WE'RE DONE WITH THREE TAILS WE'LL SEAL TWO TAILS AS WELL.
IT'LL TAKE ABOUT SIX DAYS, SO PREPARE YOURSELVES.
SIX WHOLE DAYS?!
BUT IT'S RAINING WHERE WE ARE!
HIDAN... SHUT UP.

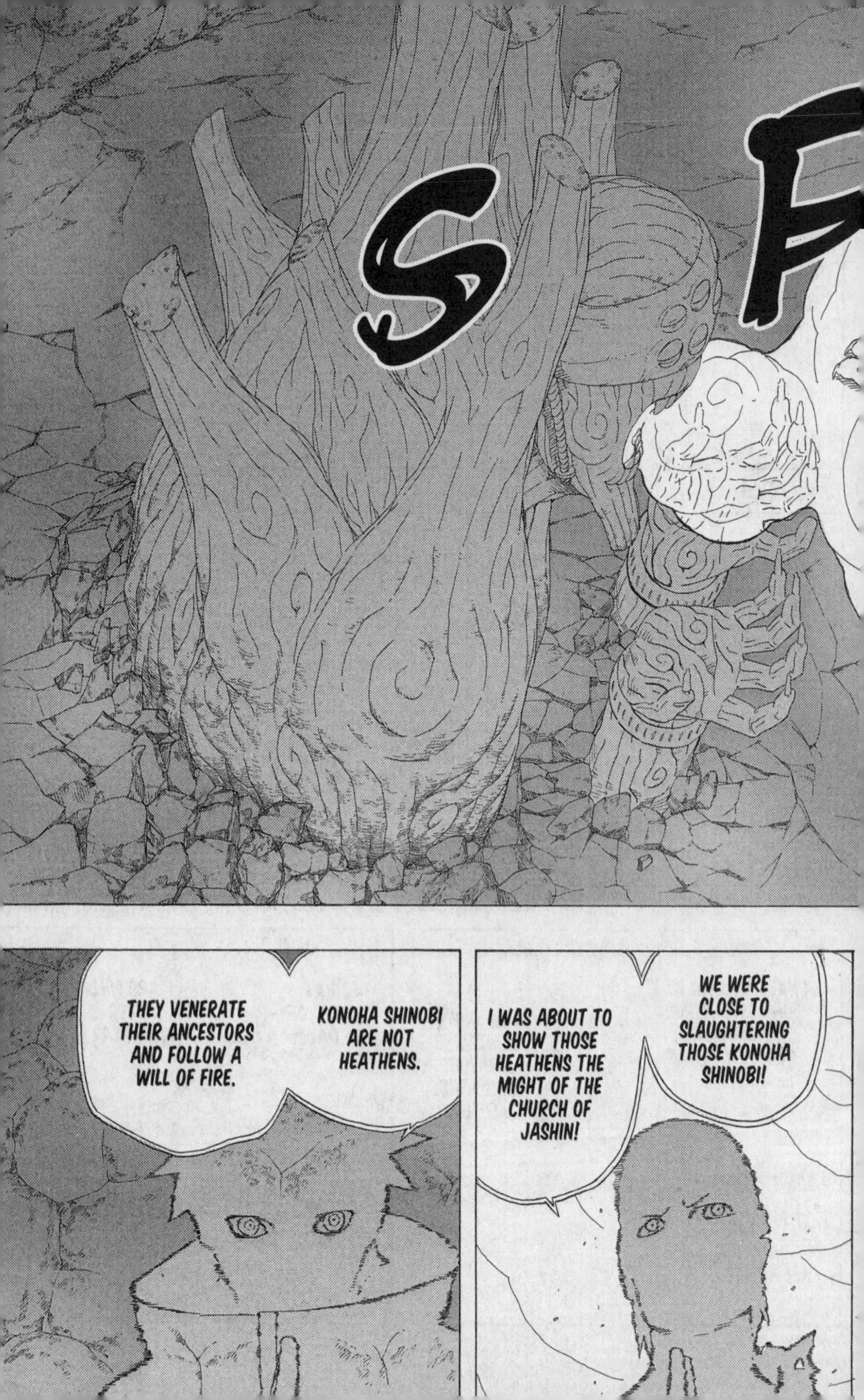
S
WE WERE CLOSE TO SLAUGHTERING THOSE KONOHA SHINOBI!
I WAS ABOUT TO SHOW THOSE HEATHENS THE MIGHT OF THE CHURCH OF JASHIN!
KONOHA SHINOBI ARE NOT HEATHENS.
THEY VENERATE THEIR ANCESTORS AND FOLLOW A WILL OF FIRE.

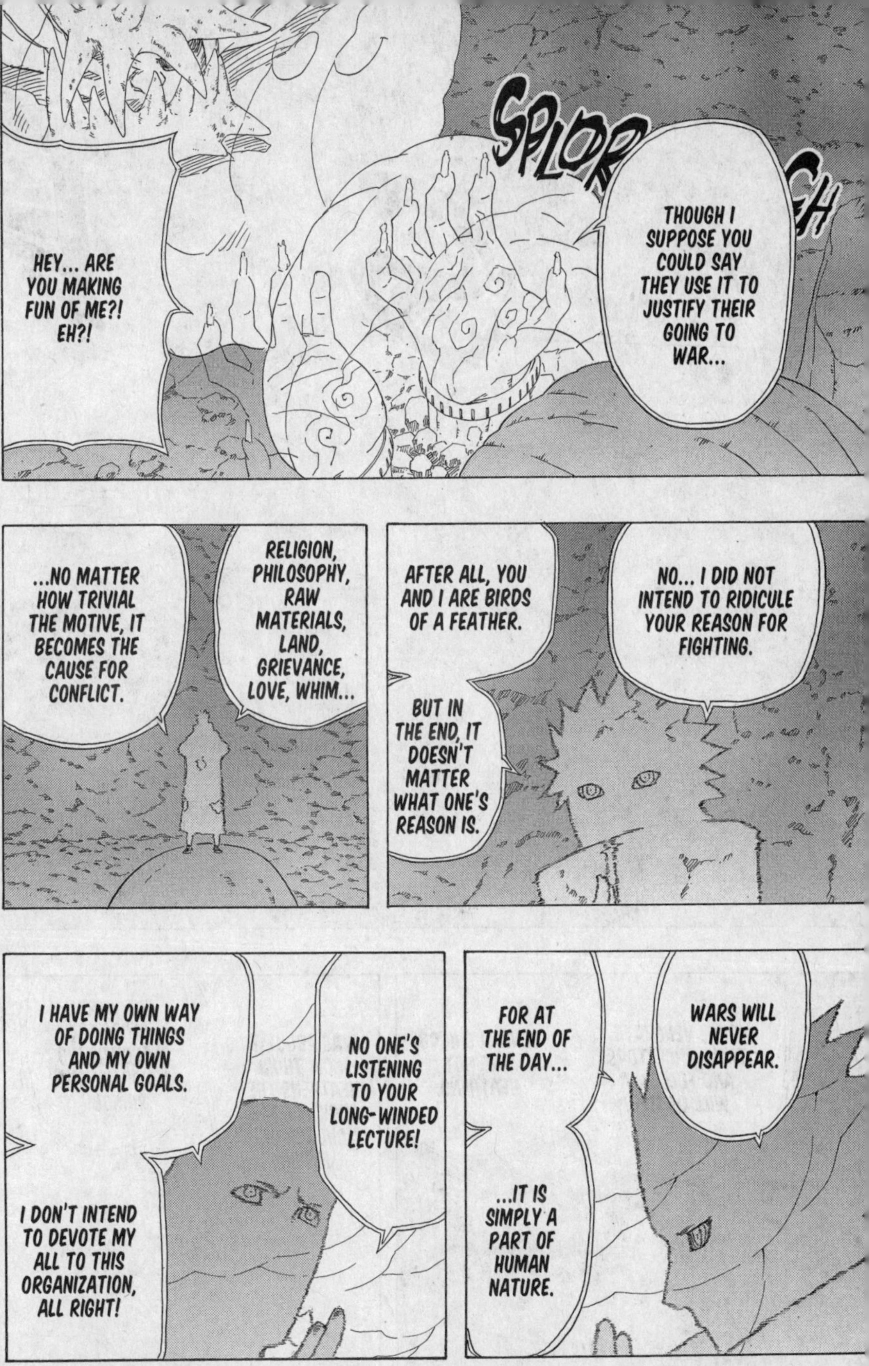
SPLOR… CH
THOUGH I SUPPOSE YOU COULD SAY THEY USE IT TO JUSTIFY THEIR GOING TO WAR...
HEY... ARE YOU MAKING FUN OF ME?! EH?!
NO... I DID NOT INTEND TO RIDICULE YOUR REASON FOR FIGHTING.
AFTER ALL, YOU AND I ARE BIRDS OF A FEATHER.
BUT IN THE END, IT DOESN'T MATTER WHAT ONE'S REASON IS.
RELIGION, PHILOSOPHY, RAW MATERIALS, LAND, GRIEVANCE, LOVE, WHIM...
...NO MATTER HOW TRIVIAL THE MOTIVE, IT BECOMES THE CAUSE FOR CONFLICT.
WARS WILL NEVER DISAPPEAR.
FOR AT THE END OF THE DAY...
...IT IS SIMPLY A PART OF HUMAN NATURE.
NO ONE'S LISTENING TO YOUR LONG-WINDED LECTURE!
I HAVE MY OWN WAY OF DOING THINGS AND MY OWN PERSONAL GOALS.
I DON'T INTEND TO DEVOTE MY ALL TO THIS ORGANIZATION, ALL RIGHT!

READ THIS WAY

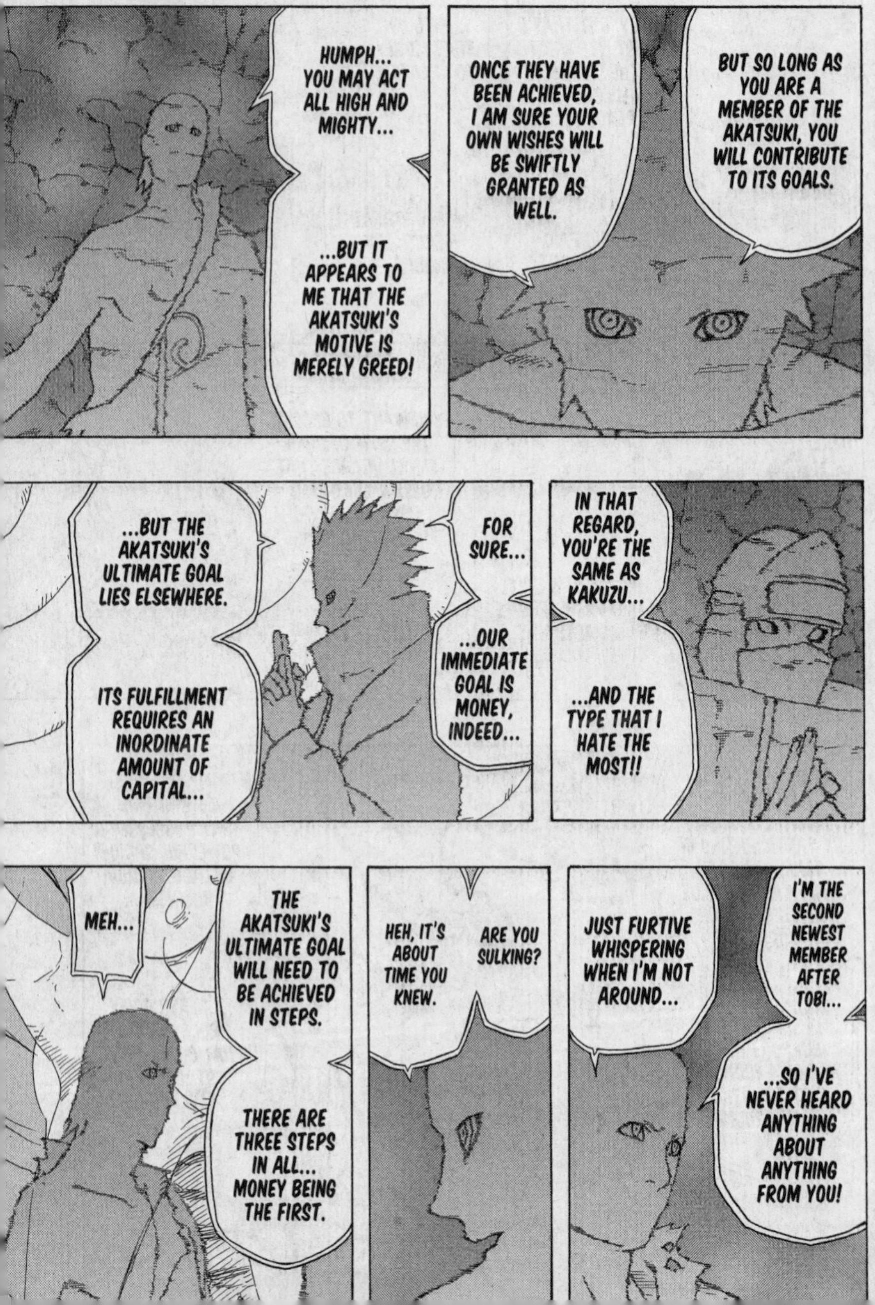

BUT SO LONG AS YOU ARE A MEMBER OF THE AKATSUKI, YOU WILL CONTRIBUTE TO ITS GOALS.
ONCE THEY HAVE BEEN ACHIEVED, I AM SURE YOUR OWN WISHES WILL BE SWIFTLY GRANTED AS WELL.
HUMPH... YOU MAY ACT ALL HIGH AND MIGHTY...
...BUT IT APPEARS TO ME THAT THE AKATSUKI'S MOTIVE IS MERELY GREED!
IN THAT REGARD, YOU'RE THE SAME AS KAKUZU...
...AND THE TYPE THAT I HATE THE MOST!!
FOR SURE...
...OUR IMMEDIATE GOAL IS MONEY, INDEED...
...BUT THE AKATSUKI'S ULTIMATE GOAL LIES ELSEWHERE.
ITS FULFILLMENT REQUIRES AN INORDINATE AMOUNT OF CAPITAL...
I'M THE SECOND NEWEST MEMBER AFTER TOBI...
JUST FURTIVE WHISPERING WHEN I'M NOT AROUND...
...SO I'VE NEVER HEARD ANYTHING ABOUT ANYTHING FROM YOU!
ARE YOU SULKING?
HEH, IT'S ABOUT TIME YOU KNEW.
THE AKATSUKI'S ULTIMATE GOAL WILL NEED TO BE ACHIEVED IN STEPS.
MEH...
THERE ARE THREE STEPS IN ALL... MONEY BEING THE FIRST.

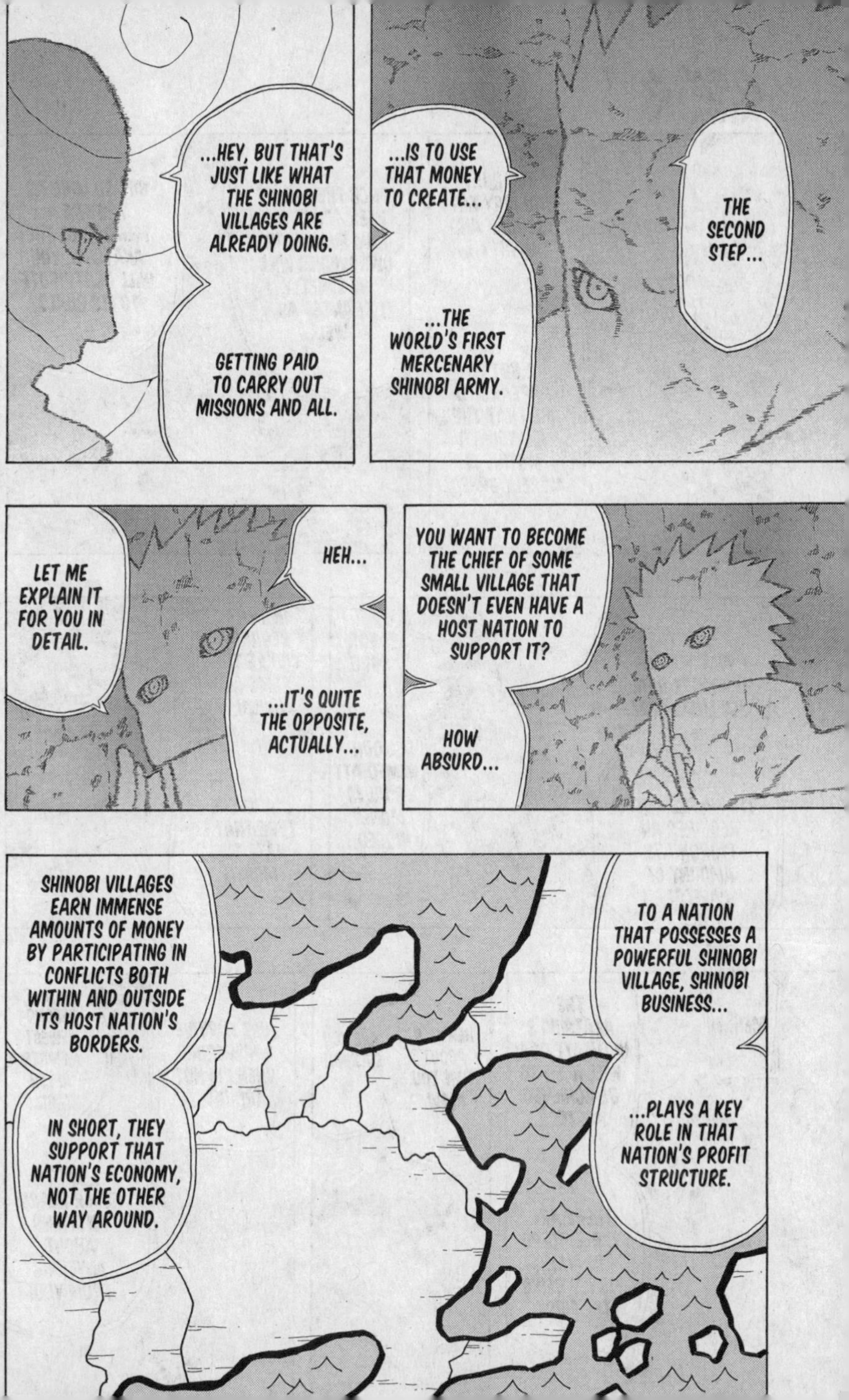
THE SECOND STEP...
...IS TO USE THAT MONEY TO CREATE...
...THE WORLD'S FIRST MERCENARY SHINOBI ARMY.
...HEY, BUT THAT'S JUST LIKE WHAT THE SHINOBI VILLAGES ARE ALREADY DOING.
GETTING PAID TO CARRY OUT MISSIONS AND ALL.
YOU WANT TO BECOME THE CHIEF OF SOME SMALL VILLAGE THAT DOESN'T EVEN HAVE A HOST NATION TO SUPPORT IT?
HOW ABSURD...
HEH...
...IT'S QUITE THE OPPOSITE, ACTUALLY...
LET ME EXPLAIN IT FOR YOU IN DETAIL.
TO A NATION THAT POSSESSES A POWERFUL SHINOBI VILLAGE, SHINOBI BUSINESS...
...PLAYS A KEY ROLE IN THAT NATION'S PROFIT STRUCTURE.
SHINOBI VILLAGES EARN IMMENSE AMOUNTS OF MONEY BY PARTICIPATING IN CONFLICTS BOTH WITHIN AND OUTSIDE ITS HOST NATION'S BORDERS.
IN SHORT, THEY SUPPORT THAT NATION'S ECONOMY, NOT THE OTHER WAY AROUND.

READ THIS WAY

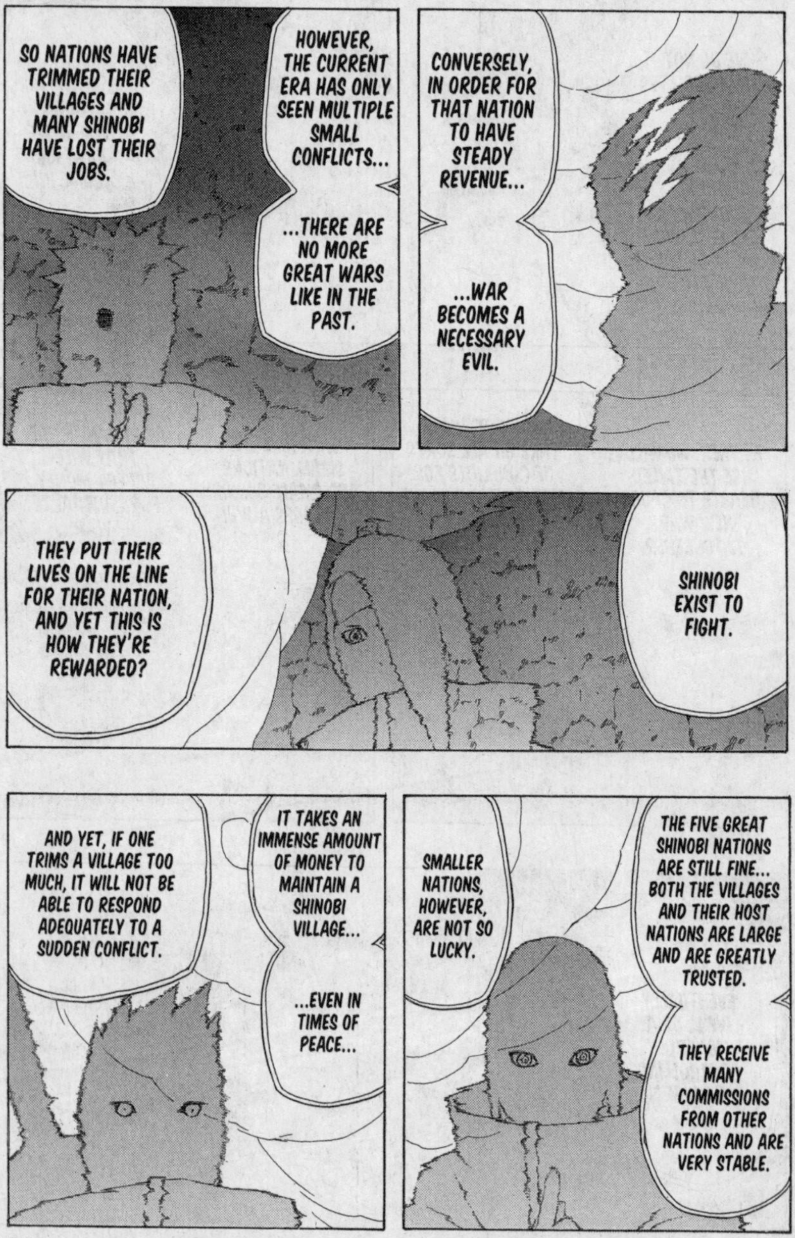
CONVERSELY, IN ORDER FOR THAT NATION TO HAVE STEADY REVENUE...
...WAR BECOMES A NECESSARY EVIL.
HOWEVER, THE CURRENT ERA HAS ONLY SEEN MULTIPLE SMALL CONFLICTS...
...THERE ARE NO MORE GREAT WARS LIKE IN THE PAST.
SO NATIONS HAVE TRIMMED THEIR VILLAGES AND MANY SHINOBI HAVE LOST THEIR JOBS.
SHINOBI EXIST TO FIGHT.
THEY PUT THEIR LIVES ON THE LINE FOR THEIR NATION, AND YET THIS IS HOW THEY'RE REWARDED?
THE FIVE GREAT SHINOBI NATIONS ARE STILL FINE... BOTH THE VILLAGES AND THEIR HOST NATIONS ARE LARGE AND ARE GREATLY TRUSTED.
THEY RECEIVE MANY COMMISSIONS FROM OTHER NATIONS AND ARE VERY STABLE.
SMALLER NATIONS, HOWEVER, ARE NOT SO LUCKY.
IT TAKES AN IMMENSE AMOUNT OF MONEY TO MAINTAIN A SHINOBI VILLAGE...
...EVEN IN TIMES OF PEACE...
AND YET, IF ONE TRIMS A VILLAGE TOO MUCH, IT WILL NOT BE ABLE TO RESPOND ADEQUATELY TO A SUDDEN CONFLICT.

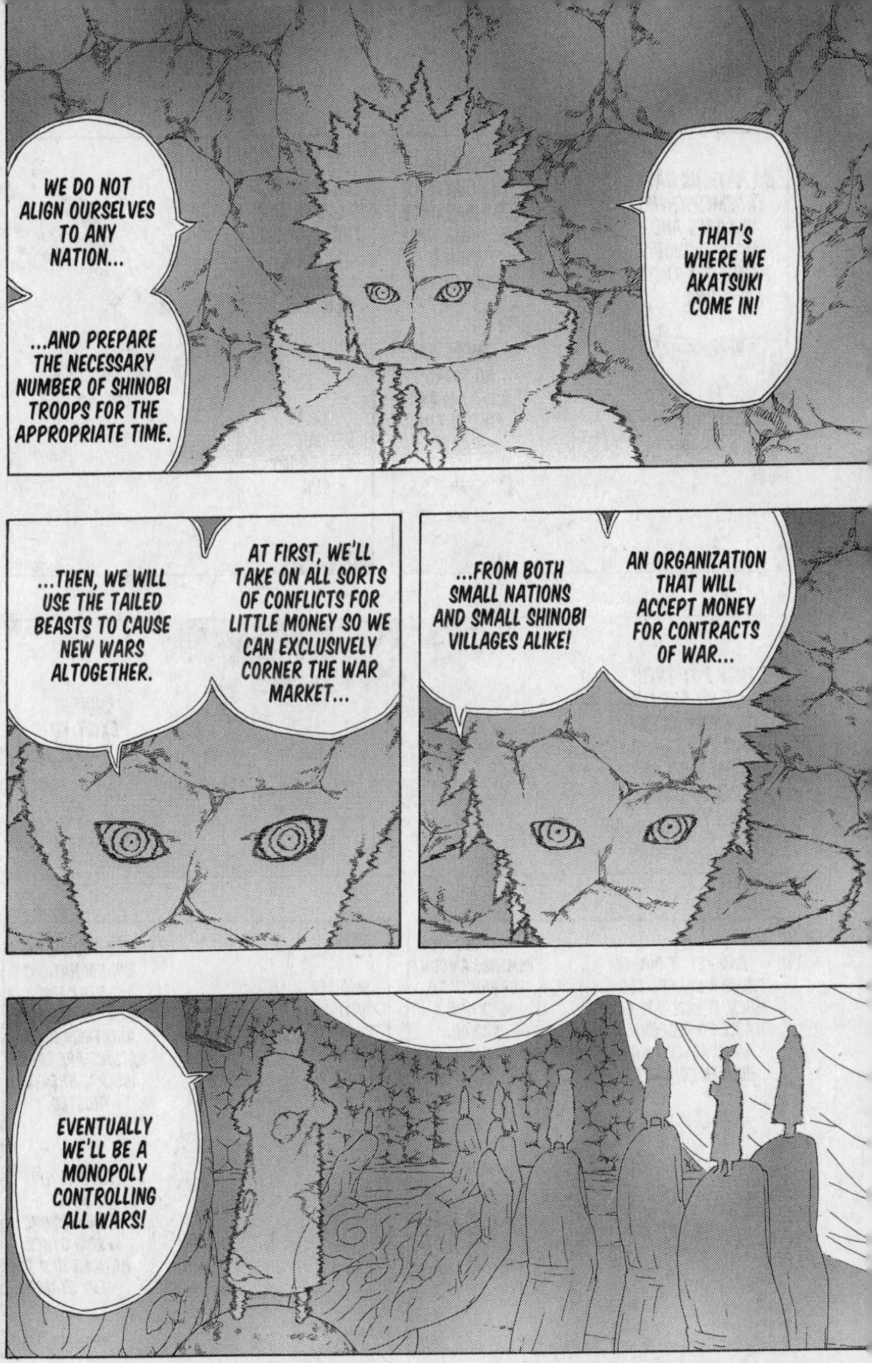
THAT'S WHERE WE AKATSUKI COME IN!
WE DO NOT ALIGN OURSELVES TO ANY NATION...
...AND PREPARE THE NECESSARY NUMBER OF SHINOBI TROOPS FOR THE APPROPRIATE TIME.
AN ORGANIZATION THAT WILL ACCEPT MONEY FOR CONTRACTS OF WAR...
...FROM BOTH SMALL NATIONS AND SMALL SHINOBI VILLAGES ALIKE!
AT FIRST, WE'LL TAKE ON ALL SORTS OF CONFLICTS FOR LITTLE MONEY SO WE CAN EXCLUSIVELY CORNER THE WAR MARKET...
...THEN, WE WILL USE THE TAILED BEASTS TO CAUSE NEW WARS ALTOGETHER.
EVENTUALLY WE'LL BE A MONOPOLY CONTROLLING ALL WARS!

READ THIS WAY

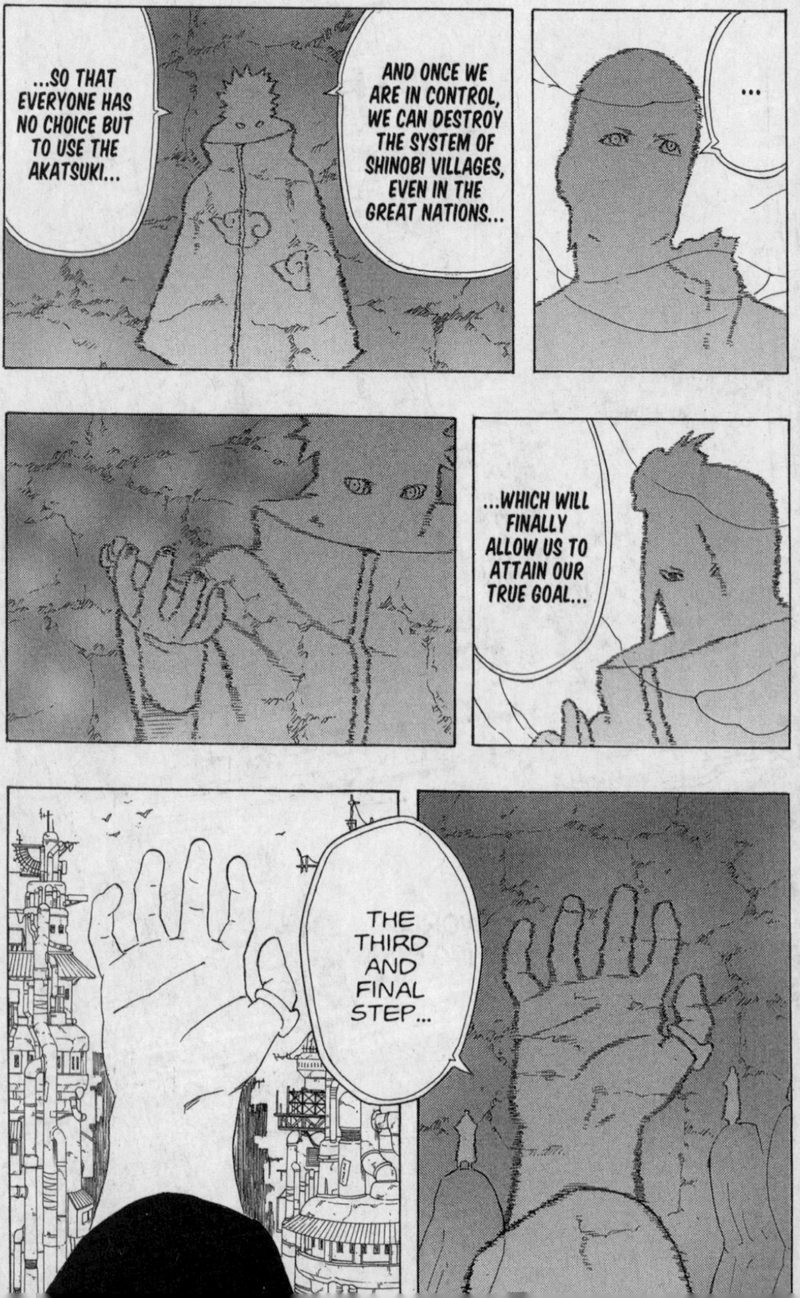
...
AND ONCE WE ARE IN CONTROL, WE CAN DESTROY THE SYSTEM OF SHINOBI VILLAGES, EVEN IN THE GREAT NATIONS...
...SO THAT EVERYONE HAS NO CHOICE BUT TO USE THE AKATSUKI...
...WHICH WILL FINALLY ALLOW US TO ATTAIN OUR TRUE GOAL...
THE THIRD AND FINAL STEP...

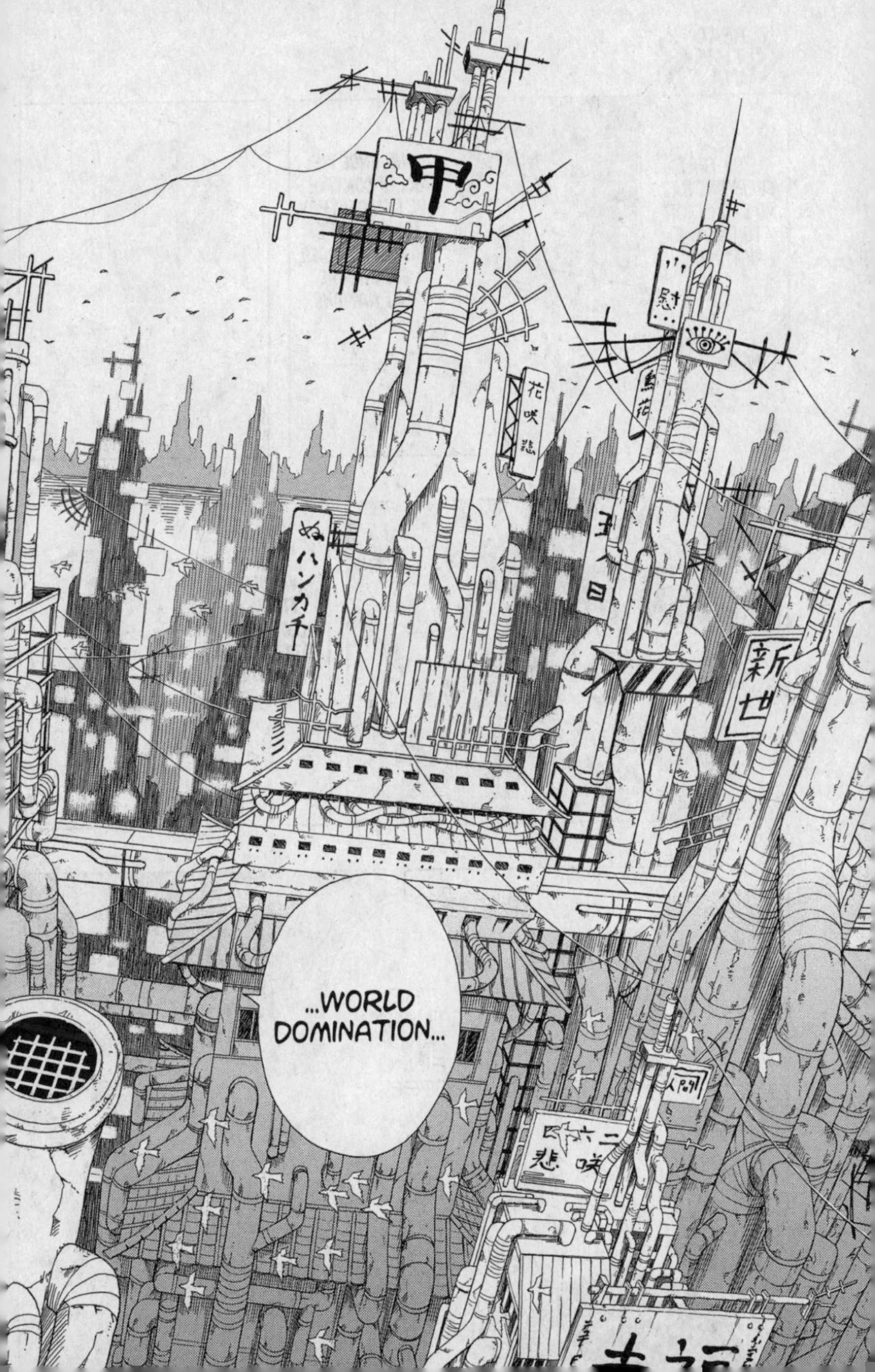
甲
花咲悲
ぬハンカチ
新世
...WORLD DOMINATION...

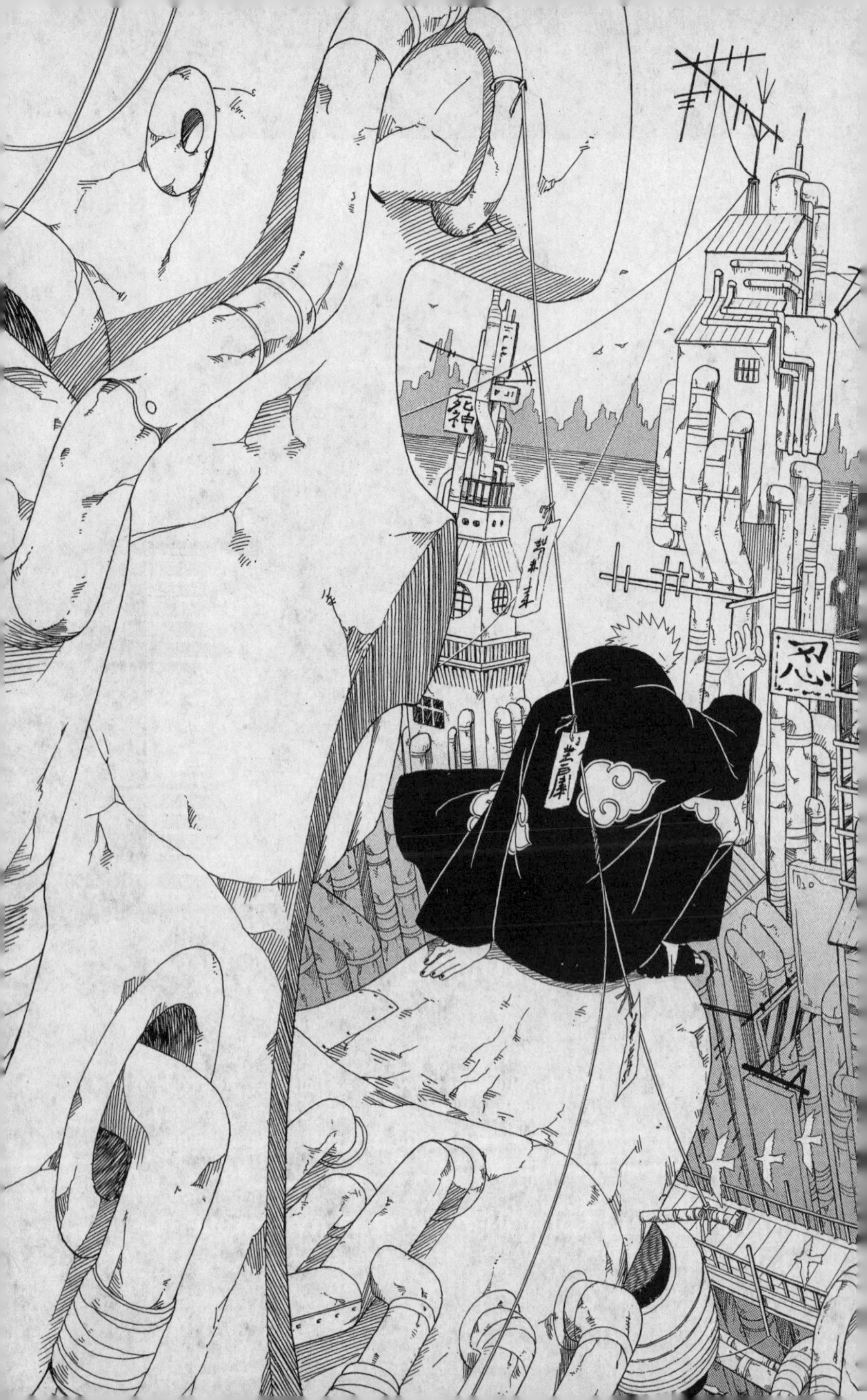
死神
忍

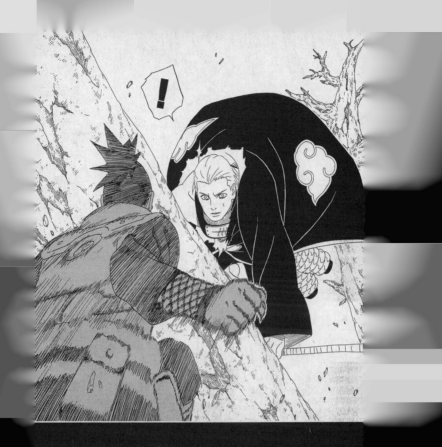

IN THE NEXT VOLUME...

MERCILESS

Shikamaru's team is out for revenge against their mentor's murderers! Tsunade tries to stop them, but Kakashi wants to help! As the divide among the ninja grows, the mysterious Akatsuki organization continue their brutal attack on the Tailed Beasts, the Biju and the young ninja who host them, including Naruto!

NARUTO 3-IN-1 EDITION VOLUME 13 AVAILABLE JANUARY 2016!

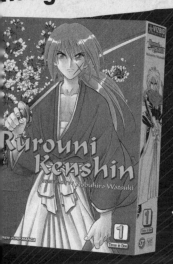
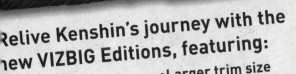

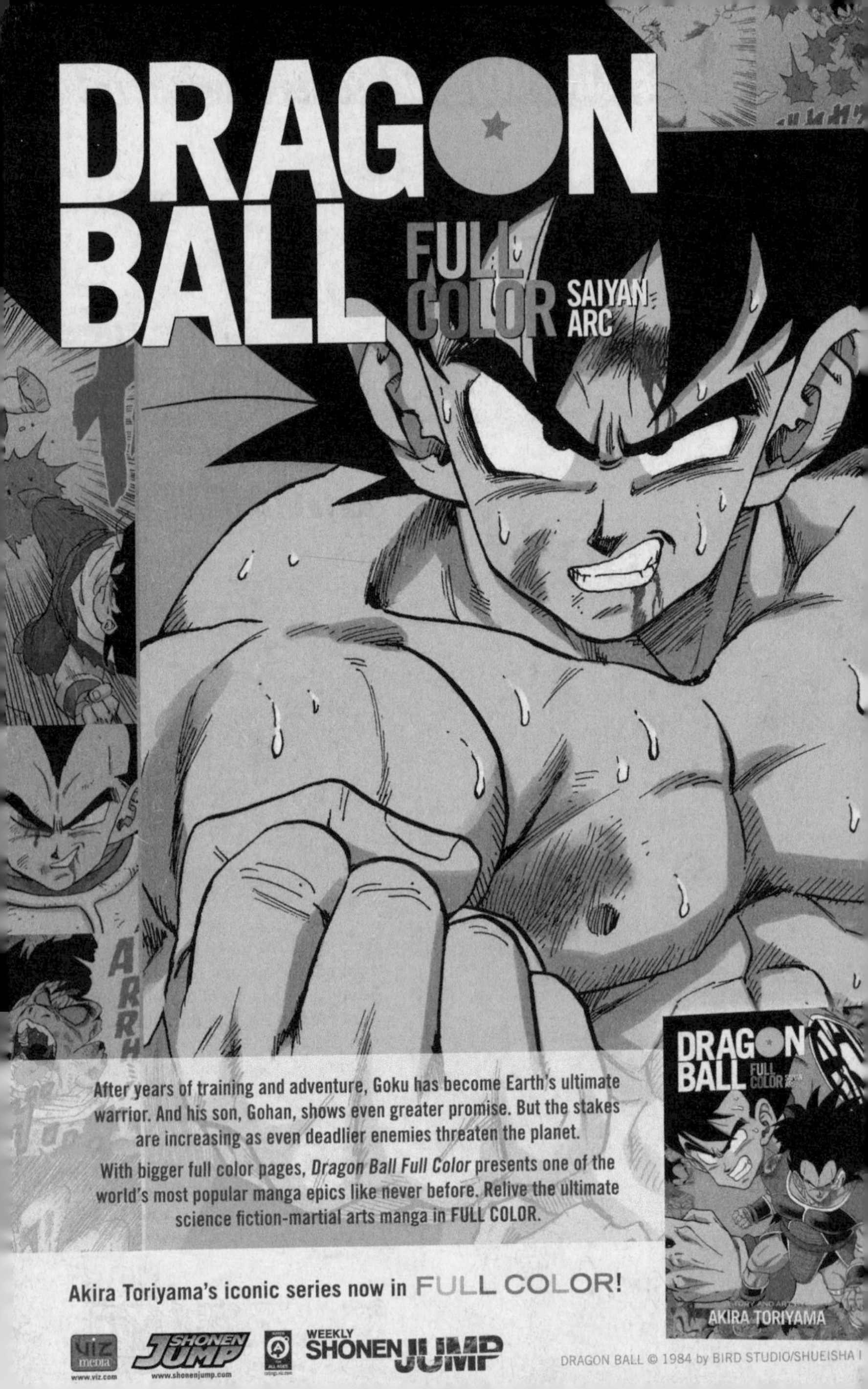

DRAGON BALL
FULL COLOR
SAIYAN ARC
After years of training and adventure, Goku has become Earth's ultimate warrior. And his son, Gohan, shows even greater promise. But the stakes are increasing as even deadlier enemies threaten the planet.
With bigger full color pages, *Dragon Ball Full Color* presents one of the world's most popular manga epics like never before. Relive the ultimate science fiction-martial arts manga in FULL COLOR.
DRAGON BALL FULL COLOR
AKIRA TORIYAMA
Akira Toriyama's iconic series now in FULL COLOR!
www.viz.com
www.shonenjump.com
WEEKLY SHONEN JUMP
DRAGON BALL © 1984 by BIRD STUDIO/SHUEISHA I

THE BEST SELLING MANGA SERIES IN THE WORLD!

ONE PIECE

Story & Art by **EIICHIRO ODA**

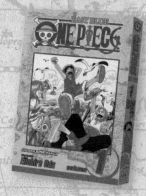

As a child, **Monkey D. Luffy** was inspired to become a pirate by listening to the tales of the buccaneer "Red-Haired" Shanks. But Luffy's life changed when he accidentally ate the Gum-Gum Devil Fruit and gained the power to stretch like rubber...at the cost of never being able to swim again! Years later, still vowing to become the king of the pirates, Luffy sets out on his adventure in search of the legendary "One Piece," said to be the greatest treasure in the world...

A PREMIUM BOX SET OF THE FIRST TWO STORY ARCS OF ONE PIECE!

A PIRATE'S TREASURE FOR ANY MANGA FAN!

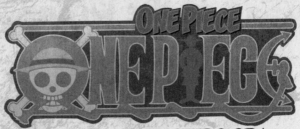

STORY AND ART BY EIICHIRO ODA

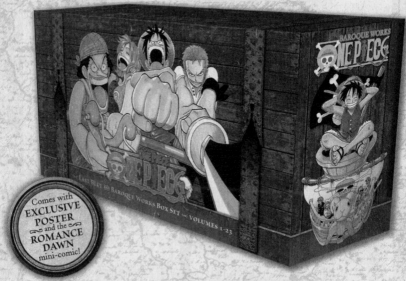

Comes with **EXCLUSIVE POSTER** and the **ROMANCE DAWN** mini-comic!

As a child, Monkey D. Luffy dreamed of becoming King of the Pirates. But his life changed when he accidentally gained the power to stretch like rubber...at the cost of never being able to swim again! Years later, Luffy sets off in search of the "One Piece," said to be the greatest treasure in the world...

This box set includes VOLUMES 1-23, which comprise the EAST BLUE and BAROQUE WORKS story arcs.

EXCLUSIVE PREMIUMS and GREAT SAVINGS over buying the individual volumes!

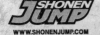

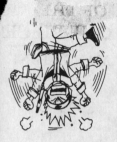

You're Reading in the Wrong Direction!!

Whoops! Guess what? You're starting at the wrong end of the comic!
...It's true! In keeping with the original Japanese format, **Naruto** is meant to be read from right to left, starting in the upper-right corner.

Unlike English, which is read from left to right, Japanese is read from right to left, meaning that action, sound effects and word-balloon order are completely reversed... something which can make readers unfamiliar with Japanese feel pretty backwards themselves. For this reason, manga or Japanese comics published in the U.S. in English have sometimes been published "flopped"—that is, printed in exact reverse order, as though seen from the other side of a mirror.

By flopping pages, U.S. publishers can avoid confusing readers, but the compromise is not without its downside. For one thing, a character in a flopped manga series who once wore in the original Japanese version a T-shirt emblazoned with "M A Y" (as in "the merry month of") now wears one which reads "Y A M"! Additionally, many manga creators in Japan are themselves unhappy with the process, as some feel the mirror-imaging of their art alters their original intentions.

We are proud to bring you Masashi Kishimoto's **Naruto** in the original unflopped format. For now, though, turn to the other side of the book and let the ninjutsu begin...!

—Editor

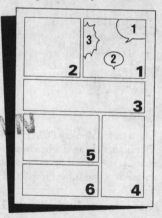